A+ Guide to Software
Managing, Maintaining, and Troubleshooting

THIRD EDITION

Jean Andrews, Ph.D.

CompTIA Certified

THOMSON

COURSE TECHNOLOGY

Australia • Canada • Mexico • Singapore • Spain • United Kingdom • United States

A+ Guide to Software: Managing, Maintaining, and Troubleshooting, Third Edition

is published by Course Technology.

Senior Editor:
Lisa Egan

Managing Editor:
William Pitkin III

Product Managers:
Manya Chylinski

Developmental Editors:
Lisa Ruffolo
Dan Seiter

Marketing Manager:
Jason Sakos

Associate Product Managers:
Mirella Misiaszek
David Rivera

Editorial Assistant:
Amanda Piantedosi

Senior Manufacturing Coordinator:
Trevor Kallop

Production Editor:
Kelly Robinson

Cover Design:
Abby Scholz

Internal Design:
Janis Owens, Books by Design

Copyeditor:
Kristen Taggart

Compositors:
Digital Publishing Solutions
GEX Publishing Services

Brief Contents

Table of Contents

A+ Operating System Technologies Examination Objectives

Introduction

A+ Guide to Software: Managing, Maintaining, and Troubleshooting, Third Edition was written to be the very best tool on the market today to prepare you to support operating systems used on personal computers. This book takes you from the just-a-user level to the I-can-fix-this level for the most common PC operating system concerns. This book achieves its goals with an unusually effective combination of tools that powerfully reinforce both concepts and hands-on, real-world experience. It also provides thorough preparation for CompTIA's revised 2003 A+ Operating System Technologies Exam. Students who use this book should first be competent computer users. An appropriate prerequisite is a general course on microcomputer applications. This book includes:

- **Comprehensive review and practice end-of-chapter material,** including a chapter summary, key terms, review questions, and hands-on projects.
- **Step-by-step instruction** on installation, maintenance, optimizing system performance, and troubleshooting.
- A **wide array of photos and screen shots** support the text, displaying in detail exactly how to best understand, purchase, install, and maintain your software.
- **In-depth, hands-on projects** at the end of each chapter are designed to assure that you not only understand the material, but can execute procedures and make decisions on your own.
- **Test preparation on CD-ROM.** Because so many instructors, students, and employers are focused on certification, we provide ample opportunity to prepare for the A+ exams. On the CD that accompanies this book, you will find over 400 test preparation questions powered by MeasureUp, a leading test preparation vendor. Additionally, there are over 1000 test preparation questions from Certblaster, which features A+ testing in 5 different testing modes. In total, there are over 1400 test preparation questions, which means students will have plenty of opportunity to practice, drill, and rehearse for the exam once they have worked through this book. **The unlock code for the A+ CertBlaster questions is: c_a+ (case sensitive)**

In addition, the carefully structured, clearly written text is accompanied by graphics that provide the visual input that is essential to learning. And for instructors using the book in a classroom, a special CD-ROM is available that includes an Instructor's Manual, an Online Testing system, and a PowerPoint presentation.

The book begins with a survey and comparison of all major operating systems. Then you learn to work from the command prompt using MS-DOS commands needed for drastic troubleshooting situations. Next you will install and learn to use each major Microsoft operating system. The chapters are organized so that you can install and learn to use and support Windows 98, then proceed to Windows 2000 with a brief coverage of Windows NT, and finally to Windows XP. You will learn about the special concerns of Windows on a network, on the Internet, and on notebook computers. You will also be introduced to Linux and the Mac OS.

This book provides thorough preparation for CompTIA's newly revised A+ OS Technologies Exam. This book maps completely to the revised certification exam objectives. This certification credential's popularity among employers is growing exponentially, and obtaining certification increases your ability to gain employment and improve your salary. To get more information on A+ Certification and its sponsoring organization, the Computing Technology Industry Association, see their Web site at *www.comptia.org*.

Features

To ensure a successful learning experience, this book includes the following pedagogical features:

- **Learning Objectives:** Every chapter opens with a list of learning objectives that sets the stage for you to absorb the lessons of the text.
- **Comprehensive Step-by-Step Troubleshooting Guidance:** Troubleshooting guidelines are included in almost every chapter.
- **Step-by-Step Procedures:** The book is chock-full of step-by-step procedures covering subjects from understanding how the latest operating system technologies work to installation and maintenance.
- **Art Program:** Numerous detailed photographs, three-dimensional art, and screenshots support the text, displaying operating system screens exactly as you will see them in your work.
- **A+ Table of Contents:** This table of contents indicates every page that relates to each certification objective. This is a valuable tool for quick reference.
- **Applying Concepts:** These sections offer practical applications for the material being discussed. Whether outlining a task, developing a scenario, or providing pointers, the Applying Concepts sections give you a chance to apply what you've learned to a typical PC problem.

NOTE

Notes: Note icons highlight additional helpful information related to the subject being discussed.

A+
OS
1.1

A+ Icons: All of the content that relates to CompTIA's A+ 2003 Certification exam, whether it's a page or a sentence, is highlighted with an A+ icon. The icon notes the exam name and the objective number. This unique feature highlights the relevant content at a glance, so you can pay extra attention to the material.

A+ Exam Tip Boxes: These boxes highlight additional insights and tips to remember if you are planning on taking the A+ Exams.

Caution Icon: This icon highlights critical safety information. Follow these instructions carefully to protect the PC and its data and for your own safety.

End-of-Chapter Material: Each chapter closes with the following features, which reinforce the material covered in the chapter and provide real-world, hands-on testing of the chapter's skill set.

CHAPTER SUMMARY

- **Chapter Summary:** This bulleted list of concise statements summarizes all major points of the chapter.

REVIEWING THE BASICS

- **Review Questions:** You can test your understanding of each chapter with a comprehensive set of review questions. The "Reviewing the Basics" questions check your understanding of fundamental concepts, while the "Thinking Critically" questions help you synthesize and apply what you've learned.

KEY TERMS

- **Key Terms:** The content of each chapter is further reinforced by an end-of-chapter key terms list. The definitions of all terms are included at the end of the book in a full-length glossary.

- **Hands-on Projects:** You get to test your real-world understanding with hands-on projects involving a full range of software and hardware problems. Each hands-on activity in this book is preceded by the Hands-on icon and a description of the exercise that follows.

Web Site: For updates to this book and information about our complete line of A+ PC Repair topics, please visit our Web site at *www.course.com/pcrepair*.

Instructor Resources

The following supplemental materials are available when this book is used in a classroom setting. All of the supplements available with this book are provided to the instructor on a single CD-ROM.

Electronic Instructor's Manual: The Instructor's Manual that accompanies this textbook includes additional instructional material to assist in class preparation, including suggestions for classroom activities, discussion topics, and additional projects.

Solutions: Answers to all end-of-chapter material, including the Review Questions, and where applicable, Hands-on Projects, are provided.

ExamView®: This textbook is accompanied by ExamView, a powerful testing software package that allows instructors to create and administer printed, computer (LAN-based), and Internet exams. ExamView includes hundreds of questions that correspond to the topics covered in this text, enabling students to generate detailed study guides that include page references for further review. The computer-based and Internet testing components allow students to take exams at their computers, and also save the instructor time by grading each exam automatically.

PowerPoint Presentations: This book comes with Microsoft® PowerPoint® slides for each chapter. These are included as a teaching aid for classroom presentation, to make available to students on the network for chapter review, or to be printed for classroom distribution. Instructors, please feel at liberty to add your own slides for additional topics you introduce to the class.

Figure Files: All of the figures in the book are reproduced on the Instructor Resources CD, in bit-mapped format. Similar to the PowerPoint presentations, these are included as a teaching aid for classroom presentation, to make available to students for review, or to be printed for classroom distribution.

Daily Lesson Planner: This free teaching tool enables instructors to use our A+ products with even greater ease! It includes detailed lecture notes and teaching instructions that incorporate all of the components of the A+ Total Solutions. User name and password are required for download. It is available on the Instructor CD and online at *www.course.com/pcrepair*.

Acknowledgments

Thank you to the wonderful people at Course Technology who continue to provide support, warm encouragement, patience, and guidance. Lisa Egan, Manya Chylinski, Mirella Misiaszek, David Rivera, Amanda Piantedosi, Kelly Robinson, and Laura Hildebrand of CT: You've truly helped make this third edition fun! Thank you Lisa Ruffolo and Dan Seiter, the Developmental Editors, for your suggestions, encouragements, attention to detail, and your genuine friendship. You were a pleasure.

Thank you to all the people who took the time to voluntarily send encouragements and suggestions for improvements to the previous editions. Your input and help is very much appreciated. Thank you to Tony Woodall of Omega Computers for your outstanding research efforts. Also, thank you to Jill West for your support here at home.

This book is dedicated to the covenant of God with man on Earth.

Jean Andrew, Ph.D.

Photo Credits

Photos courtesy of Jennifer Dark.

Read This Before You Begin

The following hardware, software, and other equipment are needed to do the hands-on projects at the end of the chapters:

- You need a working PC on which you can install an operating system.
- Compatible operating systems are Windows 98, Windows NT Workstation, Windows 2000 Professional, or Windows XP Professional.

CompTIA Authorized Curriculum Program

The logo of the CompTIA Authorized Curriculum Program and the status of this or other training material as "Authorized" under the CompTIA Authorized Curriculum Program signifies that, in CompTIA's opinion, such training material covers the content of the CompTIA's related certification exam. CompTIA has not reviewed or approved the accuracy of the contents of this training material and specifically disclaims any warranties of merchantability or fitness for a particular purpose. CompTIA makes no guarantee concerning the success of persons using any such "Authorized" or other training material in order to prepare for any CompTIA certification exam.

The contents of this training material were created for the CompTIA Operating System Technologies exam covering CompTIA certification exam objectives that were current as of November 2003.

State of the Information Technology (IT) Field

Most organizations today depend on computers and information technology to improve business processes, productivity, and efficiency. Opportunities to become global organizations and reach customers, businesses, and suppliers are a direct result of the widespread use of the Internet. Changing technology further changes how companies do business. This fundamental change in business practices has increased the need for skilled and certified IT workers across industries. This transformation moves many IT workers out of traditional IT businesses and into various IT dependent industries such as banking, government, insurance, and healthcare.

In the year 200, the U.S. Department of Labor, Bureau of Labor Statistics, reported that there were 2.1 million computer and data processing services jobs within organizations and an additional 164,000 self-employed workers. This makes the IT industry one of the largest in the economy. Even in the recent, more challenging economic times, the job opportunities for skilled and certified IT professionals remain fairly robust.

In any industry, the workforce is important to continually drive business. Having correctly skilled workers in IT is always a struggle with the ever-changing technologies. It has been estimated that technologies change approximately every 2 years. With such a quick product life cycle, IT workers must strive to keep up with these changes to continually bring value to their employer.

Certifications

Different levels of education are required for the many jobs in the IT industry. Additionally, the level of education and type of training required varies from employer to employer, but the need for qualified technicians remains constant. As technology changes and advances in the industry continue to rapidly evolve, many employers consistently look for employees that possess the skills necessary to implement these new technologies. Traditional degrees and diplomas do not identify the skills that a job applicant has. With the growth of the IT industry, companies increasingly rely on technical certifications to identify the skills a particular job applicant possesses. Technical certifications are a way for employers to ensure the quality and skill qualifications of their computer professionals, and they can offer job seekers a competitive edge over their competition. According to Thomas Regional Industrial Market Trends, one of the 15 trends that will transform the workplace over the next decade is a severe labor and skill shortage, specifically in technical fields, which are struggling to locate skilled and educated workers.

There are two types of certifications, vendor neutral and vendor specific. Vendor neutral certifications are those that test for the skills and knowledge required in specific industry job roles and do not subscribe to a specific vendor's technology solution. Vendor neutral certifications include all of the Computing Technology Industry Association's (CompTIA) certifications, Project Management Institute's certifications, and Security Certified Program certifications. Vendor specific certifications validate the skills and knowledge necessary to be successful by utilizing a specific vendor's technology solution. Some examples of vendor specific certifications include those offered by Microsoft, IBM, Novell, and Cisco.

As employers struggle to fill open IT positions with qualified candidates, certifications are a means of validating the skill sets necessary to be successful within an organization. In most careers, salary and compensation is determined by experience and education, but in IT the number and type of certifications an employee earns also determines salary and wage increases forIT staff. The Department of Labor, Bureau of Labor Statistics, reported that the computer and data processing industry has grown at a dramatic rate from 1990 to 2000 and is anticipated to grow about 86% in wages and salaries by the year 2010. Robert Half International reported that, in the U.S., starting salaries for help-desk support staff in 2001 ranged from $30,500 to $56,000 and more senior technical support salaries ranged from $48,000 to $61,000.

Certifications provide job applicants with more than just a competitive edge over their non-certified counterparts who apply for the same IT positions. Some institutions of higher education grant college credit to students who successfully pass certification exams, moving them further along in their degree programs. Certifications also give individuals who are interested in careers in the military the ability to move into higher positions more quickly. And many advanced certification programs accept, and sometimes require, entry-level certifications as part of their exams. For example, Cisco and Microsoft accept some CompTIA certifications as prerequisites for their certification programs.

A Valuable Resource: The TechCareer Compass™

Finding a career that fits a person's personality, skill set, and lifestyle is challenging and fulfilling, but can often be difficult. What are the steps individuals should take to find that dream career? Is IT interesting to you? Chances are if you are reading this book then this question has been answered. What about IT do you like? The world of work in the IT industry is vast. Some questions to ask yourself: Are you a person who likes to work alone, or do you like to work in a group? Do you like speaking directly with customers or prefer to stay behind the scenes? Does your lifestyle encourage a lot of travel, or do you need to stay in one location? All of these factors influence your decision when faced with choosing the right job. Inventory assessments are a good first step to learning more about you, your interests, work values, and abilities. There are a variety of Web sites that offer assistance with career planning and assessments.

The Computing Technology Industry Association (CompTIA) hosts an informational Web site called the TechCareer Compass™ (TCC) that defines careers in the IT industry. The TCC is located at http://tcc.comptia.org. This Web site was created by the industry and outlines over 100 industry jobs. Each defined job includes a job description, alternate job titles, critical work functions, activities and performance indicators, and skills and knowledge required by the job. In other words, it shows exactly what the job entails so that you can find one that best fits your interests and abilities. Additionally, the TCC maps over 750 technical certifications to the skills required by each specific job, allowing you the ability to research and plan your certification training. The Web site also includes a resource section, which is updated regularly with articles and links to other career Web sites. The TechCareer Compass is the one stop location for IT career information.

In addition to CompTIA's TechCareer Compass, there are many other Web sites that cover components of IT careers and career planning. Many of these sites can also be found in the TCC Resources section. Some of these other career planning sites include: YourITFuture.com, ITCompass.net, and About.com.

Tara Manzow, M Ed
Program Manager, CompTIA

Citation

Bureau of Labor Statistics, U.S. Department of Labor. *Career Guide to Industries, 2002-03 Edition, Computer and Data Processing Services.* On the Internet at http://www.bls.gov/oco/cg/cgs033.htm (visited August 14, 2003).

Bureau of Labor Statistics, U.S. Department of Labor, *Occupational Outlook Handbook, 2002-03 Edition, Computer Support Specialists and System Administrators.* On the internet at http://www.bls.gov/oco/home.htm (visited August 14, 2003).

Thomas Regional Industrial Market Trends. July 8, 2003 Newsletter: *15 Trends that Will Transform the Workforce.* On the Internet at http://www.thomasregional.com/newsarchive2.html?us=3f61ed4162269&to=5&from=0&id=1057266649 (visited September 10, 2003).

How to Become Comptia Certified

This training material can help you prepare for and pass a related CompTIA certification exam or exams. In order to achieve CompTIA certification, you must register for and pass a CompTIA certification exam or exams. In order to become CompTIA certified, you must:

(1) Select a certification exam provider. For more information please visit the following Web site: *www.comptia.org/certification/general_information/test_locations.asp.*

(2) Register for and schedule a time to take the CompTIA certification exam(s) at a convenient location.

(3) Read and sign the Candidate Agreement, which will be presented at the time of the exam(s). The text of the Candidate Agreement can be found at the following Web site: *www.comptia.org/certification/general_information/candidate_agreement.asp.*

(4) Take and pass the CompTIA certification exam(s).

For more information about CompTIA's certifications, such as their industry acceptance, benefits, or program news, please visit *www.comptia.org/certification/default.asp.*

CompTIA is a non-profit information technology (IT) trade association. CompTIA's certifications are designed by subject matter experts from across the IT industry. Each CompTIA certification is vendor-neutral, covers multiple technologies, and requires demonstration of skills and knowledge widely sought after by the IT industry.

To contact CompTIA with any questions or comments:

Please call + 1 630 268 1818

questions@comptia.org

Introducing and Comparing Operating Systems

In this chapter, you will learn:

- What an operating system does
- How DOS began and how it is used today
- About the various Windows operating systems and the differences between them
- Advantages and disadvantages of common non-Windows operating systems

Personal computers have changed the way we work, play, and do business. Everyone, no matter how young or old they are or how they make their living, encounters a personal computer in some way almost daily. No matter how experienced a computer user you are, this book can take you from the just-a-user stage to understanding what happens behind the scenes when you click a Web site link or install a new screen saver. Not only will you understand what happened, but you'll also be able to customize your operating system (OS) and applications, troubleshoot and solve problems with the OS, and optimize your system for best performance.

The goals of this book are to enable you to compare different operating systems and make wise buying decisions about them, and to empower you to understand, troubleshoot, customize, and optimize a Windows operating system. In addition, this book prepares you to pass the A+ Operating System Technologies exam, one of the two exams required by CompTIA (*www.comptia.org*) for A+ certification. Its companion book, *A+ Guide to Managing and Troubleshooting Hardware* (Course Technology 2004, ISBN 0-619-21327-2), prepares you for the A+ Core Hardware Service Technician exam, the other exam required by CompTIA for A+ certification. To begin using this book, nothing more is expected of you than to be a knowledgeable computer user.

This book is organized to make it easy for you to learn by doing. The operating systems are covered so that you can install one and learn to use, support, and troubleshoot it before moving on to the next. This first chapter starts the process by introducing you to many different operating systems and highlights what they have in common. In this chapter, you will learn what an operating system does and how it relates to the user. Operating systems continue to evolve as hardware and software technologies improve. As you read about various OSs in this chapter, you will see the evolution from DOS to Windows 9x and to Windows NT/2000/XP. You will also be introduced to alternate OSs (Unix, Linux, OS/2, and Mac OS).

What an Operating System Does

An **operating system** is a computer program that controls a computer. An OS controls the hardware components that make up a computer and also provides an interface that a user or an application can use. Figure 1-1 illustrates that an OS must relate to the user, to applications, and to various hardware components. You can also see that the OS must relate to these hardware devices by way of the **central processing unit (CPU),** also called a **microprocessor,** the most important microchip in the system, which is responsible for processing all data and instructions. The OS is the middleman between the user and applications on one side and the CPU and other hardware on the other side.

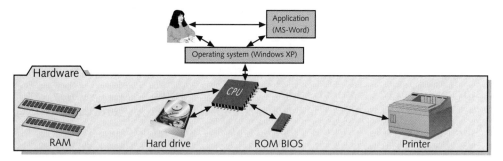

Figure 1-1   Users and applications depend on the OS to relate to all hardware components

Several applications might be installed on a computer to meet various needs of the users, but it needs only one operating system. There are several operating systems on the market, each designed to support different types of hardware systems and user needs:

- *DOS*. DOS, the disk OS, was the first OS among IBM computers and IBM-compatible computers. Because DOS was written for early PCs, it has significant limitations today. DOS was the OS used by early versions of Windows, including Windows 3.1 and Windows 3.11 (collectively referred to as Windows 3.x). Windows 3.x did not perform OS functions, but simply served as a user-friendly intermediate program between DOS and applications and the user.
- *Windows 9x*. Other early OSs that use a DOS core are Windows 95, Windows 98, and Windows Me, collectively called Windows 9x. These are true operating systems with a DOS core and provide a user-friendly interface. Even though Windows XP is slowly replacing Windows 9x, Windows 98 is still the most popular OS on desktop computers for home use. (Many people chose not to upgrade from Windows 98 to Windows Me because they did not consider it a significant enough upgrade.)
- *Windows NT, Windows 2000, and Windows XP*. Windows NT comes in two versions, Windows NT Workstation for workstations, and Windows NT Server to control a network. Windows 2000 is an upgrade of Windows NT, and Windows XP is an upgrade of Windows 2000. Windows 2000 also comes in several versions, some designed for the desktop and others designed for high-end servers. Windows 2000 Professional is popular as an OS for the corporate desktop. Windows 2000 Server, Advanced Server, and Datacenter Server are network server OSs. Windows XP also currently comes in several versions. The two most popular versions for desktop PCs are Windows XP Home and Windows XP Professional.

- *Unix*. Unix is a popular OS used to control networks and to support applications used on the Internet.
- *Linux*. Linux is a scaled-down version of Unix that is provided, in basic form, free of charge and includes open access to the programming code of the OS. It is often used for server applications.
- *OS/2*. OS/2, developed by IBM and Microsoft, is less common for home desktop PCs, but is used in certain types of networks. Microsoft developed Windows NT using some of the core components of OS/2 and intended it to replace OS/2.
- *Mac OS*. Mac OS is available only for Apple Macintosh computers and is often used for graphics applications and in educational settings.

You will learn more about each of these OSs later in this chapter. Although there are important differences among them, OSs share the following four main functions:

- *Managing hardware*

  - Managing the BIOS (programs permanently stored on hardware devices)
  - Managing memory, which is a temporary place to store data and instructions as they are being processed
  - Diagnosing problems with software and hardware
  - Interfacing between hardware and software (that is, interpreting application software needs to the hardware and interpreting hardware needs to application software)

- *Managing files*

  - Managing files on hard drives, floppy drives, CD drives, and other drives
  - Creating, storing, retrieving, deleting, and moving files

- *Providing a user interface*

  - Performing housekeeping procedures requested by the user, often concerning secondary storage devices, such as formatting new disks, deleting files, copying files, and changing the system date
  - Providing a way for the user to manage the desktop, hardware, applications, and data

- *Managing applications*

  - Installing and uninstalling applications
  - Running applications and managing the interface to the hardware on behalf of an application

Operating System Components

A+ EXAM TIP

The A+ OS exam expects you to know all the key terms found in this section.

An operating system is made up of several internal components, which you will learn about throughout this book. Every operating system has two main components: the shell and the kernel (see Figure 1-2). A **shell** is the portion of the OS that relates to the user and to applications. The shell provides a command, menu, or icon interface to the user using various interface tools such as Windows Explorer, the Control Panel, or My Computer.

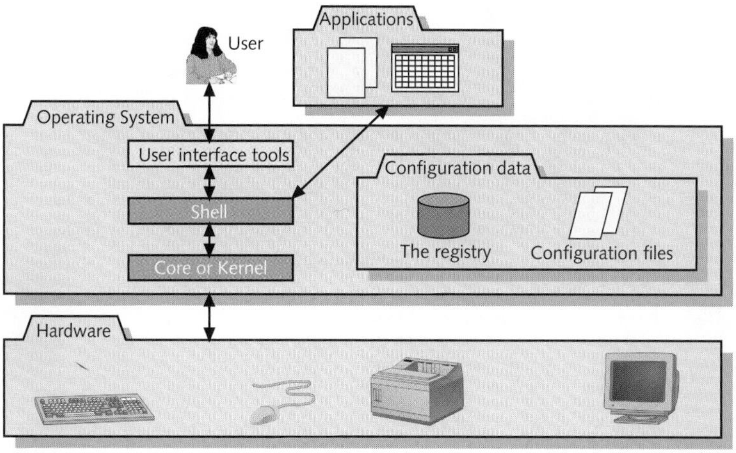

Figure 1-2   Inside an operating system, different components perform various functions

The core, or **kernel,** of the OS is responsible for interacting with hardware. It has more power to communicate with hardware devices than the shell so that applications operating under the OS cannot get to hardware devices without the shell passing those requests to the kernel. This structure provides for a more stable system.

An operating system needs a place to keep hardware and software configuration information, user preferences, and application settings that are used when the OS is first loaded and are accessed as needed by hardware, applications, and users. This information can be kept in a database or text files. Windows uses a database for most of this information, which is called the **registry.** In addition, some data is kept in text files called **initialization files,** which often have an .ini or .inf file extension.

How an OS Relates to Users

When a PC is first turned on, the operating system is loaded. After the OS is in control, it either automatically executes a program or turns to the user for its next instruction. If you are working with the OS, you see an interface on the monitor screen. This interface can be command-driven, menu-driven, or icon-driven.

Command-Driven Interfaces

A+
OS
1.1

With a command-driven interface, you type commands to tell the OS to perform operations. For example, in Figure 1-3, the VER command reports the operating system version. DOS and Unix use command-driven interfaces, and other OSs may provide access to a command-driven interface. Computer technicians who are good typists and are very familiar with DOS-like commands often prefer this kind of OS interface.

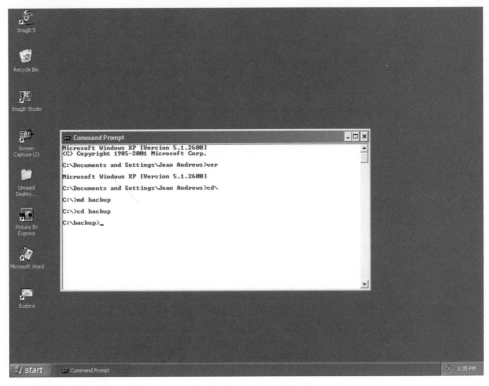

Figure 1-3   An operating system command-driven interface: a DOS box

To access this window, sometimes called a DOS box, using Windows XP, click Start, point to All Programs, point to Accessories, and then click Command Prompt. What shows in the command prompt depends on the current drive and directory.

Menu-Driven Interfaces

Some OSs allow you to choose from a list of options displayed on the screen. An example of such a menu-driven interface is Windows Explorer in Windows XP. From the drop-down menus, you can format disks, rename files, copy and delete files, and perform many other operations to manage files and storage devices (see Figure 1-4). Note that Windows Explorer uses icons as well as menus.

Icon-Driven Interfaces

Today's OSs are more likely to use an icon-driven interface than a command-driven one. With an icon-driven interface, sometimes called a **graphical user interface (GUI)**, you perform operations by selecting icons (or pictures) on the screen. When an OS is first executed, the initial screen that appears, together with its menus, commands, and icons, is called the **desktop**. Figure 1-5 shows the Windows 2000 default desktop, which has an icon-driven interface. You double-click an icon with the mouse to execute a software program or right-click an icon to see its shortcut menu. Just about all OSs today offer a combination of menu and icon-driven interfaces such as the Control Panel window in Figure 1-5, which includes both menus and icons.

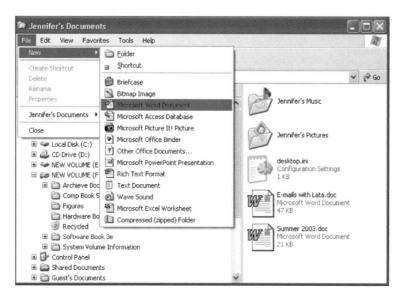

Figure 1-4   A menu-driven interface: Windows Explorer in Windows XP

Figure 1-5   An icon-driven interface: Windows 2000 desktop

Comparing Operating Systems

A+
OS
1.1

The goal of this section is to help you understand what each OS does best and how to compare features of each to make wise buying decisions and technical distinctions. It's impossible to adequately do that without discussing some technical terms. Most of these terms are covered in detail in the next chapter, but for now, here are some basic definitions. To understand the differences between OSs, you need to understand the following terms:

- Each process that a CPU is aware of is called a **thread**. For example, if the OS directs the CPU to start the process of saving a file to the hard drive, this process is one thread to the CPU.

- **16-bit mode** and **32-bit mode**, also called **real mode** and **protected mode**, respectively, have to do with whether the CPU processes 16 or 32 bits at a time. OSs, applications, and CPUs all operate in either 16-bit (real) or 32-bit (protected) modes. Because twice as much data is processed at one time, 32-bit OSs are much faster than 16-bit OSs. Some OSs, such as Windows XP 64-bit Edition, process data 64 bits at a time.

- A **file allocation table (FAT)** is a table on a hard drive or floppy disk that tracks the locations of files on a disk. A disk is composed of **tracks**, which are concentric circles on the disk surface, shown in Figure 1-6. Each track is divided into several segments, each called a **sector**. A **cluster** is the smallest unit of space on a disk for storing data and is made up of one or more sectors. The FAT contains a list of clusters and details which clusters are used for each file stored on the disk. The most recent version of FAT, FAT32, is a more efficient method of organization for large drives than FAT16 (the earlier version).

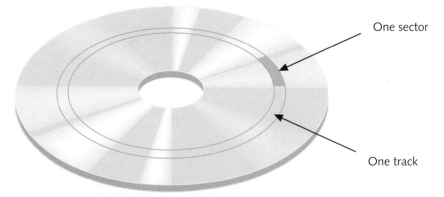

One sector

One track

Figure 1-6   A hard drive or floppy disk is divided into tracks and sectors. Several sectors make one cluster

A+
OS
1.1

- **Random access memory (RAM)** is temporary memory stored on chips inside the computer. These chips are stored on memory modules, some of which are shown in Figure 1-7. Memory is a place for the CPU to store programs and data while it is processing both; the information stored in RAM disappears when the computer is turned off.
- A computer provides several ports on the back of the computer case to connect different devices, such as a keyboard, mouse, or printer.

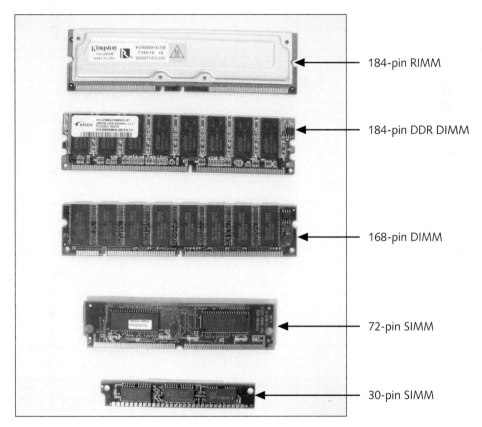

184-pin RIMM

184-pin DDR DIMM

168-pin DIMM

72-pin SIMM

30-pin SIMM

Figure 1-7   Types of RAM modules

Now that you've learned some basic terms relating to OSs, let's compare several OSs, keeping in mind the following criteria:

- What kind of interface does the OS provide for the user?
- How many and what kinds of applications are written to work with the OS?
- What are the hardware requirements to make efficient use of the OS?
- What computer ports and other hardware devices and features does the OS support?
- How does the OS perform in a network?

The following sections compare the most well-known OSs used in PCs and the OSs used in Macintoshes, including their advantages and disadvantages. As a PC technician, you will encounter many different OSs and you might be expected to service them. However, when purchasing an OS for a notebook or desktop PC, most likely your choice will be Windows XP, as it is expected to replace all Windows notebook and desktop OSs. For Macintoshes, select the latest Mac OS; for some specialized network and Internet applications, Linux might be appropriate.

As you read these sections, keep in mind the four main functions of an operating system (managing hardware, providing a user interface, working with files, and running applications), and notice how each OS performs these functions differently.

DOS (Disk Operating System)

DOS was the first OS used by IBM microcomputers. For years DOS remained the unchallenged standard for OSs used by IBM and IBM-compatible machines. It is a simple operating system, and simple often means reliable. PC technicians should be familiar with DOS because it can be very effective in troubleshooting situations when a more complex OS fails.

DOS is used in some proprietary systems where older hardware and software (sometimes called **legacy** hardware or software) are still doing the job and there is little reason to upgrade either. However, the primary use of DOS today is as a troubleshooting tool. Windows 9x uses some DOS programs as part of the underlying OS (called a DOS core), and therefore has some DOS characteristics. When the Windows 9x GUI interface fails to load, the only recourse is to fall back to the tried-and-true DOS portion of the OS stored on floppy disks or the hard drive. Also, Windows NT/2000/XP offers some form of a recovery tool that includes a command prompt where you issue DOS-like commands. You'll learn about these in future chapters.

Table 1-1 summarizes the advantages and disadvantages of DOS.

Advantages	Disadvantages
• DOS runs on small, inexpensive microcomputers with a minimum amount of memory and hard drive space. • Text-based DOS programs are faster and more compact than comparable graphics-intensive GUI programs. • Some older applications are still in use today that were written for DOS and older hardware because of the low overhead of DOS compared to more modern OSs.	• Memory management is awkward and sometimes slow. • DOS has no icon-driven interface. • DOS does only single-tasking; that is, it supports only one application running at a time. • DOS was not designed for use on networks. A separate software program is necessary for a DOS machine to access a network.

Table 1-1 (continued)

Advantages	Disadvantages
• DOS is still a viable option for some specialized applications using a dedicated computer that does not involve heavy user interaction—for example, a microcomputer dedicated to controlling an in-house phone system. • DOS can be used to boot and troubleshoot a computer when a more sophisticated OS is too cumbersome and has too much overhead.	• The last standalone version is DOS 6.22, which does not take advantage of the many new CPU features now available. • Hardly any new software is being written for DOS.

Table 1-1   Advantages and disadvantages of DOS

Windows Operating Systems

This section discusses Windows 9x, NT, 2000, and XP. As you read this section, you will learn about the evolution of Windows OSs and some of the corresponding changes in technology.

Windows 9x

Windows 95, Windows 98, and Windows Me (referred to collectively as Windows 9x) move closer to a new OS but do not completely eliminate DOS. Windows 95 introduced an improved and more automated method of installing new hardware devices, called Plug and Play (PnP). Windows 95 also introduced 32-bit programming, an early form of memory paging, networking, and many other features available in Windows NT/2000/XP. Windows 9x includes hundreds of device drivers. (**Device drivers** are programs stored on the hard drive that are designed to run an input/output hardware device, such as a monitor or a mouse. You will learn more about device drivers in the next chapter.)

Windows 98 added several new features to the OS and Windows Me added even more, but both retain the fundamental DOS core and are a blend of low-end and high-end technologies. These operating systems fulfill the Microsoft commitment to be **backward-compatible** with older software and hardware while still taking advantage of newer technology. Windows 9x is an OS that bridges two worlds (see Figure 1-8).

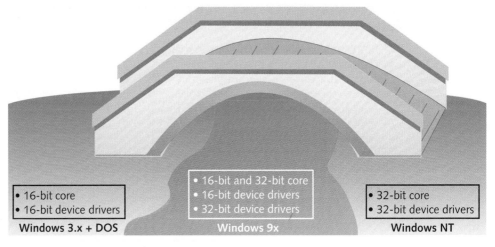

- 16-bit core
- 16-bit device drivers

Windows 3.x + DOS

- 16-bit and 32-bit core
- 16-bit device drivers
- 32-bit device drivers

Windows 9x

- 32-bit core
- 32-bit device drivers

Windows NT

Figure 1-8   Windows 9x is the bridge from DOS to Windows NT

As an example of a Windows 9x interface, Figure 1-9 shows a desktop for Windows 98 Second Edition. A window is open, showing the Control Panel, which provides a centralized location from which to administer hardware, software, and system settings, and the Start and Programs menus are open. These features will appear much the same on other Windows 9x desktops.

Figure 1-9   The Windows 98 SE desktop

Table 1-2 lists the hardware requirements of Windows 9x. Note that Table 1-2 gives the *recommended* minimum to run each version of Windows 9x. You may find different values in other documentation, because these OSs may run under lower specifications than the recommended minimums. System requirements can also change depending on whether you are installing on a new system or upgrading an older system, as well as which features you choose to install. Also, sometimes Microsoft lists the minimum requirements to *install* an OS, which might be different from the requirements to *run* an OS. (Requirements in Table 1-2 are for running the OS.) Keep these differences in mind when reviewing the lists of minimum hardware requirements for OSs throughout this chapter.

Description	Windows 95	Windows 98	Windows Me
Processor	486 or higher	Pentium	Pentium 150 MHz
RAM	8 MB	24 MB	32 MB
Free hard drive space	50 MB	195 MB	320 MB

Table 1-2   Recommended minimum hardware requirements for Windows 9x

Table 1-3 summarizes the advantages and disadvantages of Windows 9x.

Advantages	Disadvantages
• Windows 9x offers a very user-friendly and intuitive GUI interface. • Windows 9x offers almost complete back-ward-compatibility for applications written for DOS and earlier versions of Windows. • Windows 9x is a mix of older and newer OS technology and works with both older and newer software and hardware. • Disk access time under Windows 9x is improved over DOS and Windows 3.x. • Plug and Play features make installing some new hardware devices easier than with earlier OSs. • Because it is the most popular OS today, many users are comfortable with it and are reluctant to change.	• Because of the attempt to bridge older and newer technology, there are some prob-lems with failures and errors created in this hybrid environment. • Windows 9x is considered a dying OS, and Microsoft is slowly reducing its commit-ment to support it, forcing the industry to move forward to Windows XP, the replace-ment OS for Windows 9x.

Table 1-3   Advantages and disadvantages of Windows 9x

Windows 98 Upgrades

Microsoft has produced two upgrades for Windows 98: Windows 98 Second Edition (Windows 98 SE) and Windows Millennium Edition (Windows Me). Each upgrade has significant enhancements over its predecessor.

Windows 98 SE includes several patches, or fixes, for the first edition of Windows 98, updates of existing components, and some new components. Most new features involve improved networking and Internet access. Security for a dial-up connection over regular phone lines was also upgraded.

A new feature is Internet Connection Sharing (ICS), which makes it possible for a Windows 98 PC to access the Internet through another computer on a local network so that only one computer requires a direct connection to an Internet Service Provider (ISP). This feature means that several PCs on a small home network can share the same access to an ISP without incurring additional charges and without installing third-party software. Support for modems that use a USB port and additional network features are also included.

Although Windows Me is, at its core, a Windows 9x upgrade, Windows Me moves one step closer to phasing out Windows 9x and replacing it with Windows XP because Windows Me contains features from Windows 2000, the predecessor of Windows XP. Windows Me is designed for home users, not for businesses, and focuses on enhancements to multimedia features such as support for video cameras, digital cameras, scanners, and a jukebox recorder. It includes a compression utility for video files and a video editor. True to its goal as a home PC operating system, the OS is very user-friendly, including more informative error messages and troubleshooting utilities. The more technical differences among Windows 95, Windows 98, and Windows Me are covered in Chapter 4.

NOTE To learn which version of Windows is installed, right-click the My Computer icon and select Properties on the shortcut menu. When the System Properties dialog box opens, click the General tab.

Windows NT/2000/XP

✓ **A+ EXAM TIP**

The A+ OS exam expects you to be familiar with the My Computer utility, including its general purposes and how to use it. You must also be familiar with the System Properties dialog box.

Windows NT/2000/XP represents three generations of the Microsoft New Technology (NT) operating systems designed to replace Windows 9x and satisfy the growing needs of the computer industry. Windows NT was conceived when IBM and Microsoft collaborated in building OS/2. While IBM took over OS/2, Microsoft redesigned and added to the original code, calling the new OS Windows NT. The next two evolutions of the OS were called Windows 2000 and Windows XP. Versions of Windows NT and Windows 2000 are designed as server OSs. Windows NT and 2000 have many of the same objectives as Unix and are considered the primary competitors to Unix in the client/server industry. Because Windows NT and 2000 can manage access to a LAN, they are considered competitors of NetWare software by Novell, which is popular for managing LANs. Windows XP is designed for corporate desktop and home use to replace Windows 9x and Windows NT/2000 on the desktop, and Windows 2003 Server is designed to replace Windows NT/2000 as the latest server OS. For an OS to contend for so many markets, it needs to meet many goals, including those discussed next.

Goals of Windows NT/2000/XP

The following are some of the more important goals of Windows NT/2000/XP.

Eliminate the DOS Core Used by Windows 9x   Windows 95, 98, and Me all use a DOS core, which accounts for the awkward and unstable ways that Windows 9x manages memory, hard drive access, security, and applications. Windows NT/2000/XP uses an altogether new core that breaks with the past. Using this new technology, Windows NT/2000/XP can make better use of memory and other system resources, provide more security for applications and users, and improve performance. Windows 9x is a combination 16-bit and 32-bit OS, but Windows NT/2000/XP is a true 32-bit OS with no 16-bit components.

Room to Grow   Windows NT/2000/XP is designed for expandability, so it can more easily accommodate new hardware and software. The main way that the OS does this is by using a modular approach to performing tasks. For example, DOS and Windows 9x allow applications to have direct access to memory, but Windows NT/2000/XP does not allow an application direct access to memory or other hardware devices. Applications are required to pass their requests to the OS, which processes them and gives the application as much memory as it requests if that memory is not currently used by other applications. Because of this layer of protection between software and hardware, when hardware requirements change, Windows manages the change; the application is insulated from the change.

Portability to Different Platforms   Because of Windows NT/2000/XP's modular approach, it easily ports to different platforms or hardware configurations, including different CPU technologies. The Windows installation CD-ROM comes with three directories ready to accommodate three different CPU technologies. (For Intel-based CPUs, the directory on the CD is \i386.) Windows NT/2000/XP can accommodate several CPU technologies because it isolates parts of the OS from other parts in a modular fashion. The part of the OS that interacts with the hardware is the **hardware abstraction layer (HAL)**, which is the layer between the OS and the hardware. The HAL is available in different versions, each designed to address the specifics of a particular CPU technology. The HAL is the only part of the OS that has to change when platforms change. The other components of the OS need not be changed when the platform changes.

A+
OS
1.1

Compatibility with Legacy Software   Generally, as long as DOS or Windows 9x applications don't attempt to access resources directly, they can run under Windows NT/2000/XP. However, Windows NT/2000/XP gives no guarantee of backward compatibility, as Windows 9x did.

Security   Windows NT/2000/XP provides security similar to that on Unix systems, which is greater than the security in Windows 9x. Windows NT/2000/XP's security features include the following:

- Requires that a user have a logon ID and password to gain access to the PC
- Provides security between users on the same PC, so that one user can block another user from data or software
- Creates auditing trails to identify security breaches
- Protects memory between different applications loaded at the same time

Performance and Reliability   Although no OS is fault-proof, Windows NT/2000/XP provides a much more stable environment than many OSs, including Windows 9x. Windows NT/2000/XP is less likely to hang, or "lock up," than other PC OSs. If an application stalls, other loaded applications are less likely to be affected. When using powerful workstations, Windows NT/2000/XP outperforms Windows 9x.

Support for Hardware   Windows NT/2000/XP is designed for current hardware devices, and many legacy hardware devices are not supported. For this reason, before you decide to install Windows NT/2000/XP, determine if all components on your PC will work under Windows NT/2000/XP. For instance, you might have to replace a network card, modem, or video card before Windows NT/2000/XP works. To determine if a hardware component is supported by Windows NT/2000/XP, see the **hardware compatibility list (HCL)** for Windows NT/2000/XP that comes with the OS. The most recent copy is available on the Microsoft Web site at *www.microsoft.com/ whdc/hcl/search.mspx*. On the list, which you can search by hardware category or company name, are all hardware devices supported by Windows XP, Windows 2000, and Windows Me. For instance, Figure 1-10 shows the partial results of a search for video cards compatible with Windows. If a device is not on the list, ask the manufacturer if there is a driver specifically for the version of Windows you are using. If no driver exists, this device will not work under this version of Windows NT/2000/XP.

1

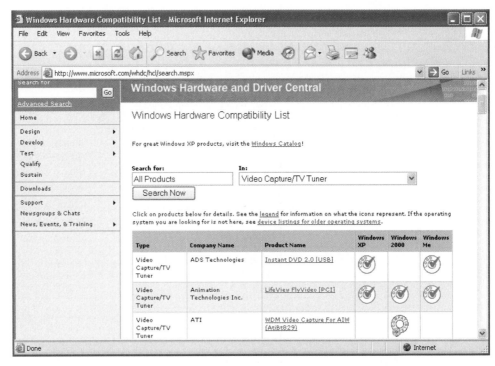

Figure 1-10   Some video capture cards compatible with Windows 2000/XP and Windows Me from the HCL

Choosing Between Windows 9x and Windows NT/2000/XP

Although many people and businesses still use Windows 9x, it is now outdated, having been superseded by Windows 2000 and Windows XP. In most situations, you should install Windows XP on a PC. (Windows NT and Windows 2000 are not good choices because they are being phased out by Microsoft, and Windows XP offers significant improvements over these older OSs.) However, in the following situations, it might be appropriate to install Windows 98 or Windows Me:

- You have legacy hardware devices that cannot be replaced, and drivers for Windows NT/2000/XP are not available from the manufacturer or Microsoft.
- The PC is not powerful or big enough to support Windows NT/2000/XP. (See the hardware requirements listed later in the chapter, and then allow extra resources for your applications.)
- The software you intend to use on the PC works better under Windows 98/Me than it does under Windows XP. Running older DOS and Windows 16-bit applications might be a problem in a Windows XP environment. Also, some 32-bit programs written for Windows 9x might not work under Windows NT/2000/XP because of differences the API calls to the operating system. An **application program interface (API)** is method by which one program calls another program to perform a task.

Table 1-4 lists the major differences between Windows NT/2000/XP and Windows 9x.

Feature	Windows 9x	Windows NT/2000/XP
Hardware requirements	Low, requiring a 486 PC with 8–16 MB of RAM	High, requiring a Pentium with 16–64 MB of RAM
Hardware compatibility	Supports most legacy devices	Supports most current devices, but does not claim backward-compatibility with legacy devices
Software compatibility	Fully backward-compatible with older DOS and Windows 3.x applications	No support for any application that attempts to access hardware directly
Performance	Often runs better on older, less powerful computers	Has significantly better performance on systems with at least 64 MB of RAM
Reliability and stability	Sometimes not stable	Very high reliability and stability; all applications run in protected memory space
Security	Allows violations of the logon process controlled from a server	Very high security down to the file level

Table 1-4   Comparing Windows NT/2000/XP to Windows 9x

Windows NT

Windows NT breaks with previous versions of Windows. Windows NT was a first step in the major evolution of Microsoft Windows operating systems terminating in Windows XP. Windows NT supports **multiprocessing** (two or more CPUs). It is also designed to work within a powerful networked environment. Computers called servers are configured to store programs and data used remotely by other computers called clients. With client-server arrangements, an organization's resources can be used more effectively, because computers are networked together to share these resources. Windows NT Workstation is designed to run on clients, and Windows NT Server to run servers.

Windows NT had many problems and was difficult to install and support. Most organizations that used Windows NT have upgraded to Windows 2000 or Windows XP, but you may still see a few Windows NT installations, so you must be familiar with this OS. Table 1-5 summarizes the advantages and disadvantages of Windows NT.

Advantages	Disadvantages
• Windows NT was designed to run in powerful client-server environments and targeted both the client and the server market. • Windows NT offered a completely new file management system, different from earlier Windows OSs. • Windows NT Workstation offered networking over a LAN and dial-up connections over phone lines. • Windows NT Server offered powerful security as a file server and for network administration. • Windows NT supported multiprocessing.	• The hardware requirements of Windows NT eliminated it as a plausible option for older, low-end PCs. • Windows NT was not compatible with some older hardware and software. • Windows NT did not use some of the technologies or newer features used by Windows 2000 and XP, such as Safe Mode, Plug and Play, USB support, Device Manager, and FAT32. • Windows NT is not currently supported by Microsoft. No new service packs (fixes or patches correcting known errors in the OS) are being released. • Windows NT Workstation has mostly been replaced by Windows 2000/XP on the desktop. Windows NT Server has been replaced by Windows 2000 Server and Windows 2003 Server as a server OS.

Table 1-5   Advantages and disadvantages of Windows NT

 A+ EXAM TIP

The A+ OS exam expects you to know that Windows NT does not have a Device Manager, Safe Mode, Plug and Play, FAT32, or support for USB devices.

The minimum hardware requirements for Windows NT on an IBM-compatible PC are included in the following list. However, even though Windows NT does run on this minimum hardware configuration, remember that you need a powerful high-end PC to experience the full benefits of Windows NT.

- Pentium-compatible processor or higher
- 16 MB of RAM (32 MB is recommended)
- 125 MB of hard disk space

While these minimum requirements refer to IBM-compatible machines, Windows NT can run on other computers, providing the same interface and functionality. The hardware platforms supported by Windows NT are included in the following list. This book focuses only on the Intel-based CPUs of IBM-compatible machines.

- Intel x86-based (486 or higher) processor
- MIPS R4x00-based processor
- Alpha AXP-based processor
- PReP-compliant PowerPC-based processor

Windows 2000

Windows 2000 is actually a suite of operating systems, each designed for a different-sized computer system. The Windows 2000 desktop (see Figure 1-11) looks much the same as that of Windows 9x and NT. Windows 2000 is built on Windows NT and was designed to ultimately replace both Windows 9x for low-end systems and Windows NT for midrange and high-end systems.

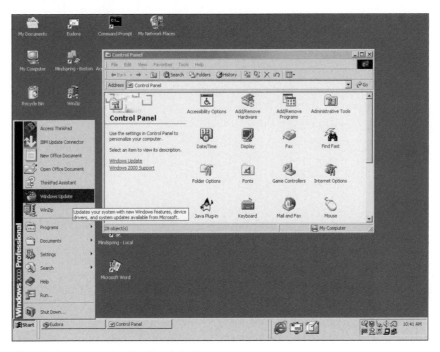

Figure 1-11   The Windows 2000 Professional desktop

As you read about the different Windows 2000 operating systems, keep in mind that all Windows 2000 versions have the same fundamental core and execute programs in the same manner. The differences among the four versions in the following list are the size of the organization they are designed to support and networking features.

- *Windows 2000 Professional* was designed to replace both Windows 9x and Windows NT Workstation as a personal computer desktop or notebook OS. It is an improved version of Windows NT Workstation, using the same new technological approach to hardware and software, and includes all the popular features of Windows 9x, including Plug and Play.
- *Windows 2000 Server* is the improved version of Windows NT Server and is designed as a network operating system for low-end servers.

- *Windows 2000 Advanced Server* is a network operating system that has the same features as Windows 2000 Server but is designed to run on more powerful servers.
- *Windows 2000 Datacenter Server* is a network operating system that is another step up from Windows 2000 Advanced Server. It is intended to be used in large enterprise centers.

Hardware and software must qualify for all the Windows 2000 products. For hardware, check the HCL at *www.microsoft.com/whdc/hcl/search.mspx*. For software applications, search the list of compatible software applications at *www.microsoft.com/windows2000/server/howtobuy/upgrading/compat/search/software.asp*.

Table 1-6 compares the hardware specifications for Windows 2000 products.

Description	Windows 2000 Professional	Windows 2000 Server	Windows 2000 Advanced Server	Windows 2000 Datacenter Server
Minimum processor required (CPU)	133 MHz Pentium-compatible	133 MHz Pentium-compatible	133 MHz Pentium-compatible	133 MHz or higher
Minimum hard drive size	2 GB	2 GB	2 GB	2 GB
Minimum hard drive free space	650 MB	1 GB	1 GB	1 GB
Minimum RAM	64 MB	128 MB minimum supported; 256 MB minimum recommended	128 MB minimum supported; 256 MB minimum recommended	256 MB
Maximum RAM supported	4 GB	4 GB	8 GB	64 GB
Maximum CPUs in one system	2	4	8	32

Table 1-6   Comparing Windows 2000 products

Windows 2000 offered several improvements over Windows NT, which are described next.

A+
OS
1.1

Reliability   Windows 2000 is more reliable than Windows NT. The Windows File Protection feature of Windows 2000 prevents Windows system files and device drivers from being overwritten by faulty application installation programs or deleted by users, which prevents corruption and improves system reliability. By contrast, earlier versions of Windows did not always ask for permission before allowing an application to alter or overwrite a critical system file. Also, Windows 2000 has some new tools to help application developers build installation disks for their products and troubleshoot application problems.

Security   Windows 2000 offers better security than previous operating systems. The **NT file system** (**NTFS**) developed for Windows NT and used by Windows 2000 and Windows XP gives better security and is improved over the Windows NT version of NTFS. Windows 2000 has its own data encryption system and uses Kerberos (a security standard) to encrypt a user ID and password as the user logs on to the network from a Windows 2000 workstation.

Personalized Start Menu   Windows 2000 includes a personalized Start menu that shows only the applications used most often, so that the menus are not cluttered with applications seldom used. See Figure 1-12. The down arrows indicate that there are more applications in the list but they are hidden from view. To see these applications, briefly hold the pointer over the menu.

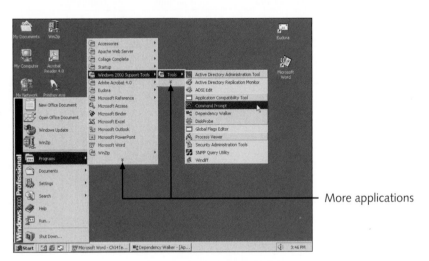

More applications

Figure 1-12   The Windows 2000 personalized Start menu does not initially show applications that are not often used

Power Use   Windows 2000 uses the **Advanced Configuration and Power Interface** (**ACPI**), which enables a computer to power down unused devices to conserve power, and gives the user much more control over power to the system. The Windows 2000 ACPI features are improved over those of Windows 98. Both require the cooperation of an ACPI-compliant motherboard. For example, on a PC with an ACPI mother-

A+
OS
1.1

board, you can set the Power Options of Windows 2000 by opening the Control Panel shown in Figure 1-13. Double-click the Power Options icon. When the Power Options Properties dialog box opens, click the Advanced tab (see Figure 1-14). From the list of power options, select what will happen when you press the power button on your computer case. For example, you can set the computer to change to Standby mode when you press the power button. On the Hibernate tab, you can also control when and how the system goes into hibernation, a state in which little power is used but open applications are restored the next time you power up.

ACPI specifications were developed by Compaq, Intel, Microsoft, Phoenix, and Toshiba to allow for reliable power management through hardware and software cooperation. For more information about ACPI, see *www.acpi.info*. You'll also learn more about ACPI later in this book.

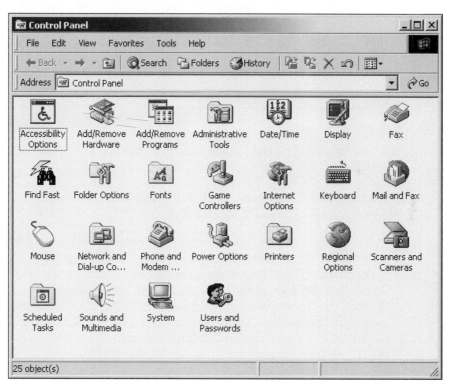

Figure 1-13   Windows 2000 Control Panel

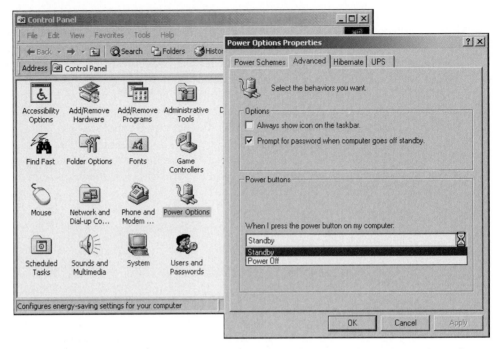

Figure 1-14   Windows 2000 offers several features to control power from the Power Options icon of
Control Panel

Added Notebook Computer Features   The following features are available for
notebook computers using Windows 2000:

- Offline Files and Folders allows you to download files and folders from a network to the computer so you can work on them offline. When the computer is
later connected to the network, the files and folders can be uploaded to the network so that any changes are kept current on the network.
- A notebook user can work from home and connect to the corporate network
over the Internet in a secure connection. To do this, Windows 2000 encrypts
data before it is transmitted over the Internet.
- The power management features of Windows 2000 are enhanced and improved
over those of Windows 98.

Table 1-7 summarizes the advantages and disadvantages of Windows 2000.

Advantages	Disadvantages
• Windows 2000 provides powerful support to a network, including advanced security for the network and the ability to organize access to network resources in a centralized location on the network called an Active Directory. • Windows 2000 is backward-compatible with all Windows NT and Windows 9x applications and most Windows 3.x and DOS applications. • Windows 2000 is really four operating systems, each targeting a different-sized computer and different computing needs, thus making the OS suite extremely versatile.	• Just as with Windows NT, Windows 2000 hardware requirements disqualify it as an option for an older, low-end PC operating system. • Windows 2000 is not scalable. Rather than having one OS that can easily handle a major computer system upgrade, the user must purchase one version of Windows 2000 for a small system and another to handle the upgraded system. • Windows 2000 is being replaced by Windows XP on the desktop and Windows 2003 Server on the server, and is therefore considered a dying OS, although it is still currently supported by Microsoft.

Table 1-7   Advantages and disadvantages of Windows 2000

Windows XP

Windows XP attempts to integrate Windows 9x and 2000, while providing added support for digital and networking technologies. The two main versions are Windows XP Home and Windows XP Professional, though other less significant editions include Windows XP Media Center Edition, Windows XP Tablet PC Edition, and Windows XP 64-bit Edition.

This book focuses on Windows XP Professional and Windows XP Home. Both editions include the following features:

- A new user interface, which is shown in Figure 1-15. Notice how different it looks from the desktops for earlier Windows versions such as Windows 9x and Windows 2000.
- The ability for two users to log on simultaneously, both with their own applications open
- Windows Media Player for Windows XP, which provides a centralized application for working with digital media
- Windows Messenger for instant messaging, conferencing, and application sharing
- An expanded Help feature
- Advanced security features

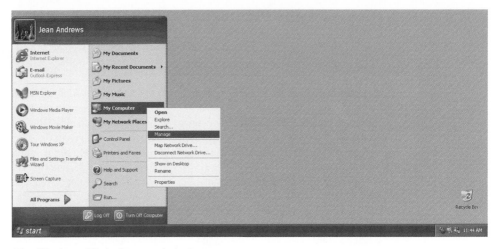

Figure 1-15   The Windows XP desktop and start menu

Here are some features that are included only with Windows XP Professional:

- Features for remote access, including remote desktop and roaming user profiles
- Additional security features
- Multilingual capabilities
- Support for new higher-performance processors

The Windows XP 64-bit Edition is designed to be used with a high-end CPU such as the Intel Itanium or the AMD Opteron. This version of Windows XP is designed mostly for servers or heavily technical workstation users who need greater amounts of memory and higher performance than standard desktop users, such as for scientific and engineering applications. For instance, an aircraft designer who needs to simulate how various conditions affect aircraft materials might use Windows XP 64-bit Edition on a system supporting resource-intensive simulation and animation applications.

Windows Internet Explorer, Windows Media Player, a firewall, and other Microsoft products are tightly integrated with the Windows XP operating system. Some users see this as a disadvantage and others see it as an advantage. Full evaluation of the integration of Microsoft software with the Windows XP operating system is beyond the scope of this overview.

NOTE

To know the Windows XP version, the CPU speed, and the amount of RAM installed on your computer, click the Start button on the Windows XP desktop and right-click My Computer. Select Properties on the shortcut menu and select the General tab.

A+
OS
1.1

The minimum requirements for Windows XP Professional are:

- A minimum of 64 MB of RAM, with 128 MB recommended
- At least 1.5 GB of free hard drive space, with 2 GB recommended
- A CPU that runs at least 233 MHz, with a 300-MHz CPU recommended. Remember that Windows XP can support two CPUs.

NOTE Remember that the requirements of an OS vary depending on which version you have installed and what applications and hardware you have installed with it.

Windows XP provides several enhancements over Windows 2000 and other earlier versions. Table 1-8 summarizes the advantages and disadvantages of Windows XP.

Advantages	Disadvantages
• Provides better integration of Windows 9x and NT than Windows 2000. • Offers significant GUI enhancements over earlier versions of Windows. • Adds features but uses only slightly more total memory for the OS than Windows 2000. • Adds advanced file sorting options, such as sorting pictures by resolution or sound files by artist. • Includes built-in support for compressed files. • Has improved troubleshooting tools and is generally more stable than previous Windows OSs.	• Requires nearly a gigabyte of hard drive space for the operating system itself, and at least a 233-MHz processor with 64 MB of RAM. • Programs used with Windows XP may require more than the minimum system specifications for the operating system. • Nearly eliminates support for device drivers not approved by Microsoft. • Security concerns with centralized storage of online information in Microsoft Passport, a repository of the user IDs and passwords you use on the Internet.

Table 1-8   Advantages and disadvantages of Windows XP

Windows XP and Previous Windows OSs

Windows XP is replacing all previous versions of Windows in the home market and for the corporate desktop. If your hardware and applications qualify, select Windows XP Home Edition for a home PC over Windows 98/Me. For a corporate environment, use Windows XP Professional over Windows NT/2000. The only exception to this is when you have compatibility issues with older hardware and software.

Other Operating Systems

✔ A+ EXAM TIP

The A+ OS exam does not cover Unix, Linux, OS/2, or the Mac OS.

As a PC technician you are likely to see a variety of operating systems on all kinds of personal computers. Windows and non-Windows operating systems share many of the same functions and goals. In this section, you will learn about Unix, Linux, OS/2, and Mac OS. Pay close attention to the advantages and disadvantages of each as well as comparisons between the technologies.

Unix

Unix originally was written for mainframe computers in the early 1970s; only in the past few years has it become available for many different kinds of computers, including PCs. It is also a popular OS for networking. Unix computers are often used for Internet support. Problems with Unix stem mostly from the lack of consistency from one vendor's version to another. Hardware requirements for Unix vary widely depending on the version—or in Unix slang, the flavor—installed.

Table 1-9 summarizes the advantages and disadvantages of the Unix OS, including comparisons of Unix and Windows.

Advantages	Disadvantages
• Unix was written for powerful microcomputer systems and has strong multiprocessing capability. • Unix manages large quantities of memory well. • Unix performs very well in a networking environment. • Unix does not require as much memory or processor time as Windows does. • Unix systems generally do not crash as frequently as Windows systems. • Design and implementation of Unix include support for remote management.	• Unix industry standards are not uniform, making it difficult for Unix developers, administrators, and users to move from one Unix vendor to another. • Unix requires a powerful, large microcomputer system. • Few business applications have been written for Unix for PCs, although several very powerful database packages are available under Unix, such as Informix and Oracle. • Unix does not automatically provide the user-friendly GUI that Windows OSs include. • Unix does not include some of the customized applications development and Web publishing features that Windows has.

Table 1-9 Advantages and disadvantages of Unix

Linux

A variation of Unix that has recently gained popularity is Linux (pronounced "Lih-nucks"), an OS created by Linus Torvalds when he was a student at the University of Helsinki in Finland. Basic versions of this OS are available for free, and all the underlying programming instructions (called source code) are also freely distributed. Like Unix, Linux is distributed by several different companies, whose versions of Linux are sometimes called **distributions**. Popular distributions of Linux include SuSE (*www.suse.com*), RedHat (*redhat.com*), Caldera (*www.caldera.com*), Mandrake (*www.linux-mandrake.com*), and TurboLinux (*www.turbolinux.com*). Linux can be used both as a server platform and a desktop platform, but its greatest popularity has come in the server market. Hardware requirements for Linux vary widely, depending on the distribution and version installed.

NOTE

For more information on Linux, see *www.linux.org* as well as the Web sites of the different distributors of Linux.

Table 1-10 summarizes the advantages and disadvantages of Linux.

Advantages	Disadvantages
• Linux rarely crashes. • Basic versions can be downloaded and installed free. • Linux distributions that include technical support and software packages are available at a lower cost than other operating systems. • Linux generally handles network connections better than Windows. • Source code is available to users, so development environments can be customized. • Linux on an inexpensive PC is an excellent training tool for learning Unix.	• Linux can be difficult to install, particularly for users who are not familiar with Unix commands. • Documentation can be spotty. • Linux can be difficult for casual users to operate. • Optimizing a Linux system can take a significant investment of time and research. • Not many applications are available for Linux on the desktop.

Table 1-10   Advantages and disadvantages of Linux

Network services such as a Web server or e-mail server often are provided by a computer running the Linux operating system. Linux is well-suited to support various types of servers. Because Linux is very reliable and does not require a lot of computing power, it is sometimes used as a desktop OS, although it is not as popular for this purpose because it is not easy to use. As a PC support technician, you should know a little about Linux, including a few basic commands, which are covered in a later chapter.

Because many users prefer a Windows-style desktop, several applications have been written to provide a GUI shell for Unix and Linux. These shells are called X Windows. A typical X Windows screen is shown in Figure 1-16.

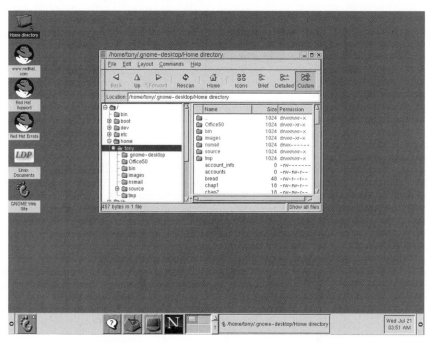

Figure 1-16 X Windows software provides a GUI shell for Linux and Unix users

OS/2

OS/2, written by IBM in cooperation with Microsoft Corporation, was designed as a replacement for DOS. OS/2 requires at least a 486 processor, 12–16 MB of RAM, and 100–300 MB of free hard drive space (depending on which features are installed). Although many airline ticketing systems, worldwide and local banks, prisons, railroad systems, and U.S. government branches use OS/2, it has never gained popularity for individual PC users. Although some people have predicted the downfall of OS/2 for years, its use continues, and applications are still being written for it. Recently, IBM adapted OS/2 for use with Web business solutions, including support for Web server software, Web protocols, and database interaction.

Table 1-11 summarizes the advantages and disadvantages of OS/2.

Advantages	Disadvantages
• OS/2 can handle large quantities of memory directly and quickly. • OS/2 runs many DOS applications better than Windows and Unix. • OS/2 has an icon-driven interface. • OS/2 works well in a networking environment. • Software designed for OS/2 sometimes runs more efficiently than comparable Windows programs.	• Relatively few applications are written for OS/2. • Many microcomputer users are not familiar with OS/2 and avoid it for that reason. • OS/2 requires a powerful computer system and large amounts of RAM and hard drive space to run efficiently.

Table 1-11　Advantages and disadvantages of OS/2

Macintosh Operating System (Mac OS)

The Mac OS is available only on Macintosh computers. Both were first introduced in 1984. Several versions of the Macintosh OS have been written since, the latest being Mac OS X (ten), which offers easy access to the Internet and allows any Macintosh computer to become a Web server for a small network. Because it is easy to use, the Mac OS has been popular in educational environments from elementary school through the university level. It also provides excellent support for graphics and multimedia applications. Mac OS X requires at least 128 MB of RAM and 1.5 GB of hard drive space.

The Mac OS X interface is significantly different from that of the Mac OS 9, including two new features called the dock and the toolbar, as shown in Figure 1-17. When a Mac is turned on, a program called the Finder is automatically launched. This is the program that provides the desktop, which functions as the GUI for the Mac OS. Generally, under normal Mac OS operation, you cannot quit the Finder program.

Windows are used to navigate among files and applications in the Mac. The Mac windows work like windows in Microsoft operating systems, in that they can be minimized or maximized, icons can be moved around within them, and the window on top is active when several are open. You can work within one window, using buttons and menu options to navigate among applications and views, or you can open each application or view in a new Finder window.

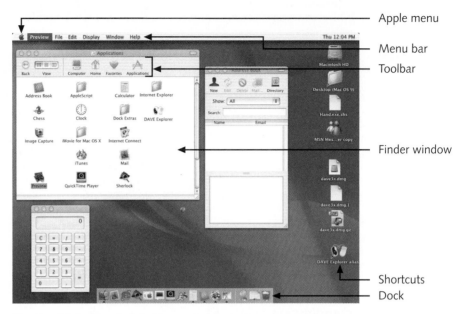

Figure 1-17   The Mac OS desktop is intuitive and easy to use

Before Apple introduced the iMac, most of the Mac OS was permanently stored in Apple ROM, and only Apple had access to that code. This prevented other companies from manufacturing computers that ran Macintosh software. With the iMac, Apple moved most of the OS code into an upgradeable file called Mac OS ROM, primarily stored on the hard drive with some startup code in a smaller ROM chip. The Mac OS X ROM file contains programs called managers that perform specific system functions like keeping track of windows, organizing menus, allocating system resources, and many others. Another important difference between Mac OS X and earlier versions is that Mac OS X provides better support for multitasking and is thus less likely to freeze when several applications are running simultaneously.

The Mac OS X tries to make user interaction with the OS as smooth and as minimal as possible by providing superior Plug and Play capabilities, so that new hardware devices can be added easily and are automatically recognized by the OS. Additionally, the Mac OS does not allow users to interact directly with the OS code as some other OSs do. This can be an advantage because the Mac OS automatically performs certain functions that the user has to perform with other OSs.

NOTE

Although the initial cost of setting up a Macintosh system is generally higher than for a comparable IBM-compatible system, the cost of support and maintenance is generally lower for the Mac.

1

Table 1-12 summarizes the advantages and disadvantages of the Mac OS.

Advantages	Disadvantages
• The Mac OS has an excellent icon-driven interface, and it is easy to learn and use. • The Mac OS has supported a GUI interface and Plug and Play devices since it was first developed. • The Mac OS manages large quantities of memory. • Many applications exist for the Mac OS to create and edit graphics, build Web sites, and manage multimedia. • Mac OS systems are generally less prone to crashing than Windows systems.	• Historically, the Macintosh was not viewed as a professional computer but rather was relegated to education and game playing. Then the Mac gained a significant place in the professional desktop publishing and graphics markets. Most recently, the availability of more powerful IBM-compatible PCs and OSs to handle the high demands of graphics has reduced the demand for the Mac. • Because IBM-compatible PCs have a larger share of the market than Macintosh computers, software compatible with the Mac OS is not always as readily available.

Table 1-12   Advantages and disadvantages of the Macintosh operating system

CHAPTER SUMMARY

▶ An operating system controls the different hardware components that make up a computer and provides an interface that a user or an application can use.

▶ Operating system functions include managing BIOS (programs permanently stored on hardware devices) and memory, interfacing between hardware and software, and performing tasks requested by the user (such as formatting disks and copying or deleting files).

▶ The two main components of an operating system are the shell and the kernel.

▶ The Windows registry and initialization files are used to store system information such as configuration settings, application settings, and user preferences.

▶ Users interact with an OS by a command-driven, menu-driven, or icon-driven interface.

▶ A thread is a process that the CPU is aware of.

▶ OSs, applications, and CPUs all operate in either 16-bit (real) mode or 32-bit (protected) mode, depending on how many bits the CPU can process at once.

▶ The most well-known OSs for microcomputers are DOS, Windows, Unix, Linux, Mac OS, and OS/2.

▶ DOS was replaced by Windows as the most popular OS, but decisions made when DOS was designed still affect Windows 9x today.

▶ Windows 95, Windows 98, and Windows Me are collectively referred to as Windows 9x.

▶ Windows 9x is a bridge between older and newer OS technologies. It can support both 16-bit and 32-bit applications.

▶ The two upgrades Microsoft released for Windows 98 are Windows 98 SE and Windows Me.

▶ Windows NT breaks with previous versions of Windows by severing the connection between Windows and DOS and not allowing applications to have direct access to system resources.

▶ Windows NT is the first fully 32-bit Windows OS. Windows 2000 and XP are also 32-bit OSs.

▶ Windows 2000 is actually a suite of operating systems: Windows 2000 Professional, Windows 2000 Server, Windows 2000 Advanced Server, and Windows 2000 Datacenter Server.

▶ Windows NT does not support Plug and Play, does not have a Safe Mode, and does not have a Device Manager. Windows 9x, Windows 2000, and Windows XP support all these.

▶ Windows XP attempts to integrate 9x and 2000, while providing added support for digital and networking technologies. The two main versions are Windows XP Home and Windows XP Professional.

▶ Unix was originally written for mainframe computers in the early 1970s. Today, it is available for other types of computers, such as servers and PCs. It is often used for Internet support.

▶ Linux is a variation of Unix that was created by Linus Torvalds. Basic versions of the OS are available for free download, and the underlying source code is openly distributed.

▶ OS/2 was written by IBM in cooperation with Microsoft and is now distributed and maintained by IBM. Systems that use OS/2 include airline ticketing systems, worldwide and local banks, and railroads. OS/2 is generally not very popular with PC users.

▶ Mac OS is available only on Macintosh computers. It has been widely used in educational markets and with graphics-intensive applications.

KEY TERMS

For explanations of key terms, see the Glossary near the end of the book.

16-bit mode
32-bit mode
Advanced Configuration and Power
    Interface (ACPI)
application program interface (API)
backward-compatible
central processing unit (CPU)
cluster
desktop
device driver

distribution
file allocation table (FAT)
graphical user interface (GUI)
hardware abstraction layer (HAL)
hardware compatibility list (HCL)
initialization file
kernel
legacy
microprocessor
multiprocessing

NTFS (NT file system)
operating system
protected mode
RAM (random access memory)
real mode
registry
sector
shell
thread
track

REVIEWING THE BASICS

1. List three well-known OSs.

2. What are the four main tasks an OS performs?

3. Name three types of user interfaces.

4. Which Microsoft operating system supports only single-tasking?

5. Which operating system was the first one used by IBM microcomputers?

6. Windows _____ used DOS as its underlying OS; Windows _____ is a true OS but bases its core functions on DOS; and Windows _____ was the first Windows version to fully sever the connection with DOS and create an altogether new OS core.

7. What is the name of the technology that allows for easy installation of hardware devices?

8. Which Windows OS uses only 16-bit processing? Some 16-bit and some 32-bit? 32-bit only?

9. A software program stored on the hard drive and designed to be used by the OS to run an input/output hardware device is called a(n) _____.

10. Windows Me is an upgrade of Windows _____.

11. Which Windows operating system does not support Plug and Play?

12. Which operating system introduced the NTFS file system?

13. What information can you find on the HCL?

14. Name the four OSs in the Windows 2000 suite.

15. What file systems used to organize a hard drive does Windows 2000 support?

16. What is the name of the Windows database used to hold configuration information?

17. Under what circumstances would Windows 98 be a better choice for a home computer user than Windows XP?

18. Name at least two advantages of Windows XP over earlier versions of Windows.

19. Name two Windows OSs that support USB ports. Name one Windows OS that does not support USB.

20. Name an Intel CPU that will work with the Windows XP 64-bit Edition.

21. In documentation, why is there sometimes a discrepancy in the hardware requirements listed for an OS?

22. What was Unix originally written for? How is it used today?

23. Which OS offers basic versions for free download and includes open access to its source code?

24. Name an OS that does not use a GUI.

25. What are two features on the Mac OS X desktop that were not present in Mac OS 9?

26. What are two popular uses for Mac OS?

THINKING CRITICALLY

1. Why does Windows NT not guarantee backward-compatibility with applications written with older Windows versions?

2. Which is a better choice for networks: Windows 9x or Windows 2000?

3. Which is the best choice for notebook computers: Windows 9x, NT, or 2000? Why?

4. Your supervisor has asked you to give him five reasons why he should upgrade the desktop OSs in your department from Windows NT to Windows XP. List your top five reasons.

HANDS-ON PROJECTS   1

PROJECT 1-1: Using the HCL

Make a list of the hardware devices installed on your computer. Check for the HCL on Microsoft's Web site (*www.microsoft.com/whdc/hcl/search.mspx*) and determine which versions of Windows you can use with the hardware you have installed. Print the results of your search of the HCL for your hardware devices. (If you are unsure what hardware devices are installed, use Device Manager. For Windows 2000 or Windows 9x, click **Start, Settings, Control Panel**, double-click the **Systems** icon, and then click the **Device Manager** tab. Installed hardware devices are listed.)

PROJECT 1-2: Comparing Interfaces

This project assumes that you are using Windows NT/2000/XP or Windows 9x. In this project, you will take screen shots of the three different types of interfaces and compare them. First, take a screen shot of your desktop, which is an example of an icon-driven interface, by completing the following steps:

1. Minimize all programs you have running so that you see your desktop with its icons showing.

2. Press the **Print Screen** key on your keyboard. (The actual label on the key may be different, depending on the keyboard you are using.) This copies an image of your screen onto the Clipboard.

3. To start the Microsoft Paint program, click **Start**, select (**All**) **Programs**, then **Accessories**, then **Paint**.

4. Click **Edit** on the menu bar, and then click **Paste**, or press the **Ctrl** key and the **V** key simultaneously (Ctrl+V) to paste the image of your screen into Paint.

5. Save the screen shot (click **Edit, Save**) with the name **icon_interface**.

6. Print the screen shot by clicking **File** on the Paint menu bar and then clicking **Print**. You now have a printed screen shot of an icon-driven interface.

7. If you have Windows 2000 or XP, click **Start**, point to (**All**) **Programs**, point to **Accessories**, and then click **Command Prompt**. If you have Windows 9x, click **Start**, point to **Programs**, and then click **MS-DOS Prompt**. Take a screen shot of the Command Prompt window using the procedure in Steps 2–4 above. Save the screen shot with the name **command_interface**, and then print it.

8. Right-click the **Start** button and select **Explore** to open Windows Explorer. Take a screen shot of Explorer using the method in Steps 2–4, save it as **menu_interface**, and then print the screen shot.

Compare the printouts of the three different types of interfaces. What are the similarities and differences among them? Besides menu-driven, what other type of interface does Windows Explorer illustrate?

PROJECT 1-3: Choosing an OS

Read the three following scenarios and determine which OS you think should be installed in each situation. Use the information given in this chapter and Web sites on the Internet to research the OSs you are considering.

A. You have two computers in your home, one running Windows 95 and one running Windows NT, and you are installing a third computer. The computers in your home have not previously been networked, and you intend to network them when you install the third one. You would like to be able to use the programs you already have installed as well as newer programs, and you want to be able to install new hardware devices easily. Which OS should you choose for the new computer? Will you keep the present OSs on the existing computers?

B. You have been asked to set up the computer for the new graphic artist at your company, who is an expert using Adobe PageMaker (*www.adobe.com*) on a Macintosh computer. In addition to running this graphics software, the new employee will need to use the same software programs as the other members of the office, including Microsoft Office (*www.microsoft.com*). Which OS would you choose for this person?

C. You are setting up a new network for a small business that has about 20 employees, and you are planning to install the same OS on everyone's computer. You need a highly efficient network that can process information quickly and can work well with the company's extensive database of customer and product information. Which OS will you choose for each personal computer on the network?

Discuss your choices for scenarios A, B, and C with your instructor and classmates, including the following questions:

1. Which OS did you choose, and why?

2. What are the advantages and disadvantages of your choice?

3. What other OSs could you have chosen for the same scenario, and how would that have changed the situation?

4. Other than the information in the chapter, what additional information do you want to know before you feel confident you can make a good decision?

PROJECT 1-4:   Researching on the Internet: Windows Updates

Visit Microsoft's Windows Web site at *www.microsoft.com/windows*. Which versions of Windows are considered current, and which are listed as previous versions? Are there any mentioned in this chapter that are not listed? Make a list of the Windows versions and their status, making use of the links on the Windows site as necessary.

CASE PROJECT

Determining Your Operating System

In the case projects in this book, you will install and uninstall several different operating systems. First, you need to determine what operating system you currently have installed. For Windows, right-click the **My Computer** icon on the desktop and then choose **Properties** on the shortcut menu. The System Properties dialog box opens, showing the OS and version.

Whenever you are installing, uninstalling, or reconfiguring hardware or software, it is a good idea to keep detailed notes of what you are doing in case you need to backtrack. This information can also be useful for troubleshooting and technical support. You will be keeping a notebook for the Case Projects throughout this book. As your first entry in the notebook, write down the information shown on the General tab of the System Properties dialog box about the system that is installed on your computer.

NOTE

This project assumes that you are beginning with a computer that has Windows 95 or later installed. If you are beginning with a blank PC, make an initial entry in your notebook about the specifications of the OS you are planning to install, such as the OS and version, the minimum hardware requirements for it, and the hardware you have in the system on which you will be installing the OS.

How an OS Works with Hardware and Other Software

In the last chapter you were introduced to many different operating systems used on personal computers. In this chapter, you'll go behind the scenes to see how these operating systems relate to the hardware they manage and the applications they support. You'll see how an OS controls several of the more significant hardware devices using the resources made available to it for interaction with these devices. You'll also see how an OS serves an application, providing the interface the application needs to command and use hardware devices. The chapter begins by introducing the more significant hardware devices that you need to be aware of. If you are already familiar with hardware, you can skip this first section.

Introducing Hardware

It's difficult to understand what an operating system does unless you know something about computer hardware, so first, you'll learn about several hardware components common to most systems.

Ports Used by External Devices

The major components in a computer system are housed inside the computer case and are called internal devices. Figure 2-1 shows a computer case with the side panel removed and the major parts labeled. Some devices, such as a keyboard, mouse, printer, and speakers, are called external devices and reside outside the case. All external and internal devices must connect to the central processing unit (CPU) inside the case. External devices connect to the case by way of a port on the back or front of the computer case.

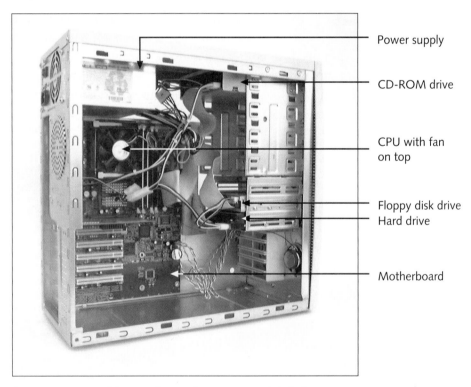

Power supply

CD-ROM drive

CPU with fan on top

Floppy disk drive
Hard drive

Motherboard

Figure 2-1   A computer case with some internal components labeled

Figure 2-2 shows the ports provided to the outside of another computer case: mouse port, keyboard port, USB port, parallel port, serial port, video port, network port, microphone port, phone line port, and speaker port. With a **serial port**, data travels serially (one bit follows the next). This port is often used for an external modem or serial mouse (a mouse that uses a serial port). A **parallel port** carries data in parallel and is most often used by a printer. A **universal serial bus (USB) port** is a newer port used by many input/output devices such as a keyboard, printer, scanner, or mouse. In later chapters, you'll learn how the OS configures and manages each of these ports and the devices that use them.

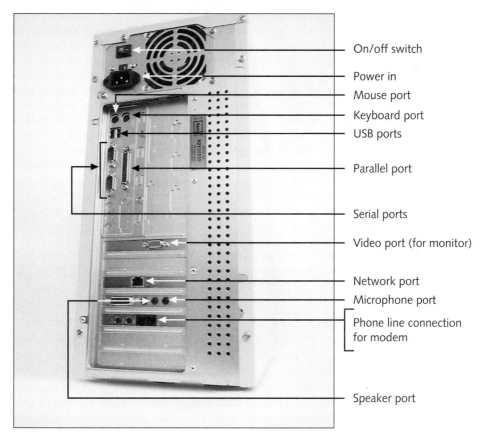

On/off switch
Power in
Mouse port
Keyboard port
USB ports
Parallel port
Serial ports
Video port (for monitor)
Network port
Microphone port
Phone line connection for modem
Speaker port

Figure 2-2 Input/output devices connect to the computer case by ports usually found on the back of the case

The **motherboard**, shown in Figure 2-3, is the largest circuit board inside a computer case and is also the most complex. Because the CPU is central to all hardware and software operations, all devices must somehow connect to the CPU, and they all do this by way of the motherboard. The motherboard provides ports for some external devices and slots for inserting expansion cards that also provide ports.

For example, a video card is inserted in a slot on the motherboard and provides a video port to which the monitor connects.

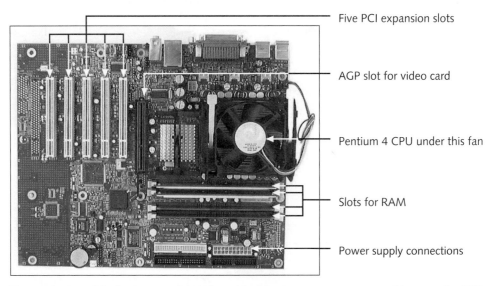

Five PCI expansion slots

AGP slot for video card

Pentium 4 CPU under this fan

Slots for RAM

Power supply connections

Figure 2-3   The motherboard is the largest circuit board inside the computer case and houses the CPU

Listed below are the major components found on all motherboards, some of which are labeled in Figure 2-3 and are discussed in detail in the sections that follow.

- CPU, the computer's most important chip
- Random access memory (RAM) used to temporarily hold data and instructions as they are processed
- Traces or wires on the motherboard used for communication
- Expansion slots to connect expansion cards to the motherboard
- Connectors for drives (for example, hard drive, floppy disk drive, CD-ROM drive)
- ROM BIOS memory chip used to permanently store instructions that control basic hardware functions (explained in detail later in the chapter)
- CMOS (complementary metal oxide semiconductor) configuration chip (also explained later in the chapter)
- Power supply connections to provide electricity to the motherboard and expansion cards

The CPU

The CPU is central to all processing done by a computer. Every command from the OS is passed to the CPU, which controls all the hardware components in the computer. The CPU is installed in a slot or socket on the motherboard (refer back to

2

Figure 2-3). All CPUs today operate in one of two modes: 16-bit or 32-bit, which are sometimes called real mode and protected mode. There are several differences between these two modes, but fundamentally, 16-bit mode, or **real mode**, means that the CPU processes 16 bits of data at one time, and in 32-bit mode, or **protected mode**, it processes 32 bits at a time.

NOTE

Several newer CPUs, such as the Intel Itanium and the AMD Opteron, operate in 64-bit mode. Windows XP 64-bit Edition is designed to use this type of CPU.

The speed of a CPU is partly determined by how much data it can process at one time and how much data it can send or receive at one time. Every CPU has lines coming to it that are embedded on the motherboard, collectively called a **bus** (see Figure 2-4). These lines are devoted to different purposes. Some lines on the bus are designated to carry data—they are called the **data bus** or **data path**. Early CPUs used a 16-bit data path and processed 16 bits at one time. Today's CPUs can use one size for the data path but another for internal processing. For example, the Pentium CPUs use a 64-bit data path coming to and going from the CPU, but internally they process 32 bits at a time. Other lines on a bus are used for addresses, control signals, and voltage.

Bus lines

Bottom of the CPU socket

Figure 2-4   On the bottom of the motherboard, you can see bus lines ending at the CPU socket

Memory or RAM

Recall from Chapter 1 that RAM is microchips used to temporarily hold data and instructions while the CPU processes both. These microchips are stored on tiny circuit boards called memory modules. Memory modules can be SIMMs, DIMMs, or RIMMs. The most common module for today's motherboards is a DIMM. A memory module is installed in memory slots on the motherboard designed to hold a particular type and speed of module.

Using Windows XP, you can see what type of CPU and how much memory you have installed. Click Start, right-click My Computer, select Properties on the shortcut menu, and click the General tab (see Figure 2-5). Also shown is the version of Windows you are using. (For Windows 2000 and Windows 9x, right-click the My Computer icon on your desktop.)

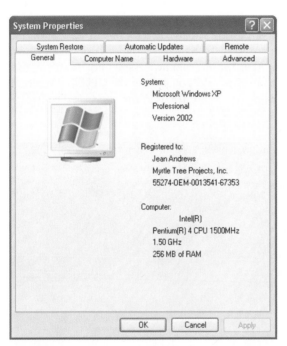

Figure 2-5   Use the System Properties dialog box to see how much memory is installed

Memory is useless to the system until it has been assigned addresses that the operating system, device drivers, and BIOS can use to communicate with it. These **memory addresses** are numbers that are assigned to each usable cell of memory, and the assignments are normally done when the OS is first loaded. How memory addresses are assigned and used is covered later in the chapter.

Buses on the Motherboard

All hardware devices are directly or indirectly connected to the motherboard because they are all dependent on the CPU on the motherboard for processing their data. Each bus provides a way for devices to connect to it and, ultimately, to the CPU. Sometimes a bus provides a port on the outside of the computer case for an external device to connect to by way of a cable or cord, or the bus might provide a slot on the motherboard into which a circuit board fits. In any case, a device always connects to a single bus on the motherboard. A motherboard can have several different buses; each type of bus has data lines, address lines, and control lines. An operating system relates to the bus, so the OS must support it in order for it to be used by the system.

Some common buses and the expansion slots they support are listed and described here:

- The first motherboards of the 1980s had only one bus, the **system bus,** which supported several **Industry Standard Architecture (ISA)** slots. The first ISA slot had only eight lines for data and was called the 8-bit ISA slot. It had 20 address lines and ran at 4.77 MHz, which means that data was transferred on the bus at a rate of 4,770,000 transfers per second. Today's system buses run up to 800 MHz, and have a 64-bit wide data path and at least a 36-bit wide address path. These system buses, sometimes called **memory buses, front-side buses,** or **local buses,** always connect directly to the CPU and memory, but are much too fast to support the slow ISA slots, which connect to the system bus by way of slower I/O buses that act as middlemen.

- Later, the 8-bit ISA slot was improved by adding 8 lines for data, and this version is known as the 16-bit ISA slot. This slot runs at 8.33 MHz and has 24 lines for the address bus. All operating systems for personal computers today support the 16-bit ISA slot although newer motherboards don't have them because they are slow and difficult to support.

- The **Peripheral Component Interconnect (PCI) bus** was invented for devices that are faster than the 16-bit ISA bus but can't run as fast as the system bus between memory and the CPU. The PCI bus runs in sync with the system bus at one-third or one-half the speed. All Windows OSs support PCI.

- The **Accelerated Graphics Port (AGP) bus** was designed to accommodate a fast video card, which is a circuit board that controls the monitor. Windows 2000/XP and Windows 9x support AGP. A motherboard has only a single AGP slot to accommodate one monitor. Figure 2-6 shows a video card installed in an AGP slot. You can also see five PCI slots in the figure.

- The USB bus is designed to support ports off the motherboard for slower external devices such as a mouse, keyboard, scanner, video camera, or digital telephone. You saw two USB ports on the back of a computer case in Figure 2-2. The USB bus supports up to 127 devices, which can be daisy-chained together and connected to a single USB port on a motherboard. Windows 95 with the USB update, Windows 98/Me, and Windows 2000/XP support USB.

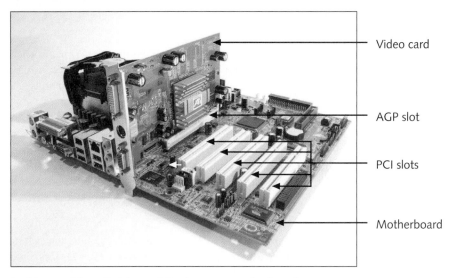

Figure 2-6   A video card installed in an AGP slot on a motherboard

- FireWire, sometimes called IEEE 1394 or simply 1394, is a very fast bus designed to connect fast external devices to a port off the motherboard called a FireWire or 1394 port. The bus was designed by the Institute of Electrical and Electronic Engineers (IEEE), led primarily by Apple Computer, which named the bus FireWire. Windows NT/2000/XP and Windows 98/Me support FireWire.

BIOS on the Motherboard and Other Circuit Boards

Some very basic instructions and data are stored on the motherboard—just enough to provide rudimentary information about the setup of the computer, to start the computer, search for an operating system stored on the system, and manage simple devices such as the floppy disk drive and keyboard. These instructions to start the computer and manage some devices are stored on special ROM (read-only memory) chips on the motherboard and are called the **basic input/output system (BIOS)**. The BIOS that the OS uses to manage simple devices is called **system BIOS** and the BIOS that is used to start the computer is called **startup BIOS**. The BIOS might support three technologies, depending on when and who manufactured the BIOS: Advanced Configuration and Power Interface (ACPI), Advanced Power Management (APM), and Plug and Play (PnP).

Advanced Configuration and Power Interface (ACPI)

Some BIOSs on the motherboard and operating systems support a power-saving feature using the standards developed by Intel, Microsoft, and Toshiba called the Advanced Configuration and Power Interface (ACPI) standards. Using ACPI, a system can be powered up by an external device such as a keyboard. Windows

2

2000/XP and Windows 9x support ACPI, as do most recent motherboard BIOS. Microsoft calls an ACPI-compliant BIOS a "good" BIOS. To see if your BIOS is ACPI compliant, check this Microsoft URL:
www.microsoft.com/windows2000/professional/howtobuy/upgrading/compat
An older BIOS power management standard is Advanced Power Management (APM) that is also supported by Windows 9x and Windows 2000/XP.

Plug and Play

Another feature of both the BIOS and the OS is **Plug and Play (PnP)**, a standard designed to make the installation of new hardware devices easier (see Figure 2-7). If the BIOS is a Plug and Play BIOS, it will begin the process of configuring hardware devices in the system. It gathers information about the devices and then passes that information to the operating system. If the operating system is also Plug and Play compliant, it will use that information to complete the hardware configuration process.

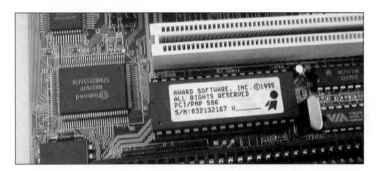

Figure 2-7   Plug and Play BIOS is found on most motherboards built after 1994

Windows 9x and Windows 2000/XP support Plug and Play, but Windows NT does not. However, Windows 2000/XP Plug and Play is more advanced than the Windows 9x version and does not use the startup BIOS to help with Plug and Play configurations, preferring to gather its own information about hardware. In fact, Microsoft suggests that you disable the Plug and Play features of your BIOS when using Windows 2000/XP.

Extended system configuration data (ESCD) Plug and Play BIOS is an enhanced version of Plug and Play that creates a list of all the things you have done manually to the configuration that Plug and Play does not do on its own. This ESCD list is written to the BIOS chip so that the next time you boot, the startup BIOS can faithfully relay that information to Windows. Windows 9x benefits from this information, but it is not important to Windows 2000/XP. The BIOS chip for ESCD BIOS is a special RAM chip called Permanent RAM, or PRAM, that can hold data written to it without the benefit of a battery, which the CMOS setup chip requires.

S Setup Chip

Another chip on the motherboard, called the **CMOS configuration chip, CMOS setup chip**, or **CMOS RAM chip**, contains a very small amount of memory, or RAM, enough to hold configuration or setup information about the computer. This chip is responsible for remembering the current date and time, which hard drives and floppy drives are present, how the serial and parallel ports are configured, and so forth. When the computer is first turned on, it looks to this CMOS chip to find out what hardware it should expect to find. The CMOS chip is powered by a trickle of electricity from a small battery located on the motherboard or computer case, usually close to the CMOS chip itself so that when the computer is turned off, the CMOS chip still retains its data.

The program to change CMOS setup is stored in the ROM BIOS chip and can be accessed during the startup process. The keystrokes to enter CMOS setup are displayed somewhere on the screen during startup in a statement such as "Press the Del key to enter setup." Different BIOSs use different keystrokes. The CMOS setup does not normally need to be changed except, for example when there is a problem with hardware, a new floppy drive is installed, or a power-saving feature needs to be disabled or enabled. The CMOS setup can also hold one or two power-on passwords to help secure a system. Know that these passwords are not the same passwords that can be required by a Windows OS at startup.

APPLYING CONCEPTS

Reboot your PC and look for the message on the first or second display screen that tells you how to enter CMOS setup. Press that key. What version of BIOS are you using? Exit setup without making any changes. The system should reboot to the Windows desktop.

Hard Drives and Other Secondary Storage Devices

A hard drive is an example of a **secondary storage** device, which is a device that can hold data and instructions, but the data and instructions can only be stored there and not processed there by the CPU. Before the instructions can be processed, they must be copied from a secondary storage device to a **primary storage** device, which is memory. In other words, you store files that contain data and programs on a hard drive, but to use these data and programs, they must be copied into memory. You'll learn more about this process later in the chapter.

Another difference between secondary and primary storage devices is that secondary devices hold data permanently, and primary devices hold data temporarily. What is stored on your hard drive remains there even when the PC is turned off, but what is stored in memory is lost as soon as you turn off your PC. Some secondary storage devices are hard drives, floppy disk drives, CD drives, DVD drives, and Zip drives. Figure 2-8 shows a hard drive subsystem.

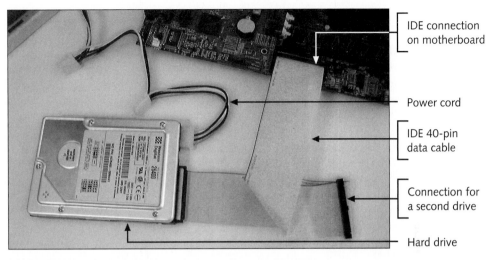

IDE connection
on motherboard

Power cord

IDE 40-pin
data cable

Connection for
a second drive

Hard drive

Figure 2-8   A PC's hard drive subsystem

Most motherboards offer two **Enhanced Integrated Drive Electronics (EIDE)** connections. **Integrated Drive Electronics (IDE)** is a group of standards that governs how a hard drive works, and EIDE is a group of standards that governs how a secondary storage device such as a hard drive, CD-ROM drive, or Zip drive can interface with a system. The computer industry most often uses the term IDE for both IDE and EIDE. The connections for the two IDE channels on the motherboard are called the primary and secondary channels. Each cable or channel can accommodate two IDE devices, such as a hard drive and a CD-ROM drive, for a total of four IDE devices in one system. Power to the hard drive comes through a power cable from the PC's power supply.

Now that you are familiar with some important hardware devices, you can turn your attention to what an operating system does and how it relates to users, applications, and hardware devices.

How an Operating System Works

Recall that an OS manages hardware, provides a user interface, manages applications, and manages files and folders. In Chapter 1, you saw the three kinds of interfaces an OS provides a user: command-driven, menu-driven, and icon-driven. This section focuses on the three other functions of an operating system.

An OS Manages Files and Folders

A+
OS
1.1
1.4

Recall from Chapter 1 that an operating system is responsible for storing the files and folders on a secondary storage device such as a CD, floppy disk, or hard drive using organizational methods called a file system. Windows uses several different file systems; the most popular are FAT and NTFS. The FAT file system is named after the file allocation table (FAT), a table on a hard drive or floppy disk that tracks the locations of files on a disk. The most recent version of FAT, FAT32, is a more efficient method of organization for large hard drives than FAT16 (the earlier version). The New Technology file system (NTFS) is supported by Windows NT/2000/XP and is designed to be used on hard drives to provide greater security than does the FAT file system.

✔ A+ EXAM TIP

The A+ OS exam expects you to know all the key terms in this section.

A floppy disk or hard drive is composed of **tracks**, which are concentric circles on the disk surface, shown in Figure 2-9. Each track is divided into several segments, each called a **sector**. A **cluster**, the smallest unit of space on a disk for storing data, is made up of one or more sectors. A file system, either FAT or NTFS, tracks how these clusters are used for each file stored on the disk.

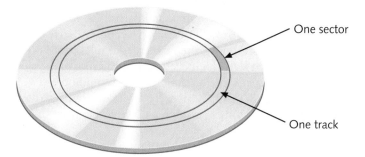

One sector

One track

Figure 2-9   A hard drive or floppy disk is divided into tracks and sectors. Several sectors make one cluster.

Files and Directories

Regardless of the file system used, every OS manages a hard drive by using directories (Windows calls these folders), subdirectories, and files. A **directory table** is a list of files and subdirectories. When a hard drive is first installed and formatted, there is a single directory table on the drive called the **root directory**. For logical drive C, the root directory is written as C:\.

NOTE

A physical hard drive can be divided into logical drives, sometimes called volumes, such as drive C or drive D. You will learn more about logical drives and volumes in Chapter 3.

2

As shown in Figure 2-10, this root directory can hold files or other directories, which can have names such as C:\Tools. These directories, called **subdirectories, child directories,** or **folders,** can, in turn, have other directories listed in them. Any directory can have files and other directories listed in it, for example, C:\wp\data \myfile.txt in Figure 2-10. The C: identifies the logical drive. If a directory is on a floppy disk, either A: or B: identifies it. When you refer to the drive and directories pointing to the location of the file, as in C:\wp\data\myfile.txt, the drive and directories are called the **path** to the file. The first part of the file before the period is called the **filename** (myfile), and the part after the period is called the **file extension** (txt), which, for Windows and DOS, always has three characters or fewer. The file extension identifies the file type, such as .doc for Microsoft Word document files or .xls for Microsoft Excel spreadsheet files.

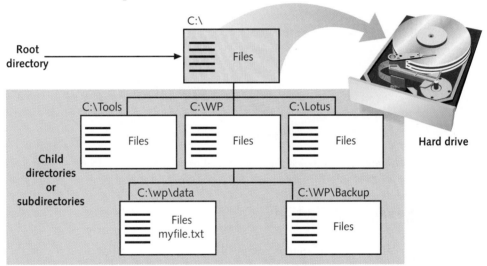

Figure 2-10   A hard drive is organized into groups of files stored in directories. The first directory is called the root directory. All directories can have sub- or child directories. Under Windows, a directory is called a folder.

Partitions and Logical Drives on a Hard Drive

A hard drive is divided into one or more **partitions.** A partition can be a primary partition or an extended partition (see Figure 2-11). A primary partition can have one logical drive, and an extended partition can have one or more logical drives. Most hard drives have one primary partition containing one logical drive called drive C: and one extended partition that can have one or more logical drives such as drive D: and drive E:. Each **logical drive,** sometimes called a **volume,** is formatted using its own file system. For example, if a hard drive is divided into two logical drives, drive C: might be formatted using the FAT32 file system, and drive D: might use the NTFS file system. Each logical drive has its own root directory and subdirectories.

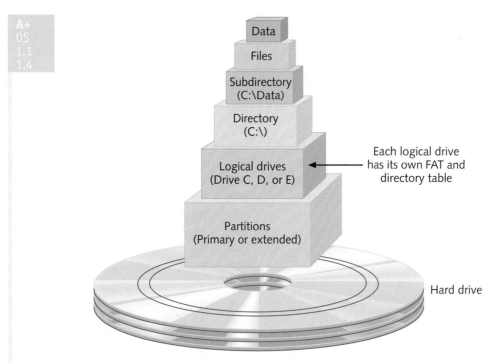

Figure 2-11   A hard drive is divided and organized at several levels

An OS Manages Applications

An operating system is responsible for managing all other software on the PC, including installing and running applications. An application depends on an OS to provide access to hardware resources, manage its data in memory and in secondary storage, and perform many other background tasks. For example, consider a situation in which Windows XP loads and executes an application. The application cannot run or even load itself without Windows XP, much as a document cannot be edited without a word-processing program. Windows XP stays available to the application for the entire time the application is running. The application passes certain functions to Windows XP, such as reading from a CD-ROM or printing.

An application written to work with one OS, such as Windows XP, does not necessarily work with another, such as a Macintosh system, with some exceptions. For instance, Windows 9x is written so that any application designed to work with DOS or Windows 3.x also works with Windows 9x, an early selling point for Windows 9x. However, to take full advantage of an operating system's power and an application's power, buy application software written specifically for your OS.

Application software is downloaded from the Internet or comes written on CD-ROMs or floppy disks; usually it must be installed on a hard drive in order to run. During the installation, the install program creates folders on the hard drive and

2

copies files to them. For Windows, it also makes entries in the Windows registry, and it can place icons on the desktop and add entries to the Start menu. Because the install program does all the work for you, installing software usually is very easy. (Installing software is covered in later chapters.)

Loading Application Software Using the Windows Desktop

Once an application is installed, Windows NT/2000/XP and Windows 9x offer four ways to execute, or load, software.

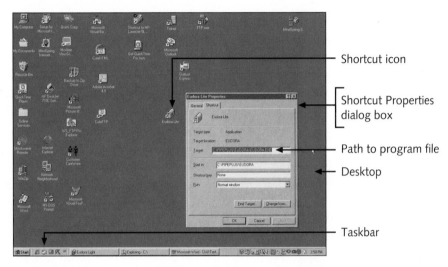

Shortcut icon

Shortcut Properties dialog box

Path to program file

Desktop

Taskbar

Figure 2-12   Windows has icons on the desktop that point to program files on the hard drive

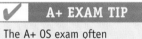
A+ EXAM TIP

The A+ OS exam often expects you to know more than one way to do something. Knowing the four ways to load an application is a good example.

- *Use a shortcut icon:* Place a shortcut icon directly on the desktop for the applications you use often and want to get to quickly. These shortcuts contain the command line used to execute the application. To view this command line, right-click an application icon on the desktop to open a shortcut menu. On the shortcut menu, select Properties. The icon's Properties dialog box appears (see Figure 2-12). In this dialog box, you can view the complete command line that the icon represents. Chapter 4 explains how to create shortcuts for Windows.
- *Use the Start menu:* Click the Start button, select Programs (or All Programs in Windows XP), and then select the program from the list of installed software.
- *Use the Run command:* Click the Start button, and then click Run to display the Run dialog box (see Figure 2-13). In this dialog box, enter a command line or click Browse to search for a program file to execute.
- *Use Windows Explorer or My Computer:* Execute a program or launch an application file by double-clicking the filename in Windows Explorer or My Computer.

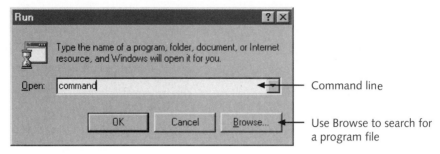

— Command line

— Use Browse to search for a program file

Figure 2-13   The Windows Run dialog box allows you to enter DOS-like commands

Real (16-Bit) and Protected (32-Bit) Operating Modes

Recall that the CPU operates in two modes: 16-bit or 32-bit, which are called real mode and protected mode. In real mode, an application has complete access to all hardware resources, but in protected mode, the OS controls how an application can access hardware. In protected mode, more than one program can run at the same time, which is a type of multitasking. In protected mode, the OS provides to each program a limited and controlled access to hardware resources. Here lies the meaning behind the two terms, real and protected. Real mode means that the software has "real" access to the hardware; protected mode means that more than one program can be running, and each one is "protected" from other programs accessing its hardware resources.

APPLYING CONCEPTS

Practice the last three ways listed to load an application. Use Microsoft Paint as your sample application. The program file is Mspaint.exe. Execute the application by using the Start menu, using the Run dialog box, and using Windows Explorer.

Even after protected mode became available, hardware and software needed to be backward compatible (able to support older technology), so today's CPUs and operating systems still support real mode. In fact, the CPU starts in real mode and must be told to switch to protected mode. For this reason, an OS starts in real mode and commands the CPU to switch to protected mode before allowing user interaction or loading an application. DOS and the MS-DOS mode of Windows 9x operate in real mode. Windows 9x and Windows NT/2000/XP start in real mode and then switch to protected mode. In protected mode, the OS allots CPU time to an application for a specified period and then preempts the processing to give the CPU to another application, in a process called **preemptive multitasking**. The result is that the computer appears to be multitasking when it really is not. Windows 95 was the first version of Windows to provide preemptive multitasking.

16-Bit and 32-Bit Software   Applications and device drivers written for
Windows 3.x are called 16-bit Windows software. Data access is 16 bits at a time, and
each program is written so that it should not infringe on the resources of other applications that might be running. Software programs written for Windows 95 and later
Windows OSs are called 32-bit drivers or 32-bit applications.

Nearly all applications and device drivers written today are 32-bit, although 16-bit
software still exists, and you must know how to support it in a Windows environment. You will learn more about supporting 16-bit applications and drivers in
Chapter 5.

An OS Manages Hardware

An operating system is responsible for communicating with hardware, but the OS
does not relate directly to the hardware. Rather, the OS uses device drivers or the
BIOS to interface with hardware. Figure 2-14 shows these relationships. Therefore,
most PC software falls into three categories:

- Device drivers or the BIOS
- Operating system
- Application software

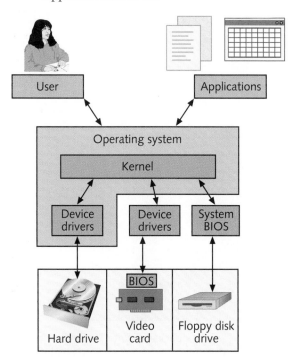

Figure 2-14   An OS relates to hardware by way of BIOS or device drivers

Recall that device drivers are small programs stored on the hard drive that tell the computer how to communicate with a hardware device such as a printer, network card, or modem. These drivers are installed on the hard drive when the device is first installed. The BIOS on the motherboard is hard-coded, or permanently coded, into a computer chip called the ROM BIOS chip. Next you look at how an OS uses device drivers and the BIOS to manage hardware.

How an OS Uses Device Drivers

Device drivers are designed to interface with specific hardware devices. They are stored on the hard drive and installed when the OS is first installed or when new hardware is added to a system. The OS provides some device drivers, and the manufacturer of the specific hardware device with which they are designed to interface provides others. In either case, unlike BIOS, device drivers are usually written for a particular OS and might need to be rewritten for use with another.

When you purchase a printer, DVD drive, Zip drive, digital camera, scanner, or other hardware device, bundled with the device is a set of floppy disks or CDs that contain the device drivers (see Figure 2-15). You must install these device drivers under the operating system so it will have the necessary software to control the device. In most cases, you install the device and then install the device drivers. There are a few exceptions, such as a digital camera using a USB port to download pictures. In this case, you install the software to drive the digital camera before you plug in the camera. See the device documentation to learn what to do first. Later chapters cover device driver installations.

Figure 2-15   A device such as this CD-ROM drive comes packaged with its device drivers stored on a floppy disk or other media. Alternately, you can use device drivers built into the OS.

Device drivers come from a number of sources. Some come with and are part of the operating system, some come with hardware devices when they are purchased, and some are provided for downloading over the Internet from a device manufacturer's Web site.

2

There are two kinds of device drivers: 16-bit real-mode drivers and 32-bit protected-mode drivers. Windows 95 and Windows 98 support both, but Windows Me and Windows NT/2000/XP use only 32-bit drivers. Windows 9x and Windows 2000/XP provide hundreds of 32-bit drivers for many different kinds of devices, and device manufacturers also provide their own 16- or 32-bit drivers, which come bundled with the device or can be downloaded from the device manufacturer's Web site.

Device Drivers Under Windows 2000/XP   Before installing a new hardware device on a Windows 2000/XP system, always check the **hardware compatibility list** (**HCL**) to determine if a driver will work under Windows 2000/XP. Go to this Microsoft Web site and search for your device:

www.microsoft.com/whdc/hcl/search.mspx

If the device does not install properly or produces errors, check the manufacturer's Web site for a driver that the manufacturer says is compatible with Windows 2000/XP. Once installed, Windows 2000/XP and Windows 9x keep information about 32-bit drivers in the Windows registry.

Sometimes, to address bugs, make improvements, or add features, manufacturers release device drivers that are more recent than those included with Windows or bundled with the device. Whenever possible, it is best to use the latest driver available for a device provided by the device manufacturer. You can usually download these updated drivers from the manufacturer's Web site. You will learn how to install, update, and troubleshoot drivers in later chapters.

APPLYING CONCEPTS

Suppose you have just borrowed a HP 995c Deskjet printer from a friend, but you forgot to borrow the CD with the printer drivers on it. You could go to the Hewlett-Packard Web site (*www.hp.com*), download the drivers to a folder on your PC, and install the drivers under Windows. Figure 2-16 shows you a Web page from the site listing downloadable drivers for ink-jet printers. Search the HP site and find the driver for your borrowed HP 995c printer.

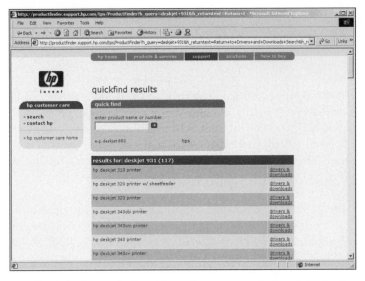

Figure 2-16   Download the latest device drivers from a manufacturer's Web site

Device Drivers Under Windows 9x   Windows 9x comes with 32-bit drivers for hundreds of hardware devices. However, Windows does not provide drivers for all older devices, so a system might sometimes need to use an older 16-bit real-mode device driver. These 16-bit drivers are loaded by entries in the **Config.sys, Autoexec.bat,** and **System.ini** files, text files used to configure DOS and Windows 3.x that Windows 9x supports for backward compatibility. In Chapter 4, you will learn how to install 32-bit and 16-bit drivers under Windows 9x.

Under DOS, a program, such as a device driver that stays in memory until the CPU needs it, is called a **terminate-and-stay-resident (TSR)** program. The term is seldom used today, except when talking about real-mode programs.

How an OS Uses System BIOS to Manage Devices

The OS communicates with simple devices, such as floppy drives or keyboards, through system BIOS. In addition, system BIOS can be used to access the hard drive. In the case of the hard drive, an OS has a choice of using system BIOS or device drivers. Most often it uses device drivers because they are faster. The trend today is to use device drivers rather than the BIOS to manage devices.

There is a good way to determine whether the BIOS or a device driver is controlling a device. If the device is configured using CMOS setup, most likely system BIOS controls it. If the device is configured using the OS, most likely a driver controls it. Sometimes you can use the Windows System Information or Device Manager utilities to find out the name of a driver controlling a device.

For example, in Figure 2-17, the setup main menu for an Award BIOS system lets you configure, or set, the system date and time, the Supervisor Password (power-on password), floppy disk drives, the hard drive, and the keyboard. Figure 2-18 shows another setup window for this same BIOS that can configure serial ports, an infrared port, and a parallel port. System BIOS can control all these devices. On the other hand, there is no setup window in this BIOS to control the DVD drive or Zip drive installed on this system. The BIOS is not aware of these devices; this means they are controlled by device drivers.

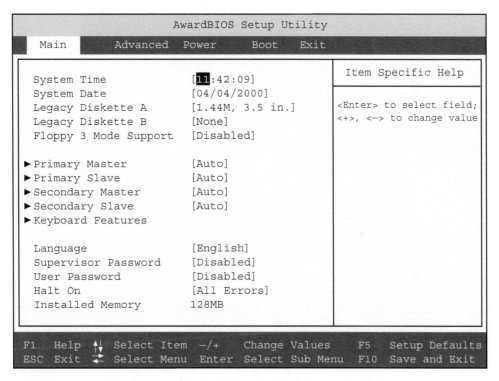

Figure 2-17   Use the BIOS setup main menu for Award BIOS to configure some of the devices controlled by system BIOS

NOTE   Recall that you can access CMOS setup windows during startup, when a system displays a message at the bottom of the screen saying something like, "Press Del to enter setup." Pressing the indicated key launches a program stored on the ROM BIOS microchip to change the contents of CMOS RAM. This BIOS setup program provides windows like those in Figures 2-17 and 2-18.

An OS uses BIOS or device drivers to manage hardware devices. The BIOS or driver communicates with a device by way of system resources on the motherboard. You next look at these resources and how they work.

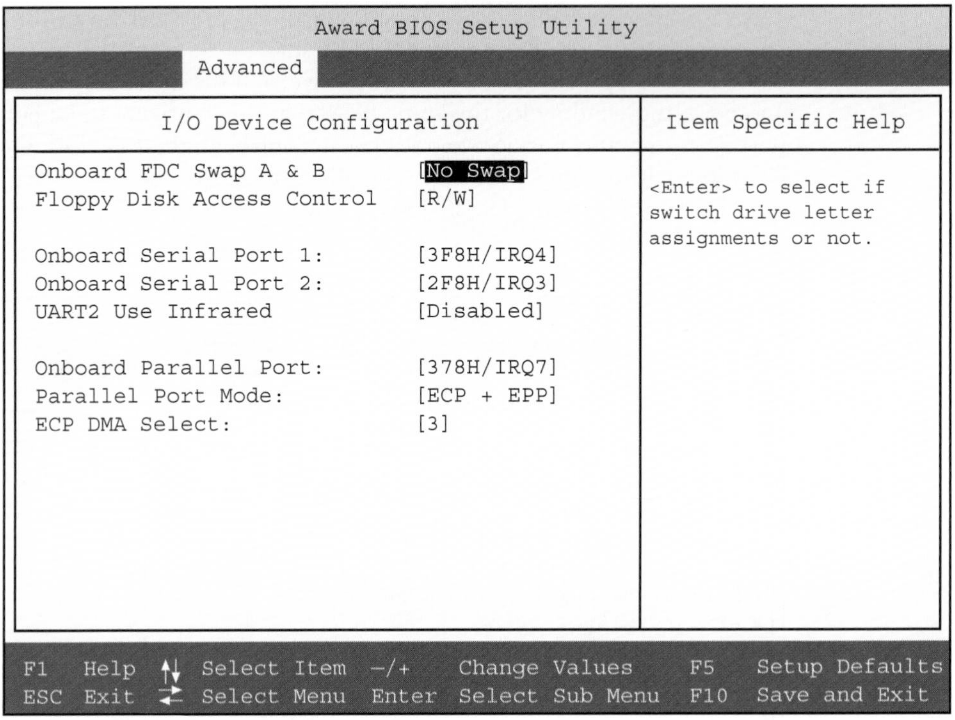

```
                        Award BIOS Setup Utility
            Advanced

           I/O Device Configuration              Item Specific Help

Onboard FDC Swap A & B          [No Swap]
Floppy Disk Access Control      [R/W]           <Enter> to select if
                                                switch drive letter
                                                assignments or not.
Onboard Serial Port 1:          [3F8H/IRQ4]
Onboard Serial Port 2:          [2F8H/IRQ3]
UART2 Use Infrared              [Disabled]

Onboard Parallel Port:          [378H/IRQ7]
Parallel Port Mode:             [ECP + EPP]
ECP DMA Select:                 [3]




F1   Help  ↑↓  Select Item   −/+   Change Values    F5   Setup Defaults
ESC  Exit  ⇄   Select Menu  Enter  Select Sub Menu  F10  Save and Exit
```

Figure 2-18   Use this Award BIOS setup window to configure several I/O devices, including the serial, parallel, and infrared ports

BIOS and Device Drivers Use System Resources

A **system resource** is a tool used by either hardware or software to communicate with the other. When the BIOS or a driver wants to send data to a device (such as when you save a file to the hard drive), or when the device needs attention (such as when you press a key on the keyboard), the device or software uses system resources to communicate. There are four types of system resources: **interrupt request (IRQs) numbers, I/O addresses,** memory addresses, and **direct memory access (DMA) channels.** Table 2-1 lists these system resources used by software and hardware and defines each.

As Table 2-1 explains, all four resources are used for communication between hardware and software. Hardware devices signal the CPU for attention using an IRQ. Software addresses a device by one of its I/O addresses. Software looks at memory as a hardware device and addresses it with memory addresses, and DMA channels pass data back and forth between a hardware device and memory.

System Resource	Definition
IRQ	A line of a motherboard bus that a hardware device can use to signal the CPU that the device needs attention. Some lines have a higher priority for attention than others. Each IRQ line is assigned a number (0 to 15) to identify it.
I/O addresses	Numbers assigned to hardware devices that software uses to send a command to a device. Each device "listens" for these numbers and responds to the ones assigned to it. I/O addresses are communicated on the address bus.
Memory addresses	Numbers assigned to physical memory located either in RAM or ROM chips. Software can access this memory by using these addresses. Memory addresses are communicated on the address bus.
DMA channel	A number designating a channel on which the device can pass data to memory without involving the CPU. Think of a DMA channel as a shortcut for data moving to and from the device and memory.

Table 2-1   System resources used by software and hardware

OS Tools to Examine a System

 A+ EXAM TIP

The A+ OS exam expects you to be familiar with all three utilities discussed in this section.

You have learned about many hardware devices, OS components, and system resources in this chapter. When installing new components or troubleshooting a system, it is important to know how to use OS tools to examine the system. This section discusses several of these tools.

Device Manager

A+
OS
1.1
1.5
3.2

Device Manager under Windows 2000/XP and Windows 9x (Windows NT does not have a Device Manager) is the primary tool used to manage hardware devices.

To access Device Manager using Windows XP: Click Start, right-click My Computer, and select Properties on the shortcut menu. The System Properties dialog box opens. Click the Hardware tab and then click Device Manager.

To access Device Manager using Windows 2000: Right-click the My Computer icon on the desktop, select Properties on the shortcut menu, click the Hardware tab, and then click the Device Manager button.

To access Device Manager using Windows 9x: Right-click the My Computer icon on the desktop, select Properties on the shortcut menu, and then click the Device Manager tab.

The Device Manager dialog box for Windows XP is shown in Figure 2-19. Click a plus sign to expand the view of an item, and click a minus sign to collapse the view. To find out more information about a device, right-click the device and select Properties on the shortcut menu. You can see the Properties dialog box for the video card in Figure 2-19.

When a device is giving you a problem, check for information in the Properties dialog box of that device. You can also update the driver for a device, enable or disable a device, change a system resource assigned to a device, and uninstall a device from this window. The steps for performing these tasks are covered in later chapters.

You can also use Device Manager to view system resources and how they are used. For example, using Windows XP, on the Device Manager menu bar, click View, and then click Resource by type (see Figure 2-20). The resulting window shows all four system resources and how they are currently used. This information can be helpful when troubleshooting a problem with a failed hardware device or bus.

You can get a printed report of system information using Device Manager, which can be useful to document the current status of a system. To print the report using Windows XP, click the printer icon on the Device Manager toolbar. There are three options for the report: System summary, Selected class or device, and All devices and system summary.

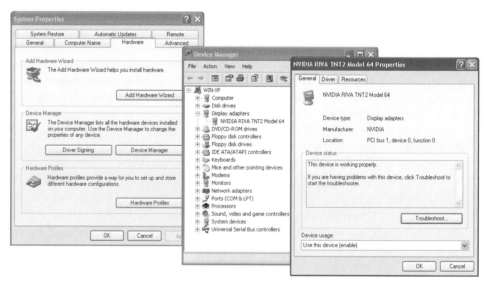

Figure 2-19   Device Manager tells you information about devices

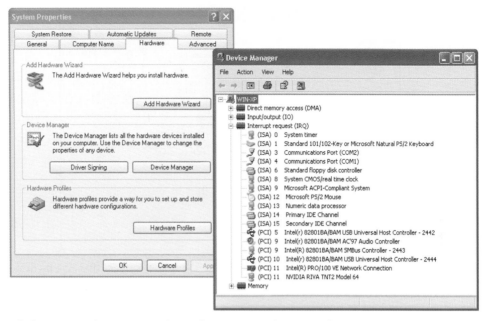

Figure 2-20   Windows XP Device Manager shows the current assignments for system resources

System Information

The System Information utility gives information similar to that given by Device Manager plus more. For example, it tells you the BIOS version you are using, the directory where the OS is installed, how system resources are used, information about drivers and their current status, and much information about software installed on the system that is not included in Device Manager.

To run System Information using Windows 2000/XP or Windows 9x: Click Start, click Run, in the Run dialog box, enter Msinfo32.exe, and then click OK. The System Information dialog box appears (see Figure 2-21).

System Information can be useful when a system is having trouble starting. Use it to get a list of drivers that loaded successfully. If you have saved the System Information report when the system was starting successfully, comparing the two reports can help identify the problem device.

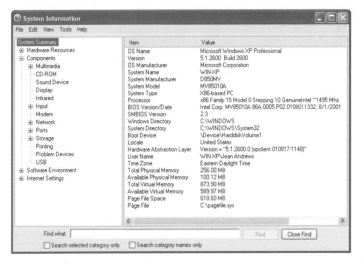

Figure 2-21   System Information gives information about your system that can be useful when troubleshooting

Microsoft Diagnostic Utility (MSD)

DOS and Windows 9x offered the Microsoft Diagnostic Utility (MSD), a utility useful to view information about the system, including information about memory, video, ports, device drivers, system resources, and other information.

To load MSD using Windows 9x: Click Start, click Run, enter MSD.EXE in the Run dialog box, and then click OK. The MSD window appears (see Figure 2-22). You will practice using MSD in a project at the end of this chapter.

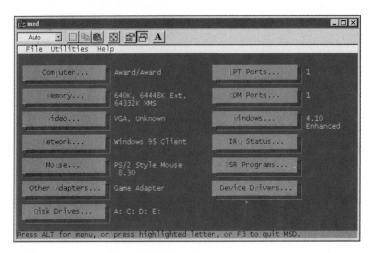

Figure 2-22   MSD opening screen

CHAPTER SUMMARY

2

▶ Ports on the motherboard include serial, parallel, USB, mouse, keyboard, and FireWire ports.

▶ The motherboard is the largest circuit board inside the computer case and holds the CPU, the most important microchip inside a computer, which is responsible for all processing done by the system.

▶ A CPU can operate in real or protected mode. In real mode, it processes 16 bits at a time, and in protected mode, it processes 32 bits at a time.

▶ Real mode runs a single program using a 16-bit data path and protected mode can multitask using a 32-bit data path.

▶ RAM (memory) temporarily holds data and programs while the CPU processes both. Common RAM modules installed on the motherboard are SIMMs, DIMMs, and RIMMs.

▶ A motherboard has several buses, each designed for a different purpose and running at a different speed. Some buses are the 8-bit and 16-bit ISA buses, the system bus, the PCI bus, the AGP bus used for a single video card, the USB bus that provides USB ports for slower I/O devices, and IEEE 1394 (FireWire) used for faster I/O devices.

▶ BIOS and an OS can support three common standards, ACPI and APM to conserve power, and Plug and Play to make device installations easier.

▶ BIOS manages a CMOS RAM chip on the motherboard that contains configuration settings for the motherboard. A program in BIOS lets you change CMOS setup at startup.

▶ Most hard drives and other secondary storage devices use IDE technology, which can support up to four drives in a system. There are two IDE connections on the motherboard, for two cables. Each cable can connect two drives.

▶ A file system is a method by which the OS organizes the files on a hard drive. The most popular file system for Windows is FAT, which can be either FAT16 or FAT32.

▶ Using FAT, clusters are listed in the FAT and filenames are listed in a directory table.

▶ Directories (folders) can contain files and other child directories or subdirectories (folders).

▶ Application software relates to the OS, which relates to BIOS and device drivers to control hardware.

▶ From the Windows desktop, programs can be launched from the Start menu, a shortcut icon on the desktop, the Run dialog box, Windows Explorer, or My Computer.

▶ Most PC software falls into three categories: Device drivers or the BIOS, operating system, and application software.

▶ Device drivers are compiled as either 16-bit or 32-bit software. Most drivers today are 32-bit protected-mode drivers that Windows loads from the registry.

▶ Windows 95/98 loads older 16-bit device drivers from Autoexec.bat, Config.sys, or System.ini to be backward compatible with DOS and Windows 3.x.

▶ Four system resources that aid in the communication between hardware and software are I/O addresses, IRQs, DMA channels, and memory addresses.

▶ An IRQ is a line on a bus that a device needing service uses to alert the CPU.

▶ The CPU places a device's I/O address on the address bus when it wants to initiate communication with the device.

▶ Memory addresses are numbers assigned to physical memory (RAM) that software can use to access this memory.

▶ A DMA channel provides a shortcut for a device to send data directly to memory, bypassing the CPU.

▶ Three Windows utilities useful for gathering information about a system are Device Manager, System Information, and Microsoft Diagnostic Utility (MSD).

KEY TERMS

For explanations of key terms, see the Glossary near the end of the book.

Accelerated Graphics Port
    (AGP) bus
Autoexec.bat
basic input/output system (BIOS)
bus
child directory
cluster
CMOS configuration chip
CMOS RAM chip
CMOS setup chip
Config.sys
data bus
data path
DMA (direct memory
    access channel)
directory table
Enhanced Integrated Drive
    Electronics (EIDE)
file extension

filename
folder
front-side bus
hardware compatibility list (HCL)
I/O address
Industry Standard Architecture
    (ISA) slot
Integrated Drive Electronics (IDE)
interrupt request (IRQ) number
local bus
logical drive
memory address
memory bus
motherboard
parallel port
partition
path
PCI (Peripheral Component
    Interconnect bus)
Plug and Play (PnP)

preemptive multitasking
primary storage
protected mode
real mode
root directory
secondary storage
sector
serial port
startup BIOS
subdirectory
system BIOS
system bus
system resource
System.ini
terminate-and-stay-resident (TSR)
track
universal serial bus (USB) port
volume

REVIEWING THE BASICS

1. What port on the back of your PC is most likely used for a printer?

2. What is the largest circuit board inside the PC case?

3. In what two modes does a CPU operate?

4. Name three types of memory modules.

5. What is the name of the dialog box in Windows 2000/XP/9x that gives the amount of RAM installed and the version of Windows currently running?

6. Current system buses run at about _____ MHz, and they have a(n) _____ bit data path and a(n) _____ bit address path.

7. Which is faster, a PCI slot or an ISA slot on a motherboard?

8. How is an AGP slot on a motherboard used?

9. What makes a BIOS a "good" BIOS, according to Microsoft?

10. Which Windows operating system does not support Plug and Play?

11. Which Windows OS uses Plug and Play but does not depend on BIOS Plug and Play to aid in the configuration process?

12. How is the CMOS RAM chip powered when the system is turned off?

13. What must happen to a program that is stored on a hard drive before it can be executed?

14. What technology standard is used to govern how drives such as CD-ROM drives, Zip drives, and hard drives can interface with a system?

15. Which file system is used by floppy disks?

16. What are two file systems used by hard drives?

17. When a hard drive is first installed and formatted, what is the name of the single directory created?

18. Directories created under other directories are called _____, _____, or _____.

19. Another name for a logical drive is a(n) _____.

20. List four ways an application can be launched from the Windows desktop.

21. Real mode operates using a(n) _____-bit data path, and protected mode uses a(n) _____-bit data path.

22. Name one way BIOS and device drivers are the same. Name one way they are different.

23. Which Microsoft operating system supports 16-bit device drivers or 32-bit device drivers?

24. A hardware device that is support by Windows 2000/XP is listed on the _____.

25. Windows keeps information about installed device drivers in the _____.

26. List three text files that Windows 9x supports for loading device drivers in order to remain backward compatible with DOS and Windows 3.x.

27. How can you determine if your BIOS is aware that a device is installed in the system?

28. List four system resources that software uses to manage hardware.

29. Name one Windows 2000/XP and Windows 9x utility that allows you to see the IRQ assignments made to devices.

30. What Windows utility is used to uninstall a device?

2

THINKING CRITICALLY

1. Name one system resource that a video card most likely will not need.

2. Is a mouse more likely to be controlled by a device driver or by system BIOS?

3. Name one device that is likely to be controlled by system BIOS.

4. If your printer is giving you trouble, what is the best way to obtain an update for the device driver?

5. Describe how you can change the contents of the CMOS RAM setup chip.

HANDS-ON PROJECTS

HANDS-ON
PROJECTS

PROJECT 2-1: Using the Windows 2000/XP System Information Utility

Windows 2000/XP has a System Information utility that gives you detailed information about your system. Using Windows 2000/XP, do the following to run the System Information utility and gather information about your system:

1. Click **Start,** click **Run,** and then type **Msinfo32.exe** in the Run dialog box. Click **OK.** The System Information dialog box appears.

2. Browse through the different levels of information in this window and answer the following questions:

   a. What OS and OS version are you using?

   b. What is your CPU speed?

   c. What is your BIOS manufacturer and version?

   d. How much RAM is installed on your video card? Explain how you got this information.

   e. What is the name of the driver file that manages your parallel port? Your serial port?

   f. How is IRQ 10 used on your system? IRQ 4?

   g. Which DMA channels are used on your system and how are they used?

PROJECT 2-2: **Using a Freeware Diagnostic Utility**

You can download many freeware diagnostic utilities from the Internet and use them to examine, troubleshoot, and benchmark a system. Do the following to download and use one utility to examine your system:

1. Go to the CNET Networks Web site at *www.cnet.com* and download the latest version of Fresh Diagnose. Web sites change often, but at the time of this writing, you would click **Downloads**, **Utilities and Drivers**, and then **Fresh Diagnose 6.0**. Save the utility to a folder on your hard drive named Downloads.

2. Double-click the file to execute the program to install the software. When given the opportunity, choose to create a shortcut to the software on your desktop.

3. Click the shortcut to run the Fresh Diagnose program.

4. Browse through the Fresh Diagnose menus and answer the same questions listed in Project 2-1 for the Windows 2000/XP System Information utility.

5. Compare the two programs, Fresh Diagnose and System Information, by answering the following questions:

   a. Which product is easiest to use and why?

   b. Which product gives the most information about your system?

   c. What is one advantage that System Information has over Fresh Diagnose?

   d. What is one advantage that Fresh Diagnose has over System Information?

   e. Which product do you prefer and why?

PROJECT 2-3: **Using Microsoft Diagnostics with Windows 9x**

DOS and Windows offer the Microsoft Diagnostics utility. This utility examines your system, displaying useful information about ports, devices, memory, and the like. The MSD.EXE utility can be found in the \TOOLS\OLDMSDOS directory on your Windows 9x installation CD. Using Windows Explorer, copy it to your hard drive, storing it in a folder named \Tools.

For Windows 9x, boot your PC to an MS-DOS prompt in real mode. To boot into real mode, press **Ctrl** or **F8** as you start the system. The Windows Startup menu appears. Select **Command prompt only**. From the DOS prompt, execute this command: **C:\TOOLS\MSD**. The MSD window appears (shown earlier in Figure 2-22).

Browse carefully through all menu options of this utility, and answer the following questions about your system:

1. List the following or print the appropriate MSD screen: manufacturer; version number; and date of your system BIOS, video BIOS, and mouse device driver.

2. What kind of video card is installed?

3. How much memory is currently installed on this PC?

4. What version of the OS is the PC running?

5. What CPU is the PC using?

Exit MSD. Save the information you noted to compare with the information that you will obtain from MSD in Windows 2000.
You need Windows 2000 installed on a PC to do the rest of this project:

1. Copy the **MSD.exe** program to a folder on your Windows 2000 PC named \Tools.

2. From within Windows 2000, open a command prompt. (Click **Start**, **Programs**, **Accessories**, **Command Prompt**).

3. From the command prompt, start MSD using this command: **\Tools\MSD**.

4. Browse through all menu options, and answer the same questions about your system as you did for Windows 9x.

PROJECT 2-4: Using Device Manager

Using Device Manager under Windows 2000/XP or Windows 9x, answer these questions about your computer. (To access Device Manager using Windows 2000/XP, from the System Properties dialog box, click the **Hardware** tab and then click **Device Manager**. For Windows 9x, right-click the **My Computer** icon on the desktop, select **Properties** on the shortcut menu, and click the **Device Manager** tab.)

1. Does your computer have a network card installed? If so, what is the name of the card?

2. What three settings can be changed under Device Manager?

3. What are all the hardware devices that Device Manager recognizes as present?

CASE PROJECT

Preparing to Install a New Operating System on a Hard Drive

Before installing a new operating system on a hard drive, you need to know the search order of drives that startup BIOS uses to search for an OS. The order might be C and then A or some other order. Enter the CMOS setup of your PC and search for the setup screen that sets the boot order. Change the order so that BIOS looks to the floppy drive (drive A) to load the OS before it looks to drive C. Answer these questions:

1. What keystroke did you press at startup to enter CMOS setup?

2. What BIOS does your motherboard use (include brand and version)?

3. List the different CMOS setup windows that can be accessed from the CMOS main menu window.

4. Access the window that gives information about serial ports. What is the name of that window?

5. What I/O addresses and IRQ does the first serial port use?

6. What I/O addresses and IRQ does the first parallel port use?

7. What is the system date reported by CMOS setup? System time?

8. What keystrokes do you press to exit CMOS setup without saving any changes?

9. What is the name of the setup menu that contains the boot sequence order?

10. What was the boot sequence order when you first entered setup?

11. What is the new boot sequence order?

Understanding the Boot Process and Command Line

In this chapter, you will learn:

- How a computer boots up and about some useful tools for troubleshooting a failed boot

- How Windows manages floppy disks and hard drives

- To use many commands at the command prompt

U nderstanding what happens when you first turn on a PC is essential to knowing what to do when problems arise with booting or when applications or hardware fail after the boot. This chapter focuses on how the hardware boots up to the point an operating system (OS) is loaded, and then spends a little less time on the loading of an OS. In later chapters, you will learn in more detail what happens when each OS is loaded, and how to troubleshoot problems when the OS fails to load correctly.

After a system boots and you are working with an OS, most often you are using the Windows desktop, which is both menu-driven and icon-driven. Using Windows Explorer or My Computer, you can copy files, create folders, and even perform some limited troubleshooting tasks when problems arise. However, if the OS is not functioning well enough to provide a desktop, a PC technician must troubleshoot the system using a command-driven interface. Learning to use the command line is important because it is the tried-and-true tool for the worst operating system problems. Knowing how to use the command prompt is essential to PC troubleshooting.

We begin the chapter by learning how a PC first boots up and about some troubleshooting tools to use when the boot fails. Next we will turn our attention to how Windows manages floppy disks and hard drives. Then we will look at some essential commands used from a command prompt when troubleshooting a failing system.

Booting Up Your Computer

The term **booting** comes from the phrase "lifting yourself up by your bootstraps" and refers to the computer bringing itself up to an operable state without user intervention. Booting refers to either a "soft boot" or "hard boot." A **hard boot**, or **cold boot**, involves turning on the power with the on/off switch. A **soft boot**, or **warm boot**, involves using the operating system to reboot. For Windows NT/2000/XP and Windows 9x, one way to soft boot is to click Start, click Shut Down, select Restart from the Shut Down menu, and then click OK. For DOS, pressing the three keys Ctrl, Alt, and Del at the same time performs a soft boot.

A+ EXAM TIP

The A+ OS exam expects you to know the difference between a hard boot and soft boot.

A hard boot is more stressful on your machine than a soft boot because of the initial power surge through the equipment. Also, a soft boot is faster. Always use the soft boot to restart unless the soft boot method doesn't work. If you must power down, avoid turning off the power switch and immediately turning it back on without a pause, because this can damage the machine. Some PCs have a reset button on the front of the case. Pressing the reset button starts the boot process at an earlier point than does the operating-system method, and is therefore a little slower, but might work when the operating-system method fails. For newer motherboards, pressing the reset button is the same as powering off and on, except that there is no stress to the system caused by the initial power surge.

In the next section, you will learn what happens when the PC is first turned on and the startup BIOS takes control, and then begins the process of loading an OS.

Startup BIOS Controls the Beginning of the Boot

A successful boot depends on the hardware, the BIOS, and the operating system all performing without errors. If errors occur, they might or might not stall or lock up the boot process. Errors are communicated as beeps or as messages on screen. Appendix A, "Error Messages and Their Meanings," lists some examples of these messages. The functions performed during the boot can be divided into four parts, as shown in the following list.

Here is a brief overview of all four parts before we look at the first three parts in detail. (The fourth part, loading and executing an application, was covered in the last chapter.) Startup BIOS is in control for the first step and the beginning of the second step, when control is turned over to the OS.

- *Step 1: Startup BIOS runs the **power-on self test (POST)** and assigns system resources.* The ROM BIOS startup program surveys hardware resources and needs, and assigns system resources to meet those needs (see Figure 3-1). The ROM BIOS startup program begins the startup process by reading configuration information stored in DIP switches, jumpers, and the CMOS

3

chip, and then comparing that information to the hardware—the CPU, video card, disk drive, hard drive, and so on. Some hardware devices have BIOSs of their own that request resources from startup BIOS, which attempts to assign these system resources as needed.

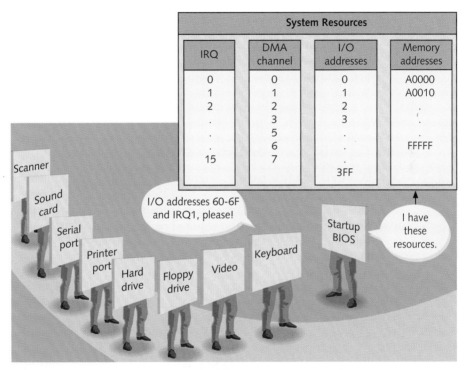

Figure 3-1   Boot Step 1: ROM BIOS startup program surveys hardware resources and needs and assigns system resources to satisfy those needs

- *Step 2: The ROM BIOS startup program searches for and loads an OS.* Most often the OS is loaded from logical drive C on the hard drive. Configuration information on the CMOS chip tells startup BIOS where to look for the OS. Most new BIOSs support loading the OS from the hard drive, a floppy disk, a CD, or a Zip drive. The BIOS turns to that device, reads the beginning files of the OS, copies them into memory, and then turns control over to the OS. This part of the loading process works the same for any operating system; only the OS files being loaded change.
- *Step 3: The OS configures the system and completes its own loading.* The OS checks some of the same things that startup BIOS checked, such as available memory and whether that memory is reliable. Then the OS loads the software to control a mouse, CD-ROM, scanner, and other peripheral devices. These devices generally have device drivers stored on the hard drive. The Windows desktop is loaded.

■ *Step 4: Application software is loaded and executed.* Sometimes an OS is configured to automatically launch application software as part of the boot process. When you tell the OS to execute an application, the OS first must find the application software on the hard drive, CD-ROM, or other secondary storage device, copy the software into memory, and then turn control over to it.

■ Finally, you can command the application software, which makes requests to the OS, which, in turn, uses the system resources, system BIOS, and device drivers to interface with and control the hardware. At this point, the user is in control.

Now let's focus on how the BIOS locates the OS and how the OS is loaded and executed.

How the BIOS Finds and Loads the OS

Once POST and the first pass at assignment of resources is complete, the next step is to load an OS. Startup BIOS looks to CMOS setup to find out which device is set to be the boot device. Most often the OS is loaded from logical drive C on the hard drive. The minimum information required on the hard drive to load an OS is shown in the following list. You can see some of these items labeled in Figure 3-2.

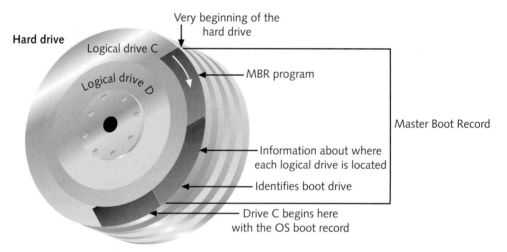

Figure 3-2 A hard drive might contain more than one logical drive; the Master Boot Record at the beginning of the drive contains information about the location of each logical drive, indicates which drive is the boot drive, and holds the master boot program that begins the process of loading an operating system

■ A small sector (512 bytes) at the very beginning of the hard drive, called the **Master Boot Record (MBR)**, contains two items. The first item is the master boot program, which is needed to locate the beginning of the OS on the drive.

3

- The second item in the MBR is a table, called the **partition table**, which contains a map to the logical drives on the hard drive. This table tells BIOS how many partitions the drive has and how each partition is divided into one or more logical drives, which partition contains the drive to be used for booting (called the **active partition**), and where each logical drive begins and ends. You'll learn more about this later in the chapter.
- At the beginning of the boot drive (usually drive C) is the OS **boot record** (also called **boot sector**), which loads the first program file of the OS. For Windows 9x, that program is **Io.sys**, and for Windows NT/2000/XP, that program is **Ntldr**.
- The boot loader program for the OS (Io.sys or Ntldr) begins the process of loading the OS into memory. For Windows 9x, **Msdos.sys** is needed next, followed by **Command.com**. These two files, plus Io.sys, are the core components of the real-mode portion of Windows 9x. Windows NT/2000/XP has a different set of startup files, which you will learn about in Chapters 5 and 6.

NOTE A **program file** contains a list of instructions for the OS to follow. Program files can be a part of the OS or applications and have a .com, .sys, .bat, or .exe file extension. Ntldr is an exception to that rule because it has no file extension.

APPLYING CONCEPTS

Suppose you turn on your PC and see a black screen with one of these error messages on it:

```
Non-system disk or disk error, press any key
Bad or missing COMMAND.COM
No operating system found
```

Don't panic! You probably have a floppy disk in the drive. Just remove the disk and press any key. Most likely you'll boot normally. Here's what happened:

The BIOS looks to CMOS setup to find out which secondary storage device should have the OS (see Figure 3-3). Setup might instruct the BIOS to look first on drive C, and, if it finds no OS there, then try drive A; or the order might be to search A then C. If BIOS looks first to drive A and finds no disk in the drive, it turns to drive C. If it looks first to drive A and finds a disk in the drive, but the disk does not contain the OS (for Windows 9x, that means the OS boot record, Io.sys, Msdos.sys, and Command.com), then one of the preceding error messages appears.

You must replace the disk with one that contains the OS or simply remove the disk and press any key to force the BIOS to continue to drive C to find the OS.

A+
OS
1.2
1.3
2.5
3.2

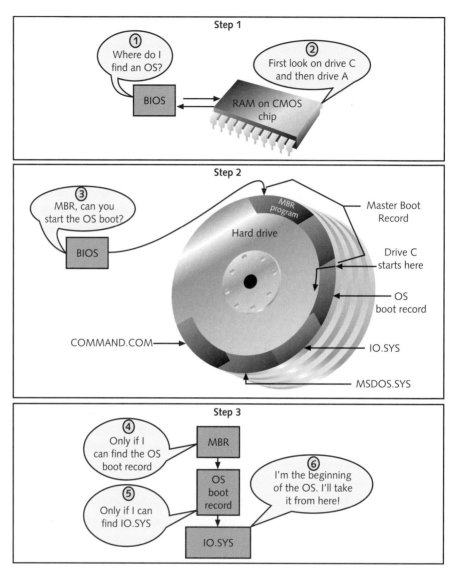

Figure 3-3
Boot Step 2: BIOS searches for and begins to load an operating system (in this example, Windows 9x is the OS)

NOTE

The order of drives that the BIOS follows when looking for an OS is called the boot sequence. You can change the boot sequence on your PC by using CMOS setup.

3

Loading the MS-DOS Core of Windows 9x

A+
OS
1.2
1.3
2.5
3.2

This section describes what first happens during booting when only the MS-DOS core of Windows 9x is loaded, which brings the OS to a real-mode command prompt similar to a DOS command prompt. It's important for a PC technician to understand this real-mode DOS core because it is often used as a troubleshooting tool when the hard drive fails. You can boot to a command prompt in several ways, including booting from a Windows startup disk or using the Windows startup menu. You'll learn how to prepare a startup disk later in the chapter. Chapter 4 covers how to use the Windows startup menu in Windows 9x.

In Step 2 of Figure 3-3, the BIOS locates the MBR on the hard drive, which looks to the partition table to determine where the logical boot drive is physically located on the drive. It then turns to the OS boot record of that logical drive.

The OS boot record is a very short program; it loads just one hidden file, which makes up the DOS core, into memory (see Figure 3-3, Step 3; and Figure 3-4). (A **hidden file** is a file that does not appear in the directory list.) The OS boot record program knows the filename, which is Io.sys. The Io.sys file contains the basic I/O software for real mode and requires that the Msdos.sys file be present. Msdos.sys is a text file that contains some parameters and switches you can set to affect the way the OS boots. You will learn about the contents of Msdos.sys and how to change it to affect the boot process in Chapter 4.

 A+ EXAM TIP

The A+ OS exam expects you to know that the three OS files necessary to boot to a command prompt in Windows 9x are Io.sys, Msdos.sys, and Command.com. Config.sys and Autoexec.bat are not required but are used if they are present.

Once Io.sys is loaded into memory, the boot record program is no longer needed, and control is turned over to Io.sys. This program looks for Msdos.sys, reads it, and uses the settings in it. Io.sys then looks on the hard drive for a file named Config.sys. This configuration file contains commands that tell Io.sys how many files it can open at any one time (Files=) and how many file buffers to create (Buffers=). (A buffer is a temporary holding area for files.) Config.sys also includes the commands to load device drivers (Device=), as well as other information. An example of a typical command in Config.sys follows; it gives real-mode Io.sys access to memory above 1 MB, called extended memory:

```
Device=himem.sys
```

Several drivers can be loaded into memory from commands in Config.sys. Io.sys puts these programs in memory wherever it chooses. However, a program can request that it be put in a certain memory location.

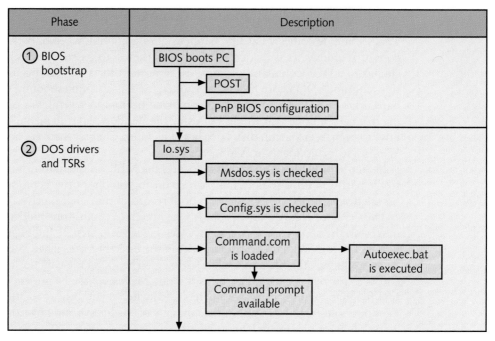

Phase	Description
① BIOS bootstrap	BIOS boots PC → POST → PnP BIOS configuration
② DOS drivers and TSRs	Io.sys → Msdos.sys is checked → Config.sys is checked → Command.com is loaded → Autoexec.bat is executed; Command.com is loaded → Command prompt available

Figure 3-4   Boot Step 3: Operating system completes the boot process; MS-DOS core is loaded and command prompt presented to user

Sometimes Config.sys is used to create a RAM drive. A **RAM drive** is an area of memory that looks and acts like a hard drive, but because it is memory, it is much faster. When booting from the Windows 9x startup disk, Windows creates a RAM drive to hold files after they have been uncompressed. This eliminates the need for hard drive access, and there is no room for the files on the floppy disk. An example of a command in Config.sys to create a RAM drive is:

```
device=ramdrive.sys 2048
```

The command tells the OS to create a RAM drive that is 2048K in size.

After Config.sys is executed, Io.sys looks for another OS file, named Command.com. This file has three parts: more code to manage I/O, programs for internal OS commands such as Copy and Dir, and a short program that looks for the Autoexec.bat file.

NOTE

Some OS commands are **internal commands**, meaning they are embedded in the Command.com file, and others are **external commands**, meaning they have their own program files. An example of an external command is Format, stored in the file Format.com.

Command.com looks for Autoexec.bat and, if found, executes it. The filename **Autoexec.bat** stands for "automatically executed batch file." A **batch file** is a text file that contains a series of commands that are executed in order. Autoexec.bat lists OS commands that execute automatically each time the OS is loaded. The following commands are examples of commands that might be found in the Autoexec.bat file:

- The following Path command lists two paths, separated by semicolons. The OS uses the paths listed in the Path command to locate program files.

```
PATH C:\;C:\Windows;
```

- The Set command is used to create and assign a value to an environmental variable that an application can later read. A software installation program might add a Set command to your Autoexec.bat file. Later, the software uses the environmental variable in the program. An example of a Set command assigning a path to the variable Mypath is:

```
Set Mypath=C:\VERT
```

- The Restart command causes the system to reboot.

```
Restart.com
```

- The Temp command lets applications know where to store temporary files. Add the Temp command to Autoexec.bat if applications are putting temporary files in strange locations. An example of a Temp command is:

```
Temp=C:\Temp
```

NOTE

By default, DOS stores temporary files in C:\Temp, Windows 9x uses C:\Windows\Temp, Windows NT uses C:\Temp, Windows 2000 uses C:\Winnt\Temp, and Windows XP uses C:\Windows\Temp.

- The Echo command turns on and off the displaying of commands and messages. Use it in a batch file to control output to the screen.

```
Echo off
```

Booting into real mode with a command prompt is completed after Autoexec.bat has finished executing. At this point, Command.com is the program in charge, displaying a command prompt and waiting for a command. On the other hand, if a program or menu was executed from Autoexec.bat, it might ask you for a command.

The command prompt indicates the drive that loaded the OS. If the OS files were loaded from a floppy disk, the command prompt is A:\> (called the A prompt). If the OS was loaded from the hard drive, the command prompt is C:\> (the C prompt).

The colon following the letter identifies the letter as the name of a drive, and the backslash identifies the directory on the drive as the root or main directory. The > symbol is the prompt symbol that the OS uses to say, "Enter your command here." This drive and root directory are now the default drive and directory, sometimes called the current or working drive or directory.

If you want to finish loading Windows 9x, use the Win command, which executes the program Win.com. Enter this command at the C prompt:

```
C:\> WIN
```

Note that commands used at a command prompt are not case sensitive; that is, you can enter *WIN*, *Win*, or *win*.

NOTE

Emergency Startup Disks

Although you normally boot from a hard drive, problems with the hard drive sometimes make booting from a floppy disk necessary. A floppy disk with enough software to load an operating system is called a **bootable disk**, or **system disk**. A bootable disk with some utility programs to troubleshoot a failed hard drive is called a **rescue disk, emergency startup disk (ESD)**, or **startup disk**. Having a rescue disk available for an emergency is very important, and a PC technician should always have one or more on hand.

Each OS provides an automated method to create a rescue disk or set of disks. Windows 9x uses a single bootable disk, and Windows 2000 uses a set of four disks. Windows XP uses a different approach to recovering from a failed boot, and does not rely on startup disks. In this section, you will learn how to create a Windows 9x startup disk and use the disk. How to troubleshoot a failed boot using Windows 2000/XP is covered in future chapters.

Windows 9x Startup Disks

A Windows 9x startup disk has everything you need to troubleshoot a failed hard drive or prepare a new hard drive for use. The disk does not need to be created on the same computer that will use it, although in most cases you should use the same version of Windows as used by the computer that will be using the disk. Follow these instructions to create a startup disk for Windows 9x.

1. Click **Start** on the taskbar, point to **Settings**, and then click **Control Panel**.

2. In the Control Panel window, double-click the **Add/Remove Programs** icon.

3. Click the **Startup Disk** tab, and then click the **Create Disk** button (see Figure 3-5).

3

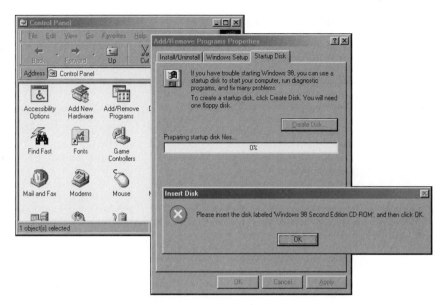

Figure 3-5   Windows might use the Windows CD to create a startup disk

> 4. Windows might need the Windows CD to create the disk. Insert the CD if it is requested. Windows then creates the startup disk.

NOTE

When Windows 9x (including Windows Me) creates a startup disk, it copies files to the disk from the \Windows\Command\EBD folder. You can also copy these files to a formatted disk to create a startup disk manually.

✓ **A+ EXAM TIP**

The A+ OS exam expects you to know each step in creating a Windows 9x startup disk.

Windows places many utility programs on the disk that you will learn to use in the next section. One file on the disk is Ebd.cab, a compressed file called a **cabinet file**, that contains several other compressed files. During startup, the contents of the cabinet file are uncompressed and copied to the RAM drive, because there is not enough space for them on the floppy disk and the startup disk assumes the hard drive might not be accessible. You can also use the Extract command to extract specific files when the RAM drive is not active.

APPLYING CONCEPTS

If you have access to a Windows 9x computer, create a startup disk and boot from the disk. What messages and questions do you see on the screen when you boot from the disk? If you have access to a Windows 2000 or Windows XP computer, boot it using the Windows 9x startup disk. What messages or questions do you see? Are there any differences?

Using a Windows 9x Startup Disk with Another OS

In some situations, it is appropriate to use a startup disk created by one OS to boot a failed system that has a different OS installed. For example, suppose Windows NT/2000/XP refuses to boot. Using a different PC, you can create a startup disk under Windows 98 and then use it to boot the Windows NT/2000/XP PC. If you can successfully boot to an A prompt (A:\>), you have demonstrated that the hard drive or files stored on it is the source of the problem. However, it is best to use recovery procedures and disks native to the installed OS.

APPLYING CONCEPTS

Many PC technicians use a Windows 9x startup disk when troubleshooting Windows NT/2000/XP computers, because the Windows 9x startup disk has a useful set of tools and resources that are not as easily available under Windows 2000/XP. Here are three situations in which you might choose to use a Windows 9x startup disk:

- You are helping someone solve a problem with their Windows NT/2000/XP system, which refuses to boot. You have your Windows 98 startup disk handy, so you boot from it and get to an A prompt. In order to get to an A prompt successfully, many subsystems in the computer must be functioning, including the motherboard, CPU, memory, floppy disk drive, power supply, and video system. In fact, you have just proven that the problem is isolated to the hard drive.
- Next, use the Windows 98 Fdisk command stored on the startup disk to examine the partition table of the hard drive. If Fdisk can see the table and describe it correctly, then you know that the partition table is not damaged. You have now isolated the problem to the file system on the hard drive. At that point, you must use tools native to Windows 2000/XP to solve the problem. (Fdisk is covered later in this chapter.)
- A Windows XP computer comes to you for repair with a failed hard drive. You install a new hard drive, but you do not have the Windows installation CD to install Windows XP on the drive. In this situation, you can use a Windows 9x startup disk to boot the system and create a partition table on the drive. This assures you that the drive is functioning properly even without installing an OS.
- Your Windows NT system will not boot, and your term paper is stored on the hard drive! If the hard drive is using the FAT file system, you might be able to use the Windows 98 startup disk to recover the file. There are special considerations for Windows NT/2000/XP. These OSs support more than one file system, and a Windows 9x startup disk supports only FAT16 or FAT32. If a Windows NT/2000/XP hard drive has a different file system installed, such as NTFS (New Technology file system), then the Windows 9x startup disk cannot read that file system. In this situation, you can work from an A prompt, but you will not be able to access the hard drive. The solution is to create rescue disks under these operating systems that can read the file system.

In order for a PC to boot from a hard drive or floppy disk, the file system on the drive or disk must be healthy. We now turn our attention to how a file system works on a disk or hard drive.

Managing Floppy Disks and Hard Drives

When a hard drive (sometimes called the HDD) is first installed, it has nothing written on it except empty track markings put there at the factory. A floppy disk is completely blank and does not have even these track markings. The OS must prepare these disks for use by putting track markings on a floppy disk and putting a file system on both the floppy disk and hard drive. In addition, the OS is responsible for managing the file system, including creating, deleting, copying, and moving directories and files. This section looks at the commands to do all this from a command prompt under Windows 9x. Except for writing a new file system to a hard drive, you can perform these same functions from within Windows NT/2000/XP or Windows 9x using Windows Explorer.

In this section, you will learn how data is organized on floppy disks and hard drives, a subject that was introduced in the last chapter. In the following section, you will learn more details about specific commands executed from a command prompt.

How Data Is Logically Stored on a Floppy Disk

A+
OS
1.1

When a floppy disk is first formatted, sector and track markings are written to the disk. Recall from Chapter 2 that tracks are concentric circles on the disk and a segment of a track, called a sector, always holds 512 bytes of data. All floppy disks, no matter what size or density, and hard drives are divided into tracks and sectors.

Recall that a cluster, sometimes called a file allocation unit, is a group of sectors that is the smallest unit on a disk used to hold a file or a portion of a file. "Sector" refers to how data is physically stored on a disk, while "cluster" describes how data is logically organized. The BIOS manages the disk as physical sectors, but the OS considers the disk only as a long list of clusters that can each hold a fixed amount of data (see Figure 3-6). The OS keeps that list of clusters in the file allocation table (FAT).

There are several variations of floppy disks, including the older 5¼-inch floppy disk, the 3½-inch double-density floppy disk, and the most current floppy disk, the 3½-inch high-density disk, which holds 1.44 MB of data. Let's see how this disk holds data.

A+
OS
1.1

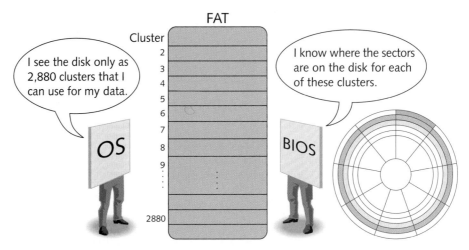

Figure 3-6 Clusters or file allocation units are managed by the OS in the file allocation table (FAT), but BIOS manages these clusters as one or two physical sectors on the disk

The 3½-inch high-density floppy disk has 80 tracks × 18 sectors per track on each side, for a total of 1,440 sectors. This type of disk has only one sector per cluster, making 1,440 × 2 sides, or 2,880 clusters. Because each cluster holds 512 bytes (one sector) of data, a 3½-inch high-density floppy disk has 2,880 × 512 = 1,474,560 bytes of data. Divide this number by 1,024 to convert bytes to kilobytes. The storage capacity of this disk is 1,440 kilobytes. Divide by 1,000 to convert kilobytes to megabytes, and the storage is 1.44 MB.

NOTE

There is a discrepancy in the computer industry regarding the definition of a megabyte. Sometimes 1 megabyte = 1,000 kilobytes; at other times, we use the relationship of 1 megabyte = 1,024 kilobytes.

Formatting a Floppy Disk

When a floppy disk is first prepared for use, it is formatted using the Format command or Windows Explorer. The following happens during formatting:

- Tracks are created and the place on each track where the first sector begins is marked.
- The boot record is created, as discussed later in this section.
- Two copies of the FAT are created. (This process is discussed in detail later in this section.)
- The root directory is created.

Next we look at the contents of the boot record, the FAT, and the root directory.

The Boot Record

A+
OS
1.1

At the beginning of each floppy disk, the first sector contains basic information about how the disk is organized, including the number of sectors, the number of sectors per cluster, the number of bits in each FAT entry, and other information that an OS or BIOS needs to read the data on the disk. This information is stored in the first sector or record on the disk, the boot record. At the end of the boot record is a small program, called the **bootstrap loader**, that can be used to boot from the disk. The boot record indicates which version of DOS or Windows was used to format the disk, names the program it searches for to load an OS (Io.sys), and is always located at the beginning of the disk at track 0, sector 1 (bottom of the disk, outermost track). This uniformity of layout and content allows any version of DOS or Windows to read any DOS or Windows disk. If Io.sys, Msdos.sys, and Command.com are on the disk, the disk is said to be bootable. All boot records, however, are the same, whether or not the disk is bootable.

APPLYING CONCEPTS

During the boot, if BIOS looks to the floppy drive for a boot device and finds a disk in the drive, the program stored in the boot record is executed. If this program does not find Io.sys, the disk is not bootable and a message appears, such as the following:

```
Non-system disk or disk error...Replace and strike any
key when ready...Disk boot failure
```

POST stops until you intervene. Only the program in the boot record can determine if the disk is bootable. Verify that the boot sequence is first drive A, then C. Then put a nonbootable disk in a floppy disk drive and boot the system. What error message do you see?

The File Allocation Table (FAT)

Recall from Chapter 2 that the FAT lists the location of files on the disk in a one-column table. Because the width of each entry in the column is 12 bits, the FAT is called a 12-bit FAT or **FAT12**. The FAT lists how each cluster or file allocation unit on the disk is currently used. A file is stored in one or more clusters that do not have to be contiguous on the disk. If a file is not stored in consecutive clusters, it is called a **fragmented file**. During formatting, if the OS finds a bad cluster, it marks the cluster in the FAT so it will not be used. An extra copy of the FAT is kept immediately following the first. If the first is damaged, sometimes you can recover your data and files by using the second copy.

The Root Directory

Recall that the root directory, or main directory, is a table listing all the files assigned to this table. The root directory contains a fixed number of rows to accommodate a predetermined number of files and subdirectories; the number of available rows depends on the disk type. A 3½-inch high-density floppy disk has 224 entries in the root directory. The root directory will later contain information about each file and subdirectory stored in it. Some important items in a directory are:

- *The filename and extension.* An entry in a directory is only big enough for an eight-character filename. For long filenames, more room in the directory is required. This room is provided by using more than one entry in the directory for a single file, enough to accommodate the length of the filename. Both the long filename and the DOS version short filename are stored in the directory.
- *Time and date of creation or last update.* The date and time come from the system date and time, which the OS gets from the real-time clock during the boot. At the command prompt, you can change these values with the Date and Time commands. Using the Windows desktop, change the date and time in the Control Panel. The earliest possible date allowed using either method is 1/1/1980.
- *The file attributes.* These are on/off switches indicating the archive, system file, hidden file, and read-only file status of the file or directory. You can use several OS commands to change the file attributes; you'll learn about many of them later in this chapter.

NOTE The archive status is a switch used to indicate whether the file has been changed since the last backup and should be backed up next time a backup is made. You will learn more about this process in Chapter 10.

The root directory and all subdirectories contain the same information about each file. Only the root directory has a limitation on the number of entries. Subdirectories can have as many entries as disk space allows. Because long filenames require more room in a directory than short filenames, assigning long filenames reduces the number of files that can be stored in the root directory.

NOTE See Appendix D, "FAT Details," for tables showing the contents of the floppy disk boot record, the root directory, and the meaning of each bit in the attribute byte.

Next we look at how a hard drive is organized to hold data.

How a Hard Drive Is Logically Organized to Hold Data

A+
OS
1.4

Recall that today's hard drives come from the factory already low-level formatted (that is, with track and sector markings already in place). During installation, after the hard drive is physically installed, the next step is to partition the drive into manageable areas. The high-level divisions are called partitions, and within the partitions, the drive is further divided into logical drives or volumes. This section discusses the different types of divisions, how they are organized and used by the OS, and how to use OS commands to partition and format a hard drive for first use.

Preparing a hard drive to hold data requires the following three steps:

1. *Low-level format.* This physically formats the hard drive and creates the tracks and sectors. For hard drives today, this step has already been done by the time you buy the drive, and does not involve an OS.

2. *Partitioning the hard drive.* Even if only one partition is used, this step is still required. The DOS and Windows 9x Fdisk program sets up a partition table at the beginning of the hard drive. Within each partition, Fdisk also creates logical drives, assigning letters to these drives. Windows NT/2000/XP uses the Diskpart program in the Recovery Console or the Disk Management utility from within Windows to create and delete partitions and logical drives.

3. *High-level format.* This must be done by the OS for each logical drive on the hard drive. As each logical drive is formatted, the OS creates a file system, either FAT16, FAT32, or NTFS. DOS and Windows 9x use the Format.com program to do the job, and Windows NT/2000/XP uses Diskpart or Disk Management.

Recall that the first sector (512 bytes) at the beginning of a hard drive holds the MBR, and that the MBR contains the following information:

- The master boot program (446 bytes) that calls the boot program to load the OS
- The partition table, which contains the description, location, and size of each of the first four partitions on the drive (16 bytes are used to describe each partition)

Although you might have a 10-GB hard drive that is only a single physical drive, an OS can divide this drive into more than one logical drive. When partitioning the drive using Fdisk, Diskpart, or Disk Management, two kinds of divisions take place. First, the physical drive is divided into one or more partitions, and then each partition is further divided into logical drives or volumes. (A logical drive is sometimes called a logical partition. Don't let the two uses of the term "partition" confuse you; partitions and logical partitions are divisions at different levels.) Figure 3-7 shows a typical example; the hard drive is divided into two partitions. The first partition contains one logical drive (drive C), and the second partition is divided into two logical drives (D and E). The partition table at the very beginning of the drive records all these divisions.

A+
OS
1.4

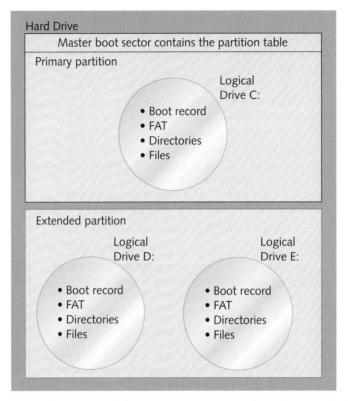

Figure 3-7 A hard drive is divided into one or more partitions that contain logical drives

During POST, the master boot program, which is stored at the beginning of the MBR, executes and checks the integrity of the partition table itself. If it finds any corruption, it refuses to continue execution, and the disk is unusable.

If the table entries are valid, the partition table program looks in the table to determine which partition is the active partition, and it executes the bootstrap loader program in the boot record of that partition.

NOTE

Suppose you try to boot your system and get the message, "Invalid drive specification." This error can be caused by a number of problems; a possibility is a **boot sector virus.** This type of virus attacks the MBR program. To replace the MBR program with a fresh one, use the Windows 9x Fdisk /MBR command or the Windows 2000/XP Fixmbr command.

Using DOS or Windows 9x, a hard drive can have only one primary partition and one extended partition, although the partition table can contain four partitions. Also, the **primary partition** can have only a single logical drive. In that case, the one logical drive in the primary partition is the only logical drive on the hard drive that can boot the operating system, and is the active partition. The **extended partition** can have several logical drives. Using Windows NT/2000/XP, a hard drive can have up to four partitions, but only one of them can be an extended partition.

How Many and What Kind of Logical Drives?

After the hard drive is formatted and ready for use, you are not usually aware that the logical drives on the hard drive all belong to the same hard drive. For example, Figure 3-8 shows three drives, C, D, and E, that are logical drives on one hard drive. If you right-click the icon for one drive, such as drive D in the figure, and select Properties on the shortcut menu, you can see the amount of space allotted to this logical drive and how much of it is currently used. Also note that in the figure drive D is formatted using the FAT32 file system. One logical drive can be formatted with one file system and other logical drives on the same hard drive can be formatted using a different file system such as FAT16 or NTFS. You'll see examples of this in future chapters.

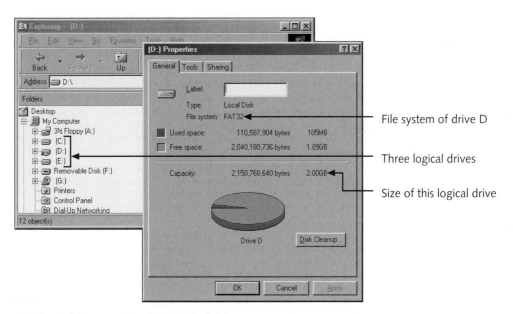

Figure 3-8   This hard drive contains three logical drives

DOS and all versions of Windows support the FAT16 file system. Windows 95 offered a slightly improved file system called VFAT that supports long filenames, and Windows 95 Service Release 2 (sometimes called Windows 95b or Windows 95 OSR2) introduced the FAT32 file system. FAT32 is supported by Windows 95 and all later versions of Windows 9x, Windows 2000, and Windows XP. Windows NT introduced the NTFS file system, which is also supported by Windows 2000 and Windows XP. You'll learn about the different versions of NTFS in later chapters. The next sections discuss FAT16, VFAT, FAT32, and NTFS. With these file systems, one goal is to reduce the size of one cluster, to avoid wasting space on the hard drive for small files that don't need large clusters.

FAT16

DOS and all versions of Windows support the FAT16 file system, which uses 16 bits for each cluster entry in the FAT. Using FAT16, the smallest cluster size is four sectors. Each cluster is 512 bytes/sector × 4 sectors/cluster, or 2,048 bytes. A one-character file takes up 2,048 bytes of space on a hard drive. For larger drives, the number of sectors in one cluster is even larger.

Virtual File Allocation (VFAT)

Windows 95 and Windows for Workgroups feature some improved methods of hard drive access, called **VFAT**, or **virtual file allocation table**. These enable Windows to use 32-bit, protected-mode device drivers for hard drive access. In Windows for Workgroups, VFAT is called 32-bit file access. Windows 95 supports filenames of up to 255 characters. Recall that the filename and extension are stored in the root directory or in a subdirectory list. Each entry in the directory is 32 bytes long, and each 32-byte entry is called a block. Long filenames require more than one block in the directory. The FAT is not affected, but still uses 16 bits per cluster entry. VFAT has been rendered obsolete by FAT32.

> Some DOS-based disk utility programs can damage the entries in a directory in these additional blocks because they are not programmed to manage the extra blocks that hold long filenames. Even a simple DEL command under DOS can leave these extra blocks unavailable for later use. The Windows 9x ScanDisk utility can recover these unreleased blocks.

FAT32

Beginning with Windows 95 OSR2, Microsoft offered a FAT that contains 32 bits per FAT entry instead of the older 12-bit or 16-bit FAT entries. Actually, only 28 of the bits are used to hold a cluster number; the remaining four bits are reserved.

FAT32 is recommended for hard drives larger than 512 MB and is efficient for drives up to 16 GB. In this range, the cluster size is 8K. After that, the cluster size increases to about 16K for drives in the 16-GB to 32-GB range. You are then reaching a hard drive size that warrants a more powerful file management system than FAT32, such as NTFS, supported by Windows NT/2000/XP.

> If you are currently using FAT16 and are considering switching to FAT32, you can use Partition-Magic by PowerQuest Corporation (*www.powerquest.com*) to scan your hard drive and tell you how much of the drive is used for slack space. Knowing this can help you decide if the change will yield more usable drive space. In Chapter 4 you will learn how to use a Windows utility to convert a FAT16 drive to FAT32.

3

NTFS   Windows NT/2000/XP supports the **New Technology file system (NTFS)**. NTFS is designed to provide more security than does the FAT file system and uses a database called the **master file table (MFT)** to hold information about files and directories and their locations on the hard drive. Whereas the FAT file system writes the FAT and root directory at the beginning of a hard drive, NTFS writes the MFT at the end of a hard drive. Use NTFS under Windows NT/2000/XP when you have a large hard drive, you are not going to install Windows 9x on the drive as a second OS, and security is a concern.

It is best to install NTFS at the same time you install Windows NT/2000/XP from the setup CD, though you can convert a FAT file system to NTFS after Windows NT/2000/XP is installed.

How Many Logical Drives?

When you partition a hard drive and create logical drives, you decide how many logical drives you want and how large each drive will be. Some people prefer to use more than one logical drive to organize their hard drives. However, the main reason you need multiple logical drives is to optimize space and access time to the drive. The larger the logical drive, the larger the cluster size, and the more slack or wasted space there is. When deciding how to allocate space to logical drives, the goal is to use as few logical drives as possible and still keep cluster size to a minimum. For Windows 9x, use FAT32 to get the smaller cluster size.

Table 3-1 helps you decide how to slice your drive. Notice that the largest logical drive possible using FAT16 is 2 GB (this limitation is rooted in the largest cluster number that can be stored in a 16-bit FAT entry). For Windows NT/2000/XP, FAT16 logical drives can be no larger than 4 GB. However, you can see from the table that, to make a drive that big, the cluster size must be huge. Also, the largest hard drive that FAT16 can support is 8.4 GB; if the drive is larger than that, you must use FAT32 or NTFS.

File System	Size of Logical Drive	Sectors Per Cluster	Bytes Per Cluster
FAT16	16 MB to 128 MB	4	2,048
	128 to 256 MB	8	4,096
	256 to 512 MB	16	8,192
	512 MB to 1 GB	32	16,384
	1 GB to 4 GB	64	32,768
FAT32	512 MB to 8 GB	8	4,096
	8 GB to 16 GB	16	8,192
	16 GB to 32 GB	32	16,384

Table 3-1 (continued)

File System	Size of Logical Drive	Sectors Per Cluster	Bytes Per Cluster
	More than 32 GB	64	32,768
NTFS	Up to 512 MB	1	512
	512 MB to 1 GB	2	1,024
	1 GB to 2 GB	4	2,408
	More than 2 GB	8	4,096

Table 3-1 Size of some logical drives compared to cluster size for FAT16, FAT32, and NTFS

The different file systems have the following size barriers:

- For DOS and Windows 9x, the largest volume (logical drive) that FAT16 supports is 2.1 GB.
- FAT16 cannot be used on hard drives (including all volumes) that exceed 8.4 GB.
- For Windows NT/2000/XP, the largest volume that FAT16 supports is 4 GB.
- Windows 2000/XP does not support a FAT32 volume larger than 32 GB.
- Windows 9x FAT32 does not support hard drives larger than 137 GB.
- Windows 2000 supports hard drives larger than 137 GB if Service Pack 3 or higher is applied, and Windows XP supports these drives if Service Pack 1 or higher is applied.

When to Partition a Drive

There are several reasons to partition a drive:

- When you first install a new hard drive, you must partition it to prepare it for use.
- If an existing hard drive is causing errors, you can repartition the drive and reformat each logical drive to begin fresh. You will destroy all data on the drive, so back up important data first.
- If you suspect a virus has attacked the drive, you can back up critical data and repartition the drive to begin with a clean one.
- If you want to wipe a hard drive clean and install a new OS, you can repartition a drive in preparation for formatting it with a new file system. If you do not want to change the size or number of partitions, you do not have to repartition the drive.

When installing Windows 9x, before you use the Windows 9x CD for Windows 9x upgrades, you can boot from a bootable disk that has the Fdisk.exe program file on it. Then use Fdisk to partition the hard drive, and install enough of a previous version of Windows to boot from it. During a Windows 9x installation, if the drive is not partitioned, the install procedure automatically executes Fdisk to partition the drive.

Many technicians prefer third-party software over Fdisk because, when Fdisk partitions a drive, it erases all data on the existing partitions that it changes or overwrites. On the other hand, PartitionMagic protects data when it changes the partitions on the drive. Also, PartitionMagic has a more user-friendly GUI interface.

NOTE

Fdisk under Windows 98 can incorrectly display the size of hard drives larger than 64 GB. The capacity will be reported as the true capacity minus 64 GB. For example, Fdisk will show a 120-GB drive to be 56 GB (120 GB – 64 GB). When using Windows 9x with drives larger than 64 GB, check with the hard drive manufacturer for freeware that you can use to partition and format the drive. For instance, Western Digital has Data Lifeguard Tools and Maxtor has MaxBlast software.

NOTE

If a hard drive has been partitioned by third-party software such as Disk Manager or SpeedStor, use this third-party software to repartition the drive.

Using Fdisk to Partition a Drive

To use Fdisk, boot from a startup disk that has the Fdisk.exe utility and enter Fdisk at the command prompt. The Fdisk opening menu appears (see Figure 3-9). Select option 1 to create the first partition. The menu in Figure 3-10 appears. Use option 1 to create the primary DOS partition. If you plan to install Windows 9x later, be sure this partition is at least 150 MB, preferably more. Make this first partition the active partition, which is the partition used to boot the OS. Fdisk automatically makes this partition drive C.

Next, use option 2 shown in Figure 3-10 to create an extended DOS partition using the remainder of the hard drive, and then use option 3 to create logical drives in the extended partition.

When you are creating logical drives, you decide how large you want each drive to be. If you have at least 512 MB available for the drive, a message appears asking, "Do you wish to enable large disk support (Y/N)?" If you respond Y, then Fdisk assigns the FAT32 file system to the drive; otherwise it uses FAT16.

Fdisk also assigns a drive letter to the logical drive. For a primary partition, drive C is assigned to the one volume and drives D, E, and so forth are assigned to volumes in the extended partition. However, if a second hard drive is installed in a system, Fdisk takes this into account when assigning drive letters. Drive D is assigned to the one volume in the primary partition of the second hard drive, leaving drive letters E, F, G, H, and so forth for the volumes in the extended partitions of both hard drives. For example, in a two hard-drive system where each hard drive has three logical

A+
OS
1.4
1.5

drives, the drive letters for the first hard drive will be C, E, and F and the drive letters for the second hard drive will be D, G, and H.

When Fdisk is completed, the hard drive has a partition table, an active and extended partition, and logical drives within these partitions. As shown in Figure 3-9, you can choose option 4 of Fdisk to display partition information (see Figure 3-11).

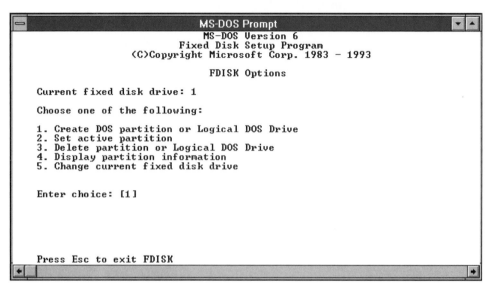

Figure 3-9 Fixed disk setup program (Fdisk) menu

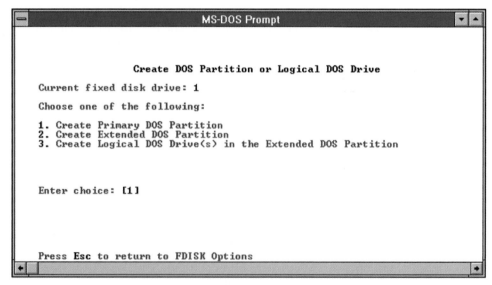

Figure 3-10 Fdisk menu to create partitions and logical drives

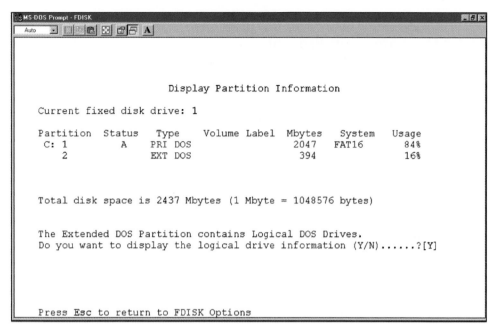

Figure 3-11   Fdisk displays partition information

After you exit the Fdisk window, reboot the PC before you format the logical drives.

Now that the hard drive is partitioned and logical drives are created and assigned drive letters, the next step is to format each logical drive. For the configuration shown back in Figure 3-8, the three commands used to format these three logical drives are:

```
Format C:/S
Format D:
Format E:
```

In the Format command line, the /S option makes the drive bootable, and the drive letter tells the OS which drive to format. Other options for the Format command are covered in the next section.

Using the Command Prompt

A+
OS
1.1
1.2
1.3
1.5

In this section, you will first learn how to access a command prompt and how to launch programs from the command prompt. Then you will learn to use several commands to manage files and folders and perform many useful utility tasks when troubleshooting a failing system. Most of the commands in this section work under Windows NT/2000/XP and Windows 9x.

When using Windows 2000/XP, you can get to a command prompt from the Windows desktop and use it to perform many utility tasks. When troubleshooting a failed boot, you can load the Recovery Console, which provides a command prompt but does not provide a Windows desktop. The Recovery Console is sometimes the only tool that is available in the worst-case situations. Many commands in this chapter also work at the Recovery Console command prompt.

Accessing a Command Prompt

There are several ways to get to a command prompt:

- Each Windows OS has a command window that you can access from the Windows desktop. For Windows XP, click Start, All Programs, Accessories, and Command Prompt. The Command Prompt window appears, as shown in Figure 3-12. To access a command prompt window in Windows 2000, click Start, Programs, Accessories, and Command Prompt. To access a command prompt window from a Windows 9x desktop, click Start, Programs, and MS-DOS Prompt. (In Windows 9x, a command prompt window is sometimes called a **DOS box**.) Using a command prompt window, you can enter the DOS-like commands discussed in this chapter. To exit the window, type Exit at the command prompt.

Figure 3-12   A Command Prompt window can be used to practice the commands given in this section

> **✔ A+ EXAM TIP**
>
> The A+ OS exam expects you to know all these ways to access a command prompt!

3

- For all versions of Windows, you can also open a command prompt window using an alternate method: click Start, click Run, and enter Command.com in the Run dialog box. To get a 32-bit version of the 16-bit Command.com program in Windows NT/2000/XP, enter Cmd.exe in the Run dialog box.
- Using Windows 2000/XP, use the four Windows 2000 startup disks or the Windows XP installation CD to boot the PC and load the Recovery Console. You will learn more about loading and using the Recovery Console in Chapter 6.
- Using Windows 9x, when you boot from a bootable disk or a Windows 9x startup disk, you get a command prompt instead of the Windows desktop.
- Using Windows 95 or Windows 98 (not Windows Me), click Start, click Shut Down, and select Restart in MS-DOS mode from the Shut Down dialog box. Using this method, you get a command prompt provided by the DOS real-mode core of Windows 95/98.
- Using Windows 9x, hold down the Ctrl key or the F8 key while booting, which causes the OS to display a startup menu. From the menu, select Command prompt only.

For convenience, you can add a command prompt icon to your Windows desktop for easy access. Locate the program file (Command.com or Cmd.exe) in Windows Explorer and, while holding down the Ctrl key, drag the icon to your desktop. Another way to create the shortcut is to click Start, point to Programs (All Programs in Windows XP), Accessories, and Command Prompt. Right-click Command Prompt and select Create Shortcut on the shortcut menu.

APPLYING CONCEPTS

For practice, try all the preceding methods of accessing a command prompt, except using the Recovery Console. Then create a command prompt icon on your desktop.

A command prompt provides information about the current drive and directory. For example, if you booted a Windows 98 PC from a bootable floppy disk into command prompt mode, you would see the A prompt (A:\>). Recall that the A: indicates the current drive. (A drive letter is always followed by a colon.) The backslash indicates the root directory, and the > symbol indicates that you can enter a new command.

A+
OS
1.1
1.2
1.3
1.5

To make the hard drive (drive C) the default drive, enter C: at the A prompt.

The prompt now changes to indicate the current directory and drive in the root directory of drive C. It looks like this:

```
C:\>
```

Launching a Program Using the Command Prompt

A+
OS
1.1
1.2
1.3
1.4
1.5
3.3

In the last chapter, you learned how to launch a program from the Windows desktop. You can also launch a program from a command prompt window. At the command prompt, when you type a single group of letters with no spaces, the OS assumes that you typed the filename of a program file you want to execute, which is stored in the current directory. The OS attempts to find the program file by that name, copies the file into RAM, and then executes the program. Let's use as our example the program Mem.exe, a Windows 9x utility that displays how memory is currently allocated. The program file Mem.exe is stored on the hard drive in the C:\Windows\command folder. Note what happens in Figure 3-13 when you type mem at the A: prompt, like this:

```
A:\>mem
```

The OS says it cannot find the program to execute. It looked only on the floppy disk (drive A) for Mem.com, Mem.exe, or Mem.bat, the three file extensions that the OS recognizes for programs. If the OS finds none of these files in the current directory, it stops looking and displays the error message:

```
Bad command or file name
```

To help the OS locate the program file, you must first change the default drive to the hard drive by giving the command:

```
A:\> C:
```

Notice in Figure 3-13 that the prompt changes to C:\>, indicating that the logical drive C on the hard drive is the default drive. Now you change the default directory on the hard drive to \Windows\Command using the **CD** (**change directory**) **command**, like this:

```
C:\>CD\windows\command
```

(Remember that DOS and Windows commands are not case sensitive, so it makes no difference whether you type CD, Cd, or cd.) The prompt now looks like this:

```
C:\WINDOWS\COMMAND>
```

A+
OS
1.1
1.2
1.3
1.4
1.5
3.3

Figure 3-13 shows what happens when you enter the mem command again. The OS locates and executes the program file. In Chapter 9, you will learn how to interpret the results of the mem command showing in Figure 3-13.

```
A:\>mem
Bad command or file name

A:\>c:

C:\>cd\windows\command

C:\WINDOWS\COMMAND>mem

Memory Type              Total      Used       Free
- - - - - - - - - -    - - - - - - - -   - - - -   - - - - - -
Conventional              640K      160K       480K
Upper                       0K        0K         0K
Reserved                    0K        0K         0K
Extended (XMS)        130,036K    2,112K   127,924K

Total memory          130,676K    2,272K   128,404K

Total under 1 MB          640K      160K       480K

Largest executable program size       479K (490, 816 bytes)
Largest free upper memory block                  (0 bytes)
MS-DOS is resident in the high memory area.

C:\WINDOWS\COMMAND>
```

Figure 3-13   Finding a program file

File and Directory Naming Conventions

When working with a command prompt, it is important to understand how to name directories and files, and how to type directory names and filenames in the command line. Under DOS, a filename can contain up to eight characters, a separating period, and a file extension of up to three characters, like this: filename.ext. This is called the 8.3 format. Characters can be the letters a through z, the numbers 0 through 9, and the following characters:

    _ ^ $ ~ ! # % & - { } ( ) @ ' `

Be sure to not use a space, period, *, ?, or \ in a filename or file extension. Acceptable file extensions for program files are .com, .sys, .bat, and .exe. For example, the DOS utility program that displays information about the system is Msd.exe.

Under Windows, directory names and filenames can be as long as 255 characters and can contain spaces. When creating subdirectories under directories, know that the maximum depth of directories you can create is dependent on the length of the directory names. When working from a command prompt and using long directory names or filenames, put double quotation marks around the name, like this: "My long filename.doc".

When using long filenames in Windows 9x, remember that the DOS portion of the system can only understand eight-character filenames with three-character extensions. When the DOS part of the system is operating, it truncates long filenames and assigns new eight-character names. For example, under DOS, the filename Mydocument.doc displays with the first few letters and a tilde (~) character:

```
Mydocum~.doc
```

If you have two documents that would have the same name when truncated in this manner, DOS also adds an identifying number. For example, if you have a document named Mydocument.doc and one named Mydocumentnew.doc, DOS truncates these:

```
Mydocu~1.doc
Mydocu~2.doc
```

When you boot using a Windows 9x startup disk or some other MS-DOS disk, be aware of this file-naming convention.

Wildcards

As you work at the command prompt, you can use two **wildcards** with filenames to execute a command on a group of files, or in an abbreviated filename if you do not know the entire name. The question mark (?) is a wildcard for one character, and the asterisk (*) is a wildcard for more than one character. For example, if you want to find all files in a directory that start with A and have a three-letter file extension, you would use the following command:

```
dir a*.???
```

Commands to Manage Disks, Hard Drives, Files, and Directories

You can use several OS commands to manage files, directories, floppy disks, and hard drives. This section describes a number of commands with some of their more common options. For more information about these and other OS commands, type the command name at a command prompt, then type /? (slash and question mark). All the commands are available using a Windows 9x startup disk, and some are available using the Windows 2000/XP Recovery Console. Also, some commands have equivalent Windows tools that are available from the Windows 2000/XP or Windows 9x desktop.

Dir

Use this command to list files and directories. Some examples are:

DIR /P	List one screen at a time.
DIR /W	Use wide format, where details are omitted and files and folders are listed in columns on the screen.
DIR *.txt	Use a wildcard character.
DIR Myfile.txt	Check that a single file is present.

APPLYING CONCEPTS

Your hard drive has failed and you boot your PC using a Windows 98 startup disk. You get to the C prompt and go to the directory containing your term paper: C:\Data\My Term Paper.doc. How will the filename appear on your screen? Find out by using Windows Explorer to create the folder and file on your hard drive. Then boot from a Windows 98 startup disk and use the CD and DIR commands to display the filename.

Type

The Type command displays the contents of a text file on your screen. Some examples are:

Type Myfile.txt	Displays file contents.
Type Myfile.txt >PRN	Redirects output to printer.
Type Myfile.txt |More	Displays output one screen at a time.

Del or Erase

The Del or Erase command erases files or groups of files. If the command does not include drive and directory information, like the following examples, the OS uses the default drive and directory when executing the command.

For example, to erase all files in the A:\DOCS directory, use the following command:

```
C:\> ERASE A:\DOCS\*.*
```

To erase all files in the current default directory, use the following command:

```
A:\DOCS> DEL *.*
```

To erase all files in the current directory that have no file extension, use the following command:

```
A:\DOCS> DEL *.
```

To erase the file named Myfile.txt, use the following command:

```
A:\>DEL MYFILE.TXT
```

Rename or Ren

The Rename command renames a file or folder. For example, to change the name of Myfile.txt to Mybackup.text, use this command:

```
Ren Myfile.txt, Mybackup.txt
```

Copy

The Copy command copies a single file or group of files. The original files are not altered.

To copy a file from one drive to another, use the following command:

```
A:\>COPY drive:\path\filename.ext drive:\path\filename.ext
```

The drive, path, and filename of the source file immediately follow the Copy command; the drive, path, and filename of the destination file follow the source filename. If you do not specify the filename of the copy, the OS assigns the file's original name. If you omit the drive or path of the source or the destination, then the OS uses the current default drive and path.

To copy the file Myfile.txt from the root directory of drive C to drive A, use the following command:

```
C:\>COPY MYFILE.TXT A:
```

Because the command does not include a drive or path before the filename Myfile.txt, the OS assumes that the file is in the default drive and path.

To copy all files in the C:\DOCS directory to the floppy disk in drive A, use the following command:

```
C:\>COPY C:\DOCS\*.* A:
```

To make a backup file named System.bak of the System.ini file in the \Windows directory of the hard drive, use the following command:

```
C:\WINDOWS>COPY SYSTEM.INI SYSTEM.BAK
```

NOTE When trying to recover a corrupted file, you can sometimes use the Copy command to copy the file to new media, such as from the hard drive to a floppy disk. During the copying process, if the Copy command reports a bad or missing sector, choose the option to ignore that sector. The copying process then continues to the next sector. The corrupted sector will be lost, but others can likely be recovered.

If you use the Copy command to duplicate multiple files, the files are assigned the names of the original files. When you duplicate multiple files, the destination portion of the command line cannot include a filename.

Xcopy /C /S /Y /D:

The Xcopy command is more powerful than the Copy command. It follows the same general command-source-destination format as the Copy command, but it offers several more options.

For example, use the /S option with the Xcopy command to copy all files in the directory \DOCS, as well as all subdirectories under \DOCS and their files, to the disk in drive A.

```
C:\>XCOPY C:\DOCS\*.* A: /S
```

To copy all files from the directory C:\DOCS created or modified on March 14, 2004, use the /D switch, as in the following command:

```
XCOPY C:\DOCS\*.* A: /D:03/14/04
```

Use the /Y option to overwrite existing files without prompting, and use the /C option to keep copying even when an error occurs.

Deltree [drive:] path

The Deltree command deletes the directory tree beginning with the subdirectory you specify, including all subdirectories and all files in all subdirectories in that tree. Use it with caution! To delete the C:\Docs folder and all its contents, use this command:

```
C:\>DELTREE C:\Docs
```

Mkdir [drive:]path or MD [drive:]path

The Mkdir command (abbreviated MD, for make directory) creates a subdirectory under a directory. To create a directory named \GAME on drive C, use this command:

```
MKDIR C:\GAME
```

The backslash indicates that the directory is under the root directory. To create a directory named CHESS under the \GAME directory, use this command:

```
MKDIR C:\GAME\CHESS
```

The OS requires that the parent directory GAME already exist before it creates the child directory CHESS.

Figure 3-14 shows the result of the Dir command on the directory \GAME. Note the two initial entries in the directory table, the . (dot) and the .. (dot, dot) entries. The Mkdir command creates these two entries when the OS initially sets up the directory. You cannot edit these entries with normal OS commands, and they must remain in the directory for the directory's lifetime. The . entry points to the subdirectory itself, and the .. entry points to the parent directory, in this case, the root directory.

<

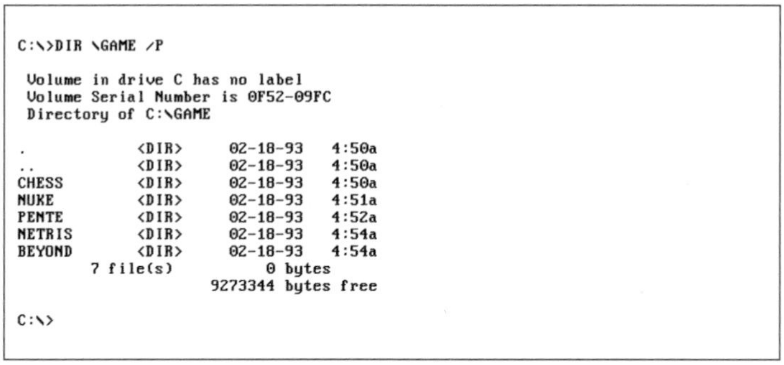

```
C:\>DIR \GAME /P

 Volume in drive C has no label
 Volume Serial Number is 0F52-09FC
 Directory of C:\GAME

.           <DIR>     02-18-93   4:50a
..          <DIR>     02-18-93   4:50a
CHESS       <DIR>     02-18-93   4:50a
NUKE        <DIR>     02-18-93   4:51a
PENTE       <DIR>     02-18-93   4:52a
NETRIS      <DIR>     02-18-93   4:54a
BEYOND      <DIR>     02-18-93   4:54a
        7 file(s)           0 bytes
                      9273344 bytes free

C:\>
```

Figure 3-14 Dir of the \GAME directory

Chdir [drive:]path or CD [drive:]path or CD..

The Chdir command (abbreviated CD, for change directory) changes the current default directory. Using its easiest form, you simply state the drive and the entire path that you want to be current:

```
CD C:\GAME\CHESS
```

The command prompt now looks like this:

```
C:\GAME\CHESS>
```

To move from a child directory to its parent directory, use the .. variation of the command:

```
C:\GAME\CHESS> CD..
C:\GAME>
```

Remember that .. always means the parent directory. You can move from a parent directory to one of its child directories simply by stating the name of the child directory:

```
C:\GAME>CD CHESS
C:\GAME\CHESS>
```

Do not put a backslash in front of the child directory name; doing so tells the OS to go to a directory named CHESS that is directly under the root directory.

Rmdir [drive:]path or RD [drive:]path

The Rmdir command (abbreviated RD, for remove directory) removes a subdirectory. Before you can use the Rmdir command, three things must be true:

- The directory must contain no files.
- The directory must contain no subdirectories.
- The directory must not be the current directory.

The . and .. entries are present when a directory is ready for removal. For example, to remove the \GAME directory in the preceding example, the CHESS directory must first be removed:

```
C:\>RMDIR C:\GAME\CHESS
```

Or, if the \GAME directory is the current directory, use this command:

```
C:\GAME>RD CHESS
```

Once you remove the CHESS directory, you can remove the \GAME directory. You must first leave the \GAME directory like this:

```
C:\GAME>CD..
C:\>RD \GAME
```

Attrib

The Attrib command displays or changes the read-only, archive, system, and hidden attributes assigned to files. To display the attributes of the file MYFILE.TXT, use this command:

```
ATTRIB MYFILE.TXT
```

To hide the file, use this command:

```
ATTRIB +H MYFILE.TXT
```

To remove the hidden status of the file, use this command:

```
ATTRIB -H MYFILE.TXT
```

To make the file a read-only file, use this command:

```
ATTRIB +R MYFILE.TXT
```

To remove the read-only status of the file, use this command:

```
ATTRIB -R MYFILE.TXT
```

To turn on the archive bit, use this command:

```
ATTRIB +A MYFILE.TXT
```

To turn off the archive bit, use this command:

```
ATTRIB -A MYFILE.TXT
```

The archive bit is used to determine if a file has changed since the last backup.

Sys Drive:

The Sys command copies the system files needed to boot to a disk or hard drive. Use the command if the system files on a drive are corrupt. You can access the drive, but you cannot boot from it. The command to copy system files to the hard drive is:

```
SYS C:
```

Chkdsk [drive:] /F /V

A+
OS
1.3

The Chkdsk command reports information about a disk. Use the /F option to have Chkdsk fix errors it finds, including errors in the FAT caused by clusters marked as being used but not belonging to a particular file (called lost allocation units) and clusters marked in the FAT as belonging to more than one file (called cross-linked clusters). To check the hard drive for errors and repair them, use this command:

```
CHKDSK C: /F
```

To redirect the output from the Chkdsk command to a file that you can later print, use this command:

```
CHKDSK C: >Myfile.txt
```

The /V option of the Chkdsk command displays all path and filename information for all files on a disk:

```
CHKDSK C: /V
```

For Windows 2000/XP, Chkdsk is best used in the Recovery Console, and for Windows 9x, Chkdsk is useful when using a startup disk. From the Windows desktop, rather than use Chkdsk, use other error-checking tools such as ScanDisk for Windows 9x or Error-checking for Windows 2000/XP. (These Windows tools are discussed in future chapters.)

Scandisk Drive: /A /N /P

A+
OS
1.3
1.5

The Scandisk command scans a hard drive for errors and repairs them if possible. Scandisk checks the FAT, long filenames, lost and cross-linked clusters, directory tree structure, bad sectors, and compressed structure, if the drive has been compressed using Windows DriveSpace or DoubleSpace. The /A parameter is used to scan all non-removable local drives. Use this command only to display information without fixing the drive:

```
SCANDISK C: /P
```

Use this command to display information and fix errors:

```
SCANDISK C:
```

Use this command to start and stop Scandisk automatically:

```
SCANDISK C: /N
```

If you use the preceding command, Scandisk still stops to report errors.

Windows 9x offers Scandisk from the command prompt and from the desktop. It is not available under Windows NT/2000/XP.

Scanreg /Restore /Fix /Backup

The Scanreg command restores or repairs the Windows 98 registry. It uses backups of the registry that Windows 98 Registry Checker automatically makes each day. To restore the registry from a previous backup, use this command:

```
SCANREG /RESTORE
```

A menu appears asking you which backup to use.
To repair a corrupted registry, use this command:

```
SCANREG /FIX
```

To create a new backup of the registry, use this command:

```
SCANREG /BACKUP
```

Don't use this last command if you are having problems with the registry.

Defrag Drive: /S

The Defrag command examines a hard drive or disk for **fragmented files** (files written to a disk in noncontiguous clusters) and rewrites these files to the disk or drive in contiguous clusters. Use this command to optimize a hard drive's performance.
Use the /S:N option to sort the files on the disk in alphabetical order by filename.

```
DEFRAG C: /S:N
```

Use the /S:D option to sort the files on the disk by date and time.

```
DEFRAG C: /S:D
```

The Defrag command works under Windows 9x. It is not available from the Windows 2000/XP Recovery Console.

Ver

Use the Ver command to display the version of the operating system in use. It works under Windows 2000/XP and Windows 9x.

Setver

You can execute this command from Autoexec.bat to tell DOS applications that the version of DOS they are looking for is the version they are using. The command allows some older DOS applications to run that might otherwise hang.

Extract filename.cab file1.ext /D

The Extract command extracts files from a cabinet file such as the Ebd.cab file on the Windows 98 startup disk. To list the files contained in the cabinet file, use this command:

```
EXTRACT EBD.CAB /D
```

To extract the file Debug.exe from the Ebd.cab file, use this command:

```
EXTRACT EBD.CAB DEBUG.EXE
```

To extract all files from the Ebd.cab cabinet file, use this command:

```
EXTRACT EBD.CAB *.*
```

This command is available under Windows 9x. For Windows 2000/XP, use the Expand command, which is available under the Recovery Console.

Debug

The Debug program is an editor that can view and manipulate the components of a file system on floppy disks and hard drives, including the FAT, directories, and boot records. You can also use Debug to view the contents of memory and hexadecimal memory addresses. To access Debug, enter the command Debug at the command prompt.

Edit [path][filename]

The Edit program (Edit.com) is a handy, "quick and dirty" way to edit text files while working at a command prompt. To edit the Autoexec.bat file on a floppy disk, use this command:

```
EDIT A:\AUTOEXEC.BAT
```

If the file does not already exist, Edit creates it. For the Autoexec.bat file on the Windows 98 startup disk, your screen should be similar to the one shown in Figure 3-15. After you have made your changes and want to exit from the editor, press the Alt key to activate the menus, and choose Exit from the File menu. When asked if you want to save your changes, respond Yes to exit the editor and save changes.

The Edit command is available under Windows 9x, but not Windows 2000/XP.

A+
OS
1.3
.1.5

```
 File  Edit  Search  View  Options  Help
                   a:\AUTOEXEC.BAT
@ECHO OFF
set EXPAND=YES
SET DIRCMD=/O:N
set LglDrv=27 * 26 Z 25 Y 24 X 23 W 22 V 21 U 20 T 19 S 18 R 17 Q 16 P 15
set LglDrv=%LglDrv% O 14 N 13 M 12 L 11 K 10 J 9 I 8 H 7 G 6 F 5 E 4 D 3 C
cls
call setramd.bat %LglDrv%
set temp=c:\
set tmp=c:\
path=%RAMD%:\;a:\;%CDROM%:\
copy command.com %RAMD%:\ > NUL
set comspec=%RAMD%:\command.com
copy extract.exe %RAMD%:\ > NUL
copy readme.txt %RAMD%:\ > NUL

:ERROR
IF EXIST ebd.cab GOTO EXT
echo Please insert Windows 98 Startup Disk 2
echo.
pause
GOTO ERROR

 F1=Help                                    Line:1    Col:1
```

Figure 3-15   Edit Autoexec.bat

NOTE

In older versions of DOS, Qbasic.exe was required for Edit.com to work correctly.

Editing Autoexec.bat and Config.sys   If you make a mistake when editing Autoexec.bat or Config.sys, you can cause a boot problem. Before editing these files on your hard drive, always make a rescue disk. If you are editing one of these files on a rescue disk, you can make a backup copy of the file before you edit it or have a second rescue disk ready just in case.

Do not use word-processing software, such as Word or WordPerfect, to edit Autoexec.bat or Config.sys, unless you save the file as a text (ASCII) file. Word-processing applications place control characters in their document files that prevent the OS from interpreting the file correctly.

NOTE

When working from a command prompt, you can reboot your computer (Ctrl + Alt + Del) to execute the new Autoexec.bat file, or you can type Autoexec.bat at the command prompt. If the computer stalls during the boot, use another startup disk to reboot. You can also press the F5 key to bypass the startup files during the boot.

Fdisk /Status /MBR

The Fdisk command is used to prepare a hard drive for first use. It creates partitions and logical drives on the hard drive, displays partition information, and restores a damaged Master Boot Record. Table 3-2 shows options for this command.

Fdisk Command Option	Description
/MBR	Repairs a damaged MBR program stored at the beginning of the partition table
/Status	Displays partition information for all hard drives in the system

Table 3-2   Options for the Fdisk command

Fdisk works under Windows 9x, and is useful when booting from a Windows 9x startup disk to examine the partition table on a malfunctioning hard drive, or to prepare a hard drive for first use. Windows 2000/XP has a different tool, called Disk Management, which works from the Windows desktop to prepare a hard drive for first use. Using the Windows 2000/XP Recovery Console, the command similar to Fdisk /MBR is Fixmbr and the command similar to Fdisk is Diskpart.

Format Drive: /S /V:Volumename /Q /U /Autotest

Recall that the Format command is used to format a disk or a hard drive. For a hard drive using Windows 9x, first run Fdisk to partition the drive and create each logical drive. Then use Format to format each logical drive. Table 3-3 shows options for this command. Format works under Windows 2000/XP Recovery Console and under Windows 9x.

Format Command Option	Description
/V	Allows you to enter a volume label only once when formatting several disks. The same volume label is used for all disks. A volume label appears at the top of the directory list to help you identify the disk.
/S	Stores the system files on the disk after formatting. Writes the two hidden files and Command.com to the disk, making the disk bootable.
/Q	Re-creates the root directory and FATs if you want to quickly format a previously formatted disk that is in good condition. /Q does not read or write to any other part of the disk.
/F:size	Specifies the size of a floppy disk. If the size is not specified, the default for that drive is used. The common values for size are: /F:360 is 360K, double-density 5¼-inch disk /F:1.2 is 1.2 MB, high-density 5¼-inch disk /F:720 is 720K, double-density 3½-inch disk /F:1.44 is 1.44 MB, high-density 3½-inch disk

Table 3-3 (continued)

3

Format Command Option	Description
/U	Allows an unconditional format of the disk, which formats the disk more thoroughly by erasing all data. Use this option when you have been getting read/write errors on the disk.
/Autotest	Does not prompt the user before and during the format.

Table 3-3   Options for the Format command

Unformat

The Unformat command might be able to reverse the effect of an accidental format. To unformat a disk, use this command:

```
UNFORMAT C:
```

Using Batch Files

Suppose you have a list of OS commands that you want to execute several times. Perhaps you have some data files to distribute to several PCs in your office, but you have no LAN, so you must walk from one PC to another, repeatedly doing the same job. A solution is to store the list of commands in a batch file on disk and then execute the batch file at each PC. Windows requires that the batch file have a .bat file extension. For example, store these five OS commands on a disk in a file named MYLOAD.BAT:

```
C:
MD\UTILITY
MD\UTILITY\TOOLS
CD\UTILITY\TOOLS
COPY A:\TOOLS\*.*
```

From the command prompt, you execute the batch file just as you do other program files, by entering the filename, with or without the file extension:

```
A:\>MYLOAD
```

All commands listed in the file will execute, beginning at the top of the list. The preceding batch file creates a subdirectory under the C drive called Utility\Tools, changes that directory to the default directory, and copies all files from the \Tools directory in drive A into that new subdirectory. Any good book on DOS provides examples of the very useful ways you can implement batch files, including adding user menus.

CHAPTER SUMMARY

3

▶ The boot process can be divided into four parts: POST, loading the OS, the OS initializing itself, and loading and executing an application.

▶ Startup BIOS is in control of the beginning of the boot process, after which it turns control over to the OS.

▶ The Master Boot Record (MBR) program is a small program at the very beginning of the hard drive that is needed to locate the beginning of the OS on the drive.

▶ A hard drive can be partitioned into one or more logical drives. The partition table contains a map to the logical drives on the hard drive, including an indication of which drive is the boot drive.

▶ A hidden file is a file not displayed in the directory list. One example is Io.sys, which contains the basic I/O software for Windows 9x real mode.

▶ A RAM drive is an area of memory that looks and acts like a hard drive, only it performs much faster. It is sometimes used to hold program files when the hard drive is not accessible.

▶ The file Command.com has three parts: code to manage I/O, programs for internal OS commands such as Copy and Dir, and a short program that looks for the Autoexec.bat file.

▶ When the OS loads from a hard drive, the BIOS first executes the MBR program, which executes the OS boot record. The OS boot record, in turn, loads the first program file of the OS. For Windows 9x, this file is Io.sys.

▶ Io.sys, which uses Msdos.sys, and Command.com form the core of real-mode Windows 9x. These three files are necessary to boot to a command prompt. Config.sys and Autoexec.bat are not required, but are used if they are present. Other files are needed to load the GUI desktop and run GUI applications.

▶ Autoexec.bat and Config.sys are two files that contain commands used to customize the 16-bit portion of the Windows 9x load process.

▶ A floppy disk that has enough software to load an operating system is called a bootable disk, or system disk. A bootable disk that has some utility programs to troubleshoot a failed hard drive is called a rescue disk, emergency startup disk (ESD), or startup disk.

▶ Create a startup disk in Windows 9x using the Add/Remove Programs icon in the Control Panel.

▶ You can access a command prompt window, sometimes called a DOS box, in Windows 9x by clicking Start, Programs, and MS-DOS Prompt. You can also access it by clicking Start, then Run, and typing Command.com in the Run dialog box.

▶ When a hard drive is first installed, it has nothing written on it except the track and sector markings put there at the factory. A floppy disk is completely blank and does not even have any track and sector markings. The OS is responsible for formatting and managing both hard drives and floppy disks.

▶ Tracks are concentric circles on a disk. A segment of a track is called a sector and always holds 512 bytes of data.

▶ On a floppy disk, the Format command creates tracks and sectors, the boot record, two copies of the file allocation table (FAT), and the root directory.

▶ Basic information about how a floppy disk is organized is stored in the first sector of the disk, called the boot sector or the boot record. At the end of a boot record is a small program called the bootstrap loader that can be used to boot from the disk.

▶ The FAT lists the location of files on a disk in a one-column table. For the file systems FAT12, FAT16, and FAT32, the number after FAT indicates the bit width of each entry in the column. FAT12 is a file system for floppy disks.

▶ VFAT is an improvement over FAT16 that was introduced in Windows 95; it supports long filenames. FAT32, which made VFAT obsolete, was introduced in Windows 95 Second Edition. NTFS was introduced with Windows NT.

▶ After a drive is physically installed, the next step is to partition the drive into manageable areas. The high-level divisions are called partitions, and within the partitions, the drive is further divided into logical drives or volumes.

▶ The Fdisk command is used to partition a hard drive. If a drive has been partitioned using third-party software such as Disk Manager or SpeedStor, you may not be able to use Fdisk. You must use the third-party software to change the partitions on the drive.

▶ The largest drive that FAT16 can support is 8.4 GB. FAT32 is recommended for hard drives larger than 512 MB and is efficient for drives up to 16 GB.

▶ The Format command is used to format floppy disks and logical drives. The /S option with the Format command makes a drive bootable. The Unformat command attempts to reverse the effect of an accidental format.

▶ The Del or Erase command deletes files or groups of files.

▶ The Copy command copies a single file or group of files. The Xcopy command is more powerful than the Copy command and supports copying subdirectories.

▶ The Sys command copies the system files needed to boot to a disk or drive.

▶ Mkdir creates a subdirectory, Chdir changes the current directory, and Rmdir removes a subdirectory.

▶ The Attrib command displays or changes the read-only, archive, system, and hidden attributes assigned to files.

▶ Chkdsk and Scandisk both check drives for errors and repair them. Scandisk does a more thorough scan and basically replaces Chkdsk.

▶ The Scanreg command restores or repairs the Windows 98 registry.

3

KEY TERMS

For explanations of key terms, see the Glossary near the end of the book.

active partition	emergency startup disk (ESD)	Ntldr
Autoexec.bat	extended partition	partition table
batch file	external command	power-on self test (POST)
booting	FAT12	primary partition
boot record	fragmented file	program file
boot sector	hard boot	RAM drive
boot sector virus	hidden file	rescue disk
bootable disk	internal command	soft boot
bootstrap loader	Io.sys	startup disk
cabinet file	master file table (MFT)	system disk
CD (change directory) command	Master Boot Record (MBR)	virtual file allocation table (VFAT)
cold boot	Msdos.sys	warm boot
Command.com	New Technology file system (NTFS)	wildcards
DOS box		

REVIEWING THE BASICS

1. What three keys can you press to perform a soft boot when using DOS?

2. What are the four main parts of the boot process?

3. Name the program that is needed to locate the beginning of the OS on a drive.

4. List three types of information contained in a hard drive's partition table.

5. Which file systems for a hard drive does Windows 98 support?

6. Which file system does Windows NT/2000/XP support that Windows 98 does not support?

7. Which version of Windows introduced the VFAT file system? The FAT32 file system?

8. What three OS files are necessary to boot to MS-DOS mode? What is the function of each? What additional two files are not required but are used if they are present?

9. Why is it important not to edit Autoexec.bat with word-processing software such as Microsoft Word or WordPerfect?

10. What is the name of the Windows NT/2000/XP boot loader program?

11. How many bytes are contained in a sector?

12. What is the name of the first sector on a floppy disk? What information is contained in this sector?

13. FAT32 is recommended for hard drives larger than _____ and is efficient for drives up to _____.

14. When using Fdisk, what question does the software ask that will cause it to use the FAT32 file system if you respond "Y" for yes?

15. What are two Windows 2000/XP program files that can provide a Command Prompt window?

16. What are the two wildcard characters that can be used in command lines?

17. What is the /S switch used for with the Format command? The /V switch? The /F:size switch?

18. What is the name of the single directory created when a floppy disk or logical drive is first formatted?

19. Name the Windows 98 command that is used to partition a hard drive.

20. The _____ command erases files or groups of files.

21. What command is used to create a subdirectory? To change the current directory? To remove a subdirectory?

22. The _____ command displays or changes the read-only, archive, system, and hidden characteristics of files.

23. What is a hidden file? Name a Windows 9x file that is hidden.

24. The _____ Console in Windows 2000 can be used to execute commands when troubleshooting a failed boot.

25. What is the purpose of the Ebd.cab file on the Windows 98 startup disk?

26. What icon in the Windows 98 Control Panel is used to create a startup disk?

27. List the steps to add a shortcut to your Windows desktop to access a command prompt window.

28. At a command prompt, how must you type long filenames that contain spaces?

29. When using a real-mode command prompt, how will DOS display the filename Mydocument.doc?

30. What is the batch file used by Windows 98 to control loading 16-bit programs?

3

THINKING CRITICALLY

1. If a PC boots first to the hard drive before checking the floppy disk for an OS, how do you change this boot sequence so that it first looks on the floppy disk for an OS?

2. A PC continues to reboot. You try to solve the problem by booting from a Windows 98 startup disk. You boot to the A prompt and look on the hard drive. Which of the following options is a possible source of the problem? If this is the source, describe how to fix the problem.

   a. The Restart command is in the Autoexec.bat file on the hard drive.

   b. The files to load the Windows desktop have been deleted.

   c. The hard drive has five partitions and two of the five partitions have been designated the active partition.

3. Explain the difference between the Copy command and the Xcopy command.

4. Explain the difference between the Chkdsk and Scandisk commands.

5. You need to make 10 duplicates of one floppy disk. Describe how to do this using two different methods. Which method is better and why?

PROJECT 3-1: Observing the Boot Process

1. If your computer has a reset button, press it and then watch what happens. If your computer does not have a reset button, turn it off, wait a few seconds, and then turn it back on. Try to note every beep, every light that goes on or off, and every message you see on the screen. Compare your notes to those of others to verify that you did not overlook something.

2. Answer these questions from observing the boot process:

    a. What type of video card are you using?

    b. Who is the BIOS vendor, and what version of the BIOS are you using?

    c. As the computer boots, memory is counted. Observe the memory count and record the amount of memory detected. What number system is used to count this memory?

3. Unplug the keyboard and reboot the computer. What is different about the boot process? Write down your observations.

4. Plug in the keyboard again, unplug the monitor, and reboot. After you reboot, plug in the monitor. Did the computer know the monitor was missing?

5. Put a floppy disk that is not bootable in drive A, and reboot. Write down what you observe. If the PC booted to the desktop as usual, why didn't it look to the floppy disk to load the OS?

PROJECT 3-2: Creating a Startup Disk Using Windows 9x

Using directions in the chapter, create a startup disk in Windows 9x, and then test it by rebooting the computer with the disk still in the drive. Answer these questions using the Readme.txt file on the startup disk:

1. What command line is recommended to check your hard drive for errors?

2. At what point in the boot process is the RAM drive created?

3. If you reboot your PC after booting from the startup disk, will the RAM drive remain in memory?

4. Using a second disk, create a system disk using Windows Explorer. Compare the contents of the two disks.

PROJECT 3-3: Researching MS-DOS Commands Using Windows 2000/XP

In this chapter you learned about several important MS-DOS commands, but there are more commands. Do the following to find out more about the commands in the chapter and to investigate other commands.

First, access the Help feature of the OS. For Windows XP, do the following:

▶ Click **Start,** and then click **Help and Support.** The Help and Support Center window appears. In the Search box, type **Command-line reference A-Z** and then click **Go.**

For Windows 2000, do the following:

▶ Click **Start,** and then click **Help.** The Windows 2000 Help window appears. Click the **Search** tab. In the search box, type **Windows 2000 Command Reference.** Click **List Topics.** Click **Windows 2000 Command Reference Main Page,** and then click **Display.**

Use this reference tool to answer the following questions:

1. What are some parameters to the Chkdsk command that you can only use for an NTFS volume?

2. How does Chkdsk handle the situation in which a file is open (that is, currently in use by another program)?

3. Describe the Diskcomp command. What is its purpose? When would you use it?

4. Describe the Find command. What are three parameters you can use with the command? Describe a situation in which it would be useful.

5. What is the purpose of the Assoc command? What is the command to send the output of the Assoc command to a file named MyResults.txt?

PROJECT 3-4: How Large Is a Cluster?

Remember that each entry in a FAT tracks the use of one cluster. The number of sectors per cluster varies from one file system to another. The Chkdsk command displays the size of one cluster. There is another way to determine the size of a cluster with a simple test. Do the following:

1. Use the Dir command and note how much space is available on your hard drive.

2. Using Edit or Notepad, create a text file containing only a single character.

3. Use the Dir command again to note how much disk space is available and compare the two values, before and after a one-character file is written to the disk. The difference in the two values is the size of one cluster, which is the smallest amount that can be allocated to a file.

4. Verify your calculations using Chkdsk.

PROJECT 3-5: Practicing Commands

Go to a command prompt and do the following. Write down the commands you use.

1. Create a folder on your hard drive named **/testme**.

2. Make that folder the current folder.

3. Select a file in the Program Files folder on your hard drive. What is the name of the file? What is its size in bytes?

4. Copy the file to the /testme folder.

5. Format a floppy disk, making it bootable.

6. Display on the screen the amount of free bytes on the floppy disk. How many bytes are free?

7. Copy the file from the /testme folder to the floppy disk.

8. Make the floppy disk the current drive. What prompt do you now see?

9. Make the file on the floppy disk a hidden file.

10. Display on the screen the amount of free bytes on the floppy disk. How many bytes are free? Calculate how many bytes were used on the floppy disk to hold the file.

11. Unhide the hidden file on the floppy disk.

12. Rename the file **myfile.xxx**. What message appears when you rename the file?

13. Display a list of all files on the floppy disk that begin with the letter M.

PROJECT 3-6: Observing Windows 9x in Real Mode

Using Windows 9x, boot into MS-DOS real mode and then do the following.

1. From the command prompt, make a bootable disk using either of the following commands. If the disk is already formatted, but has no files stored on it, use this command:

```
C:\> Sys A:
```

To format the disk and also make it bootable, use this command:

```
C:\> Format A:/S
```

2. Your disk should now contain a boot record, the two hidden files, and Command.com. Use the Dir command to see them (**DIR A:**). Compare the bytes available on the disk to a disk that is not bootable. Calculate how many bytes must be in the two hidden files.

3. Does the hard drive contain Autoexec.bat and Config.sys files in the root directory? If so, print them using a local printer (not a network printer). Use one of the following methods:

```
C:\> TYPE filename.ext>PRN or C:\> COPY filename.ext LPT1
```

4. Test your bootable disk by inserting it in drive A and doing a soft boot. What prompt do you see on the screen?

5. At the DOS prompt, enter the Prompt command that is used to customize the DOS command prompt, where the space between P and $ can contain any text:

```
PROMPT $P $G
```

What prompt did you get?

6. By examining the prompt, guess what $P in the command line accomplishes and what $G accomplishes. Test your theory by changing the Prompt command, leaving first $P and then $G out of the command line.

7. Using Edit, create an Autoexec.bat file on your bootable disk. Create a Prompt command to include your first name. Test the command by booting from this disk.

8. Without the appropriate Path command in your active Autoexec.bat file, you cannot execute software stored on drive C from the A prompt. Test this theory by trying to execute some application software that you know is stored on your hard drive. For example, if you have MSD on your hard drive, try to execute the software at the A prompt by using the following command:

```
A:\> MSD
```

What error did you get? Why?

PROJECT 3-7: Challenge Project

Using Windows 9x, create your own bootable disk that loads the 16-bit real-mode drivers to use a mouse. Test the mouse by booting from the disk and using the mouse with the EDIT text editor.

Hint: First locate a 16-bit mouse driver file such as Mouse.sys. Load the driver file using a Device= command in Config.sys.

CASE PROJECT

Preparing a Hard Drive for the Installation of Windows 9x

 NOTE   This project requires that you completely erase everything on your hard drive. If you have important data on the drive, don't do this project!

Do the following to prepare a hard drive for a new installation of Windows 9x, which you will perform in the next chapter:

1. Boot from a Windows 9x startup disk, and then use Fdisk to create primary and extended partitions on the drive. The primary partition will contain drive C. If there is room on the drive, create two logical drives in the extended partition.

2. Format all three logical drives, placing system files on drive C.

3. Verify that you can boot to drive C and get a C prompt and that all three drives are accessible.

4. Use the Dir command to print a directory of each drive to a local printer. Use these or similar commands: DIR C:>PRN, DIR D:>PRN, and DIR E:>PRN.

5. Using ScanDisk, scan each logical drive disk surface for errors.

Supporting Windows 9x

As a PC support technician, you need to know how to install, use, and troubleshoot the Windows OSs commonly used today. You need a general knowledge of how hardware, Windows, and applications work. In Chapter 2, you learned how hardware and software work together, and in Chapter 3, you were introduced to the DOS portion of Windows 9x. This chapter covers how Windows 9x is structured, how it is used, how it works with various software programs and hardware devices, and how to troubleshoot it. Although Windows 9x is gradually being replaced by Windows XP, it is still in use, and it is important that you know how to use it effectively.

Windows 9x has had several releases, including Windows 95, Windows 95 Service Release 2 (also known as Windows 95 SR2, Windows 95 Rev B, Windows 95B, and Windows 95 OSR2), Windows 98, Windows 98 Second Edition (SE), and Windows Me (Millennium Edition). Each of these OSs uses the same basic architecture, and each release improves on previous versions and adds new features.

NOTE

To learn which version of Windows is installed, right-click the My Computer icon and select Properties from the shortcut menu. The System Properties window opens. Click the General tab.

Windows 9x Architecture

Like other OSs, Windows 9x has a shell and a kernel. A **shell** is the portion of the OS that relates to the user and to applications. The shell provides a command, menu, or icon interface to the user using various interface tools such as Windows Explorer, the Control Panel, or My Computer.

The core, or **kernel**, of the OS is responsible for interacting with hardware. It has more power to communicate with hardware devices than the shell, so that applications operating under the OS cannot get to hardware devices without the shell passing those requests to the kernel. This structure provides a more stable system.

The two most important parts of the shell are the user component and the GDI. The **user component** manages input from the keyboard and other user devices, output from the user interface, and the **GDI** (**Graphics Device Interface**). The GDI is a component of the OS responsible for presenting the graphical interface to the user and providing graphics support to output devices. The purposes of each component are listed in Table 4-1.

Component Name	Main Files Holding the Component	Functions
Kernel	Kernel32.dll, Krnl386.exe	Handles the basic OS functions such as managing memory, file I/O, and loading and executing programs
User	User32.dll, User.exe	Controls the mouse, keyboard, ports, and desktop, including the position of windows, icons, and dialog boxes
GDI	GDI32.dll, GDI.exe	Draws screens, graphics, and lines, and manages printing

Table 4-1   Core components of Windows 9x

As you learned in Chapter 1, Windows 9x is a compromise OS that bridges two worlds. In Figure 4-1, you can see that DOS was a 16-bit OS, used only 16-bit device drivers, and managed base, upper, and extended memory. Windows NT/2000/XP is a true 32-bit OS. In compromise, the core components of Windows 9x (kernel, user, and GDI) are compiled as a combination of 16-bit and 32-bit code, and Windows 9x accepts both 16-bit and 32-bit drivers. It manages memory the same way that DOS does, and uses memory paging and virtual memory as does Windows NT/2000/XP. Chapter 9 covers Windows 9x memory management in detail.

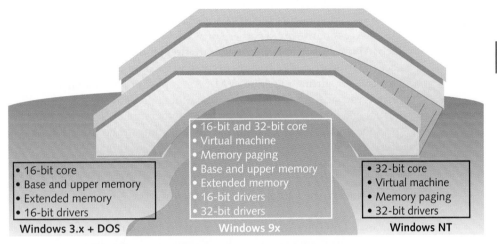

Figure 4-1   Windows 9x is the bridge from DOS to Windows NT/2000/XP

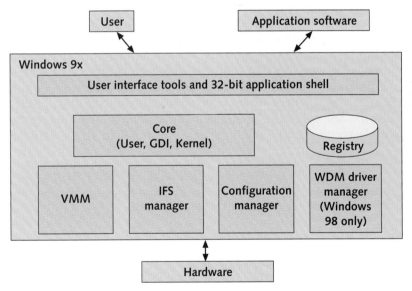

Figure 4-2   The Windows 9x architecture as it relates to the user, software, and hardware

The Windows 9x core relates to users, software, and hardware by way of several modules, as seen in Figure 4-2. Configuration data is primarily stored in the Windows 9x registry, a database that also contains the initialization information for applications, a database of hardware and software settings, Windows configuration settings, user parameters, and application settings. In addition, some data are kept in text files called initialization files, which often have an .ini or .inf file extension.

Virtual Machines

Before we look at the different components in Figure 4-2, you need to understand how these components relate to applications and hardware. Applications call on the OS to access hardware or other software by using an **application programming interface (API) call**. When applications are first loaded by Windows 9x, the methods to access hardware and software are made available to the software through an interface called a **virtual machine (VM)**. An application sees a virtual machine as a set of resources made available to it through these predefined APIs. An OS can provide a virtual machine to a single application that commands all the resources of that virtual machine, or the OS can assign a virtual machine to be shared by two or more applications. Think of virtual machines as multiple logical machines within one physical machine, similar in concept to several logical drives within one physical drive.

Figure 4-3 shows several virtual machines that Windows 9x can provide. In the figure, the system virtual machine (system VM) is the most important VM under Windows 9x, and is where all OS processes run. It can also support 32-bit and 16-bit Windows applications, but DOS programs run in their own virtual machines.

A DOS program expects to directly control the hardware of the entire PC, memory included. If a DOS program begins to use memory addresses not assigned to it, errors occur in a multitasking environment. Windows 9x solves this problem by providing the DOS program with its own virtual machine. In effect, the application says, "I want all of the memory and all of this and all of that." Windows 9x says, "OK, here they are," and gives the program its own PC, including all the virtual memory addresses it wants from 0 to 4 GB as well as its own virtual hardware! As far as the DOS program is concerned, it can go anywhere and do anything within its own PC. The DOS program does not try to communicate with any other application or to access the data of another program, because it thinks there are no other programs; it controls its entire world, and is the only program in it. That's a virtual machine.

One important result of running DOS programs in individual virtual machines is that when a DOS program makes an error, the virtual machine it is using hangs, but other programs and the OS are isolated from the problem and thus are not affected.

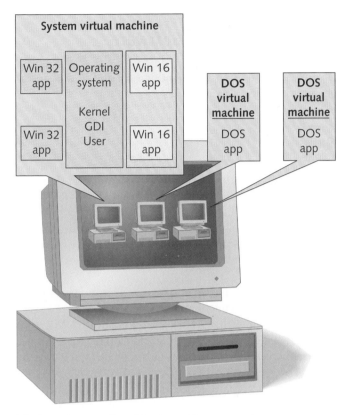

Figure 4-3   Windows 9x uses the virtual machine concept

Windows 16-bit applications offer a slightly different challenge to Windows 9x. These programs make some of the same mistakes that DOS programs do and can cause the system to hang. However, they also sometimes expect to access other programs and their data. The 16-bit Windows programs don't expect to control the hardware directly and are content to route their requests to Windows. Windows 9x places these programs within the system virtual machine because they communicate with hardware through the OS, but Windows 9x puts these programs together in their own memory space so they can share memory addresses.

The result of this arrangement is that when a 16-bit Windows program causes an error called a Windows Protection Error or a General Protection Fault, it can disturb other 16-bit programs, causing them to fail. However, it does not disturb DOS programs in their own virtual machines or 32-bit programs that don't share their virtual memory addresses.

Installing Windows 9x, Hardware, and Software

In this section, you learn how to install Windows 9x and how to install hardware and applications with Windows 9x.

Installing Windows 9x

Remember as you proceed with Windows 9x installation that there are separate CDs for installing Windows 9x on a PC without Windows (Microsoft labels the OS as Windows 9x for a New PC) and for installing Windows 9x on a PC with an earlier version of Windows (Microsoft labels the OS as Windows 9x Upgrade). The CDs for installing Windows on a new PC are significantly more expensive than the upgrade CDs. To use the upgrade CDs, a previous version of Windows must be installed on your hard drive.

A problem arises if you have just replaced a failed hard drive with a new hard drive and you want to do a fresh installation using a Windows 9x Upgrade CD. During the OS installation, the upgrade CD asks you to provide a Microsoft floppy disk or CD from an earlier version of Windows. If you cannot provide the CD or floppy, the upgrade installation terminates and you must use the more expensive version, Windows 9x for a New PC.

First, let's look at how to prepare your hard drive for installation.

Preparing for Installation

Before installing Windows 9x, verify that your system meets requirements for the OS. Check the following:

A+
OS
2.1
2.2

- Verify that the minimum and recommended hardware requirements for Windows 9x are met. Table 4-2 lists these requirements. In order for Windows 9x to perform satisfactorily, the PC should meet the recommended requirements.
- Windows 95/98 claims that it supports legacy hardware devices, but does not. To check whether a particular hardware product has been tested for use with Windows Me, go to *www.microsoft.com/whdc/hcl/search.mspx*.
- You also need to check software packages and programs for compatibility. You can do this by checking the documentation or the manufacturer's Web site for each program.

NOTE

Windows Me does not support 16-bit legacy drivers that work under Windows 95/98, so it's important to verify that your hardware devices are compatible with Windows Me.

Description	Windows 95	Windows 98	Windows Me
Processor	486—25 MHz or higher	486DX—66 MHz (Pentium is recommended)	Pentium 150 MHz
RAM	4 MB (8 MB is recommended)	16 MB (24 MB is recommended)	32 MB
Free hard drive space	50 MB	195 MB (315 MB is recommended)	320 MB

Table 4-2 Minimum and recommended hardware requirements for Windows 9x

Windows 9x is most likely to be installed as an upgrade from Windows 95 to Windows 98 or to Windows Me, or on a clean hard drive. If you are having problems with your current operating system and applications, consider doing a clean install rather than an upgrade. A **clean install** ignores any settings in the currently installed OS, including information about installed hardware or software. Therefore, after the clean install, you must reinstall all hardware and applications.

NOTE
Before deciding to do a clean install, verify that you have all the application software installation CDs or floppy disks and then back up all data on the drive. Also take time to verify that the backups are good and that you have all device driver software. Before installing Windows Me, verify that all your hardware devices qualify for Windows Me.

You do not need to format the hard drive before you begin the installation, although you should delete all folders on the hard drive used for the OS or applications, including the \Windows folder, files, and subfolders. This forces Setup to perform a clean install and make certain that no corrupted system files or applications remain, but still retain any data files that might be on the drive. If you like, you can also format the hard drive. Do this if you suspect a virus is present. If you suspect a boot sector virus is present, use the Fdisk/MBR command (discussed in Chapter 3) to rewrite the master boot sector program. Then do the clean install.

After Windows 9x is installed, reinstall all the application software. Then, if you formatted the hard drive, restore the data from backups. This method takes longer than an upgrade, but gives you the advantage of a fresh start. Any problems with corrupted applications or system settings will not cause you problems in the new installation.

An **upgrade install** carries forward as much information as it can about what the current OS knows concerning installed hardware and software, user preferences, and other settings. An upgrade is faster than a clean install because you don't need to reinstall software and hardware. However, problems with an old installation sometimes carry forward into the upgrade.

You can perform an upgrade or a clean install with either the Windows 9x for a New PC CD or the Windows 9x Upgrade CD. If you are doing an upgrade, the old operating system must be in good enough shape to boot up, because you must begin an upgrade from within the currently installed OS.

Installing Windows 9x as a Clean Installation

Recall from Chapter 2 that you can change CMOS settings to specify the order in which system BIOS looks for an OS on the drives on your PC. You might need to change the boot order in CMOS, depending on how you plan to load the OS. Older PCs could boot only from a hard drive or floppy disk. This meant that to use a CD-ROM drive, you first had to boot these PCs from floppy disks and then install the CD-ROM drivers. There are more choices with newer PCs, some of which can boot from a hard drive, floppy drive, Zip drive, CD-ROM drive, or other type of drive. These newer PCs have drivers for drive types other than hard drives and floppy drives written into their BIOS, allowing you to boot from a different medium.

NOTE
If the PC is on a network, it is possible to install the OS from another computer on the network. However, if you want to do an upgrade, you must begin the upgrade from within the current OS. Therefore, if you are performing an installation across a network, you are forced to do a clean install.

After you have verified that the system qualifies and decided to perform a clean installation, do the following to prepare your system:

- If you have important data on your hard drive, back it up to another medium. How to perform a backup is covered in Chapter 10.
- If your system BIOS runs a program to protect the boot sector of your hard drive from viruses, enter CMOS setup and disable the program because it might interfere with the installation. After the installation you can turn the program back on. While you're in CMOS setup, verify that the boot sequence is first the floppy disk or CD-ROM, depending on the media that you have for the Windows 9x setup.
- For a new hard drive, recall from Chapter 3 that the drive is partitioned using Fdisk and formatted using the Format command before an OS is installed. The Windows 9x installation will do this for you, or you can do it prior to the installation.

NOTE
Your CD-ROM drive might be configured to run a CD automatically when it is first inserted. This Autoplay feature causes the Setup opening menu to appear without your entering the Setup command (see Figure 4-4). To disable the feature, hold down the Shift key while inserting the CD.

You are now ready to perform the installation. Do the following to begin:

Windows 9x comes on a set of floppy disks or on a CD. If you are installing the OS from floppy disks, you can boot from the hard drive or floppy disk. To boot from the floppy disk, insert the Windows 9x Disk 1, which is bootable, and boot the

PC. At the A prompt, enter the command Setup.exe. You can also boot from a hard drive; go to a C prompt, and insert the Windows 9x Disk 1 in the floppy disk drive. Enter the command A:\Setup to execute the Setup program on the floppy disk. Either way, the Windows 9x setup screen appears. Follow the directions on the screen.

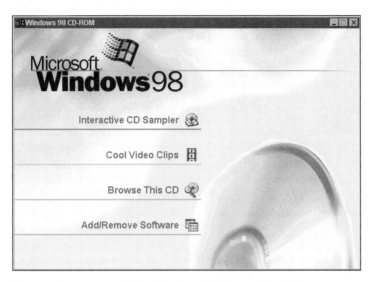

Figure 4-4   The opening screen of the Windows 98 CD provides links you can use to navigate the CD

If you are installing Windows 98 or Windows Me from a CD (and your PC can boot from a CD-ROM drive), insert the CD in the drive and reboot. If your PC cannot boot from a CD, boot from a floppy disk or hard drive, then insert the CD in the CD-ROM drive, and enter the command D:\Setup.exe, substituting the drive letter of your CD-ROM drive for *D* if necessary. The Windows 95 setup CD is not bootable, so you will need a bootable floppy disk to begin the Windows 95 installation.

NOTE

To speed up the installation, you can copy the files and folders on the Windows 9x CD to a folder on your hard drive and run the Setup program from that folder. Also, having the Windows 9x CD files on your hard drive makes it easier to access the files later when adding Windows components or updating drivers.

Installing Windows 9x as an Upgrade

If you are doing an upgrade, do the following to prepare your system before you begin the installation, in addition to the items listed previously:

- Verify that you have enough space on the hard drive. Delete files in the Recycle Bin and temporary directories.
- Run ScanDisk to check and repair errors on the hard drive. From Windows 9x, click Start, Programs, Accessories, System Tools, and ScanDisk, and then scan

each logical drive in the system. From a Windows startup disk, enter the command Scandisk at the command prompt.

- Run a current version of antivirus software to check for viruses.
- Check Config.sys and Autoexec.bat for potential problems. Verify that any hardware devices using device drivers loaded from these files work under the old OS, so you know your starting point if problems occur under the new OS.
- The Windows 9x upgrade process moves commands in Autoexec.bat that are used to load terminate-and-stay resident programs (TSRs) required for 16-bit Windows drivers and applications to Winstart.bat. Look for the Winstart.bat file in the root directory after the installation is done. If setup does not find any TSRs to put in the file, it will not be created.
- If TSRs such as QEMM386 (a memory manager by Quarterdeck) are loaded from Config.sys or Autoexec.bat, and problems arise because they run during the installation, disable them by converting these lines to remarks or comments —type *REM* at the beginning of the command lines. Later, after the installation, you can activate these lines again by removing the REMs.
- If you are connected to a network, verify that the connection works. If it does, Windows setup should be able to reestablish the connection correctly at the end of the installation.
- Create a Windows 9x rescue disk for use in the event that the installation fails.
- Decide if you want to use FAT16 or FAT32 for your file system. If you choose FAT16, you can later convert to FAT32 using the Windows Drive Converter. To access the Converter after Windows 98 is installed, click Start, Programs, Accessories, System Tools, and Drive Converter (FAT32). As an alternative, you can use the Run dialog box. For the 16-bit version, enter cvt.exe, and for the 32-bit version, enter cvt1.exe, and then click OK. The Drive Converter Wizard steps you through the process.
- If you are installing Windows 98 on a compressed drive, be aware that the registry can reside on any compressed drive, but the swap file can reside on a compressed drive only if the drive is compressed using protected-mode software such as DriveSpace. (Compressed drives, discussed in Chapter 10, are hard drives that have a portion of their data compressed in order to save space on the drive.) DriveSpace marks the area for the swap file as uncompressible. If your drive is compressed with real-mode compression software, such as DoubleSpace, then know that you cannot put the swap file on this compressed drive. The best practice is to back up the data and then uncompress the drive. You can later compress it using Windows 98 DriveSpace.
- Windows Me will not install on a compressed drive, so you must uncompress any portions of your hard drive that are compressed. If you are not sure whether your hard drive is compressed, run ScanDisk, which will tell you.
- Uninstall power management tools and disk management tools.

4

Sometimes Microsoft releases last-minute documentation on the setup CD. Check the Readme.txt file for any setup information provided. Now that everything is ready for the installation, do the following to get to the setup screen:

1. Start the PC, loading the current operating system.

2. Close all open applications, including any antivirus software that is running. Close any icons that are open in the System Tray.

3. Insert the CD in the CD-ROM drive or the floppy disk in the floppy drive. Open the Run dialog box and enter the command **D:\Setup.exe**, substituting the drive letter for your CD-ROM drive or floppy drive for D if necessary. Click **OK**.

4. Follow the instructions on the setup screen. When you have the opportunity to select the folder to install Windows, select the folder that the current OS is installed in; most likely that is \Windows. If you use the same folder, Setup uses whatever settings it finds there.

Installation Process from the Setup Screen

After you get to the setup screen, the installation process is the same, no matter whether you are doing an upgrade or a clean install. When installing Windows 9x, you have the option of creating the Startup disk, as discussed earlier. Be sure to do so to help prepare for emergencies. During the installation, you are also asked to choose from four setup options:

- *Typical.* This option installs all components that are usually installed with Windows 9x. Most often, this is the option to choose.
- *Portable.* Use this option when installing Windows 9x on a notebook computer.
- *Compact.* Use this option if you are short on hard drive space and want the smallest possible installation. No optional components are installed. After the installation, if you need a component, you can install it by double-clicking the Add/Remove Programs applet in the Control Panel.
- *Custom.* Use this option if you know you need components not normally installed under the Typical installation. You have the opportunity to select any group of components to include in the installation.

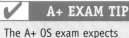 **A+ EXAM TIP**

The A+ OS exam expects you to know about all four setup options.

During the installation, Setup records information in log files. The primary log file is Setuplog.txt, a text file that Windows uses when recovering from a crash to determine how far it got in the installation. Figure 4-5 shows a portion of Setuplog.txt in which the system ran a virus check on CMOS and began checking drives. The Detection Log (Detlog.txt) keeps a record of hardware detected, as shown in Figure 4-6.

A+ OS 2.1 2.2

```
fsCmosAVCheck: Attempting CMOS Anti Virus Test
fsCmosAVCheck: CMOS Anti Virus Test SUCCEEDED
Drive=:A:, Host=::, Flags=:0x107:
Drive=:B:, Host=::, Flags=:0x107:
Drive=:C:, Host=::, Flags=:0xd:
Drive=:D:, Host=::, Flags=:0xd:
Drive=:E:, Host=::, Flags=:0x205:
vfs.boot=:C:, vfs.boothost=::
FSLog: BIOS Heads=:255:, BootPart Heads=:255:
batch settings:
[Setup]
InstallType=1
Customise=0
Express=0
ChangeDir=1
Network=1
OptionalComponents=1
System=1
MBR=1
Reboot=1
CCP=1
EBD=0
CleanBoot=0
Win31FileSystem=-8531
CopyFiles=1
```

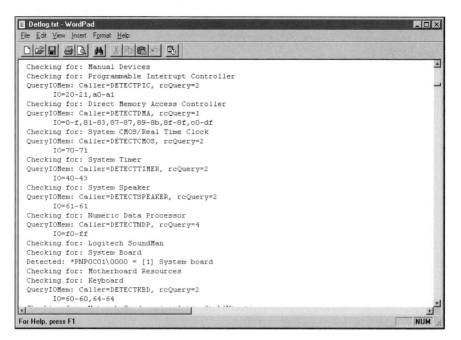

Figure 4-5 Windows records information about the setup process in Setuplog.txt

```
Checking for: Manual Devices
Checking for: Programmable Interrupt Controller
QueryIOMem: Caller=DETECTPIC, rcQuery=2
      IO=20-21,a0-a1
Checking for: Direct Memory Access Controller
QueryIOMem: Caller=DETECTDMA, rcQuery=1
      IO=0-f,81-83,87-87,89-8b,8f-8f,c0-df
Checking for: System CMOS/Real Time Clock
QueryIOMem: Caller=DETECTCMOS, rcQuery=2
      IO=70-71
Checking for: System Timer
QueryIOMem: Caller=DETECTTIMER, rcQuery=2
      IO=40-43
Checking for: System Speaker
QueryIOMem: Caller=DETECTSPEAKER, rcQuery=2
      IO=61-61
Checking for: Numeric Data Processor
QueryIOMem: Caller=DETECTNDP, rcQuery=4
      IO=f0-ff
Checking for: Logitech SoundMan
Checking for: System Board
Detected: *PNP0C01\0000 = [1] System board
Checking for: Motherboard Resources
Checking for: Keyboard
QueryIOMem: Caller=DETECTKBD, rcQuery=2
      IO=60-60,64-64
```

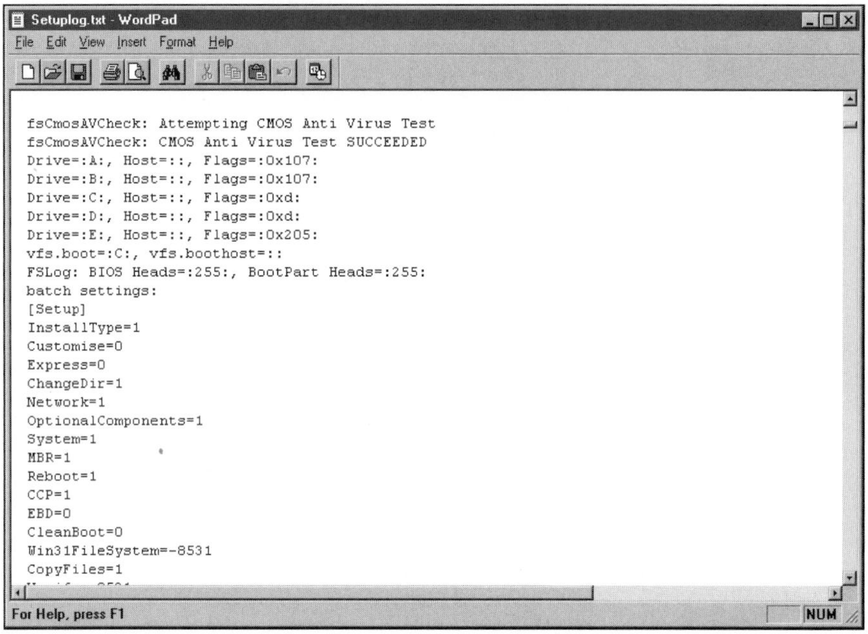

Figure 4-6 The Detlog.txt file shows what hardware has been detected

4

If the system fails to respond during the hardware detection phase, an entry is recorded in Detcrash.log, a binary file Windows uses to help recover from a crash caused by a hardware problem. Windows does not use the contents of Detlog.txt; it is created only for the benefit of the user.

For example, if Setup suspects that a network card is present, because it sees a network driver installed in Config.sys, it records in Setuplog.txt and Detlog.txt that it is about to look for the card. If it finds the card, it records the success in Detlog.txt. However, if an error occurs while Setup searches for the card, an entry is made in the Detcrash.log file.

If the system crashes while trying to detect the network card and Setup is then restarted, it looks at Detcrash.log and Setuplog.txt to determine what it was trying to do at the time of the crash. It skips that step and goes to the next step, so it doesn't make the same mistake twice.

Although Setup might crash several times during the installation, progress is still being made. By reading the content of the log files, Setup is able to skip steps that cause a problem and move forward.

NOTE

Be careful not to delete the log files during the installation, especially if you've just experienced a crash. Also, restart by using the power on/power off method so that the ISA bus is fully initialized, which does not always happen during a warm boot.

In certain situations you might want to force Setup to begin installation at the beginning instead of looking to Setuplog.txt for the entry point—for example, when you think you might have resolved a problem with hardware and want Setup to attempt to find the hardware again. To do this, delete Setuplog.txt to force a full restart.

Once the installation is complete, do the following:

- Go to the Control Panel and verify that the system date and time are correct. If they are not correct, make the change in CMOS setup.
- Using the Control Panel, open the Add/Remove Programs applet, click the Windows Setup tab, and install any additional Windows components.
- Access the Internet and go to the Microsoft Web site (*support.microsoft.com*). Download and install any available **service packs** or **patches**, which are updates and fixes to the OS released by Microsoft.
- If this is an upgrade installation, open and test the applications you already had installed under Windows 9x. Any problem you have with a particular application may be solved by uninstalling and then reinstalling it, or installing any patches necessary to make it work with the new OS. Check the application manufacturer's Web site for available updates.

Downloading and Installing Updates for Windows 9x

Between releases of OS versions, Microsoft often produce OS updates in the form of patches or service packs that add features, fix bugs, or address security issues. The Microsoft Web site, *windowsupdate.microsoft.com*, provides a list of updates available for your OS. In Windows 98 and Windows Me, you can access this page by clicking Windows Update on the Start menu. The update process examines your system and recommends available updates for you to select, download, and install following directions on the screen.

Configuring the Windows 9x Startup with Msdos.sys

In Windows 9x, the text file Msdos.sys contains several parameters that affect how the OS boots. You can change some entries in this file to customize the boot process. The file is a hidden, read-only, system file, so before you can edit it, you must first use the Attrib command at the command prompt to make the file available for editing. (Note that you can change the hidden and read-only attributes using Windows Explorer, but not the system attribute.) Also, make a backup copy of the file in case you want to revert to the form it was in before changes were made.

Follow these steps to change the options in Msdos.sys:

✔ A+ EXAM TIP

The A+ OS exam expects you to know how and why to use each of the commands in the following procedure to edit Msdos.sys.

1. Go to an OS command prompt.

2. Go to the root directory of your hard drive by entering:

   ```
   CD\
   ```

3. Make the file available for editing by entering:

   ```
   ATTRIB -R -H -S MSDOS.SYS
   ```

4. Make a backup copy of the file by entering:

   ```
   COPY MSDOS.SYS MSDOS.BK
   ```

5. Use Edit.com to edit the file by entering:

   ```
   EDIT MSDOS.SYS
   ```

6. Save the file and return it to a hidden, read-only, system file by entering:

   ```
   ATTRIB +R +H +S MSDOS.SYS
   ```

A+
OS
1.2
2.1

Table 4-3 lists each entry in the Msdos.sys file and its purpose. You can refer to this table as you read about the different options available when installing and configuring Windows 9x.

4

Command Line Variable Name	Purpose of the Values Assigned to the Variable
AutoScan	0 = Computer does not scan hard drive. 1 = Default. Prompts the user before running ScanDisk on the hard drive when booting up after the computer was not shut down properly. 2 = Automatically scans without prompting the user.
BootMulti	0 = Default. Boot only to Windows 9x. 1 = Allows for a dual boot.
BootWin	1 = Default. Boot to Windows 9x. 0 = Boot to previous version of DOS.
BootGUI	1 = Default. Boot to Windows 9x with the graphic user interface. 0 = Boot only to the command prompt for DOS 7.0 (the DOS core of Windows 95) or 7.1 (the DOS core of Windows 98). Autoexec.bat and Config.sys will be executed, and you will be in real-mode DOS.
BootMenu	0 = Default. Don't display the startup menu. 1 = Display the startup menu.
BootMenuDefault	1 through 8 = The value selected from the startup menu by default. (Normally this value should be 1.)
BootMenuDelay	n = Number of seconds delay before the default value in the startup menu is automatically selected.
BootKeys	1 = Default. The function keys work during the boot process (F4, F5, F6, F8, Shift + F5, Ctrl + F5, Shift + F8). 0 = Disable the function keys during the boot process. (This option can be used to help secure a workstation.)
BootDelay	n = Number of seconds the boot process waits (when it displays the message "Starting Windows 95" or "Starting Windows 98") for the user to press F8 to get the startup menu (default is 2 seconds).

Table 4-3 (continued)

Command Line Variable Name	Purpose of the Values Assigned to the Variable
Logo	1 = Default. Display the Windows 9x logo screen.
	0 = Leave the screen in text mode.
Drvspace	1 = Default. Load Drvspace.bin, used for disk compression, if it is present.
	0 = Don't load Drvspace.bin.
DoubleBuffer	1 = Default. When you have a SCSI drive, enables double buffering for the drive. (See the drive documentation.)
	0 = Don't use double buffering for the SCSI drive.
Network	1 = If network components are installed, include the option "Safe Mode with network support" in the startup menu.
	0 = Don't include the option on the startup menu. (This is normally set to 0 if the PC has no network components installed. The startup menu is renumbered from this point forward in the menu.)
BootFailSafe	1 = Default. Include Safe Mode in the startup menu.
	0 = Don't include Safe Mode in the startup menu.
BootWarn	1 = Default. Display the warning message when Windows 9x boots into Safe Mode.
	0 = Don't display the warning message.
LoadTop	1 = Default. Load Command.com at the top of conventional memory.
	0 = Don't load Command.com at the top of conventional memory.
	(Use this option when there is a memory conflict with this area of memory.)

Table 4-3   Contents of the Msdos.sys file options section

Figure 4-7 shows a sample Msdos.sys file. The lines containing Xs at the bottom of the file are used to ensure that the file size is compatible with other programs.

```
[Paths]
WinDir=C:\WIN95
WinBootDir=C:\WIN95
HostWinBootDrv=C

[Options]
BootMulti=1
BootGUI=1
BootMenu=1
Network=0
;
;The following lines are required for compatibility with other programs.
;Do not remove them (MSDOS.SYS needs to be >1024 bytes).
;xxxxxxxxxxxxxxxxxxxxxxxxxxxxxxxxxxxxxxxxxxxxxxxxxxxxxxxxxxxxxxxxxxxxxxa
;xxxxxxxxxxxxxxxxxxxxxxxxxxxxxxxxxxxxxxxxxxxxxxxxxxxxxxxxxxxxxxxxxxxxxxb
;xxxxxxxxxxxxxxxxxxxxxxxxxxxxxxxxxxxxxxxxxxxxxxxxxxxxxxxxxxxxxxxxxxxxc
;xxxxxxxxxxxxxxxxxxxxxxxxxxxxxxxxxxxxxxxxxxxxxxxxxxxxxxxxxxxxxxxxxxxd
;xxxxxxxxxxxxxxxxxxxxxxxxxxxxxxxxxxxxxxxxxxxxxxxxxxxxxxxxxxxxxxxxxxe
;xxxxxxxxxxxxxxxxxxxxxxxxxxxxxxxxxxxxxxxxxxxxxxxxxxxxxxxxxxxxxxxxxf
;xxxxxxxxxxxxxxxxxxxxxxxxxxxxxxxxxxxxxxxxxxxxxxxxxxxxxxxxxxxxxxxxg
;xxxxxxxxxxxxxxxxxxxxxxxxxxxxxxxxxxxxxxxxxxxxxxxxxxxxxxxxxxxxxxxh
;xxxxxxxxxxxxxxxxxxxxxxxxxxxxxxxxxxxxxxxxxxxxxxxxxxxxxxxxxxxxxxi
;xxxxxxxxxxxxxxxxxxxxxxxxxxxxxxxxxxxxxxxxxxxxxxxxxxxxxxxxxxxxxj
;xxxxxxxxxxxxxxxxxxxxxxxxxxxxxxxxxxxxxxxxxxxxxxxxxxxxxxxxxxxxk
;xxxxxxxxxxxxxxxxxxxxxxxxxxxxxxxxxxxxxxxxxxxxxxxxxxxxxxxxxxxl
;xxxxxxxxxxxxxxxxxxxxxxxxxxxxxxxxxxxxxxxxxxxxxxxxxxxxxxxxxxm
;xxxxxxxxxxxxxxxxxxxxxxxxxxxxxxxxxxxxxxxxxxxxxxxxxxxxxxxxxn
;xxxxxxxxxxxxxxxxxxxxxxxxxxxxxxxxxxxxxxxxxxxxxxxxxxxxxxxxo
;xxxxxxxxxxxxxxxxxxxxxxxxxxxxxxxxxxxxxxxxxxxxxxxxxxxxxxxp
;xxxxxxxxxxxxxxxxxxxxxxxxxxxxxxxxxxxxxxxxxxxxxxxxxxxxxxq
;xxxxxxxxxxxxxxxxxxxxxxxxxxxxxxxxxxxxxxxxxxxxxxxxxxxxxr
;xxxxxxxxxxxxxxxxxxxxxxxxxxxxxxxxxxxxxxxxxxxxxxxxxxxxs
```

Figure 4-7   A sample Msdos.sys file

Installing Hardware with Windows 9x

After a hardware device is physically installed in a system, the next step is to install the software necessary to interface with it. This software, called a device driver, is written to interface with a specific device and operating system. Knowing how to install and troubleshoot device drivers is an essential skill of a PC support technician.

When a new device is installed and you power up the PC, Windows recognizes it and immediately launches the Found New Hardware Wizard. If the wizard does not launch automatically, you can start it manually. Go to the Control Panel and double-click the Add New Hardware icon, which launches the wizard. Alternately, you can run an installation setup program on the floppy disk or CD that came bundled with the device. Look for and run a setup program named setup.exe or install.exe. Also, if you download a driver file from the Internet, double-click on the file to launch the setup program.

One step in the Found New Hardware wizard is to select the hardware device from a list of devices. If you click OK, Windows uses a Windows driver for the device, or you can click Have Disk to use your own drivers (see Figure 4-8). If you have a driver on a floppy disk or CD or you downloaded a driver from the Internet to a folder on your hard drive, click Have Disk and point the wizard to the disk, CD, or folder that contains the driver. Sometimes you must select a folder on the disk or CD for the operating system to use, such as \Win98 to locate the drivers to install under Windows 98 (or \Win2k for Windows 2000 or \WinXP for Windows XP).

> The Control Panel contains several applets, or small programs, that are used to manage Windows. You can view these applets in a list or as icons. Use the View menu in the Control Panel to change their appearance.

NOTE

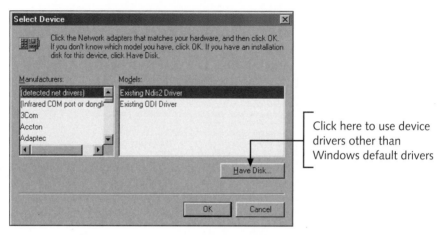

Click here to use device drivers other than Windows default drivers

Figure 4-8   To use device drivers supplied by the device manufacturer, click Have Disk

Viewing and Changing Current Device Drivers

You can view and change current device drivers from the Control Panel. For example, to view the current video driver in Windows 98, click Start, Settings, Control Panel, and then double-click Display. Click the Settings tab to view the currently installed display driver, as shown in Figure 4-9.

To change the video card driver, click Advanced, click the Adapter tab, and then click the Change button. You see the Windows 98 Update Device Driver Wizard. Click Next to see the dialog box in Figure 4-10, which includes options to let Windows 98 search for a new driver from its list of Windows drivers or to display a list of all the drivers in a specific location, so you can select the driver you want. To provide your own driver, click the second option and then click Next. Then click Have Disk to provide the new driver from a floppy disk, a CD, or a file downloaded from the Internet.

A+
OS
1.1
2.4

If the new driver fails, try uninstalling and then reinstalling the device. To uninstall a device, access Device Manager. (Click Start, Settings, Control Panel, double-click System, and then click Device Manager.) Select the device and then click Remove (see Figure 4-11). Then reboot the PC and allow the Found New Hardware Wizard to launch.

4

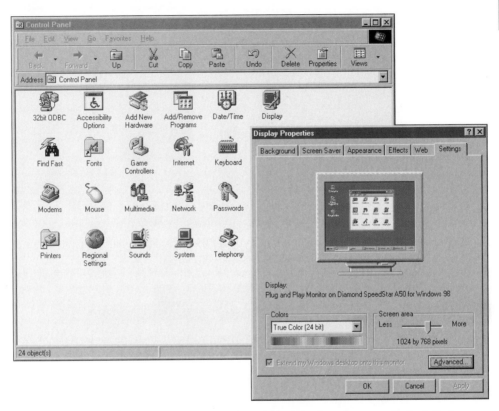

Figure 4-9   Use the Settings tab of the Display Properties window to view the currently installed display driver

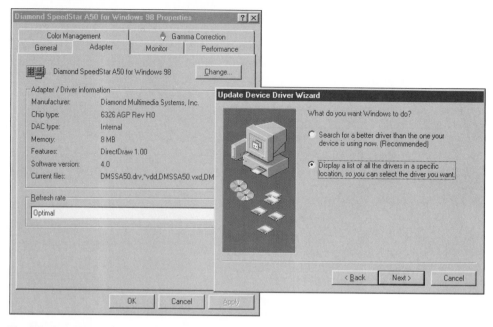

Figure 4-10   The Windows 98 Update Device Driver Wizard enables you to install a new device driver for a previously installed device

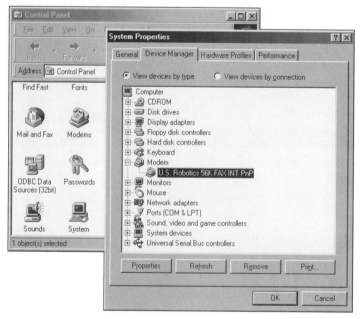

Figure 4-11   Use Device Manager to uninstall a device

Plug and Play and Hardware Installations

Remember from Chapter 1 that Plug and Play (PnP) is a set of design specifications for both hardware and software that works to make hardware installations effortless. For a system to be truly Plug and Play, it must meet these criteria:

- The system BIOS must be PnP. (To know if your BIOS is PnP, you can use MSD, a 16-bit command-line diagnostic utility.)
- All hardware devices and expansion cards must be PnP-compliant.
- The OS must be Windows 9x or another OS that supports PnP.
- A 32-bit device driver must be available (from the device manufacturer or Windows).

If all these things are true, hardware installation should be just a matter of installing the new hardware device, turning on the PC, and perhaps providing the 32-bit driver, if it is not included with Windows 9x. During the boot process, Windows 9x surveys the devices and their needs for resources and allocates resources to each device. Windows 9x is free to assign these resources to the devices and avoids assigning the same resource to two devices. For PnP to work, each device in the system must be able to use whatever resources the OS assigns to it.

NOTE   Keep in mind that Windows 9x is a compromise OS, attempting to bridge the 16-bit world and the 32-bit world. It makes many compromises between these two worlds.

Although it supports 16-bit device drivers and applications, Windows 9x works better using 32-bit drivers and 32-bit applications. If you are using older 16-bit drivers under Windows 9x, search for 32-bit drivers to replace them. Look on the device manufacturer's Web site or the Microsoft Web site.

NOTE   To learn whether a driver is 16-bit or 32-bit, look at how Windows loads it. If the driver is a 32-bit driver written for Windows 9x, it is loaded from the registry. System.ini can contain both 16-bit and 32-bit drivers. If the driver is loaded from Autoexec.bat or Config.sys, it is a 16-bit driver written for DOS. Also look in Device Manager for an exclamation point beside the device, which indicates that the driver has a problem. This might indicate that the driver is a 16-bit driver.

During the Windows 95/98 installation, Windows setup tries to substitute 32-bit drivers for all 16-bit drivers it finds in use, and, if it can, eliminates the Autoexec.bat and Config.sys files altogether. However, if it can't substitute a 32-bit driver for an older 16-bit driver, it puts (or keeps) the proper lines in the Config.sys file and sets itself up to use the older driver. Windows Me does not support 16-bit drivers, and therefore does not allow them to be loaded from Autoexec.bat or Config.sys.

4

Installing Applications in Windows 9x

As the bridge between earlier and later versions of Windows, Windows 9x can use both 16-bit and 32-bit software. This section shows you how to install both.

Preparing for Software Installation

As with installing hardware, you can do several things to prepare your system and to increase the likelihood that installing software on Windows 9x will be successful:

- *Check available resources.* Check your computer resources to make sure you have (1) enough space on your hard drive, (2) the minimum requirements for memory, and (3) the proper CPU and video monitor. Read the documentation for the software you are installing, and make sure you can fulfill any other requirements of the particular software program. The minimum requirements for the software should be listed in the installation manual. Remember that you should not completely fill your hard drive with software and data, because the operating system needs extra space for temporary files and for the swap file, which changes size depending on how much space is needed.

NOTE   For best performance with Windows 9x, allow a minimum of 100 MB of unused hard drive space for working with temporary files used by applications.

- *Protect the original software.* After the installation is complete, put the original floppy disks or CDs from which you installed the software in a safe place. If you have the original software handy, reinstalling it will be easier should something go wrong with the installed software.
- *Back up the registry and system configuration files.* Many older software packages edit Config.sys, Autoexec.bat, Win.ini, and System.ini files during the installation. Newer software might add its own entries to the Windows registry. Before you begin the installation, make backup copies of all these files so that you can backtrack if you want to. (You will learn more about backing up the registry later in the chapter.)

Installing Software

To install software designed for Windows 9x, access the Control Panel and double-click the Add/Remove Programs icon. Insert the software CD in the CD-ROM drive or the floppy disk in the floppy disk drive, and then click the Install button. Follow directions on the setup screen. If the CD-ROM drive is set to Autorun, a setup screen might appear automatically as soon as you insert the software installation CD in the drive. For older software, click Start and Run to display the Run dialog box. Enter the drive and name of the installation program, for example, A:Install or D:Setup. Either way, the installation program loads and begins executing. If the installation program asks you a question you cannot answer, you can always abandon the installation and try again later.

Most software asks you for a serial number unique to your copy of the software. The number is probably written on the CD or on the first floppy disk, or it might be stamped on the documentation. If necessary, write the serial number on the floppy disk, on the label side of the CD, or on the CD case, so that you have it if you lose the documentation later. Copyright agreements often allow you to install the software on only one computer at a time. This serial number identifies the copy of the software that you have installed on this machine.

After the installation is complete and the software is working, update your backup copies of Autoexec.bat, Config.sys, System.ini, Win.ini, and the registry so that they reflect the changes the application software made to these configuration files.

Troubleshooting Software Installations

If you have difficulty installing software in Windows 9x, try the following:

- If an application locks up when you first open it, try deleting all files and folders under \Windows\Temp. A software installation sometimes leaves files and folders in the Windows temporary directories. To conserve space on the hard drive, delete all files and folders under \Windows\Temp.
- Look at the Readme.htm hypertext file in the \Windows directory, which will point you to the Programs.txt file, also in the \Windows directory. If there is a software problem that was known when Windows shipped, information about the problem and what to do about it might be in these text files. You can also check the Web site of the software manufacturer or the Microsoft Web site for additional insight.

NOTE   A **hypertext** file is a text file that contains hypertext tags to format the file and create hyperlinks to different points in the file or to other files. Hypertext files are used on the World Wide Web and are read and displayed using a Web browser such as Microsoft Internet Explorer or Netscape Navigator. To read a hypertext file using Windows Explorer, double-click the filename; your default browser will open the file.

Supporting DOS Applications Under Windows 9x

Windows 3.x used **PIF (program information file)** files to manage the virtual machine environment for DOS applications and provided a PIF editor to alter these files. Each application had its own PIF file that was used to specify the DOS environment that Windows 3.x created for it. If an application had no PIF file, Windows 3.x used the settings in the _Default.pif file in the \Windows\System folder.

Windows 9x manages the environment for DOS applications in a slightly different fashion. The Apps.inf file has a section named [PIF95] that contains a master list of settings to be used for all DOS applications listed in the file.

If you want to customize the settings for a DOS application, use the Properties feature of the DOS program file, which creates an individual PIF for the program file and serves as the PIF editor. Right-click the program filename, and select Properties from the menu that appears. Windows searches for the program's PIF file and, if none is found, creates one using default values. If Windows 9x was installed over Windows 3.x, then _Default.pif still exists in the \Windows\System directory and default values are read from it. Regardless of where the default values come from, any changes are stored in the PIF for the application. To make the changes, use Explorer to right-click the program filename and select Properties from the shortcut menu. Click the Program tab, as shown in Figure 4-12. (Note that the Program tab will not be present for Windows applications.)

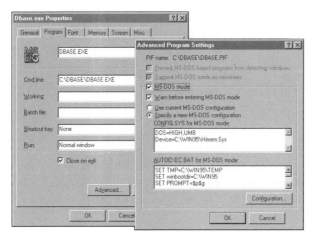

Figure 4-12   Properties sheets for a DOS application affect the way Windows 9x provides an environment for the application

If you select "Use current MS-DOS configuration", Windows executes the contents of Dosstart.bat, stored in the Windows folder. **Dosstart.bat** is a type of Autoexec.bat file that executes in two situations: when you select "Restart the computer in MS-DOS mode" from the shutdown menu, or when you run a program in MS-DOS mode. This file can be used to load real-mode device drivers, but Set commands are not executed.

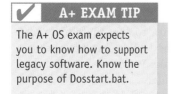

A+ EXAM TIP

The A+ OS exam expects you to know how to support legacy software. Know the purpose of Dosstart.bat.

If you select "Specify a new MS-DOS configuration", you can change the Autoexec.bat and Config.sys files used for this MS-DOS mode only. For example, if the application runs slowly in DOS mode and does a lot of disk accessing, you can add entries to run real-mode SmartDrive here. SmartDrive is a 16-bit driver used to manage disk caching. It is not normally run under Windows 9x, having been replaced by the faster 32-bit Vcache, which is built into Windows 9x. In this situation, because Windows 9x does not manage disk access in MS-DOS mode, loading SmartDrive from the Advanced Program Settings window is appropriate, because Vcache will not be running.

Using Windows 9x

Windows 9x offers a variety of methods and tools to manage the OS. This section shows you how to use keystroke shortcuts, how to manage the desktop, and how to use Windows Explorer and Device Manager.

4

Keystroke Shortcuts in Windows

Table 4-4 lists a few handy keystrokes to use when working with Windows, including the function keys you can use during startup. You can also use the mouse to accomplish some of these tasks, but keystrokes are faster for experienced typists. Also, in some troubleshooting situations, the mouse is not usable. At those times, knowing these keystrokes is very valuable.

General Action	Keystrokes	Description
While loading Windows	F4	Load previous version of DOS.
	F5	Start in Safe Mode.
	F8 or Ctrl	Display startup menu.
	Shift + F8	Step-by-step confirmation.
Working with text anywhere in Windows	Ctrl + C	Shortcuts for Copy.
	Ctrl + Ins	
	Ctrl + A	Shortcut for selecting all text.
	Ctrl + X	Shortcut for Cut.
	Ctrl + V	Shortcut for Paste.
	Shift + Ins	
	Shift + arrow keys	Hold down the Shift key, and use the arrow keys to select text, character by character.
Managing programs	Alt + Tab	Hold down the Alt key and press Tab to move from one loaded application to another.
	Ctrl + Esc	Display Start menu.
	Alt + F4	Close a program window, or, if no window is open, shut down Windows.

Table 4-4 (continued)

General Action	Keystrokes	Description
	Double-click	Double-click an icon or program name to execute the program.
	Ctrl + Alt + Del	Display the Task List, which you can use to switch to another application, end a task, or shut down Windows.
Managing files, folders, icons, and shortcuts	Ctrl + Shift while dragging a file	Create a shortcut.
	Ctrl while dragging a file	Copy a file.
	Shift + Delete	Delete a file without placing it in the Recycle Bin.
	F2	Rename an item.
	Alt + Enter	Display an item's Properties window.
Selecting items	Shift + click	To select multiple entries in a list (such as filenames in Explorer), click the first item, hold down the Shift key, and click the last item you want to select in the list. All items between the first and last are selected.
	Ctrl + click	To select several non-sequential items in a list, click the first item to select it. Hold down the Ctrl key and click other items anywhere in the list. All items you click are selected.
Using menus	Alt	Press the Alt key to activate the menu bar.
	Alt, letter	After the menu bar is activated, press a letter to select a menu option. The letter must be underlined in the menu.
	Alt, arrow keys	After the menu bar is activated, use the arrow keys to move over the menu tree.

Table 4-4 (continued)

4

General Action	Keystrokes	Description
	Alt, arrow keys, Enter	After the menu bar is activated and the correct option is highlighted, press Enter to select the option.
	Esc	Press Escape to exit a menu without making a selection.
Managing the desktop	Print Screen	Copy the desktop into the Clipboard.
	Ctrl + Esc	Display the Start menu and move the focus to the menu. (Use the arrow keys to move over the menu.)
	Alt + M	After the focus is on the Start menu, minimize all windows and move the focus to the desktop.
Working with windows	Ctrl + Tab and Ctrl + Shift + Tab	Move through tabbed pages in a dialog box.
	Shift + Close (X) button on a window	Close current folder and its parent folders.
	F5	Refresh the contents of a window.
Using the Windows key (key labeled with the Windows flag icon)	Win	Display the Start menu.
	Win + E	Start Windows Explorer.
	Win + M	Minimize all windows.
	Win + Tab	Move through items on taskbar.
	Win + R	Display the Run dialog box.
	Win + Break	Display the System Properties window.
Using the Applications shortcut menu (key labeled with a box and arrow icon).	Application key	When an item is selected, display its key

Table 4-4   Keystrokes that make working with Windows easier

Managing the Windows 9x Desktop

A+
OS
1.1

From the Windows 9x desktop you can make applications automatically load at startup, create shortcuts to files and applications, and make the environment more user-friendly. In this section, you will learn some ways to manage the Windows 9x desktop.

To control display settings, right-click anywhere on the desktop and select Properties from the shortcut menu. The Display Properties window appears as shown in Figure 4-13.

✔ **A+ EXAM TIP**

Because you can't always depend on the mouse working, the A+ OS exam expects you to know how to troubleshoot using keystrokes. It's a good idea to practice using these keystrokes before taking the exam. A project at the end of this chapter will help you practice.

Some of the more common things you can do from each tab on the window are:

- *Background*. Select desktop wallpaper or a pattern.
- *Screen Saver*. Select a screen saver and change its settings; change power settings for the monitor.
- *Appearance*. Pick and customize a color scheme for the desktop.
- *Effects*. Specify icon settings.
- *Web*. Set Active Desktop properties.
- *Settings*. Change the color range and display size.

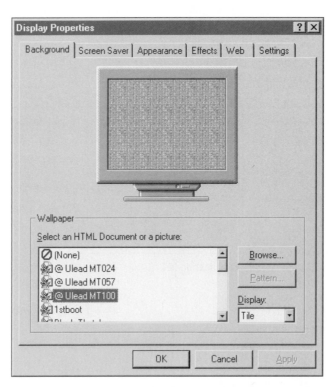

Figure 4-13   The Display Properties window lets you change settings for your desktop

A+
OS
1.1

You can also hide and unhide the taskbar at the bottom of the desktop. Click Start, Settings, Taskbar, and Start Menu. The Taskbar Properties window appears. (You can also reach this window by right-clicking the taskbar and selecting Properties from the shortcut menu.) Then click the Taskbar Options tab, and select Auto hide (see Figure 4-14).

4

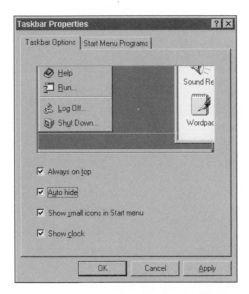

Figure 4-14   Use the Taskbar Properties window to change taskbar settings

Working with Shortcuts

A **shortcut** on the desktop is an icon that points to a program you can execute, or to a file or folder. The user double-clicks the icon to load the software. You can create a shortcut in several ways; one way is through the Start Menu Programs tab on the Taskbar Properties window you saw in Figure 4-14.

From here, click the Add button. The Create Shortcut Wizard appears, as shown in Figure 4-15. Enter the name of the program to which you want to create a shortcut, or browse for the file on your computer. In this example, we are creating a desktop shortcut to the Notepad application.

Once you enter or select the name of the program for which you want to create a shortcut, click Next. You then have the option to select where to place the shortcut. Select Desktop at the top of the folder list to create a desktop shortcut, and then click Next. Follow the directions in the wizard to complete the process. Remember that you can create a shortcut for a program or a data file, name it, and select where to place it (either on the desktop or on the Start menu). If you want a program to load whenever Windows 9x starts, create a shortcut and put it in the StartUp folder of the

Start menu. All items in the StartUp folder execute automatically when Windows 9x starts.

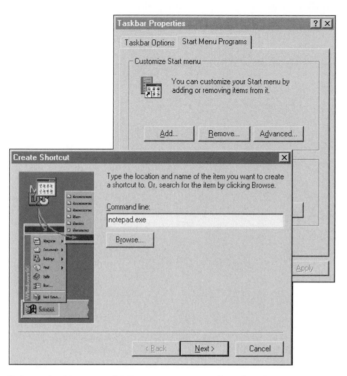

Figure 4-15   Select the item to which you want to point the shortcut

Here are some other ways to create a shortcut:

- Select the file, folder, or program in Explorer or in a My Computer window. From the File menu, select Create Shortcut.
- From the File menu in Explorer, click New and then click Create Shortcut.
- Right-click the file, folder, or program to which you want to create a shortcut, and select Create Shortcut from the menu.

A+
OS
1.1

- Drag the file, folder, or program to the desktop.
- Right-click the file, folder, or program and hold down the mouse button while dragging the item to the desktop. When you release it, a dialog box appears. Choose Create Shortcut(s) Here.

NOTE

To edit a shortcut, right-click it and select Properties from the menu. To delete a shortcut, select Delete from this same menu.

4

Managing Icons

An icon on the desktop can be a shortcut to an application, or it can represent a file that belongs to an application. The telltale sign of the difference is the small, bent-arrow shortcut symbol on the icon, as seen in Figure 4-16. The icon on the right represents the document file MyLetter1.doc stored in the \Windows\Desktop folder, and the icon on the left is a shortcut to the file MyLetter2.doc, which can be stored anywhere on the drive. Also shown in Figure 4-16 are the contents of the \Windows \Desktop folder as seen by Explorer. You can add an icon to the desktop by putting a file in this folder. One way to delete an icon on the desktop is to delete the corresponding file in this folder; however, as you will see, this method can cause problems.

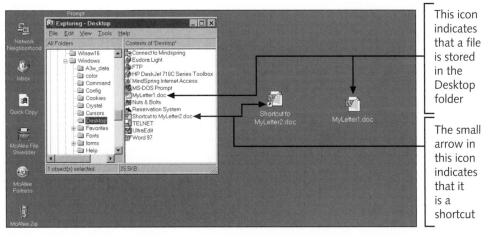

This icon indicates that a file is stored in the Desktop folder

The small arrow in this icon indicates that it is a shortcut

Figure 4-16   One icon is a shortcut, and the other icon represents a file stored in the Desktop folder

If you delete a shortcut icon from the desktop or the \Windows\Desktop folder, such as Shortcut to MyLetter2.doc, the shortcut is gone, but the actual file that the shortcut points to is not deleted. If you delete a document icon, such as MyLetter1.doc, the document itself is deleted.

An error can occur if the actual document file, MyLetter2.doc, is deleted, but the shortcut to the deleted document remains on the desktop. Figure 4-17 shows a sample error message that occurs when this shortcut is used.

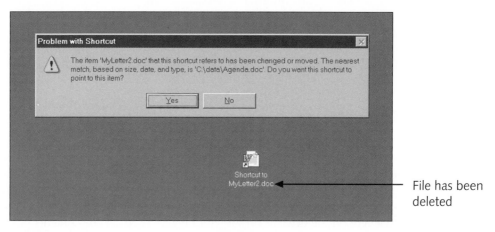

File has been deleted

Figure 4-17   The file that the shortcut points to has been deleted, which causes an error when the shortcut is used

Windows Explorer

In this section, you learn how to use Windows Explorer to manage floppy disks and hard drives in Windows 9x. You can open Windows Explorer using several methods:

- Click Start, Programs, and Windows Explorer.
- Right-click My Computer and select Explore from the menu.
- Right-click Start and select Explore from the menu.
- Open My Computer and then click the View menu, Explorer Bar, and Folders.

Figure 4-18 shows computer resources in the My Computer folder as seen when using Windows Explorer. (You can also access My Computer by double-clicking the desktop icon in Windows 9x.)

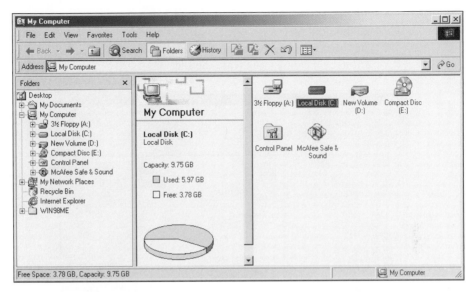

4

Figure 4-18   The My Computer view in Windows Explorer

Shortcut Menu Options

The easiest way to manage drives, disks, folders, and files in Windows Explorer is to use the shortcut menus. To access a shortcut menu, right-click the icon representing the item you want to work with. Figure 4-19 shows the shortcut menu for the floppy drive as an example.

Here are some tasks you can perform from a shortcut menu.

- If you select Explore, you can see the contents of the selected disk or folder in the current Explorer window. If you select Open, the contents of the disk or folder appear in a separate window.
- The Create Shortcut option creates a shortcut icon for the selected item.
- Selecting the Properties option brings up a dialog box showing information about the selected item and allows you to change settings for the item.
- If you selected a disk or drive, the shortcut menu contains a Format option. Recall that you can use Explorer to format a floppy disk by selecting Format from the shortcut menu.
- The Backup option enables you to make a backup of a disk, and the Sharing option enables you to share a drive, folders, or files with other users on your network.
- For floppy drives, if you select Copy Disk, the dialog box shown in Figure 4-20 opens, where the disk listed under "Copy from" is the source disk and the disk listed under "Copy to" is the target disk. Click Start to copy the disk.

- The shortcut menu for files gives you additional options such as printing and emailing the file.
- The shortcut menu for a folder allows you to create a file. The menu lists applications you can use to create the file.

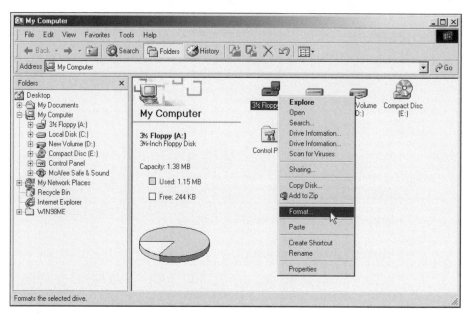

Figure 4-19   Use the shortcut menu to manage items in Explorer

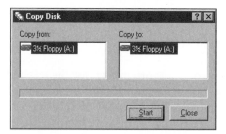

Figure 4-20   Copying a disk using Windows

As you can see, some options on shortcut menus are the same for files, folders, drives, and disks; others are specific to particular items. The additional shortcut menu options may differ, depending on what programs you have installed to work with a particular item.

Now let's look in more detail at ways to use Windows 9x Explorer to work with files and folders on your floppy disk or hard drive.

A+
OS
1.1
1.3
1.4
1.5

Creating a Folder

To create a folder, first select the folder you want to be the parent folder by clicking the folder's name. For example, to create a folder named Games under the folder named Download, first click the Download folder. Then click the File menu, select New, and select Folder from the submenu that appears. The new folder will be created under Download, but its name will be New Folder. The name New Folder is automatically selected and highlighted for the user to type a new name. Type Games to change the folder name, as shown in Figure 4-21. The maximum depth of folders under folders depends on the length of the folder names. Recall from Chapter 3 that you can also create a folder using the MD command from a command prompt.

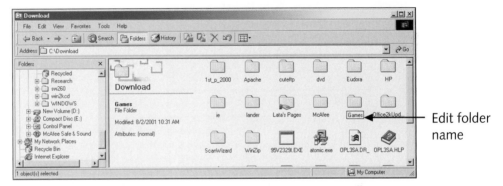

Edit folder name

Figure 4-21   Edit the new folder's name

Deleting a Folder

To delete a folder from Explorer, right-click the folder and select Delete from the shortcut menu. A confirmation dialog box asks if you are sure you want to delete the folder. If you click Yes, you send the folder and all its contents, including subfolders, to the Recycle Bin. Empty the Recycle Bin to free your disk space. Files and folders sent to the Recycle Bin are not deleted until you empty it. Recall from Chapter 3 that you can also delete a folder using the RD command from a command prompt.

File Attributes

Using Explorer, you can view and change the file attributes. From Explorer, right-click a file and select Properties from the shortcut menu. The Properties window shown in Figure 4-22 appears. From the Properties window, you can change the read-only, hidden, and archive attributes (but not the system attribute) of the file. Recall from Chapter 3 that you can change all the attributes of a file or folder using the Attrib command from a command prompt.

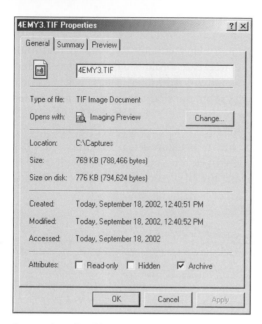

Figure 4-22   Properties of a file in Windows

Folder Properties

You can also view and change the properties assigned to folders. Select the folder, and then click the Explorer menu, click Tools, Folder Options, and click the View tab. From this window you can change how and when files appear in the folder.

Windows identifies file types primarily by the file extension. In Windows Explorer, by default, Windows 9x hides the extensions of files if it knows which application to use to open or execute the file. For example, just after installation, it hides .exe, .com, .sys, and .txt file extensions but does not hide .doc, .ppt, or .xls files until the software to open these files has been installed. To display all file extensions, open the View tab in the Folder Options window, and uncheck "Hide file extensions for known file types".

Device Manager

Device Manager gives a graphical view of hardware devices configured under Windows and the resources and drivers they use. Using Device Manager, you can make changes, update drivers, and uninstall device drivers. You can also use Device Manager to print a report of system configuration. When a device driver is being installed, Windows 9x might inform you of a resource conflict, or the device simply might not work. Use Device Manager as a useful fact-finding tool for resolving the problem.

Device Manager is one tab on the System Properties window. To access System Properties, right-click the My Computer icon on the desktop and select Properties from the shortcut menu, or double-click the System icon in the Control Panel. From the System Properties window, click the Device Manager tab. The list of devices appears, as seen in Figure 4-23.

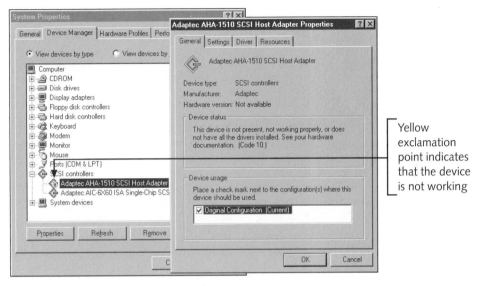

4

Yellow exclamation point indicates that the device is not working

Figure 4-23 The Properties window of an installed device that is not working

A + sign next to the device name indicates that you can click the sign for a list of manufacturers and models installed. The open diamond symbol indicates a SCSI device, and the three-forked symbol is used for USB. Symbols that indicate a device's status are:

- A red X through the device name indicates a disabled device.
- An exclamation point on a yellow background indicates a problem with the device. (The device might still be functioning.)
- A blue I on a white field indicates that automatic settings were not used and resources have been manually assigned. It does not indicate a problem with the device.
- For Windows Me, a green question mark indicates a compatible driver is installed (not the driver designed for the device), which means the device might not be fully functional.

For a better explanation of a problem, click the device and select Properties. The Device Properties dialog box that opens can give you helpful information about solving problems with I/O addresses, DMA channels, and IRQs used by the device, as well as the names of devices that are also attempting to use the same resources.

In fact, before you start hardware installation, you might want to use Device Manager to print a summary of all hardware installed on the PC and resources being used. This printout can be a record of your starting point before the installation, as well as a tool to help resolve conflicts during the installation. To print this summary, access Device Manager and click Print. From the Print dialog box, select All Devices and System Summary for a complete listing.

NOTE If you have a problem with an installed device, use Device Manager to uninstall the device. Select the device and click the Uninstall button. Then reboot and reinstall the device, looking for problems during the installation that point to the source of the problem. Sometimes reinstalling a device is all that is needed to solve the problem.

Booting Windows 9x

In Chapter 3, you learned how to boot to a command prompt. In this section, you will learn about the startup process in Windows 9x, including the differences between booting Windows 95 and booting Windows 98/Me. Finally, you will learn how to cause an application to load at startup. First, however, you'll learn more about important files that Windows 9x uses when booting.

Files Used to Customize the Startup Process

Windows 9x uses several files to control the startup process. Recall that DOS requires Io.sys, Msdos.sys, and Command.com in the root directory of the boot device in order to load. In addition, Autoexec.bat and Config.sys are text files that can contain settings for environmental variables and commands to load drivers and TSRs. Windows 9x supports Autoexec.bat and Config.sys for backward compatibility with DOS.

If Autoexec.bat or Config.sys files are present in the root directory, the command lines in them are executed during the boot. They are used to customize the loading process. Just as DOS uses text files to hold information about what is loaded, Windows 3.x also uses text files to hold custom settings that help control the loading process. These files are called **initialization files**, and some entries in them are read and used by Windows 9x. However, most Windows 9x settings are stored in the Windows registry rather than in text files.

You can edit these text files with the Edit.com program from the command prompt or any text editor from within Windows. The Windows System Configuration Editor (Sysedit) is a handy Windows text editor designed to be used with these files. To use Sysedit, type sysedit in the Run dialog box. These files automatically appear for editing: Autoexec.bat, Config.sys, **Win.ini**, **System.ini**, and **Protocol.ini** (see Figure 4-24).

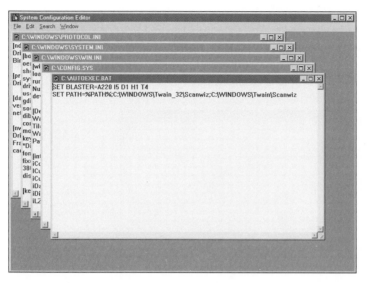

Figure 4-24   Sysedit can be used to edit Windows system files

Recall that an initialization file, which has an .ini file extension, is used by Windows and application software to store configuration information needed when they are first loaded. An application can have its own .ini files and registry, and can also store its information in the Windows .ini files and the Windows registry. Table 4-5 shows Windows .ini files, which Windows 9x supports for backward compatibility with Windows 3.x.

Windows Initialization File	General Purpose of the File
System.ini	Contains hardware settings and multitasking options for Windows. The [386Enh] section loads protected mode (32-bit) drivers for older applications, which may cause problems in more recent operating systems.
Progman.ini	Contains information about Program Manager groups
Win.ini	Contains information about user settings, including printer, fonts, file associations, and settings made by applications
Control.ini	Contains information about the user's desktop, including color selections, wallpaper, and screen saver options
Mouse.ini	Contains settings for the mouse
Protocol.ini	Contains information about the configuration of the network

Table 4-5   Windows .ini files

System.ini and Win.ini are used by both Windows 3.x and Windows 9x. A sample Windows 9x System.ini file is shown in Figure 4-25. The two sections required for the boot process are [boot] and [386Enh]. Windows 3.x kept many more entries in these sections than does Windows 9x, which really only uses these files for backward compatibility with older applications.

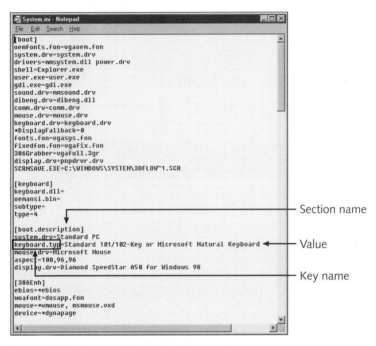

Figure 4-25   A sample Windows 98 System.ini file

Initialization files are only read when Windows or an application using .ini files starts up. If you change the .ini file for an application, you must restart the software for the change to take effect. If you want the application to ignore a line in the .ini file, you can turn the line into a **comment** line by putting a semicolon or the letters REM at the beginning of the line.

Sometimes it is necessary to manually edit an .ini file that belongs to an application, but you should normally not edit System.ini or other Windows 9x initialization files. Incorrect changes to these files might result in Windows not running correctly, and Windows sometimes overwrites these files when changes are made to it through the Control Panel.

We now turn our attention to the Windows 9x startup process, in which these and other files are used.

The Windows 9x Startup Process

A+
OS
2.3

Windows 9x first loads in real mode and then switches to protected mode. With DOS, the two core real-mode system files responsible for starting up the OS, Io.sys and Msdos.sys, remain in memory, running even after the OS is loaded. With Windows 9x, Io.sys is responsible only for the initial startup process performed in real mode. Then control is turned over to Vmm32.vxd, which works in protected mode, and Io.sys is terminated. Recall that Windows 9x includes a file named Msdos.sys, but it is only a text file that contains some parameters and switches you can set to affect the way the OS boots.

Startup in Windows 9x is a five-phase process, as shown in Figure 4-26. We will look at each phase.

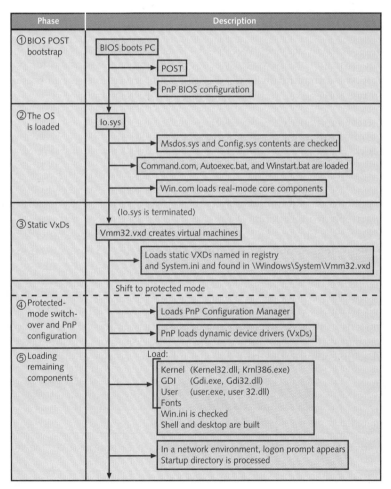

Figure 4-26   Windows 9x core components and the loading process

Phase 1: BIOS POST and Bootstrap

Startup BIOS begins the process. If the BIOS is a Plug and Play (PnP) BIOS, it examines the devices on the system and determines which are PnP-compliant. BIOS first enables the devices that are not PnP and then tries to make the PnP devices use the leftover resources. It also looks to permanent RAM for information about hardware, and uses that information to help configure PnP devices that have their configuration information recorded there. It performs POST and saves information that Windows uses later to complete the hardware configuration.

BIOS looks for a device (hard drive, floppy disk, CD-ROM drive, and so forth) containing the OS and loads Windows 9x. The MBR program on the boot device executes the bootstrap loader, which looks for the initial hidden file of Windows 9x (Io.sys).

Phase 2: The OS Is Loaded

In Phase 2, BIOS turns control over to Io.sys, which creates a real-mode operating system environment. Next, Io.sys checks the text file Msdos.sys for boot parameters. Then Io.sys automatically loads the following drivers if they are present: Himem.sys, Ifshlp.sys, Setver.exe, and Drvspace.bin (or Dblspace.bin).

- Himem.sys provides access to extended memory.
- 16-bit programs use Ifshlp.sys to access the file system.
- Setver.exe is included for backward compatibility with DOS applications that expect all DOS components to be from the same version. Setver.exe "asks" the DOS application what version of DOS it expects to use and presents DOS components to that application as if they were all from that version, even if they are actually from different versions.
- Drvspace.bin and Dblspace.bin provide disk compression. One of these two files is loaded only if Io.sys finds Dlbspace.ini or Drvspace.ini in the root directory of the boot drive.

Io.sys also sets several environmental variables to default settings. In DOS, these default settings were loaded from Config.sys. Entries in Io.sys cannot be edited, but an entry in Config.sys overrides the default entry in Io.sys. Therefore, if you want to use settings different from the default, put the command in Config.sys, which is executed at this point in the load. The default Io.sys entries are listed in Table 4-6.

Entry	Description
Buffers=30	The number of file buffers to create.
DOS=HIGH	The DOS core of Windows 9x is loaded into the high memory area (HMA).
Files=60	The number of files that can be open at one time under 16-bit applications.

Table 4-6 (continued)

Entry	Description
Himem.sys	Himem.sys is loaded to manage extended memory in Windows 9x.
Lastdrive=Z	The last letter that can be assigned to a logical drive.
Setver.exe	A program that tells DOS applications that the version of DOS they are looking for is the version they are using. The program allows some older DOS applications to run that might otherwise hang.
Shell=Command.com /P	Loads Command.com and executes Autoexec.bat.
Stacks=9,256	The number of frames of instructions that can be held in memory in a queue at one time. Used for backward compatibility with older applications.

Table 4-6   Entries in Io.sys that once were in Config.sys

Next, Io.sys loads Command.com and follows instructions stored in Autoexec.bat and Winstart.bat. The default assignments made to environmental variables that were stored in Autoexec.bat in DOS are shown in the following list:

- Tmp=c:\windows\temp
- Temp=c:\windows\temp
- Prompt=pg
- Path=c:\windows;c:\windows\command

The Tmp and Temp variables are used by some software to locate where to put their temporary files. You can change any of these variables by making an entry in Autoexec.bat. Next, Io.sys loads Win.com. Then Win.com loads other real-mode core components.

Phase 3: Static VxDs

In Phase 3, Io.sys relinquishes control to the virtual machine manager (VMM) component housed in Vmm32.vxd along with some virtual device drivers. A **virtual device driver (VxD)** works with a virtual machine to provide access to hardware for software running in the VM. Under Windows 3.x, these VxDs were loaded from System.ini and had a .386 file extension. Under Windows 9x, if stored in individual files, they have a .vxd file extension. They are called **static VxDs** because once they are loaded into memory, they remain there. (Conversely, **dynamic VxDs** are loaded into and unloaded from memory as needed.)

Vmm32.vxd is built specifically for a particular computer when Windows 9x is installed and contains some VxDs critical for a successful boot; each installation of Windows will have a different build of this file. (The VxD drivers now included in Vmm32.vxd were listed in the [386enh] section of System.ini under Windows 3.x.) Vmm32.vxd terminates Io.sys and, while still in real mode, loads static VxD device drivers as identified in four different locations. They can be embedded in Vmm32.vxd, named in the registry or System.ini, or stored in the .vxd files in the \Windows\System\Vmm32 directory.

If you suspect a problem with a VxD that is part of the Vmm32.vxd file, then store a new version of the .vxd file in the \Windows\System\Vmm32 directory. If Windows finds a VxD driver there, it uses that driver instead of the one embedded in Vmm32.vxd. Also, VxD drivers are listed in the registry and in System.ini. Normally, the entries are the same, and entries are only listed in System.ini for backward compatibility. However, if an entry in System.ini differs from an entry in the registry, the value in System.ini is used.

Phase 4: Protected-Mode Switchover and PnP Configuration

At the beginning of Phase 4, Vmm32.vxd switches to protected mode and loads Configuration Manager. Configuration Manager is responsible for configuring legacy and PnP devices. It uses any information that PnP BIOS might have left for it and loads the 32-bit VxDs for the PnP devices.

Phase 5: Loading the Remaining Components

In Phase 5, with Vmm32.vxd still in control, the three core components are loaded, then fonts and other associated resources are loaded. Win.ini is checked and commands stored there are executed to allow backward compatibility. The shell and user desktop are loaded. If the computer is working in a networked environment, a logon dialog box is displayed, and the user can log on to Windows 9x and the network. Finally, any processes stored in the Startup directory are performed.

Differences Between the Windows 95 and Windows 98/Me Boot Process

Windows 98 made some minor changes in what happens during startup to speed up the boot process. For instance, Windows 95 waits two seconds, displaying "Starting Windows 95" so that you can press a key to alter the boot process. Windows 98 eliminated this two-second wait and, in its place, allows you to press and hold the Ctrl key as it loads. If you do, you see the startup menu that is also available with Windows 95.

APPLYING CONCEPTS

Loading an Application at Startup

If you want an application to load automatically at startup, you can:

- Place a shortcut in the folder C:\Windows\All Users\Startup Menu\Programs\StartUp.
- Put the name of the program file in the Load= or Run= line in Win.ini.
- Manually edit the registry key HKEY_LOCAL_MACHINE\SOFTWARE\ Microsoft\Windows\CurrentVersion\Run.

Try one of these methods yourself.

Troubleshooting Tools for Windows 9x

NOTE

Tools new with Windows Me are System Restore and System File Protection. System Restore automatically backs up the registry and other system files when the system is idle. System File Protection is similar to Windows 2000 System File Protection; it prevents system files from being accidentally deleted and prevents application installations from overwriting newer DLL files with older or nonstandard versions.

Now let's look at some support tools that are useful for troubleshooting problems with the OS during or after the boot. Table 4-7 lists several tools that monitor and improve system performance, control the OS, and help with troubleshooting. Several major tools are covered in this section; in the next section, you will see how to use these tools in troubleshooting situations.

✓ A+ EXAM TIP

To prepare for the A+ OS exam, know the purpose of all the utilities in Table 4-7 and the program filename of the utility.

Tool	Win 95	Win 98/ME	Description
Automatic Skip Driver Agent Filename: Asd.exe Location: \Windows		X	Automatically skips drivers that prevent Windows from loading and records problems encountered in the log file Asd.log. To run, select Automatic Skip Driver Agent from the Tools menu of the System Information window.
Microsoft System Information Filename: MSInfo32.exe Location: \Program Files\ Common files\Microsoft shared\Msinfo	X	X	Displays system information, including installed hardware and device drivers. To run, click Start, Programs, Accessories, System Tools, and System Information, or type Msinfo32.exe in the Run dialog box.
Hardware Diagnostic tool (Hwinfo.exe)		X	Displays the same information as System Information, but in text form. Enter hwinfo /ui in the Run dialog box.
Registry Checker Filename: Scanreg.exe Location: \Windows\Command		X	Backs up, verifies, and recovers the registry. To run, select Registry Checker from the Tools menu of the System Information window.
Windows Update Filename: Iexplore.exe Location: *www.microsoft.com/ windowsupdate*	X	X	Downloads service packs (fixes) for Windows from the Microsoft Web site.
System options in Control Panel	X	X	Several applets in the Control Panel can be used to monitor and tweak system performance.
System Configuration Utility Filename: MsConfig.exe Location: \Windows\System		X	Allows you to temporarily modify the system configuration to help with troubleshooting. To run, select System Configuration Utility from the Tools menu of the System Information window or type **Msconfig** in the Run dialog box.

Table 4-7 (continued)

A+
OS
1.5
3.1
3.2

4

Tool	Win 95	Win 98/ME	Description
System File Checker Filename: Sfc.exe Location: \Windows\System		X	Verifies system files. This tool scans for changed, deleted, or corrupted system files and restores them from the originals on the Windows CD. To run, select System File Checker from the Tools menu of the System Information window.
System Monitor Filename: Sysmon.exe Location: \Windows		X	System Monitor tracks the performance of some important system components. To run, click Start, Programs, Accessories, System Tools, and System Monitor.
Microsoft Backup Filename: Msbackup.exe Location: \Program Files\ Accessories\Backup\)	X	X	Backs up files and folders to prevent loss when your hard drive fails. To run, click Start, Programs, Accessories, System Tools, and Backup. The utility is covered in Chapter 10.
System Recovery Filename: pcrestor.bat Location: On the Windows 98/Me CD in \Tools\Sysrec		X	Uses a full system backup created by Microsoft Backup to reinstall Windows and restore the system to its state as of the last backup.
Dr. Watson Filename: Drwatson.exe Location: \Windows		X	Traps errors in log files created by applications and takes a snapshot of the system to use for troubleshooting.
Scheduled Task Wizard Filename: Mstask.exe Location: \Windows\System	X	X	Schedules tasks such as MS Backup to run at predetermined times.
Version Conflict Manager Filename: Vcmui.exe Location: \Windows		X	Replaces an older Windows file with a newer file that was saved when Windows or an application was installed.
System Configuration Editor Filename: Sysedit.exe Location: \Windows\System	X	X	Text editor to edit files that configure how Windows loads. To run it, enter Sysedit.exe in the Run dialog box. Sysedit automatically opens Protocol.ini, System.ini, Win.ini, Config.sys, and Autoexec.bat for editing.

Table 4-7 (continued)

Tool	Win 95	Win 98/ME	Description
Task Manager Filename: Taskman.exe Location: \Windows	X	X	Run, switch, and end applications, and access the Shutdown menu. To run it, type Taskman in the Run dialog box.
Signature Verification Tool Filename: sigverif.exe Location: \Windows		X	Checks system drivers for digital signatures given to them by Microsoft, which ensures they have been tested by Microsoft. To run it, use the System Information window.
Digital Signature Check		X	Identifies drivers that have been digitally signed by Microsoft to verify their integrity. To use it, enable this key in the registry: HKEY_LOCAL_MACHINE\Software \Microsoft\Driver Signing.

Table 4-7   Windows 9x system performance and troubleshooting tools

System Applet in the Control Panel

One useful applet in troubleshooting a system is the System Properties window. To access the System applet, right-click My Computer and select Properties from the shortcut menu, or click the System icon in the Control Panel. The applet offers several tools for performance monitoring and troubleshooting. For example, the Performance tab in Figure 4-27 shows a performance report from two computers, one in need of performance tuning and one running at optimal performance. Key messages to look for on this screen (see Figure 4-27a) are "Some drives are using MS-DOS compatibility" under File System, and "MS-DOS compatibility mode" under Virtual Memory. These messages mean that real-mode drivers are being used, which can slow down performance, especially when used with hard drive access. Figure 4-27b indicates that both these components are using 32-bit protected-mode drivers.

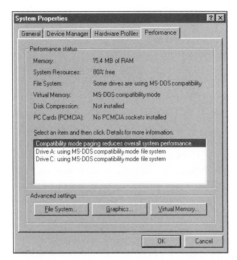 

a. Adjustments are needed in order to use 32-bit protected-mode resource

b. System running at optimal performance

Figure 4-27   The Performance tab under System Properties in the Control Panel can tell you if your file system and virtual memory are running at optimal performance

Whenever you see MS-DOS mode (real mode) drivers being used, do whatever you can to see that these drivers are replaced with 32-bit protected-mode drivers. One important tool to use for this process is the text file Ios.ini, which contains the Windows 9x Safe Driver List. Windows 9x uses this list to determine if it can safely substitute a protected-mode driver for a real-mode one. Also, if it attempts to make the substitution but fails, it often records the problem in another file, Ios.log. Check this file for information about the problem.

If a real-mode driver is being used, and you believe that a protected-mode driver should be used in its place, first check Ios.log for any error messages. If you don't find an error message, add the real-mode driver name to the safe driver list in the Ios.ini file. Anything following the semicolon on the line is a comment. You can also use REM to comment out a line.

Sample lines in the Ios.ini file are:

```
[SafeList]
386max.sys ; Qualitas
extrados.pro; Qualitas Memory Manager
extrados.max; Qualitas Memory Manager
4dos.com ; 4DOS shell program
ad-dos.com ; Afterdark
ad-wrap.com ; Afterdark
adi2.com ; Afterdark
aspi3x70.sys; DTC SCSI driver
```

System Monitor

System Monitor allows you to monitor how system resources are being used by applications. It can monitor the file system, memory, the kernel, printer sharing services, and network performance data.

APPLYING CONCEPTS

System Monitor is not automatically installed in a typical installation. To install it, go to the Control Panel, and select Add/Remove Programs. Click Windows Setup, and then select Accessories. To run System Monitor, click Start, point to Programs, Accessories, System Tools, and then click System Monitor.

Figure 4-28 shows System Monitor tracking the kernel and disk cache hits and misses. Under the File menu, you can add and delete items the monitor is tracking. Use System Monitor to help determine if an application is using an inordinate amount of resources or has a memory leak. A memory leak occurs when you exit software and it unloads from memory, but it does not release the memory addresses that it was using for its data back to the OS. Memory leaks can occur when software is corrupted, poorly written, or plagued with a virus. You notice memory leaks when your system gets sluggish after you have launched and exited an application several times before rebooting the system. A reboot releases all memory addresses.

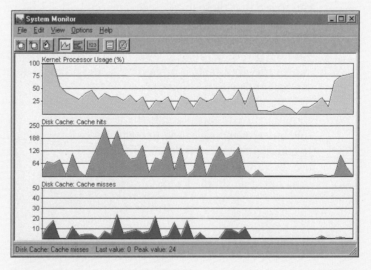

Figure 4-28   System Monitor can track the performance of several system resources

System Configuration Utility

A+
OS
1.5

Like loading Windows in Safe Mode, the System Configuration Utility (Msconfig.exe) reduces the startup process to its essentials. If starting Windows in this condition eliminates the problem you are troubleshooting, you can use this utility to add items back one at a time until the problem occurs; the source of the problem is related to the last item you added. To use the utility, do the following:

4

1. To access the utility, click **Start**, point to **Programs, Accessories, System Tools,** and then click **System Information**. The Microsoft System Information window opens.

2. From the **Tools** menu, select **System Configuration Utility** (see Figure 4-29). The System Configuration Utility dialog box opens, as shown in Figure 4-30. Another way to access the utility is to type **Msconfig** in the Run dialog box.

3. To diagnose a problem, select **Diagnostic startup – interactively load device drivers and software,** and then click **OK** to restart your computer.

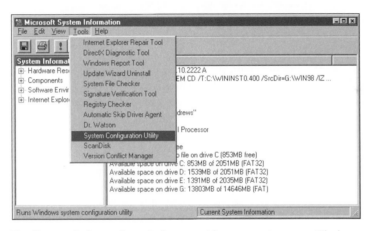

Figure 4-29   The System Information window provides access to many Windows support tools

Figure 4-30   The Windows 98 System Configuration Utility helps troubleshoot Windows configuration problems

4. If this solves the problem, then the clean start was successful. Next, select **Selective startup** from the dialog box shown in Figure 4-30 and methodically select first one item and then another to restore, until the problem reappears. Begin by restoring all entries in Autoexec.bat and Config.sys, to determine if real-mode drivers and programs loaded from these files are the source of the problem.

5. If the problem still occurs, even with the clean boot, then try the following:

- If you have not already done so, scan for a virus, using a current version of antivirus software.
- Use Registry Checker to check for corrupted system files.
- Use System File Checker to check for corrupted system files.
- Check the CMOS setup screen for wrong settings.

Dr. Watson

A troubleshooting tool you can use when you have problems running an application is Dr. Watson. **Dr. Watson** is a Windows utility that can record detailed information about the system, errors that occur, and the programs that caused them in a log file named \Windows\Drwatson\WatsonXX.wlg, where XX is an incrementing number. Start Dr. Watson (see Figure 4-31), and then reproduce the application error.

A+
OS
3.1
3.2

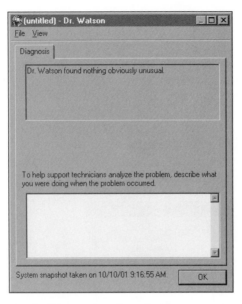

4

Figure 4-31   The Dr. Watson opening window

Next, look at the events logged in the Dr. Watson window under the Diagnosis tab. Use this information to check the Microsoft Web site, *support.microsoft.com*, for the problem and solution. For errors that you cannot reproduce at will, you can load Dr. Watson each time Windows starts by creating a shortcut to Drwatson.exe in the StartUp folder.

The Windows 9x Registry

A+
OS
1.1
1.2
1.3
1.5
3.1

In supporting and troubleshooting Windows 9x, you need to understand the role of the registry and .ini files. The registry is a database of configuration information and settings for users, hardware, applications, and the OS. Starting with Windows 9x, the registry takes over the essential functions of .ini files. However, Windows 9x still supports .ini files for compatibility with Windows 3.x and legacy software and hardware devices. Entries that 16-bit Windows applications make in Win.ini and System.ini are not added to the registry because these applications cannot access the registry. Entries made in .ini files by applications that can access the registry are copied into the registry. In this section, you will examine how the registry is organized, what kinds of information are in the registry, how and why you might edit the registry, and how to recover from a corrupted registry.

How the Registry Is Organized

The registry organizes information in a hierarchical database with a treelike, top-to-bottom design. The Windows 9x System.ini file contains setup parameters.

A+
OS
1.1
1.2
1.3
1.5
3.1

Figure 4-25 shows a portion of the System.ini file. Notice that section names appear in square brackets, key names to the left of the equal signs, and values assigned to these key names to the right of the equal signs. The Windows 9x registry takes on a similar but enhanced design that allows for keys to cascade to several levels on the tree. Figure 4-32 shows a portion of a Windows 9x registry. Consider names on the left of the window as similar to section names in System.ini; these names are called **keys** by Windows 9x. On the right of the window are value names, such as Screen-SaveTime, and to the right of each name is the **value data** assigned to that name, such as "60". The value names, called values by Windows 9x, are similar to the key names in System.ini, and the value data is similar to the values assigned to key names in System.ini.

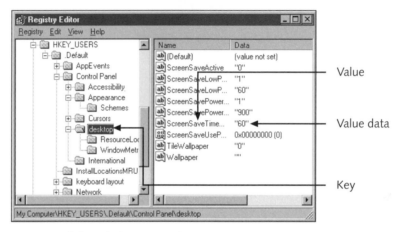

Figure 4-32   Structure of the Windows 9x registry

The registry is organized into the six major branches, or keys, listed in Table 4-8. The registry is contained in two files, System.dat and User.dat, located in the Windows directory as hidden, read-only, system files, although the information forms only a single database.

Key	Description
HKEY_CLASSES_ROOT	Contains information about file associations and OLE data. (This branch of the tree is a mirror of HKEY_LOCAL_MACHINE\ Software\Classes.)
HKEY_USERS	Includes user preferences, including desktop configuration and network connections.
HKEY_CURRENT_USER	If there is only one user of the system, this is a duplicate of HKEY_USERS. For a multiuser system, this key contains information about the current user preferences.

Table 4-8 (continued)

Key	Description
HKEY_LOCAL_MACHINE	Contains information about hardware and installed software.
HKEY_CURRENT_CONFIG	Contains the same information in HKEY_LOCAL_MACHINE\Config and has information about printers and display fonts.
HKEY_DYN_DATA	Keeps information about Windows performance and Plug-and-Play information.

4

Table 4-8   Six major branches, or keys, of the Windows 9x registry

Recovering from a Corrupted Registry

Windows 95 has a way to recover from a corrupted registry that is different from the method used by Windows 98/Me. These methods are discussed next.

Windows 95 Backup of the Registry   Windows 95 maintains a backup copy of the two registry files and names the backup files System.da0 and User.da0. Each time Windows 95 boots successfully, it makes a new backup of the two registry files. If Windows 95 has trouble loading and must start in Safe Mode, it does not back up the registry.

If Windows 95 does not find a System.dat file when it starts, it automatically replaces it with the backup System.da0. If both System.dat and User.dat are missing, or if the WinDir= command is missing in Msdos.sys, Windows 9x tells you that the registry files are missing and starts in Safe Mode. It then displays the Registry Problem dialog box. Click the Restore From Backup and Restart buttons to restore the registry files from System.da0 and User.da0. If these files are also missing, the registry cannot easily be restored. You can either restore the files from your own backups or run Windows 9x Setup. There is another option. Look for the file System.1st in the root directory of the hard drive. This is the System.dat file created when Windows 9x was first installed. In an emergency, you can revert to this file.

Windows 98/Me Registry Checker   Windows 98/Me offers a utility called the Registry Checker, which is not available with Windows 95. It automatically backs up the registry each day, and by default, it keeps the last five days of backups. In an emergency, you can recover the registry from one of these backups. You can also tell Registry Checker to make an additional backup on demand, for example, when you make changes to the registry and want to back them up before you make new changes.

To access Registry Checker, select Start, point to Programs, Accessories, System Tools, and then click System Information. The Microsoft System Information window opens (see Figure 4-33). From the menu bar, select Tools and then Registry Checker. Registry Checker tells you if the registry is corrupted and fixes it, if allowed. You can also create a new backup at this time.

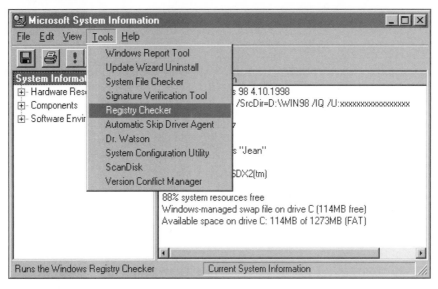

Figure 4-33   The Registry Checker is available under Programs, Accessories, System Tools, System
Information; it is used to back up, restore, and repair the Windows 98 registry

Backups are kept in cabinet files in the \Windows\Sysbckup folder as rb001.cab,
rb002.cab, and so on. To revert to one of these backups, you must first be in
MS-DOS mode. For Windows Me, boot from a bootable disk. For Windows 98,
boot from a bootable disk or boot to an MS-DOS prompt from the Windows 98
startup menu. (Windows Me does not have this option on the startup menu.) From
the MS-DOS prompt (not a DOS box within a Windows session), use the commands
in Table 4-9 to repair or recover the registry.

Command	Purpose
Scanreg /Restore	Restores the registry from a previous backup. A screen appears asking you which backup to use.
Scanreg /Fix	Repairs the corrupted registry. If the problem is inherent to the registry itself, this might work. If you want to undo a successful change to the registry, then use the Restore option instead.
Scanreg /Backup	Creates a new backup of the registry at the DOS prompt. Don't do this if the registry is giving you problems.

Table 4-9 (continued)

Command	Purpose
Scanreg /Opt	Optimizes the registry. ScanReg looks for and deletes information in the registry that is no longer used. This reduces the size of the registry, which might speed up booting.
Scanreg /?	Help feature of ScanReg.

Table 4-9   Commands used to repair or recover the Windows 98 or Windows Me registry

Modifying the Registry

When you make a change in the Control Panel, Device Manager, or many other places in Windows 9x, the registry is modified automatically. This is the only way most users will ever change the registry. However, on rare occasions you might need to edit the registry manually. For example, if a virus infected your registry, an antivirus technical staff person or directions downloaded from an antivirus Web site might direct you to edit the registry and delete any entries added by the virus. The first step in editing the registry is to back up the two registry files System.dat and User.dat. The next step is to use Regedit.exe, located in the Windows folder. You can use Explorer to locate the file, then double-click it, or you can click Start, then Run, and type Regedit in the Run dialog box. When you do, the window in Figure 4-34 opens. Open one branch of the tree by clicking the + sign to the left of the key, and close the branch by clicking the – sign. To search for an entry in the registry, click the Edit menu and then click Find.

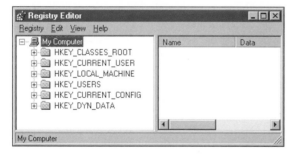

Figure 4-34   The six major branches, or keys, of the registry seen in the Registry Editor

Troubleshooting Windows 9x

This section covers Windows 9x troubleshooting. It is important for you to know how to troubleshoot problems that occur during a Windows installation, problems that occur during the boot process, and problems that occur during normal Windows operations.

Troubleshooting Windows 9x Installations

A+
OS
2.1

Table 4-10 lists some problems that might occur while installing Windows 9x and what to do about them.

Symptom	Description and Solution
An error message about BIOS appears during installation.	This is most likely caused by BIOS not allowing changes to the boot sector to protect it from viruses. Disable the feature in CMOS setup.
Windows 9x stalls during the first restart after installation.	This is probably caused by legacy hardware that is not configured correctly. Try the following: • Remark (REM) out all entries in Config.sys and Autoexec.bat. • Disable the ISA enumerator by commenting out this line in System.ini: Device=ISAPNP.386.
During the first restart after installation, an error message appears with information about a bad or missing file.	This is probably cause d by an error in Config.sys or Autoexec.bat. Try renaming both files so they are not executed. If this solves the problem, then comment out each line in the file, one at a time, until you know which line caused the problem.
During the first restart after the installation, you get an error message about a missing or damaged VxD file.	Run Windows setup again and select the option to verify or replace the missing VxD (virtual device driver).
After upgrading from Windows 95 to Windows 98, the startup screen still says Windows 95.	This can be caused by one of two problems. First, the Io.sys file might not have been updated. If so, use the Sys C: command to replace it. Or, the file Logo.sys is in the root directory, which overrides the logo screen embedded in Io.sys. Delete or rename the file.
"Invalid system disk" error appears during setup.	• Suspect a boot sector virus. Run a current version of antivirus software. • If this error occurs while installing Windows when disk management software such as DiskPro is running, Windows might have damaged the hard drive MBR. To recover from this problem, see the documentation for the disk management software.

Table 4-10 Some problems and solutions when installing Windows 9x

NOTE For specific error messages that occur during installation and what to do about them, go to the Microsoft Web site *support.microsoft.com* and search for the error message.

Troubleshooting the Windows 9x Boot Process

4

A+
OS
2.3
3.1

When the boot process does not complete correctly, you can go through these basic steps to troubleshoot it:

1. Check and address any error messages that occur during a normal boot.

2. If you cannot boot to a normal desktop, boot in Safe Mode and begin troubleshooting there. If you can boot to Safe Mode but cannot boot normally, you probably have a driver problem of some kind, because the main difference between Safe Mode and normal booting is the drivers that are loaded.

3. If you cannot boot using Safe Mode, the GUI portion of the OS is not functioning. Boot to the command prompt using the startup menu. Use commands at the C prompt for troubleshooting.

4. If the startup menu is not accessible, the MS-DOS core of the OS is not functioning. Boot from an emergency startup disk, and try to access drive C.

5. If you cannot access drive C, then the hard drive is not accessible. Try Fdisk. If Fdisk does not work, treat the problem as a hardware problem.

Error Messages Received While Loading Windows 9x

Error messages are your first indications that something is going wrong with the Windows 9x boot process. You can use these messages to figure out how to solve some Windows 9x boot problems. Table 4-11 shows error messages that Windows 9x might produce and gives advice about what to do when you see them. Specific errors are covered later in this section.

Error Message or Problem	What to Do
MS-DOS compatibility mode	• Windows is using real-mode drivers to access the hard drive rather than the preferred 32-bit drivers. After backing up the Config.sys and System.ini files, remove any references to real-mode drivers for the hard drive in these files.

Table 4-11 (continued)

Error Message or Problem	What to Do
	• The problem might be due to an outdated mother-board BIOS. Consider updating the BIOS.
Bad or missing file Real-mode driver missing or damaged Error in config.sys line xx	• Verify that Config.sys, Autoexec.bat (root directory of the hard drive), and System.ini (Windows folder) are present and in the right location. • Check Config.sys and Autoexec.bat for errors using the step-by-step confirmation option from the Windows 9x startup menu. To check System.ini, rename the file so that it will not be used and boot with a bare-bones version of the file. • Look in the Win.ini file for applications that are attempting to load at startup but have been deleted or uninstalled. Check the Load= or Run= lines.
Cannot open file *.inf	• This error is caused by insufficient memory. Disable any TSRs running in Autoexec.bat. • Close any applications that are running or remove them from the Start folder.
Insufficient disk space	Run ScanDisk and Defragmenter. Check free space on the hard drive.
Invalid system disk	Suspect a boot sector virus. Run a current version of antivirus software.
Bad or missing command.com	Io.sys could be missing or corrupted. Restore the file from a backup or an emergency startup disk. To restore all real-mode files needed to begin loading Windows 9x, do the following: (1) boot from a Windows 9x emergency startup disk, (2) restore Io.sys, Msdos.sys, Drvspace.bin, and Command.com by executing the command SYS C:, and (3) remove the floppy disk and reboot.
Invalid VxD dynamic link call from IFSMGR	This error is caused by a missing or corrupted Msdos.sys file. Restore the file from a backup or from an emergency startup disk.
Missing system files	Run the SYS C: command.
System Registry file missing	Either System.dat or User.dat is corrupted or missing. For Windows 95, restore them by using either System.da0 or User.da0. For Windows 98/Me, run ScanReg.

Table 4-11 (continued)

Error Message or Problem	What to Do
VxD error returns to command prompt	A VxD file is missing or corrupted. Run Windows Setup from the Windows 9x CD, and choose Verify installed components.
Error containing the text "Kernel32.dll"	An error that contains this text probably indicates a corrupted kernel. Try restoring system files. If that doesn't work, reinstall Windows. Note that this error may appear at other times, not just during the boot process.

4

Table 4-11   Error messages received while loading Windows 9x

Windows has several tools you can use to help troubleshoot problems with booting:

- Use the System Configuration Utility (Msconfig.exe) to limit what loads during the boot in order to attain the cleanest possible boot.
- Use Device Manager to disable a device that you think is causing a problem.
- Use Automatic Skip Driver Agent (ASDA) to keep Windows from installing a driver that might be corrupted, including built-in Windows drivers.
- The Windows 9x startup menu includes Safe Mode, the command prompt, and other troubleshooting options.

Windows 9x Startup Menu Options

Normally, when you load Windows, the message "Starting Windows" appears and then the OS loads. However, you can force the startup menu to appear rather than the "Starting Windows" message by pressing the F8 key or holding down the Ctrl key during the boot.

The Windows 9x startup menu options are:

1. Normal

2. Logged (\Bootlog.txt)

3. Safe Mode

4. Safe Mode with network support

5. Step-by-step confirmation

6. Command prompt only

7. Safe Mode command prompt only

8. Previous version of MS-DOS

What to expect when you select each menu option is described next. Option 4 appears if the OS is configured for a network, and Option 8 appears if a previous version of DOS was retained during the Windows 9x installation. Option 6 is not available with Windows Me.

Normal   In Msdos.sys, if BootGUI=1, then this option starts Windows 9x. If BootGUI=0, then this option boots to the DOS 7.0 or DOS 7.1 prompt (the DOS core of Windows 9x). Either way, the commands in Autoexec.bat and Config.sys are executed.

If a problem appears when you boot in Normal Mode but does not appear when you boot in Safe Mode, then suspect that Config.sys, Autoexec.bat, System.ini, Win.ini are the source of your problem. To eliminate Config.sys or Autoexec.bat as the source of the problem, boot using the Step-by-step confirmation option on the startup menu. To eliminate Win.ini or System.ini as the source of the problem, use the following procedure:

1. Change the name of the System.ini file in the Windows folder to System.sav.

2. Find the System.cb file in the Windows folder, and make a copy of it. Rename the copy System.ini. Do not rename the original System.cb file because you may need it at another time.

3. In the [boot] section of the System.ini file, add this line and then save the file: drivers=mmsystem.dll

4. Change the name of the Win.ini file in the Windows folder to Win.sav.

5. Restart your computer.

If this works, the problem was in the Win.ini or System.ini files, and you can reexamine these files in detail to determine the exact source of the problem.

If your mouse stops working when you copy the System.cb file and rename it System.ini, add the following lines in the specified sections of the new System.ini file:

```
[boot]
mouse.drv=mouse.drv
[386Enh]
mouse=*vmouse,imsmouse.vxd
```

Logged (\Bootlog.txt)   This option is the same as Normal, except that Windows 9x tracks the load and startup activities and logs them to the Bootlog.txt file. A portion of a sample Bootlog.txt file is shown in Figure 4-35. Notice that this file contains information about which components loaded successfully and which did not. This file can be a helpful tool when troubleshooting.

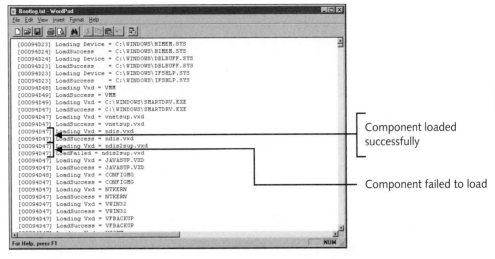

A+
OS
2.3
3.1

4

Component loaded
successfully

Component failed to load

Figure 4-35   The Bootlog.txt file contains information about successful and unsuccessful boot activities

Safe Mode (Press F5 While Loading)   When you have problems with the
Windows 9x boot process but no error message appears during the boot, you can use
Safe Mode to troubleshoot the problems. You can reach Safe Mode either from the
startup menu or by pressing F5 while Windows is loading. Figure 4-36 shows Win-
dows 98 booted into Safe Mode. Safe Mode does not execute entries in the registry,
Config.sys, Autoexec.bat, and the [boot] and [386Enh] sections of System.ini. Also,
when you enter Safe Mode, Windows 98/Me includes support for networks, but
Windows 95 does not.

Safe Mode starts Windows 9x with a minimum default configuration to give you
an opportunity to correct an error in the configuration. For example, if you selected
a video driver that is incompatible with your system, Windows 9x detects the problem when it starts and enters Safe Mode with a standard VGA driver selected. You
can then go to Device Manager, select the correct driver, and restart Windows.

From the startup menu, you can choose to enter Safe Mode if you know of a problem you want to correct. For example, if you selected a group of background and
foreground colors that makes reading the screens impossible, you can reboot and
choose Safe Mode. Safe Mode gives you the standard color scheme along with the
VGA mode. Go to Display Properties, make the necessary corrections, and reboot.

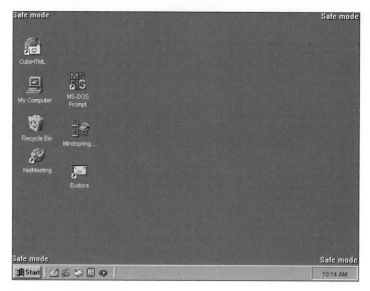

Figure 4-36   Windows 98 Safe Mode

Sometimes you will use Safe Mode for troubleshooting when you don't know exactly what the problem is. In that situation, once you are in Safe Mode, use the following checklist:

- Use a current version of antivirus software to scan for a virus.
- Sometimes loading in Safe Mode is all that is needed. Try to reboot the PC in Normal Mode.
- If the Safe Recovery dialog box appears, select the option of Use Safe Recovery. Windows 9x then attempts to recover from previous boot problems. Try to boot again.
- If you had problems with a device installation before the Windows failure, disable or remove the device in Device Manager. Reboot after disabling each device that you suspect to be a problem.
- If you have just made configuration changes, undo the changes and reboot.
- Look for real-mode drivers or TSRs (programs loaded in Config.sys, Autoexec.bat, or System.ini) that might be causing a problem, and disable them by inserting a semicolon or a REM at the beginning of the command line.
- Try to boot again. If the problem is still not solved, restore the registry. For Windows 95, make backups of System.dat and User.dat. Then overwrite them with System.da0 and User.da0. For Windows 98/Me, use ScanReg to restore the registry from backups. (ScanReg was covered earlier in the chapter.)
- Run ScanDisk to repair errors on the hard drive and optimize it. While in Safe Mode, select Start, Programs, Accessories, System Tools, and ScanDisk. Under Type of Test, select Thorough. (See Figure 4-37.)

4

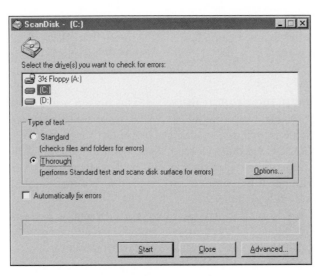

Figure 4-37 Use ScanDisk to check the hard drive for errors

- Run the Defragmenter utility to optimize the drive (covered in Chapter 10).
- For Windows 98, run System File Checker to verify system files.
- For Windows 98/Me, run Automatic Skip Driver Agent to skip loading any driver that causes a problem. Reboot and examine the Asd.log file for recorded errors.
- For Windows 98/Me, use the System Configuration Utility to reduce the system to essentials and reboot. If the problem goes away, restore one item at a time until the problem returns. Then you can identify the item that is the source of the problem.
- Using Explorer, search for files in system folders that have changed recently. To sort file and folder names by date last modified using Explorer, click the Modified column heading. To reverse the sort order, hold down the Ctrl key while clicking the Modified column heading. If software or drivers have been installed recently, suspect that they might be the source of the problem.

Safe Mode with Network Support   This option allows you access to the network when booting into Safe Mode. It is useful if Windows 95 is stored on a network server and you need to download changes to your PC in Safe Mode. This option is not available on the startup menu in Windows 98/Me, which automatically includes network support.

To eliminate the network connection as a source of a boot problem you are troubleshooting, first boot in Safe Mode without network support and then boot in Safe Mode with network support. If the boot without network support succeeds but the boot with network support gives errors, then suspect that the network drivers might be the source of the problem. For Windows 98/Me, disable the network card in Device Manager to eliminate the network drivers as the source of the problem.

Step-by-Step Confirmation   This option asks for confirmation before executing each command in Io.sys, Config.sys, and Autoexec.bat. You can accomplish the same thing by pressing Shift + F8 when the message "Starting Windows 95/98" appears.

The A+ OS exam expects you to know how Win.com is used.

Command Prompt Only   This option is not available with Windows Me. Under Windows 95/98, it executes the contents of Autoexec.bat and Config.sys but doesn't start Windows 95/98. You get a DOS prompt instead. Type WIN to load Windows 95/98. This command executes the file Win.com. You can use several switches with the WIN command when troubleshooting the OS. Table 4-12 lists these switches.

In a troubleshooting situation, try each switch until you find one that works. You can then identify the source of the problem, and can sometimes put entries in the System.ini file to make the switch a permanent part of the load.

Command/Switch	Purpose
WIN /D:M	Starts Windows in Safe Mode
WIN /D:F	Turns off 32-bit disk access; use this option if there appears to be a problem with hard drive access
WIN /D:S	Instructs Windows not to use memory address F000:0, which is used by BIOS
WIN /D:V	Instructs Windows that the system BIOS should be used to access the hard drive rather than the OS
WIN /D:X	Excludes all upper memory addresses from real-mode drivers

Table 4-12   Switches used with the WIN command

Safe Mode Command Prompt Only   This option does not execute the commands in Autoexec.bat or Config.sys. You get a DOS prompt.

Previous Version of MS-DOS   This option loads a previous version of DOS if one is present. You can get the same results by pressing F4 when the message "Starting Windows 95/98" appears. This option is not available in Windows 98 SE or Windows Me.

Troubleshooting with the Startup Menu

If you tried using the tools recommended in the previous sections, but have not yet identified the source of the problem, use the following checklist to troubleshoot using the startup menu.

- Try a hard boot. A soft boot might not do the trick, because TSRs are not always "kicked out" of RAM with a soft boot.
- If you have not already done so, try Safe Mode next.
- Try the Step-by-step confirmation option next. Look for error messages caused by a missing or corrupted driver file. Try not allowing real-mode drivers to load. After the problem command within Autoexec.bat or Config.sys is identified, you can eliminate the command or troubleshoot it. Specific commands in these files and their purposes were covered in Chapter 3.
- Use the Logged option next, and examine the Bootlog.txt file that is created to see if it identifies the problem.
- Try booting using the Command prompt only option. From the command prompt, run the real-mode version of ScanDisk, which you can find in the \Windows\Command folder, to scan the hard drive for errors. From a command prompt, enter this command: C:\Windows\Command\Scandisk. If the Scandisk.exe program on the hard drive is corrupted, use the one on the emergency startup disk.
- From the command prompt in Windows 98/Me, type Scanreg/Fix and try to reboot.
- Next, type Scanreg/Restore and select the latest known good backup of the Windows 9x registry. Try to reboot.
- From the command prompt, you can use the WIN command with the switches listed in Table 4-12. If one of these commands solves the problem, look for real-mode drivers that might be in conflict, eliminating those that you can. Examine Bootlog.txt for errors and try booting from Safe Mode again.
- Try booting with the Safe Mode command prompt only. Remember that when you are in Safe Mode, the registry is not executed. If you suspect a corrupted registry, restore it to its last saved version as you learned to do earlier. Then try the WIN command with or without the switches, as necessary.

Using the Startup Disk for Troubleshooting

If you cannot solve the boot problems by using the troubleshooting utilities within Windows or on the startup menu, use an emergency startup disk to recover from the failed boot. If you do not have an emergency startup disk, create one on another computer and use it to work with the computer that has the problem. Before using the startup disk, it is a good idea to check it for viruses on a working computer by scanning it with antivirus software. If you find a virus on the emergency startup disk, destroy the disk and use a working computer to create a new one.

To use the emergency startup disk, place it in the floppy disk drive and turn on the PC. It will boot to a startup menu or to an A prompt, depending on the version of Windows 9x you are using. Figure 4-38 shows the startup menu.

If you are using a version for which the startup disk boots to a menu, select the first option, which is to start the PC with CD-ROM support. The OS then examines the system for problems and provides an A prompt where you can enter commands.

4

If the system failed to boot from the hard drive, the first step in troubleshooting at this point is to see if you can access the hard drive. Enter DIR C: at the A prompt. If this step works, then the problem lies in the software used on the hard drive to boot, including the OS boot record, OS hidden files, and command interface files. If you cannot access the hard drive, the problem is with the partition table, the Master Boot Record, the hard drive, its cabling, or its power source. In this case, you need to examine the hard drive for errors.

Use Fdisk to examine the partition table. If the table is corrupted, most likely you have lost everything on your hard drive. Try using the Fdisk /MBR command to restore the Master Boot Record on the drive. If this does not work, try creating new partitions on the drive and formatting the drive. All data and software on the drive will be lost. If you cannot use Fdisk on the drive, treat the problem as a hardware problem.

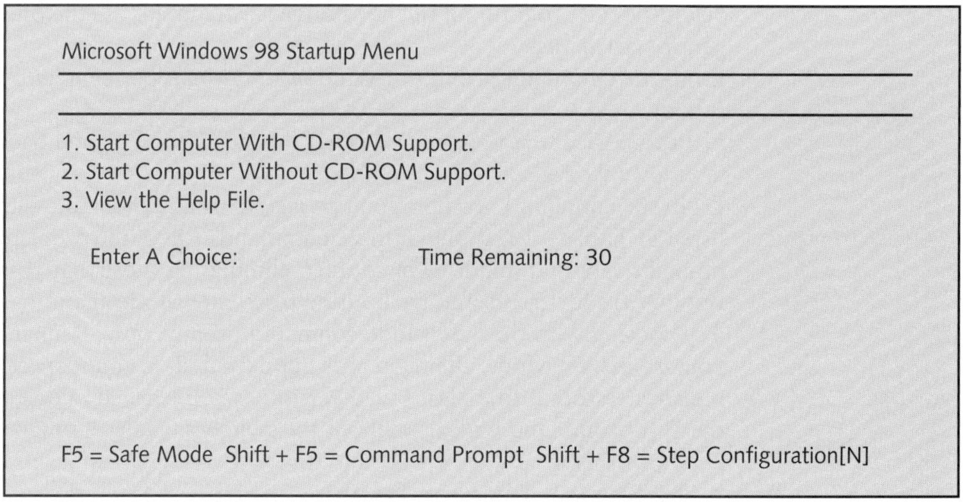

```
Microsoft Windows 98 Startup Menu
_____

_____

1. Start Computer With CD-ROM Support.
2. Start Computer Without CD-ROM Support.
3. View the Help File.

    Enter A Choice:                    Time Remaining: 30




F5 = Safe Mode  Shift + F5 = Command Prompt  Shift + F8 = Step Configuration[N]
```

Figure 4-38   Windows 98 rescue disk startup menu

After you complete troubleshooting the hard drive, eliminating physical problems with the hard drive subsystem, CMOS, and the partition table, the next step is to run the Windows 9x Setup program. When given the opportunity, select Verify installed components. Setup then restores damaged or missing system files.

Accessing the CD-ROM Drive when Booting from a Floppy Disk   Because Windows is normally loaded from a CD, your emergency startup disk should include the drivers necessary to access the CD-ROM drive. When you are recovering from a failed hard drive, you will not have access to the 32-bit Windows CD-ROM drivers on the hard drive. Windows 98 and later versions of Windows automatically add the real-mode CD-ROM device drivers to their rescue disks, but Windows 95 does not. This section explains how to add this function to a Windows 95 rescue disk.

4

Two files are required to access a CD-ROM drive while in real mode: the 16-bit device driver provided by the manufacturer of the CD-ROM drive (or a generic real-mode driver that works with the drive), and the 16-bit real-mode OS interface to the driver, Mscdex.exe. The device driver is loaded from Config.sys, and Mscdex.exe is loaded from Autoexec.bat.

For example, let's say your CD-ROM drive comes with a floppy disk that includes the following files:

- *Install.exe.* CD-ROM installation program
- *Cdtech.sys.* CD-ROM device driver
- Instruction files and documentation

To make your Windows 95 rescue disk capable of accessing the CD-ROM drive when you boot from this disk, first you need to copy two files to the root directory of the rescue disk: Mscdex.exe from the C:\Windows \Command folder and Cdtech.sys from the floppy disk bundled with your CD-ROM drive. Then add the following command or a similar one to the Config.sys file (the parameters in the command lines are explained in the following list):

```
DEVICE = A:\CDTECH.SYS /D:MSCD001
```

Put the following command or a similar one in your Autoexec.bat file on the floppy disk:

```
MSCDEX.EXE /D:MSCD001 /L:E /M:10
```

The explanations of these command lines are as follows:

- When the program Mscdex.exe executes, it uses the MSCD001 entry as a tag back to the Config.sys file to learn which device driver is being used to interface with the drive. In this case it is Cdtech.sys.
- To Mscdex.exe, the drive is named MSCD001 and is being managed by the driver Cdtech.sys.
- Mscdex.exe will use Cdtech.sys as its "go-between" to access the drive.
- Mscdex.exe also assigns a drive letter to the drive. If you want to specify a drive letter, use the /L: option in the command line. In our example, the CD-ROM drive will be drive E. If you don't use the /L: option, then the next available drive letter is used.
- The /M: option controls the number of memory buffers.
- If the files referenced in these two commands are stored on the floppy disk in a different directory from the root directory, then include the path to the file in front of the filename.

Troubleshooting Windows 9x Hardware and Software

Now that you know about some of the tools used for troubleshooting, you can learn about the general approaches you should take to troubleshooting problems.

Troubleshooting a PC problem begins with isolating it into one of two categories: problems that prevent the PC from booting and problems that occur after a successful boot. Begin by asking the user questions like the following to learn as much as you can:

- When did the problem start?
- Were there any error messages or unusual displays on the screen?
- What programs or software were you using?
- Did you move your computer system recently?
- Has there been a recent thunderstorm or electrical problem?
- Have you made any hardware, software, or configuration changes?
- Has someone else been using your computer recently?
- Can you show me exactly what you did when this problem occurred? (Have the user reproduce the problem and watch each step.)
- Next, ask whether the PC boots properly. If not, then begin troubleshooting the failed boot.

Here are some general tips for troubleshooting hardware:

- Try rebooting the computer. The problem with the device may disappear when Windows redetects it.
- Frequent system lockups and General Protection Faults might indicate corrupted memory modules. Try using memory-testing software to check for intermittent memory errors, which indicate the module needs replacing. An example of memory-testing software is DocMemory by CST, Inc. (*www.docmemory.com*).
- For external devices such as monitors, printers, and scanners, try turning on the device before turning on the computer. If your computer is on and you are rebooting, leave the device on and online.
- If a device doesn't work with one application, try it with another. If the problem only occurs with one application, the problem is probably not with the hardware device but with that application.
- Check Device Manager for errors it reports about the device. If it reports errors, use the Hardware Troubleshooter in Device Manager to help resolve the problem or go to the Microsoft Web site and search for the error message.
- The driver might be corrupted or need updating. Look on the Web for updated device drivers. Search the device manufacturer's Web site or the Microsoft Web site for information about problems with the device and solutions.
- Use Device Manager to uninstall the device and then reinstall it. If you uninstall the device and then reboot, Windows should recognize an uninstalled device and automatically launch the Found New Hardware Wizard. If it doesn't launch, then chances are the device is not working or is not PnP.

■ For PnP devices on expansion cards such as sound cards, modems, and network cards, if you uninstall the device in Device Manager and Windows does not recognize the device when you reboot, the device might not be working. The expansion card needs to be reseated or moved to a different expansion slot. If that doesn't work, the card needs replacing.

■ If none of these things work, ask yourself what changed since the device last worked. For example, maybe you added another hardware device that conflicts with the one you are using, or maybe you have added software that conflicts with the software that the problem device is using. Try disabling other devices or try uninstalling software that you suspect is causing the problem. Use Automatic Skip Driver Agent to eliminate other devices that might prevent the problem driver from working.

For application software problems, try the following:

■ Address any error messages that appear when using the software.

■ If you don't understand the error message, write it down or print it, and then look it up on the Microsoft support Web site or the product manufacturer's Web site. Follow the directions given on the Web sites to resolve the problem.

■ Read the documentation that came with the application and documents on the manufacturer's Web site. Perhaps you are using a function incorrectly.

■ A virus might be the source of the problem. Run current antivirus software.

■ Consider that data files might be corrupted. Try creating new data files used by the software.

■ Consider that the hardware the software is using might have a problem. For the hard drive, run ScanDisk and Defrag and check for free disk space. Delete files in the \Windows\Temp folder. For a device other than the hard drive, try using another application to access the device.

■ Try uninstalling and reinstalling the software. Back up the data first.

■ Launch Dr. Watson and then try to reproduce the error with the application. Look in the Dr. Watson log files for clues and search the Microsoft Web site.

■ Perhaps the application depends on OS files that are corrupted. Try restoring Windows system files. Check the Microsoft Web site for Windows 9x service packs that might resolve the problem. Install all Windows service packs. You might have to reinstall Windows.

■ Ask yourself, "When was the last time the software worked?" What happened differently then? Did you get an error message that seemed insignificant at the time? What has happened to your computer since the software last worked? Have you added more software or changed the hardware configuration?

■ A configuration file, which contains software settings, might be corrupted. Look for a file with a file extension of .ini, .inf, or .cfg.

4

A+
OS
3.3

If the system is performing slowly, try the following:

- The problem might be caused by lack of resources. If your system is running low on memory or has too many applications open, it might not be able to support a device. A corrupted Windows system file or registry can also cause problems with hardware devices. Try verifying system files or restoring the registry from backup.
- Check the hard drive. Run ScanDisk and Defrag. Delete unneeded files and empty the Recycle Bin. Generally clean up the hard drive, making plenty of room for the swap file and temporary files used by applications.
- Suspect a virus. Run a current version of antivirus software. Clean or delete all files that contain viruses. Restore system files.
- Check for applications loaded at startup that use system resources. Close applications not currently in use.
- Look for icons in the **System Tray,** the small area on the right side of the taskbar at the bottom of the screen. These icons represent small applets that are loaded at startup and take system resources. Keep these icons to a minimum.
- Clean up the registry using the Scanreg /opt command.
- Remove extraneous software such as fancy screen savers and desktop wallpaper and photos.
- Verify that Windows is using optimum caching on the hard drive and CD-ROM drive. Go to the System Properties window and click the Performance tab. Click File System. The File System Properties window appears (see Figure 4-39). On the Hard Disk tab, select Full Read-ahead optimization, and on the CD-ROM tab, select Large cache size.

NOTE

If an application locks up, press Ctrl + Alt + Del and select the program in the Close Program dialog box. Click End Task.

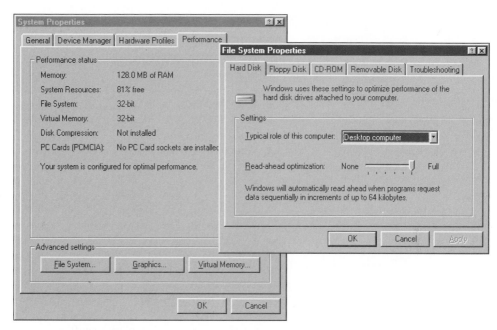

A+
OS
3.3

Figure 4-39   Verify that the hard drive is set for optimal caching

Windows Help and the Microsoft Web Site

A+
OS
3.2

Windows Help might provide useful information when you try to resolve a problem. To access the Troubleshooting tool of Windows Help, click Start, click Help, and then click Troubleshooting. The Help information includes suggestions that can lead you to a solution. For example, in Figure 4-40, the Hardware Troubleshooter suggests that you check to see that the device is not listed twice in Device Manager. If this is the case, you should remove the second occurrence of the device.

Also, the Microsoft Web site, *support.microsoft.com* (see Figure 4-41), has lots of information on troubleshooting. Search for the device, an error message, a Windows utility, a symptom, a software application, an update version number, or key words that lead you to articles about problems and solutions. You can also go to *www.microsoft.com* to browse for links on hardware and software compatibility. Other sources of help are application and device user installation manuals, training materials, and the Web sites of application and device manufacturers.

NOTE

For those who are serious about learning to provide professional sup port for Windows 95 or Windows 98, two good books are *Microsoft Windows 95 Resource Kit* and *Microsoft Windows 98 Resource Kit*, both by Microsoft Press.

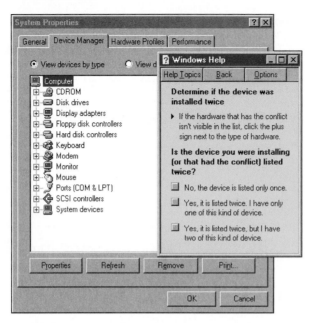

Figure 4-40   Troubleshooter making a suggestion to resolve a hardware conflict

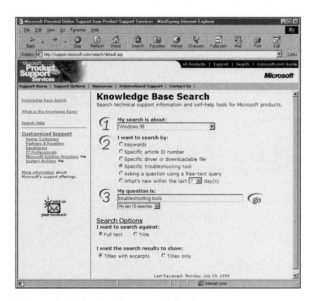

Figure 4-41   Microsoft Technical Support Web site

CHAPTER SUMMARY

4

▶ Windows 9x has a shell and kernel; the Windows 9x core consists of the kernel, the user, and the GDI.

▶ Virtual machines (VMs) are multiple logical machines within one physical machine. If an application crashes or produces another type of error within a VM, only that VM is affected, instead of the entire system.

▶ Although Windows 95/98 supports 16-bit drivers, using 32-bit drivers whenever possible is better.

▶ Before installing Windows 9x as an upgrade, verify that you have enough hard drive space, run ScanDisk or Chkdsk, run antivirus software, back up critical system files, disable TSRs that might cause problems if they run during installation, verify that any network connections work, make sure that the swap file is on a drive compressed with protected-mode software, and decide whether you want to use FAT16 or FAT32.

▶ If Windows is already installed and you want to do a clean install, use the setup screen to install the new OS in a different folder than the one used by the currently installed OS, which is probably \Windows.

▶ Before performing a Windows 98/Me upgrade, check hardware and software compatibility, run antivirus software, and back up your system. The Setup Wizard on the Windows 98 CD will guide you through the setup process. After setup is complete, test installed applications and back up your system again.

▶ When adding new hardware to Windows 9x, use the Add New Hardware Wizard. Select the hardware from a list of devices to use a Windows driver, or click Have Disk to use your own drivers (from a manufacturer's disk or downloaded from the Internet to a folder on your hard drive). Alternatively, you can run the setup program provided by the device manufacturer.

▶ For a Windows 9x system to be truly Plug and Play (PnP), the system BIOS must be PnP, all hardware devices and expansion cards must be PnP-compliant, and a 32-bit device driver must be available for any installed hardware device.

▶ Dosstart.bat is a type of Autoexec.bat file that executes when you restart the computer in MS-DOS mode or when you run a program in MS-DOS mode.

▶ An OS that supports protected mode can create a virtual real mode for a 16-bit application so that the application thinks it is the only program running, has all memory available to it, and accesses data using a 16-bit data path. Windows 9x ordinarily runs a 16-bit DOS application in a virtual DOS machine.

▶ Windows keystroke shortcuts are useful for experienced typists who may find them faster than the mouse; they are also useful in troubleshooting situations when the mouse does not work.

▶ In the Display Properties window, you can change the background, screen saver, appearance, icon effects, Active Desktop settings, color range, and display size for the desktop.

▶ Starting with Windows 9x, the Windows registry takes over the essential functions of .ini files. However, Windows 9x still supports System.ini and Win.ini for backward compatibility with legacy hardware devices and legacy software applications.

▶ The registry is contained in two files, System.dat and User.dat. Windows 95 maintains backups of these files, called System.da0 and User.da0, that you can use when troubleshooting. Windows 98/Me keeps compressed backups of the registry and system files in cabinet files named rb000.cab, rb001.cab, and so forth.

▶ Changes in the Control Panel, Device Manager, and other locations in Windows 9x can change the registry automatically. The Regedit utility is used to edit the registry manually.

▶ The Registry Checker (Scanreg.exe) backs up, verifies, and recovers the registry. It automatically backs up the registry every day and keeps the last five days of backups.

▶ The System Configuration Utility (Msconfig.exe) allows you to modify the system configuration temporarily to help with troubleshooting. It reduces the startup process to essentials.

▶ The Dr. Watson utility (Drwatson.exe) helps you troubleshoot applications by trapping errors in log files and taking a snapshot of the system.

▶ The System Configuration Editor (Sysedit.exe) is a text editor used to edit system files. When you run Sysedit, it automatically opens Protocol.ini, System.ini, Win.ini, Config.sys, and Autoexec.bat.

▶ Device Manager lists hardware devices installed on a system. For more information about a specific device in Device Manager, click the device and select Properties.

▶ The five phases of the Windows 9x boot process are BIOS POST and bootstrap, loading the OS, the loading of real-mode VxDs, protected-mode switchover and PnP configuration, and loading remaining components.

▶ Applications are loaded at startup by a shortcut in the StartUp folder, the name of the program file in the Load= or Run= line in Win.ini, or an entry in the registry.

▶ When troubleshooting Windows 9x boot problems, first check error messages, then boot in Safe Mode, then boot to the command prompt using the startup menu, and finally try booting from an emergency startup disk.

▶ To force the Windows 9x startup menu to appear, hold down either the Ctrl key or the F8 key during the boot.

▶ In Logged mode, Windows tracks startup activities and logs them to the Bootlog.txt file.

▶ You can reach Safe Mode either from the Windows startup menu or by pressing F5 while Windows is loading.

▶ Safe Mode starts Windows 9x with a minimum default configuration to give you an opportunity to correct an error in the configuration.

▶ Choosing Command Prompt Only from the startup menu executes the contents of Autoexec.bat and Config.sys but does not start Windows. Instead it brings you to a DOS prompt. Use the WIN command to load Windows 9x.

▶ Use the startup disk to recover from a failed boot when you cannot solve the problem using the startup menu or cannot boot from the hard drive. If you do not have a startup disk or the one you have has a virus, use a working computer to create a new disk.

4

KEY TERMS

For explanations of key terms, see the Glossary near the end of the book.

application programming interface (API) call	kernel	System.ini
clean install	keys	System Tray
comment	patch	upgrade install
Dosstart.bat	PIF (program information file)	user component
Dr. Watson	Protocol.ini	value data
dynamic VxD	service pack	virtual device driver (VxD)
GDI (Graphics Device Interface)	shell	virtual machine (VM)
hypertext	shortcut	Win.ini
initialization files	static VxD	
	Sysedit	

REVIEWING THE BASICS

1. What are the three core components of Windows 9x?

2. Which are preferable to use: 32-bit drivers or 16-bit drivers?

3. What is the function of the Autorun.inf file included on the Windows 9x installation CD? The Setup.exe file? The Readme.txt file?

4. List at least five things you need to do to prepare your hard drive for an upgrade installation of Windows 9x.

5. What are the four types of installations that you can choose during setup of Windows 9x?

6. What are the log files Setuplog.txt, Detlog.txt, and Detcrash.log used for?

7. What type of disk should you always create when prompted to do so during Windows 9x setup? Why is this such an important step?

8. Give two situations in which Windows keyboard shortcuts might be useful.

9. What is the Windows keyboard shortcut to display the startup menu while Windows is loading? To go through step-by-step confirmation of startup? To move from one loaded application to another?

10. How do you access the Display Properties window? What are two settings you can change from this window?

11. When adding hardware to Windows 9x, how do you indicate that you want to use a Windows driver? A manufacturer-provided or downloaded driver?

12. Use the _____ applet in the Control Panel when installing 32-bit software designed for Windows 9x. Use the _____ option on the Start menu when installing older 16-bit software.

13. What is a comment line? How is a comment line noted within a file?

14. Explain the purpose of the System Configuration Utility. How would you use it in troubleshooting?

15. Name four configuration files that Windows 9x includes for backward compatibility with legacy software and hardware.

16. The Windows registry is contained in two files, _____ and _____. The Windows 95 backups of these files are called _____ and _____.

17. Which version of Windows includes the Registry Checker? How often does this utility back up the registry?

18. Explain the difference between the Regedit and Scanreg utilities.

19. Name the files that Sysedit automatically displays for editing. Give a short description of each.

20. List the five phases of the Windows 9x boot process and give a short description of each.

21. Explain how the file Setver.exe is used in Windows 9x.

22. What Msdos.sys entry can be used to backtrack from a Windows 9x installation to the underlying version of DOS? What happens when this entry is set to =0? To =1?

23. List the options on the Windows 9x startup menu and give a short description of each. Which option appears for Windows 95 but not for Windows 98, and why? Which option appears for Windows 95/98, but not for Windows Me?

24. Which startup menu options execute Autoexec.bat and Config.sys? Which do not?

25. What Windows utility allows you to control what drivers are loaded during Windows startup?

26. _____ is a Windows utility that can record detailed information about the system, errors that occur, and the programs that caused them in a log file.

27. What parts of the Windows load does Safe Mode not execute?

28. Name two ways to end an application that is hung without rebooting the PC.

29. After using the Windows 98 startup menu to boot the system to a command prompt, what command can you use to load the Windows desktop?

30. What function key do you press during bootup to start Windows 98 in Safe Mode?

4

THINKING CRITICALLY

1. An application loads at startup. List the steps you would take to stop an application from loading at this time.

2. Place these tools in the order you would use them when troubleshooting the Windows 9x boot process: emergency startup disk, Safe Mode, error messages, and the command prompt.

3. You attempt to install a new hardware device, but Windows 98 locks up during the boot. You remove the device and try to reboot, but Windows 98 still locks up. Which tools do you use to solve the problem and what do you do with them? (Note you might use more than one of these tools.)

   a. Device Manager

   b. System Information utility

   c. Windows 98 startup disk

   d. Scanreg

   e. Registry Checker

HANDS-ON PROJECTS

HANDS-ON
PROJECTS

PROJECT 4-1: Practicing Keystrokes

Disconnect your mouse and reboot your PC, then practice using the keyboard in case you must troubleshoot a system when the mouse does not work.

1. Open Explorer and select the file Io.sys in the root directory of the hard drive. The file will be hidden, so you must unhide it. From the View menu, select Folder Options, click the View tab, and then select Show all files. List the keys you needed to do this step.

2. What is the exact size of the file in bytes, and the date and time the file was last modified?

3. Which key do you press to move down through the logical drives listed in Explorer?

4. Which key do you press to move down through files listed in a folder in Explorer?

PROJECT 4-2: **Installing a Windows Component**

Using the Add/Remove Programs applet in the Control Panel, look for Windows components that are not installed and install one. You need access to the Windows 98 CD, or the files on the CD must be copied to the hard drive or a network drive.

PROJECT 4-3: **Using Shortcuts**

Create a shortcut on your desktop to Notepad (Notepad.exe), a text editor. Using a second method for creating shortcuts, add a shortcut to the Windows command prompt (Command.com). First, locate the two program files on your hard drive by clicking Start, Find, and using the Find dialog box. Then create the shortcuts. List the steps you took to create each shortcut.

PROJECT 4-4: **Using the Windows 9x Startup Menu**

As soon as your computer displays the message "Starting Windows 95/98" during the boot process, press the **F8** function key. Select **Logged(\Bootlog.txt)**. After the boot is complete, open the file **Bootlog.txt** and print its contents. Shut down Windows, reboot the computer, and then press **F8** again. Select the **Safe Mode** option, and note the differences in the screen's appearance. Shut down Windows, reboot the computer, and then press **F8** again. This time choose the **Step-by-step confirmation** option. Write down each command that executes.

PROJECT 4-5: **Using Windows Utilities and Files**

1. Place a shortcut to Task Manager on your desktop. Print a screen shot of the Properties window of the shortcut. Test the shortcut.

2. Cause Sysedit to launch automatically at startup. Print the screen showing how you did this.

3. Edit Msdos.sys so that it automatically displays the startup menu when loading Windows. Print the contents of the file.

PROJECT 4-6: Troubleshooting a Boot Problem

Edit the Config.sys file on your PC. If you are using an installation of Windows 9x that does not use a Config.sys file, then create one. Enter a command line in the file that you know will cause an error. Boot the PC. Press **F8** during the boot, and walk through the boot process to demonstrate how this procedure can help you diagnose a problem with startup files.

Correct the command line in Config.sys, reboot, and walk through each command in the boot process.

PROJECT 4-7: Tools for Troubleshooting a Device Driver

Using Automatic Skip Driver Agent (ASDA), disable one or more devices at startup. Print a screen shot of ASDA showing the disabled devices. Reboot and verify that the devices are not available. Using ASDA, enable the devices, reboot, and verify that the devices work.

Be sure you have the drivers for the devices available on the hard drive, floppy disk, or CD. Using Device Manager, uninstall a device. Print a screen shot of Device Manager showing that the device is not installed. Reinstall the device and verify that it is working.

PROJECT 4-8: Preparing a Hard Drive for the Installation of Windows 9x

CAUTION

This project requires that you completely erase everything on your hard drive. If you have important data on the drive, don't do this project!

Do the following to prepare a hard drive for a new installation of Windows 9x:

1. Boot from a Windows 9x startup disk, and then use Fdisk to create primary and extended partitions on the drive. The primary partition will contain drive C. If there is room on the drive, create two logical drives in the extended partition.

2. Format all three logical drives, placing system files on drive C.

3. Verify that you can boot to drive C, get a C prompt, and access all three drives.

4. Use the DIR command to print a directory of each drive to a local printer. Use these or similar commands: DIR C:>PRN, DIR D:>PRN, and DIR E:>PRN.

5. Using ScanDisk, scan each logical drive disk surface for errors.

CASE PROJECT

Installing Windows 9x

Follow the instructions in this chapter to install Windows 9x using a Typical installation. Create the rescue disk when prompted to do so. Write down each decision you have to make as you perform the installation. If you get any error messages during the installation, write them down and list the steps you took to recover from the error. How long did the installation take?

4

Understanding and Installing Windows 2000 and Windows NT

Windows NT, Windows 2000, and Windows XP share the same basic Windows architecture and have similar characteristics. Windows NT introduced a new file system, NTFS, that represents a break with past Windows operating systems; Windows 2000 and Windows XP use it as well. Windows 2000 is the culmination of the evolution of Microsoft operating systems from the 16-bit DOS operating system to a true 32-bit, module-oriented operating system, complete with desktop functionality, user-friendly Plug and Play installations, and other easy-to-use features. Windows XP includes additional support for multimedia, Plug and Play, and legacy software, making the final step for Microsoft to announce the merging of Windows 9x and Windows NT operating systems into a single OS. (There will be no future updates to Windows 9x, as Microsoft considers this OS a legacy technology.) This chapter lays the foundation for understanding the architecture of Windows NT/2000/XP and then shows you how to install Windows 2000 Professional. You will also learn how to install hardware and software under Windows 2000. Because a PC support technician occasionally sees Windows NT still used, the last part of the chapter covers Windows NT installation and support.

Windows NT/2000/XP Architecture

For the corporate desktop or home PC, in most cases you would choose Windows XP rather than Windows 2000. However, if you must select between Windows 98 and Windows 2000, Windows 2000 is the better choice for the corporate desktop. Because of its improved power management, Windows 2000 is also a better choice for notebook computers. For the business environment, Windows 2000 is more secure and reliable and offers better support for very large hard drives. Windows 98 is the better choice for the home PC. Windows 98 works better than Windows 2000 with games, music, and video, and supports the widest variety of hardware and software products.

Windows 2000 includes four operating systems:

> **A+ EXAM TIP**
>
> Microsoft offers several operating systems designed to run on servers, including Windows NT Server, Windows 2000 Server, and Windows 2003 Server. None of the server operating systems is covered on the A+ exams.

- *Windows 2000 Professional* was designed to replace both Windows 9x and Windows NT Workstation as a personal computer desktop or notebook OS. It is an improved version of Windows NT Workstation, using the same new technological approach to hardware and software, and has all the popular features of Windows 9x, including Plug and Play.
- *Windows 2000 Server* is the improved version of Windows NT Server and is designed as a network operating system for low-end servers.
- *Windows 2000 Advanced Server* is a network operating system that has the same features as Windows 2000 Server but is designed to run on more powerful servers.
- *Windows 2000 Datacenter Server* is a network operating system that is a step up from Windows 2000 Advanced Server. It is intended for use in large enterprise operations centers.

Now let's look at the architecture of Windows NT/2000/XP in more detail, including how the OS relates to applications, networking features, and the management of hard drives and memory.

Windows NT/2000/XP Modes

Windows NT/2000/XP operates in two modes, user mode and kernel mode, which each take advantage of different CPU functions and abilities (see Figure 5-1). This section explains both modes.

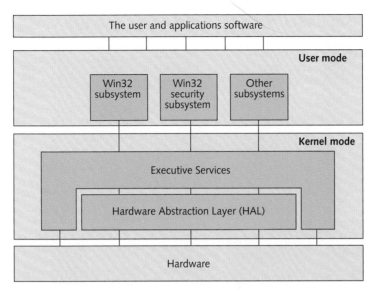

Figure 5-1 User mode and kernel mode in Windows NT/2000/XP and how they relate to users, application software, and hardware

User Mode

User mode is a processor mode in which programs have only limited access to system information and can access hardware only through other OS services. The OS has several **subsystems,** or OS modules, that use this mode and interface with the user and with applications. The Windows tools you use, such as Windows Explorer, run primarily in user mode. In Figure 5-1, note the Win32 subsystem, which is probably the most important user mode subsystem because it manages and provides an environment for all 32-bit programs, including the user interface (such as the one for Explorer). The Win32 security subsystem provides logon to the system and other security functions, including privileges for file access.

All applications relate to Windows NT/2000/XP by way of the Win32 subsystem, either directly or indirectly. Figure 5-2 shows how various programs that run under Windows NT/2000/XP interact with subsystems. For instance, each legacy DOS application resides in its own NTVDM. An **NTVDM (NT virtual DOS machine)** is a carefully controlled environment that Windows NT/2000/XP provides. In it a DOS application can interface with only one subsystem and cannot relate to anything outside the system, so it is similar to the Windows 9x virtual DOS machine introduced in Chapter 4. All 16-bit Windows 3.x applications reside in a **Win16 on Win32 (WOW)** environment. Within the WOW, these 16-bit applications can communicate with one another and the WOW, but that's as far as their world goes. Figure 5-2 shows three 16-bit Windows 3.x applications residing in a WOW that resides in one NTVDM. Because each DOS application expects to run as the only application on a PC, each has its own NTVDM.

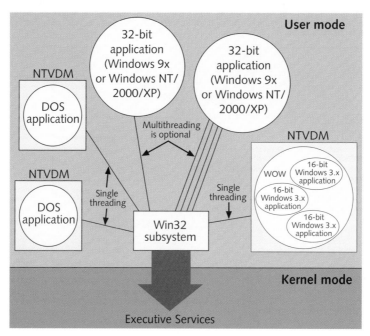

Figure 5-2   Environment subsystems in Windows NT/2000/XP user mode include NTVDMs for DOS and Windows 3.x applications and optional multithreading for 32-bit applications

You can see in Figure 5-2 that 32-bit applications do not require an NTVDM and can relate to the Win32 subsystem directly, because they are written to run in protected mode. They can also use a single line of communication (called single-threading) with the Win32 subsystem or multiple lines for interfacing (called **multithreading**) with the Win32 subsystem, depending on what the process requests. A **thread** is a single task that the process requests from the kernel, such as the task of printing a file. A **process** is a program or group of programs that is running, together with the system resources assigned to it, such as memory addresses, environmental variables, and other resources. Sometimes a process is called an instance, such as when you say, "Open two instances of Internet Explorer." Technically, you are saying to open two Internet Explorer processes. An example of multithreading is Microsoft Word requesting that the subsystem read a large file from the hard drive and print a job at the same time. Single-threading happens when the application does not expect both processes to be performed at the same time but simply passes one request followed by another.

Kernel Mode

Kernel mode is a processor mode in which programs have extensive access to system information and hardware. Kernel mode is used by two main components: the HAL and a group of components collectively called executive services. The **HAL** (**hardware abstraction layer**) is the layer between the OS and the hardware. The HAL is available in different versions, each designed to address the specifics of a particular

CPU technology. **Executive services** interface between the subsystems in user mode and the HAL. Executive services components manage hardware resources by way of the HAL and device drivers. Windows NT/2000/XP was designed to port easily to different hardware platforms. Because only the components operating in kernel mode actually interact with hardware, they are the only parts that need to be changed when Windows NT/2000/XP moves from one hardware platform to another.

Applications in user mode have no access to hardware resources. In kernel mode, executive services have limited access to hardware resources, but the HAL primarily interacts with hardware. Limiting access to hardware, mainly to the HAL, increases OS integrity because more control is possible. With this isolation, an application cannot cause a system to hang by making illegal demands on hardware. Overall performance is increased because the HAL and executive services can operate independently of the slower, less-efficient applications using them.

5

Networking Features

A+
OS
4.1

A workstation running Windows NT/2000/XP can be configured to work as one node in a workgroup or one node on a domain. A **workgroup** is a logical group of computers and users that share resources (such as the scanner, printer, spreadsheet, and Word document in Figure 5-3), where administration, resources, and security on a workstation are controlled by that workstation. Each computer maintains a list of users and their rights on that particular PC. A Windows **domain** is a group of networked computers that share a centralized directory database of user account information and security for the entire set of computers (Figure 5-4). A workgroup uses a **peer-to-peer** networking model, and a domain uses a **client/server** networking model. Using the client/server model, the directory database is controlled by a Network Operating System (NOS). Popular NOSs are Windows Server 2003, Windows 2000 Server, Novell NetWare, Unix, Linux, and Mac OS. Windows for the desktop has network client software built in for Windows (Microsoft Client), Mac (AppleTalk Client), and Novell NetWare (Client for NetWare). Alternately, for Novell NetWare, you can install Novell's version of its client software. You should also know that Windows XP does not include AppleTalk Client.

✔ A+ EXAM TIP

The A+ OS exam expects you to know all the key terms in this section.

In a Windows NT Server, Windows 2000 Server, or Windows Server 2003 domain, a network administrator manages access to the network through a centralized database. In Figure 5-4, you see the possible different components of a Windows domain. Every domain has a **domain controller**, which stores and controls a database of (1) user accounts, (2) group accounts, and (3) computer accounts. This database is called the directory database or the **security accounts manager (SAM)** database.

Because the domain controller database is so important, Windows allows backup copies of the database to exist on more than one computer in the domain. Under Windows NT, a network can have a primary domain controller and one or more backup domain controllers. The **primary domain controller (PDC)** holds the original directory database, and read-only copies are stored on **backup domain controllers**

A+
OS
4.1

(BDCs). An administrator can update the database on the PDC from any computer on the network, and the BDCs later get a copy of the updated database.

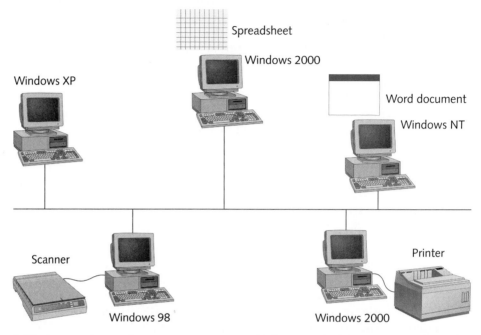

Figure 5-3   A Windows workgroup is a peer-to-peer network where no single computer controls the network and each computer controls its own resources

With Windows 2000, a network can have any number of domain controllers, each keeping a copy of the directory that can be edited. An administrator can update the directory on any one of these domain controllers, which will then communicate the change to the other domain controllers.

When Windows NT and Windows 2000 domain controllers are on the same network, conflicts can result because of the differences in the way the domain controllers work in each OS. For this reason, Windows 2000 runs in two modes: native mode and mixed mode. **Native mode** is used when no Windows NT domain controllers are present, and **mixed mode** is used when there is at least one Windows NT domain controller on the network. Mixed mode is necessary when a large network is being upgraded from Windows NT to Windows 2000, and some servers have been upgraded but others have not. When you install Windows 2000 Server, the default mode is mixed mode. After the installation, an administrator can choose to migrate to native mode by using the Computer Management console, which you will learn about in the next chapter. Once you change a domain to native mode, you cannot change it back to mixed mode.

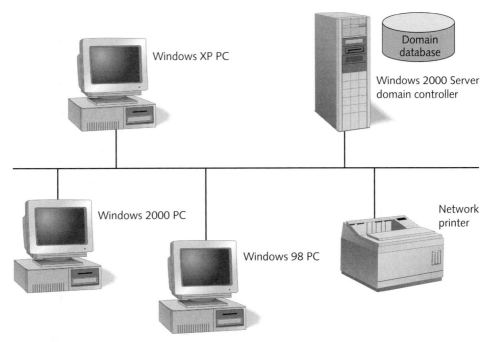

Figure 5-4   A Windows domain is a client/server network where security on each PC or other device is controlled by a centralized database on a domain controller

In addition to native mode and mixed mode, another networking feature new to Windows 2000 is **Active Directory**, a directory database and service that allows for a single administration point for all shared resources on a network. In Windows 2000, the security accounts manager (SAM) database is part of Active Directory. Active Directory can track file locations, databases, Web sites, users, services, and peripheral devices, including printers, scanners, and other hardware. It uses a locating method similar to that used by the Internet. Windows 2000 Server versions provide Active Directory, and Windows 2000 Professional acts as an Active Directory client, or user, of the directory.

Windows NT/2000/XP Logon

Regardless of whether Windows NT/2000/XP computers are networked or not, every Windows NT/2000/XP workstation has an **administrator account** by default. An administrator has rights and permissions to all computer software and hardware resources and is responsible for setting up other user accounts and assigning them privileges. During the Windows NT/2000/XP installation, you enter a password to the default administrator account. When the workstation is part of a Windows work-group, you can log on as an administrator after the OS is installed and create local user accounts. If the workstation is part of a domain, a network administrator sets up global user accounts that apply to the entire domain, including giving access to

A+
OS
4.1

the local workstations. Local user accounts, as well as other ways to secure a work-station, are covered in Chapter 8.

When Windows NT/2000/XP starts up, you must log on before you can use the OS. For Windows NT/2000, you see the logon screen when you press Ctrl + Alt + Del. Windows XP displays a logon screen by default. To log on, enter a user name and password, and click OK. Windows NT/2000/XP tracks which user is logged on to the system and grants rights and permissions according to the user's group or to specific permissions granted this user by the administrator. If you do not enter a valid account name and password, Windows NT/2000/XP does not allow you access to the system.

How Windows NT/2000/XP Manages Hard Drives

A+
OS
1.4
2.1

Windows NT incorporated new ways of managing hard drives that are also used in Windows 2000 and Windows XP. Windows NT/2000/XP assigns two different functions to hard drive partitions holding the OS (see Figure 5-5). The **system partition**, normally drive C, is the active partition of the hard drive. This is the partition that contains the OS boot record. Remember that the MBR program looks to this OS boot record for the boot program as the first step in turning the PC over to an OS. The other partition, called the **boot partition**, is the partition where the Windows NT/2000/XP operating system is stored.

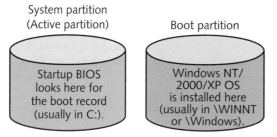

Figure 5-5   Two types of Windows NT/2000/XP hard drive partitions

NOTE

Don't be confused by the terminology here. It is really true that, according to Windows NT/2000/XP terminology, the Windows OS is on the boot partition, and the boot record is on the system partition, although that might seem backward. The PC boots from the system partition and loads the Windows NT/2000/XP operating system from the boot partition.

The system partition and the boot partition can be the same partition or separate partitions. Windows NT/2000/XP is designed to use two partitions in this way so that the Windows system files do not have to be stored on the same partition used to boot the OS. For Windows NT, both partitions can be formatted with either FAT16 or NTFS. Windows 2000/XP uses NTFS, FAT16, or FAT32, although NTFS under Windows NT is not compatible with an NTFS volume under Windows 2000/XP.

A+
OS
1.4
2.1

Know that Windows 9x and DOS cannot read files stored on an NTFS volume. If you want these OSs to access the volume, use the FAT16 file system.

Recall that Windows 9x can use Fdisk to create two partitions: a primary partition and an extended partition. The primary partition contains drive C, and the extended partition can contain several volumes or logical drives. Also recall that each FAT16 volume can be no larger than 2 GB. Using Windows NT/2000/XP, you can have up to four partitions. The first partition must be a primary partition and, if it is the boot device, can have only a single drive C. There can be up to four primary partitions on the drive, each containing a single logical drive. However, one of the four partitions can be an extended partition, which means it can have several volumes or logical drives. Because of the way Windows NT/2000/XP uses the FAT, each FAT16 volume can be up to 4 GB. However, to make the volume compatible with Windows 9x, limit the size to 2 GB.

Now that you've seen how partitions work in Windows NT/2000/XP, let's look at how file systems work.

A Choice of File Systems

Table 5-1 summarizes which file systems are supported by which operating systems. You need this information to plan your Windows NT/2000/XP installation. Windows versions not discussed in this chapter are included for comparison. Windows NT/2000/XP does not support the High Performance File System (HPFS) used by OS/2. If a hard drive is using HPFS, use the Windows NT/2000/XP Convert.exe utility to convert an HPFS partition to an NTFS partition. This program can also convert a FAT16 partition to NTFS.

	DOS	Windows 95	Windows 98	Windows NT	Windows 2000	Windows XP
FAT16	X	X	X	X	X	X
FAT32		X (for OSR2)	X		X	X
NTFS				X	X	X

Table 5-1   Operating system support for file systems

Although Windows NT 4.0 does not support FAT32, you can use third-party utility software packages such as FAT32 for Windows NT 4.0 by Winternals (*www.winternals.com*) to manage the interface, making it possible for Windows NT to read from and write to FAT32.

When a hard drive is formatted for NTFS, each cluster can range from 512 bytes on smaller disks to 4K on larger disks. Clusters are numbered sequentially by logical cluster numbers (LCN) from the beginning to the end of the disk. Each cluster number is stored in a 64-bit entry, compared to either 16 bits for FAT16 or 32 bits for FAT32.

The FAT file system uses three components to manage data on a logical drive: the FAT, directories, and data files. In contrast, the NTFS file system uses a database called the **master file table (MFT)** as its core component. The MFT tracks the contents of a logical drive using one or more rows in the table for each file or directory on the drive. As shown in Figure 5-6, the MFT contains information about each file in one record, or row, including header information (abbreviated H in Microsoft documentation); standard information (SI) about the file, including date and time; filename (FN); security information about the file, called the security descriptor (SD); and data about the location of the file. Entries in the MFT are ordered alphabetically by filename to speed up a search for a file listed in the table.

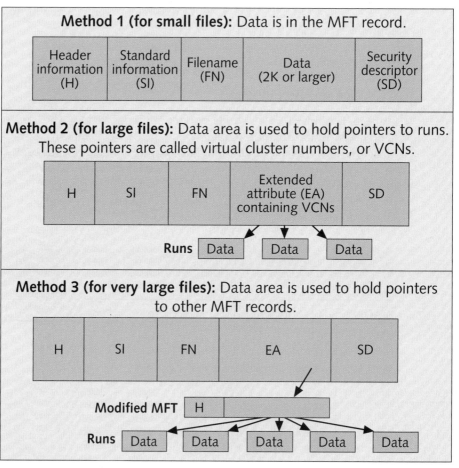

Figure 5-6   The Windows NT/2000/XP file system Master File Table uses three methods to store files, depending on the file size

Referring again to Figure 5-6, note that the data area in the MFT record is 2K for small hard drives but can be larger for larger hard drives. For small files, if the data can fit into the 2K area, the file description and the file's data are fully contained within the MFT.

If the file is moderately large and the data does not fit into the MFT, the data area in the MFT becomes an extended attribute (EA) of the file, which points to the location of the data. The data itself is moved outside the table to clusters called runs. The record in the MFT for this moderately large file contains pointers to these runs. Each data run, or cluster, assigned to the file is given a 64-bit virtual cluster number (VCN). The MFT maps the VCNs for the file onto the LCNs for the drive. This mapping is stored in the area of the MFT record that would have contained the data if the file had been small enough. If the file is so large that the pointers to all the VCNs cannot be contained in one MFT record, then additional MFT records are used. The first MFT record is called the base file record and holds the location of the other MFT records for this file.

Advantages of NTFS and FAT

When choosing between the NTFS file system and the FAT16 or FAT32 file system, consider the advantages that NTFS offers over FAT:

- NTFS is a recoverable file system. NTFS retains copies of its critical file system data and automatically recovers a failed file system, using this information the first time the disk is accessed after a file system failure.
- NTFS under Windows 2000/XP supports encryption (encoding files so they can't be deciphered by others) and disk quotas (limiting the hard drive space available to a user). Windows NT NTFS does not support these features.
- NTFS supports compression (reducing the size of files and folders). Windows 9x supports compression of an entire logical drive but not compression of individual files or folders.
- NTFS provides added security in the event you boot from floppy disks:

  - If you boot a PC using a DOS or Windows 9x boot disk, you can access the hard drive of a Windows NT/2000/XP system that uses the FAT file system, but you cannot access an NTFS file system.
  - If you boot a PC using the Windows 2000/XP Recovery Console or the three Windows NT startup disks, you can only access the NTFS file system if you provide an administrator account and password. In fact, if the administrator forgets his or her password to the OS, the hard drive is not accessible; when using Windows tools, the only recourse is to reload the OS.

NOTE

Third-party utility software can sometimes help you recover a forgotten administrator password. For example, ERD Commander 2003 by Winternals (*www.winternals.com*) is a bootable operating system on CD that contains Locksmith, a utility that lets you reset a forgotten administrator password. Boot a Windows NT/2000/XP system from the ERD Commander 2003 CD to launch a Windows-like desktop from which you can use several recovery tools.

- NTFS supports mirroring drives, meaning that two copies of data can be kept on two different drives to protect against permanent data loss in case of a hard drive crash. This feature makes the NTFS an important alternative for file servers.
- NTFS uses smaller cluster sizes than FAT16 or FAT32, making more efficient use of hard drive space when small files are stored.
- NTFS supports large-volume drives. NTFS uses 64-bit cluster numbers, whereas FAT16 uses 16-bit cluster numbers and FAT32 uses 32-bit cluster numbers. Because the number of bits assigned to hold each cluster number is so large, the cluster number itself can be large, and the table can accommodate very large drives with many clusters. Overall, NTFS is a more effective file system for drives larger than 1 GB and offers more robust drive compression, allowing compression of individual folders and files.

The advantages of the FAT file system over NTFS include:

- The FAT file system has less overhead than the NTFS file system, and therefore works best for hard drives that are less than 500 MB.
- The FAT file system is compatible with Windows 9x and DOS operating systems. If you plan to use either DOS or Windows 9x on the same hard drive as Windows NT/2000/XP, use the FAT file system so that DOS and Windows 9x can access files used by Windows NT/2000/XP.
- In the event of a serious problem with Windows NT/2000/XP, if you are using FAT on the active partition of the drive, you can boot the PC from a DOS or Windows 9x startup disk and access the drive.

You can choose to have Windows NT/2000/XP use NTFS by directing it to convert the hard drive from FAT to NTFS, or by having Windows NT/2000/XP partition a drive so that one partition of the drive uses the FAT format and the other uses the NTFS format. Windows NT/2000/XP allows you to format logical drives with either FAT or NTFS on the same extended partition.

Installing Windows 2000 Professional

This section explains how to install Windows 2000 on a system with a newly installed hard drive, called a clean install, and how to install Windows 2000 as an upgrade from Windows 9x or Windows NT, called an upgrade installation. Just as with Windows NT and Windows XP, Windows 2000 can be installed to be dual-booted with another OS. Before any type of installation, verify that your system meets the minimum requirements for Windows 2000. You must have at least 650 MB of free space on your hard drive, at least 64 MB of RAM, and a 133-MHz Pentium-compatible CPU or higher.

Planning the Installation

A+
OS
2.1
2.2
2.3

Before you install Windows 2000, you need to select a file system (NTFS, FAT16, or FAT32) and verify that your computer, your peripheral hardware devices, and your software qualify for Windows 2000. The best way to verify compatibility in these three areas is to check the Microsoft Web site at *www.microsoft.com/windows2000/ professional/howtobuy/upgrading/compat* (see Figure 5-7). The following is a brief explanation of why you must verify all three components.

5

- Windows NT/2000/XP does not use system BIOS to interface with hardware devices. For that reason, a hardware device must be specifically designed to interact with Windows NT/2000/XP. Don't assume that because a device is compatible with Windows NT, it works with Windows 2000. In some instances this is not the case, so check the HCL for Windows 2000 to be sure.

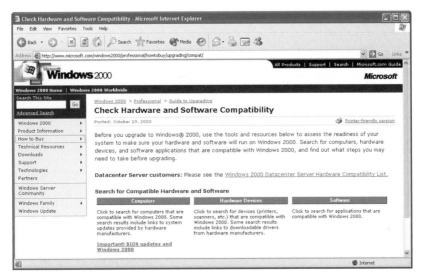

Figure 5-7   Use the Microsoft Web site to verify that your computer, peripheral devices, and applications all qualify for Windows 2000

- Software applications must also qualify for Windows 2000. If an application is not listed on the Microsoft Web site, it might still work with Windows 2000. You can verify compatibility by checking with the application manufacturer's Web site or technical support, or you can just install the application under Windows 2000 and test it yourself.
- Your motherboard BIOS must meet the **Advanced Configuration and Power Interface (ACPI)** standards developed by Intel, Microsoft, and Toshiba, which apply to system BIOS, the OS, and certain hardware devices and software to control when a device goes into an inactive state in order to conserve power. To take full advantage of Windows 2000 power management abilities, your system

A+
OS
2.1
2.2
2.3

BIOS must be ACPI-compliant. If your BIOS is not ACPI-compliant and you install Windows, Windows does not install ACPI support but installs an older HAL that does not support ACPI. If you later flash your BIOS to make it ACPI-compliant, you have to reinstall Windows to include ACPI support.

NOTE

If you have problems with Windows 2000 or NT detecting your hard drive, the problem might be out-of-date system BIOS. Try flashing BIOS and then try the Windows installation again.

Microsoft calls a BIOS that is ACPI-compliant a "good BIOS" and puts it on the Good BIOS list. The Microsoft site allows you to search for ACPI-compliant computers by model and manufacturer. The Microsoft Web site tells you if a system is compatible with Windows 2000 and sometimes provides a link to the BIOS Web site where you can download an upgrade to the BIOS. If you are upgrading BIOS, do that before you begin the Windows 2000 installation. You can install Windows 2000 on a system that is not ACPI-compliant, but you cannot use some of its power management features.

Installing Windows 2000 on Networked Computers

 A+ EXAM TIP

The A+ OS exam expects you to know about unattended installations and about the convenience of putting the Windows setup files in the \i386 directory on a file server. A server used in this way is called a **distribution server**.

If you are installing Windows 2000 on a networked PC, consider where the Windows 2000 installation files are stored. You can install the OS from a CD in the computer's CD-ROM drive, or you can store the files on a file server on the network and perform the installation from the file server. If you will be doing multiple installations on the network, consider using a file server. Copy all the files from the \i386 folder on the Windows 2000 CD to a folder on the file server and then share that folder on the network. During the installation, when you are ready for the CD, point the setup program to the file server folder instead.

Windows 2000 offers a number of options for installation that can be automated so you don't need to sit at the computer responding to the questions that setup asks during installation. One method, called an **unattended installation**, is performed by storing the answers to installation questions in a text file or script that Windows 2000 calls an **answer file**. A sample answer file is stored on the Windows 2000 CD. If you must perform many installations on computers that have the same Windows 2000 setup, it might be worth your time to develop an answer file to perform unattended installations. How to set up unattended installations is beyond the scope of this chapter.

NOTE

To learn how to create an unattended installation of Windows 2000, go to the Microsoft Support Web site (*support.microsoft.com*) and search for the Microsoft Knowledge Base article 216258. You can also search the Web site for other articles on this subject.

A+
OS
2.1
2.2
2.3

Another option is **drive imaging**, sometimes called **disk cloning** or disk imaging, which replicates the drive to a new computer or to another drive on the same computer. All contents of the drive, including the OS, applications, and data, get duplicated to the new drive. To clone a drive after the installation, use the Sysprep.exe utility to remove configuration settings such as the computer name that uniquely identifies the PC. Then clone the entire hard drive to a new PC using third-party drive-imaging software. Examples of drive-imaging software are Drive Image by PowerQuest (*www.powerquest.com*), ImageCast by Innovative Software (*www.imagecast.com*), and Norton Ghost by Symantec Corp. (*www.symantec.com*).

✔ A+ EXAM TIP

The A+ OS exam expects you to know about drive imaging.

When installing Windows 2000 on a network, just as with other operating systems, you need to know how to configure the computer to access the network. You should know these things before you begin the installation:

- The computer name and workgroup name for a peer-to-peer network
- The username, user password, computer name, and domain name for a domain network
- For TCP/IP networks, how the IP address is assigned, either dynamically (gets its IP address from a DHCP server when it first connects to the network) or statically (IP address is permanently assigned to the workstation). If the IP address is statically assigned, you need the IP address for the workstation. (DHCP servers, which are used to assign IP addresses when a computer connects to a network, are covered in Chapters 11 and 12.)

Upgrade or Clean Install?

If you are installing Windows 2000 on a new hard drive, then you are doing a clean install. If Windows 9x or Windows NT is already installed on the hard drive, then you have three choices:

- You can perform a clean install, overwriting the existing operating system and applications.
- You can perform an upgrade installation.
- You can install Windows 2000 in a second partition on the hard drive and create a dual boot situation.

Each of these options has advantages and disadvantages.

Clean Install, Overwriting the Existing Installations   A clean install that overwrites the existing installation has some advantages; one advantage is that you get a fresh start. With an upgrade, problems with applications or the OS might follow you into the Windows 2000 load. If you erase everything (format the hard drive), then you are assured that the registry as well as all applications are as clean as possible. The disadvantage is that, after Windows 2000 is installed, you must reinstall application software on the hard drive and restore the data from backups. If you do a clean install, you can choose to format the hard drive first, or simply do a clean install on top of the existing installation. If you don't format the drive, the data will

A+
OS
2.1
2.2
2.3

still be on the drive, but the previous operating system settings and applications will be lost.

If you decide to do a clean install, verify that you have all the application software CDs or floppy disks and software documentation. Back up all the data, and verify that the backups are good. Then, and only then, format the hard drive or begin the clean install without formatting the drive. If you don't format the hard drive, be sure to run a current version of antivirus software before you begin the installation.

Perform an Upgrade Installation System   All versions of Windows 9x and Windows NT Workstation 3.51 and higher can be upgraded to Windows 2000. The advantages of upgrading are that all applications and data and most OS settings are carried forward into the new Windows 2000 environment, and the installation is faster. If you perform an upgrade, you must begin the installation while you are in the current OS. If you are working from a remote location on the network, you cannot do an upgrade.

NOTE   You cannot upgrade a compressed Windows 9x drive. You must uncompress it before you can upgrade to Windows 2000 Professional.

✔ **A+ EXAM TIP**

The A+ OS exam expects you to know how to make decisions about a dual boot that require you to understand the different file systems and partition requirements for each OS.

Create a Dual Boot   The ability to boot from both Windows NT/2000 and another OS, such as DOS or Windows 9x, is called a **dual boot**. Don't create a dual boot unless you need two operating systems, such as when you need to verify that applications and hardware work under Windows NT/2000 before you delete the old OS. Windows NT/2000 does not support a second operating system on the same partition, so you must have at least two partitions on the hard drive. All applications must be installed on each partition to be used by each OS.

NOTE   Recall that Windows NT/2000/XP can support up to four partitions on a hard drive. All four can be primary partitions (which can have only one logical drive), or one of the partitions can be an extended partition (which can have several logical drives). For the first primary partition, the active partition, that drive is drive C. For a dual boot with Windows 2000, one OS is installed in the active partition on drive C, and the other OS is installed on another partition's logical drive.

You must decide what file system to use for the Windows 2000 partition: FAT16, FAT32, or NTFS. If you choose to use a dual boot with DOS, use FAT16 for the Windows 2000 partition so that DOS can read the partition. For Windows 9x, use either the FAT16 or FAT32 file system, not NTFS, so that Windows 9x can read the Windows 2000 partition.

Windows 2000 uses the latest version of NTFS, the one introduced by Windows NT Server 4.0, NTFS Version 5.0 (NTFS5). NTFS4 is used by Windows NT

Workstation 4.0. The NTFS5 version includes numerous enhancements over previous versions but cannot be read by Windows NT Workstation 4.0 unless Windows NT 4.0 Service Pack 4 is applied. For this reason, if you create a dual boot between Windows 2000 and Windows NT using NTFS for both operating systems, you can encounter the following problems:

- The file system data structures might not be the same.
- Disk utilities, such as Chkdsk under Windows NT, might not work on the drive.
- Windows NT cannot read encrypted files and folders.
- You cannot use Windows 2000 to repair a damaged Windows NT 4.0 NTFS partition. Windows NT 4.0 only allows access to an NTFS drive from within Windows NT 4.0 and not from any other OS.

For these reasons, using a dual boot between Windows 2000 and Windows NT is not recommended.

Planning an Upgrade from Windows 9x to Windows 2000

Because the Windows 9x registry and the Windows 2000 registry are not compatible, transfer of information from one to the other will not be as complete as with an upgrade from Windows NT to Windows 2000, where information in the registry is easily ported into the new OS. Until you perform the upgrade, you cannot know exactly what Windows 2000 was able to import from Windows 9x, although Setup might inform you or ask for additional help in some cases.

To test your system and be alerted to potential problems, running the Check Upgrade Only mode of Windows 2000 Setup is a good idea. This does not actually install Windows 2000 but instead just checks for compatibility and reports any upgrade issues with hardware or software. Run the utility to produce the report, Upgrade.txt, which is stored in the C:\Windows directory.

Hardware Compatibility

One issue to consider in upgrading from Windows 9x to Windows 2000 is that Windows 2000 does not import drivers from Windows 9x, because they are generally not compatible. As you learned earlier, a hardware device must be designed to be compatible with Windows 2000. If you want to install a device but its driver is not included in Windows 2000, you might have to download a driver from either the Microsoft site or the manufacturer's Web site. Check for compatibility and make sure you have all the required device drivers before you begin your Windows 9x–to–Windows 2000 upgrade. Windows 2000 attempts to carry over installed hardware devices that are compatible with Windows 2000, asking for new drivers where necessary; it ignores and does not install incompatible devices. If Setup cannot find a critical driver such as the driver to control a hard drive, it cancels the upgrade.

Another thing you need to know is that Windows 2000 deletes all the Windows 9x system files and replaces them with Windows 2000 system files in the same directory.

5

Software Compatibility   Basically, the main advantage of performing an upgrade from Windows 9x to Windows 2000 rather than doing a clean install of Windows 2000 is that you do not have to reinstall software that is compatible with Windows 2000. If an application was written for Windows 9x, it might or might not be compatible with Windows 2000. Windows 9x applications store registry data differently from Windows 2000 applications and may rely on APIs specific to Windows 9x. If an application doesn't work after you upgrade to Windows 2000, try reinstalling it. If that doesn't work, check the software manufacturer's Web site for a patch or upgrade.

Planning an Upgrade from Windows NT to Windows 2000

Upgrading to Windows 2000 from Windows NT is much easier than upgrading from Windows 9x. However, you need to be aware of some considerations before performing the upgrade:

- If you are upgrading from Windows NT using NTFS, Setup automatically upgrades to the Windows 2000 version of NTFS.
- If you are upgrading from Windows NT using FAT16 or Windows NT with third-party software installed that allows Windows NT to use FAT32, Setup asks you whether you want to upgrade to NTFS.

Hardware Compatibility   Generally, most hardware devices and their corresponding drivers that worked under Windows NT work under Windows 2000 as well, although some third-party drivers might need to be updated for Windows 2000. As always, it is a good idea to check the HCL on the Microsoft Web site or run the Check Upgrade Only mode of Windows 2000 Setup.

Software Compatibility   Nearly all applications that run with Windows NT Workstation 3.51 and later will run with Windows 2000 without modification. Here are some exceptions:

- Antivirus software and third-party network software, both of which must be removed before upgrading to Windows 2000
- Some disk management tools
- Custom tools for power management, which are replaced in Windows 2000 by ACPI. Windows 2000 also provides minimal support for APM (Advanced Power Management), which must be removed before the upgrade. Windows 2000 considers APM a legacy tool, uses it only on notebook computers, and uses only enough APM features to support a notebook computer's battery. With ACPI-compliant BIOS, the BIOS senses information about the system and turns that information over to the OS to make decisions about the system's power management functions.

A+
OS
2.1
2.2
2.3

- Custom solutions that are workarounds for Windows NT not supporting Plug and Play, which are unnecessary in Windows 2000 because it provides complete support for Plug and Play
- Software to monitor and control a UPS (uninterruptible power supply)

Now that you know about advantages and disadvantages of installing Windows 2000 as a clean install and as an upgrade, including issues to consider with specific upgrades, let's look at step-by-step procedures for how to do both.

Steps to Install Windows 2000

You can use two programs to install Windows 2000: Winnt.exe and Winnt32.exe. Winnt.exe is the 16-bit version of the setup program and Winnt32.exe is the 32-bit version. Both are located in the \i386 directory. You can use Winnt.exe for a clean install on a computer running MS-DOS, but not to perform an upgrade. Use Winnt32.exe for a clean install or an upgrade on a computer running Windows. Regardless of whether you use Winnt.exe or Winnt32.exe, the program executed is called Setup in Windows documentation. Here are the situations in which you can perform a clean install or upgrade:

✔ **A+ EXAM TIP**

The A+ OS exam expects you to know when Winnt.exe and Winnt32.exe are used for the setup process, and to know the upgrade paths for Windows 2000.

- To perform a clean install when working at the local computer, you can boot from the Windows CD or run Winnt32.exe or Winnt.exe from a command prompt. Run Winnt.exe only if you have booted into MS-DOS.
- If you want to perform an upgrade, you must be working at the local PC. You can boot from the Windows CD or run the Winnt32.exe program from within Windows 9x or Windows NT Version 4.0. You cannot perform an upgrade for earlier versions of Windows NT.
- When installing Windows from across the network to a remote PC, you can only do a clean install. In this situation, run Winnt32.exe on the local Windows computer to perform a clean install on the remote PC.

A+
OS
2.1
2.2
2.3

Also, before you begin any OS installation, access CMOS setup and verify these settings:

- If you want to begin the installation by booting from the Windows CD, verify that the boot sequence is first the CD-ROM, then the hard drive.
- Disable any virus protection setting that prevents the boot sector from being altered.
- Also, because Windows 2000 prefers to handle its own Plug and Play hardware installations without the help of BIOS, Microsoft recommends that you disable the Plug and Play feature of your motherboard BIOS.

Next we look at the step-by-step procedures for clean installations and upgrades.

NOTE

If you are having problems with Windows Setup detecting your hard drive, the problem might be out-of-date BIOS. Try flashing BIOS and then attempting the Windows installation again.

Clean Installation

The Windows 2000 package comes with documentation and a CD. For U.S. distributions, the package includes a floppy disk to provide 128-bit data encryption. (This disk is not included in distributions to other countries because of laws that prohibit 128-bit data encryption software from leaving the United States.)

If your PC is capable of booting from a CD, then insert the CD and turn on the PC. The Welcome to the Windows 2000 Setup Wizard appears (see Figure 5-8). Select "Install a new copy of Windows 2000," click Next, and proceed to Step 6 in the following procedure. However, if your PC does not boot from a CD and you have a clean, empty hard drive, first create a set of Windows 2000 setup disks to boot the PC and to begin the installation. The remaining installation is done from the CD.

To make the four setup disks, follow these directions:

1. Using a working PC, format four floppy disks.

2. Place the Windows 2000 CD in the CD-ROM drive and a formatted floppy disk in the floppy disk drive. For Windows 9x, click **Start,** then **Run,** and enter this command in the Run dialog box:

   ```
   D:\bootdisk\makeboot.exe A:
   ```

   Substitute the letter of the CD-ROM drive for D: and the letter of the floppy drive for A:, if necessary.

3. Insert new disks in the drive as requested. Label the disks Windows 2000 Setup Disks 1, 2, 3, and 4.

A+
OS
2.1
2.2
2.3

4. Now begin the Windows 2000 installation. Boot the PC from the first setup disk created earlier. You will be asked to insert each of the four disks in turn and then asked to insert the Windows 2000 CD.

5. The Windows 2000 license agreement appears. Accept the agreement and the Welcome screen appears, as shown in Figure 5-8. The setup process is now identical to that of booting directly from the CD. Save the four setup floppy disks in case you have future problems with Windows 2000.

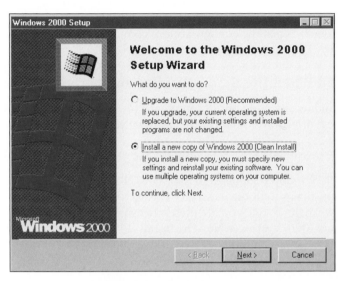

Figure 5-8　　Using the Setup Wizard, you can do an upgrade, do a clean install, or create a dual boot

6. Windows 2000 searches the hard drive for partitions and asks which partition to use. If the partitions are not created, it creates them for you. You are asked to decide which file system to use. If the hard drive has already been formatted with the FAT16 or FAT32 file system, you are asked if you want to upgrade to the NTFS file system. Be aware that if you convert the file system to NTFS, you cannot revert to FAT16 or FAT32. You can also convert from FAT16 or FAT32 to NTFS after the installation is complete. If the hard drive is already partitioned and contains a partition larger than 2 GB, and you select the FAT file system, then Windows 2000 automatically formats the drive using the FAT32 file system. It puts the entire partition in one logical FAT32 drive.

7. During installation, you are given the opportunity to change your keyboard settings for different languages, enter your name and company name, and enter the product key found on the CD case. You are also given the opportunity to enter date and time settings and an administrator password. Be sure to remember the password. It is required when you log on to the system later to set up new users and perform other administrative tasks. If you forget it and no one else has administrator privileges, you might have to reinstall Windows 2000.

8. If Setup recognizes that you are connected to a network, it provides the Networking Settings window to configure the computer to access the network. If you select Typical settings, then Setup automatically configures the OS for your network. If the configuration is not correct after the installation, you can make changes.

9. At this point in the installation, you are asked to remove the Windows 2000 CD and click **Finish**. The computer then restarts. After Windows 2000 loads, it completes the process of connecting to the network. You are asked questions about the type of network. (For example, does the network use a domain or workgroup?) When the configuration is complete, verify that you have access to the network if there is one.

Clean Install When the Hard Drive Has an Operating System Installed

If you use Windows 9x and your PC automatically detects a CD in the CD-ROM drive, follow these directions to do a clean install when another OS is already installed:

1. Using antivirus software, scan memory and your hard drive for viruses.

2. Insert the Windows 2000 CD in the CD-ROM drive. If your PC detects the CD, a window opens with the message "This CD-ROM contains a newer version of Windows than the one you are presently using. Would you like to upgrade to Windows 2000?" Answer **No**. The Install Windows 2000 window appears (see Figure 5-9).

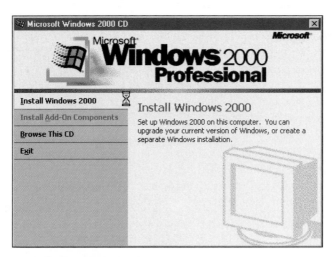

Figure 5-9   Windows 2000 Setup window

3. Click **Install Windows 2000**. The Windows Setup Wizard opens, as shown in Figure 5-8. Select **Install a new copy of Windows 2000 (Clean Install)**. Windows displays the license agreement and asks you to accept it. Enter the

A+
OS
2.1
2.2
2.3

product key from the back of the CD case, and you will be given the opportunity to select special options.

4. After a reboot, the installation continues as described earlier.

If your PC does not automatically recognize a CD, then insert the CD in the CD-ROM drive and do the following:

1. Click **Start** and then click **Run**. In the Run dialog box, enter the command **D:\i386\ winnt32.exe**. Substitute the drive letter of the CD-ROM drive for D:, if necessary.

2. The Windows 2000 Setup Wizard appears, as shown earlier in Figure 5-8. Select **Install a new copy of Windows 2000 (Clean Install)**. The installation continues as described earlier.

Upgrade Installation

To upgrade your operating system from Windows 9x or Windows NT using the Windows 2000 CD, first prepare for the installation:

1. Verify that all devices and applications are Windows 2000 compatible. Download and install any patches or upgrades from hardware or software manufacturers.

2. Using antivirus software, scan memory and your hard drive for viruses.

3. Back up all critical system files and data files. Back up the registry in case you need to backtrack to the current installation. If you have important data on your hard drive, back up the data.

4. Close all applications and disable any virus-scanning software. If the hard drive is compressed, decompress the drive.

You are now ready to perform the upgrade. Do the following:

1. Insert the Windows 2000 CD in the CD-ROM drive. If your system is set to detect the CD automatically, it runs the setup program and shows a message asking if you want to upgrade your computer to Windows 2000. Answer **Yes** and the installation begins. If Windows does not detect the CD, click **Start**, then **Run**, enter **D:\i386\winnt32.exe** in the Run dialog box, and then click **OK**. Substitute the drive letter of the CD-ROM drive for D:, if necessary. On the Welcome to Windows 2000 Setup Wizard window, select **Upgrade to Windows 2000 (Recommended)**. Follow the directions on the screen.

2. Windows 2000 Setup performs the upgrade in two major stages: the Report phase and the Setup phase. During the Report phase, Windows 2000 Setup scans the hardware, device drivers, current operating system, and applications for compatibility. In this phase, you are given the opportunity to provide third-party DLL files that make a device driver or application Windows 2000

A+
OS
2.1
2.2
2.3

compatible, if Setup recognizes that the device driver or application will not work without the fix. Next, Setup generates a report of its findings. If its findings indicate that an unsuccessful installation is likely, you can abandon the installation and perhaps check with hardware and software manufacturers for fixes. In the Report phase, Setup also creates an answer file that it uses during the Setup phase, installs the Windows 2000 boot loader, and copies Windows 2000 installation files to the hard drive.

3. The PC reboots and the Setup phase begins, which has two parts: the Text mode and the GUI mode. In the Text mode, Setup installs a Windows 2000 base in the same folder that the old OS is in, usually C:\Windows for Windows 9x and C:\WINNT for Windows NT. The target folder cannot be changed at this point. Setup then moves the Windows registry and profile information to %windir%\setup\temp, where %windir% is the path to the Windows folder, most likely C:\Windows\setup\temp.

4. The PC reboots again and the GUI mode of Setup begins. Setup reads information that it saved about the old Windows system and makes appropriate changes to the Windows 2000 registry. It then migrates application DLLs to Windows 2000 and reboots for the last time. The upgrade is complete.

NOTE

During installation, Windows 2000 records information about the installation to a file called Setuplog.txt. This file is useful when troubleshooting any problems that occur during installation.

After the Installation: Backing Up the System State

A+
OS
1.5
2.1
2.2
2.3
2.4

After you have completed installing Windows 2000, do the following:

1. Access the Internet and download and install all OS service packs, updates, and patches.

2. Verify that all hardware works and install additional devices, such as printers, as needed.

3. Create user accounts for Windows 2000. (Chapter 8 covers creating user accounts.)

4. Install additional Windows components and install applications. (Don't attempt to install applications and components before you first download and install service packs and patches.)

5. Verify that the system functions properly, and back up the system state. This backup of the system can later help you recover the OS in the event of system failure. (You will learn more about recovering from system failure in the next chapter.)

APPLYING CONCEPTS

A+
OS
1.5
2.1
2.2
2.3
2.4

Windows 2000 calls the files critical to a successful operating system load the **system state data.** This includes all files necessary to boot the OS, the Windows 2000 registry, and all system files in the %SystemRoot% folder, the folder in which Windows 2000 is installed. For an upgrade, the folder will most likely be C:\Windows, the original Windows folder before the upgrade. For a clean install, the default folder is C:\WINNT. When you back up the system state data, you cannot select which files you want to back up because Windows 2000 always backs up all of them. Here is the process:

1. Click **Start**, point to **Programs**, **Accessories**, **System Tools**, and then click **Backup**. The Backup dialog box opens. Click the **Backup** tab (see Figure 5-10).
2. Check the **System State** box in the list of items you can back up. Notice in Figure 5-10 that the system state includes the boot files and the registry. It also includes the COM+ (Component Object Model) Registration Database, which contains information about applications and includes files in the Windows folders.
3. Select the destination for the backup. You can back up to any media, including a folder on the hard drive, Zip drive, tape drive, or network drive. Click **Start Backup** to begin the process.

Later, if you have problems with a corrupted Windows 2000 installation, you can click the Restore tab in the Backup dialog box illustrated in Figure 5-10. Use this Restore window to restore the system to its state at the last backup.

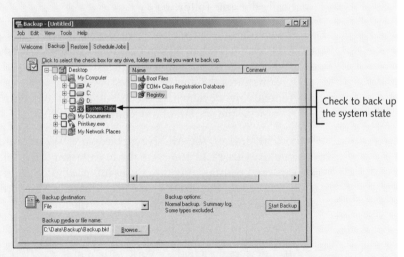

Check to back up the system state

Figure 5-10   Back up the Windows 2000 registry and all critical system files

A+
OS
1.5
2.1
2.2
2.3
2.4

NOTE When you back up the system state, the registry is also backed up to the folder %SystemRoot%\repair\RegBack. If you later have a corrupted registry, you can copy files from this folder to the registry folder, which is %SystemRoot%\System32\Config.

Installing Hardware and Applications Under Windows 2000

A+
OS
2.1
2.4

This section discusses how to install hardware and software with Windows 2000 and includes special considerations for legacy hardware. As with Windows 98, Windows 2000 has an Add New Hardware Wizard that automatically launches when new hardware is detected. Software is best installed from the Add/Remove Programs icon in the Control Panel.

Installing Hardware

Windows 2000 can automatically detect and install Plug and Play (PnP) devices, as long as you also have PnP-compliant drivers. If a device is PnP, Windows 2000 automatically does the following:

- Identifies the device you are installing
- Determines what system resources the device needs and assigns them so that there are no conflicts with other devices
- Configures the device as necessary
- Loads any device drivers needed to run the device
- Informs the system of any configuration changes

For PnP devices, the Add New Hardware Wizard automatically launches at startup. Any user can complete the installation if the following are true: The device drivers can be installed without user input, all files necessary for a complete installation are present, the drivers have been digitally signed (**digital signatures** are digital codes used to authenticate the source of files), and there are no errors during installation. If one of these conditions is not met, the installation is abandoned until someone with administrator privileges logs on.

Most devices designed to work with Windows 2000 are PnP-compatible. If a device is not PnP and you are logged on with administrator privileges, you can use the Add/Remove Hardware applet in the Control Panel to install the device.

If you are using the Add/Remove Hardware Wizard, you have to provide information such as where the driver for the device is located. Some devices that don't work with Windows 2000 may be completely incompatible and will not work at all. If you

A+
OS
2.1
2.4

install a device and have a problem with it, you can attempt to update the device driver as follows:

1. In the Control Panel, double-click the **System** icon. The System Properties dialog box opens. Select the **Hardware** tab (see Figure 5-11).

2. Click the **Device Manager** button. The Device Manager opens, as shown in Figure 5-11. Expand the device class tree by clicking the plus sign, and locate the device for which you want to update a driver. For this example, we are using the floppy disk drive.

3. Right-click the floppy drive and select **Properties** from the shortcut menu (see Figure 5-11).

4. The Floppy disk drive Properties dialog box opens (see Figure 5-12). On the **Driver** tab, click **Update Driver**. The Update Device Driver Wizard appears. If an update exists, follow directions on the screen to update the driver.

NOTE

You must be logged on with administrator privileges to make changes from Device Manager.

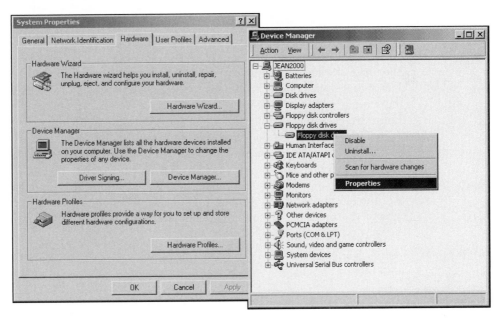

Figure 5-11   Use Device Manager to access a device's properties

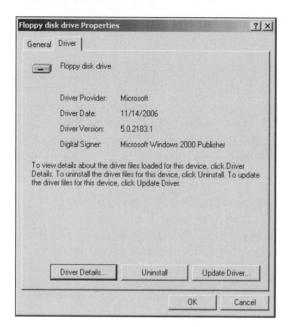

Figure 5-12   A device's Properties window provides a way to update its drivers

Installing Applications

The process of installing applications in Windows 2000 is not much different than that of earlier versions of Windows. If you are familiar with the installation wizards and setup programs used with Windows 9x, you should recognize all but a few minor details of these same components in Windows 2000.

The Windows 2000 Add/Remove Programs utility looks significantly different than in Windows 9x, and it provides more options. From the Windows 2000 Add/Remove Programs window, you can change or remove presently installed programs (see Figure 5-13); add new programs from a CD, a floppy disk, or from Microsoft over the Internet; and add or remove Windows components. In Figure 5-13, note the expanded drop-down menu in the upper-right corner, which shows how you can sort the view of presently installed programs.

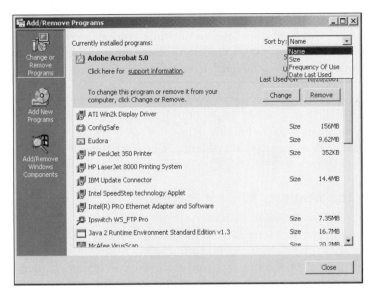

Figure 5-13   Making changes to currently installed programs

Supporting Windows NT

A+
OS
2.1
2.3
3.1
3.2

Though Windows 2000 and Windows XP are gradually replacing Windows NT, Windows NT is still around; therefore, knowing how to support it is important. Much of what you learn in this section carries over to later Windows OSs. First we will look at different ways to install Windows NT, and then we'll look at how to troubleshoot the Windows NT boot process.

Installing Windows NT as the Only OS

A+ EXAM TIP

The A+ OS exam does not have extensive coverage of Windows NT, but you should know about installing it and supporting the boot process.

Windows NT comes with three disks that contain a simplified version of Windows NT, enough to boot a PC. If the hard drive does not contain an OS, the installation begins by booting from these three disks. After Windows NT is loaded from these three disks, it can access the CD-ROM drive, and installation continues from the CD. The program on the CD executed at that point is Winnt.exe, a 16-bit program. A faster version of Winnt.exe on the CD named Winnt32.exe, a 32-bit program, can be used instead of Winnt.exe in certain situations. Winnt32.exe can be run only after Windows NT has already been installed for the first time; it is used to upgrade from an older NT version to a newer version or to reinstall a corrupted version. It must be executed from within Windows NT.

The three startup disks can later be used to boot the PC if files on the hard drive become corrupted. You can also create a new set of bootable disks.

A+
OS
2.1
2.3
3.1
3.2

The Windows NT installation files are stored in the \i386 directory on the CD-ROM drive. If hard drive space is plentiful, you can copy the contents of the \i386 directory and its subdirectories to the hard drive and install from there, which is faster because access to the hard drive is faster than access to the CD-ROM drive. If the computer is connected to a network, the contents of the \i386 directory can be copied to a network server, and the Winnt.exe program can be executed from the server to install Windows NT on the PC, if certain conditions exist. (Installations from servers are not covered in this chapter.) To perform an upgrade to Windows NT, boot the OS and execute the Winnt.exe program on the Windows NT CD.

Troubleshooting the Windows NT Boot Process

In this section, you will learn how to troubleshoot the Windows NT boot process and about some diagnostic tools that you can use for maintenance and troubleshooting. Many general troubleshooting tips you learned in earlier chapters apply to Windows NT as well. Troubleshooting the Windows 2000 boot process is covered in Chapter 6.

The following list includes things you can do and the order in which you should do them to troubleshoot a failed Windows NT boot. You will learn more about these tools and processes later in this section. Windows NT does not have a Safe Mode as does Windows 9x, nor does it have several of the useful troubleshooting utilities of Windows 9x that you learned about in the last chapter.

As Windows NT/2000/XP is booting, if it thinks there is a problem you should know about or the system is set for a dual boot, a **boot loader menu** appears and gives you options such as which OS you want to load or how you want to handle a problem.

APPLYING CONCEPTS

To recover from a failed Windows NT boot:

- If the Windows NT boot loader menu appears, use the Last Known Good configuration to return to the last registry values that allowed for a successful boot. Any configuration changes since the last good boot will be lost.
- If you cannot boot from the hard drive, boot using the three boot disks that came with the OS. If you don't have these three disks, you can create them on a working PC. Check for corrupted boot and system files that you can replace. (How to create the three boot disks is covered later in this section.)
- Boot from the three disks, and select the option "To repair a damaged Windows NT version 4.0 installation."

- Try reinstalling Windows NT in the same folder it currently uses. Tell the Setup program this is an upgrade.
- As a last resort, if you are using the NTFS file system and you must recover data on the hard drive, move the hard drive to another system that runs Windows NT and install the drive as a secondary drive. You might then be able to recover the data.

Last Known Good Configuration

5

Each time Windows NT boots and the first logon is made with no errors, the OS saves a copy of the hardware configuration from the registry, which is called the **Last Known Good configuration**. (All hardware configuration sets stored in the registry, including the Last Known Good, are called control sets.) If an error occurs the next time the PC boots, it can use the Last Known Good configuration. The key in the registry that contains the Last Known Good configuration is HKEY_LOCAL_MACHINE\HARDWARE.

If Windows NT detects the possibility of a problem, it adds the Last Known Good option to the Windows NT boot loader menu. You can select this Last Known Good option to revert to the control set used for the last good boot. For example, if you install a new device driver, restart Windows NT, and find that the system hangs, you can use the Last Known Good option to revert to the previous configuration.

Because the configuration information is not saved to the Last Known Good control set until after the logon, don't attempt to log on if you have trouble with the boot. Doing so causes the Last Known Good to be replaced by the current control set, which might have errors.

For example, if you install a new video driver, restart Windows, and find the screen very difficult to read, don't log on. Instead, press the reset button to reboot the PC. When given the choice, select Last Known Good from the boot loader menu.

To prevent hard drive corruption, if you have problems booting Windows NT, wait for all disk activity to stop before pressing the reset button or turning off the PC, especially if you are using the FAT file system.

If you accidentally disable a critical device, Windows NT decides to revert to the Last Known Good for you. You are not provided with a menu choice.

Reverting to the Last Known Good causes the loss of any changes made to the hardware configuration since the Last Known Good was saved. Therefore, it is wise to make one hardware configuration change at a time and reboot after each change. That way, if problems during booting are encountered, only the most recent change is lost. When installing several hardware devices, install them one at a time, rebooting each time.

NOTE

If you have problems booting in Windows NT, don't log on. If you do, you will overwrite your previous Last Known Good.

Windows NT Boot Disks

With Windows 9x and DOS, any single floppy disk could be formatted as a boot disk or system disk. Windows NT is different. It requires three disks to hold enough of Windows NT to boot. However, just as with Windows 9x, you can use Explorer to format a single disk just to hold data or software, but you cannot make the disk a startup disk, as is the case with Windows 9x.

If you try to boot from a disk that has been formatted by Windows NT, this error message appears:

```
BOOT: Couldn't find NTLDR
Please insert another disk
```

If the original three disks to boot Windows NT become corrupted or are lost, you can make extra copies using Winnt32.exe if you are running Windows NT, or using Winnt.exe if you are running another OS, such as DOS or Windows 9x. You do not have to be working on the PC where you intend to use the disks in order to make them, because the disks don't contain unique information for a specific PC.

Creating Windows NT Boot Disks   Do the following to create boot disks using Windows NT:

1. Click **Start**, click **Run,** and then enter one of the following commands in the Run dialog box. Substitute the letter of your CD drive for E in the command line, if necessary.

   ```
   E:\i386\winnt32.exe /ox
   E:\i386\winnt.exe /ox
   ```

   The /OX parameters cause the program to create only the set of three disks, without performing a complete installation. In Figure 5-14, you can see the command line from within Windows NT used to create the disks when drive E contains the Windows NT installation CD.

2. The program asks for the location of the installation files. In this example, you would enter E:\i386. You are then prompted to insert three disks. The program creates the disks beginning with disk 3, then 2, then 1.

Windows NT does not have a Safe Mode as does Windows 9x, so if the PC later cannot boot Windows NT from the hard drive, these three disks can be used to load Windows NT, which loads using a generic VGA mode. After Windows NT is loaded, use a fourth disk—the Emergency Repair Disk (ERD)—to restore critical system files to their state at the time the last update was made to the ERD.

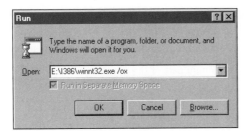

Figure 5-14 Using Winnt32.exe to create a set of boot disks

5

The Windows NT Emergency Repair Disk

The **Emergency Repair Disk (ERD)** contains information unique to your OS and hard drive. You are given the opportunity to create the disk during installation. Always create this disk, because it is your record of critical information about your system that can be used to fix a problem with the OS.

The ERD enables restoration on your hard drive of the Windows registry, which contains all the configuration information for Windows. In addition, the disk includes information used to build a command window to run DOS-like commands. The files on the ERD are listed in Table 5-2. Files stored on the ERD are also written to the hard drive during the installation. Using Explorer, you can see the files listed in the *winnt_root*\repair folder.

In Microsoft documentation, *winnt_root*\ is the folder that Windows NT is installed in, which most likely is C:\Winnt\.

NOTE

After the installation, you can create a new ERD or update the current one by using the Rdisk.exe utility in the *winnt_root*\system32 folder. You should update the disk any time you make any major changes to the system, for example, when you install hardware or software. To use the Rdisk.exe utility, click Start, then Run, and then either click Browse or enter the path to the utility. Add the /S option so that the utility also updates the registry.

File	Description
Setup.log	A read-only, hidden system file used to verify the files installed on a system
System._	A compressed file containing part of the registry
Sam._	A compressed file containing some of the security part of the registry
Security._	A compressed file containing some of the security part of the registry
Software._	A compressed file containing software information in the registry
Default._	A compressed file containing part of the registry
Config.nt	The Windows NT version of Config.sys used in creating a command window
Autoexec.nt	The Windows NT version of Autoexec.bat
Ntuser.da	A compressed file containing information about authorized users of the system

Table 5-2   Files on the Windows NT Emergency Repair Disk

If Windows NT is stored on drive D, the command line is:

```
D:\Winnt\System32\rdisk.exe /s
```

First, files are updated in the D:\Winnt\Repair directory, then you are given the opportunity to create a new ERD.

Using the Boot Disks and the ERD to Recover from a Failed Boot

In case of problems with the OS, you can do several things to attempt to load Windows NT from the hard drive, which are beyond the scope of this book. However, in the case of a hard drive failure, you can boot from the three boot disks that come with the Windows NT CD or that you made using either Winnt.exe or Winnt32.exe. The Windows NT programs on these disks may also request that you provide the ERD. Insert the first boot disk, and reboot. You will be prompted to insert disk 2, followed by disk 3. The Setup menu in Figure 5-15 then appears. Select the option to repair a damaged installation by pressing R, and follow directions on the screen.

A+
OS
2.1
2.3
3.1
3.2

```
Windows NT Workstation Setup

Welcome to Setup.
The Setup program for the Microsoft(R) Windows NT(TM) OS version 4.0
prepares Windows NT to run on your computer.

      *To learn more about Windows NT Setup before continuing, press F1
      *To set up Windows NT now, press ENTER
      *To repair a damaged Windows NT version 4.0 installation, press R
      *To quit Setup without installing Windows NT, press F3
```

Figure 5-15   Windows NT Workstation Setup menu

NOTE   Windows NT does not have a Device Manager. When installing and troubleshooting hardware, look for individual icons in the Control Panel to manage hardware devices. For a detailed report of the system configuration, use the WinMSD command. At a command prompt enter Winmsd /a /f. The command creates the report in the current directory.

CHAPTER SUMMARY

▶ Windows 2000 is actually a suite of operating systems: Windows 2000 Professional, Windows 2000 Server, Windows 2000 Advanced Server, and Windows 2000 Datacenter Server.

▶ The two architectural modes of Windows NT/2000/XP are user mode and kernel mode. Kernel mode is further divided into two components: executive services and the hardware abstraction layer (HAL).

▶ A process is a unique instance of a program running together with the program resources and other programs it may use. A thread is one task that the process requests from the kernel, such as the task of printing a file.

▶ An NTVDM provides a DOS-like environment for DOS and Windows 3.x applications.

▶ Windows 3.x 16-bit applications run in a WOW.

▶ A workgroup is a group of computers and users sharing resources. Each computer maintains a list of users and their rights on that particular PC. A domain is a group of networked computers that share a centralized directory database of user account information and security.

▶ Of all Windows NT/2000/XP accounts, the administrator account has the most privileges and rights. It can create user accounts and assign them rights.

▸ Windows 2000 can run in native mode and mixed mode. Native mode is used when all domain servers are Windows 2000 servers. Mixed mode is used when a domain has both Windows 2000 and Windows NT servers controlling the domain.

▸ Windows NT can operate using two different file systems: FAT16 and NTFS. NTFS offers more security and power than FAT16, but FAT16 is backward-compatible with older OSs. Windows 2000/XP supports FAT16, FAT32, and NTFS. NTFS under Windows 2000/XP is not compatible with NTFS under Windows NT.

▸ Windows NT/2000/XP offers a clean install and an upgrade installation. A clean install overwrites all information from previous operating system installations on the hard drive.

▸ System BIOS, hardware, and software must be compatible with Windows 2000. Check the HCL and the Compatible Software Applications list on the Microsoft Web site before beginning an installation. If you need to flash BIOS, do it before you begin the installation.

▸ A PC can be configured to dual boot between Windows NT or 2000 and another OS, such as Windows 9x or DOS.

▸ Windows 2000/NT supports a dual boot, but each operating system must be installed in its own partition, and an application must be installed twice, once for each OS.

▸ A Windows 2000 upgrade installation is done in two phases, the Report phase and the Setup phase.

▸ Windows 2000 supports Plug and Play and automatically launches the Add New Hardware Wizard when it senses a new device has been installed on the system. Windows NT does not support Plug and Play.

▸ Windows 2000 has a Device Manager to view, uninstall, and update devices, but Windows NT does not have a Device Manager. In Windows NT, hardware devices are managed from applets in the Control Panel.

▸ Applications can be installed in Windows 2000 using the Add/Remove Programs applet in the Control Panel.

▸ Four disks are important in recovering from a failed Windows NT boot. Three disks are required to boot Windows NT, and an Emergency Repair Disk (ERD) can be prepared to recover critical system files on the hard drive.

KEY TERMS

For explanations of key terms, see the Glossary near the end of the book.

ACPI (Advanced Configuration
   and Power Interface)
Active Directory
administrator account
answer file
backup domain controller (BDC)
boot loader menu
boot partition
client/server
digital signature
disk cloning
distribution server
domain
domain controller

drive imaging
dual boot
Emergency Repair Disk (ERD)
executive services
HAL (hardware abstraction layer)
kernel mode
Last Known Good configuration
master file table (MFT)
mixed mode
multithreading
native mode
NTVDM (NT virtual DOS
   machine)

peer-to-peer
primary domain controller
   (PDC)
process
security accounts manager
   (SAM)
subsystem
system partition
system state data
thread
unattended installation
user mode
Win16 on Win32 (WOW)
workgroup

5

REVIEWING THE BASICS

1. What layer of Windows NT/2000/XP is most responsible for interacting with hardware?

2. What is one reason that interaction with hardware is limited to only one or two components of Windows NT/2000/XP?

3. What are the two modes of the Windows NT/2000/XP architecture?

4. Which of these two modes contains the NTVDM?

5. What is the name of the folder on the Windows NT/2000 CD where the installation files are stored?

6. Before you install Windows 2000, how can you determine if the OS supports all the hardware on your PC?

7. What is one reason not to upgrade from Windows 98 to Windows NT?

8. What file systems does Windows NT support? Windows 2000?

9. If you have Windows 98 installed on a PC using FAT32 and you are creating a dual boot with Windows NT, what must you do first so that Windows NT can access the entire hard drive?

10. How many bits are used to store a cluster number in the Windows NT NTFS file system?

11. What is the file system that is common to DOS, Windows 9x, and Windows NT?

12. Which of the two Windows 2000 setup programs is a 32-bit program? A 16-bit program?

13. What must you know in order to log on to the Windows 2000 Recovery Console?

14. Windows NT/2000/XP is installed using a system partition and a boot partition. Which of these partitions must be the active partition of the hard drive?

15. In a Windows NT/2000/XP workgroup, where is access to an individual workstation on the network controlled?

16. In a Windows NT/2000/XP domain, where is access to an individual workstation on the network controlled?

17. What is the first Windows NT/2000/XP program that is loaded and run when Windows NT is booted?

18. What is required before Windows 2000 can provide full power management functionality?

19. Name three manufacturers responsible for the initial development of ACPI.

20. Explain the difference between Windows 2000 native mode and mixed mode.

21. If you are installing Windows 2000 on a new hard drive and your system cannot boot from a CD, how do you begin the installation?

22. If you install Windows 2000 on an 8-GB hard drive, use a single partition for the drive, and choose not to use the NTFS file system, what file system will Windows 2000 automatically use?

23. What is the command to create a set of Windows 2000 boot disks?

24. If your BIOS is not ACPI-compliant, what should you do before you install Windows 2000?

25. If an administrator is concerned about security on a system, which file system is appropriate?

26. Can you perform an upgrade of Windows 2000 from a remote computer on the network? Explain your answer.

27. For a person to be able to install hardware, what privileges or permissions must be assigned to his or her user account?

28. How many floppy disks are needed in order to boot Windows NT from disk?

29. When there is a problem booting to Windows NT and the Last Known Good configuration is used, what is lost?

30. What Windows NT utility program is used to create the Windows NT ERD?

THINKING CRITICALLY

1. You are planning an upgrade from Windows 98 to Windows 2000 Professional. Your system uses a modem card that you don't find listed on the Microsoft Windows 2000 list of compatible devices. What do you do next?

   a. Abandon the upgrade and continue to use Windows 98.

   b. Check the Web site of the modem manufacturer for a Windows 2000 driver.

   c. Buy a new modem card.

   d. Install a dual boot for Windows 98 and Windows 2000 and only use the modem when you have Windows 98 loaded.

2. You have just installed Windows 2000 and now attempt to install your favorite game, which worked fine under Windows 98. When you attempt the installation, you get an error. What is your best next step?

   a. Purchase a new version of your game, one that is compatible with Windows 2000.

   b. Download any service packs or patches to Windows 2000.

   c. Reinstall Windows 98.

3. You have a critically important, irreplaceable data file stored on your Windows NT hard drive, which uses the NTFS file system, and you have not made a backup of the file. When you boot up the system, you see a blue screen with a strange error message that you have never seen and don't understand. You have another Windows NT system that is working that might be of help to you. What is your next step?

   a. Step back from the problem, take a deep breath, and carefully consider your options.

   b. Use your three boot disks to boot the nonworking system and attempt to repair the Windows NT installation.

   c. Format the hard drive and perform a fresh installation of Windows NT.

   d. Remove the hard drive from the nonworking system, install it as a second drive in the working system, and attempt to rescue the critical data file.

HANDS-ON PROJECTS

HANDS-ON PROJECTS

PROJECT 5-1: Preparing for Windows 2000

Use the Microsoft Web site *www.microsoft.com/windows2000/professional/ howtobuy/upgrading/compat* to research whether your home or lab PC qualifies for Windows 2000. Fill in the following table and print the Web pages showing whether each hardware device and application installed on your PC qualifies for Windows 2000.

Hardware Device or Application	Specific Device Name or Application Name and Version	Does It Qualify for Windows 2000?
Motherboard BIOS		
Video card		
Modem card (if present)		
Sound card (if present)		
Printer (if present)		
Network card (if present)		
CD-ROM drive (if present)		
DVD drive (if present)		
SCSI hard drive (if present)		
Other device		
Application 1		
Application 2		
Application 3		

PROJECT 5-2: Listing Windows Components

After installing Windows 2000, list the Windows components included under the Add/Remove Programs applet in the Control Panel that Windows 2000 Setup did not install on your PC.

PROJECT 5-3:   **Backing Up the System State**

Back up the Windows 2000 system state to a folder named C:\MyBackup. You will use this backup in the next chapter in a recovery process. Print a screen shot of Explorer showing the size of the backup file in the MyBackup folder.

PROJECT 5-4:   **Using the Internet for Problem Solving**

Access the *support.microsoft.com* Web site for Windows NT Workstation support. Print one example of an article from the Knowledge Base that addresses a problem with booting Windows NT.

PROJECT 5-5:   **Using the Internet for Research**

You want to install Windows NT on a PC using a dual boot with Windows 98. The Windows 98 logical drive is using FAT32, and you want Windows NT to be able to access the data files on this logical drive. Use the Internet to answer these questions:

1. What third-party software allows Windows NT to read from FAT32 volumes? How much does it cost? What URL did you use to answer the question?

2. What third-party software allows Windows NT to write to FAT32 volumes? How much does it cost? What URL did you use to answer the question?

5

Managing and Troubleshooting Windows 2000

In the last chapter, you learned about the Windows NT/2000/XP architecture and how to install Windows 2000 and Windows NT. You also learned how to troubleshoot the Windows NT boot process. Recall that Windows NT does not provide many support tools to aid in trouble shooting when the OS does not boot correctly. Windows 2000 and Windows XP have more troubleshooting tools and options. Some of these tools and options work with both Windows 2000 and Windows XP, and some work with only one OS or the other. In this chapter, you learn about the details of the Windows NT/2000/XP boot process, and specifically how to troubleshoot the Windows 2000 boot process. In addition, this chapter covers supporting and troubleshooting Windows 2000 after it boots, including problems you might have with system errors and performance. In the next two chapters, you will learn about Windows XP.

Understanding the Windows NT/2000/XP Boot Process

A+
OS
1.2
2.3

Understanding the boot process and making changes to it are critical when supporting Windows NT/2000/XP. In this section you learn what happens during the boot process, as well as how to solve boot problems. The following is a look behind the scenes, with a description of each step in the boot process. As you read, refer to Table 6-1 for an outline of the boot sequence for Intel-based computers.

1. *BIOS executes POST.* First, startup BIOS performs POST, which executes regardless of which OS is present. After POST, BIOS turns to the hard drive to load an OS. Remember from earlier chapters that BIOS looks for the partition information at the beginning of the hard drive.

2. *BIOS executes the MBR program.* The first thing on the hardware that BIOS needs is the master boot program. Remember that the master boot program is the very first thing written in the first sector of a hard drive. The master boot program is followed by the partition table itself, and both are stored in the Master Boot Record. BIOS executes this master boot program, which examines the partition table, looking for the location of the active partition on the drive, and then turns to the first sector of the active partition to find and load the program in the boot sector of that active partition. So far in the boot process, nothing is different between Windows NT/2000/XP and other OSs.

Step Performed by	Description
1. Startup BIOS	POST (power-on self test) is executed.
2. Startup BIOS	MBR (Master Boot Record) is loaded, and the master boot program within the MBR is run. (The master boot program is at the very beginning of the hard drive, before the partition table information. The program searches for and loads the OS boot record of the active partition.)
3. MBR program	The boot sector from the active partition is loaded, and the program in this boot sector is run.
4. Boot sector program	Ntldr (NT Loader) file is loaded and run.
5. Windows NT/2000/XP loader	The processor is changed from real mode to flat memory mode, in which 32-bit code can be executed.
6. Windows NT/2000/XP loader	Minifile system drivers (described following) are started so files can be read.
7. Windows NT/2000/XP loader	Read Boot.ini file and build the boot loader menu described in the file. (This menu is discussed in Chapter 7.)

Table 6-1 (continued)

Step Performed by	Description
8. Windows NT/2000/XP loader	If the user chooses Windows NT/2000/XP, then the loader runs Ntdetect.com to detect hardware present; otherwise, it runs Bootsect.dos.
9. Windows NT/2000/XP loader	Ntldr reads information from the registry about device drivers and loads them. Also loads the Hal.dll and Ntoskrnl.exe.
10. Windows NT/2000/XP loader (the last step performed by the loader)	Ntldr passes control to Ntoskrnl.exe; load is complete.

Table 6-1 Steps in the Intel-based CPU boot process

6

3. *The MBR program executes the OS boot program.* Remember that when DOS or Windows 9x boots, the OS boot sector contains the name of the initial OS load program, Io.sys. When Windows NT/2000/XP is installed, it edits this boot sector of the active partition, instructing it to load the Windows NT/2000/XP program Ntldr at startup, instead of Io.sys. (It does this even when the PC is configured for a dual boot.)

4. *The boot program executes Ntldr.* With the execution of Ntldr, Windows NT/2000/XP then starts its boot sequence. This program is responsible for loading Windows NT/2000/XP and performing several chores to complete the loading process. It then passes control to the OS.

5. *Ntldr changes the processor mode and loads a file system.* Up to this point, the CPU has been processing in real mode. Windows NT/2000/XP does not process in real mode. Ntldr is a 32-bit program that begins by changing the CPU mode from real mode to a 32-bit mode called **32-bit flat memory mode** in order to run its 32-bit code. Next a temporary, simplified file system called the **minifile system** is started so that Ntldr can read files from either a FAT or an NTFS file system.

6. *Ntldr reads and loads the boot loader menu.* Ntldr then is able to read the **Boot.ini** file, a hidden text file that contains information needed to build the boot loader menu. The user can make a selection from this menu or accept the default selection by waiting for the preset time to expire.

7. *Ntldr uses Ntdetect.com.* If Ntldr is to load Windows NT/2000/XP as the OS, Ntldr runs the program Ntdetect.com, which checks the hardware devices present and passes the information back to Ntldr. This information is used later to update the Windows NT/2000/XP registry concerning the Last Known Good hardware profile used.

8. *Ntldr loads the OS and device drivers.* Ntldr then loads Ntoskrnl.exe, Hal.dll, and the System hive. The System hive is a portion of the Windows NT/2000/XP

A+
OS
1.2
2.3

registry that includes hardware information used to load the proper device drivers for the hardware present. You will learn more about the System hive in Chapter 8.

9. *Ntldr passes control to Ntoskrnl.exe.* Ntldr then passes control to Ntoskrnl.exe, and the boot sequence is complete.

10. *An operating system other than Windows NT/2000/XP is chosen.* If a selection was made from the boot loader menu to load an OS other than Windows NT/2000/XP, such as DOS or Windows 9x, Ntldr does not load Ntdetect.com or complete the remaining chores to load Windows NT/2000/XP. Instead, Ntldr loads and passes control to the program Bootsect.dos, which is responsible for loading the other OS.

NOTE When repairing a corrupted hard drive, a support person often copies files from one PC to another. However, the Bootsect.dos file contains information from the partition table for a particular hard drive and cannot be copied from another PC.

The files needed to boot Windows NT/2000/XP successfully are listed in Table 6-2. (In the table, references to *winnt_root* follow Microsoft documentation conventions and mean the name of the directory where Windows NT/2000/XP is stored, which is \\Winnt by default. Also, Microsoft sometimes refers to this root folder as %SystemRoot%.)

File	Location
Ntldr	Root folder of the system partition (usually C:\\)
Boot.ini	Root folder of the system partition (usually C:\\)
Bootsect.dos	Root folder of the system partition (usually C:\\)
Ntdetect.com	Root folder of the system partition (usually C:\\)
Ntbootdd.sys*	Root folder of the system partition (usually C:\\)
Ntoskrnl.exe	*winnt_root*\\system32 folder of the boot partition
Hal.dll	*winnt_root*\\system32 folder of the boot partition
System	*winnt_root*\\system32\\config folder of the boot partition
Device drivers	*winnt_root*\\system32\\drivers folder of the boot partition

*Ntbootdd.sys is used only with a SCSI boot device.

Table 6-2   Files needed to boot Windows NT/2000/XP successfully

Customizing the Windows NT/2000/XP Boot Process

A+
OS
2.3

The Boot.ini file contains information about how the Windows NT/2000/XP boot is configured and can be used to customize the boot process. As you learned earlier in this chapter, Ntldr reads this file and uses it to see what operating systems are available and how to set up the boot. Figure 6-1 shows an example of a Boot.ini file for Windows 2000.

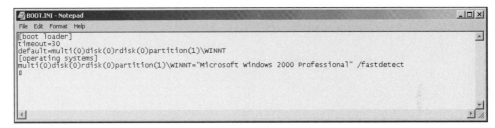

```
BOOT.INI - Notepad
File  Edit  Format  Help
[boot loader]
timeout=30
default=multi(0)disk(0)rdisk(0)partition(1)\WINNT
[operating systems]
multi(0)disk(0)rdisk(0)partition(1)\WINNT="Microsoft Windows 2000 Professional" /fastdetect
```

Figure 6-1   A sample Boot.ini file

There are two main sections in Boot.ini: the [boot loader] section and the [operating systems] section. The [boot loader] section contains the number of seconds the system gives the user to select an operating system before it loads the default operating system; this is called a timeout. In Figure 6-1, the timeout is set to 30 seconds. If the system is set for a dual boot, the path to the default operating system is also listed in the [boot loader] section.

The [operating systems] section of the Boot.ini file provides a list of operating systems that can be loaded, including the path to the boot partition of each operating system. Here is the meaning of each entry in Figure 6-1 that points to the location of the OS:

- *Multi(0).* Use the first hard drive controller.
- *Disk(0).* Used only when booting from a SCSI hard drive.
- *Rdisk(0).* Use the first hard drive.
- *Partition(1).* Use the first partition on the drive.

You can add switches to the [operating systems] section of the Boot.ini file, either by editing the file manually or through the System Properties dialog box. In Figure 6-1, the only switch used in this Boot.ini file is /fastdetect, which causes the OS not to attempt to inspect any peripherals connected to a COM port at startup.

The recommended way to change Boot.ini settings is through the System Properties dialog box, which is easier and safer than editing the file manually. For Windows 2000, do the following:

1. On the Start menu, point to **Settings** and then click **Control Panel**.

2. Double-click the **System** icon.

3. The System Properties dialog box opens. Click the **Advanced** tab (see Figure 6-2).

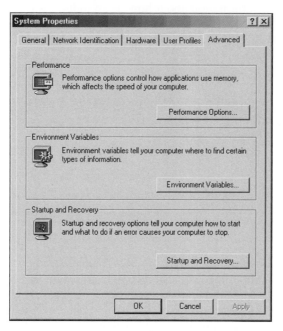

Figure 6-2 You can access startup and recovery options from the System Properties window

4. Click the **Startup and Recovery** button.

5. The Startup and Recovery window opens (see Figure 6-3). Change settings as desired and then click **OK** to save them (or click Cancel if you do not want to save them).

NOTE

To view or edit the Boot.ini file using a text editor such as Notepad, you must first change the folder options to view hidden system files. Open Windows Explorer, select the root directory, click Tools on the menu bar, click Folder Options, and then select the View tab. Uncheck the option "Hide protected operating system files."

A+
OS
2.3

Figure 6-3   Changing the default operating system and timeout value in the Startup and Recovery window changes the Boot.ini settings

Troubleshooting the Windows 2000 Boot Process

A+
OS
2.3
3.1
3.2
3.3

When problems arise with booting, as with all PC problems, try the simple things first. Turn off the power and restart the system. Check for loose cables, switches that are not on, stuck keys on the keyboard, a wall outlet switch that has been turned off, and similar easy-to-solve problems. The next step is to determine at what point in the boot process the system fails. Ask what has happened since the last successful boot.

Has new hardware or software been installed? Has there been a power surge or electrical storm? Has a user tinkered with the system? If you cannot pinpoint the source of the problem, then several tools can help you troubleshoot the boot process. Windows 2000 offers an Advanced Options menu, which includes starting the computer in Safe Mode. Use this option to prevent many device drivers and system services that normally load during the boot process from loading. You can then fix or disable these devices or services once the OS loads. The second utility, called the Recovery Console, is new in Windows 2000. Its command-line interface lets you perform maintenance and repairs to the hard drive. Another tool is the emergency repair disk, which is used to recover from problems with corrupted or missing operating system files or a corrupted hard drive boot sector. These three tools are discussed next.

✔ **A+ EXAM TIP**

The A+ OS exam expects you to be able to select the appropriate next step in troubleshooting a failed boot when given a specific scenario. As you study the tools in this section, pay attention to how a tool affects the installed OS, applications, and data. The idea is to fix the problem by using the tool that least affects the OS, applications, and data.

Advanced Options Menu

A+
OS
2.3
3.1
3.2
3.3

As a PC boots and the "Starting Windows" message appears at the bottom of the screen, press the F8 key to display the Windows 2000 **Advanced Options menu**, shown in Figure 6-4. As with the Windows 9x startup menu, this menu can be used to diagnose and fix problems when booting Windows 2000. The purpose of each menu option is outlined in the following sections.

```
Windows 2000 Advanced Options Menu
Please select an option:

        Safe Mode
        Safe Mode with Networking
        Safe Mode with Command Prompt

        Enable Boot Logging
        Enable VGA Mode
        Last Known Good Configuration
        Directory Services Restore Mode (Windows 2000 domain controllers only)
        Debugging Mode

        Boot Normally

Use ↑ and ↓ to move the highlight to your choice.
Press Enter to choose.
```

Figure 6-4   Press the F8 key at startup to display the Windows 2000 Advanced Options menu

Safe Mode

Safe Mode boots the OS with a minimum configuration and can be used to solve problems with a new hardware installation or problems caused by user settings. Safe Mode boots with the mouse, monitor (with basic video), keyboard, and mass storage drivers loaded. It uses the default system services (it does not load any extra services) and does not provide network access. When you boot in Safe Mode, you see "Safe Mode" in all four corners of your screen. You have a GUI interface in Safe Mode. The screen resolution is 600 × 800 and the desktop wallpaper (background) is black. After the OS loads in Safe Mode, you can disable the problem device, scan for viruses, run diagnostic software, or take other appropriate action to diagnose and solve problems. When you load Windows 2000 in Safe Mode, all files used for the load are recorded in the Ntbtlog.txt file.

Safe Mode with Networking

Use this option when you are solving a problem with booting and need access to the network to solve the problem. For example, if you have just attempted to install a printer, which causes the OS to hang when it boots, and the printer drivers are down-loaded from the network, boot into Safe Mode with Networking. Uninstall the printer and then install it again from the network. Also use this mode when the

Windows 2000 installation files are available on the network, rather than the Windows 2000 installation CD, and you need to access these files.

Safe Mode with Command Prompt

This Safe Mode option does not load a GUI desktop automatically. Use it to get a command prompt. If the first Safe Mode option does not load the OS, then try this option.

Enable Boot Logging

When you boot with this option, Windows 2000 loads normally and you access the regular desktop. However, all files used during the load process are recorded in a file, Ntbtlog.txt. Use this option to see what did and did not load during the boot process. If you have a problem getting a device to work, check Ntbtlog.txt to see what driver files loaded. Boot logging is much more effective if you have a copy of Ntbtlog.txt that was made when everything worked as it should. Then you can compare the good load to the bad load, looking for differences.

Enable VGA Mode

Use this option when the video setting does not allow you to see the screen well enough to fix a bad setting. This can happen because of a corrupted video driver or when a user creates a desktop with black fonts on a black background, or something similar. Booting in this mode gives you a very plain VGA video. Go to the Display settings, correct the problem, and reboot normally.

Last Known Good Configuration

Just as with Windows NT, Windows 2000 keeps the Last Known Good configuration in the registry. Use this option if you suspect the system was configured incorrectly. It restores Windows 2000 to the settings of the last successful boot, and all system setting changes made after this last successful boot are lost.

NOTE

Each time the system boots completely and the user logs on, the Last Known Good configuration is saved. If you have booted several times since a problem started, the Last Known Good will not help you recover from the problem, because all saved versions of the Last Known Good reflect the problem.

Directory Services Restore Mode (Windows 2000 Domain Controllers Only)

This option applies only to domain controllers and is used as one step in the process of recovering from a corrupted Active Directory. Recall that Active Directory is the domain database managed by a domain controller that tracks users and resources on the domain. The details of how all this works are beyond the scope of this chapter.

A+
OS
2.3
3.1
3.2
3.3

Debugging Mode

This mode gives you the opportunity to move system boot logs from the failing computer to another computer for evaluation. Connect another computer to the failing computer by way of the serial port. In this mode, Windows 2000 sends all the boot information to the serial port. For more details, see the *Windows 2000 Professional Resource Kit* (Microsoft Press).

Recovery Console

The Advanced Options menu can help if the problem is a faulty device driver or system service. However, if the problem goes deeper than that, the next tool to use is the **Recovery Console**. Use it when Windows 2000/XP does not start properly or hangs during the load. The Recovery Console is a command-driven operating system that does not use a GUI. With it you can access the FAT16, FAT32, and NTFS file systems.

The purpose of the Recovery Console is to allow you to repair a damaged registry, system files, or file system on the hard drive. You must enter the Administrator password in order to use the Console and access an NTFS volume. You are not allowed into all folders, and you cannot copy files from the hard drive to a floppy disk without setting certain parameters. If the registry is so corrupted that the Recovery Console cannot read the password in order to validate it, you are not asked for the password, but you are limited in what you can do at the Console.

APPLYING CONCEPTS

The Recovery Console software is on the Windows 2000 CD and the four Windows 2000 setup disks. You can launch the Recovery Console from the CD or four disks, or manually install the Recovery Console on the hard drive and launch it from there. If you have not already created the Windows 2000 setup disks, you can go to a working Windows 2000 PC and create the disks by following the directions given in Chapter 5. Follow these steps to load Windows 2000 from the disks and access the Recovery Console:

1. Insert the first of the four setup disks, and restart the PC. You are directed to insert each of the four disks in turn, and then the Setup screen appears as shown in Figure 6-5.

```
Windows 2000 Professional Setup
─────────────────────────────────────────────────────────────

   Welcome to Setup

   This portion of the Setup program prepares Microsoft®
   Windows 2000 ( TM ) to run on your computer.

            • To set up Windows 2000 now, press ENTER.
            • To repair a Windows 2000 installation, press R.
            • To quit Setup without installing Windows 2000, press F3.




   ─────────────────────────────────────────────────────────
   ENTER=Continue    R=Repair    F3=Quit
```

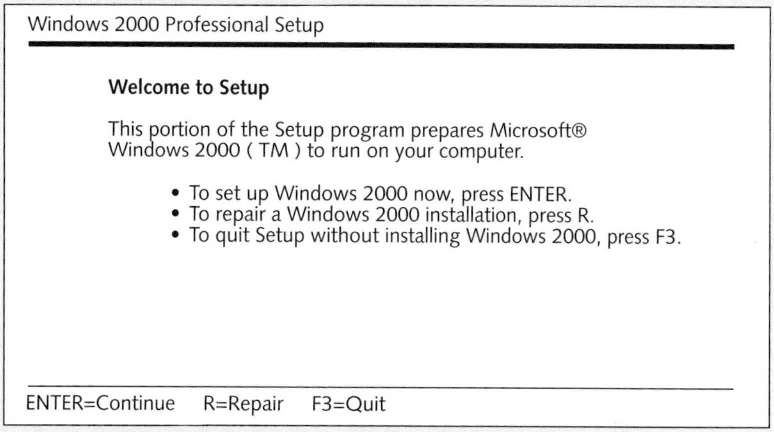

Figure 6-5   Use this Windows Setup screen to access the Recovery Console

2. Type **R** to select the "To repair a Windows 2000 installation" option. The Windows 2000 Repair Options window opens (see Figure 6-6). Type **C** to select the Recovery Console.

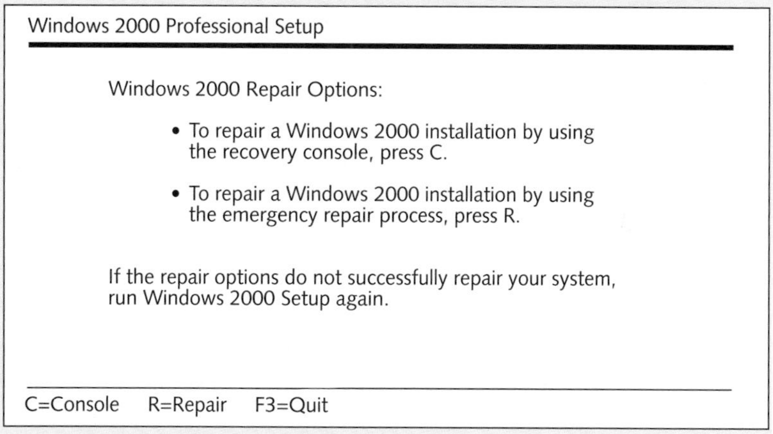

```
Windows 2000 Professional Setup
─────────────────────────────────────────────────────────────

        Windows 2000 Repair Options:

              • To repair a Windows 2000 installation by using
                the recovery console, press C.

              • To repair a Windows 2000 installation by using
                the emergency repair process, press R.

        If the repair options do not successfully repair your system,
        run Windows 2000 Setup again.



   ─────────────────────────────────────────────────────────
   C=Console    R=Repair    F3=Quit
```

Figure 6-6   Windows 2000 offers two repair options

3. The Windows 2000 Recovery Console window opens (see Figure 6-7). The Recovery Console looked at the hard drive and determined that only a single Windows 2000 installation was on the drive installed in the C:\Winnt folder. (The Winnt folder might be on a different drive on your machine.) Press 1 and then press Enter to select that installation.

> Microsoft Windows 2000 (TM) Recovery Console.
>
> The Recovery Console provides system repair and recovery functionality.
>
> Type EXIT to quit the Recovery Console and restart the computer.
>
> 1: C:\WINNT
>
> Which Windows 2000 installation would you like to log onto
> (To cancel, press ENTER)? 1
> Type the Administrator password:
> C:\WINNT>

Figure 6-7   The Windows 2000 Recovery Console command prompt

4. Enter the Administrator password, and press **Enter**. If you don't know the password, you cannot use the console.

5. You now have a command prompt. You can use a limited group of DOS-like commands at this point to recover a failed system. These commands are listed and described in Table 6-3. To leave the Recovery Console and start Windows 2000, type **Exit** at the command prompt.

NOTE   To retrieve the last command, press F3 at the command prompt. To retrieve the command one character at a time, press the F1 key.

Command	Description
Attrib	Changes the attributes of a file or folder, and works the same as the DOS version, as in the following example: `Attrib -r -h -s filename` Removes the read, hidden, and system attributes from the file.
Batch	Carries out commands stored in a batch file: `Batch file1 file2`. The commands stored in file1 are executed, and the results written to file2. If no file2 is specified, results are written to the screen.
Cd	Displays or changes the current directory.

Table 6-3 (continued)

Command	Description
Chkdsk	Checks a disk and repairs or recovers the data.
Cls	Clears the screen.

Copy	Copies a single uncompressed file. For example,
	`Copy A:\File1`
	
	`C:\Winnt\File2`
	copies the file named File1 on the floppy disk to the hard drive's Winnt folder, naming the file File2. Use the command to replace corrupted files.

Del	Deletes a file: `Del File1`.
Dir	Lists files and folders.
Disable	Used when a service or driver starts and prevents the system from booting properly: `Disable servicename` Disables a Windows 2000 system service or driver, restarts the computer without it, and helps you determine the problem.
Diskpart	Creates and deletes partitions on the hard drive. Enter the command with no arguments to display a user interface.
Enable	Enables a Windows 2000 system service or driver: `Enable servicename`.
Exit	Quits the Recovery Console and restarts the computer.
Expand	Expands a compressed file and copies it from a floppy disk or a CD to the destination folder; for example: `Expand A:\File1 C:\Winnt` Expands the file on the floppy disk and copies it to the hard drive.
Fixboot	Rewrites the OS boot sector on the hard drive. If a drive letter is not specified, the system drive is assumed. Type the `Fixboot C:` command when the boot sector is damaged.
Fixmbr	Rewrites the Master Boot Record boot program. This command is the same as `Fdisk/MBR`. Use this command when the Master Boot Record is damaged.
Format	Formats a logical drive. If no file system is specified, NTFS is assumed.

Table 6-3 (continued)

6

Command	Description
	Type `Format C:/fs:FAT32` to use the FAT32 file system.
	Type `Format C:/fs:FAT` to use the FAT16 file system.
Help	Help utility appears for the given command: `Help Fixboot`.
Listsvc	Lists all available services.
Logon	Allows you to log on to an installation with the Administrator password.
Map	Lists all drive letters and file system types.
Md or Mkdir	Creates a directory: `MD C:\TEMP`.
More or Type	Displays a text file on screen: `TYPE filename.txt`.
Rd or Rmdir	Deletes a directory: `RD C:\TEMP`.
Rename or Ren	Renames a file: `Rename File1.txt File2.txt`.
Set	Displays or sets Recovery Console environmental variables.
Systemroot	Sets the current directory to the directory where Windows 2000 is installed.
Type	Displays contents of a text file: `Type File1.txt`.

Table 6-3   Commands available from the Recovery Console

Using the Recovery Console to Restore the Registry

If you suspect that the Windows 2000 registry is damaged, you can use the Recovery Console commands to restore the registry from the last backup that you created. (This process also works for the Windows XP registry.) The registry consists of five files—Default, Sam, Security, Software, and System—which are stored in the %SystemRoot%\System32\Config folder. A backup of the registry is stored in the %SystemRoot%\repair\RegBack folder every time you back up the system state (see Figure 6-8).

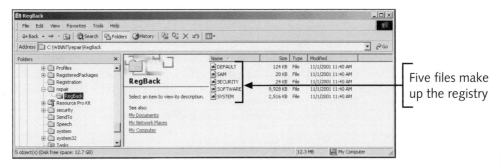

Five files make up the registry

Figure 6-8   Windows puts a backup of the registry in the C:\WINNT\repair\RegBack folder

6

To restore the registry from this backup using the Recovery Console, first rename the registry files so that you can backtrack if necessary. From the Recovery Console command prompt, perform the steps outlined in Table 6-4. These actions restore the registry to its state at the time of the last backup.

Command	Description
1. Systemroot	Makes the Windows folder the current folder.
2. CD System32\Config	Makes the Windows registry folder the current folder.
3. Ren Default Default.save Ren Sam Sam.save Ren Security Security.save Ren Software Software.save Ren System System.save	Renames the five registry files.
4. Systemroot	Returns to the Windows folder.
5. CD repair\RegBack	Makes the registry backup folder the current folder.
6. Copy default C:\Winnt\system32\config Copy Sam C:\Winnt\system32\config Copy Security C:\Winnt\system32\config Copy Software C:\Winnt\system32\config Copy System C:\Winnt\system32\config	Copies the five registry files from the backup folder to the registry folder.

Table 6-4   Steps to restore the Windows 2000/XP registry

Installing the Recovery Console

A+
OS
2.3
3.1
3.2
3.3

Although the Recovery Console is often launched from the Windows CD to recover from system failure, you can also install it on your working system so it appears on the OS boot loader menu. Use it to address less drastic problems that occur when you can boot from the hard drive. To install the Recovery Console:

1. Open a command window in Windows 2000.

2. Change from the current directory to the \i386 folder on the Windows 2000 CD.

3. Enter the command **winnt32 /cmdcons**. The Recovery Console is installed.

4. Restart your computer. Recovery Console should now be shown with the list of available operating systems on the OS boot loader menu.

Emergency Repair Process

If options on the Advanced Options menu fail to recover the system and the Recovery Console fails as well, your next option is the **Emergency Repair Process**. Use this option only as a last resort because it restores the system to the state it was in immediately after the Windows 2000 installation. All changes since the installation are lost. The process uses an Emergency Repair Disk (ERD), but the disk does not contain the same information as the Windows NT ERD (Windows NT Emergency Repair Disk).

Recall that the Windows NT ERD contains a copy of the registry and that you should update the disk any time you make significant changes to the registry. You can then use the disk to repair a corrupted registry, restoring it to the state it was in when you last updated the ERD.

The Windows 2000 ERD contains information about your current installation but does not contain a copy of the registry because it is too large to fit on a single floppy disk. The Windows 2000 ERD points to a folder on the hard drive where the registry was backed up when Windows 2000 was installed. This folder is %SystemRoot%\repair, which most likely is C:\Winnt\repair.

APPLYING CONCEPTS

Using the Windows 2000 ERD to recover from a corrupted registry returns you to the installation version of the registry, and you lose all changes to the registry since that time. Because of the way the ERD works, you do not need to update the disk once you've created it. Before a problem occurs, follow these directions to create the disk:

1. Click **Start**, point to **Programs**, **Accessories**, and **System Tools**, and then click **Backup**. The Backup window appears with the Welcome tab selected (see Figure 6-9). Select **Emergency Repair Disk**.

2. The Backup tab and the Emergency Repair Diskette dialog box open. If you check the box shown in Figure 6-10, the system backs up your registry to a folder under the Repair folder %SystemRoot%\repair\RegBack.

3. Click **OK** to create the disk. Label the disk "Windows 2000 Emergency Repair Disk", and keep it in a safe place.

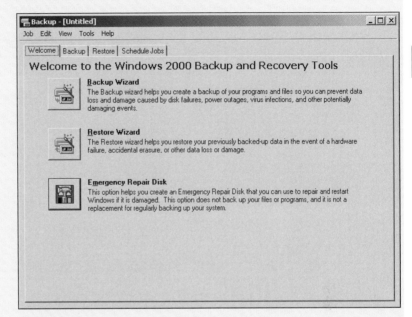

Figure 6-9   Use the Backup window to back up the registry and create an emergency repair disk

If your hard drive fails, you can use the ERD to restore the system, including system files, boot files, and the registry, to the state it was in at the end of the Windows 2000 installation. Follow these steps:

1. Boot the PC from the four Windows 2000 setup disks. The Setup menu appears (refer back to Figure 6-5). Select option **R**.

2. When the Windows 2000 Repair Options window opens (refer back to Figure 6-6), select option **R**.

3. You are instructed to insert the Emergency Repair Disk. Follow the instructions on the screen to repair the installation.

If this process does not work, then your next option is to reinstall Windows 2000. If you have access to a Windows 98 startup disk, it is a good idea to use Windows 98 ScanDisk to scan the hard disk surface for errors before you do the installation. If you suspect that a virus damaged the file system, also use the Fixmbr command or the Fdisk /MBR command discussed

A+
OS
2.3
3.1
3.2
3.3

in earlier chapters to replace the master boot program in case it has been corrupted by the virus. Windows 2000 also offers a utility called InoculateIT Antivirus AVBoot, a command-line tool that can scan memory, the MBR sector, and OS boot sectors for viruses. You will learn to use the utility in a project at the end of the chapter.

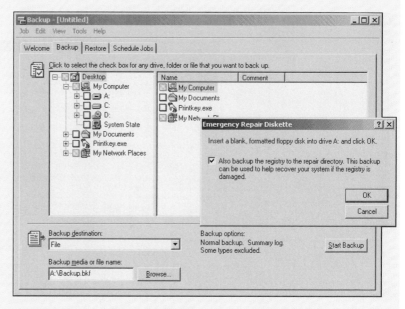

Figure 6-10   Create an ERD and back up the registry to the hard drive

Tools For Maintenance and Troubleshooting

A+
OS
1.5

In this section, you will learn about many tools you can use for maintenance and troubleshooting in Windows 2000. You learned about some tools earlier in this chapter, as well as in previous chapters on other versions of Windows. All tools discussed in this section work under Windows XP, although in some cases, the menus have changed slightly. Of the tools discussed in this section, all except Windows File Protection, Microsoft Management Console, and automated Windows Update are available under Windows NT. In this section, you will learn how to use tools to manage hard disks, applications, system processes, and other Windows components.

Using the Backup Tool to Restore the System State

A+
OS
1.5

In Chapter 5, you learned how to back up the system state after installing Windows 2000 and verifying that the system is working. To use the backup (Ntbackup.exe) to restore the system state after the system fails or the registry becomes corrupted, begin the same way you did to make the backup by clicking Start, pointing to Programs, Accessories, and System Tools, and then clicking Backup. The dialog box opens showing the Backup tab. Click the Restore tab, which is shown in Figure 6-11.

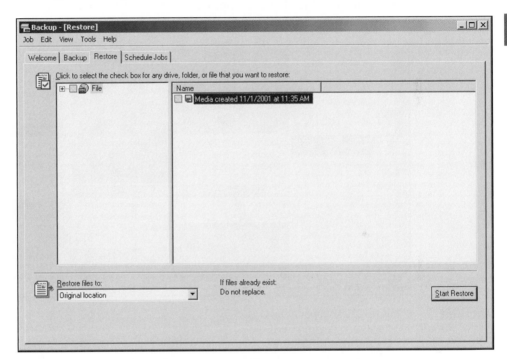

Figure 6-11   Restore the system state from the Restore tab of the Backup window

From the Restore tab, first select the backup you want to restore. Then, in the list box in the lower-left corner, select the location to which the backup is to be restored. Click the Start Restore button in the lower-right corner to start the process. Remember that you can restore the system state as a way of restoring the registry.

Windows 2000 Support Tools

A+
OS
3.3

Windows 2000 offers several support tools that you can install. They are located in the \Support\Tools folder on the Windows 2000 CD. To install them, run the Setup program located in that folder. Enter this command in the Run dialog box:

```
D:\Support\Tools\Setup.exe
```

Substitute the drive letter of your CD-ROM drive for D in the command line, if necessary. The list of tools installed is shown in Figure 6-12.

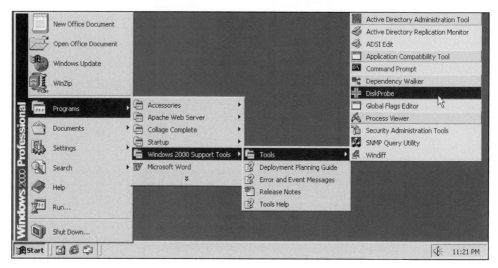

Figure 6-12   Windows 2000 support tools

One of these utilities is Dependency Walker (Depends.exe), which lists all the files used by an application. It can be useful when troubleshooting a failed application installation if you have a report of files used by the application on a computer where the installation is good, or to help resolve General Protection Faults. Compare the reports, looking for DLL files that are missing on the bad installation, are not the correct size, or are incorrectly date-stamped. Software applications often use DLL files for added functionality and to relate to the operating system. To use the utility, click Start, point to Programs, Windows 2000 Support Tools, and Tools, and then click Dependency Walker. Figure 6-13 shows a Dependency Walker window. Click File on the menu bar, click Open, and then select the main executable file for an application. In the figure, Apache.exe is selected. Apache is a popular Web server application. The window lists all supporting files that Apache.exe uses and shows how they depend on one another.

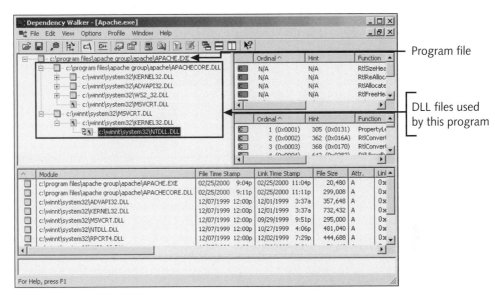

Figure 6-13　You can use Dependency Walker to solve problems with applications

Windows File Protection

Windows 2000 provides a feature called **WFP** (**Windows File Protection**) to protect system files from modification. Files protected have a .sys, .dll, .ttf, .fon, .ocs, or .exe file extension. Earlier versions of Windows sometimes allowed these files to be over-written by unsigned, non-Microsoft versions during program installations. Changes to shared system files can cause errors within a program, incompatibility between two or more programs, mismatches between file versions, or even system instability.

WFP prevents these problems and protects files from modification through two tools. One is a background process that notifies WFP when a protected file is modified. WFP then checks the file signature to see whether it is the correct Microsoft version of the file. If the file version is not correct, WFP looks in the Dllcache folder, which contains cached copies of system files, or asks that the Windows 2000 CD be inserted so that WFP can find the file and restore it from the CD. Replacing incorrect system files with correct ones from the Windows 2000 CD requires administrative permissions. If a nonadministrator user is logged on when WFP activates, WFP does not prompt that user to insert the Windows 2000 CD, but waits until an administrator logs on to request the CD and replace the file.

NOTE

If a file has been modified, is correctly signed as a Microsoft-approved version, and is not present in the Dllcache folder, WFP adds it to that folder to be used as the correct version on future scans.

A+
OS
2.4
3.3

When WFP restores a file, it shows the following message by default, replacing *file_name* with the name of the system file it restored:

```
A file replacement was attempted on the protected system
file file_name. To maintain system stability, the file
has been restored to the correct Microsoft version. If
problems occur with your application, please contact the
application vendor for support.
```

If you see this message, carefully note what application was working at the time and what happened just before the message. In addition to software installations, viruses, and software applications, errors can cause attempted modifications to system files. It is important to have as much information as possible to figure out which applications might need to be scanned for viruses or replaced altogether.

The other tool that WFP provides is the **SFC (System File Checker)**. (The program filename is Sfc.exe.) The system or an administrator might use this tool in several situations. If the administrator set the system to perform an unattended installation, the SFC checks all protected system files after Setup is completed to see whether they were modified by programs added during the installation, as well as the catalog files that contain the file signatures. If any incorrect modifications have been made or if any important system files are unsigned, WFP retrieves a copy of the file from the Dllcache folder or requests it from the Windows 2000 CD.

An administrator can also activate the SFC manually from a command prompt and use it to verify that the system is using correct versions of all protected system files, either as a preventative maintenance measure or when it is suspected that system files have become corrupted or deleted. To use System File Checker, the administrator types Sfc.exe from the command prompt with one of the switches listed in Table 6-5. You can also access the Run dialog box from the Start menu and type C:\Winnt \system32\sfc.exe /scannow (or another switch).

Switch	Function
/cachesize=x	Sets the size of the file cache, in megabytes
/cancel	Discontinues scans of protected system files
/enable	Enables normal operation of WFP
/purgecache	Empties the file cache and immediately scans all protected system files, populating the Dllcache folder with confirmed correct versions of system files (may require insertion of the Windows 2000 CD as the source for correct versions)
/quiet	Replaces incorrect versions of system files with correct ones without prompting the user
/scanboot	Performs a scan of protected system files every time the system boots

Table 6-5 (continued)

Switch	Function
/scannow	Performs an immediate scan of protected system files
/scanonce	Performs a scan of protected system files the next time the system boots
/?	Displays a list of available switches for the sfc command

Table 6-5   Switches for the Sfc.exe utility

6

Computer Management

Computer Management is a window that consolidates several Windows 2000 administrative tools that you can use to manage the local PC or other computers on the network. To use most of these tools, you must be logged on as an administrator, although you can view certain settings and configurations in Computer Management if you are logged on with lesser privileges. To access Computer Management, open the Control Panel, open the Administrative Tools window, and then double-click the Computer Management icon. The Computer Management window appears (see Figure 6-14). Some tasks you can perform from this window include monitoring problems with hardware, software, and security. You can share folders, view device configurations, add new device drivers, start and stop services, and manage server applications.

NOTE By default, the Administrative Tools group is located in the Control Panel. In addition, you can add the Administrative Tools group to appear in the Start menu when you click Start, Programs, and Administrative Tools. To do that, right-click the taskbar and select Properties. On the Taskbar and Start Menu Properties dialog box, select the Advanced tab. Check Display Administrative Tools, and click OK.

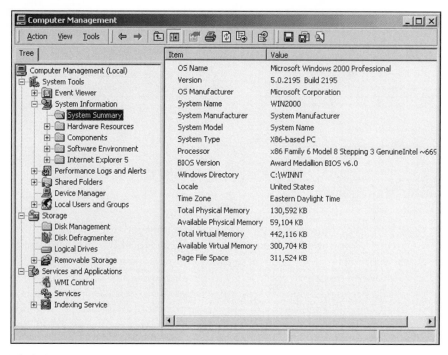

Figure 6-14 Windows 2000 Computer Management combines several administrative tools into a single easy-to-access window

Disk Management

A+ EXAM TIP

The A+ OS exam expects you to be able to use the Computer Management window. Disk Management is one of the more important tools in this window.

The Computer Management console contains a tool called **Disk Management** that you can use to create partitions on basic disks or volumes on dynamic disks, and to convert a basic disk to a dynamic disk. This graphical, user-friendly utility replaces the Fdisk utility of earlier Windows OSs. To access the utility, select Disk Management in the Computer Management console or enter Diskmgmt.msc in the Run dialog box. When Disk Management first loads, it examines the drive configuration for the system and displays all drives in a graphical format so you can see how each drive is allocated.

The Disk Management window shown in Figure 6-15 displays three drives. Disk 0 is a basic hard drive using the NTFS file system. Disk 1 is a dynamic hard drive that has not yet been allocated into volumes. The third drive is a CD-ROM drive shown with a CD in the drive.

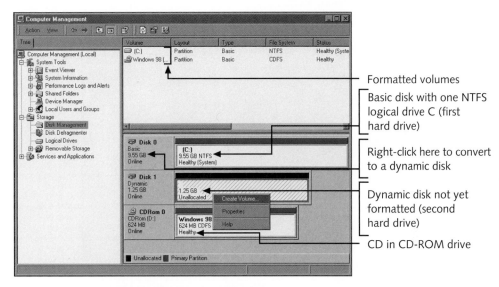

Formatted volumes

Basic disk with one NTFS
logical drive C (first
hard drive)

Right-click here to convert
to a dynamic disk

Dynamic disk not yet
formatted (second
hard drive)

CD in CD-ROM drive

Figure 6-15   Create a volume on an unallocated dynamic disk

After you install a new second hard drive in the system, and then first access Disk Management, it asks if you want to create a basic disk or dynamic disk using the new drive. Disk Management displays the new disk with unallocated space, as shown in Figure 6-15. This second hard drive has been designated as a dynamic disk.

To create a volume on this dynamic disk:

1. Right-click an unallocated area of the drive, and select **Create Volume** on the shortcut menu (see Figure 6-15).

2. The Create Volume Wizard launches. Click **Next** to continue.

3. On the next screen (see Figure 6-16), select a volume type, either Simple volume, Spanned volume, or Striped volume. In our example, only Simple volume is available, because we are working with only one dynamic drive. You need to have more than one dynamic drive to specify a volume as striped or spanned. Click **Next** to continue.

4. Follow the wizard through the process of specifying the volume size, a drive letter, file system (NTFS, FAT, or FAT32), and allocation unit size (default is 512 bytes). The wizard then creates the dynamic volume.

The process for creating a partition on a basic disk is similar; the main difference is that the wizard is called the Create Partition Wizard. Access it by right-clicking the unallocated portion of the basic disk, selecting Create Partition, and following the directions in the wizard.

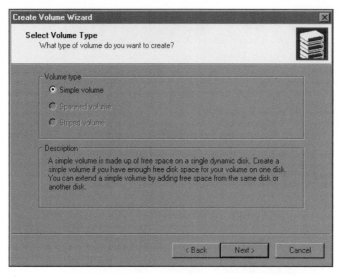

Figure 6-16 Disk Management provides the Create Volume Wizard to help you create volumes

Microsoft Management Console

When Windows combines several administrative tools in a single window, the window is called a **console**. Individual tools within the console are called **snap-ins**. An example of a console is Computer Management. Event Viewer and System Information are two snap-ins in that console. Another example of a console is Recovery Console, introduced earlier in the chapter. Windows 2000/XP offers a way for you to create your own customized consoles using the console-building utility **Microsoft Management Console** (**MMC**). Table 6-6 lists some available snap-ins for MMC.

> ✔ **A+ EXAM TIP**
>
> The A+ OS exam expects you to be able to use Microsoft Management Console to create a customized console.

Snap-in	Description
ActiveX Control	Enables you to add ActiveX controls to your system
Certificates	Provides certificate management at the user, service, or computer level
Component Services	Links to the Component Services management tool, which is located on the Control Panel

Table 6-6 (continued)

Snap-in	Description
Computer Management	Links to the Computer Management tools on the Control Panel
Device Manager	Lets you see what hardware devices you have on your system and configure device properties
Disk Defragmenter	Links to the Disk Defragmenter utility (Defrag.exe)
Disk Management	Links to the Disk Management tool
Event Viewer	Links to the Event Viewer tool, which displays event logs for the system
Fax Service Management	Enables you to manage fax settings and devices
Folder	Enables you to add a folder to manage from MMC
Group Policy	Provides a tool to manage group policy settings
Indexing Service	Searches files and folders using specified parameters
IP Security Policy Management	Manages Internet communication security
Link to Web Address	Enables you to link to a specified Web site
Local Users and Groups	Provides a tool to manage settings for local users and groups
Performance Logs and Alerts	Gives you an interface from which to set up and manage logs of and Alerts performance information and alerts about system performance
Removable Storage Management	Enables you to manage settings and configuration information for removable storage devices such as Zip drives and tape backup drives
Security Configuration and Analysis	Enables you to manage configuration of security settings for computers and Analysis that use security template files
Services	Provides a centralized interface for starting, stopping, and configuring system services
Shared Folders	Provides information about shared folders, open files, and current sessions
System Information	Contains information about the system that you can use when troubleshooting

Table 6-6   Some MMC snap-ins

Creating a Customized Console

As with the Computer Management console, you must have administrative privileges to perform most tasks from the MMC. You can use MMC to create your own customized consoles. You can also save a console in a file, which is assigned an .msc file extension. Store the file in the C:\Documents and Settings*user*\StartMenu\Programs \Administrative Tools folder to make it appear as a program when you click Start, Programs, and Administrative Tools. In the path, substitute the name of the user. For example, for the Administrator, the path to the .msc file is C:\Documents and Settings \Administrator\Start Menu\Programs\Administrative Tools.

NOTE   After you create a console, you can copy the .msc file to any computer or place a shortcut to it on the desktop.

Follow these directions to open MMC and create a console that contains some popular utility tools:

1. Click **Start**, click **Run**, enter **MMC** in the Run dialog box, and then click **OK**. An empty console window appears, as shown in Figure 6-17.

2. Click **Console** on the menu bar, and then click **Add/Remove Snap-in**. The Add/ Remove Snap-in window opens. The window illustrated in Figure 6-18 is empty because no snap-ins have been added to the console.

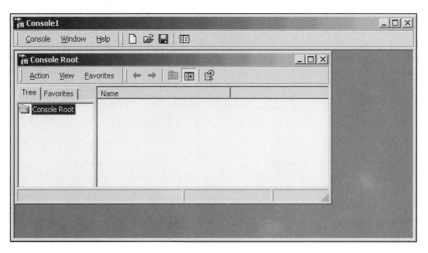

Figure 6-17   An empty console

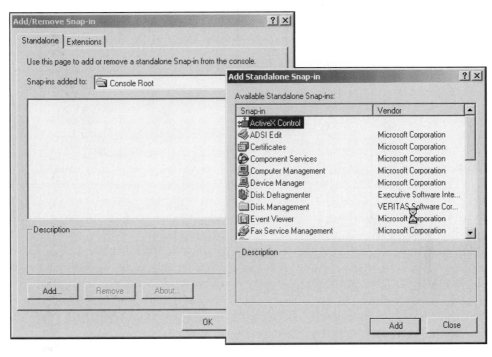

6

Figure 6-18 List of snap-ins available to be added to a console

3. Click **Add**. You see a list of snap-ins that can be added to a console, as shown in Figure 6-18. Select a snap-in and then click **Add**.

4. A dialog box opens that allows you to set the parameters for the snap-in. The dialog box offers different selections, depending on the snap-in being added. When you have made your selections, click **Finish**. The new snap-in appears in the Add/Remove Snap-in window.

5. Repeat Steps 3 and 4 to add all the snap-ins that you want to the console. When you finish, click **Close** from the Add Standalone Snap-in window illustrated in Figure 6-18, then click **OK**.

6. Figure 6-19 shows a console with four snap-ins added. To save the console, click **Console** on the menu bar, and then click **Save As**. The Save As dialog box opens.

7. The default location for the console file is shown in Figure 6-19. This is the location that ensures the console appears as an option under Administrative Tools on the Start menu. Select this location for the file, name the file, and click **Save**.

8. Close the console window by clicking **Console** on the menu bar, and then clicking **Exit**.

A+
OS
1.1
1.5

To use the console, click Start, Programs, and Administrative Tools, and then select the console.

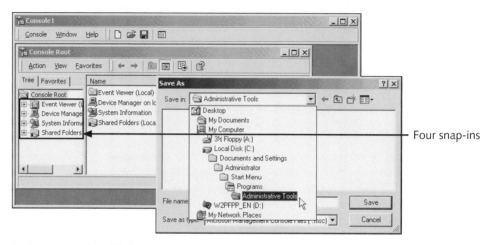

Figure 6-19   Saving a console with four snap-ins

Event Viewer

A+
OS
1.5
3.1
3.2
3.3

The Event Viewer MMC snap-in connects to the Event Viewer tool, which displays logs about significant system events that occur in Windows NT/2000/XP or in applications running under these OSs, such as a hardware or network failure, OS error messages, a device or service that has failed to start, or General Protection Faults. Three different logs are shown in Event Viewer, and are displayed in Windows 2000, as shown in Figure 6-20:

- *The application log* records application events that the developer of the program sets to trigger a log entry. One type of event recorded in this log is an error recorded by the Dr. Watson utility, which you will learn about later in the chapter.
- *The security log* records events based on audit policies, which an administrator setsto monitor user activity such as successful or unsuccessful attempts to access a file or log on to the system. Only an administrator can view this log.
- *The system log* records events triggered by Windows components, such as a device driver failing to load during the boot process. Windows NT/2000/XP sets which events are recorded in this log. All users can access this log file.

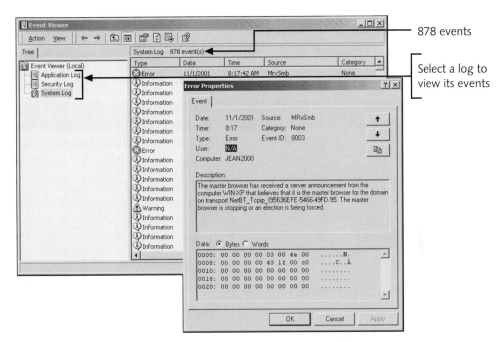

Figure 6-20   Use Event Viewer to see information about security audits in the security log and error, warning, or information events for the system and application logs

Three types of events are recorded in the system and application logs:

- *Information* events are recorded when a driver, service, or application functions successfully.
- *Warning* events are recorded when something happens that may indicate a future problem but does not necessarily indicate that something is presently wrong with the system. For example, low disk space might trigger a warning event.
- *Error* events are recorded when something goes wrong with the system, such as a necessary component failing to load, data getting lost or becoming corrupted, or a system or application function ceasing to operate.

You can open Event Viewer from the Computer Management console, or you can locate it by double-clicking the Administrative Tools icon in the Control Panel. To view a log within Event Viewer, click the log that you want to view in the left pane. This generates a summary of events that appears in the right pane. Double-click a specific event to see details about it (see Figure 6-20).

Notice in the figure that 878 events are listed in the system log. You may only want to view certain events and not the entire list to find what you're looking for. To filter events, right-click a log in the left pane, and select Filter on the shortcut menu. To filter events, you can use several criteria, which are listed in Table 6-7.

Property	Description
Category	The category that the event falls under, such as an attempt to log on to the system or access a program
Computer	The name of a computer on the system
Event ID	A number that identifies the event and makes tracking events easier for support personnel
Event source	The application, driver, or service that triggered the event
Event type	The type of event, such as information, error, or warning
From: To:	The range of events that you want to view. You can view the events from first to last event, or you can view all events that occurred on a specific date and in a specific time range.
User	The logon name for a user

Table 6-7   Log properties that can be used to filter events

Another way you can avoid a ballooning log file is to set a size limit and specify what happens when the log reaches this limit. If you right-click a log, select Properties on the shortcut menu, and click the General tab, you can set the maximum size of the log in megabytes (as well as view general information about the log). You can set the log to overwrite events as needed, overwrite events that are more than a specified number of days old, or not overwrite events at all. Select this last option when system security is high and you do not want to lose any event information. If you select this option, the system simply stops recording events when the log file reaches the maximum size (see Figure 6-21).

To allow the system to record events in the log after a log reaches maximum size, you have to review the events and clear the log manually, either by clicking the Clear Log button in the Properties dialog box or selecting Clear All Events from the Action menu. Before clearing the log, Event Viewer gives you a chance to save it.

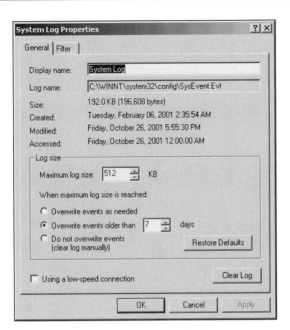

Figure 6-21   View information about a log, including maximum size of the log file, in the Log Properties window

Performance Monitoring and Optimization

Maintaining optimal performance, or addressing performance problems when they develop, involves a three-part process in which you analyze data provided by monitoring tools such as Task Manager and System Monitor, determine areas in which performance is below the baseline, and identify and take the steps necessary to correct the problem.

Principles for Optimizing Performance

Here are some principles to remember when trying to optimize performance on your Windows NT/2000/XP system:

■ One of the most important things you can do is establish a **baseline** of acceptable performance for your system, defining what you consider normal performance under a typical workload. Baselines can be created when the OS is first installed, when major changes are made, and on a periodic basis such as once a month. Figure out what resources the system uses when you are running all required programs and services. That will help you decide whether you need to add more resources (such as more RAM) to the system. Heavily used Windows 2000 computers may benefit from having as much as 512 MB of RAM, whereas machines used more moderately may only need 128 MB of RAM.

- If you add RAM, remember that you also need to increase the size of the paging file. You might also increase paging file size if the peak usage of the paging file is too close to the limit.
- Replacing one component may not help much if other components have not been upgraded. For example, if you install a faster CPU, you need to look at the amount of RAM and the size of the hard drive as well.
- Each application is assigned a priority level, which determines its position in the queue for CPU resources. This priority level can be changed for applications that are already loaded by using Task Manager. If an application performs slowly, increase its priority. You should only do this with very important applications, because giving an application higher priority than certain background system processes can sometimes interfere with the operating system.
- In general, upgrading an existing PC is recommended as long as the cost of the upgrade stays below half the cost of buying a new machine. Even if you just keep the case, power supply, and an expansion card or two, buying a new motherboard and hard drive can be almost like having a whole new system at a lower cost.

The rest of this section discusses two tools that you can use to monitor system performance: Task Manager and System Monitor.

Task Manager

A+
OS
1.5
3.2

Task Manager (Taskman.exe) allows you to view the applications and processes running on your computer as well as performance information for the processor and the memory.

There are three ways that you can access Task Manager:

- Press Ctrl+Alt+Del. The Windows Security window opens. Click the Task Manager button.
- Right-click a blank area on the taskbar, and then select Task Manager on the shortcut menu.
- Press Ctrl+Shift+Esc.

Task Manager has three tabs: Applications, Processes, and Performance. On the Applications tab (see Figure 6-22), each application loaded can have one of two states: Running or Not Responding. If an application is listed as Not Responding, you can end it by selecting it and clicking the End Task button at the bottom of the window. You will lose any unsaved information in the application.

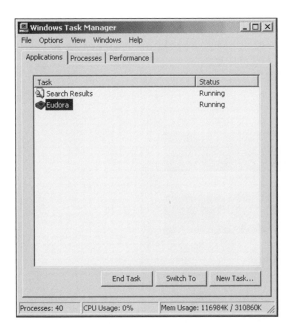

Figure 6-22   The Applications tab in Task Manager shows the status of active applications

The Processes tab lists system services and other processes associated with applications, together with how much CPU time and memory the process uses. This information can help you determine which applications are slowing down your system. The Performance tab, shown in Figure 6-23, provides more detail about how a program uses system resources. You can use these views to identify which applications and processes use the most CPU time.

On the Performance tab, note the four frames at the bottom of the window. These frames give the following information:

- The *Totals* frame indicates how much the system is currently being used by counting handles (indicates a device or file is being accessed), threads (unit of activity within a process), and processes (programs running). Use these entries to know how heavily the system is used.
- The *Physical Memory* frame lists Total (amount of RAM), Available (RAM not used), and System Cache (RAM in use). Use these entries to know if you must upgrade RAM.
- The *Commit Charge* frame lists Total (current size of virtual memory, also called the page file or swap file), Limit (how much of the paging file can be allocated to applications before the size of the paging file must be increased), and Peak (maximum amount of virtual memory used in this session). Use these entries to learn if you must increase the size of the paging file.
- The *Kernel Memory* frame indicates how much RAM and virtual memory the OS uses. This frame lists Total (sum of RAM and virtual memory), Paged (how much of the paging file the OS uses), and Nonpaged (how much RAM the OS

A+
OS
1.5
3.2

uses). Use this frame to learn how much memory the OS is using. If usage is high, look for OS processes you can eliminate.

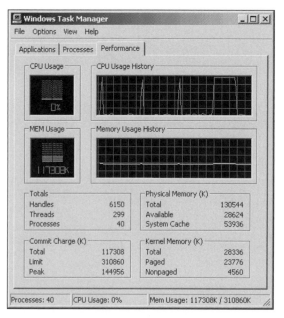

Figure 6-23   The Performance tab shows more detail about how system resources are being used

By reading the information in the frames in Figure 6-23, you can see that the OS is using about 28 MB of memory. The system contains about 130 MB of RAM, and the maximum paging file size is set to about 311 MB. How to change the maximum and initial size of the paging file is covered in Chapter 9.

NOTE

If your desktop locks up, you can use Task Manager to refresh it. Press Ctrl+Alt+Del and then click Task Manager. Click the Processes tab. Select Explorer.exe (the process that provides the desktop) and then click End Process. Click Yes. Then click the Applications tab. Click New Task. Enter Explorer.exe in the Create New Task dialog box and click OK. Your desktop will be refreshed and any running programs will still be open.

System Monitor

In most cases, you can find the information you need from Task Manager to determine if the system needs performance tuning or upgrading. If this information is not detailed enough, use System Monitor, which provides more system performance detail than Task Manager. There are three components of System Monitor: objects, instances, and counters. Objects are hardware or software system components, and instances are multiples of objects. For example, Microsoft Word is an object, but if you have Word open in two separate windows on the desktop, then two instances of this one object are running. Counters show information on specific characteristics of an object and constantly gather data and update the counter display. You can specify which counters to show for an object.

Important objects to monitor using System Monitor include Memory, Paging File, Processor, and Physical Disk (the hard drive). In the following example, you will access System Monitor and then add and view counters for the Memory object.

1. In the Control Panel, double-click the **Administrative Tools** icon.

2. In the Administrative Tools window, double-click the **Performance** icon.

3. The Performance window opens (see Figure 6-24). System Monitor is highlighted and the System Monitor details pane appears on the right. The pane is blank because no objects are being monitored. Right-click the pane and select **Add Counters** on the shortcut menu (see Figure 6-24).

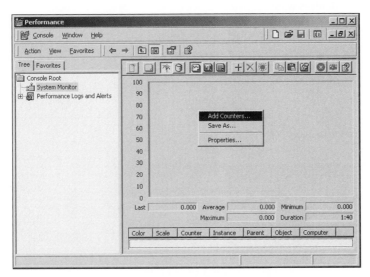

Figure 6-24   Access System Monitor through the Performance window

4. The Add Counters window opens (see Figure 6-25). From the Performance object drop-down list, select the **Memory** object.

5. You have the option to view all counters, but that makes a messy, hard-to-read display. By default, the "Select counters from list" option is selected. Locate and click the **Available Bytes** counter, which tells you how much physical memory remains. Click **Add**.

6. Scroll down the list until you see the **Page Faults/sec** counter. This tells you how many pages were requested but not immediately available in memory. Click **Add**.

7. Click **Close** to close the Add Counters window.

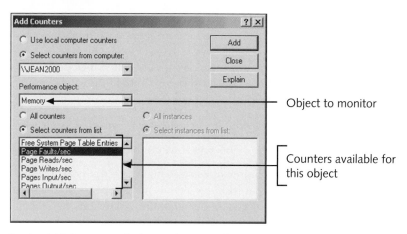

Figure 6-25   In the Add Counters window, select a performance object and counters to monitor

Figure 6-26 shows System Monitor in the process of monitoring the two counters you selected. The lines tracking the counters are color-coded to match the counters listed at the bottom of the graph. Look at the left side of the graph. The line representing Page Faults/sec begins at 0 and spikes when an application is opened. The line representing Available Bytes begins at 30 and dips lower, showing fewer bytes are available when applications are active. The vertical line on the right moves to the right as monitoring continues.

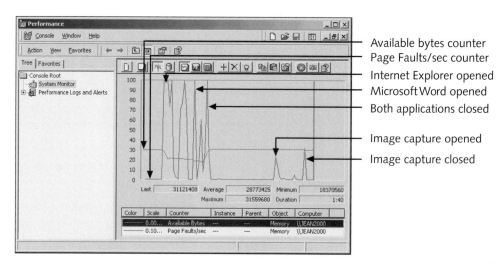

Figure 6-26   System Monitor shows how changes in system activity affect the selected object and counters

Dr. Watson and Memory Dumps

A+
OS
3.1
3.2

Two tools that can produce text output useful in diagnosing problems with the OS and applications are Dr. Watson and memory dumps. Recall from Chapter 4 that Dr. Watson is used to debug errors in applications by recording error events to a log file. It can help solve problems such as when an application fails to install or load, when the system locks, or when error messages appear. In Windows 2000, these events are recorded in the Drwtsn32.log file. Dr. Watson automatically launches when an application error occurs, or you can launch it manually by entering Drwtsn32.exe in the Run dialog box or at a command prompt. The log file is written to the \Documents and Settings*user*\Documents\DrWatson folder.

Another tool that helps you understand what happened when an error occurs is a **memory dump**. It saves the contents of memory at the time a stop error halts the system in a file called a **dump file**. A **stop error** is an error so severe that the operating system stops all processes. How to capture and interpret memory dumps is beyond the scope of this book.

6

Windows Update

A+
OS
2.2
3.2

In the process of maintaining and troubleshooting Windows 2000, remember that the Microsoft Web site offers patches, fixes, and updates for known problems and has an extensive knowledge base documenting problems and their solutions. You learned how to download a Windows update in Chapter 4; the process is basically the same for Windows 2000 as it is for Windows 9x. You can access Windows Update by going to the Microsoft site *v4.windowsupdate.microsoft.com*, or you can click Windows Update on your Start menu, which takes you directly to the site.

 A+ EXAM TIP

The A+ OS exam expects you to know that applying the latest OS service packs, patches, and updates is always done as one of the last steps after installing or upgrading an OS.

If you think you might later want to uninstall a critical update or service pack, select the option to Save uninstall information. Later, to uninstall the fix, again execute the downloaded file. When given the option, select "Uninstall a previously installed service pack."

In addition to critical updates and service packs that Microsoft creates to address known problems with Windows, the Windows Update tool also uses ActiveX controls to scan your system, find your device drivers and system files, and compare these files to the ones on the Windows Update server. If you do not already have Active Setup and the Active X controls installed on your computer, a prompt to install them appears when you access the site. After Windows Update scans your system and locates update packages and new versions of drivers and system files, it offers you the option of selecting files for download.

In addition to the information in this chapter, other important sources of information about Windows 2000 are the Microsoft Web site at *support.microsoft.com* and the *Windows 2000 Professional Resource Kit* by Microsoft Press. The *Resource Kit* includes a CD that contains additional Windows 2000 utilities. These resources can

A+
OS
2.2
3.2

further help you understand Windows 2000 and solve problems with the OS. Also remember that user manuals are an excellent source of information, as well as the Web, training manuals, and product installation documentation.

Because ActiveX controls have open access to the Windows operating system, there is some risk of an ActiveX control causing damage to data or software on your computer. Some system administrators require that ActiveX controls be disabled when they are not specifically needed for tasks such as Windows Update downloads.

In addition to the support tools described here, third-party diagnostic software can be of help. For example, ConfigSafe by imagineLAN, Inc. (*www.imaginelan.com*) is a utility that tracks configuration changes to Windows 9x or Windows NT/2000/XP and can restore the system to a previously saved configuration.

CHAPTER SUMMARY

▶ The boot process for Windows NT, Windows 2000, and Windows XP works the same under each OS, although the tools to troubleshoot a failed boot are slightly different for each OS.

▶ The boot process can be customized with entries in Boot.ini. The Boot.ini file can be edited with a text editor, but it is best to change the file using the System Properties dialog box.

▶ Tools to use to troubleshoot problems with loading Windows 2000 are the Advanced Options menu, the Recovery Console, and the Emergency Repair Process.

▶ To access the Advanced Options menu, press F8 when starting Windows 2000.

▶ The Advanced Options menu includes Safe Mode, Safe Mode with Networking, Safe Mode with Command Prompt, Enable Boot Logging, Enable VGA Mode, Last Known Good Configuration, Directory Services Restore Mode, and Debugging Mode.

▶ The Recovery Console is a command interface with a limited number of commands available to troubleshoot a failing Windows 2000 load. The console requires that you enter the Administrator password.

▶ Access the Recovery Console by first booting from the Windows 2000 CD or from the four setup disks, or install the console under the boot loader menu and access it from there.

▶ Using the Recovery Console, you can restore the registry to the state it was in at the time of the last backup of the registry.

▶ The Emergency Repair Process lets you restore the system to its state at the end of the Windows 2000 installation. Don't use it unless all other methods fail, because you will lose all changes made to the system since the installation. The Emergency Repair Process requires the emergency repair disk.

▶ Back up the Windows 2000 system state on a regular basis using the Backup utility. This backup includes system files, files to load the OS, and the registry. Back up the system state before editing the registry.

▶ Windows 2000 Support Tools can be installed from the Windows 2000 CD and include several utilities to support hardware and applications.

▶ Windows File Protection (WFP) protects the system files against an application, a virus, or a user changing or deleting them. System File Checker is part of the WFP system.

▶ Disk Management is a tool found in the Computer Management console. Disk Management replaces Fdisk in older Windows OSs, and is used to partition and format a hard drive and to convert a basic disk to a dynamic disk.

▶ Microsoft Management Console (MMC) can be used to create customized consoles to manage the OS.

▶ Event Viewer is used to view system, application, and security events.

▶ When monitoring performance, begin by establishing a baseline that helps determine what performance should be expected of a system.

▶ Task Manager is used to measure performance, giving information about the processor, memory, the hard drive, and virtual memory.

▶ System Monitor gives more detail than Task Manager, and can be used to monitor object and instance performance over time by using counters that you select for monitoring.

▶ Information about application errors and stop errors can be recorded by Dr. Watson and memory dumps.

▶ Windows Update uses the Microsoft Web site to download patches and fixes to Microsoft OSs and applications.

▶ Additional sources of support for Windows 2000 include the Microsoft support Web site at *support.microsoft.com* and the *Windows 2000 Professional Resource Kit* by Microsoft.

KEY TERMS

For explanations of key terms, see the Glossary near the end of the book.

32-bit flat memory mode	dump file	Recovery Console
Advanced Options menu	Emergency Repair Process	SFC (System File Checker)
baseline	memory dump	snap-ins
Boot.ini	Microsoft Management Console (MMC)	stop error
console	minifile system	WFP (Windows File Protection)
Disk Management		

REVIEWING THE BASICS

1. In the Windows NT/2000/XP boot process, what file reads and loads the boot menu?

2. Where is the Boot.ini file stored?

3. What does %SystemRoot% mean?

4. List the steps to restore the Windows 2000 system state from the backup made with the Backup utility.

5. In what folder does Windows 2000 store a backup of the registry when backing up the system state?

6. Under what circumstances would you use the Enable VGA Mode option on the Advanced Options menu?

7. What key do you press to display the Advanced Options menu during startup?

8. When you look at a Windows desktop, how can you tell if the system has been booted into Safe Mode?

9. What is the purpose of Safe Mode with Networking under the Advanced Options menu?

10. What is the name of the log file that Windows 2000 uses when booting in Safe Mode?

11. List the steps to load the Recovery Console when using the four Windows 2000 rescue disks.

12. Why is the Administrator password required in order to use the Recovery Console?

13. In Question 12, under what circumstances is the password not required?

14. What is the purpose of the Systemroot command under the Recovery Console?

15. Under the Recovery Console, what is the command that gives the same results as Fdisk/MBR?

16. What is the command to install the Recovery Console on the boot loader menu?

17. Before you can perform the Windows 2000 Emergency Repair Process, what disk must you have? What is contained on the disk?

18. When would you use System File Checker? What is the command to execute it?

19. What is the command to install the Windows 2000 Support Tools?

20. What is the name of the log file created by Dr. Watson?

21. Name two Windows utilities that can be used to monitor OS performance.

22. What tool can you use to create a console containing Device Manager and Event Viewer?

23. What is the file extension assigned to a console file?

24. Name one snap-in contained in the Computer Management console.

25. What is the program filename for System File Checker?

26. List three ways to access the Task Manager.

27. List the steps used to end an application when it refuses to respond to keystrokes or the mouse action.

28. What are the three logs kept by Event Viewer?

29. In what folder do you put a console file that you want displayed when you are logged on as an administrator and then click Start, Programs, and Administrative Tools?

30. Before clearing the Event Viewer log, explain how you can save the log for later viewing.

THINKING CRITICALLY

1. Your Windows 2000 system boots to a blue screen and no desktop. What do you do first?

    a. Reinstall Windows 2000.

    b. Attempt to boot into the Advanced Options menu.

    c. Attempt to boot into the Recovery Console.

    d. Attempt to use the Emergency Repair Process.

2. You were unable to use the Emergency Repair Process to restore a failed Windows 2000 system, but there is a very important data file on the hard drive that you need to recover. The hard drive is using the NTFS file system. What do you do?

   a. Boot using a Windows 98 startup disk and use the Copy command to attempt to recover the file.

   b. Boot to the Recovery Console using the Windows 2000 setup CD and attempt to recover the file.

   c. Reinstall Windows 2000 and then recover the file.

   d. Boot to the Advanced Options menu and use Safe Mode to recover the file.

3. You need to install a customized console on 10 computers. What is the best way to do that?

   a. When installing the console on the first computer, write down each step to make it easier to do the same chore on the other nine.

   b. Create the console on one computer and copy the .mmc file to the other nine.

   c. Create the console on one computer and copy the .msc file to the other nine.

HANDS-ON PROJECTS

HANDS-ON PROJECTS

PROJECT 6-1: **Using the Microsoft Knowledge Base**

Using the Microsoft support Web site (*support.microsoft.com*), print information about the following:

▸ Troubleshooting IEEE 1394 devices running under Windows 2000 Professional

▸ How to set up Windows 2000 to support multiple CPUs

▸ How to set up and troubleshoot multiple monitors with Windows 2000 Professional

PROJECT 6-2: **Using DiskProbe to Back Up the MBR**

Windows 2000 DiskProbe edits individual sectors on a hard drive and can edit the MBR, boot sectors, and the FAT16, FAT32, and NTFS file system tables, as well as data files. Research DiskProbe and find directions that show you how to back up the MBR, which contains the partition table. Follow these directions and answer these questions:

1. In the C:\ProgramFiles\Support Tools folder, find the document Dskprtrb.doc, which describes how to use DiskProbe. Print the page from the document that describes how to save the MBR record on a floppy disk.

2. If the Windows 2000 Support Tools are not installed, install them now.

3. Run DiskProbe (click **Start,** point to **Programs, Windows 2000 Support Tools,** and **Tools,** and then click **DiskProbe**).

4. Follow the directions to save the MBR, including the partition table, to a floppy disk.

5. How many bytes of data are included in the MBR? What is the file size?

6. What is the disadvantage of using DiskProbe to restore the MBR in the event it becomes corrupted?

PROJECT 6-3: **Creating a Windows 2000 Antivirus Boot Disk**

Windows 2000 offers an antivirus program that can scan memory, the MBR sector, and OS boot sectors for viruses. Follow these directions to create the boot disk and scan your system for viruses. Use the disk when you suspect that a virus has attacked your Windows 2000 hard drive.

1. Insert the Windows 2000 CD in the CD-ROM drive, and insert an empty floppy disk in the floppy disk drive.

2. Click **Start** and then click **Run.** In the Run dialog box, enter the following command, substituting the drive letter of your CD-ROM drive for D, if necessary: **D:\VALUEADD\3RDPARTY\CA_ANTIV\Makedisk.bat**

3. Label the disk Windows 2000 AVBoot.

4. Boot from the floppy disk. When the scan finishes, Windows 2000 automatically loads.

Note: If your PC is not set to boot from a floppy disk before booting from the hard drive, change the boot sequence in CMOS setup.

PROJECT 6-4: Using Dependency Walker

Follow these steps to use Dependency Walker to list the files used by Internet Explorer:

1. If the Windows 2000 Support Tools are not installed, install them now.

2. Run Dependency Walker (click **Start**, point to **Programs, Windows 2000 Support Tools,** and **Tools,** and then click **Dependency Walker**).

3. Set Dependency Walker to show all supporting files used by Internet Explorer.

4. List the files or print the screen showing them.

PROJECT 6-5: Creating Baselines for Your System

A+ EXAM TIP

The A+ OS exam expects you to know filenames of Windows utility programs so that you can run the utility from a command prompt.

In this chapter, you learned about several tools you can use to establish baselines for a system before a problem occurs. One tool to help establish a baseline is the boot log. Using the Windows 2000 Advanced Options menu, boot with Enable Boot Logging. Print the Ntbtlog.txt file created. Then boot with Safe Mode. Again print the Ntbtlog.txt file. Compare the two files and mark the differences. Keep these two reports in case you ever have problems booting this system, because they can provide a picture of what a normal boot should be.

PROJECT 6-6: Finding Windows 2000 Utilities

The following table lists some important Windows utilities covered in this chapter. Fill in the right side of the table with the filename and path of each utility. (*Hint*: You can use Windows Explorer or Search to locate files.)

Utility	Filename and Path
System File Checker	
Disk Defragmenter	
Command window	
Chkdsk	
System Information	
Task Manager	

Installing and Using Windows XP Professional

In this chapter, you will learn:

- About the features and architecture of Windows XP
- How to install Windows XP
- How to use Windows XP
- How to install hardware and applications with Windows XP

Windows XP is the latest generation of Microsoft operating systems. Windows XP currently comes in several varieties: Windows XP Professional, Windows XP Home Edition, Windows XP Media Center Edition, Windows XP Tablet PC Edition, and Windows XP 64-Bit Edition. This chapter focuses on Windows XP Professional, which is the upgrade from Windows 2000 Professional. Features of Windows XP that you already learned about in chapters on earlier versions of Windows are not covered in detail, where they have not changed in Windows XP; more discussion is given to new features or changes to existing ones. This chapter builds the foundation you will need to manage and provide technical support for Windows XP, the focus of the next chapter.

Features and Architecture of Windows XP

Windows XP integrates features of Windows 9x and Windows 2000, while providing added support for multimedia and networking technologies. The look and feel of Windows XP differs slightly from its predecessors, and utilities and functions are organized differently under menus and windows. You'll learn about many of these differences in this chapter.

NOTE   Windows XP is replacing all previous versions of Windows in the home market and for the corporate desktop. If your hardware and applications qualify, select Windows XP Home Edition for a home PC over Windows 98/Me. For a corporate environment, choose Windows XP Professional over Windows NT/2000. The only possible trouble with switching operating systems is compatibility issues with older hardware and software.

Windows XP Features

Windows XP Home Edition and Windows XP Professional have these features, among others:

- A new user interface, shown in Figure 7-1. Notice how different it looks from the desktops of earlier Windows versions such as Windows 98 and Windows 2000.
- The ability for two or more users to be logged on simultaneously. Each user has a separate profile, and Windows XP can switch between users, keeping a separate set of applications open for each user.
- Windows Media Player for Windows XP, a centralized application for working with digital media
- Windows Messenger for instant messaging, conferencing, and application sharing
- The ability to burn a CD simply by dragging and dropping a folder or file onto the CD-R device icon
- An expanded Help feature
- Advanced security features

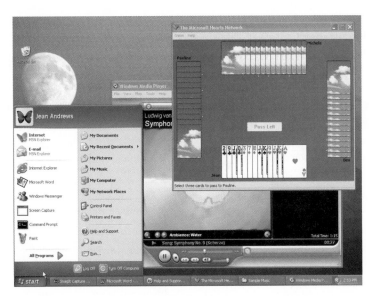

7

Figure 7-1 The Windows XP desktop and Start menu

In addition to these features of Windows XP Home Edition, Windows XP Professional offers:

- A way for someone to remotely control your computer, called Remote Desktop
- A way for an administrator to manage user profiles from a server (roaming profiles)
- Additional security features
- Multilingual capabilities
- Support for new higher-performance processors

Windows XP Media Center Edition is an enhanced version of Windows XP Professional, and includes additional support for digital entertainment hardware such as video recording integrated with TV input. It's designed for the high-end PC home market and is only available when preinstalled on a high-end PC manufactured by a Microsoft partner. Windows XP Tablet PC Edition is also built on Windows XP Professional with additional support for tablet PCs.

There is also Windows XP 64-Bit Edition, designed to be used with a high-end 64-bit CPU such as the Intel Itanium or AMD Opteron. This Windows XP version is designed mostly for servers or heavily technical workstations that run scientific and engineering applications and need greater amounts of memory and higher performance than standard desktop PCs. For example, an aircraft designer who uses software to simulate how various conditions affect aircraft materials might use Windows XP 64-Bit Edition on a system that supports resource-intensive simulation and animation applications.

Windows Internet Explorer, Windows Media Player, a firewall, and other Microsoft products are tightly integrated with the Windows XP operating system. Some users see this as a disadvantage, and others see it as an advantage. Tight integration allows applications to interact easily with other applications and the OS, but makes it more difficult for third-party software to compete with Microsoft applications.

Windows XP provides several enhancements over Windows 2000 and other earlier versions. Table 7-1 summarizes the advantages and disadvantages of Windows XP.

Advantages	Disadvantages
Provides better integration of Windows 9x and NT than Windows 2000 did	Requires nearly a gigabyte of hard drive space for the operating system itself, and at least a 233-MHz processor with 64 MB of RAM
Offers significant GUI enhancements over earlier versions of Windows	Programs used with Windows XP may need more than the minimum system requirements for the operating system
Adds features but uses only slightly more total memory for the OS than Windows 2000	Nearly eliminates support for device drivers not approved by Microsoft
Adds advanced file sorting options, such as sorting pictures by resolution or sound files by artist	Security concerns with centralized storage of online information in Microsoft Passport, a repository of the user IDs and passwords you use on the Internet
Includes built-in support for compressed files	
Has improved troubleshooting tools and is generally more stable than previous Windows OSs	

Table 7-1   Advantages and disadvantages of Windows XP

Windows XP Architecture

Windows XP uses the same kernel architecture as Windows NT and Windows 2000, with components operating in either user mode or kernel mode. Figure 7-2 shows how the different OS components relate. Notice in the figure that some low-level device drivers such as those that access the hard drive have direct access to hardware, just as they do with Windows NT and Windows 2000. All 16-bit and 32-bit applications relate to the kernel by way of the Win32 subsystem operating in user mode. As you will learn in the next chapter, the boot process is also the same, and the files needed for a successful boot are the same as those for Windows NT/2000.

Windows XP is generally more stable than Windows NT and Windows 2000. It was designed to avoid situations that occurred with Windows NT/2000, which caused drivers and applications to bring these systems down. Installing Windows XP should also be easier than installing Windows NT or Windows 2000. In addition, Windows XP has increased security, including a built-in Internet firewall designed to protect a home PC connected directly to the Internet by way of an always-on

A+
OS
1.1

connection such as a cable modem or DSL. Firewalls, cable modems, and DSL are covered in Chapters 11 and 12.

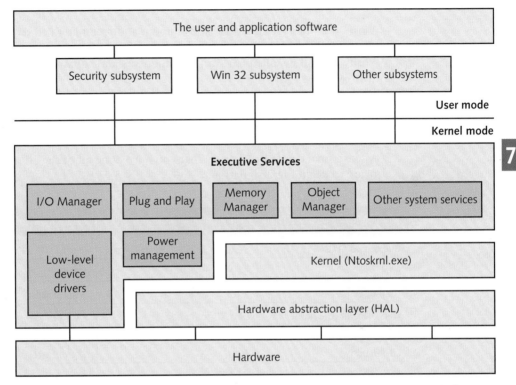

Figure 7-2 The Windows XP architecture uses the same basic structure and components as Windows NT and Windows 2000

Installing Windows XP

A+
OS
2.1
2.2

Installing Windows XP involves many of the same considerations and decisions that you learned about when installing Windows 2000. In this section, you learn how to install Windows XP as a clean install and as an upgrade, including how to set up a dual boot.

Planning the Installation

A+
OS
2.1
2.2

Before installing Windows XP, do the following:

- Verify that the system meets the minimum and recommended requirements shown in Table 7-2.
- Verify that all installed hardware components and software are compatible with Windows XP.
- Decide how you will partition your hard drive and what file system you will use.
- For a PC on a network, decide whether the PC will be configured as a workstation in a workgroup or as part of a domain. (Workgroups and domains were covered in Chapter 5.)
- Make a final checklist to verify that you have done all of the above and are ready to begin the installation.

Component or Device	Minimum Requirement	Recommended Requirement
One or two CPUs	Pentium II 233 MHz or better	Pentium II 300 MHz or better
RAM	64 MB	128 MB up to 4 GB
Hard drive partition	2 GB	2 GB or more
Free space on the hard drive partition	640 MB (bare bones)	2 GB or more
CD-ROM drive	12x	12x or faster
Accessories	Keyboard and mouse or other pointing device	Keyboard and mouse or other pointing device

Table 7-2 Minimum and recommended requirements for Windows XP Professional

Remember that the requirements of an OS vary depending on which version you have installed and what applications and hardware you have installed with it.

NOTE

APPLYING CONCEPTS

Minimum Requirements and Hardware Compatibility

Recall from earlier chapters that you can use the My Computer icon on the Windows desktop to determine the current CPU and available RAM. To see how much hard drive space is available, open Windows Explorer, right-click the drive letter, and select Properties from the shortcut menu. Part of the installation process for an upgrade is to clean up the hard drive, which might free some hard drive space. Even though Windows XP requires only 640 MB to install, you cannot achieve acceptable results unless you have at least 1.5 GB of free hard drive space on the volume that holds Windows XP.

There are several ways you can verify that software and hardware qualify for Windows XP. One way is to run the Readiness Analyzer. Use the following command from the Windows XP CD, substituting the drive letter of your CD-ROM drive for D in the command line, if necessary:

```
D:\I386\Winnt32 /checkupgradeonly
```

Depending on the release of Windows XP, your path might be different. The process takes about 10 minutes to run and displays a report that you can save and later print. The default name and path of the report is C:\Windows\compat.txt. The report is important if you have software you are not sure will work under Windows XP. If the analyzer reports that your software will not work under Windows XP, you might choose to upgrade the software or set up a dual boot with your old OS and Windows XP. (Dual-boot setup is covered later in the chapter.)

Readiness Analyzer also checks hardware compatibility. Another way to verify your hardware is to go to the Microsoft Web site and search on each hardware device by type. The process is different from that of Windows 2000. Begin at the Windows Catalog page (*www.microsoft.com/windows/catalog*). Click the Hardware tab. A list of hardware device categories appears on the left side of the screen. Select a category or use the search utility on the page. Figure 7-3 shows the beginning of the list of qualifying modem cards. There might be a copy of the Windows XP Professional HCL in the hcl.txt file on the Windows XP CD in the support folder. But for the most up-to-date information, use the Microsoft Web site.

If your hardware does not qualify for Windows XP, check the hardware manufacturer's Web site for an upgrade and download the upgraded drivers before you begin the installation. If you plan to erase the hard drive as part of the installation, store these drivers on floppy disks or on a network drive until you're ready to install them under Windows XP. If you cannot find an upgrade, sometimes a device will work if you substitute a Windows driver written for a similar device. Check the documentation for your device, looking for information about other devices it can emulate. It is especially important to know that your network card or modem card qualifies for Windows XP before you install the OS, because you need the card to access the Internet to get upgrades. If you are not sure an important hardware component qualifies, then install Windows XP as a dual boot with your current OS. Later, when you get the component working under Windows XP, you can uninstall the other OS.

7

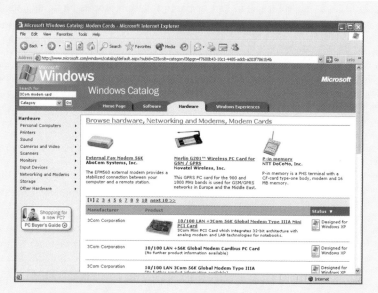

Figure 7-3   To see if your hardware device qualifies for Windows XP, search by hardware category, manufacturer name, or product name

Hard Drive Partitions and File Systems

Windows XP needs at least a 2-GB partition for the installation and should have about 1.5 GB of free space on that partition. You can install Windows XP on the same partition as another OS, but Windows XP overwrites the existing OS on that partition. If you do not have a free 2-GB partition for the installation, you must delete smaller partitions and repartition the drive. Deleting a partition erases all data on it, so be sure to create backups first. Follow these general directions to ensure that partitions on the hard drive are adequate to install Windows XP:

- For Windows 9x, use Fdisk at the command prompt, and for Windows 2000, use Disk Management to determine what partitions are on the drive, how large they are, what logical drives are assigned to them, and how much free space on the drive is not yet partitioned.
- If existing partitions are too small, look at the free space on the drive. If there is enough free space that is not yet partitioned, use that free space to create a new partition that is at least 2 GB.

- If you cannot create a 2-GB or larger partition, back up your data, delete the smaller partitions, and create a 2-GB or larger active partition on the drive.
- If you have free space on the drive for other partitions, don't partition them at this time. First install Windows XP and then use Disk Management under Windows XP to partition the remaining free space on the drive.

The same concerns about selecting a file system for Windows 2000 apply to Windows XP. The file systems supported by Windows XP are the same as those supported by Windows 2000: FAT16, FAT32, and NTFS. Recall that the NTFS file system used by Windows 2000 is incompatible with the Windows NT NTFS file system, causing a potential problem when installing Windows 2000 and Windows NT on the same PC as a dual boot. Because the Windows XP NTFS file system is the same as the Windows 2000 NTFS file system, a dual boot between these two OSs should be no problem. Here are the general directions for selecting a file system:

- Use the NTFS file system if you are interested in file and folder security, file compression, control over how much disk space a user is allowed, or file encryption.
- Use the FAT32 file system if you are setting up a dual boot with Windows 9x and each OS must access all partitions.
- Use the FAT16 file system if you are setting up a dual boot with MS-DOS or Windows NT and each OS must access all partitions.

Joining a Workgroup or a Domain

If you are installing Windows XP on a network, you must decide how you will access the network. If you have fewer than 10 computers networked together, Microsoft recommends that you join these computers in a workgroup, in which each computer controls its own resources. In this case, each user account is set up on the local computer, independently from user accounts on other PCs. There is no centralized control of resources. For more than 10 computers, Microsoft recommends that you use a domain controller running a network operating system such as Windows Server 2003 to control network resources. (Windows XP Professional installed on a workstation can then be a client on this Windows network.) You will also want to use a domain controller if you want to administer and secure the network from a centralized location, or if several centralized resources on the network are shared by many users. How to manage workgroups is covered in Chapter 11, but managing a domain controller is beyond the scope of this book.

NOTE

Windows XP Home Edition does not support joining a domain. If you plan to use a domain controller on your network, install Windows XP Professional.

7

Upgrade or Clean Install?

If you plan to set up a dual boot, then you will perform a clean install for Windows XP. If you already have an OS installed and you do not plan a dual boot, then you have a choice between an upgrade and a clean install. Things to consider when making this decision are:

- You can use the less expensive upgrade version of Windows XP Professional to upgrade from Windows 98, Windows Me, Windows NT 4.0, and Windows 2000 to Windows XP Professional.
- You can use the less expensive upgrade version of Windows XP Home Edition to upgrade from Windows 98 or Windows Me to Windows XP Home Edition.
- If you currently have Windows 95 installed, you must do a clean install using the more expensive "For a New PC" version of Windows XP Professional or Windows XP Home Edition.
- Regardless of whether you have an OS currently installed, you can still choose to do a clean install if you want a fresh start. Unless you erase your hard drive, reformat it, or delete partitions before the upgrade, data on the hard drive is not erased even if you convert to a new file system during the installation. However , OS settings and installed software do not carry forward into the new installation.

Final Checklist

Before you begin the installation, complete the final checklist shown in Table 7-3 to verify that you are ready.

Things to Do	Further Information
Does the PC meet the minimum or recommended hardware requirement?	CPU: RAM: Hard drive size: Free space on the hard drive:
Have you run the Readiness Analyzer or checked the Microsoft Web site to verify that all your hardware and software qualify?	List hardware and software that need to be upgraded:
Do you have the product key available?	Product key:
Have you decided how you will join a network?	Workgroup name: Domain name: Computer name:

Table 7-3 (continued)

Things to Do	Further Information
Will you do an upgrade or clean install?	Current operating system:
	Does the old OS qualify for an upgrade?
Is your hard drive ready?	Size of the hard drive partition:
	Free space on the partition:
	File system you plan to use:
For a clean install, will you set up a dual boot?	List reasons for a dual boot:
	For a dual boot
	Size of the second partition:
	Free space on the second partition:
	File system you plan to use:
Have you backed up important data on your hard drive?	Location of backup:

Table 7-3   Checklist to complete before installing Windows XP

Installation Process

Follow these general directions to perform a clean install of Windows XP on a PC that does not already have an OS installed:

1. Boot from the Windows XP CD, which displays the menu shown in Figure 7-4. This menu might change slightly from one Windows XP release to another. Select the first option and press Enter. If your PC does not boot from a CD, go to a command prompt and enter the command **D:\i386\Winnt.exe**, substituting the drive letter of your CD-ROM drive for D, if necessary. (The path might vary depending on the release of Windows XP.) The End-User License agreement appears. Accept the agreement.

2. Setup lists all partitions that it finds on the hard drive, the file system of each partition, and the size of the partition. It also lists any unpartitioned free space on the drive. From this screen, you can create and delete partitions and select the partition on which you want to install Windows XP. If you plan to have more than one partition on the drive, create only one partition at this time. The partition must be at least 2 GB in size and have 1.5 GB free. After the installation, you can use Disk Management to create the other partitions. Figure 7-5 shows an example of the list provided by Setup when the entire hard drive has not yet been partitioned.

```
Windows XP Professional Setup
=========================

    Welcome to Setup.

    This portion of the Setup program prepares Microsoft ( R )
    Windows ( R ) XP to run on your computer.

        •    To set up Windows XP now, press ENTER.

        •    To repair a Windows XP installation using Recovery Console,
             press R.

        •    To quit Setup without installing Windows XP, press F3.


ENTER=Continue  R=Repair  F3=Quit
```

Figure 7-4   Windows XP Setup opening menu

3. If you created a partition in Step 2, Setup asks which file system you want to use to format the partition, NTFS or FAT. If the partition is at least 2 GB in size, the FAT file system will be FAT32. Select a file system for the partition. The Setup program formats the drive, completes the text-based portion of setup, and loads the graphical interface for the rest of the installation. The PC then restarts.

4. Select your geographical location from the list provided. Windows XP will use it to decide how to display dates, times, numbers, and currency. Select your keyboard layout. Different keyboards can be used to accommodate special characters for other languages.

5. Enter your name, the name of your organization, and your product key.

6. Enter the computer name and the password for the Administrator account. This password is stored in the security database on this PC. If you are joining a domain, the computer name is the name assigned to this computer by the network administrator managing the domain controller.

It is *very* important that you remember the Administrator password. You cannot log on to the system without it.

7. Select the date, time, and time zone. The PC might reboot.

A+
OS
2.1
2.2

```
Windows XP Professional Setup
==========================

    The following list shows the existing partitions and
    unpartitioned space on this computer.

    Use the UP and DOWN ARROW keys to select an item in the list.

        •   To set up Windows XP on the selected item, press ENTER.

        •   To create a partition in the unpartitioned space, press C.

        •   To delete the selected partition, press D.


    ┌──────────────────────────────────────────────────────┐
    │  28663 MB Disk 0 at Id 0 on bus 0 on atapi [MBR]     │
    │                                                      │
    │    Unpartitioned space                  28663 MB    │
    │                                                      │
    │                                                      │
    │                                                      │
    └──────────────────────────────────────────────────────┘



  ENTER=Install     C=Create Partition     F3=Quit
```

Figure 7-5   During Setup, you can create and delete partitions and select a partition on which to install Windows XP

8. If you are connected to a network, you will be asked to choose how to config-ure your network settings. The Typical setting installs Client for Microsoft Networks, File and Printer Sharing, and TCP/IP using dynamically assigned IP addresses. The Custom setting allows you to configure the network differently. If you are not sure which to use, choose the Typical settings. You can change them later. How networks are configured is covered in Chapter 11.

9. Enter a workgroup or domain name. If you are joining a domain, the network administrator will have given you specific directions on how to configure user accounts on the domain.

NOTE   During a normal Windows XP installation, setup causes the system to reboot three times.

For a clean install on a PC that already has an OS installed, follow these general directions:

1. Close any open applications. Close any boot management software or antivirus software that might be running in the background.

2. Insert the Windows XP CD in the CD-ROM drive. Autorun launches the opening window shown in Figure 7-6.

3. Select the option to **Install Windows XP**. On the next screen, under Installation Type, select **New Installation**. Read and accept the licensing agreement. The installation process works the same as in the preceding procedure, resuming with Step 3.

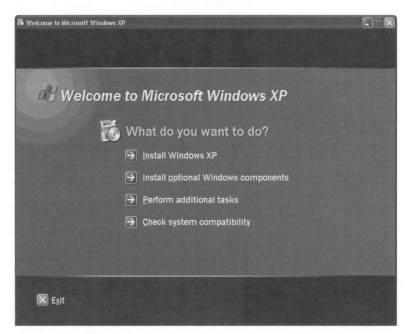

Figure 7-6   Windows XP Setup menu

When performing an upgrade to Windows XP, follow these general directions:

1. Before you begin the installation, do the following to prepare the system:

   ▪ Clean up the hard drive: erase unneeded or temporary files, empty the Recycle Bin, run Disk Defragmenter, and do a ScanDisk of the drive.
   ▪ If you have determined that you must upgrade hardware or software and that these upgrades are compatible with your old OS, perform the upgrades and verify that the hardware or software is working.
   ▪ If you do not have the latest BIOS for your motherboard, flash your BIOS.

A+
OS
2.1
2.2

- Back up important files.
- Scan the hard drive for viruses using a current version of antivirus software.
- If you have a compressed hard drive, uncompress the drive. The only exception is that if you are using Windows NT file compression on an NTFS drive, you do not need to uncompress it.
- Uninstall any hardware or software that you know is not compatible with Windows XP and for which you have no available upgrade.

2. Insert the Windows XP Upgrade CD in the CD-ROM drive. The Autorun feature should launch the Setup program, with the menu shown in Figure 7-6. Select the option to **Install Windows XP**.

3. If the Setup menu does not appear, you can enter the Setup command in the Run dialog box. Recall that the command is D:\i386\Winnt.exe, where you substitute the drive letter of your CD-ROM drive for D, if necessary.

4. On the next screen, under Installation Type, select **Upgrade**. The menu gives you two options:

- *Express Upgrade*. This upgrade uses existing Windows folders and all the existing settings it can.
- *Custom Upgrade*. This upgrade allows you to change the installation folder and the language options. Using this option, you can also change the file system to NTFS.

5. Select the type of upgrade, and accept the licensing agreement.

6. Select the partition on which to install Windows XP. If the drive is configured as FAT and you want to convert to NTFS, specify that now. Note that Windows XP has an uninstall utility that allows you to revert to Windows 98 if necessary. This uninstall tool does not work if you convert FAT to NTFS.

7. Setup performs an analysis of the system and reports any compatibility problems. Stop the installation if the problems indicate that you will not be able to operate the system after the installation.

8. For an upgrade from Windows 98 or Windows Me to Windows XP, the Setup program converts whatever information it can in the registry to Windows XP. At the end of the installation process, you are given the opportunity to join a domain. For Windows NT and Windows 2000 upgrades, almost all registry entries are carried forward into the new OS; the information about a domain is not requested because it is copied from the old OS into Windows XP.

7

Upgrading from Windows NT or Windows 2000 to Windows XP is the easiest type of upgrade because these operating systems all have similar registries and support applications and devices in the same way. Nearly all applications that run on Windows NT or Windows 2000 will run on Windows XP. When you upgrade from Windows NT to Windows XP, the NTFS file system is automatically converted to the Windows XP version.

> Antivirus software designed to be used with the Windows NT NTFS file system might not run under the Windows XP NTFS file system because of the way some antivirus programs filter software as it accesses the file system. You might have to upgrade your antivirus software after Windows XP is installed.

Setting Up a Dual Boot

You can configure Windows XP to set up a dual boot with another operating system. Start the installation as you would for a clean install on a PC with another operating system already installed. When given the opportunity, choose to install Windows XP on a different partition than the other OS. Windows XP recognizes that another OS is installed and sets up the startup menu to offer it as an option for booting. After the installation, when you boot with a dual boot, the **boot loader menu** automatically appears and asks you to select an operating system, as shown in Figure 7-7.

> ✔ **A+ EXAM TIP**
>
> The A+ OS exam expects you to be familiar with a dual boot and how to set one up.

The first active partition (drive C) must be set up with a file system that both operating systems understand. For example, for a dual boot with Windows 98, use the FAT32 file system. For a dual boot with Windows 2000, use either the FAT32 or the NTFS file system. You should install the other operating system first, and then you can install Windows XP in a different partition. When you install Windows XP on another active partition or an extended partition, it places only the files necessary to boot in the first active partition, which it calls the system partition. This causes Windows XP to initiate the boot rather than the other OS. The rest of Windows XP is installed on a second partition, which Windows XP calls the boot partition. This is the same way that Windows NT and Windows 2000 manage a dual boot with an older OS.

> When setting up a dual boot, always install the older operating system first.

Earlier Windows operating systems were not aware of applications installed under the other OS in a dual boot. For example, in a dual boot with Windows 98 and Windows 2000, an application had to be installed twice, once under Windows 98 and once under Windows 2000. However, Windows XP is able to use an application installed under the other OS in a dual boot. For example, if you set up a dual boot with Windows XP and Windows 98, an application installed under Windows 98 can be executed from Windows XP. This application might be listed under the Start menu of Windows XP. If it is not, you can use Windows XP Explorer to locate the program file. Double-click the application to run it from Windows XP. This makes implementing a dual boot easier because you don't have to install an application under both OSs.

Please select the operating system to start:

   Microsoft Windows XP Professional
   Microsoft Windows 98

Use the up and down arrow keys to move the highlight to your choice.
Seconds until highlighted choice will be started automatically: xx
Press ENTER to choose.

For troubleshooting and advanced startup options for Windows, press F8.

Figure 7-7   Menu displayed for a dual boot

After the Installation

Immediately after you have installed Windows XP, there are several things to do to activate the OS, prepare it for use, and back up the hard drive in preparation for a disaster. These steps are discussed next.

Product Activation

Product activation is a method used by Microsoft to prevent unlicensed use of its software so that you must purchase a Windows XP license for each installation of Windows XP. The license was introduced with Microsoft Office XP, and Microsoft says it will continue using product activation in all future Microsoft products. The first time you log on to the system after the installation, the Activate Windows dialog box appears with these three options (see Figure 7-8):

- Yes, let's activate Windows over the Internet now
- Yes, I want to telephone a customer service representative to activate Windows
- No, remind me to activate Windows every few days

If you choose to activate Windows over the Internet and are connected to the Internet at the time, the process is almost instant. Windows XP sends a numeric identifier to a Microsoft server, which sends a certificate activating the product on your PC. You have up to 30 days after installation to activate Windows XP; after that the system will not boot. If you install Windows XP from the same CD on a different computer and you attempt to activate Windows from the new PC, a dialog box appears telling you of the suspected violation of the license agreement. You can call a Microsoft operator and explain what caused the discrepancy. If your explanation is reasonable (for example, you uninstalled Windows XP from one PC and installed it on another), the operator can issue you a valid certificate. You can then type the certificate value into a dialog box to complete the boot process.

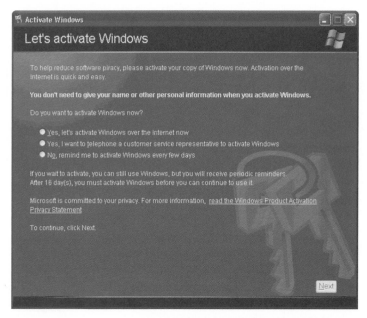

Figure 7-8   Product activation is a strategy used by Microsoft to prevent software piracy

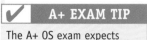 **A+ EXAM TIP**

The A+ OS exam expects you to know that it's important to install service packs and additional Windows components after you have installed an OS.

Now access the Internet and download any service packs, updates, or patches for the OS from the Microsoft Web site. You can also install any additional Windows components at this time.

Transferring User Files and Preferences to a New PC

Windows XP offers a utility that helps you transfer user files and preferences from one computer to another that has just had Windows XP installed. The **User State Migration Tool (USMT)** transfers user files and folders, display properties, taskbar options, and browser and email settings from a Windows 9x or Windows NT/2000/XP computer. This utility can help make a smooth transition because a user who is moving from one PC to another does not have to copy files and reconfigure OS settings. The process involves three steps:

1. Use a Windows XP computer to create a disk that contains the Files and Settings Transfer Wizard. This PC does not need to be the same PC that will later receive the transfer.

2. Use the disk on the source computer (the user's old computer) to run the wizard and copy the user state to a server hard drive or removable media such as a Zip drive.

3. On the destination computer (the user's new computer), use the wizard to transfer the user state to this computer.

To begin the process, use the Files and Settings Transfer Wizard to create the disk. To access the wizard, click Start, All Programs, Accessories, System Tools, and Files and Settings Transfer Wizard. The wizard's Welcome window opens. When you click Next, the wizard asks if this is the New computer or Old computer. Select New computer and then click Next. Figure 7-9 shows the next screen, with which you can choose to create the disk or declare that you are ready to put the information on the new computer. On the screen, note that you can also use the Windows XP CD to launch the wizard on the old computer rather than creating the disk.

After you have created the disk or chosen to use the Windows XP CD, go to the old computer, launch the wizard, and retrieve the files and settings. Then return to this screen on the new computer, and choose to put the information on the new computer.

Instead of using the wizard, you can also use two commands at the command prompt. Scanstate copies the information to a server or removable media, and Loadstate copies the information to the destination computer. These utilities can be included in batch files and executed automatically when implementing Windows XP over a large number of computers in an enterprise. For details on how to use the command lines in a batch file, see the *Windows XP Resource Kit* by Microsoft Press.

7

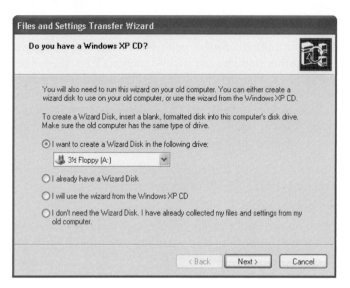

Figure 7-9   The first step in using the Files and Settings Transfer Wizard is to create the wizard disk

Preparing for Later Problems with the OS

After the installation is complete, hardware and software are installed, and user preferences are set, it is a good idea to guard against later problems with the OS by creating a backup of the hard drive. Windows XP offers a utility called **Automated System Recovery (ASR)** that allows you to restore an entire hard drive volume or logical drive to its state at the time the backup of the volume was made. This process creates the backup and creates an ASR floppy disk that allows you to use the backup to recover the system later. You will learn how to recover a failed system using a backup in the next chapter. In this section, you learn how to create the backup.

The backup file created will be just as large as the contents of the hard drive volume, so you will need a massive backup medium such as another partition on the same hard drive, on another local hard drive or file server, a tape drive, or a writeable CD-R or CD-RW drive.

CAUTION

Do not back up the logical drive or volume to a folder on the same volume. The ASR backup process allows you to do this, but restoring later from this backup does not work. Also, to better protect your installation, back up to a different hard drive or other media.

NOTE

By default, Windows XP Home Edition does not include the Backup utility. To install it manually, go to the \VALUEADD\MSFT\NTBACKUP folder on your Windows XP setup CD and double-click Ntbackup.msi. The installation wizard will complete the installation.

A+
OS
3.2

Follow these directions to create the backup and the ASR floppy disk:

1. Click **Start, All Programs, Accessories, System Tools,** and **Backup.** The Backup or Restore Wizard appears (see Figure 7-10).

Figure 7-10   Use the Backup or Restore Wizard to back up the hard drive partition after the Windows XP installation is complete

2. Click the **Advanced Mode** link. The Backup Utility window appears. Click **Automated System Recovery Wizard.** On the following screen, click **Next.**

3. The Backup Destination window appears. Select the location of the medium to receive the backup and insert a disk into the floppy disk drive. This disk will become the ASR disk. Click **Next.**

4. Click **Finish.** The backup process shows its progress, as shown in Figure 7-11.

5. When the backup is finished, label the ASR disk with the name of the disk, the date it was created, and the computer's name, and put the disk in a safe place.

NOTE

Just as with Windows 2000, you can back up the system state as discussed in Chapter 5. If you back up the system state when you complete an installation and a failure occurs in the future, you can restore the system state without overwriting user data on the hard drive. This is less drastic than the Automated System Recovery process that restores the entire volume.

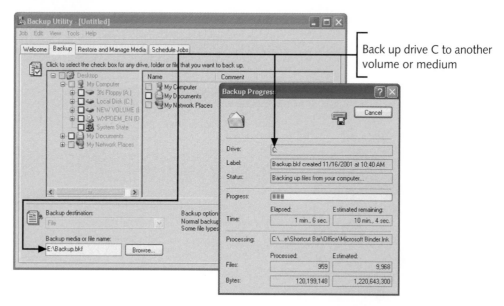

Back up drive C to another volume or medium

Figure 7-11   The Backup utility can create a backup of drive C and an ASR disk to be used later for the Automated System Recovery utility

Using Windows XP

Now that you have learned how to install Windows XP successfully and guard the system against potential failure, let's take a closer look at how it works and what it can do. One difference you will note immediately when using Windows XP for the first time is the desktop shown in Figure 7-12. When the OS is first installed, the Recycle Bin is the only shortcut on the desktop. Also note that the Start menu is organized with a more graphical look. Notice in Figure 7-12 that the username for the person currently logged on shows at the top of the Start menu. Applications at the top of the Start menu are said to be "pinned" to the menu and are permanently listed there until you change them in a Start menu setting. Applications that are used often are listed below the pinned applications and can change from time to time. The programs in the white column on the left side of the Start menu are user-oriented, and the programs in the dark column on the right side of the menu are OS-oriented.

When you click All Programs, the list of currently installed software appears. Figure 7-13 shows the default entries that appear when you click Accessories and then System Tools. You have already seen two of these tools: Backup, and Files and Settings Transfer Wizard. Also, after Windows is installed, you can use the Activate Windows option on this menu to activate Windows XP. You will learn about other options on this menu later in this chapter and in the next chapter.

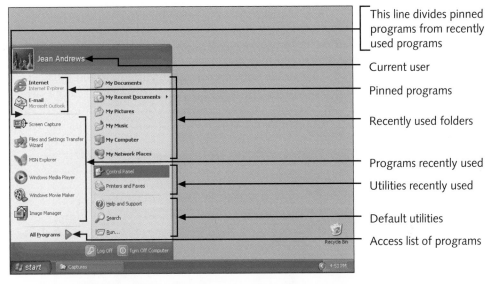

This line divides pinned programs from recently used programs

Current user

Pinned programs

Recently used folders

Programs recently used

Utilities recently used

Default utilities

Access list of programs

Figure 7-12   The Windows XP desktop and Start menu

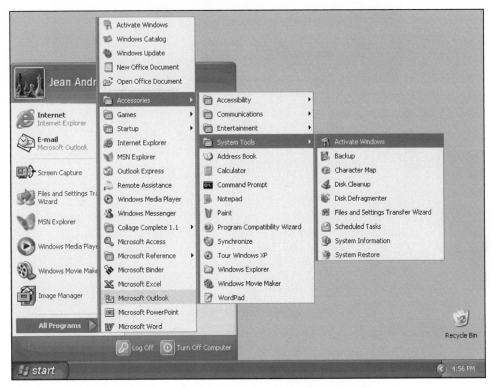

Figure 7-13   Click Start, All Programs to view the list of currently installed software

A+
OS
1.1

When you scroll down to windows and menus on these windows, you will notice you have more control over how and where things appear. Overall, if you are familiar with earlier versions of Windows, learning to use Windows XP is easy and intuitive. One example of how you can change the way a window appears is through the Control Panel. To access the Control Panel, click Start and then click Control Panel. Figure 7-14 shows the Control Panel in Category View. Select a category to see the applets in that category, or click Switch to Classic View to see the applets when you first open the Control Panel, as you did with earlier versions of Windows.

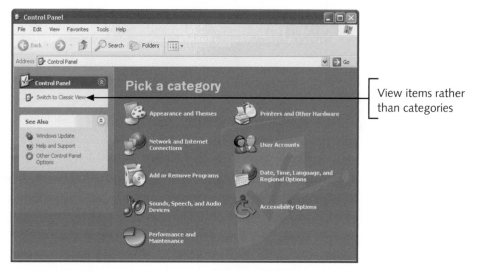

View items rather than categories

Figure 7-14   The Control Panel is organized by category, although you can easily switch to Classic View

Customizing the Windows XP Desktop

You can do several things to customize the Windows XP desktop. For example, you can change the background on the desktop (called the wallpaper), create shortcuts, and control what goes in the system tray. This section looks at each of these ways to make the desktop look and work the way you want it to.

NOTE

Each user account has a different desktop configuration, so if you want to create a customized desktop for a user, you must first log on to the system under that user account.

Managing Shortcuts

When you first install Windows XP, only the Recycle Bin shows on the desktop by default. To add other shortcuts that normally were on the Windows 2000 desktop, right-click anywhere on the desktop and select Properties from the shortcut menu.

(You can also select the Display icon in the Control Panel.) The Display Properties window appears (see Figure 7-15). Click the Desktop tab.

Click Customize Desktop to display the Desktop Items window, also shown in Figure 7-15. You can check My Documents, My Computer, My Network Places, and Internet Explorer to add these icons to the desktop. Also notice on this window the option to have Windows clean up your desktop by moving any shortcuts that you have not used in the last 60 days to a separate folder.

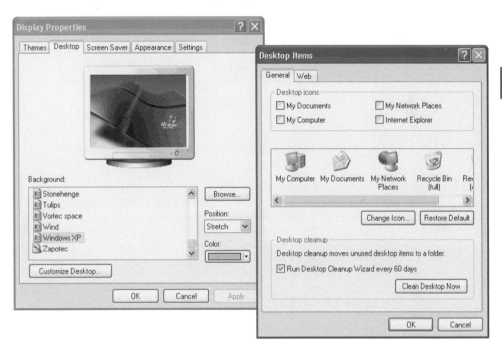

Figure 7-15   Managing the Windows XP desktop

You can add a program shortcut to the desktop by clicking Start, clicking All Programs, right-clicking a program name in the list that appears, and then selecting Copy from the shortcut menu. Then right-click anywhere on the desktop and select Paste from the shortcut menu. A shortcut is created and placed on the desktop. You can also use Windows Explorer to create a shortcut. From Explorer, right-click a program filename or the filename of a document or data file, and then select Create Shortcut from the shortcut menu (see Figure 7-16). Then, drag the shortcut created to the desktop. Chapter 4 listed several other ways to create shortcuts in Windows 9x, which also work for Windows XP.

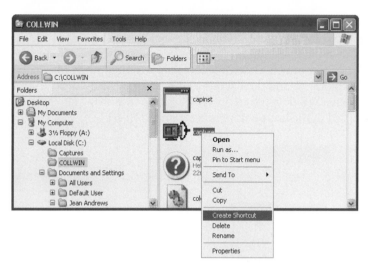

Figure 7-16   Create a shortcut to a file using the file's shortcut menu in Explorer

NOTE

Changing the wallpaper (desktop background) is easy in Windows XP. Right-click the desktop and select Properties. In the Display Properties dialog box, click the Desktop tab. Select the wallpaper and click Apply. Any photographs you have stored in C:\Documents and Settings\%username%\My Documents\My Pictures appear in the list for you to use as wallpaper. You can also use photographs you have stored in other folders as your wallpaper. Using Explorer, right-click the photograph and select Set as Desktop Background from the shortcut menu.

Windows XP Taskbar and System Tray

You can control the taskbar from the Taskbar and Start Menu windows. Access these windows by using the Taskbar and Start menu icon in the Control Panel or by right-clicking the taskbar and selecting Properties. Either way, the window in Figure 7-17 appears. From it you can add items to and remove items from the Start menu, control how the taskbar manages items in the system tray, and specify how the taskbar is displayed.

You might want to display frequently used programs as icons in the taskbar. To do that, right-click the taskbar, select Toolbars, and then click Quick Launch. Also, the system tray can sometimes become cluttered with several icons for running services such as the volume control and network connectivity. Windows XP automatically hides these icons. To display them, click the left arrow on the right side of the taskbar. In addition, by using the options on the taskbar shortcut menu, you can add

A+
OS
1.1

programs to the Quick Launch toolbar, customize taskbar properties, and add new toolbars to the taskbar.

7

Figure 7-17 Use the Taskbar and Start Menu Properties window to control what appears in the Start menu and Taskbar

Windows Messenger

When Windows XP starts, it loads Windows Messenger by default, which consumes system resources even if you are not using it. To stop Windows Messenger from loading at startup, click Start, All Programs, and Windows Messenger. Click Tools on the menu bar, and then click Options. The Options window opens, as shown in Figure 7-18. Click the Preferences tab and uncheck "Run this program when Windows starts." Click OK.

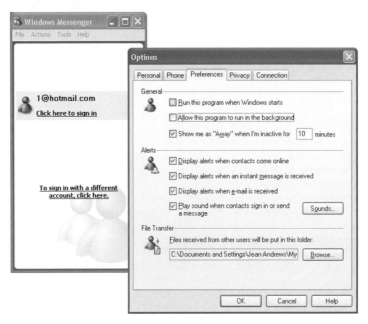

Figure 7-18   Disable Windows Messenger at startup

Managing Audio and Video

Windows XP has several built-in features to manage audio and video, including support for inputting images from digital cameras and scanners, a Windows Movie Maker for editing video, and Windows Media Player, Version 8. (Windows Me has Media Player, Version 7.) With Media Player you can play DVDs, CDs, and Internet radio. There's a jukebox for organizing audio files, including MP3 files used on music CDs. You can also burn your own music CDs using Media Player with a CD-R or CD-RW drive. To access the Media Player, click Start, All Programs, and Windows Media Player. Figure 7-19 shows the Media Player window.

As with older versions of Windows, you can record and manage sound from the Entertainment group of Windows and manage sounds for Windows events from the Sounds applet in the Control Panel. If you have a microphone connected to a sound card, you can record sound by clicking Start, All Programs, Accessories, Entertainment, and Sound Recorder. The Sound Recorder appears, as shown in Figure 7-20. Click the Record button (the red dot in the lower-right corner) to record and save a sound, such as your own voice, in a sound file. There are several types of sound files, including MP3 files (with the .mp3 file extension), which can be used on audio CDs, and Wave files (with the .wav file extension). Windows uses .wav files to record sound. Later, you can substitute this .wav file for one of the Windows sounds that plays when you open or close applications, shut down Windows, or perform many other Windows activities that can be accompanied by sound. To change the sounds for various Windows events, go to the Control Panel, open the Sounds and Audio Devices applet, and select the Sounds tab.

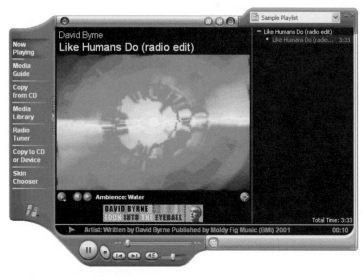

Figure 7-19   Windows Media Player

Figure 7-20   Record sounds using Windows Sound Recorder

Media Player has its own volume control, but there is another way to adjust sound. From the Control Panel, open the Sounds and Audio Devices applet and select the Volume tab. If you check "Place volume icon in the taskbar," you can easily adjust the sound from the taskbar.

NOTE

Two ways to control sound volume are to use the Windows controls or use the manual controls on an amplifier or speaker. In addition, notebooks often have manual volume controls.

Multiple Logins and Remote Assistance

Windows XP allows more than one user to be logged in at the same time. To switch from one account to another, click Start and then click Log Off. The Log Off Windows dialog box opens, giving you two choices: Switch User and Log Off. Click Switch User and then select a new account from the list of user accounts. After you enter a password, the screen goes blank and then the desktop configured for the new user appears. Each user can have his or her own set of applications open at the same time. When users switch back and forth, Windows keeps separate instances of applications open for each user.

Windows XP also offers a new feature called **Remote Assistance**. Using this utility, a user sitting at the PC can give a support technician at a remote location full access to the desktop. The technician can use the desktop just as she would if sitting in front of the PC. This is useful when an inexperienced user has trouble following the technician's directions as the technician investigates and troubleshoots problems with Windows XP.

Installing Hardware and Applications

In this section, you will learn how to install hardware and applications under Windows XP, and you will also learn several ways to solve problems with both. Later in this chapter and the next chapter, you will learn about more tools and procedures you can use to troubleshoot a failed system, program, or hardware device. We will first look at how to install hardware.

Installing Hardware

If your hardware device comes bundled with drivers for Windows XP on CD or floppy disk, use those drivers. If the drivers are not written for Windows XP, go to the manufacturer's Web site to download Windows XP drivers or visit the Microsoft Web site *(www.microsoft.com/technet)* and search on the driver or device. Have the drivers compatible with Windows XP available and then install the device.

After the device is installed and Windows XP first starts, it automatically launches the Found New Hardware Wizard, as with earlier Windows operating systems. The wizard gives you two options:

- Install the software automatically (Recommended)
- Install from a list or specific location (Advanced)

Select the option to install the software automatically, and then click Next. During the installation process, you can click Have Disk to provide a driver supplied by the manufacturer, rather than selecting the device from a list, which results in using a

A+
OS
2.4

Windows driver. Also, Windows XP might proceed with the installation using Microsoft drivers without displaying a dialog box that contains the Have Disk button. To prevent this from happening, run the setup program on the manufacturer's CD that is bundled with the device before installing it. Later, after the device is installed, Windows will use the manufacturer's installed drivers for the device.

When installing a device, Windows XP verifies that Microsoft has digitally signed the drivers. If the drivers have been written for Windows XP, even though they are not certified by Microsoft, they should still work in a Windows XP system.

Windows XP offers three processes that help solve problems with devices:

- Providing a way to automatically find an update for a driver
- Rolling back a driver in case an updated driver fails
- Verifying that the driver is certified by Microsoft

These processes are all available from Device Manager.

Using Device Manager

A+
OS
1.1
2.4
3.2
3.3

After a device is installed, you can use Device Manager to verify that Windows XP sees no problems with the device. There is more than one way to access Device Manager:

- Click Start, right-click My Computer, and then select Manage from the shortcut menu. The Computer Management window appears (see Figure 7-21). Under System Tools, click Device Manager.
- Open the System applet in the Control Panel, select the Hardware tab, and click Device Manager.
- Enter Devmgmt.msc in the Run dialog box.

Using Device Manager, you can verify that there are no resource conflicts with the device and that it works properly as viewed by Windows XP. From Device Manager, Windows XP offers a way to update a driver using the Update Device Driver Wizard. Right-click a device and select Properties from the shortcut menu. The Properties window for that device appears (see Figure 7-22). Select the Driver tab, click Update Driver to launch the wizard, and follow directions on the screen. The wizard goes to the Microsoft Web site, searches for updates to the driver, informs you if there is an update, and asks permission to install the update. Windows XP suggests an update only if the hardware ID of the device exactly matches the hardware ID of the update. A hardware ID is a number assigned to a device by the manufacturer that uniquely identifies the product.

NOTE

If you do not have an always-on connection to the Internet, connect to the Internet before you launch the Update Device Driver Wizard.

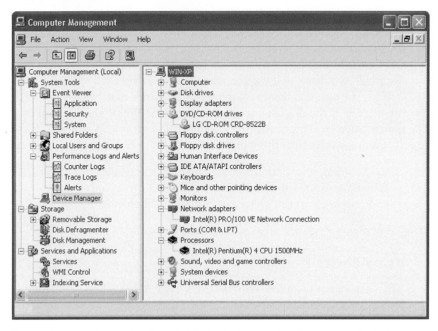

Figure 7-21 Device Manager is one tool available in the Computer Management window

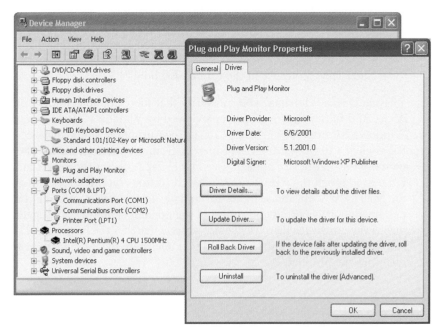

Figure 7-22 Use the Properties window for a device to obtain an updated driver from the Microsoft Web site

If you update a driver and the new driver does not perform as expected, you can revert to the old driver by using the Driver Rollback feature. To revert to a previous driver, open the Properties window for the device (see Figure 7-22), and click Roll Back Driver. If a previous driver is available, it will be installed. In many cases, when a driver is updated, Windows saves the old driver in case you want to revert to it. Note that Windows does not save printer drivers when they are updated and does not save drivers that are not functioning properly at the time of an update.

You can also copy an older driver from another PC or a backup medium to this PC for a rollback. Two files are needed: a .sys file and an .inf file. The .sys file is the actual driver, and the .inf file contains information about the driver. Put these files in the %systemroot%\ system32\reinstallbackups\ folder, and then perform the rollback.

By default, Device Manager hides legacy devices and devices that are no longer installed (including Plug and Play). To view these devices, click the View menu of Device Manager, and check Show hidden devices (see Figure 7-23).

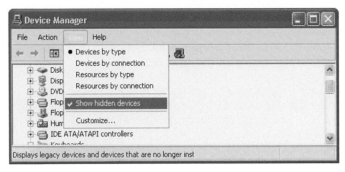

Figure 7-23   By default, Windows XP does not display legacy devices and devices that are no longer installed in Device Manager. Show these hidden devices by using the View menu.

Verify that Drivers Are Certified by Microsoft

Windows 2000 and Windows XP support the verification of digital signatures assigned to device drivers and application files, which certifies that the driver or other software has been tested and approved by Microsoft's Windows Hardware Quality Labs (WHQL) for Windows 2000 or Windows XP. If you suspect a problem with a driver, do one of the following to verify that it is digitally signed by Microsoft:

✔ A+ EXAM TIP

The A+ OS exam expects you to be familiar with methods to verify that drivers and applications are signed.

- *Use the File Signature Verification tool*. Enter the command Sigverif.exe in the Run dialog box. This command displays information about digitally signed files, including device driver files and application files, and logs information to *systemroot*\Sigverif.txt.
- *Use the Driver Query tool*. To direct output to a file, including information about digital signatures, enter this command in the Run dialog box:

```
Driverquery /si > myfile.txt
```

- *Use Device Manager*. In a device's Properties dialog box, click the Driver tab and then click Driver Details. In the Driver File Details window under Digital Signer, look for Microsoft Windows XP Publisher (for Microsoft drivers) or Microsoft WHQL (for manufacturer drivers).

NOTE   Use the Driver Query tool to save information about your system to a file when the system is healthy. Later, if you have a problem with drivers, you can compare a report to one created then to help identify the problem driver.

If a driver is not digitally signed, you can control how Windows handles it during the hardware device installation by using the Hardware tab of the System Properties window.

Installing Applications

Applications are installed under Windows XP as they are under other Windows OSs. You can use the Add or Remove Programs icon in the Control Panel, or you can run the application's setup program from the Run dialog box. You can only install software if you have Administrator privileges. An installed program is normally made available to all users when they log on. If a program is not available to all users, try installing the program files in the C:\Documents and Settings\All Users folder.

Software is uninstalled using the Add or Remove Programs applet in the Control Panel. Open the applet and select the software to uninstall (see Figure 7-24). Then click the Change/Remove icon. If other users are logged on to the system, the Warning message in Figure 7-24 appears. Log everyone off and then uninstall the software.

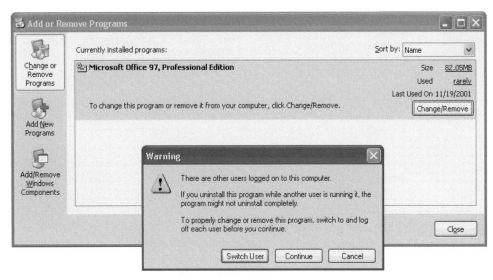

Figure 7-24   To uninstall software using the Add or Remove Programs applet, only one user, an administrator, should be logged on to the system

NOTE

You can cause a program to launch automatically each time you start Windows by putting a shortcut to the program in the Startup menu folder for the user. For each user, this folder is C:\Documents and Settings*Username*\Start Menu\Programs\Startup. If you want the software to start up automatically for all users, put the shortcut in this folder: C:\Documents and Settings \All Users\Start Menu\Programs\Startup.

Installing Legacy Software

DOS and Windows 9x applications that would not work under Windows NT and Windows 2000 are more likely to work under Windows XP. Some legacy applications that you should not attempt to run under Windows XP are older versions of antivirus software, and maintenance and cleanup utilities. In these cases, it is best to upgrade your software to versions designed to work under Windows XP.

If a legacy application does not start up and run successfully after you have installed it, try the following:

■ Check the Microsoft Web site for updates to Windows XP or the Microsoft application (*windowsupdate.microsoft.com*). How to perform Windows XP updates is covered in the next chapter.

■ Check the software manufacturer's Web site for updates or suggestions on how to run the software under Windows XP.

■ Consider upgrading the software to a later version.

■ Use the Windows XP Compatibility Mode utility.

A+
OS
3.3

The **Compatibility Mode utility** provides an application with the environment it expects from the operating system it was designed for, including Windows 95, Windows 98, Windows Me, Windows NT, and Windows 2000. (Compatibility mode does not apply to DOS applications.) There is more than one way to use the utility, but the easiest way is to create a shortcut on the desktop to an installed application and then set the properties of the shortcut to use compatibility mode. After you create the shortcut to the application, right-click it and select Properties from the shortcut menu. The Properties window appears (see Figure 7-25). Select the Compatibility tab, check "Run this program in compatibility mode for", and then select the operating system that you want Windows XP to emulate. Click Apply to apply the change. Run the software to find out whether the problem is solved.

If it is not solved, you can provide Microsoft with information that might help it fix the problem in some future Windows XP update. To provide the information, run the Program Compatibility Wizard. Click Start, All Programs, Accessories, and Program Compatibility Wizard. Follow directions on the wizard screen to locate the program file. After you locate the program file, you are asked to test the application and then respond to the questions shown in Figure 7-26.

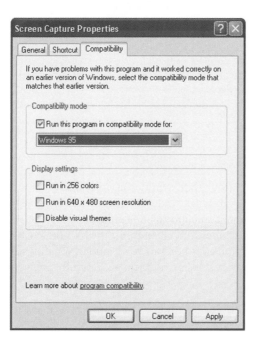

Figure 7-25   Setting Windows XP to run a legacy program in compatibility mode

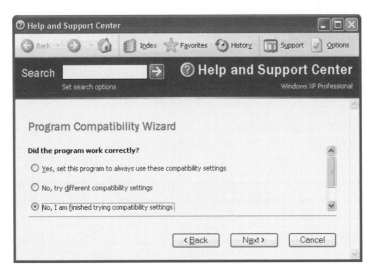

Figure 7-26   Using the Program Compatibility Wizard

If you answer, "No, I am finished trying compatibility settings," then the screen in Figure 7-27 appears. If you respond Yes to the question, "Would you like to send this information to Microsoft?", then the information needed to help Microsoft solve problems with the application is transmitted to the Microsoft Web site over the Internet.

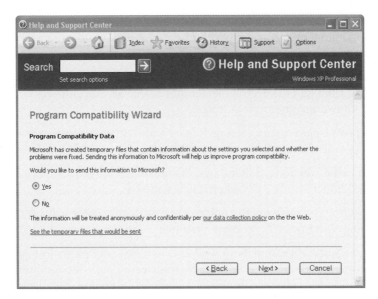

Figure 7-27   If running a legacy program in compatibility mode does not solve the problem, you can send helpful information to Microsoft

7

CHAPTER SUMMARY

▸ There are presently five versions of Windows XP: Windows XP Home Edition, Windows XP Professional, Windows XP Media Center Edition, Windows XP Tablet PC Edition, and Windows XP 64-Bit Edition.

▸ Windows XP integrates features of Windows 9x and 2000, while providing added support for multimedia and networking technologies.

▸ Although the Windows XP interface looks different from that of earlier versions of Windows and the OS organizes some utilities and functions differently, Windows XP is built on the same basic architecture as Windows NT and Windows 2000 and has the same basic kernel structure.

▸ Windows XP requires only 640 MB of free hard drive space for installation; however, acceptable performance cannot be achieved without 1.5 GB of free space on the Windows XP partition.

▸ Windows XP supports the same file systems as Windows 2000: FAT16, FAT32, and NTFS.

▸ You can install Windows XP as a dual boot with Windows 2000, because they both use the same version of NTFS. To dual boot Windows XP with Windows 9x or Windows NT, you must use FAT32 or FAT16. Always install the other OS first, and install Windows XP on a different partition than another OS.

▸ A clean install is required if you plan to dual boot Windows XP with another OS. Perform an upgrade if you have another version of Windows installed and you do not plan to dual boot.

▸ Before upgrading to Windows XP, clean up the hard drive by deleting unnecessary files and running Disk Defragmenter and ScanDisk, uncompress the drive, and delete known incompatible software.

▸ An Express Upgrade uses existing folders and settings as much as possible. A Custom Upgrade allows you to change folders, language, and the file system.

▸ Unlike earlier versions of Windows, Windows XP is aware of applications installed under another OS when it is installed as a dual boot.

▸ Microsoft uses product activation to prevent the use of its software products, including Windows XP, on more than one computer.

▸ The User State Migration Tool (USMT) enables a user to make a smooth transition from one computer to another by transferring user files and settings. The Scanstate and Loadstate commands accomplish the same thing from the command prompt.

▶ Differences in the Windows XP desktop from earlier versions include the absence (by default) of any shortcuts other than the Recycle Bin and the more graphical organization of the Start menu.

▶ Windows XP allows more than one user to be logged on at the same time, each with their own instances of open applications.

▶ Windows XP offers processes to help find updates for a driver, roll back a driver if an update fails, and verify that a driver is certified by Microsoft.

▶ The Computer Management, Disk Management, and Device Manager tools work much the same way in Windows XP as they did in Windows 2000.

▶ Windows XP Device Manager hides legacy devices (non—Plug and Play devices) by default.

▶ You can install software in Windows XP only if you have Administrator privileges.

▶ DOS applications and older Windows applications that did not work under earlier versions of Windows are more likely to work under Windows XP.

▶ Compatibility mode in Windows XP provides an application written for Windows 9x or later with the environment for which it was designed.

KEY TERMS

For explanations of key terms, see the Glossary near the end of the book.

Automated System Recovery (ASR)
boot loader menu

Compatibility Mode utility
product activation

Remote Assistance
User State Migration Tool (USMT)

REVIEWING THE BASICS

1. Name the five versions of Windows XP.

2. What are at least three similarities between Windows XP and Windows 2000? At least three differences?

3. How much free space on a partition does Windows XP require for installation? How much does it require for acceptable operation?

4. How much memory is required to install Windows XP? How much is recommended to run applications under Windows XP?

5. When you are trying to determine if your computer can support Windows XP, list the steps to know how much RAM is currently installed.

6. Which version of Windows XP must be installed on a system that is using the Intel Itanium processor? Why?

7. How many processors in a system can Windows XP support?

8. List two ways to check hardware and software compatibility for Windows XP.

9. What file system do you use if you are installing Windows XP as a dual boot with Windows 9x? Windows NT? Windows 2000?

10. Name at least four things you should do before performing an upgrade to Windows XP.

11. What are the two upgrade options for Windows XP? Explain the difference between them.

12. How long do you have to activate Windows XP? What happens if you don't?

13. What is the first Microsoft product to use product activation?

14. Explain the purpose of the USMT utility and list the three steps needed to use it.

15. What two commands can you use from the command prompt to perform the same functions as the Files and Settings Transfer Wizard?

16. How are the Windows XP desktop and Start menu different from those in Windows 2000?

17. Give two ways to create shortcuts in Windows XP.

18. What are two ways you can access the Windows XP Device Manager?

19. Name the two files that are needed to copy an older driver from another PC or a backup medium to your Windows XP PC for a device driver rollback.

20. What is the path for the report file created when you run Readiness Analyzer?

21. Which OS are DOS applications more likely to work under: Windows 2000 or Windows XP?

22. List at least three things you can do if a legacy application does not start up and run correctly after you install it under Windows XP.

23. What legacy applications should you not attempt to run under Windows XP?

24. Where should you place a shortcut if you want the associated application to start automatically on startup for all users? Give the entire path.

25. What command launches the Driver Query tool?

THINKING CRITICALLY

1. If you find out that one of your applications is not supported by Windows XP and you still want to use XP, what can you do to solve this incompatibility problem?

2. Is it possible to install Windows XP on a system that does not have a CD-ROM drive or other optical drive? Explain your answer.

3. You connect to the Internet using a telephone line and modem and you want to upgrade your system from Windows 98 to Windows XP. You search the Microsoft Web site for your modem, but don't find it. What is your best next step?

   a. Install Windows XP as a dual boot with Windows 98.

   b. Buy and install a new modem.

   c. Install Windows XP and then buy a new modem.

   d. Check the modem's Web site for Windows XP drivers.

4. You have upgraded from Windows 98 to Windows XP. You want to install a Web camera on your PC, but the drivers that came bundled with your camera are written for Windows 98 and Windows 2000. What is your best next step?

   a. Buy a new Web camera.

   b. Reinstall Windows 98.

   c. Check the camera manufacturer's Web site for Windows XP drivers.

   d. Check the Microsoft Web site for your Web camera drivers.

HANDS-ON
PROJECTS

HANDS-ON PROJECTS

PROJECT 7-1: Using Shortcuts

Create a shortcut on your desktop to Notepad (Notepad.exe), a text editor. Using a second method for creating shortcuts, add a shortcut to the Windows command prompt (Cmd.exe). First, locate the two program files on your hard drive by clicking Start, clicking Search, and using the Search dialog box. Then create the shortcuts. List the steps you took to create each shortcut.

PROJECT 7-2: Preparing for an Upgrade

On a PC with Windows 2000 or an earlier version of Windows installed, run the Readiness Analyzer from the Windows XP CD to determine whether the PC is ready for Windows XP installation. Make a list of any hardware or software components found incompatible with Windows XP, and draw up a plan for getting the system ready for an XP upgrade.

PROJECT 7-3: Updating Windows

On a Windows XP system connected to the Internet, click **Start, All Programs,** and **Windows Update.** This takes you to the Microsoft Web site, which searches your system and recommends Windows XP updates. Print the Web page showing a list of recommended updates. For a lab PC, don't perform the updates unless you have your instructor's permission.

CASE PROJECT

Installing Windows 9x

CAUTION

This project will erase everything on your hard drive. Do not do it if you have important data on the hard drive.

Prepare your hard drive for a clean installation of Windows XP by formatting the hard drive. Follow the instructions in the chapter to install Windows XP. Put Windows XP in a 2-GB partition. Write down each decision you had to make as you performed the installation. If you get any error messages during the installation, write them down and list the steps you took to recover from the error. How long did the installation take?

Once you have installed Windows XP, use Disk Management to partition and format the remainder of the hard drive. Print a screen shot of Disk Management showing the two partitions. Create an ASR backup of the system partition in the second partition. Print a screen shot showing the files on the ASR floppy disk, using Windows Explorer to view the files.

Managing and Supporting Windows XP

In this chapter, you will learn:

- How to use Windows XP features to secure the PC and protect users and their data

- About the Windows NT/2000/XP registry

- About tools for troubleshooting and maintaining Windows XP

- How to troubleshoot the Windows XP boot process

You were introduced to Windows XP in the last chapter and learned how to install and use it. This chapter takes you further in learning to support this OS. You will learn about security features that protect the Windows XP system, its users, and their data. You'll also learn how the Windows NT/2000/XP registry is organized and how to edit it, and about many troubleshooting tools available under Windows XP. Finally, you will learn how to troubleshoot the Windows XP boot process. In later chapters, you will learn more about how Windows XP is used on networks and about additional security features it has when networked.

Security Using Windows NT/2000/XP

A+
OS
1.4
2.4

Security under Windows NT/2000/XP is much improved over Windows 9x and has two goals: to secure the system resources including hardware and software from improper use, and to secure users' data from improper access. In this section you will learn about some features of Windows NT/2000/XP that support these goals. At the heart of Windows NT/2000/XP security is the concept of user accounts.

User Accounts and Profiles

A **user account** defines a user to Windows and records information about the user including the username, password used to access the account, groups that the account belongs to, and the rights and permissions assigned to the account. Permissions assigned to a user account control what the user can and cannot do and access in Windows. There are three types of user accounts in Windows NT/2000/XP:

■ **Global user accounts**, sometimes called domain user accounts, are used at the domain level, created by an administrator, and stored in the SAM (security accounts manager) database on a domain controller. A user can log on to any computer on the networked domain using a global user account, and the information about a global user account's rights and permissions apply to each workstation in the domain. The centralized SAM database is part of Active Directory, a repository of information used to manage a Windows network that is itself managed by Windows 2000 Server or Windows 2003 Server.

■ A **local user account** is created on a local computer and allows a user access to only that one computer. An administrator creates a local user account, assigns a username and password to the account, and gives the account rights and permissions. As a general rule, a user account should have no more rights than a user needs to do his or her job. For example, an administrator responsible for setting up and maintaining user accounts in an office workgroup can set the permissions on a user account to deny the user the right to install a printer, install software, or do any other chores that change the PC software or hardware environment.

■ Every Windows XP workstation has two **built-in user accounts** that are set up when the OS is first installed: an administrator account and a guest account. An administrator has rights and permissions to all computer software, data, and hardware resources. Under Windows NT/2000/XP, the administrator can create other user accounts and assign corresponding rights and permissions to individual accounts, to groups of selected accounts, or to all accounts that use the computer. A guest account has very limited privileges and gives someone who does not have a user account access to a computer. The guest account is

A+
OS
1.4
2.4

useful in a business environment where many people use a single computer for limited purposes and it is not practical for all of them to have unique user accounts.

How user accounts are set up depends on whether the computer is a standalone workstation (not networked), belongs to a workgroup, or belongs to a domain. Recall from Chapter 5 that in a workgroup, each computer manages the security for its own resources. Each local user account is set up on the local computer independent of other accounts on other PCs, and there is no centralized control of resources. If a user on one computer needs access to resources on another computer in the workgroup, the other computer must have the same user account and password that the first computer does. This chapter focuses on setting up security for standalone workstations and for workstations in a workgroup. It does not cover managing user accounts at the domain level.

After an administrator creates a local user account and the user logs on for the first time, the system creates a **user profile** for that user. When the user changes settings to customize his or her computer and then logs off, the user profile is updated so that settings can be restored the next time the user logs on.

If the computer is networked to other computers in a Windows workgroup, the administrator must create a user account on each computer in the workgroup that this user needs to access. When the user logs on to each computer in the workgroup, he or she would have to reestablish the user profile at each computer, re-creating desktop settings and application settings for each computer unless the administrator implements a feature called roaming user profiles. With **roaming user profiles**, settings established by a user at one computer are stored in a file on a file server on the network and shared with all computers in the workgroup. When a user moves from one computer to another computer in the workgroup, the roaming profile follows the user so that he or she does not have to redo settings at each computer.

Another type of profile used with workgroups is a **mandatory user profile**. This profile is a roaming user profile that applies to all users in a user group, and individual users cannot change that profile. It is used in situations where users perform only specific job-related tasks. A profile that applies to a group of users is called a **group profile**. An administrator creates roaming and mandatory profiles using the Computer Management console under the Administrative Tools applet in the Control Panel.

To view all profiles stored on a Windows XP computer, use the System Properties window. Click Start and then right-click My Computer. Select Properties and then click the Advanced tab. Under User Profiles, click the Settings button (see Figure 8-1).

Next, we turn our attention to how to create and manage local user accounts.

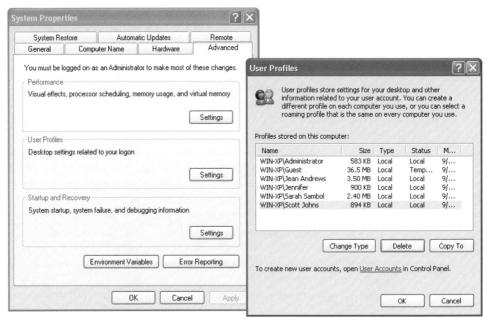

Figure 8-1   View all user profiles stored on this PC using the System Properties window

Administering Local User Accounts

When setting up accounts for users where security is a concern, you should follow a few guidelines about passwords for both users and administrators:

- Usernames for Windows NT/2000/XP logon can consist of up to 15 characters.
- Passwords can be up to 127 characters.
- Do not use a password that is easy to guess, such as one consisting of real words, your telephone number, or the name of your pet.
- The most secure type of password is a combination of letters, numbers, and even nonalphanumeric characters.
- User accounts can be set up with or without passwords. Passwords provide greater security. Where security is a concern, always set a password for the administrator account.
- Passwords can be controlled by the administrator, but generally, users should be allowed to change their own passwords.

APPLYING CONCEPTS

As an administrator, you can create a user account using the Computer Management console or the User Accounts applet in the Control Panel. If the account is created in Computer Management it will have Limited privileges. If it is created using the Control Panel, it will have

Administrator privileges. To create a local user account using Computer Management, follow these steps:

1. Log on to the computer as the administrator.
2. Click **Start** and then right-click **My Computer**. Select **Manage** on the shortcut menu. The Computer Management console window opens. (Note that you can also access Computer Management by way of the Control Panel, Administrative Tools applet.)
3. Expand **Local Users and Groups** by clicking the plus sign to its left. Right-click **Users** and then select **New User** on the shortcut menu. The New User window opens (see Figure 8-2). Enter the User name, enter the password twice, and check the boxes to decide how and when the password can be changed. You can also enter values for the Full name and Description to help identify the user. Click **Create**.

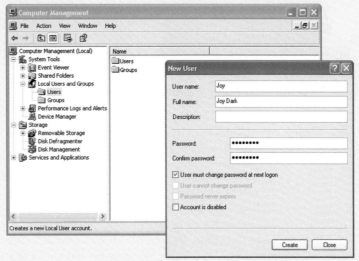

Figure 8-2   Create a user account using either Computer Management or the User Account applet in Control Panel

4. The account is created with the default type Limited, which means the account cannot create, delete, or change other accounts; make system-wide changes; or install software. If you want to give the account Administrator privileges, then open the **Control Panel** and double-click the **User Accounts** applet.
5. The User Accounts window opens listing all accounts. To make changes to an account, click **Change an account**, and then click the account you want to change.
6. In the next window, you can choose to change the name of the account, change the password, remove a password, change the picture icon associated with the account, change the account type, or delete the account. Click **Change the account type**.
7. In the next window, select **Computer administrator** and click **Change Account Type**. Click **Back** twice on the menu bar to return to the opening window.

8

Sometimes a user forgets his or her password or the password is compromised. If this happens and you have Administrator privileges, you can access the account through the Control Panel or the Computer Management Console to provide the user with a new password. This action is called resetting the password. However, resetting a password under Windows XP causes the OS to lock the user out from using encrypted email or files or using Internet passwords stored on the computer.

For this reason, each new user should create a **forgotten password floppy disk** for use in the event the user forgets the password. To create the disk, open the User Accounts applet in the Control Panel, click your account, and select "Prevent a forgotten password" under Related Tasks in the left pane of this window. Follow the wizard to create the disk. If a user enters a wrong password at logon, he or she has the opportunity to use the forgotten password floppy disk to log on.

NOTE

The forgotten password floppy disk should be kept in a protected place so that others cannot use it to gain unauthorized access to the computer.

Controlling How a User Logs On

With Windows NT/2000, there was only one way to log on to the system: pressing the Ctrl+Alt+Del keys to open the logon window. In a Windows XP workgroup, you have some options as to how logging on works:

- *Welcome screen.* The default option is a Welcome screen that appears when the PC is first booted or comes back from a sleep state. All users are listed on the Welcome screen along with a picture (which can be the user's photograph); a user clicks his or her user name and enters the password.
- *Logon window.* Instead of the Welcome screen, the user must press Ctrl+Alt +Del to get to a logon window similar to Windows NT/2000.
- *Fast User Switching.* Fast User Switching enables more than one user to be logged on to the system. If this option is disabled, only one user can log on at a time. If the option is enabled, when a user clicks Start, Log Off, then the Log Off Windows dialog box offers three options: Switch User, Log Off, and Cancel. When Fast User Switching is disabled, the Switch User option does not appear. Disable Fast User Switching when you want to conserve resources because performance is poor when several users leave applications open.

To change the way a user logs on, from Control Panel, open the User Accounts applet. Click "Change the way users log on or off" (see Figure 8-3). Make your selections and then click Apply Options to close the dialog box.

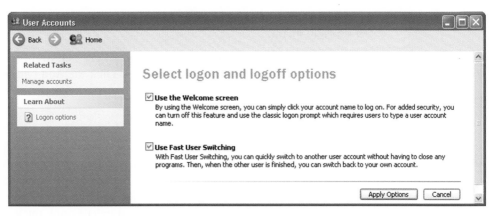

Figure 8-3   Options to change the way users log on or off

User Groups

User groups are an efficient way for an administrator to manage multiple user accounts that require the same privileges and similar profiles. When installed, Windows XP sets up several user groups including:

- **Administrators,** who have access to all parts of the system, can install or uninstall devices and applications, and can perform all administrative tasks.
- **Backup Operators** can back up and restore any files on the system regardless of their access privileges to these files.
- **Power Users** can read from and write to parts of the system other than their own local drive, install applications, and perform limited administrative tasks.
- **Limited Users** (known as Users in Windows NT/2000) have read-write access only on their own folders, read-only access to most system folders, and no access to other users' data. They cannot install applications or carry out any administrative responsibilities.
- **Guests** use a workstation once or occasionally and have limited access to files and resources. A guest account has permission to shut down a computer.

Creating a New User Group

You can also create your own user group and customize the permissions and profiles for this group of users. To create a new group:

1. Click **Start,** right-click **My Computer,** and select **Manage** on the shortcut menu.

2. The Computer Management console opens. Expand **Local Users and Groups** by clicking the plus sign.

A+
OS
1.4
2.4

3. To create a new group, right-click the **Groups** folder and select **New Group** on the shortcut menu.

4. The New Group window opens, as shown in Figure 8-4. In this window, enter a name and description of the new group and click the **Add** button to find and select users to add to this group. When finished, click **Create** to finish creating the group.

You can also change the policy settings assigned to users in a group. For example, to control what a user or a user group can do, including the ability to change the system date and time, go to the Control Panel and access the Administrative Tools applet. Double-click the Local Security Policy icon. The Local Security Settings window appears (see Figure 8-5). Under Local Policies, the User Rights Assignment group lists several activities, which can be managed by changing the user groups that have the right to do these activities. Right-click "Change the system time," and then select Properties on the shortcut menu. The Change the system time Properties dialog box appears, as shown in Figure 8-5. From this dialog box, you can add and remove the user groups that have the right to change the system time.

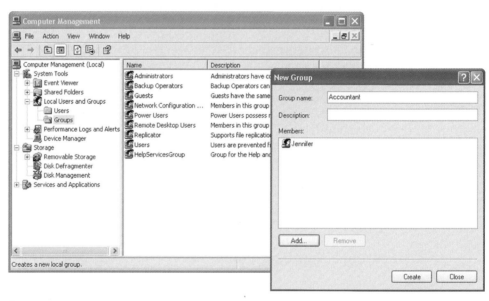

Figure 8-4   Create a new user group

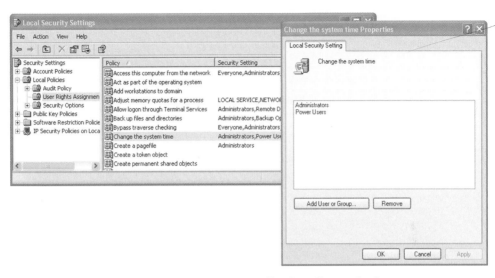

A+
OS
1.4
2.4

Figure 8-5   Local policies can be assigned to a user group, affecting all users in the group

Group Policy

Another way to control how the system can be used is by applying settings called a
Group Policy. Group Policy is normally intended to be used on a domain where
group polices are managed by Active Directory, although you can use it on a
standalone computer or a computer in a workgroup. Group Policy can be applied
to your computer, regardless of the currently logged-on user (called Computer
Configuration) or can be applied to each user who logs on (called User
Configuration). Computer-based policies are applied just before the logon window is
displayed, and user-based policies are applied after a user logs on. The Group Policy
console is a Microsoft Management Console (MMC) snap-in that can be accessed by
typing gpedit.msc in the Run dialog box. From the console you can control such
things as how Media Player, Internet Explorer, and NetMeeting work, as well as
many Windows settings and components. For a standalone computer or a computer
in a workgroup, use Computer Configuration instead of User Configuration to
implement Group Policy settings.

Disk Quotas

An administrator can set **disk quotas,** which limit how much disk space a user can
access. This is important when two or more users are using a single computer and
need to share its storage capacity. A disk quota does not specify where a user's files
must be located; it just specifies how much total space the user can take up on a volume. The disk quota set applies to all users. You can set disk quotas only if you are
using NTFS.

APPLYING CONCEPTS

To set disk quotas:

1. Log on as an administrator, and open **My Computer**.
2. Find the partition that you want to set a disk quota on. Right-click it and select **Properties** on the shortcut menu.
3. Click the **Quota** tab and the **Enable quota management** check box. See Figure 8-6.

In this view, you can specify that users have unlimited access to disk space, you can specify the amount of space for users, and you can set a level of disk space used that will trigger a warning message to a user. For this example, all users are restricted to 500 MB of storage space and warned when they have used 400 MB.

Figure 8-6   Setting disk quotas

4. Click the **Limit disk space to** radio button, enter **500** in the box next to it, and select **MB** from the drop-down menu to the right of the box.
5. In the box next to **Set warning level to**, enter **400**, and then select **MB** from the drop-down menu. This warns users when they have used 400 MB of their allotted 500 MB of storage space.
6. Click **Deny disk space to users exceeding quota limit** so that no user can use more than the specified amount of disk space.

7. Click **OK**. You are prompted to enable disk quotas. Click **OK** to respond to the prompt (see Figure 8-7).

Figure 8-7   The prompt at the end of the quota-setting process gives you information about enabling quotas

8

EFS (Encrypted File System)

A+
OS
1.4

Another Windows 2000/XP security feature is the **Encrypted File System** (EFS). EFS applies only to the Windows 2000/XP NTFS file system. In the past, it was possible to bypass an existing operating system's security measures by installing a new operating system or booting from a startup disk. In Windows 98, a password could be put on a file using a FAT file system, but you could boot from a startup disk, get to the file at the command prompt, copy it to a floppy disk, and access the file without using the password. That method does not work with EFS, which protects encrypted data even when someone who is not authorized to view those files or folders has full access to a computer's data storage. When an unauthorized user attempts to access a file encrypted using EFS, he receives the error "Access Denied."

✔ **A+ EXAM TIP**

The A+ OS exam expects you to know how to use file encryption under Windows XP.

Encryption is the process of putting readable data into code that must be translated before it can be accessed, usually by using a **key** that encrypts the data and also provides a way to "unlock" the code and translate it back into readable data.

Do not confuse the term *key* as it is used in encryption with the term *registry key*, which applies to information placed in the registry.

NOTE

To ensure that a file can be accessed if a user is not available or forgets the password to log on to the system, an administrator for the OS can decrypt a file. In this case, the administrator is called a data recovery agent (DRA).

How to Use Encryption

A user does not have to go through a complex process of encryption to use EFS; from a user's perspective, it's just a matter of placing a file in a folder marked for encryption. Encryption can be implemented at either the folder or file level. If a folder is marked for encryption, every file created in the folder or copied to the folder will be encrypted. At the file level, each file must be encrypted individually. Encrypting with EFS at the folder level is encouraged and considered a best practice because it provides greater security: any file placed in an encrypted folder is automatically encrypted so the user doesn't have to remember to encrypt it. An encrypted file remains encrypted if you move it from an encrypted folder to an unencrypted folder on the same or another NTFS logical drive.

APPLYING CONCEPTS

In the following example, you encrypt the My Documents folder for an existing user named User2, create a file in that folder that automatically becomes encrypted because the folder is encrypted, and decrypt the folder so that others can access it.

1. In Windows Explorer, locate the My Documents folder for User2. In this example, the correct path is C:\Documents and Settings\User2\My Documents.

2. Right-click the **My Documents** folder, and choose **Properties** on the shortcut menu. The My Documents Properties dialog box appears (see Figure 8-8).

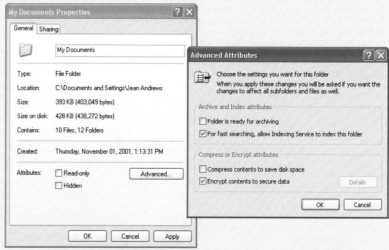

Figure 8-8   Encrypt folder contents

3. On the **General** tab, click the **Advanced** button. The Advanced Attributes dialog box appears.

4. Check the box labeled **Encrypt contents to secure data**, and click **OK** (see Figure 8-8).

5. Click **Apply**. This causes the Confirm Attribute Changes dialog box to open if any files or folders exist in the selected folder (see Figure 8-9).

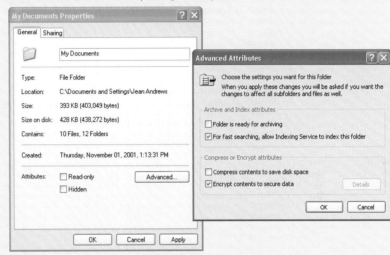

Figure 8-9   Apply changes to all folder contents

6. In this example, the subfolder My Pictures exists within the My Documents folder. If necessary, click the **Apply changes to this folder, subfolders, and files** radio button to encrypt any objects in this folder and its subfolders. (If you do not want to apply the changes to all subfolders and files, you select "Apply changes to this folder only".) Click **OK**.

7. Open Microsoft Word, type some text in a file, and save the file in User2's My Documents folder. This file is automatically encrypted, because the My Documents folder is encrypted. If an unauthorized user attempts to access the encrypted document, the user receives an error message.

Here are three ways to decrypt a file or folder to allow others to view it:

- From the file's Properties dialog box, click the Advanced button. On the Advanced Attributes dialog box, uncheck "Encrypt contents to secure data".
- Encryption is removed automatically when a file or folder is moved to a FAT logical drive (volume) because the FAT file system does not support encryption.
- Use the Cipher command discussed next.

8

The Cipher Command

A+
OS
1.4

If you are encrypting a large number of files or folders from a command prompt or using a batch file, you can use the Cipher command:

```
CIPHER [/E, /D] [/S:dir] [pathname [...]]
```

- /E encrypts the specified files or folders.
- /D decrypts the specified files or folders.
- /S: dir applies the action to the specified folder (directory) and all its subfolders.
- Pathname is the path to and the name of the file or folder that is to be encrypted or decrypted.

For example, at the command prompt, to decrypt all files in the C:\Public folder, use this command:

```
Cipher /D C:\Public\*.*
```

Internet Connection Firewall

A+
OS
4.2

Windows 2000/XP offers several security features that protect the system from unauthorized access over a network or over the Internet, which you will learn about in later chapters. One feature new to Windows XP is Internet Connection Firewall. A **firewall** is hardware or software that protects a computer or network from unauthorized access. **Internet Connection Firewall (ICF)** is Windows XP software designed to protect a PC from unauthorized access from the Internet when the PC is connected directly to the Internet.

NOTE

You should not use ICF on a PC that has Internet access from a LAN (local area network) because it can prevent others on the LAN from accessing resources on the PC.

ICF works by examining every communication that comes to the PC to determine if the communication has been initiated by the PC or is being initiated by an outside device or computer. If the communication is initiated by some source other than the PC, it is refused. With ICF, you can browse the Web, but those on the Web cannot initiate a communication with your PC in order to gain unauthorized access to data stored there.

To enable ICF, open the Network Connections applet in Control Panel, right-click the network connection icon that you use to connect to the Internet, and then select Properties on the shortcut menu. This might be a connection to the Internet by way of a dial-up modem, a cable modem, or a DSL connection. (All these connection types are covered in later chapters.) The connection Properties dialog box opens as shown in Figure 8-10 for a modem connection. Click the Advanced tab and select

"Protect my computer and network by limiting or preventing access to this computer from the Internet". If you would like the firewall to record dropped packets in a log file, click Log Dropped Packets. Click OK. Remember, don't do this for a regular network connection if you want others on the network to have access to resources on your PC.

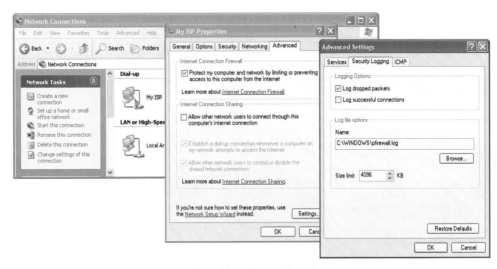

Figure 8-10   Enable Internet Connection Firewall and log dropped packets

We now turn our attention to several utilities that allow you to customize and troubleshoot Windows XP. We begin by looking at the Windows NT/2000/XP registry and learning how to edit it.

The Windows NT/2000/XP Registry

The Windows NT/2000/XP registry is a hierarchical database containing information about all the hardware, software, device drivers, network protocols, and user configuration needed by the OS and applications. Many components depend on this information, and the registry provides a secure and stable location for it. Table 8-1 lists ways in which some components use the registry. Information about the registry in this section applies to Windows NT, Windows 2000, and Windows XP.

The next section looks at how the registry is organized, how to view the contents of the registry, how to back up and recover the registry, and how Windows makes changes to the registry.

Component	Description
Setup programs for devices and applications	Setup programs can record configuration information in the registry and query the registry for information needed to install drivers and applications.
User profiles maintained and used by the OS	Windows maintains a profile for each user that determines the user's environment. User profiles are kept in files, but, when a user logs on, the profile information is written to the registry, where changes are recorded, and then later written back to the user profile file. The OS uses this profile to control user settings and other configuration information specific to this user.
Files active when Ntldr is loading the OS	During the boot process, NTDetect.com surveys present hardware devices and records that information in the registry. Ntldr loads and initializes device drivers using information from the registry, including the order in which to load them.
Device drivers	Device drivers read and write configuration information from and to the registry each time they load. The drivers write hardware configuration information to the registry and read it to determine the proper way to load.
Hardware profiles	Windows can maintain more than one set of hardware configuration information (called a **hardware profile**) for one PC. The data is kept in the registry. An example of a computer that has more than one hardware profile is a notebook that has a docking station. Two hardware profiles describe the notebook, one docked and the other undocked. This information is kept in the registry.
Application programs	Many application programs read the registry for information about the location of files the program uses and various other parameters that were stored in .ini files under Windows 9x.

Table 8-1   Components that use the Windows NT/2000/XP registry

How the Registry Is Organized

When studying how the registry is organized, keep in mind that there are two ways to look at this organization: physical and logical.

Logically, the organization of the registry looks like an upside-down tree with five branches, called keys or subtrees (see Figure 8-11), which are categories of information stored in the registry. Each key is made up of several subkeys that may also have subkeys, and subkeys hold, or contain, values. Each value has a name and data assigned to it. Data in the registry is always stored in values, the lowest level of the tree.

Logical Organization of the Registry

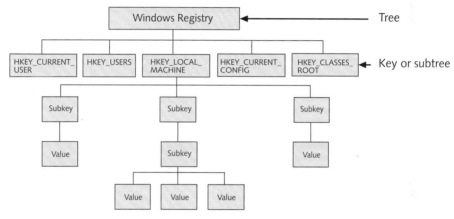

Figure 8-11   The Windows NT/2000/XP registry is logically organized in an upside-down tree structure of keys, subkeys, and values

Figure 8-12 shows the Windows Registry Editor, the window you see when you first open the editor: there are five high levels, one for each key or subtree. Notice in the figure that the HKEY_CURRENT_USER subtree has been opened to show subkeys under it; several subkeys have their own subkeys. If you click a subkey that has a value assigned to it, that value appears on the right side of the window. Later in this section, you will see how to edit values in the registry.

8

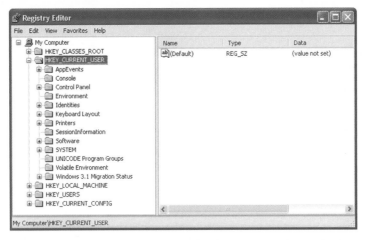

Figure 8-12   Windows Registry Editor shows the five high-level subtrees in the Windows NT/2000/XP registry

The five subtrees of the registry, shown in Figure 8-12, are listed in Table 8-2 together with their primary functions. As the table shows, the HKEY_LOCAL_MACHINE subtree is the mainstay key of the registry.

Subtree (Main Keys)	Primary Function
HKEY_CURRENT_USER	Contains information about the currently logged-on user
HKEY_CLASSES_ROOT	Contains information about software and the way software is configured. This key points to data stored in HKEY_LOCAL_MACHINE.
HKEY_CURRENT_CONFIG	Contains information about the active hardware configuration, which is extracted from the data stored in the HKEY_LOCAL_ MACHINE subkeys called SOFTWARE and SYSTEM
HKEY_USERS	Contains information used to build the logon screen and the ID of the currently logged-on user
HKEY_LOCAL_MACHINE	Contains all configuration data about the computer, including information about device drivers and devices used at startup. The information in this key does not change when different users log on.

Table 8-2   The five subtrees of the Windows NT/2000/XP registry

Physical Organization of the Registry

The physical organization of the registry is quite different from the logical organization. Physically, the registry is stored in five files called **hives**. There is no one-to-one relationship between the subtrees and these five files, even though there are five of each. Figure 8-13 shows the way the subtrees are stored in hives as follows.

A+
OS
1.1
1.2
1.5

- HKEY_LOCAL_MACHINE consists of four hives: the SAM hive, the Security hive, the Software hive, and the System hive.
- HKEY_CURRENT_CONFIG data is kept in portions of two hives: the Software hive and the System hive.
- HKEY_CLASSES_ROOT data is kept in a portion of the Software hive.
- HKEY_USERS data is kept in the Default hive.
- HKEY_CURRENT_USER data is kept in a portion of the Default hive.

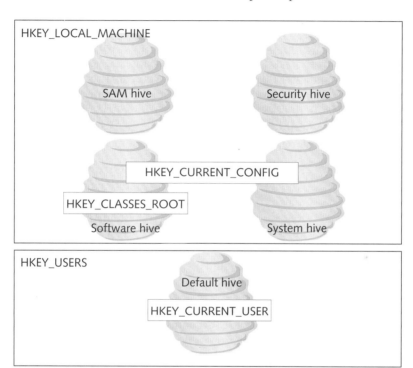

Figure 8-13   The relationship between registry subtrees (keys) and hives

From Figure 8-13, you can also see that some subtrees use data contained in other subtrees. For instance, the HKEY_CURRENT_USER data is a subset of the data in the HKEY_USERS subtree. HKEY_CURRENT_CONFIG and HKEY_CLASSES_ROOT subtrees use data contained in the HKEY_LOCAL_MACHINE subtree. However, don't let this physical relationship cloud your view of the logical relationship among these subtrees. Although data is shared among the different subtrees, logically speaking, none of the five subtrees is subordinate to any other.

The registry hives are stored in the \%SystemRoot%\system32\config folder as a group of files. In a physical sense, each hive is a file. Each hive is backed up with a log file and a backup file, which are also stored in the \%SystemRoot%\system32\config folder.

Editing the Registry

A+
OS
1.1
1.2
1.5

When you make a change in the Control Panel, Device Manager, or many other places in Windows NT/2000/XP, the registry is modified automatically. This is the only way most users will ever change the registry. However, on rare occasions you might need to edit the registry manually, for example, when you are following the directions of Microsoft technical support staff to delete references in the registry to viruses or worms. Changes to the registry take effect immediately and are permanent.

Before you edit the registry, you should back it up so that you can restore it if something goes wrong. Backing up the system state, which you learned to do in Chapter 5, is one way to back up the registry. In Chapter 5, you backed up the system state after a Windows 2000 installation, but you can also back up the system state at any time. When the system state is backed up, the Backup utility also puts a copy of the registry files in the %SystemRoot%\repair folder.

Windows NT/2000 offers two registry editors, each with a slightly different look and feel, and with some slight differences:

- Regedt32.exe located in the \%SystemRoot%\system32 folder, which shows each key in a separate window. Use it to edit the registry.
- Regedit.exe located in the \%SystemRoot% folder, which shows all keys in the same window and has a look and feel similar to Explorer. Use it to search and view the registry. Regedt32 only uses FIND to find a given key, whereas a more robust Regedt searches for keys, values, and data by using all or part of a word.

Regedt32.exe has a Security menu that allows you to apply permissions to keys and subkeys to control which user accounts have access to these keys. Under the Options menu, you have the option to work in read-only mode. Unlike Regedt, Regedt32 does not support importing and exporting the registry. Regedt, however, does have the disadvantage that it cannot display the registry values longer than 256 characters.

To access a registry editor, type the program name in the Run dialog box. With Windows XP, typing either Regedt32 or Regedit in the Run dialog box launches the Regedit.exe program.

The following example uses Regedit.exe under Windows XP to view the registry and look at registry values. To access Regedit.exe, double-click the filename in Windows Explorer or enter the filename in the Run dialog box. Figure 8-14 shows a detailed view of the registry.

A+
OS
1.1
1.2
1.5

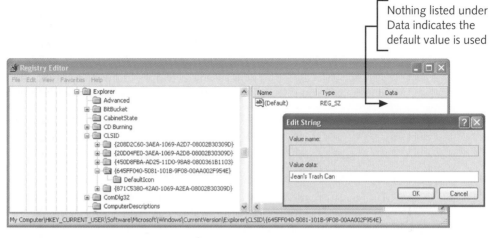

Nothing listed under Data indicates the default value is used

Figure 8-14   Editing a registry subkey value

Let's look at one example of editing the registry. Follow these directions to first back up the system state before editing the registry:

1. Click **Start**, **All Programs**, **Accessories**, **System Tools**, **Backup**. The Backup or Restore Wizard appears.

2. Click **Advanced Mode**. The Backup Utility window appears. Click the **Backup** tab.

3. Check the **System State** box, and under **Backup media or file name**, select the location to store the backup.

4. Click **Start Backup**. In the dialog box that appears, click **Start Backup** again to confirm the action. After the backup is done, click **Close** to close the Backup utility.

To change the name of the Recycle Bin on the Windows XP desktop for the currently logged-on user, do the following:

1. To open Registry Editor, click **Start**, **Run**, and then type **Regedit** in the Run dialog box. Click **OK**. The Registry Editor window appears.

2. Locate the following subkey, which is the name of the Recycle Bin on the Windows desktop, by double-clicking the yellow folder icon of each subkey, moving down through the tree to the lowest subkey value. As you move down the tree, if the currently selected subkey has a value, that value appears in the right pane of the window.

HKEY_CURRENT_USER\Software\Microsoft\Windows\CurrentVersion\
Explorer\CLSID\645FF040-5081-101B-9F08-00AA002F954E

8

A+
OS
1.1
1.2
1.5

3. Figure 8-14 shows the subkey. The right pane shows nothing listed under Data, so the default value is used, which is the value for Recycle Bin. Position the window on the screen so that you can see the Recycle Bin icon.

4. Double-click the name of the value in the right pane. The Edit String dialog box appears. The Value data should be empty in the dialog box. If a value is present, you selected the wrong value. Check your work and try again.

5. Enter a new name for the Recycle Bin. For example, in Figure 8-14, the new name is "Jean's Trash Can." Click **OK**.

6. To see your change, right-click the desktop and select **Refresh** on the shortcut menu. The name of the Recycle Bin changes.

7. To restore the name to the default value, on the Registry Editor window, again double-click the name of the value. The Edit String dialog box appears. Delete your entry and click **OK**.

8. To verify the change is made, right-click the desktop and select **Refresh** on the shortcut menu. The Recycle Bin name should return to its default value.

From these directions, you can see that changes made to the registry take effect immediately. Therefore, take extra care when editing the registry. If you make a mistake and don't know how to correct a problem you create, then you can restore the system state to recover.

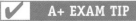

Other Maintenance and Troubleshooting Tools

A+
OS
3.1
3.2

This section discusses other commonly used tools that Windows XP provides for maintenance and troubleshooting. Some tools are new or changed in Windows XP, and some operate just as they do in Windows 2000. Table 8-3 lists several tools and their functions. Some tools are executed from a command line (have an .exe file extension), others are Microsoft Management Console snap-ins (have an .msc file extension), and others are tools built into Windows XP (such as Safe Mode). MMC was discussed in Chapter 6. MMC snap-ins are executed from the Run dialog box or can sometimes be accessed using Windows menus. Some command-line programs can be executed from the Run dialog box, and all can be executed from a command prompt window.

✔ **A+ EXAM TIP**

The A+ OS exam expects you to know the program filename of important Windows utilities.

Several tools listed in the table are discussed later in the chapter. For more extensive information about any of these tools, search Help and Support on your Windows XP computer, search the Microsoft Knowledge Base at *support.microsoft.com*, or see the book, *Microsoft Windows XP Professional Resource Kit Documentation* by Microsoft Press. In addition, to get help about a command-line tool, from a command prompt, enter the tool name followed by /?. For example, to get help about Defrag, enter Defrag /?.

Tool	Description
Add or Remove Programs	From the Control Panel, uninstalls software that is causing a problem
Automated System Recovery (ASR)	Drastically recovers a failed system. Use only as a last resort, because the logical drive on which Windows is installed is formatted and restored from the most recent backup. All data and applications written to the drive since the last backup are lost.
Backup (Ntbackup.exe)	Backs up and restores data and software
Boot logging	An option on the Advanced Options startup menu to log events to the Ntbtlog.txt file
Bootcfg (Bootcfg.exe)	Views and edits the contents of the Boot.ini file used to hold startup settings
Cacls.exe	Changes access control lists (ACLs) assigned to a file or group of files to control which users have access to a file and the type of access they have (read, write, change, or full). For more information on CACLS, type Help Cacls at a command prompt.
Chkdsk (Chkdsk.exe)	Checks and repairs errors on a logical drive
Cipher.exe	Displays and changes the encryptions applied to files and folders using the NTFS file system
Compact.exe	Displays and changes the compressions applied to files and folders using the NTFS file system
Computer Management (Compmgmt.msc)	Console provides access to several snap-ins used to manage and troubleshoot a system
Convert.exe	Converts a FAT16 or a FAT32 logical drive to NTFS
Defrag.exe	A command-line tool to defragment a logical drive or floppy disk, it is similar to the graphic tool, Disk Defragmenter.
Dependency Walker (Depends.exe)	Provides a list of files needed for an application to load
Device Driver Roll Back	Replaces a driver with the one that worked before the current driver was installed
Device Manager (Devmgmt.msc)	Displays and changes device drivers and other hardware settings

8

Table 8-3 (continued)

Tool	Description
DirectX Diagnostic Tool (Dxdiag.exe)	Used to troubleshoot problems with the DirectX application programming interface (API) used by Microsoft
Disk Cleanup (Cleanmgr.exe)	Deletes unused files to make more disk space available
Disk Defragmenter (Dfrg.msc)	Defragments a logical drive or floppy disk
Disk Management (Diskmgmt.msc)	Displays and changes partitions on hard drives and formats drives
DiskPart (Diskpart.exe)	A command-line tool to manage partitions and volumes of a hard drive similar to the graphic tool, Disk Management. Use DiskPart to write scripts to automate disk management tasks. It's also a handy way to assign drive letters to IDE devices.
Dr. Watson (Drwtsn32.exe)	Records errors and information about those errors when applications fail. Errors are recorded in a log file named **Drwatson.log**. Note this is a different name than the log filename in Windows 2000, which is Drwtsn32.log.
Driver Signing and Digital Signatures (Sigverif.exe)	Verifies that drivers, system files, and software have been approved by Microsoft
Error Reporting	Produces an error report and sends it to Microsoft when the error occurs and the PC is connected to the Internet
Event Viewer (Eventvwr.msc)	Records and displays system problems
Expand.exe	Extracts a file from a cabinet file or compressed file
Fsutil (Fsutil.exe)	Displays information about drives and file systems and does advanced management tasks on those drives
Getmac (Getmac.exe)	Displays the MAC address for the installed network adapter (discussed in Chapter 11)
Group Policy (Gpedit.msc)	Displays and changes policies controlling users and the computer

Table 8-3 (continued)

A+
OS
3.1
3.2

Tool	Description
Group Policy Result (Gpresult.exe)	Displays currently applied group policies (also know as Resultant Set of Policies, or RSoP), which helps to determine which of several policies are active for computers and users.
Group Policy Update (Gpupdate.exe)	Immediately puts into effect changes you have just made to local group policies
Help and Support	Provides helpful information, connects to Windows newsgroups, enables Remote Assistance, and steps you through many other troubleshooting tasks
Last Known Good Configuration	A startup option used when normal or Safe Mode does not work. Using this tool, you can revert the system back to before a driver or application that is causing problems was installed.
Performance Monitor (Perfmon.msc)	Reports information about performance problems
Program Compatibility Wizard	Looks at legacy software and attempts to resolve issues that prevent the software from working in Windows XP
Recovery Console	Provides a command line to perform troubleshooting tasks when the desktop will not load
Registry Editor (Regedit.exe)	Displays and changes entries in the registry
Remote Assistance	Allows a user to share his computer with a support technician at a remote location so that the technician can control the computer
Remote Desktop	Allows a support technician to control a Windows XP computer remotely
Runas.exe	Runs a program using different permissions than those assigned to the currently logged-on user
Safe Mode	Loads the Windows desktop with a minimum configuration and then is used to troubleshoot problems with device drivers, display settings, and other startup options that are causing problems
SC (Sc.exe)	Communicates commands to the Service Controller, which starts, stops, and manages programs that run in the background such as device drivers or Internet Connection Firewall

8

Table 8-3 (continued)

Tool	Description
Services (Services.msc)	Graphical version of SC
System Configuration Utility (Msconfig.exe)	Controls settings used to troubleshoot a failing system
System File Checker (Sfc.exe)	Verifies the version of all system files when Windows loads
System Information (Msinfo32.exe)	Displays information about hardware, applications, and Windows that is useful when troubleshooting. Figure 8-15 shows a view of the System Information window.
System Information (Systeminfo.exe)	A version of System Information to be used from a command-prompt window. Information is listed on screen as text only. To direct that information to a file, use the command Systeminfo.exe >Myfile.txt. Later the file can be printed and used to document information about the system.
System Restore	Used to restore the system to a previously working condition, it restores the registry, some system files, and some application files.
Task Killing Utility (Tskill.exe)	Stops a process or program currently running. Useful when managing background services such as an email server or Web server.
Task Lister (Tasklist.exe)	Lists currently running processes similar to the list provided by Task Manager
Task Manager (Taskman.exe)	Lists and stops currently running processes. Use Task Manager to stop a locked-up application.
Uninstall Windows XP Professional	Used to uninstall Windows XP and revert back to a previously installed OS
Windows File Protection	Protects system files and restores overwritten system files as needed
Windows Update (Wupdmgr.exe)	Updates Windows by examining the system, comparing it to available updates on the Microsoft Web site, and recommending appropriate updates

Table 8-3   Windows XP maintenance and troubleshooting tools

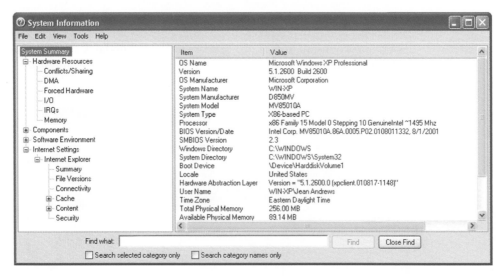

Figure 8-15   The System Information window displays important information about the system's hardware, software, and environment

Help on the Web

Microsoft offers help and updates on the Web. In earlier chapters, you learned to use the Microsoft Knowledge Base at *support.microsoft.com*. This section shows you how to access the Windows Update feature and Windows XP newsgroups.

Windows Update

A+
OS
2.2

Windows XP has an automated way to update the OS, applications, and device drivers made available on the Microsoft Web site. If no user interaction is required, anyone can perform the update, but if decisions must be made during the update, only someone with administrator privileges can perform the update.

To do an update including updating the OS, software and drivers, click Start, All Programs, and Windows Update. The Update Wizard takes you to the Microsoft Windows Update Web site (see Figure 8-16). Click "Scan for updates" and follow the directions onscreen. This update process includes updating drivers, a process that can also be started from Device Manager, as you learned in the last chapter.

If an update is available for your computer, a window similar to the one shown in Figure 8-17 appears. Note in the figure that the update process found one critical update, nine updates to Windows XP that it does not consider critical, and no updates for drivers. To view information about these updates, click them. In this example, the critical update was designed to solve a problem with security, and the nine noncritical updates were about running Java applets, connecting to a UPS (uninterruptible power supply) service, using a CD burner, running legacy applications using compatibility mode, problems with the Files and Settings Transfer Wizard,

A+
OS
2.2

problems using Remote Assistance across a firewall, and problems with Windows Messenger and Movie Maker. By default, only the critical update is selected for installing. To install noncritical updates, select the updates you want and then click Add. After you have selected what to update, click "Review and install updates" and follow directions on the screen.

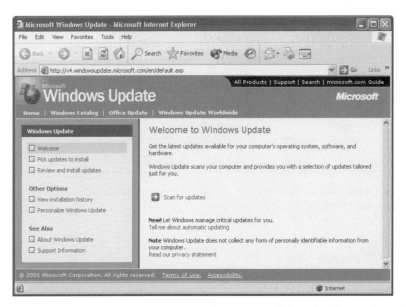

Figure 8-16 The Windows Update utility manages the process of downloading updates from the Microsoft Web site

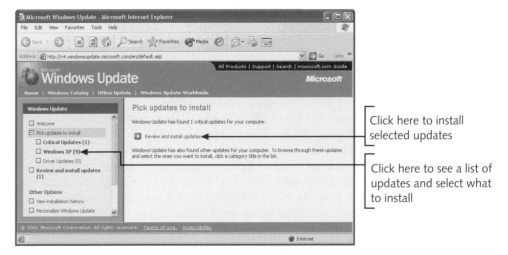

Click here to install selected updates

Click here to see a list of updates and select what to install

Figure 8-17 Windows Update process found updates appropriate to this computer

A+
OS
2.2

Sometimes errors occur during the update process or a later patch will corrupt an earlier patch. Microsoft offers a tool, Qfecheck.exe, that can be downloaded from the Microsoft Web site. You use Qfecheck.exe to scan a system for patches and report whether these patches or hotfixes are installed correctly. The tool examines the registry for patches that it thinks are installed and then verifies that these patches are installed and working correctly. To learn more about Qfecheck.exe and to download it, go to the Microsoft support site at *support.microsoft.com* and search for Knowledge Base Article 282784.

NOTE Windows XP does not ship with support for USB 2.0 (USB Hi-Speed). If you have a USB 2.0 port on your PC, the Update Wizard will recommend that you update the USB driver to support USB 2.0 unless you have already installed a third-party USB 2.0 driver. If you want to download the Microsoft USB 2.0 driver, first uninstall the third-party driver and then perform Windows Update.

8

Windows Newsgroups

If you have exhausted your sources of information and still have not resolved a problem, sometimes you can get help from a Windows newsgroup.

To access a newsgroup, click Start, and then Help and Support. On the Help and Support window, click "Get support, or find information in Windows XP newsgroups." Then click "Go to a Windows Web site forum." Click "Go to Windows Newsgroups." In the forum, you can post a question or read questions and answers posted by other users. Microsoft does not support this forum, so be careful about following the advice of users posting answers to questions on the forum.

In addition to newsgroups and the Microsoft Web site, many good Windows support Web sites exist. To get a very long list of these sites, go to a search engine on the Web such as *www.google.com* and enter Windows Help in the search box.

Troubleshooting the Boot Process

A+
OS
2.3
3.1
3.2
3.3

The Windows XP boot process works the same way as the Windows NT and Windows 2000 boot process. Refer to Chapter 6 for a review of the process and the files required for a successful boot. Many tools you learned about in Chapter 6 to recover from a failed Windows 2000 boot also work under Windows XP. They are briefly mentioned in this section to make the troubleshooting process complete. In addition, Windows XP has added two tools for solving problems with the boot process: System Restore and Automated System Recovery. The tools to use when troubleshooting a failed boot are listed here in the order you should use them. Each tool discussed is more drastic than the one before it, affecting more of the system, installed hardware and software, and user data.

- Last Known Good Configuration and, in certain situations, Driver Rollback
- Safe Mode on the Advanced Options menu
- System Restore
- Windows 2000/XP Boot Disk
- Recovery Console
- Automated System Recovery
- Reinstall Windows XP using the Windows XP CD

You learned how to use the Last Known Good Configuration for Windows NT and Windows 2000 in Chapter 6. In addition, you can use Driver Rollback discussed in Chapter 7 if you suspect that a single device driver is the source of the problem. The Windows XP Advanced Options menu, shown in Figure 8-18, is also similar to that of Windows 2000. Refer to Chapter 6 for a discussion of each of the options on the menu and how to use them. Try Safe Mode with Networking first. If that doesn't work, try Safe Mode.

```
Windows Advanced Options Menu
Please select an option:

    Safe Mode
    Safe Mode with Networking
    Safe Mode with Command Prompt

    Enable Boot Logging
    Enable VGA Mode
    Last Known Good Configuration (your most recent settings that worked)
    Directory Services Restore Mode (Windows domain controllers only)
    Debugging Mode

    Start Windows Normally
    Reboot
    Return to OS Choices Menu

Use the up and down arrow keys to move the highlight to your choice.
```

Figure 8-18   Windows XP Advanced Options menu

To access the Advanced Options menu, press F8 while Windows is loading.

NOTE

The next tool to use if these don't work is System Restore, a tool new to Windows XP, which is discussed next. If that doesn't work, then try a Windows XP boot disk that you must manually create. If this disk doesn't work, the next tool to use is the Recovery Console. Commands for the Recovery Console for Windows XP are the

A+
OS
2.3
3.1
3.2
3.3

same as for Windows 2000 and were covered in Chapter 6. If the Recovery Console fails, then use the Automated System Recovery process to restore the hard drive to its state as of the last ASR backup. If you don't have an ASR backup, then your only recourse is to reinstall Windows XP following directions given in the last chapter. Be sure to scan for viruses before you reinstall.

System Restore

The **System Restore** utility is new to Windows XP. It is similar to ScanReg used on previous versions of Windows; however, System Restore cannot be executed from a command prompt. ScanReg is not included in Windows XP. If you can load Windows XP, then you can use System Restore to restore the system state to its condition at the time a snapshot was taken of the system settings and configuration. The restore process does not affect user data on the hard drive but can affect installed software and hardware, user settings, and OS configuration settings. Also, the restore process cannot help you recover from a virus or worm infection. The restoration is taken from a snapshot of the system state, called a **restore point,** that was created earlier. The system automatically creates a restore point before you install new software or hardware or make other changes to the system. You can also manually create a restore point at any time.

NOTE

The main difference between System Restore and Automated System Recovery is that System Restore does not affect user data on the hard drive, but Automated System Recovery does. To recover a failed system without destroying data, make it a habit to always create a restore point every time you make a change to the system.

APPLYING CONCEPTS

To manually create a restore point:

1. Click **Start, All Programs, Accessories, System Tools,** and **System Restore**. The System Restore window appears.
2. The System Restore window gives you two choices: Restore my computer to an earlier time and Create a restore point. Select **Create a restore point**, and then click **Next**.
3. Type a description of the restore point such as "Just before I updated the video driver." The system automatically assigns the current date and time to the restore point.
4. Click **Create** and then **Close**. The restore point is saved.

Before using System Restore to undo a change, if the change was made to a hardware device, first try Driver Rollback so that as few changes as possible to the system are lost. If

8

A+
OS
2.3
3.1
3.2
3.3

Driver Rollback does not work or is not appropriate, do the following to revert the system back to the restore point:

1. Click **Start**, **All Programs**, **Accessories**, **System Tools**, and **System Restore**.
2. If necessary, click **Restore my computer to an earlier time**, and then click **Next**. A window appears as shown in Figure 8-19. Notice the two restore points in the figure, one created by the system and one created manually.

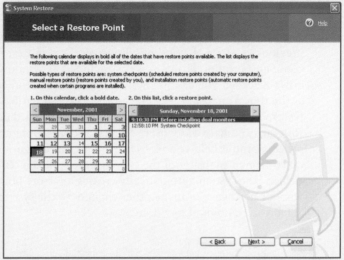

Figure 8-19   Restore points are automatically created daily and every time software or hardware is installed

3. Select the date and time and the specific restore point. Click **Next** twice.

Windows XP reboots and restores the system state to the settings saved in the restore point. Changes to user data are not affected but any installation or configuration changes made after the restore point are lost.

NOTE

To roll back the system to a Windows XP System Restore point using Windows XP requires that you can boot from the hard drive. However, there are other options using third-party utility software. For example, ERD Commander 2003 by Winternals (*www.winternals.com*) is an operating system that can be loaded from CD. Boot from the ERD Commander 2003 CD, which loads a GUI interface that looks like Windows XP. Using this Winternals desktop, you can access the registry, event logs, and Disk Management console and reset a forgotten administrator password. You can also roll back the Windows XP system to a System Restore point.

A+
OS
2.3
3.1
3.2
3.3

When selecting a restore point, select a point as close to the present as you can so that as few changes to the system as possible are lost. Accessing System Restore using the previous process assumes you can boot to a Windows desktop. If you can't do that, first try booting into Safe Mode and then use the previous procedure from the Safe Mode desktop. If that doesn't work, try booting to the Advanced Options menu.

From the Advanced Options menu, select Safe Mode. When you do that, Windows XP asks if you want to go directly to System Restore rather than to Safe Mode. Choose to go directly to System Restore.

✔ **A+ EXAM TIP**

The A+ OS exam expects you to know how to boot to a system restore point.

MS-DOS Startup Disk

Using Windows Explorer, you can create an MS-DOS startup disk that can be used to boot into MS-DOS mode, giving you an A prompt. This bootable disk is sometimes needed when following a BIOS manufacturer's procedure to flash BIOS. Also, the disk can be useful if the system will not boot, the hard drive is not using the NTFS file system, and you need to access the drive to recover data files. You cannot launch Windows XP using the startup disk or use it to recover from a failed installation.

To create a startup disk, using Windows Explorer, right-click drive A and select Format on the shortcut menu. The Format dialog box opens, as shown in Figure 8-20. Check "Create an MS-DOS startup disk," and then click Start. The unhidden files that Windows puts on the startup disk are shown in Figure 8-21. In addition to these files, Autoexec.bat, Config.sys, and the Windows 98 versions of Io.sys and Msdos.sys are also placed on the disk as hidden files.

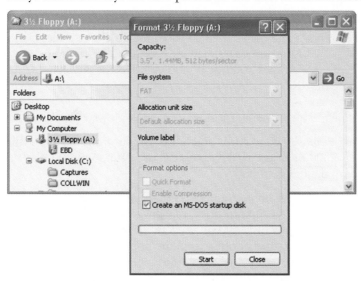

Figure 8-20   Windows XP gives you the ability to create an MS-DOS startup disk

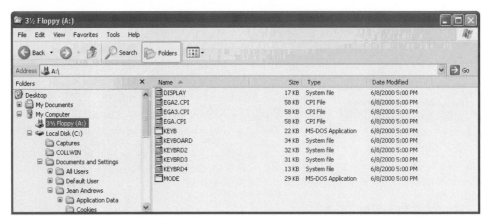

Figure 8-21   Files on the MS-DOS startup disk created by Windows XP

Windows XP Boot Disk

When troubleshooting a failed boot, if System Restore does not work, the next tool to try is the Windows XP boot disk. (You can also create and use a Windows 2000 boot disk to troubleshoot a failed Windows 2000 system.) If you boot from the disk and the Windows 2000/XP desktop loads successfully, then the problem is associated with a missing or damaged boot sector, master boot record, partition table, Ntldr file, Ntdetect.com file, Ntbootdd.sys (if it exists), boot.ini file, or a virus infection. However, a boot disk cannot be used to troubleshoot problems associated with unstable device drivers or those that occur after the Windows 2000 or Windows XP logon screen is displayed.

You first create the boot disk by formatting the disk using a working Windows 2000/XP computer and then copying files to the disk. These files can be copied from a Windows 2000/XP setup CD or a Windows 2000/XP computer that is using the same version of Windows 2000 or Windows XP as the problem PC. Do the following to create the disk:

1. Obtain a floppy disk and format it on a Windows 2000/XP computer.

2. Using Explorer, copy Ntldr and Ntdetect.com from the \i386 folder on the Windows 2000 or Windows XP setup CD or a Windows 2000/XP computer to the root of the floppy disk.

3. If your computer boots from a SCSI hard drive, then obtain a device driver (*.sys) for your SCSI hard drive, rename it Ntbootdd.sys, and copy it to the root of the floppy disk. (If you used an incorrect device driver, then you will receive an error after booting from the floppy disk. The error will mention a "computer disk hardware configuration problem" and that it "could not read from the selected boot disk." If this occurs, contact your computer

manufacturer for the correct version of the SCSI hard drive device driver for your computer.)

4. After viewing Boot.ini on the problem computer, obtain an identical copy from another known good computer (or create your own) and copy it to the root of the floppy disk.

If the problem computer is booting from an IDE hard drive then its Boot.ini should be similar to:

```
[boot loader]
timeout=30
default=multi(0)disk(0)rdisk(0)partition(1)\WINDOWS
[operating systems]
multi(0)disk(0)rdisk(0)partition(1)\WINDOWS="Microsoft
Windows XP Professional" /fastdetect
```

Note that there is a carriage return after the /fastdetect switch.

5. Write-protect the floppy disk so it cannot become infected with a virus.

NOTE

To learn more about the Windows XP boot disk, see the Microsoft Knowledge Base Articles 305595 and 314503 at the Microsoft Web site *support.microsoft.com*. To learn more about the Windows NT/2000 boot disk, see the Microsoft Knowledge Base Article 301680.

You have now created the Windows XP boot disk. Check CMOS setup to make sure the first boot device is set to the floppy disk, and then insert the boot disk and reboot your computer. If you did not enter Windows XP successfully by using the boot disk, then the next tool to try is the Recovery Console.

If you loaded Windows XP successfully, but with error messages, then do the following to attempt to repair the Windows XP installation:

- Load the Recovery Console and use the Fixmbr and Fixboot commands to repair the MBR and the boot sector.
- Run antivirus software.
- Use Disk Management to verify that the hard drive partition table is correct.
- Defragment your hard drive.
- Copy Ntldr, Ntdetect.com, and Boot.ini from your floppy disk to the root of the hard drive.
- If you're using a SCSI hard drive, copy Ntbootdd.sys from your floppy disk to the root of the hard drive.

Automated System Recovery

After you finish a Windows XP installation, if you create the Automated System Recovery disk set, you can use this or a later set of the recovery disks to restore the

A+
OS
2.3
3.1
3.2
3.3

system partition to the state it was in when the backup was made. You will lose any changes made to the volume or logical drive holding Windows XP since the backup. Everything on the volume since the ASR backup and disk were made is lost, including software and device drivers installed, user data, and any changes to the system configuration. For this reason, it's a good idea to make fresh copies of the ASR disk set periodically. You learned how to make this backup and disk in the previous chapter.

If you use the Automated System Recovery process, know that you will lose all data stored on the Windows XP volume since the last backup was made.

To restore the hard drive to the state it was in when the last ASR disk set was made, do the following:

1. Insert the Windows XP CD in the CD-ROM drive and hard boot the PC.

2. A message says "Press any key to boot from CD." Press any key.

3. A blue screen appears with the message, "Press F6 to load RAID or SCSI drivers." If your system uses RAID or SCSI, press **F6**.

4. At the bottom of the blue screen, a message says, "Press F2 to run the Automated System Recovery process." Press **F2**.

5. The screen shown in Figure 8-22 appears, instructing you to insert the ASR floppy disk. Insert the disk and then press **Enter**.

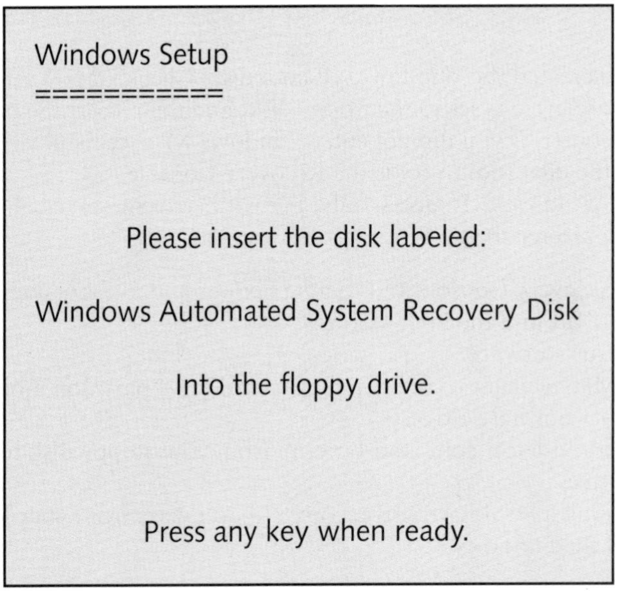

```
Windows Setup
============



            Please insert the disk labeled:

    Windows Automated System Recovery Disk

              Into the floppy drive.




            Press any key when ready.
```

Figure 8-22   Automatic System Recovery process must have the ASR floppy disk

A+
OS
2.3
3.1
3.2
3.3

Windows XP Setup does the following:

- Loads files it needs to run
- Repartitions and reformats the drive
- Installs Windows from the Windows XP CD
- Launches the Automatic System Recovery Wizard to restore the Windows system state, applications, and data to what they were at the time of the last ASR backup

The ASR recovery process erases everything on the volume being restored. Figure 8-23 shows one of the previous steps in the recovery process, in which you reformat the logical drive just before the Windows XP installation process begins.

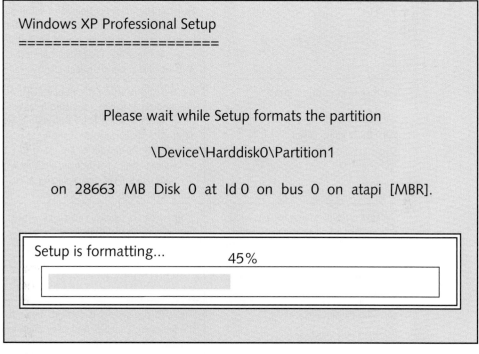

8

Windows XP Professional Setup
=========================

Please wait while Setup formats the partition

\Device\Harddisk0\Partition1

on 28663 MB Disk 0 at Id 0 on bus 0 on atapi [MBR].

Setup is formatting... 45%

Figure 8-23   As part of the Automatic System Recovery process, Windows XP Setup repartitions and reformats the volume holding Windows XP

Error Messages and Their Meanings

A+
OS
2.3
3.1
3.2
3.3

Table 8-4 lists some Windows XP error messages and what they mean. Most of these errors occur when booting.

Error Message	What It Means and What to Do About It
Invalid partition table Error loading operating system Missing operating system	The program in the MBR displays these messages when it cannot find the active partition on the hard drive or the boot sector on that partition. Use Fdisk or Diskpart from a command prompt to check the hard drive partition table for errors. Sometimes Fdisk/mbr solves the problem. Third-party recovery software such as PartitionMagic might help. If a setup program came bundled with the hard drive (such as Data Lifeguard from Western Digital or MaxBlast from Maxtor), use it to examine the drive. Check the hard drive manufacturer's Web site for other diagnostic software.
A disk read error occurred NTLDR is missing NTLDR is compressed	A disk is probably in the floppy disk drive. Remove the disk and reboot. When booting from the hard drive, these errors occur if Ntldr has been moved, renamed, or deleted, or is corrupted; if the boot sector on the active partition is corrupted; or you have just tried to install an older version of Windows, such as Windows 98, on the hard drive. First try replacing Ntldr. Then check Boot.ini settings.
A text error message appears on a blue screen and then the system halts. These Windows NT/2000/XP errors are called **stop errors** or **blue screens (BSOD)**. Some stop errors follow.	Stop errors are usually caused by viruses, errors in the file system, a corrupted hard drive, or a hardware problem.
Stop 0x00000024 or NTFS_File_System	The NTFS file system is corrupt. Immediately boot into the Recovery Console, and copy important data files that have not been backed up to another media before attempting to recover the system.
Stop 0x00000050 or Page_Fault_in_Nonpaged_Area	Most likely RAM is defective.
Stop 0x00000077 or Kernel_Stack_Inpage_Error	Bad sectors are on the hard drive, there is a hard drive hardware problem, or RAM is defective. Try running Chkdsk or, for the FAT file system, run ScanDisk using a Windows 98 startup disk.

Table 8-4 (continued)

Error Message	What It Means and What to Do About It
Stop 0x0000007A or Kernel_Data_Inpage_Error	There is a bad sector on the hard drive where the paging file is stored; there is a virus or defective RAM. Try running Chkdsk or Scandisk.
Stop 0x0000007B or Inaccessible_Boot_Device	There is a boot sector virus or failing hardware. Try Fdisk/mbr or fixmbr.
Black screen with no error messages	This is likely to be a corrupted MBR, partition table, boot sector, or Ntldr file. Boot the PC using a Windows XP boot disk and then try the fixmbr and fixboot commands from the Recovery Console. You might have to reinstall Windows.

Table 8-4   Windows XP error messages and their meanings

8

CHAPTER SUMMARY

▶ Windows NT/2000/XP requires a valid user account before you can use Windows. The user account identifies the user to Windows. Permissions assigned to a user account control what the user can and cannot do and access in Windows.

▶ Local user accounts apply to a single standalone computer or a single computer in a workgroup, and global user accounts are managed from a domain controller and apply to every computer in the domain.

▶ When using Windows in a domain, global user account information is stored in the SAM, which is part of Active Directory in Windows 2000 Server and Windows 2003 Server.

▶ When a user makes changes to the system, the changes are often recorded in the user profile, so the next time the user logs on, these changes automatically take effect.

▶ Methods that administrators can use to manage and secure multiple computers and users include roaming user profiles, mandatory user profiles, and group profiles.

▶ Passwords on user accounts are needed to secure computers and their resources. Passwords should not be easy to guess and should be a combination of letters, numbers, and nonalphanumeric characters.

▶ An administrator can create a user account using the Computer Management console or the User Accounts applet in Control Panel.

▶ Resetting a password under Windows XP causes the OS to lock out the user from using encrypted email or files or using Internet passwords stored on the computer. For that reason, it is a good idea for a user to create a Windows XP forgotten password floppy disk.

▶ In Windows NT/2000, you can only log on to the system by pressing Ctrl+Alt+Del to open the logon window. In a Windows XP workgroup, you can use the logon window, Welcome screen, or Fast User Switching.

▶ Windows XP user groups include Administrators, Backup Operators, Power Users, Limited Users, and Guests. In this list, each group has fewer permissions and rights than the previous group.

▶ Using disk quotas, an administrator can limit the amount of hard drive space a user can use.

▶ File and folder encryption and disk quotas in Windows 2000/XP require using the NTFS file system.

▶ Internet Connection Firewall (ICF) prevents communication from the Internet from accessing the system if the communication has not been initiated by the local computer.

▶ The Windows NT/2000/XP registry is organized logically into five subtrees or keys and organized physically into five files called hives. There is no one-to-one correspondence between the subtrees and the hives.

▶ The registry is edited using a registry editor, which is accessed by entering Regedit in the Run dialog box. Changes to the registry are immediate, so always make a backup of the system state before editing the registry.

▶ Windows XP offers many troubleshooting and maintenance tools. Some are available from the command line. Others are Microsoft Management Console (MMC) snap-ins, and still others are built into Windows XP.

▶ You can get help on the Web for Windows XP. Microsoft offers Windows Update and Microsoft Knowledge Base. There are also Windows newsgroups and other Web sites where you can get help.

▶ Two recovery tools new to Windows XP are Automated System Recovery and System Restore.

▶ The Automated System Recovery (ASR) process creates a backup and an ASR floppy disk that can be used to restore the backup of the volume or logical drive holding Windows XP.

▶ The Windows XP System Restore utility is similar to ScanReg in earlier versions of Windows but cannot be executed at a command prompt. System Restore restores the system state using restore points, which are snapshots of the system state.

KEY TERMS

For explanations of key terms, see the Glossary near the end of the book.

Backup Operator
blue screen (BSOD)
built-in user account
disk quota
Drwatson.log
Encrypted File System (EFS)
encryption
firewall
forgotten password floppy disk
global user account

Group Policy
group profile
Guest
hardware profile
hive
Internet Connection Firewall (ICF)
key
Limited User

local user account
mandatory user profile
Power User
restore point
roaming user profile
stop error
System Restore
user account
user profile

8

REVIEWING THE BASICS

1. Which operating system has the most security: Windows 9x or Windows XP?

2. What is the difference between joining a workgroup and joining a domain?

3. Where is user account information stored on a Windows 2000/2003 domain?

4. When is the local user profile created?

5. How are a roaming profile and a mandatory profile the same? How are they different?

6. What is the difference between the tools ASR and System Restore?

7. What are two important criteria that make for a good password?

8. What can a user do to keep from having the administrator reset a forgotten password?

9. Which user group has more rights, Power Users or Administrators?

10. When using Group Policy on a computer in a workgroup, which type of configuration do you use?

11. What do you implement to control how much disk space a user can take up?

12. Explain how to decrypt a file using My Computer.

13. What command can you use at the command prompt to encrypt a file?

14. Which applet in Control Panel is used to enable and disable Internet Connection Firewall?

15. Which Windows registry subtree contains information about the currently logged-on user?

16. Which Windows registry subtree gets all its information from the HKEY_LOCAL_MACHINE subtree?

17. In Windows NT/2000/XP, a file that contains part of the Windows registry is called a(n) _____.

18. What is the Windows XP command to access the registry editor?

19. What is the name of the utility program that allows you to view and edit Boot.ini?

20. How is Dr. Watson different in Windows XP from how it was in Windows 2000?

21. How is the registry editor different in Windows XP from how it was in Windows 2000?

22. What is the name of the snap-in file for Disk Defragmenter?

23. Looking at a program filename and file extension, how can you tell if the program is a MMC snap-in or a command-line program?

24. What is the name of the log file created when boot logging is enabled from the Advanced Options startup menu?

25. What is a restore point, and what is it used for?

26. ScanReg has been replaced by System Restore in Windows XP. What is the main advantage that ScanReg has over System Restore?

27. Can you use an MS-DOS startup disk to launch Windows XP? To recover data files? To recover from a failed installation of Windows XP?

28. What are two recovery tools new to Windows XP that are used to recover from a failed boot?

29. When trying to restore a failed system, what should you do next if Recovery Console does not work?

30. Place these tools in the order in which you should try them when troubleshooting the boot process: Recovery Console, Advanced Options menu, System Restore.

THINKING CRITICALLY

1. Suppose a user has encrypted important data files and now is no longer working for your company. How do you decrypt these files so they can be read?

2. If your computer at home is connected to the Internet by way of your spouse's computer, which is connected to the Internet using cable modem, which computer should have Internet Connection Firewall enabled?

3. Your Windows XP system locks up occasionally. What are some probable causes and solutions? *Note:* This question combines skills learned in this and other chapters.

    a. The hard drive has errors. Run _____ to correct file system errors.

    b. An application might not be compatible with Windows XP. To find out if you have applications installed that are not certified by Microsoft for Windows XP, run the _____ utility.

    c. The hard drive might be full. To find out use _____.

    d. The system might have a virus. To eliminate that possibility, use _____.

4. You are attempting to upload images from your digital camera to your Windows XP system using a USB connection, but you get errors. Select the appropriate task or tasks to solve the problem. List the selected tasks in the order you should perform them.

    a. Update Windows XP with service packs or patches.

    b. Reinstall the digital camera software.

    c. Reboot your system.

    d. Verify the camera is turned on.

HANDS-ON PROJECTS

PROJECT 8-1: Problem-Solving Using the Microsoft Knowledge Base

Your hard drive has been attacked by a malicious virus, and you have decided to restore it from the last backup made by the ASR backup process. You cannot find the ASR floppy disk required for the restore process. Search the Microsoft Knowledge Base for the steps to re-create the ASR floppy disk when the ASR backup is available. Print the Knowledge Base article.

PROJECT 8-2: Using the Microsoft Management Console

Microsoft Management Console under Windows XP works the same as it does under Windows 2000. Follow the step-by-step directions in Chapter 6 to create a customized console in Windows XP. Put two snap-ins in the console: Device Manager and Event Viewer.

PROJECT 8-3: Using System Restore

Create a restore point. Make a change to the display settings. Restore the system using System Restore. Are the changes still in effect? Why or why not?

PROJECT 8-4: Using the ASR Process

Create an ASR backup following directions in the chapter. Add a few data files to the hard drive. Restore the system using the ASR process. Do the data files still exist on the hard drive? Why or why not?

PROJECT 8-4: Exploring the Internet Connection Firewall

Using the Windows XP Help and Support Center, answer these questions about Internet Connection Firewall:

1. List the steps to view the contents of the log file that ICF uses to record dropped packets.

2. What is the filename of this log file?

3. What applet in Control Panel can you use to change the location of this file?

4. Which version of Windows XP does not include ICF? Why do you think this is so?

5. Explain how you could use ICF to record when others on your local network access your Windows XP computer.

Managing Memory

In earlier chapters, you learned about the different operating systems, and how to install, support, and troubleshoot them. This chapter looks at an important component in every computer system, memory or RAM, and examines how Windows 9x and Windows NT/2000/XP manage it. You will first learn how DOS and Windows 9x manage memory and then see how managing memory was greatly improved when Windows NT introduced an entirely different approach. This new approach is used by Windows NT/2000/XP. In the next chapter, you will learn how to manage another important PC component, hard drives.

OS Memory Management Evolution

Memory management under DOS and Windows 9x can seem complicated because of the way the process has evolved over the past 20 years or so. Like an old house that has been added to and remodeled several times, the present-day design is not as efficient as that of a brand new house. Decisions made by IBM and Microsoft in the early 1980s still significantly affect, and in some cases limit, the way memory is used under Windows 9x. Because Windows NT, followed by Windows 2000 and Windows XP, have had the luxury of being designed from the ground up, they are free of those limitations.

Early CPUs had only 20 lines on the bus available to handle addresses, so the largest memory address the CPU could use was 11111111111111111111, which is 1,048,575, or 1,024K or 1 MB of memory. This 1 MB of memory was used by DOS and divided up according to the scheme shown in Table 9-1.

Range of Memory Addresses	Range Using Hex Terminology	Type of Memory
0 to 640K	0 to A0000	Conventional or base memory
640K to 1024K	A0000 to FFFFF	Upper memory (A through F ranges)
Above 1024K	100000 and up	Extended memory

Table 9-1   Division of memory under DOS and Windows 9x

The first 640K of memory was used by DOS and applications, and the addresses from 640K up to 1024K were used by the BIOS and device drivers. Then newer CPUs and motherboards were developed with 24 address lines and more, so that memory addresses above 1024K became available; they were called **extended memory**. Windows 9x still uses these same divisions of memory, although it makes the most use of extended memory. Memory addresses are expressed using hexadecimal notation. Because the hex numbers in upper memory begin with A through F, the divisions of upper memory are often referred to as the A range, B range, and so on, up to the F range.

APPLYING CONCEPTS

Using Windows 9x Device Manager, you can see how the first 1 MB of memory addresses are assigned (see Figure 9-1). To view the list, select Computer and click Properties, then click Memory. Notice in the figure that the system BIOS has been assigned memory addresses in the F range of upper memory. This F range is always reserved for motherboard BIOS and is never requested by other programs. When the CPU is first turned on and needs a program to know how to boot up, it begins with the instructions stored on the ROM BIOS chip that are assigned to these memory addresses.

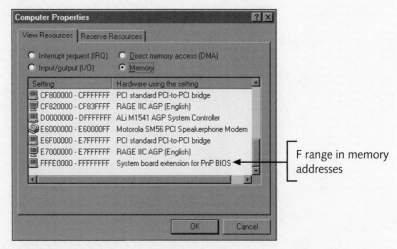

Figure 9-1   Computer Properties window shows how the first megabyte of memory addresses are assigned

How Memory Addresses Are Used

A+
OS
1.1

Once memory addresses have been assigned to memory, they can be used for communication with all software layers. Device drivers, the OS, and application software are all working when a computer is running. During output operations, application software must pass information to the OS, which in turn passes that information to a device driver. The device drivers managing input devices must pass information to the OS, which passes it to the application software. These layers of software all identify the data they want to share by referring to the memory address of the data (see Figure 9-2).

Recall that Windows 95 became the first OS in the evolution of Windows operating systems to support 32-bit, protected-mode application software. However, it still allows 16-bit, real-mode device drivers, and 16-bit software to run in a **virtual DOS machine (VDM)** or to run in real mode. A VDM is an environment that a 32-bit, protected-mode OS provides for a real-mode program to operate in.

9

Figure 9-2   Applications, the OS, and drivers pass data among them by communicating the address of memory holding the data

If Windows 9x forces all software to run in 32-bit, protected mode or in a VDM, then it can control how software accesses hardware. For example, in Figure 9-3, you can see that the 16-bit program running in real mode has direct access to RAM. But in protected mode, more than one program can run, and the programs must depend on the OS to access RAM. This arrangement also allows the OS some latitude in how it uses RAM. If the OS is low on RAM, it can store some data on the hard drive. This method of using the hard drive as though it were RAM is called **virtual memory**, and data stored in virtual memory is stored in a file on the hard drive called a **swap file** or **page file**. The OS manages the entire process, and the applications know nothing about this substitution of hardware resources for RAM.

Windows NT made a break with the past. It requires that all device drivers be 32-bit drivers. It does not allow other software to operate in real mode, but only in a virtual real mode, which it tightly controls. This makes Windows NT a much more stable OS than Windows 9x. (Note that Windows 95 and Windows 98 support 16-bit or 32-bit drivers, but Windows Me only supports 32-bit drivers.)

Table 9-2 summarizes the evolution of operating systems and software as it applies to memory. Notice that Windows NT is the first Microsoft OS to resolve many issues involving real mode, particularly the 1024K limitation imposed by real mode. With DOS, this limitation directly affected memory resource management; in some cases, it can still be significant with Windows 9x.

RAM

16-bit
program

Real mode: One program has direct access to hardware

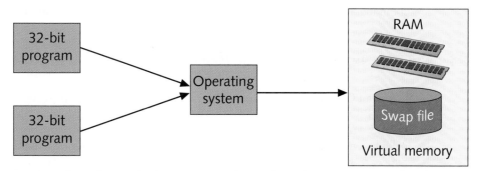

32-bit
program

32-bit
program

Operating
system

RAM

Swap file

Virtual memory

Protected mode: Multiple programs depend on the OS to access hardware

Figure 9-3   Protected mode allows more than one program to run, each protected from the other by the operating system

Operating System	Real Mode	Protected Mode
DOS	Operates totally in real mode, but later offered Himem.sys, a device driver that allows programs access to extended memory.	NA
Windows 95/98	Allows real-mode drivers to be loaded during startup; 16-bit DOS applications are allowed a real-mode session.	Switches back and forth between real mode and protected mode as necessary; supports both 16-bit and 32-bit applications in a virtual machine.
Windows NT/2000/XP	NA	All work is done in protected mode. Supports 32-bit applications. 16-bit applications can operate in a virtual machine only.

Table 9-2   Summary of how operating systems have evolved in managing memory

We now look at how each OS manages memory, beginning with DOS and Windows 9x and then turning our attention to Windows NT/2000/XP.

Windows 9x Memory Management

Windows 9x views and manages memory addresses as DOS did. However, because Windows 9x runs in protected mode and uses virtual memory, it can do a better job of managing extended memory than DOS. This section first looks at how Windows 9x manages memory addresses and then at how it manages virtual memory.

How Windows 9x and DOS Manage Memory Addressing

When a PC is first booted, many programs demand memory addresses, including ROM BIOS programs on the motherboard and some circuit boards, device drivers, the OS, and applications. This process of assigning memory addresses to programs is called memory mapping. Sometimes older ROM BIOS programs and device drivers expect to be assigned certain memory addresses and will not work otherwise. Windows 9x is committed to maintain backward compatibility with these old programs. This fact is probably the greatest limitation of Windows 9x today.

There are several types of memory that the OS manages: conventional, upper, and extended memory. To get a clear picture of this memory-addressing schema, consider the memory map shown in Figure 9-4. The first 640K of memory addresses are called **conventional memory,** or base memory. The memory addresses from 640K up to 1024K are called **upper memory.** Memory above 1024K is called extended memory. The first 64K of extended memory is called the **high memory area (HMA).**

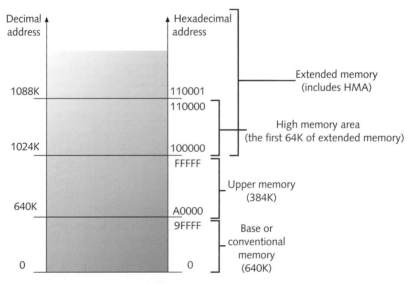

Figure 9-4   Memory address map (not to scale) showing the starting and ending addresses of conventional, upper, and extended memory, including the high memory area

Conventional Memory

In the early 1980s, when IBM and Microsoft were designing the original PCs, they decided to make 640K of memory addresses available to the user, thinking that this was plenty for anything the user would ever want to do. This 640K of addresses was intended to hold the OS, the application software, and the data being processed. At that time, 640K of memory addresses was more than enough to handle all the applications available. Today, 640K of memory addresses is grossly inadequate.

The problem caused by restricting the number of memory addresses available to the user to only 640K could have been solved by simply providing more addresses to the user in future versions of DOS. However, another original design decision ruled this out. The next group of memory addresses, the 384K above conventional memory, called upper memory, were assigned to utility operations for the system. The system requires memory addresses to communicate with peripherals. The programs (such as BIOS on a video card or on the motherboard) and data are assigned memory addresses in this upper memory area. For example, the video BIOS and its data are placed in the very first part of upper memory, the area from 640K to 768K. All video ROM written for DOS-based computers assumes that these programs and data are stored in this area. Also, many DOS and Windows applications interact directly with video ROM and RAM in this address range.

Programs almost always expect data to be written into memory directly above the addresses for the program itself, an important fact for understanding memory management. Thus, if a program begins storing its data above its location in conventional memory, eventually it will "hit the ceiling," the beginning of upper memory assigned to video ROM. The major reason that applications have a 640K memory limit is that video ROM begins at 640K. If DOS and Windows 9x allowed applications into these upper memory addresses, all DOS-compatible video ROM would need to be rewritten, and many DOS applications that access these video addresses would not work. The 32-bit device drivers and applications under Windows 9x don't have this problem because they can run from extended memory and turn to the OS to access video.

Upper Memory

The memory map in Figure 9-4 shows that the memory addresses from 640K up to (but not including) 1024K are called upper memory. In the hexadecimal number system (see Appendix C), upper memory begins at A0000 and goes through FFFFF. Video ROM and RAM are stored in the first part of upper memory, hex A0000 through CFFFF (the A, B, and C areas of memory). Sixteen-bit BIOS programs for other legacy expansion boards are assigned memory addresses in the remaining portions of upper memory. BIOS on the motherboard (system BIOS) is assigned the top part of upper memory, from F0000 through FFFFF (the F area of upper memory). Upper memory often has unassigned addresses, depending on which boards are present in the system. Managing memory effectively involves gaining access to these unused addresses in upper memory and using them to store device drivers and TSR (terminate-and-stay-resident) programs.

Extended Memory and the High Memory Area

Memory above 1 MB is called extended memory. The first 64K of extended memory is called the high memory area, which exists because a bug in the programming for the older Intel 286 CPU (the first CPU to use extended memory) produced this small pocket of unused memory addresses. Beginning with DOS 5, the OS capitalized on this bug by storing portions of itself in the high memory area, thus freeing some conventional memory where DOS had been stored. This method of storing part of DOS in the high memory area is called "loading DOS high." You will see how to do this later in the chapter.

Extended memory is actually managed by the OS as a device (the device is memory) that is controlled by a device driver. To access extended memory, you need the device driver (called a memory extender) that controls it, and you must use applications that have been written to use the extended memory. The amount of extended memory you can have on your computer is limited by the amount of RAM that can be installed on your motherboard and the number of memory addresses the CPU and the memory bus can support.

Utilities that Manage Memory

The two utilities used by Windows 9x to manage memory above 640K are Himem.sys and Emm386.exe. **Himem.sys** is the device driver for all memory above 640K. The program file **Emm386.exe** contains the software that loads device drivers and other programs into upper memory. Himem.sys is automatically loaded by Windows 9x during the boot process, but can also be loaded by an entry in Config.sys. Emm386.exe is not loaded automatically by Windows 9x, but you can load it by an entry in Config.sys.

> ✔ **A+ EXAM TIP**
>
> The A+ OS exam expects you to know how and when to use Himem.sys and Emm386.exe to manage upper and extended memory.

Using Himem.sys

Himem.sys is considered a device driver because it manages memory as a device. It can be executed by the Device= command in Config.sys. Figure 9-5 shows an example of a very simple Config.sys file on a floppy disk that loads Himem.sys. The Config.sys file is being edited by the Edit.com text editor utility.

To create the file on a floppy disk, you can use either of these two methods:

- Make drive A the default drive and enter this command:

  ```
  A:\> Edit Config.sys
  ```

- Make drive C the default drive and enter this command:

  ```
  C:\> Edit A:Config.sys
  ```

File   Edit   Search   View   Options   Help
A:\CONFIG.SYS
```
device=himem.sys
device=A:\util\mouse.sys
device=A:\util\ansi.sys
files=99
buffers=40
```

F1=Help   Line:6   Col:1

Figure 9-5   Config.sys set to use memory above 640K

9

The second line in the Config.sys file, device=A:\util\mouse.sys, tells DOS to load into memory a device driver from the \Util directory on the floppy disk. This driver allows you to use the mouse while in MS-DOS mode.

The third line in the Config.sys file, device=A:\util\ansi.sys, tells DOS to load the device driver Ansi.sys into memory. Ansi.sys helps control the keyboard and monitor, providing color on the monitor and an additional set of characters to the ASCII character set. For more information about ASCII and ANSI, see Appendix B.

Using Emm386.exe

In DOS and Windows 9x, Emm386.exe manages the memory addresses in upper memory. Before we see how to use it, let's begin by examining memory when upper memory addresses are not available. To do that, we use the MEM command, which lets us view how memory is currently allocated. Use the /C option to get a complete list and include the |MORE option to page the results on your screen. Figure 9-6 was produced using this command:

```
MEM /C |MORE
```

In Figure 9-6 the first column shows the programs currently loaded in memory. The second column shows the total amount of memory used by each program. The columns labeled Conventional and Upper Memory show the amount of memory being used by each program in each of these categories. This PC is not making use of upper memory for any of its programs. At the bottom of the screen is the total amount of free conventional memory (544,720 bytes) that is available to new programs to be loaded. Making this value as high as possible is the subject of this section.

```
Modules using memory below 1 MB:

  Name          Total              Conventional        Upper Memory
  --------    ----------------    ----------------    ----------------
  MSDOS        18,672   (18K)      18,672   (18K)            0    (0K)
  HIMEM         1,168    (1K)       1,168    (1K)            0    (0K)
  DBLBUFF       2,976    (3K)       2,976    (3K)            0    (0K)
  IFSHLP        2,864    (3K)       2,864    (3K)            0    (0K)
  WIN           3,616    (4K)       3,616    (4K)            0    (0K)
  COMMAND       8,416    (8K)       8,416    (8K)            0    (0K)
  SAVE         72,768   (71K)      72,768   (71K)            0    (0K)
  Free        544,720  (532K)     544,720  (532K)            0    (0K)

Memory Summary:

  Type of Memory       Total         Used          Free
  ----------------   -----------   -----------   -----------
  Conventional         655,360       110,640       544,720
  Upper                      0             0             0
  Reserved                   0             0             0
  Extended (XMS)   133,156,864        69,632   133,087,232
  ----------------   -----------   -----------   -----------
-- More --
```

Figure 9-6   MEM report with /C option on a PC not using upper memory

Creating and Using Upper Memory Blocks

Figure 9-7 shows an example of a Config.sys file that is set to use upper memory addresses. The first line loads the Himem.sys driver. The second line loads the Emm386.exe file. Emm386.exe assigns addresses in upper memory to memory made available by the Himem.sys driver. The NOEMS switch at the end of the command line says to Windows, "Do not create any simulated expanded memory." Expanded memory is an older type of memory above 1 MB that is no longer used by software. The command to load Emm386.exe must appear after the command to load Himem.sys in the Config.sys file.

The command DOS=HIGH,UMB serves two purposes. The one command line can be broken into two commands like this:

```
DOS=HIGH
DOS=UMB
```

The DOS=HIGH portion tells the OS to load part of the DOS core into the high memory area ("loading DOS high"). Remember that the high memory area is the first 64K of extended memory. This memory is usually unused unless we choose to store part of DOS in it with this command line. Including this command in Config.sys frees some conventional memory that would have been used by the OS.

```
   File  Edit  Search  View  Options  Help
                      A:\CONFIG.SYS
device=himem.sys
device=emm386.exe noems
dos=high,umb
devicehigh=A:\util\mouse.sys
files=99
buffers=40



F1=Help                                Line:1    Col:1
```

Figure 9-7   Config.sys set to use upper memory

The second part of the command, DOS=UMB, creates upper memory blocks. An **upper memory block (UMB)** is a group of consecutive memory addresses in the upper memory area that has had physical memory assigned to it. The OS identifies blocks that are not currently being used by system ROM or expansion boards, and the memory manager makes these blocks available for use. This command, DOS=UMB, enables the OS to access these upper memory blocks. After the UMBs are created, they can be used in these ways:

- `Devicehigh` = command in Config.sys
- `Loadhigh` command in Autoexec.bat
- `Loadhigh` command at the command prompt (explained in the next section)

The fourth line in the Config.sys file in Figure 9-7 uses a UMB. The command Devicehigh=A:\Util\Mouse.sys tells the OS to load the mouse device driver into one of the upper memory blocks created and made available by the previous three lines. This process of loading a program into upper memory addresses is called loading high.

Loading Device Drivers High

Using the Devicehigh= command in Config.sys, rather than the Device= command, causes the driver to load high. With the Devicehigh= command, the OS stores these drivers in UMBs using the largest UMB first, then the next largest, and so on until all are loaded. Therefore, to make sure there is enough room to hold them all in upper memory, order the Devicehigh= command lines in Config.sys so that the largest drivers are loaded first.

You can determine the amount of memory a device driver allocates for itself and its data by using the MEM command with the /M filename option:

```
MEM /M filename
```

The filename is the name of the device driver without the file extension.

9

You can also use a UMB from Autoexec.bat using the Loadhigh (LH) command. For example, to load high Mscdex.exe, a utility to access a CD-ROM drive, use either command:

```
LH Mscdex.exe
Loadhigh Mscdex.exe
```

In either case, the program is loaded into the largest UMB available and does not use up more precious conventional memory. Note that before the Loadhigh command will work, the program files Himem.sys and Emm386.exe must be available to the OS, and these three lines must be added to Config.sys and executed by booting the computer:

```
Device=HIMEM.SYS
Device=EMM386.EXE NOEMS
DOS=UMB
```

If the Himem.sys and Emm386.exe files are not in the root directory of the boot device, you must include the path to the filename in the Device= line, like this:

```
Device=C:\DOS\HIMEM.SYS
```

NOTE When a program is loaded high, two things can go wrong. Either the program might not work from upper memory, causing problems during execution, or there might not be enough room in upper memory for the program and its data. If the program causes the computer to hang when you attempt to run it, or if it simply refuses to work correctly, remove it from upper memory.

Windows 9x, which is mostly a 32-bit OS, "lives" in extended memory together with its device drivers and applications, and uses only base and upper memory for 16-bit components. If you are using all 32-bit drivers and applications in a Windows 9x environment, then you do not need to be concerned about managing base and upper memory. We now turn our attention to how Windows 9x manages virtual memory.

How Windows 9x Manages Virtual Memory

Virtual memory uses hard drive space so that it acts like memory. Windows stores virtual memory in a file called a swap file. The purpose of virtual memory is to increase the amount of memory available. Of course, because a hard drive is much slower than RAM, virtual memory works considerably slower than real memory. For example, a hard drive may have a data access time of 10 milliseconds (10 millionths of a second, abbreviated 10 ms), whereas RAM speed may be 60 nanoseconds (60 billionths of a second or 60 ns).

Windows 9x automates virtual memory management, and Microsoft recommends that you allow it to do so. To see what virtual memory options Windows 9x offers, click Start, point to Settings, click Control Panel, select System, and then select the Performance tab. Click Virtual Memory and the dialog box in Figure 9-8 appears. These settings are used to tell Windows how to manage the swap file. Unless you have good reason to do otherwise, check "Let Windows manage my virtual memory settings."

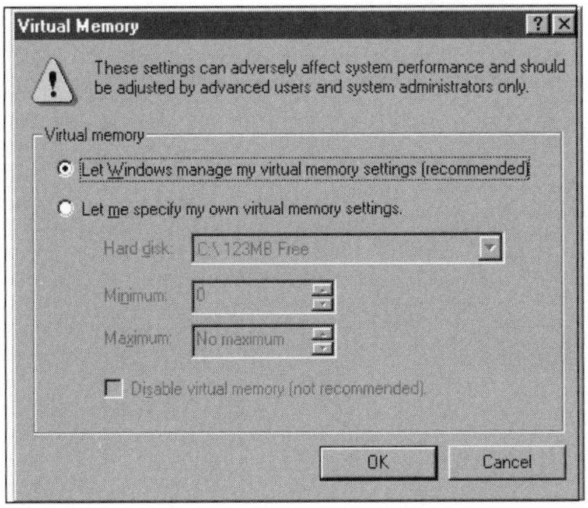

Figure 9-8   Options for managing virtual memory in Windows 9x

One reason you might want to manage virtual memory yourself is to make the file size permanent to prevent Windows from resizing the file, which can slow down performance. To improve performance, first defragment the hard drive so there is plenty of unfragmented space for the file. Then set the maximum and minimum file sizes to the same value, which forces the size not to change. If you have the available hard drive space, set the size to about 2.5 times the amount of RAM.

Notice in Figure 9-8 that you can specify the location of the swap file. The name of the swap file in Windows 9x is **Win386.swp,** and its default location is C:\Windows. You can choose to put the swap file on a compressed drive, but Windows does not compress the swap file itself, to better ensure the file's safety.

Memory Paging

A+ EXAM TIP

The A+ OS exam expects you to know the names of each OS's swap file.

Windows 9x stores virtual memory in the swap file and manages that memory for application programs. The Windows component called the Virtual Memory Manager (VMM) controls this process, moving 4K segments, called **pages**, in and out of physical RAM, a process called **memory paging**. If RAM is full, the manager takes a page and moves it to the swap file.

If RAM is full much of the time, the VMM might spend excessive time moving pages in and out of RAM. That can cause excessive hard drive use, decrease overall system performance, and even cause the system to lock up or applications to fail. This situation, sometimes called **disk thrashing**, can cause premature hard drive failure. Symptoms of excessive memory paging are:

- Very high CPU use
- Very slow system response
- Constant hard drive use

To avoid excessive memory paging, leave fewer applications open at the same time or install more RAM.

Windows NT/2000/XP Memory Management

As you have seen, managing memory under DOS and Windows 9x can be complicated because of having to deal with conventional, upper, and extended memory for backward compatibility. Windows NT/2000/XP eliminates that complexity, because memory is simply memory; in other words, all memory addresses are used the same way. This approach also causes Windows NT/2000/XP to lose some backward compatibility with legacy software and devices.

The Windows NT/2000/XP memory management model is illustrated in Figure 9-9, which shows the object-oriented approach to memory management. The application or device driver only says, "I want memory." It cannot tell Windows which physical memory or which memory addresses it wants, or even the range of addresses it wants to fall within. Windows uses its virtual memory manager to interface between the application or driver and the physical and virtual memory that it controls. Memory is allocated in 4K segments or pages. Applications and devices written for Windows NT/2000/XP only know how many pages they have. The virtual memory manager takes care of the rest. It is free to store these pages in RAM or on the hard drive in the swap file named **Pagefile.sys** (see Figure 9-9).

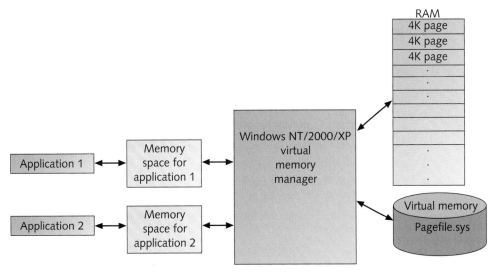

Figure 9-9   Windows NT/2000/XP memory management

How Windows 2000/XP Manages Virtual Memory

Under Windows 2000/XP, the default size of the paging file is set to 1.5 times the amount of RAM installed. You might need to change the paging file to improve system performance. Here are some guidelines to remember in managing paging files:

- Set the initial and maximum sizes of the file to the same value. This prevents disk fragmentation that might result from setting them to two different values. Windows 2000/XP does not normally need to change the size of the paging file during processing.
- When changing the size of a paging file, remember that you need to balance the file size with disk space usage and that Windows 2000/XP requires at least 5 MB of free space on a disk. In other words, don't make the file too large, especially when the disk it is stored on is active or has limited space. Test performance as you change paging file size and make changes gradually.
- Moving the paging file to a volume other than the boot volume can help conserve disk space on the boot volume and optimize performance, especially when a system has multiple hard disks.
- When deciding where to put the paging file, know that memory dumps (covered in Chapter 6) cannot be captured if the paging file is on a different physical disk from the operating system.

A+
OS
2.5

APPLYING CONCEPTS

To change virtual memory settings and paging file size in Windows 2000/XP, do the following:

1. Right-click **My Computer** and select **Properties** from the shortcut menu.
2. The System Properties window opens. Click the **Advanced** tab.
3. For Windows XP, click **Settings** under Performance. For Windows 2000, click the **Performance Options** button.
4. The Performance Options window opens. For Windows XP, click the **Advanced** tab and then click the **Change** button. For Windows 2000, click the **Change** button.
5. The Virtual Memory window opens. In this window, you can change the paging file size and view information about the paging file and the registry. Figure 9-10 shows all three windows for Windows XP.

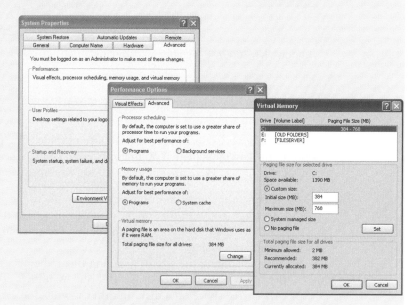

Figure 9-10   Use the System Properties window to change paging file settings

NOTE

You can also access the Windows 2000/XP Performance Options window from the Computer Management window. Open the Computer Management window, right-click Computer Management (Local), and select Properties from the shortcut menu.

Troubleshooting Memory

A+
OS
3.1
3.3

Recurring errors or lockups during normal operations can mean unreliable memory. If the system locks up or you regularly receive error messages about illegal operations and **General Protection Faults (GPF)** such as "exception fault 0E at >>0137:BFF9z5d0" during normal operation, and you have not just upgraded memory, do the following:

- Run a current version of antivirus software to check for viruses.
- The problem might be with the OS or applications. Download the latest patch for the OS or the application from the manufacturer's Web site.
- Memory modules might be faulty. You can run utility software such as Memtest86 to test memory. Check the Web site *www.memtest86.com* to download this program.
- You might not have enough memory installed. To determine how much memory your system has, right-click My Computer and select Properties from the menu. In the System Properties window, click the General tab.

NOTE

How much memory do you need? With the demands that today's software places on memory, the answer is probably "All you can get." Windows 95 and Windows 98 need 16 MB to 32 MB of memory. Windows 2000 and Windows XP require 64 MB of RAM. But for best performance, install 128 MB into a Windows 9x system and 256 MB or more into a Windows 2000/XP system.

9

CHAPTER SUMMARY

- Early limitations on the number of memory addresses available to the CPU were rooted in the fact that older motherboards had 20 lines on the bus for memory addresses, yielding a total of 1 MB of memory addresses.

- DOS and Windows 9x divide memory into base (conventional), upper, and extended memory.

- DOS and Windows 9x use the Himem.sys memory manager extension to allow access to extended memory (memory addresses above 1 MB). DOS and Windows 9x use Himem.sys, along with Emm386.exe, to manage memory above 640K. Emm386.exe contains the software that loads 16-bit device drivers and other programs into upper memory.

- You can use a UMB (upper memory block) from Autoexec.bat with the Loadhigh (LH) command.

▶ The MEM command with the appropriate parameters shows exactly where in upper memory the UMBs are located and what software has been assigned addresses in upper memory.

▶ Windows 95/98 uses 16-bit and 32-bit drivers. Windows Me and Windows NT/2000/XP use only 32-bit drivers. Windows 95/98 16-bit drivers use conventional and upper memory, and 32-bit drivers use extended memory. In Windows NT/2000/XP, there are no divisions of memory. All 32-bit drivers just use memory without requesting particular memory addresses.

▶ Virtual memory uses hard drive space as memory to increase the total amount of memory available. In Windows, virtual memory is stored in the swap file. The Windows 9x swap file is Win386.swp and the Windows 2000/XP swap file is Pagefile.sys.

▶ Virtual memory is managed in Windows 2000/XP from the System Properties window.

▶ To know how much memory is installed, right-click My Computer, select Properties from the menu, and click the General tab.

KEY TERMS

For explanations of key terms, see the Glossary near the end of the book.

conventional memory	Himem.sys	upper memory
disk thrashing	memory paging	upper memory block (UMB)
Emm386.exe	page	virtual DOS machine (VDM)
extended memory	page file	virtual memory
General Protection Fault (GPF)	Pagefile.sys	Win386.swp
high memory area (HMA)	swap file	

REVIEWING THE BASICS

1. List two operating systems that allow 16-bit drivers.

2. List four operating systems that allow only 32-bit drivers.

3. What are the three types of memory addresses that Windows 9x manages? What are the memory address ranges for each?

4. What is the hexadecimal address range for upper memory?

5. Name the two utilities that Windows uses to manage memory above 640K. Give a brief description of each.

6. Define memory paging. What problem can excessive memory paging cause? What are some symptoms of this problem?

7. Give one reason you should make the paging file maximum size the same as the paging file initial size.

8. What is the name of the Windows 9x swap file?

9. What is the name of the Windows 2000/XP swap file?

10. By default, Windows 2000/XP makes the paging file how large compared to the amount of RAM installed?

11. List the steps in Windows 2000 to change the size of the paging file.

12. What might be a symptom in Windows of unreliable memory on a motherboard?

13. List at least three things you can do if you receive memory errors during normal operation when you have not recently upgraded memory.

14. What Windows utility can report the amount of RAM installed in a system?

15. How much RAM is required in a Windows 2000/XP system? How much is recommended?

9

THINKING CRITICALLY

1. Why is it necessary to understand how to create and use upper memory blocks in Windows 9x?

2. What is the DOS=HIGH,UMB command used for? Explain both parts of the command.

3. Can an application or device driver specify which physical memory or memory addresses it wants in Windows NT/2000/XP? Why or why not?

PROJECT 9-1: Using Himem.sys and Emm386.exe

Using DOS or Windows 9x, practice using Himem.sys and Emm386.exe:

1. Make a bootable disk that does not contain an Autoexec.bat or Config.sys file, and boot from the disk.

2. Use the **Mem** command to display a memory report showing that upper memory is currently not used.

3. Load a mouse driver into upper memory as you saw done in the chapter (see Figure 9-5).

4. Reboot the PC and use the **Mem** command to demonstrate that the mouse driver is loaded high.

5. Print the contents of your Config.sys file.

6. List a directory of your floppy disk to the printer. What files on your disk are necessary to make the mouse work when loaded high?

PROJECT 9-2: Examining How Windows 9x Memory is Configured

Examine two or three different Windows 9x systems and answer these questions for each system.

1. Does the system have an Autoexec.bat file or Config.sys file in the root directory of the hard drive?

2. What commands are in each of these files to manage memory? Explain the purpose of each command.

PROJECT 9-3: Using a Memory Diagnostic Utility

Go to the Memtest86 Web site at *www.memtest86.com* and download the Memtest86 software. Use it to test the RAM installed on your system. Did the software detect any errors?

PROJECT 9-4:   **Windows 2000/XP Virtual Memory Settings**

Using Windows 2000/XP, answer these questions about your virtual memory settings:

1. What is the initial size of the paging file?

2. What is the maximum size of the paging file?

3. What is the current size of the paging file?

4. On what volume is the paging file stored?

9

Supporting Hard Drives

In this chapter, you will learn:

- About supporting hard drives and making backups

- About viruses and other computer infestations, and how to protect against them

- How to troubleshoot hard drives

So far this book has concentrated on specific operating systems, which will be your focus as a software technician. Many functions are common to all Windows operating systems, and this chapter is a consolidation of several of these functions. You will learn about supporting hard drives, including how to protect them against different types of viruses. This chapter also covers utilities to check a hard drive for errors, drive compression, caching for hard drives, and ways to create hard drive backups. Finally, you will learn how to troubleshoot problems that software can cause for hard drives.

Managing Hard Drives

The hard drive is the most important secondary storage device in your computer. In this section, you learn how to keep the drive clean and free from errors, about drive compression and disk caching, and how to make backups.

Defrag and Windows Disk Defragmenter

A+
OS
1.3
1.5
2.5

The Defrag command detects and repairs fragmentation. **Fragmentation** occurs when a single file is placed in several cluster locations that are not directly next to each other. The clusters that make up a file are together called a **chain**. When a hard drive is new and freshly formatted, the OS writes files to the drive beginning with cluster 2, placing the data in consecutive clusters. Each new file begins with the next available cluster. Later, after a file has been deleted, the OS writes a new file to the drive, beginning with the first available cluster in the FAT. If the OS encounters used clusters as it writes the file, it simply skips these clusters and uses the next available one. In this way, after many files have been deleted and added to the drive, files become fragmented. On a well-used hard drive, it is possible to have a file stored in clusters at 40 or more locations. Fragmentation is undesirable because when the OS has to access many different locations on the drive to read a file, access time slows down, and if the file becomes corrupted, recovering a fragmented file is more complicated than recovering a file in one continuous chain.

For these reasons, one routine maintenance task is to **defragment** the hard drive periodically. To do this, you can run the Defrag command from a command prompt or use a graphical Disk Defragmenter utility available from the Windows desktop. With Windows NT, you must use third-party software, as Windows NT does not include a defragmenter command. Regardless of the method used, you should defragment your hard drive every month or so as part of a good maintenance plan.

To use Windows XP Disk Defragmenter, first close all open applications. Then choose Start, All Programs, Accessories, and System Tools. Click Disk Defragmenter. From the Disk Defragmenter dialog box (see Figure 10-1) you can select a drive and defragment it. To use Windows 9x or Windows 2000 Disk Defragmenter, choose Start, Programs, Accessories, and then System Tools.

NOTE

Defragmenting a large hard drive may take a long time, so plan for this before you begin. For Windows 9x, if you want to watch the progress as it moves through the FAT, click Show Details in the Disk Defragmenter dialog box.

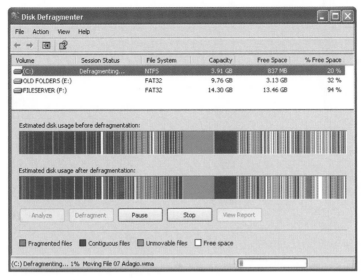

Figure 10-1   Windows XP defragmenting a volume

10

Using ScanDisk to Correct Cross-Linked and Lost Clusters

As you learned in Chapter 3, a directory on a floppy disk or hard drive is a table holding information about files in that directory or folder. The directory contains the number of the first cluster in the file. The FAT holds the map to all the other clusters in the file. Occasionally, the mapping in the FAT becomes corrupted, resulting either in lost clusters or cross-linked clusters, as shown in Figure 10-2. Here, File 3 has lost direction and points to a cluster chain that belongs to File 4. Clusters 29 through 31 are called **cross-linked clusters** because more than one file points to them, and clusters 15 through 17 and 28 are called **lost clusters** or **lost allocation units** because no file in the FAT points to them.

In Chapter 3, you learned about the Chkdsk and Scandisk commands. You can use Chkdsk /F to repair cross-linked and lost clusters. The Chkdsk command is supported by all versions of Windows. For Windows 9x, use it from any command prompt. For Windows 2000/XP, use Chkdsk from a Windows command prompt or from the Recovery Console. The Windows 9x ScanDisk utility is an improvement over Chkdsk and was designed to replace it. ScanDisk can repair cross-linked and lost clusters, check the FAT for other problems with long filenames and the directory tree, scan the disk for bad sectors, and repair problems with the structure of a hard drive that has been compressed using Windows DriveSpace or DoubleSpace.

A+
OS
1.3
1.5
2.5

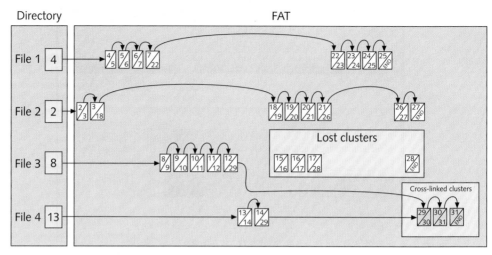

Figure 10-2   Lost and cross-linked clusters

Windows 2000/XP uses a different method to repair a file system. For Windows 2000/XP, open Windows Explorer, right-click the drive, and select Properties from the shortcut menu. Click the Tools tab and click Check Now under Error-checking (see Figure 10-3). Check the two boxes "Automatically fix file system errors" and "Scan for and attempt recovery of bad sectors."

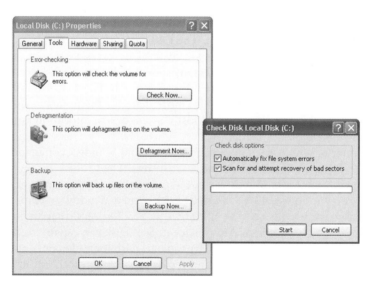

Figure 10-3   Windows XP repairs hard drive errors under the drive's Properties window using Windows Explorer

You can use ScanDisk from a command prompt or from the Windows desktop using Windows 9x. To use ScanDisk from the Windows 9x desktop, click

A+
OS
1.3
1.5
2.5

Start, Programs, Accessories, System Tools, and then ScanDisk. The ScanDisk utility first asks which drive you want to scan and gives you the choice of a Standard or Thorough scan (see Figure 10-4). The Standard scan checks files and folders for errors. The Thorough scan does all that the Standard scan does and also checks the disk surface for bad sectors. Click Start to begin the scan.

In command mode, such as when you've booted from a Windows 9x startup disk, enter the command Scandisk. The screen in Figure 10-5 appears. When the program finishes scanning the disk, it returns you to a command prompt.

10

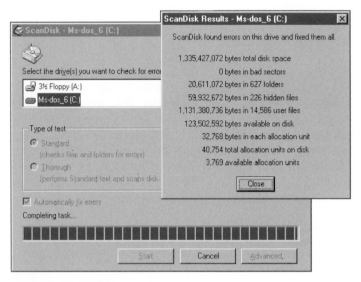

Figure 10-4   ScanDisk results

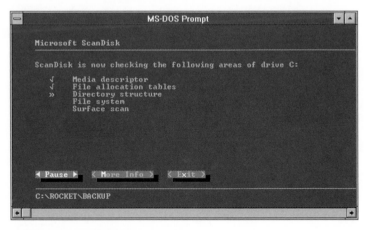

Figure 10-5   ScanDisk in MS-DOS mode

Use ScanDisk from a Windows 9x startup disk or from the desktop for both troubleshooting and maintenance. Like Defrag, ScanDisk is a good tool to run occasionally to check the health of the drive and possibly avert future problems.

Disk Cleanup

A+
OS
1.3
1.4
2.5

Disk Cleanup is a convenient way to delete temporary files on a hard drive, freeing up space and sometimes improving performance. To access Disk Cleanup under Windows 2000/XP and Windows 9x, right-click the drive in Windows Explorer and select Properties from the shortcut menu. The Disk Properties window appears (see Figure 10-6). On the General tab, click Disk Cleanup. From this view, you can select nonessential files to delete in order to save drive space. Disk Cleanup tells you how much total space you can save and how much space each type of removable file is taking; it also describes each type of file. Included in the list are temporary files created by applications that the applications no longer need.

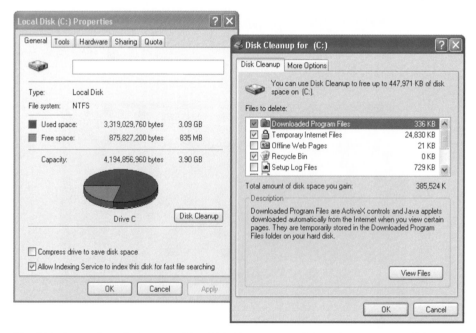

Figure 10-6   The Disk Properties window provides Disk Cleanup, a quick and easy way to delete temporary files on a hard drive

Disk Compression

A+
OS
1.4

Disk compression software can help meet the ever-increasing demand for more space on hard drives to hold software and data. Software packages requiring 200 to 250 MB of hard drive space were unheard of three or four years ago but are now common. Hard drive sizes have increased proportionately. Even so, we often seek ways to cram more onto nearly full hard drives.

Software to manage disk compression works by (1) storing data on your hard drive in one big file and managing the writing of data and programs to that file, and (2) rewriting data in files in a mathematically coded format that uses less space. Most disk compression programs combine these two methods. This section covers disk compression methods in several versions of Windows.

NOTE

Disk compression does save hard drive space, but you need to carefully consider the risks involved as well as performance issues such as longer disk access time. If you do choose to use disk compression, keep good backups of both the data and the software. If the data and software on your drive are especially valuable, you may want to invest in a larger hard drive instead of using compression.

10

Disk Compression in Windows XP and Windows 2000

Using the NTFS file system in Windows 2000/XP, you can compress a single file or folder or you can compress the entire NTFS volume. When you place a file or folder on a compressed volume, it will be compressed automatically. When you read a compressed file from a compressed volume, it will be decompressed automatically and then will be recompressed when you save it back to the compressed volume.

To compress an NTFS volume:

1. Open Windows Explorer.

2. Locate and right-click the root folder for the volume you want to compress. You will find it in the left pane of Windows Explorer.

3. Select **Properties** from the shortcut menu. The Properties dialog box appears.

4. If necessary, click the **General** tab (see Figure 10-7). This window displays the file system used (NTFS), the size of the volume, and the amount of free space. To compress the volume, click the check box labeled **Compress drive to save disk space**. Click **OK**.

5. The Confirm Attribute Changes dialog box appears. Indicate whether you want to compress only the root folder or the entire volume, and then click **OK** to begin compression.

A+
OS
1.4

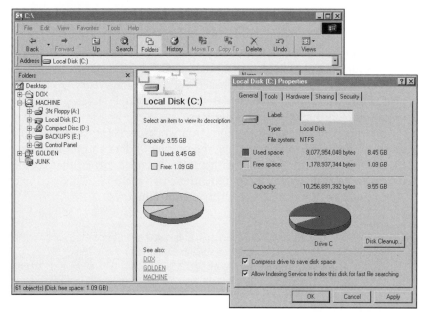

Figure 10-7   Compressing an NTFS volume

NOTE

The Disk Properties window for a FAT32 volume under Windows 2000/XP will not display the check box to compress the volume.

To compress a single folder or file on a Windows 2000/XP NTFS volume, right-click the folder or file and select Properties from the shortcut menu. Click the General tab, and then click Advanced. In the Advanced Attributes window, check "Compress contents to save disk space." For a FAT32 volume, files and folders cannot be compressed and the General tab does not have an Advanced button.

Disk Compression in Windows 9x

Windows 95 and Windows 98 support drive compression (Windows Me does not) using the **DriveSpace** utility on a FAT16 file system. However, the compressed volume is somewhat unstable and should not be used if important data is on the volume. Use it with caution!

NOTE

If a Windows 9x utility such as DriveSpace is missing from a menu list, the component might not have been installed when Windows was installed. To install a Windows component after Windows is installed, go to the Control Panel, select Add/Remove Programs, and click the Windows Setup tab.

A+
OS
1.4

To compress a FAT16 volume in Windows 95/98 using DriveSpace, first back up the data. Then click Start, Programs, Accessories, and System Tools. Select DriveSpace and follow the steps to select and compress the drive. Once the drive is compressed, never trust important data to it.

Disk Caching

A+
OS
2.5

A **disk cache** is a temporary storage area in RAM for data being read from or written to a hard drive, and is used to speed up access time to the drive. The process of disk caching works like this:

1. The CPU asks for data from a hard drive.

2. The hard drive controller sends instructions to the drive to read the data and then sends the data to the CPU.

3. The CPU requests more data, quite often data that immediately follows the previously read data on the hard drive.

4. The controller reads the requested data from the drive and sends it to the CPU.

Without a cache, each CPU request requires that data be read from the hard drive, as indicated in the top part of Figure 10-8.

10

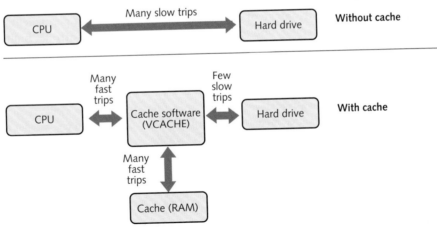

Figure 10-8   A CPU asking a hard drive for data without cache (upper part) and with cache (lower part)

With a hard drive cache, the cache software handles the requests for data, as shown in the lower part of Figure 10-8. The cache program reads ahead of the CPU requests by guessing what data the CPU will request next. Because most data that the CPU requests is in consecutive areas on the drive, the cache program guesses correctly most of the time. The program stores the read-ahead data in memory (RAM). When the CPU requests the next set of data, if the cache program guessed right, the

A+
OS
2.5

program can send that data to the CPU from memory without having to go back to the hard drive. Some cache software caches entire tracks at a time; other software caches groups of sectors.

Hardware Cache or Software Cache

There are two kinds of hard drive caches: hardware and software. Some hard drive controllers have a **hardware cache** built right into the controller circuit board. The BIOS on the controller contains the cache program, and RAM chips on the controller hold the cache.

A **software cache** is a cache program stored on the hard drive like other software, and is usually loaded into memory when a computer is booted. The software cache program uses system RAM to hold the cache.

There are advantages and disadvantages to both kinds of hard drive cache. A hardware cache does not use RAM on the motherboard, but a software cache uses RAM for both the cache program itself and the data being cached. Therefore, a disadvantage of a software cache is that it uses RAM that might otherwise be used for application software and its data.

On the other hand, a software cache is faster because of where the data is stored. Because data is stored in RAM, when the CPU is ready for the data, it only needs to travel from RAM to the CPU on the system bus, the fastest bus on the motherboard. Because the hardware cache is on the controller board, when the CPU is ready for data stored in this cache, the data must travel from the controller board over one or more buses to the CPU.

Another disadvantage of a hardware cache is that it is a permanent part of the hard drive controller, and today's hard drives have the controller built into the drive housing. Exchanging hard drives to upgrade to a faster hardware cache is impractical, whereas upgrading to a faster software cache is a viable option.

NOTE

When buying a new hard drive, check whether it includes hardware caches as an option. A controller with its own hardware cache is slightly more expensive than one without a cache. In hard drive ads, the cache is sometimes called a buffer.

How Disk Caching Methods Have Changed

As operating system technologies have changed, so have software disk caching methods. Here is a summary of how different OSs have accomplished disk caching.

- *DOS.* Before disk caching came along, DOS used buffers to speed disk access. A **buffer** is an area in memory where data waiting to be read or written is temporarily stored. Disk caches do a better job of speeding disk access than buffers, so the only reason to use buffers today is to satisfy the requirements of older software that uses them. Buffers are implemented by putting the

Buffers=[*number*] command in Config.sys. This command specifies how many buffers DOS is to make available for use while data is being read.

■ *DOS with Windows 3.x*. DOS with Windows 3.x used **SMARTDrive**, a 16-bit, real-mode software cache utility. SMARTDrive caches data both being read from and written to the hard drive, and caches data being read from floppy disks.

■ *Windows 9x*. Windows 9x has a built-in 32-bit, protected-mode software cache called **VCACHE**, which is automatically loaded by Windows 9x without entries in Config.sys or Autoexec.bat. VCACHE doesn't take conventional memory or upper memory space the way SMARTDrive does, and it does a much better job of caching.

■ *Windows NT/2000/XP*. Versions of Windows after Windows 9x use automated disk caching as an inherited Windows component. When working with caching under these versions of Windows, you can monitor physical disk performance using counters.

To verify that disk caching for write operations is enabled for Windows XP, open Windows Explorer, right-click drive C, and select Properties from the shortcut menu. Click the Hardware tab and then click Properties. In the drive's Properties window, click the Policies tab and verify that "Enable write caching on the disk" is checked (see Figure 10-9). For Windows 2000, open the drive's Properties window, click the Disk Properties tab, and verify that Write cache enabled is checked.

10

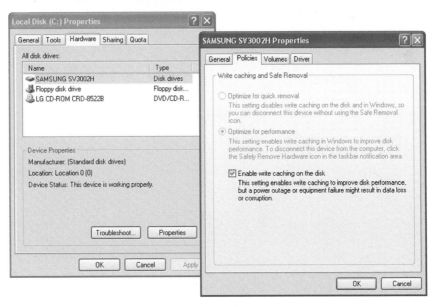

Figure 10-9   Verify that Windows XP disk caching is enabled

Making Backups

A **backup** is an extra copy of a data or software file that you can use if the original file becomes damaged or destroyed. Losing data due to system failure, a virus, file corruption, or some other problem really makes you appreciate the importance of having backups. This section covers the hardware and software needed to make backups of data and software from a hard drive. Windows 9x and Windows NT/2000/XP offer backup tools, which are also covered in this section.

NOTE   With data and software, here's a good rule of thumb: If you can't get along without it, back it up.

You can use sophisticated methods to create backups in which the backup process is selective, backing up only what's changed, what has not been recently backed up, and so forth. Traditionally, these methods all involve backing up to tapes, because a tape is most likely large enough to contain an entire backup of a hard drive and they are inexpensive. In the following discussions of specific backup methods, tape is our medium. These backup methods are designed to reuse tapes and to make the backup process more efficient. On a network, often the backup medium is a device such as another hard drive or a tape drive on a computer somewhere on the network. Full, incremental, and differential backup methods speed up the backup process, and scheduled backups minimize the inconvenience to users. Selective backups only back up data that changes often on the hard drive. By selecting only certain critical folders on the drive to back up, the backup routine goes much faster, and recovery of lost data is much easier.

The Child, Parent, Grandparent Method

Before you perform routine hard drive backups, devise a backup plan or procedure. One common plan, called the **child, parent, grandparent backup method,** makes it easy to reuse tapes. This method is explained in Table 10-1. Put the plan in writing, and keep a log of backups performed.

Name of Backup	How Often Performed	Storage Location	Description
Child backup	Daily	On-site	Keep four daily backup tapes, and rotate them each week. Label the four tapes Monday, Tuesday, Wednesday, and Thursday. A Friday daily (child) backup is not made, because on Friday you make the parent backup.
Parent backup	Weekly	Off-site	Perform the weekly backup on Friday. Keep five weekly backup tapes, one for each Friday of the month, and rotate them each month. Label the tapes Friday 1, Friday 2, Friday 3, Friday 4, and Friday 5.
Grandparent backup	Monthly	Off-site, in a fireproof vault	Perform the monthly backup on the last Friday of the month. Keep 12 tapes, one for each month. Rotate them each year. Label the tapes January, February, and so on.

Table 10-1   The child, parent, grandparent backup method

10

Full, Incremental, and Differential Backups

Some backup methods are more efficient because they do not always create a complete backup of all data. A **full backup** backs up all data from the hard drive or an area of the hard drive. An **incremental backup** backs up only files that have changed or been created since the last backup, whether that backup is itself an incremental or full backup. **Differential backups** back up files that have changed or been created since the last full backup.

Begin by performing a full backup. The next time you back up, choose the incremental method to back up only files that have changed or been created since the full backup. The second time you perform an incremental backup, you back up only the files that have changed or been created since the last incremental backup.

For example, using the child, parent, grandparent method, you can perform a full backup each Friday. Monday through Thursday, you perform incremental backups. The advantage of this method is that incremental backups are faster and require less storage space than full backups. The disadvantage is that, to recover data, you must begin with the last full backup and work your way forward through each incremental backup until the time that the data was lost. This process can be time-consuming. Plan to make a full backup after at least every sixth or seventh incremental backup. The Windows NT/2000/XP and Windows 9x backup utilities support incremental backups.

If you create differential backups with the child, parent, grandparent method, create a full backup on Fridays. On Monday, do a differential backup to back up all files that have changed since Friday. On Tuesday, a differential backup also backs up all files that have changed since Friday (the full backup). Differential backups don't consider whether other differential backups have been performed. Instead, they compare data only to the last full backup, which is how differential backups and incremental backups differ. Another difference is that incremental backups mark files as having been backed up, but differential backups do not. The advantage of differential backups over incremental ones is that if you need to recover data, you only need to recover from the last full backup and the last differential backup. Differential backups are not supported by Windows 95 but are supported by Windows 98 and Windows NT/2000/XP.

Scheduling Backups

Backups can be performed manually by a user sitting at the computer or can be scheduled to run automatically without user interaction. A scheduled backup is performed automatically by software when the computer is not commonly in use, such as during the middle of the night. Windows 98 and Windows NT/2000/XP support scheduling any program (including backup tasks) to execute at designated dates and times without user intervention.

Using Windows 98, do the following to create a program called Batch.bat to run a backup and schedule it to run at 11:59 p.m. every Monday night:

1. Using Notepad or WordPad, type the following command line, where the tape drive is E and the /S parameter tells the OS to include subdirectories when copying (hidden files are not copied, but data is not usually hidden):

   ```
   Xcopy C:\Data\*.* E: /S
   ```

2. Save the file as **\Data\Batch.bat**, and exit the text editor.

3. Double-click **My Computer** on the desktop, and then double-click **Scheduled Tasks** to open the Scheduled Tasks window (see Figure 10-10).

4. Double-click **Add Scheduled Task**. The Scheduled Task Wizard appears. Select the program to schedule; click **Browse**, find and click the **Batch.bat** file in the \Data folder, and then click **Open**.

5. Enter a name for the scheduled task, select how often to perform the task, and then click **Next** (see Figure 10-11).

6. Enter the start time and select the day of the week for the task to execute. For example, enter **11:59 PM every Monday**. Click **Next**.

7. The wizard reports the scheduled task parameters. Click **Finish**.

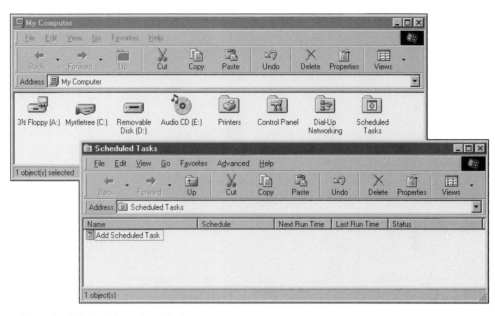

Figure 10-10 Add a scheduled task under Windows 98

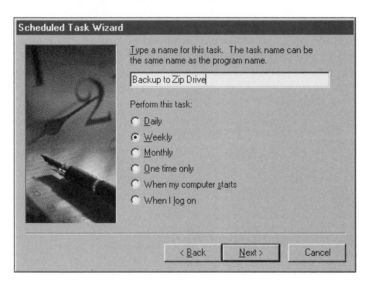

Figure 10-11 Name the scheduled task and select how often it runs

8. To change settings for a scheduled task, double-click **My Computer**, double-click **Scheduled Tasks**, and then right-click the task in the Scheduled Tasks window. Select **Properties** from the shortcut menu. The task Properties dialog box opens (see Figure 10-12).

10

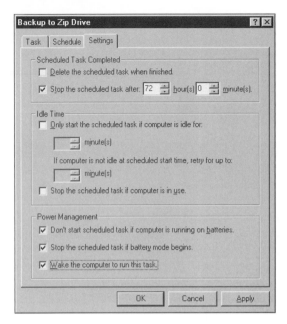

Figure 10-12 With some computers, the task scheduler can power up the computer to run the task

9. Click the **Settings** tab to change the task settings. Notice at the bottom of the Settings sheet that you can direct the scheduler to wake the computer to perform the task. This feature requires a motherboard that supports the option for software to power up the PC. To learn if your motherboard supports the feature, see CMOS setup or the motherboard documentation. If not, then the PC must be turned on for the scheduler to work.

You have just learned how to use a batch file to execute a scheduled backup. Windows offers a more powerful and sophisticated utility called Windows Scripting Host (WSH), which uses Windows commands to execute scripts written in a scripting language such as VBScript or JScript. This utility is also good for making backups. The script is stored in a file that can be placed as an icon on the desktop. To run the script, type the word *wscript.exe filename* in the Run dialog box, substituting the name of the script file for *filename*, or double-click the desktop icon. You can also make a script file run as a scheduled task.

Backup Software

Most tape drives come with some backup software. You can also purchase third-party backup software or use Windows NT/2000/XP or Windows 9x backup utilities for backing up your hard drive. Because the software only backs up files that are not currently in use, close all files before performing a backup.

APPLYING CONCEPTS

To perform a backup for Windows 2000/XP (using Ntbackup.exe), follow these steps. The procedure is for Windows XP, but Windows 2000 steps are similar:

1. For Windows XP, click **Start**, point to **All Programs**, **Accessories**, **System Tools**, and click **Backup**. The Backup Wizard appears. Click **Advanced Mode**. For Windows 2000, click **Start**, **Programs**, **Accessories**, **System Tools**, and **Backup**.

2. The Backup utility opens. Click the **Backup** tab (see Figure 10-13). If you want to perform a backup immediately, check the drive and subfolders to back up. Note the box labeled **Backup media or file name** in the lower-left corner, which says where to back up to. Click the **Start Backup** button in the lower-right corner to perform the backup.

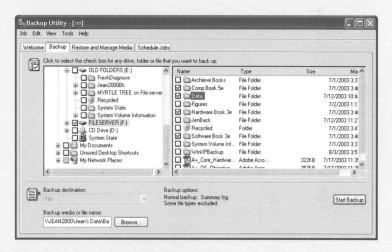

Figure 10-13   You can perform an immediate backup from the Backup tab

3. To perform a scheduled backup, begin by clicking the **Schedule Jobs** tab. Select a date on which you want to schedule a backup, and then click the **Add Job** button.

4. The Backup Wizard opens. On the first screen, click **Next**. Select **Backup selected files, drives, or network data** and click **Next**.

5. On the next screen, select what you want to back up, and then click **Next**.

6. Follow the steps through the wizard to choose where you want to save your backup, give a name to the backup, and select the type of backup (Normal, Copy, Incremental, Differential, or Daily). You can also specify how to verify the data, and specify if the data is to be appended to an existing backup or replaces an existing backup.

7. When asked if you want to perform the backup now or later, select **Later** and give the backup a name. Click the **Set Schedule** button.

8. The Schedule Job dialog box appears, as shown in Figure 10-14. Schedule how often the backup is to occur, and then click **OK**.

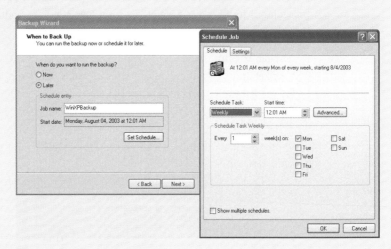

Figure 10-14   Schedule repeated backups

9. Click **Next** in the wizard, and follow the remaining instructions to complete the backup. At the end of the process, the wizard gives you an onscreen report summarizing information about the backup.

 NOTE By default, Windows XP Home Edition does not include the Backup utility. To install it manually, go to the \VALUEADD\MSFT\NTBACKUP folder on your Windows XP setup CD and double-click Ntbackup.msi. The installation wizard will complete the installation.

To recover files, folders, or the entire drive from backup using the Windows 2000/XP Backup utility, click the Restore and Manage Media tab on the Backup Utility window (see Figure 10-13). Select the backup job to use for the restore process. The Backup utility displays the folders and files that were backed up with this job. You can select the ones that you want to restore.

Windows 9x Backup Utility   Windows 9x offers a Microsoft Backup utility (Msbackup.exe) that can back up to removable disks and tape drives. Windows 98 supports many popular backup devices that Windows 95 did not, including those using parallel ports, IDE/ATAPI devices, and SCSI devices. To use drives and tapes not supported by Windows 9x, use third-party backup software.

10

✔ **A+ EXAM TIP**

The A+ OS exam expects you to know when and how to use the Windows 2000/XP utility, Ntbackup.exe, and the Windows 9x utility Msbackup.exe.

To use Windows 98 Microsoft Backup, click Start, point to Programs, Accessories, System Tools, and then click Backup. Follow the Backup Wizard as it steps you through the process of selecting the backup medium and the files, folders, or logical drives you want to back up. To select what to back up, the wizard takes you to a backup window similar to the Windows 2000/XP Backup window.

Disk Cloning Software

A+
OS
2.1

You can back up a hard drive by replicating it to a different computer or to another drive on the same computer, such as when you deploy a new operating system with application software on multiple computers in a corporate or educational lab. This process, called **disk cloning**, **disk imaging**, or **drive imaging** is best done with software designed for that purpose. Examples of disk imaging software are Drive Image by PowerQuest (*www.powerquest.com*), ImageCast by Innovative Software (*www.imagecast.com*), and Norton Ghost by Symantec Corp (*www.symantec.com*).

APPLYING CONCEPTS

Dave was well on his way to building a successful career as a PC repair technician. His PC repair shop was doing well and he was excited about his future. But one bad decision changed everything. He was called to repair a server at a small accounting firm. The call was on the weekend when he was normally off, so he was in a hurry to get the job done. He arrived at the accounting firm and saw that the problem was an easy one to fix, so he decided not to do a backup before working on the system. During his repairs, the hard drive crashed and all data on the drive was lost—four million dollars worth! The firm sued, Dave's business license was stripped, and he was ordered to pay the money the company lost. A little extra time to back up the system would have saved his whole future.

Planning for Disaster Recovery

The time to prepare for disaster is before it occurs. If you have not prepared, the damage from a disaster will most likely be greater than if you had made and followed disaster plans. Suppose the hard drive on your PC stopped working and you lost all its data. What would be the impact? Are you prepared for this event? Backups are important, but you should also know how to use them to recover lost data. Also know when the backup was made and what to do to recover information entered since the last backup. Here's where careful recordkeeping pays off.

When you perform a backup for the first time or set up a scheduled backup, verify that you can use the backup tape or disks to successfully recover the data. This is a very important step in preparing to recover lost data. After you create a backup, erase a file on the hard drive, and use the recovery procedures to verify that you can re-create the file from the backup. This verifies that the backup medium works, that the recovery software is effective, and that you know how to use it. After you are convinced that the recovery works, document how to perform it.

NOTE

Verify that your recovery plan works by practicing it before disaster occurs.

Always record your regular backups in a table with the following information:

- Folders or drives backed up
- Date of the backup
- Type of backup
- Label identifying the tape, disk, or other media

If you discover that data has been lost days or weeks ago, you can use this table to help you recover the data. Keep the records in a notebook. You can also store the records in a log file (a file where events are logged or recorded) each time you back up. Store the file on a floppy disk or another PC.

Viruses and Other Computer Infestations

A+
OS
3.3

Statistics show that in 2001, one in 10 corporate desktop computers was infected with a computer infestation, and the rate of infestation is increasing 15 percent each year. A computer support person needs to know how to protect computers against computer infestations (including viruses), how to recognize them, and how to get rid of them. Understanding what infestations are, how they work, and where they hide helps technicians deal with them successfully. A computer **infestation** is any unwanted program transmitted to a computer without the knowledge of the user or owner, and is designed to do varying degrees of damage to data and software. Computer infestations do not damage PC hardware. However, when boot sector information is destroyed on a hard drive, the hard drive can appear to be physically damaged. What most people call viruses really fall into four categories of computer infestations: viruses, worms, Trojan horses, and logic bombs. The four types of infestations differ in the way they spread, the damage they do, and the way they hide.

Because viruses are by far the most common kind of computer infestation, one of the most important defenses against them is **antivirus (AV) software**, designed to discover and remove a virus. This section looks at several AV programs and how to use them effectively.

Understanding Computer Infestations

A **virus** is a program that replicates by attaching itself to other programs. The infected program must be executed for a virus to run. The virus might then simply replicate or also do damage by immediately performing some harmful action. A virus might be programmed to perform a negative action in the future, such as on a particular date (for instance, Friday the 13th), or when some logic within the host program is activated. A virus differs from a **worm**, a program that spreads copies of itself throughout a network or the Internet without a host program. A worm creates problems by overloading the network as it replicates. Worms do damage by their presence rather than by performing a specific damaging act, as a virus does. A worm overloads memory or hard drive space by replicating repeatedly. When a worm (for example, W32.Sobig.F@mm) is loose on the Internet, it can do damage such as sending mass emailings.

A **Trojan horse** is a third type of computer infestation that, like a worm, does not need a host program to work; rather it substitutes itself for a legitimate program. Most Trojan horses cannot replicate themselves, although there are some exceptions. One Trojan horse program was disguised as an automatic backup utility downloadable from the Internet. When used, it created backups and replicated itself to the backups. It was programmed to damage several systems on Friday the 13th. In this case, the Trojan horse program is also considered a virus because of its ability to replicate. Because Trojan horse infestations generally cannot replicate and require human intervention to move from one location to another, they are not as common as viruses.

A **logic bomb** is dormant code added to software and triggered at a predetermined time or by a predetermined event. For example, an employee might put code in a program to destroy important files if his or her name is ever removed from the payroll file. Also, viruses, worms, Trojan horses, and logic bombs can occur in combination, such as when a virus gains access to a network by way of a Trojan horse. The virus can plant a logic bomb within application software on the network that sets off a worm when the application executes.

10

Where Viruses Hide

A program is called a virus for three reasons: (1) it has an incubation period (does not do damage immediately), (2) it is contagious (can replicate itself), and (3) it is destructive. There are several types of viruses and methods that viruses use to avoid detection by antivirus software.

Boot Sector Virus   A **boot sector virus** hides in a boot sector program. It can hide on a hard drive either in the program code of the Master Boot Record or in the boot record program that loads the OS on the active partition of the hard drive. On a floppy disk, a boot sector virus hides in the boot program of the boot sector. One of the most common ways a virus spreads is from a floppy disk used to boot a PC.

When the boot program is loaded into memory, so is the virus, which can then spread to other programs.

Many CMOS setups have an option that can protect against some boot sector viruses. It prevents writing to the boot sector of the hard drive. This feature must be turned off before installing Windows 9x or Windows NT/2000/XP, which must write to the boot sector during installation. Windows 9x does not tell you that you must turn the feature off and start the installation over until about halfway through the installation.

File Viruses   A **file virus** hides in an executable (.exe, .com, or .sys) program or in a word-processing document that contains a macro. A **macro** is a small program contained in a document that can be automatically executed when the document is first loaded or later by pressing a key combination. For example, a word-processing macro might automatically read the system date and copy it into a document when you open the document. Viruses that hide in macros of document files are called macro viruses. **Macro viruses** are the most common viruses spread by email, hiding in macros of attached document files.

One well-known example of a macro virus is Melissa, first introduced in 1999 in a Word 97 macro. The virus spread around the world within one working day. The email that initially spread Melissa looked like this:

> From: (name of infected user)
> Subject: Important Message From (name of infected user)
> To: (50 names from alias list)
> Here is that document you asked for ... don't show anyone else ;-)
> Attachment: LIST.DOC

When the recipient opened the document, a macro executed and immediately emailed the List.doc to 50 email addresses listed in the user's address book. The virus infected other Word documents, which, when emailed, also spread the virus.

One type of file virus searches a hard drive for files with .exe extensions and then creates another file with the same filename and a .com file extension, and stores itself there. When the user launches a program, the OS first looks for the program name with the .com file extension. It then finds and executes the virus. The virus is loaded into memory and loads the program with the .exe extension. The user appears to have launched the desired program. The virus is then free to do damage or spread itself to other programs.

Multipartite Viruses   A **multipartite virus** is a combination of a boot sector virus and a file virus. It can hide in either type of program.

Cloaking Techniques

A virus is programmed to attempt to hide from antivirus (AV) software. AV software can only detect viruses identical or similar to those it has been programmed to search for and recognize. AV software detects a known virus by looking for distinguishing characteristics called **virus signatures**, which is why it is important to update your AV software.

> Antivirus software cannot detect a virus it does not know to look for. Therefore, upgrade your AV software regularly to keep your protection current as new viruses are discovered.

NOTE

A virus attempts to hide from AV software in two ways: by changing its distinguishing characteristics (its signature) and by attempting to mask its presence. Three types of viruses categorized according to their cloaking techniques are polymorphic, encrypting, and stealth viruses.

Polymorphic Viruses   A **polymorphic virus** changes its distinguishing characteristics as it replicates. Mutating in this way makes it more difficult for AV software to recognize the presence of the virus.

Encrypting Viruses   One key symptom AV software looks for is a program that can replicate itself. An **encrypting virus** can transform itself into a nonreplicating program to avoid detection. However, it must revert to a replicating program to spread or replicate, and can then be detected by AV software.

Stealth Viruses   A **stealth virus** actively conceals itself, using one or more of the following techniques:

- Because AV software can detect a virus by noting the difference between a program's file size before the virus infects it and after the virus is present, the virus alters OS information to mask the size of the file it hides in.
- The virus monitors when files are opened or closed. When it sees that the file it is hiding in is about to be opened, it temporarily removes itself or substitutes a copy of the file that does not include the virus. The virus keeps a copy of this uninfected file on the hard drive just for this purpose.

The Damage an Infestation Can Cause

Viruses, worms, and Trojan horses have not been known to physically damage a hard drive or other hardware device. The damage they do ranges from minor, such as displaying bugs crawling around on a screen, to major, such as erasing everything written on a hard drive. Infestation damage is called the payload and can be accomplished in a variety of ways. A virus can be programmed to drop its payload only in response to a triggering event such as a date, opening a certain file, or pressing a certain key. Figure 10-15 shows the results of a harmless virus that simply displays garbage on the screen.

10

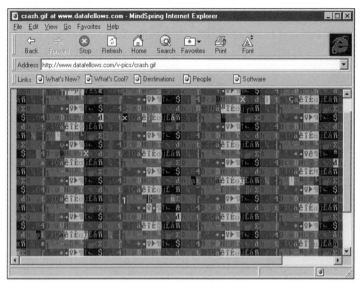

Figure 10-15   The crash virus appears to be destructive, making the screen show only garbage, but does no damage to hard drive data

How Infestations Spread

Understanding how infestations spread is essential to understanding how to protect your computer against them. Some computers are more vulnerable than others, depending on user habits. Here is a list of user activities that make a computer susceptible to infestations.

- Executing attachments to email messages without first scanning them for viruses
- Trading floppy disks containing program files
- Connecting the computer to an unprotected network
- Buying software from unreliable sources
- Downloading programs from the Internet
- Using floppy disks from unknown sources
- Using shared network programs
- Using used, preformatted floppy disks
- Reading email that automatically executes a word processor to read attached files
- Not write-protecting original program disks

How a Virus Replicates   Once a program containing a virus is copied to your PC, the virus can spread only when the infected program executes. The process is shown in Figure 10-16. The first step in executing a program, whether it is stored in a program file or in a boot sector, is to load the program into memory. Viruses hidden in a program can then be executed from memory. A virus can either be a **memory-resident virus** and stay in memory, still working even after the host program terminates, or a **non-memory-resident virus** that is terminated when the host program is closed.

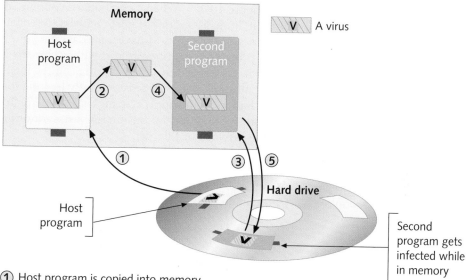

① Host program is copied into memory.

② The virus may or may not move itself to a new location in memory.

③ A second program is opened and copied into memory.

④ The virus copies itself to the second program in memory.

⑤ The newly infected second program is written back to the hard drive.

Figure 10-16 How a virus replicates

After a virus is loaded into memory, it looks for other programs loaded into memory. When it finds one, it copies itself there and into that same program file on disk. In Figure 10-16, you can see that a virus becomes more dangerous the longer it stays loaded into memory and the more programs that are opened while it is there. For this reason, if you want to use a computer that has been used by other people, such as in a computer lab, always reboot before you begin work to clear memory of programs. Use a hard boot, not just a soft boot, to erase all memory-resident programs (including a memory-resident virus) from memory.

How a Trojan Horse Gets into Your Computer   A Trojan horse is an infestation masquerading as a legitimate program. One interesting example of a Trojan horse is the AOL4FREE program. Originally this illegal program could provide unauthorized access to America Online. After AOL blocked the program's usefulness, a new program emerged, also called AOL4FREE. It was not an online access program but a destructive Trojan horse. People passed the program around, thinking that it would provide illegal access to AOL; however, if executed, it actually erased files on their hard drives.

A+
OS
3.3

How a Worm Gets into Your Computer   Most worms come to your computer or network through the Internet. A computer communicates with other computers on the Internet by using identifying numbers called ports, which are similar to post office box numbers (see Figure 10-17). When a computer is configured for network or Internet communication, it opens a series of port numbers to send and receive messages. One computer will say to the other, "I have a message for your port 25." If the receiving computer is not protected against worms, it will receive any message from any computer to any port it has opened to service. Worms on the Internet routinely perform "port scanning," meaning that they are constantly looking for open, unprotected ports through which they can invade a system. Once they are in the computer, they are free to move to other computers on the internal network or produce mass emailings to bog down the network or Internet.

Recall from Chapter 8 that the best way to defend against worms is to use a firewall, which is software or hardware that prevents worms or hackers from using open ports or services. A Windows XP firewall is discussed in Chapter 8. You will learn more about Internet communication, ports, and firewalls in Chapter 12.

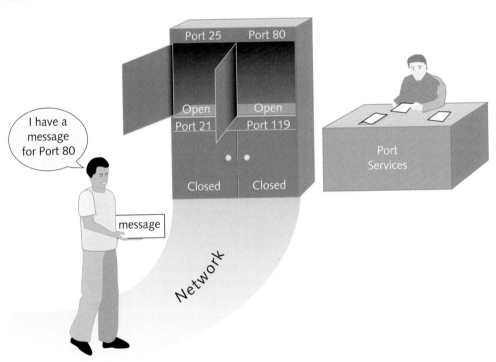

Figure 10-17   A computer receives communication over a network by way of ports or numbers that identify a communication service

Virus Hoaxes

A+
OS
3.3

A virus hoax is an email warning about a nonexistent virus. The warning is itself a pest because it overloads network traffic. Here's an example of a virus hoax email message I received:

> There is a new virus going around in the last couple of days!! DO NOT open or even look at any mail that you get that says: "Returned or Unable to Deliver." The virus will erase your whole hard drive and attach itself to your computer components and render them useless. Immediately delete any mail items that say this. AOL has indicated this is a very dangerous virus, and there is NO remedy for it at this time. Please be careful and forward to all your online friends ASAP. This is a new email virus and not a lot of people know about it; just let everyone know, so they won't be a victim. Please forward this email to your friends!!!

Viruses grow more powerful every day, but it is unlikely that this message is accurate. It is unlikely that a virus can render computer components useless. No virus has been known to do actual physical damage to hardware, although viruses can make a PC useless by destroying programs or data, and a few viruses have been able to attack system BIOS code on the motherboard. However, some can hide in macros in word-processing documents attached to email messages, and a few viruses are able to hide in Web pages transmitted as email messages and interpreted by email software when you first open the messages.

What's most important is not to be gullible and take the bait by forwarding the message to someone else. The potential damage a hoax like this can do is to overload an email system with useless traffic, which is the real intent of the hoax. When I received this email, more than a hundred names were on the distribution list.

Before forwarding a virus warning, you can check the Web sites of virus software manufacturers such as the ones listed later in this section. In addition, here are some Web sites that specialize in debunking virus hoaxes:

- *hoaxbusters.ciac.org* by Computer Incident Advisory Capability
- *www.hoaxinfo.com* by Jeff Richards
- *www.hoaxkill.com* by Oxcart Software
- *www.viruslist.com* by Kaspersky Lab
- *www.vmyths.com* by Rhode Island Soft Systems, Inc.

There are many sources for checking for virus hoaxes. Using a search engine, type the words *virus hoax*, a similar phrase, or the name of the virus or virus warning, and you'll find a wealth of information. Always check before sending!

10

Protecting Against Computer Infestations

A+
OS
3.3

You can do a lot to protect your computer against viruses and other infestations. Your first line of defense is to make backups, use antivirus software regularly, keep Windows current with updates and patches, and implement a firewall. After that, use wisdom when managing programs. Here are some general guidelines:

- Buy antivirus software and set your computer to run the AV program automatically at startup.
- Keep your AV software current by periodically downloading upgrades from the Internet. Many antivirus programs now offer an automatic update feature.
- Set a virus scan program to automatically scan word-processing documents and other email attachments when they are opened. Some Web-based email clients, such as Yahoo! Mail, offer the option to scan attachments before downloading them.
- Implement a firewall. Chapter 12 discusses how to use software or hardware firewalls.
- Keep Windows updated on your computer using the Microsoft Web site *windowsupdate.microsoft.com*. Microsoft is continually solving security problems with patches and service packs for the OS.
- Establish and faithfully execute a plan to make scheduled backups of your hard drive to protect against potential infestation damage.
- Only buy software from reputable vendors.
- Don't trade program files on floppy disks.
- Don't use floppy disks from unknown sources, and always scan floppy disks for viruses, no matter where they came from.
- Download software from the Internet sparingly, and then always scan program files for viruses before executing them.
- Never use pirated software.
- Format floppy disks before first use.
- Write-protect original program floppy disks, or use CDs to install programs.
- In a business environment, adopt strict company policies against using unauthorized software.
- Before using a running computer that others have used, hard-boot the computer.
- Set your computer CMOS settings to boot from drive C, then drive A.
- Turn on antivirus protection for your MBR in the CMOS settings, if available.

Virus Symptoms

A+
OS
3.3

Here are some warnings that suggest a virus is at work:

- A message appears that a downloaded document contains macros, or an application asks whether it should run macros in a document. (It is best to disable macros if you cannot verify that they are from a trusted source and that they are free of viruses or worms.)
- A program takes longer than normal to load.
- The number and length of disk accesses seem excessive for simple tasks.
- Unusual error messages occur regularly.
- Less memory than usual is available.
- Files mysteriously disappear or appear.
- Strange graphics appear on your computer monitor, or the computer makes strange noises.
- There is a noticeable reduction in disk space.
- The system cannot recognize the hard drive when you boot from a floppy disk.
- The system cannot recognize the CD-ROM drive, although it worked earlier.
- Executable files have changed size.
- Executable files that once worked no longer work and give unexpected error messages.
- The access lights on the hard drive and floppy drive turn on when there should be no activity on that device. (However, sometimes an OS performs routine maintenance on the drive when the system has been inactive for a while.)
- Files constantly become corrupted.
- Strange or bizarre error messages appear.
- Windows error messages about the FAT or partition table appear.
- The hard drive boots but hangs before getting a Windows desktop.
- File extensions or file attributes change without reason.
- The virus scanner software displays a message.
- You receive email messages that you have sent someone an infected message.
- The number of bad sectors on the hard drive continues to increase.
- Task Manager reveals unfamiliar processes running.
- The Sigverif command reveals that uncertified software is installed.

10

What to Do When You Suspect a Virus Infestation

If you suspect a virus, run a virus scan program to detect and delete the virus. If the antivirus software is not already installed, you can still use it. Consult the documentation for instructions on how to proceed. In many cases, the installation process detects the virus and eliminates it before continuing the installation. However, if the AV software does not recognize the virus or if the virus successfully hides, the AV program cannot detect the virus. If the AV software found nothing, but you still suspect a virus, get the latest upgrade of your AV software and try it or another AV program. Also download recent virus definitions; these are usually part of automatic AV software updates.

A+
OS
3.3

If you know the name of the virus or worm, check the Web site of the antivirus software for information about the infestation and how to remove it. The antivirus software vendor might instruct you to download a special program to remove a particular virus or worm. Instructions might tell you to first reboot into Windows Safe Mode or to disable certain services before executing the removal software.

Table 10-2 lists popular antivirus software and Web sites that provide information about viruses.

Antivirus Software	Web Site
Norton AntiVirus by Symantec, Inc.	www.symantec.com
Dr. Solomon's Software	www.drsolomon.com
McAfee VirusScan by McAfee Associates, Inc.	www.mcafee.com
ESafe by Aladdin Knowledge Systems, Ltd.	www.esafe.com
F-Prot by Frisk Software International	www.f-prot.com
Command AntiVirus by Command Software	www.commandcom.com
PC-cillin by Trend Micro (for home use)	www.antivirus.com
NeaTSuite by Trend Micro (for networks)	www.antivirus.com

Table 10-2   Antivirus software and information

When selecting antivirus software, find out if it can:

- Download new software upgrades and virus definitions from the Internet so that your software knows about new viruses
- Automatically execute at startup
- Detect macros in a word-processing document as it is loaded by the word processor
- Automatically monitor files being downloaded from the Internet, including email attachments and attachments sent during a chat session, such as when using AOL Instant Messenger
- Send virus alerts to your email address to inform you of a dangerous virus and the need to update your antivirus software
- Scan both automatically and manually for viruses

Using Antivirus Software

Antivirus software can work at different times to scan your hard drive or a floppy disk for viruses. Most AV software can be configured to scan memory and the boot sector of your hard drive for viruses each time your PC boots. Often it's not practical to have AV software scan the entire hard drive each time you boot, because that

A+
OS
3.3

takes too much time. Consider scheduling the AV software to run at the same time every day, such as during lunch hour.

Some AV software can run continuously in the background and scan all programs that execute. However, the software can cause problems with other software, especially during installations. If you have a problem installing a new application, try terminating your AV software.

Set your AV software to scan files as they are downloaded from the Internet or a network, and to scan documents for macro viruses each time a document is opened by a word processor.

Troubleshooting Hard Drives

A+
OS
3.2

Although the hard drive itself is a hardware component, problems with hard drives can be caused by software as well. Problems can also be categorized as those that prevent the hard drive from booting and those that prevent data from being accessed. In this section, you will learn about software problems with hard drives.

When a user brings a problem to you, begin troubleshooting by interviewing the user, being sure to include these questions:

10

- Can you describe the problem and show me how to reproduce it?
- Was the computer recently moved?
- Was any new hardware or software recently installed?
- Was any software recently reconfigured or upgraded?
- Did someone else use your computer recently?
- Does the computer have a history of similar problems?

Once you gather this basic information, you can begin diagnosing and addressing the hard drive problems.

If a hard drive is not functioning and data is not accessible, setting priorities helps focus your work. For most users, data is the first priority unless they have a recent backup. Software can also be a priority if it is not backed up. Reloading software from the original installation disks or CD can be time-consuming, especially if the configuration is complex or you have written software macros or scripts but did not back them up.

If you have good backups of both data and software, hardware might be your priority. It could be expensive to replace, but downtime can be costly, too. The point is, when trouble arises, determine your main priority and start by focusing on that.

Be aware of the resources available to help you resolve a problem:

- Documentation often lists error messages and their meanings.
- The Internet can also help you diagnose hardware and software problems. Go to the Web site of the product manufacturer and search for the FAQs (frequently asked questions) list or bulletin board. It's likely that others have

encountered the same problem and posted the question and answer. If you search and cannot find your answer, then you can post a new question.

- Technical support from the ROM BIOS, hardware, and software manufacturers can help you interpret an error message, or it can provide general support in diagnosing a problem. Most technical support is available during working hours by telephone. Check your documentation for telephone numbers. An experienced computer troubleshooter once said, "The people who solve computer problems do it by trying something and making phone calls, trying something else and making more phone calls, and so on, until the problem is solved."

NOTE

Remember one last thing. After making a reasonable and diligent effort to resolve a problem, getting the problem fixed could become more important than resolving it yourself. There comes a time when you might need to turn the problem over to a more experienced technician.

Troubleshooting Hard Drives with Third-Party Software

To troubleshoot hard drive problems, you might need to use third-party utility software. Three popular utility programs are Norton Utilities, SpinRite, and Partition-Magic. The following descriptions tell you what to expect from this software when a hard drive fails. Note that these are *not* complete listings of the utility software functions, nor of all available software. See specific software documentation for more details.

- *Norton Utilities* by Symantec (*www.symantec.com*) offers several easy-to-use tools to prevent damage to a hard drive, recover data from a damaged hard drive, and improve system performance. Many functions of these tools have been taken over and improved by utilities included with recent versions of Windows. The most commonly used Norton Utilities tools now are the recovery tools. Two examples are Norton Disk Doctor, which automatically repairs many hard drive and floppy disk problems, and UnErase Wizard, which allows you to retrieve accidentally deleted files. When using Norton Utilities, be certain you use the version of the software for the operating system you have installed. Using Norton with the wrong OS can do damage.
- *PartitionMagic* by PowerQuest Corporation (*www.powerquest.com*) lets you manage partitions on a hard drive more quickly and easily than with Fdisk for Windows 9x or Disk Management for Windows NT/2000/XP. You can create new partitions, change the size of partitions, and move partitions without losing data or moving the data to another hard drive while you work. You can switch between FAT16 and FAT32 without disturbing your data, and you can hide and show partitions to secure your data.
- *SpinRite* by Gibson Research (*www.grc.com*) is hard drive utility software that has been around for years. Still a DOS application without a sophisticated GUI interface, SpinRite has been updated to adjust to new drive technologies. It

supports FAT32, SCSI, Zip drives, and Jaz drives. You can boot your PC from a floppy disk and run SpinRite from a floppy, which means that it doesn't require much system overhead. Because it is written in a language closer to the binary code that the computer understands, it is more likely to detect underlying hard drive problems than software that uses Windows, which can stand as a masking layer between the software and the hard drive. SpinRite analyzes the entire hard drive surface, performing data recovery of corrupted files and file system information. Sometimes, SpinRite can recover data from a failing hard drive when other software fails.

NOTE Always check compatibility between utility software and the operating system with which you plan to use it. One place you can check is the service and support section of the software manufacturer's Web site.

Software Problems with Hard Drives

A+
OS
3.3

Here are some general software causes of hard drive problems. The root cause of many of these problems is a virus:

- Corrupted OS files
- Corrupted partition table, boot record, or root directory, making all data on the hard drive inaccessible
- Corrupted area of the FAT that points to the data, the data's directory table, or the sector markings where the data is located
- Corrupted data

Resolving Hard Drive and Data Access Problems

Software problems can prevent data or programs on the hard drive from being accessible. For a hard drive and its data to be accessible by DOS or Windows, the following items, listed in the order they are accessed, must be intact for a FAT file system: the partition table, the boot record, the FAT, and directory, the system files, and data and program files.

- *Partition table.* When the partition table is damaged, BIOS tries to load the OS, first reading the master boot program at the beginning of the partition table information on the hard drive. If the partition table is damaged, this error message appears:

  ```
  Invalid drive or drive specification
  ```

  In this case, you should still be able to boot from a floppy disk. When you get to the A prompt and try to access the hard drive by entering C:, you get the same error. To restore the boot program at the very beginning of the partition table in the Master Boot Record information, use this command for Windows 9x or Windows NT:

```
A> Fdisk /Mbr
```

For Windows 2000/XP, use this command from the Recovery Console:

```
Fixmbr
```

Often, these commands solve the problem of a damaged partition table.

NOTE

There is a danger in using the Fdisk/MBR command. Some viruses detect when the MBR is altered or when an attempt is made to alter it, and do further damage at that time. Also, some third-party drive encryption software alters the MBR. If Fdisk/MBR overwrites the data encryption program in the MBR, encrypted data on the hard drive might not be readable. If you have important data on the drive that is not backed up, try to recover the data before using Fdisk/MBR.

- *Boot record.* If the OS boot record on a hard drive is damaged, you cannot boot from the hard drive. After you boot from a floppy disk and try to access the hard drive, you might get one of these error messages:

```
Invalid media type
Non-DOS disk
Unable to read from Drive C
```

If the OS boot record is damaged, the best solution is to recover it from the backup copy you made when you first became responsible for the PC. (You can use Norton Utilities to make the backup.) If you don't have a backup, try to repair the boot record using Norton Disk Doctor or SpinRite.

- *FAT and root directory.* The partition table and boot record are easily backed up to disk; they do not change unless the drive is repartitioned or reformatted. Always back them up as soon as you can after you buy a new computer or become responsible for a working one. Unlike the partition table and the boot record, the FAT and the root directory change often and are more difficult to back up. The success of Windows or third-party utilities in repairing a damaged FAT or root directory depends on the degree of damage to the tables. If these tables are damaged, you may receive this error message:

```
Sector not found reading drive C, Abort, Retry, Ignore,
Fail?
```

Try copying important files on the drive to another medium. If you encounter the error, type I to ignore the bad sector and continue copying. Norton Disk Doctor might be able to repair the FAT or root directory.

- *System files*. If the two OS hidden files (Io.sys and Msdos.sys) are missing or corrupted, you should see one of these error messages:

```
Non system disk or disk error...
Invalid system disk...
```

  Use the following command to copy the two hidden files and the Command.com file from a rescue disk to the hard drive:

```
A:\> Sys C:
```

- *Data and program files*. Data and program files can become corrupted for many reasons, ranging from power spikes to user error. If the corrupted file is a program file, the simplest solution might be to reinstall the software or recover the file from a previous backup. Restoring a data file that is not backed up is covered in the next section, along with problems that can cause data and program file corruption.

Data and Program File Corruption

To restore a data file that is not backed up, you have three options:

- Use operating system tools and commands to recover the file.
- Use third-party software such as Norton Utilities or SpinRite to recover the file.
- If neither of these approaches works, you can turn to a professional data recovery service. These services can be expensive, but, depending on how valuable the data is, the cost might be justified.

When a data file or program file is damaged, portions of the file may still be intact. The basic approach to recovering data in this situation is to create a new file on another disk or on the hard drive, containing all the sectors from the original file that can be read from the damaged disk or hard drive. Use the Copy command and when you get an error message, try to move on to the next sector. Some of the file might be copied to the new medium. Then edit the newly created file to replace the missing data.

How successfully an OS recovers data depends on how badly damaged the file is. A few examples of how data commonly becomes damaged and what can be done to recover it are discussed in the following list. If a file has been accidentally erased, or the disk or hard drive is otherwise damaged, remember these two things:

- Don't write anything to the disk or hard drive, because you might overwrite data that you could otherwise recover.
- If you are recovering data from a floppy disk, use Diskcopy in DOS or Copy Disk in Windows Explorer to make a copy of the disk before you do anything else. If Copy Disk or Diskcopy doesn't work, try copying the disk with a third-party program such as Norton Utilities.

10

Here are some problems you may experience with files and the file system:

- *Corrupted file header.* If an application cannot open or read one of its data files, the file header might be corrupted. Many applications place header information (called the file header) at the beginning of the file. This data follows a different format from the rest of the file. The application uses it to identify the file and its contents. If the file header is lost or corrupted and an application needs that header to read the file, you can sometimes recover the contents by treating the file as an ASCII text file.

NOTE

Most applications let you import a text file and then convert it to the application's format. Read your application's documentation to learn how to import a text file.

- *Lost clusters.* A disk can develop lost clusters (lost allocation units) if a program cannot properly close a file it has opened. For example, if you boot your computer while an application is running (not a good thing to do for this very reason), the application does not have the opportunity to close a file and may lose clusters. Clusters can also be lost if you remove a floppy disk from a drive while the drive light is still on (also not a good thing to do). Some older applications, such as early versions of MS Access, might not complete writing a file to a floppy disk until the application is closed or another data file is opened. In this case, you must close the application or open a new file before it is safe to remove the floppy disk.

  Lost clusters are clusters that are not incorporated into a file. The Chkdsk and Scandisk commands turn the clusters into a file with the name File0000.chk or a similar filename with a higher number, and store the file in the root directory. To use this utility at a command prompt to access lost clusters, use the command with the /F option, like this:

  ```
  C:\> Chkdsk A:/F
  ```

  Often the file created can be used by the application that it belongs to, although you might have to change the file extension so the application will recognize the file. You can also use Windows 9x ScanDisk to accomplish the same results. If the drive is compressed, try booting to a command prompt and using Scan-Disk to recover the compressed data. Include the name of the compressed volume file on the host drive, like this:

  ```
  Scandisk drvspace.nnn
  ```

  or

  ```
  Scandisk dblspace.nnn
  ```

Substitute the file extension for the compressed volume file on the host drive (for example, Drvspace.001 or Dblspace.001).

- *Erased file.* A deleted file can sometimes be recovered. First look for the file in the Recycle Bin. If it's not there, try the Unerase or Undelete command at a command prompt, which recovers some erased files.

NOTE Viruses cause many file system problems. When you have a problem with a corrupted system file, program file, or data file, run a current version of antivirus software. The software will probably not help recover the file but might prevent other files from becoming infected.

CHAPTER SUMMARY

- To improve hard drive performance, use Disk Defragmenter regularly. If a drive is giving errors, use Windows 9x ScanDisk or Windows 2000/XP drive properties to check for errors and fix them.

- Windows 9x disk compression works by storing data on a drive in one big file and should not be trusted with valuable data.

- Volumes can be compressed under Windows 2000/XP as long as they are using NTFS.

- Disk caching uses temporary storage to speed up access to hard drive data and can be controlled either by hardware or software.

- DOS uses buffers rather than disk caching. Windows 3.x and 9x use built-in caching programs. Windows NT/2000/XP uses automated caching.

- The child, parent, grandparent backup method involves reusing tapes by making daily, weekly, and monthly backups.

- A full backup backs up all data from a hard drive. A differential backup backs up files that have changed or been created since the last full backup. An incremental backup backs up only files that have changed or been created since the last backup, whether or not it was a full backup.

- You can create backups using utilities included with tape drives or with Windows, or you can purchase third-party software.

- Disk cloning replicates a hard drive to a new computer.

- For disaster recovery, it is important to create and test a plan that includes keeping records of backups and recovery procedures.

10

▶ Viruses, which replicate by attaching themselves to other programs, are the most common type of computer infestation. Other types include worms, Trojan horses, and logic bombs.

▶ Viruses can hide in the boot sector, files, macros within files, or in both the boot sector and a file.

▶ Types of viruses that attempt to hide from antivirus software are polymorphic viruses, encrypting viruses, and stealth viruses.

▶ Damage from viruses ranges from an altered monitor display to the erasure of files or even an entire hard drive.

▶ Use antivirus software regularly both to clean out known viruses and to scan for undetected and unmanifested ones.

▶ Hard drive problems can be caused by hardware or software problems, and tend to fall into two categories: those that prevent the hard drive from booting and those that prevent data from being accessed.

▶ Three third-party utility software programs used to work with hard drives are Norton Utilities, SpinRite, and PartitionMagic.

▶ Common hard drive problems are corruption in OS files, the partition table, the boot record, the root directory, the FAT, sector markings, or data itself.

▶ For DOS or Windows to access a hard drive using the FAT file system, the following items must be intact, listed in the order in which they are accessed: the partition table, the boot record, the FAT and directory, the system files, and data and program files.

▶ You can use ScanDisk and Chkdsk to recover lost allocation units caused when files are not properly closed by the application creating them.

▶ When data is lost on a hard drive, don't write anything to the drive if you intend to try to recover the data.

KEY TERMS

For explanations of key terms, see the Glossary near the end of the book.

antivirus (AV) software
backup
boot sector virus
buffer
chain
child, parent, grandparent
    backup method
cross-linked clusters
defragment
differential backup
disk cache
disk cloning
disk compression
disk imaging

drive imaging
DriveSpace
encrypting virus
file virus
fragmentation
full backup
hardware cache
incremental backup
infestation
logic bomb
lost allocation units
lost clusters
macro

macro virus
memory-resident virus
multipartite virus
non-memory-resident virus
polymorphic virus
SMARTDrive
software cache
stealth virus
Trojan horse
VCACHE
virus
virus signature
worm

10

REVIEWING THE BASICS

1. What is the difference between a cross-linked cluster and a lost cluster? What can cause them?

2. What are two tools that Windows 9x uses to check for cross-linked and lost clusters?

3. What are two tools that Windows 2000/XP uses to check for cross-linked and lost clusters?

4. Of the two tools used by Windows 2000/XP to check for cross-linked and lost clusters, which tool is available from the Recovery Console?

5. Explain two disadvantages of data compression.

6. What file system is necessary to use if a volume is to be compressed under Windows 2000?

7. What is the name of the drive compression utility used by Windows 95/98?

8. How is a hardware cache different from a software cache?

9. Name and define the method DOS used to speed up disk access.

10. How is disk caching accomplished in Windows XP? Windows 9x? Windows 3.x with DOS?

11. What is the difference between an incremental backup and a differential backup?

12. What versions of Windows support incremental backups? Differential backups?

13. What is the Windows Scripting Host utility used for, and what is the command line to execute it?

14. Explain the child, parent, grandparent method of making backups.

15. What must you do before you can use the Windows Backup utility on a Windows XP Home Edition PC?

16. What process is used to replicate a hard drive to a new computer? When might you use this process, and what are some examples of software designed to perform it?

17. Why should you create a disaster recovery plan? What type of information would you include in it?

18. Define and explain the differences between viruses, worms, Trojan horses, and logic bombs.

19. Where can viruses hide?

20. What is the best way to protect a computer or network against worms?

21. What is the best way to determine if an email message warning about a virus is a hoax?

22. Name three ways that a virus can hide from antivirus software.

23. Are boot sector viruses limited to hard drives? Explain.

24. What is the most likely way that a virus will get access to your computer?

25. List three third-party utility programs used to support hard drives.

26. List at least four causes of hard drive problems.

27. What items must be intact in order for DOS or Windows to be able to access a hard drive using the FAT file system? List them in the order in which they are accessed.

28. What error message might appear if the partition table is damaged? The boot record? The FAT? The system files?

29. If a file header is lost or corrupted and an application needs that header to read the file, how can you recover the contents of the file?

30. If an erased file is not found in the Recycle Bin, what command can you use at a command prompt to attempt to recover the file?

THINKING CRITICALLY

1. You have an 8-GB hard drive and are using Windows 98. You need to use this system to store a commercial database that will be updated daily. The database will include photographs of products and you expect the data to take up about 10 GB of space. What do you do to solve the problem of too much data and not enough space?

   a. Compress the drive using Windows 98 DriveSpace.

   b. Compress the drive using third-party compression software.

   c. Install a new hard drive to hold the data.

2. You have an important FoxPro database stored on your hard drive. The drive has been giving bad sector errors for several weeks. You kept meaning to back up the data, but have not gotten around to it. Now you attempt to access the database and FoxPro tells you it cannot open the file. What do you try first? Second? Third?

   a. Reenter all the data and promise yourself you'll be more faithful about backups.

   b. Use SpinRite software to attempt to recover the file.

   c. Use ScanDisk to correct the bad sectors.

   d. Change the file extension of the database file to .txt and tell FoxPro to attempt to open the file as an ASCII text file.

3. Your system is very sluggish and takes a long time to boot and to load applications. Applications move very slowly as well. List three possible solutions that were described in this chapter.

10

PROJECT 10-1: Using a Windows Command Prompt to Manage a Hard Drive

On a Windows 2000/XP computer, do the following:

1. Boot to the Recovery Console and use the Chkdsk command to check the hard drive for errors and correct them. What is the Chkdsk command line that you used?

2. Boot to the Windows 2000/XP desktop. From a Command window, use the Defrag command to defragment the hard drive. What command line did you use?

On a Windows 9x computer, do the following:

1. Print the contents of Scandisk.ini in the \Windows\Command directory of your hard drive. Scandisk.ini contains settings that ScanDisk reads and uses when it executes.

2. What setting allows ScanDisk to delete the contents of a lost cluster without prompting you first?

3. From the .ini file information, can ScanDisk repair a damaged boot sector of a compressed drive?

4. From a command prompt, type **DEFRAG**. Follow the directions to defragment a disk or hard drive.

5. Reboot using a Windows 9x startup disk. Run **Scandisk** from the command prompt. What errors did it find?

PROJECT 10-2: Using Windows to Back Up Files and Folders

This exercise lets you practice using Windows Backup and see how the Backup utility manages several situations.

Part I

1. Using Windows Explorer, create a folder called **Backtest** on a hard drive.

2. Use Explorer to find a .txt file, and copy it to the new folder. Copy two other files to the Backtest folder. Make a subfolder called **Subfolder** in Backtest and copy a fourth file to C:\backtest\subfolder.

3. Right-click the .txt file and rename it **Overwrite.txt**. Right-click the second file and rename it **Delete.txt**. Rename the third file **NoChange.txt**. Leave the fourth file alone for now. Use Explorer and write down the file sizes before the backup.

4. Click **Start, Programs, Accessories, System Tools,** and **Backup.**

5. Use the directions provided in this chapter to back up the Backtest folder to a floppy disk. Use Explorer and compare the backup file sizes to the original file sizes. How are they different?

6. Delete the file **Delete.txt.** Edit and change the contents of Overwrite.txt. Make no changes to No Change.txt. Delete **Subfolder.**

7. Using Windows Backup, restore the files from the backup to their original folder.

   a. What did Backup do with the Delete.txt file?

   b. What did Backup do with the Overwrite.txt file?

   c. What did Backup do with the NoChange.txt file?

   d. What did Backup do with the missing subfolder and missing file?

   e. What is the name of the backup file on the floppy disk?

   f. What are the name and path to the error log created by Backup?

   g. Print the error log.

10

Part II

8. Use Windows Explorer to copy the Backtest folder to a second floppy disk.

9. Delete all files in the Backtest folder on the hard drive.

10. Use Windows Explorer to copy the three files back to the Backtest folder.

11. Delete the files in the Backtest folder on the hard drive.

12. Open the Recycle Bin and restore the three files to the Backtest folder by high-lighting them and using the **File, Restore** option. Did they return to the correct folder?

13. Once again, delete the files in the Backtest folder on the hard drive.

14. Highlight the three files in the Recycle Bin, and click **File, Delete.** Can you still restore the files?

PROJECT 10-3: Using the Internet to Learn About Viruses

One source of information about viruses on the Web is F-Secure Corporation. Go to the Web site *www.f-secure.com/v-descs* shown in Figure 10-18 for information about viruses; the viruses are listed alphabetically with complete descriptions, including any known sources of the viruses.

Figure 10-18   For complete virus information, see the F-Secure Web site

Print a description of three viruses from this Web site:

▶ One virus that destroys data on a hard drive

▶ One harmless virus that displays only garbage on the screen

▶ One virus that hides in a boot sector

The site also lists information about the most recent viruses. Search the Web site at *www.fsecure.com*, list five recent viruses, and describe their payload.

PROJECT 10-4: Downloading the Latest Update of AV Software

If you own antivirus software, download the latest antivirus (AV) definition list from the Internet. For example, for Norton AntiVirus, follow these directions:

1. Log on to the AV site: *www.symantec.com/downloads*.

2. Click **Virus Definition Updates** and then click **Download Virus Definitions**. Select your Norton Antivirus product and operating system.

3. Follow the directions to download the latest update and signature list for the particular version of your AV software.

4. While online, see if the site offers information on virus hoaxes and create a list of hoaxes if it does.

PROJECT 10-5: Troubleshooting a Hard Drive Problem over the Phone

A friend calls you to say that her hard drive does not work. She is using Windows 98 and has a rescue disk. Over the phone, walk her through the process of booting from the rescue disk and using the utilities on the disk to examine the hard drive. List the utilities on the rescue disk that she should use, in the order that she should use them, and write down what she should do with each utility.

In a lab environment, you can simulate this phone call by sitting with your back to a user sitting at a PC. Talk the user through the process without turning around and looking at the PC screen.

10

Windows on a Network

This chapter discusses how to use Windows to connect PCs in networks. You'll learn about the different technologies used to connect PCs in networks. You'll learn how to support PCs connected to a network, how computers are identified on a network, how to share computer resources over a network, and how to troubleshoot a network connection. In the next chapter, you'll learn how to connect to the Internet and how to use the resources on it.

Physical Network Architectures

Connecting devices on a **LAN** (**local area network**) provides a way for workstations, servers, printers, and other devices to communicate and share resources. There are several LAN architectures, or ways of connecting nodes on a network. (A **node**, or **host**, is one device on the network such as a workstation, server, or printer.) The four most popular physical network architectures (sometimes called hardware protocols) for local networks are Ethernet, wireless LAN, Token Ring, and FDDI. An older type of network technology is Attached Resource Computer network (ARCnet), which is seldom seen today. This section introduces the most popular LAN architectures, Ethernet and wireless.

Ethernet

Ethernet is the most popular network architecture used today. The three variations of Ethernet are primarily distinguished from one another by speed: 10-Mbps Ethernet, 100-Mbps or Fast Ethernet, and Gigabit Ethernet.

Most Ethernet networks are arranged in a star configuration with a hub in the center (see Figure 11-1). In a star arrangement, a hub passes all data that flows to it to every device connected to it. Think of a **hub** as just a pass-through and distribution point for every device connected to it, without regard for what kind of data is passing through and where the data might be going.

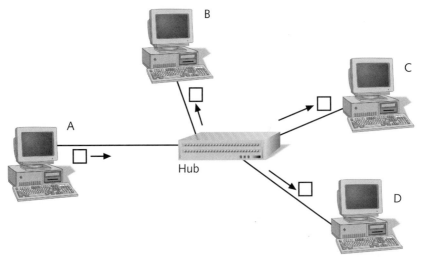

Figure 11-1   Any data received by a hub is replicated and passed on to every device connected to it

Figure 11-2 shows a hub that has two types of connectors. The more common **RJ-45 connector** uses twisted-pair cable, the most common type of cable. A less commonly used and heavier coaxial cable uses a BNC connector, also available on this hub. A hub is not required on a network; you can connect computers together in a line. This arrangement is called a bus formation, a less common type of network that typically uses coaxial cable.

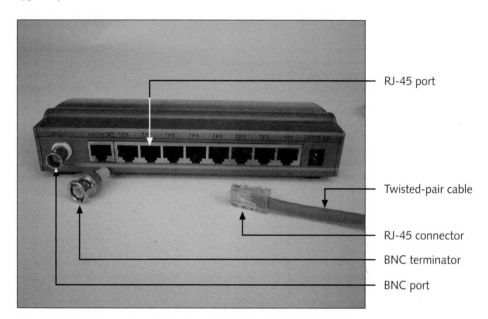

RJ-45 port

Twisted-pair cable

RJ-45 connector

BNC terminator

BNC port

11

Figure 11-2   A hub is a pass-through device to connect nodes on a network

Wireless LANs

Wireless LAN (WLAN) technology, as the name implies, uses radio waves or infrared light instead of cables or wires to connect computers or other devices. Connections are made using a wireless network interface card, which includes an antenna to send and receive signals. Wireless LANs are popular in places where networking cables are difficult to install, such as outdoors or in a historic building with wiring restrictions, or where there are many mobile users, such as on a college campus. Wireless devices can communicate directly (such as a handheld device communicating with a PC via an infrared connection), or they can connect to a LAN by way of a wireless **access point (AP)**, as shown in Figure 11-3. Access points are placed so that nodes can access at least one access point from anywhere in the covered area. When devices use an access point, they communicate through the access point instead of communicating directly.

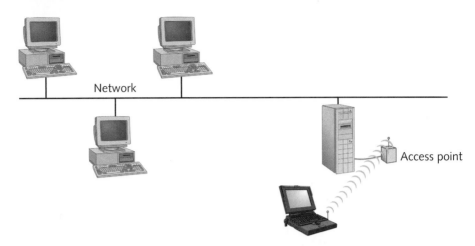

Figure 11-3   Nodes on a wireless LAN connect to a cabled network by way of an access point

NOTE

A LAN is often depicted in a logic diagram as a straight line with devices connecting to it. This method merely shows that devices are connected and is a nondescriptive way of drawing a LAN that might use a hub for communication.

The first IEEE standard that outlined wireless LAN specifications was IEEE 802.11, published in 1990. Most current wireless LAN devices operate under the 1999 IEEE **802.11b** standard. This standard is also called **Wi-Fi,** and called **AirPort** by Apple Computers, although there are other wireless technologies available, such as **Bluetooth.** 802.11b uses a frequency range of 2.4 GHz in the radio band and has a distance range of about 100 meters. 802.11b is a popular and inexpensive network solution for home and office. As a home network, it has the disadvantage that many cordless phones use the 2.4-GHz frequency range and cause network interference. Two other IEEE wireless standards are 802.11a and 802.11g.

How NICs Work

A PC connects to a network by way of a **network adapter,** which is most often an expansion card called a **network interface card (NIC),** using a PCI slot. However, the adapter can also be an external device providing a network port or wireless connection. The device can connect to the PC using a USB port, SCSI external port, or serial port. In addition, the adapter can be embedded on the motherboard, which provides the network port. In any case, the adapter must match the type and speed of the physical network being used, and the network port must match the type of connectors used on the network. Laptops can make connections to a network through a PC Card NIC, a built-in network port, a wireless connection, or an external device that connects to the laptop by way of a USB port.

An internal NIC plugs into a motherboard expansion slot, provides a port or ports (or antenna in the case of a wireless NIC) for connection to a network, and manages the communication and hardware network protocol for the PC. An external NIC provides the same functions and can use a PC Card slot or USB port. An individual NIC can be designed to support Ethernet, Token Ring, FDDI, or wireless architectures, but only one architecture at a time. However, it might be designed to handle more than one cabling system. The network card and the device drivers controlling it are the only components in the PC that are aware of the type of physical network being used. In other words, the type of network in use is transparent to the applications using it.

Some Ethernet NICs have more than one type of port on the back of the card, in order to accommodate different cabling media. This type of Ethernet card is called a **combo card** (see Figure 11-4).

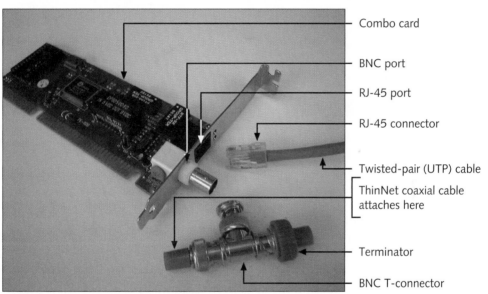

11

Combo card

BNC port

RJ-45 port

RJ-45 connector

Twisted-pair (UTP) cable

ThinNet coaxial cable attaches here

Terminator

BNC T-connector

Figure 11-4   This Ethernet combo card can use either a BNC or RJ-45 connection, depending on the cabling system used

Different networks have different ways of identifying network nodes. Ethernet, WLAN, and Token Ring cards have MAC addresses hard-coded on the card by their manufacturers. Called **MAC (Media Access Control) addresses, hardware addresses, physical addresses, adapter addresses,** or Ethernet addresses, they are 6-byte (48-bit) hex addresses unique to each card. Part of the MAC address refers to the manufacturer; therefore, no two adapters should have the same MAC address.

The next section looks at the different OS networking protocols, how they work, and how to configure a computer to use them.

Windows Networking

As a system of interlinked computers, a network needs both software and hardware to work. Software includes an operating system installed on each computer on the network, and perhaps **network operating sytem (NOS)** to control the entire network and its resources. If the network is small (fewer than 10 computers), it can be a **peer-to-peer network,** in which each computer on the network has the same authority as the other computers. Recall from Chapter 5 that a Windows peer-to-peer network is called a workgroup. Larger networks use the **client/server** model, in which access to a network is controlled by an NOS using a centralized database. A **client** computer provides a user ID and password to a **server** that validates the data against the security database. In a Windows network, this server is called the domain controller, and the network model is called a domain. Popular network operating systems are Windows Server 2003, Windows 2000 Server, Novell NetWare, Unix, and Linux. Windows 9x and Windows NT/2000/XP have client software built in for Windows and Novell NetWare servers. Alternately, for Novell NetWare, you can install Novell client software.

A+ EXAM TIP

The A+ Core and OS exams expect you to understand the differences between a peer-to-peer network and a client/server network.

A network can have more than one workgroup or domain in operation, and some computers might not belong to any workgroup or domain. A computer joins a workgroup or domain in order to share resources with other computers and devices in the group or domain. Company policy controls how many workgroups or domains can exist within the company network based on user needs, security concerns, and administrative overhead required to manage the groups.

At the physical network level, Windows supports Ethernet, ATM, Token Ring, and other networking protocols. At the operating system level, Windows supports the three suites of protocols shown in Figure 11-5 and described in the following list. AppleTalk, which is shown in the figure but not listed here, is a networking protocol for Macintosh computers. The figure also shows the different ways a computer or other device on the network can be addressed. Use this figure as a reference point throughout this section to understand the way the protocols and addresses relate on the network.

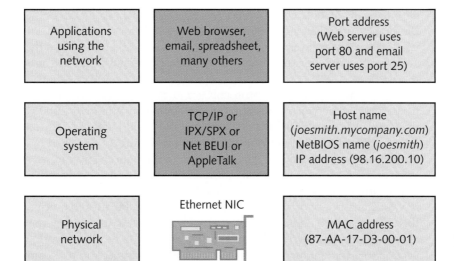

A+
OS
4.1

Figure 11-5　An operating system can use more than one method to address a computer on the network, but at the network level, a MAC address is always used to address a device on the network

A+ EXAM TIP

The A+ Core and OS exams expect you to be familiar with the protocols listed and described here.

- **TCP/IP (Transmission Control Protocol/Internet Protocol)** is the protocol suite used on the Internet and so should be your choice if you want to connect your network to the Internet, with each workstation having Internet access. Novell NetWare, Linux, Unix, and Mac OS also support TCP/IP.

- **IPX/SPX (Internetwork Packet Exchange/Sequenced Packet Exchange)** is a networking protocol suite designed for use with the Novell NetWare operating system. Novell NetWare is an OS designed to control access to resources on a network, similar to Windows 2003 Server. An OS designed to manage a network is called an NOS. IPX/SPX is similar to TCP/IP but is not supported on the Internet.

- **NetBEUI (NetBIOS Extended User Interface)** is a proprietary Windows protocol suite used only by Windows computers. NetBEUI is faster than TCP/IP and easier to configure but does not support routing to other networks, and therefore is not supported on the Internet. It should only be used on an isolated network. Windows XP does not automatically install NetBEUI, as Microsoft considers it a legacy protocol.

To use one of these protocols on a network, the first step is to physically connect the computer to the network by installing the NIC in the computer and connecting the network cable to the hub or other network device. (For wireless LANs, after installing the NIC, you put the computer within range of an access point.) The next step is to install the protocol in the operating system. Once the protocol is installed, it

A+
OS
4.1

automatically associates itself with any NICs it finds, in a process called binding. **Binding** occurs when an operating system-level protocol such as TCP/IP associates itself with a lower-level hardware protocol such as Ethernet. When the two protocols are bound, communication continues between them until they are unbound, or released.

You can determine which protocols are installed in Windows by looking at the properties of a network connection. For example, in Windows 2000 you can open the Control Panel and double-click the Network and Dial-up Connections icon. Then right-click the Local Area Connection icon (see Figure 11-6). The Local Area Connection Properties dialog box opens, as shown in the figure. You can see that two of the three protocols provided with Windows 2000 are installed because they are checked. In this situation, the PC is using a TCP/IP network, but one network printer uses IPX/SPX and does not support TCP/IP. Because the PC uses that printer, it must have IPX/SPX installed. (A **network printer** is a printer that any user on the network can access, through its own network card and connection to the network, through a connection to a standalone print server, or through a connection to a computer as a local printer, which is shared on the network.) There is no problem with more than one operating system protocol operating on the network at the same time.

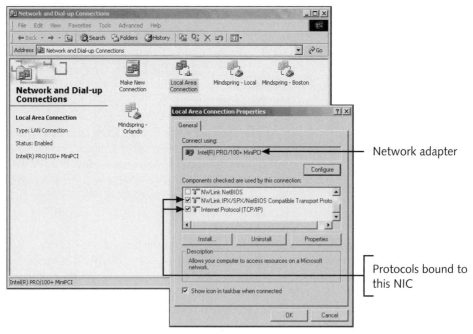

Figure 11-6   Two of three Windows 2000 network protocols are installed and bound to this network adapter

Addressing on a Network

A+
OS
4.1
4.2

Every device on a network has a unique address. Part of learning about a network is learning how a device (such as a computer or a printer) or a program (such as a Web server) is identified on the network. On a network, four methods are used to identify devices and programs:

✔ **A+ EXAM TIP**

The A+ Core and OS exams expect you to know each of the methods of identifying devices and programs on a network.

- *Using a MAC address.* As you learned earlier, a MAC address is a unique address permanently embedded in a NIC and identifying a device on a LAN. A MAC address is a value expressed as six pairs of hexadecimal numbers and letters, often separated by hyphens. The MAC address is used only by devices inside the local network, and is not used outside the LAN.
- *Using an IP address.* An **IP address** is a 32-bit address consisting of a series of four 8-bit numbers separated by periods. An IP address identifies a computer, printer, or other device on a TCP/IP network such as the Internet or an intranet. (An **intranet** is a company network that uses TCP/IP.) Because the largest possible 8-bit number is 255, each of the four numbers can be no larger than 255. An example of an IP address is 109.168.0.104. Consider a MAC address, a local address, and an IP address a long-distance address.
- *Using character-based names.* Character-based names include domain names, **host names**, and **NetBIOS (Network Basic Input/Output System)** names used to identify a PC on a network with easy-to-remember letters rather than numbers. (Host names and NetBIOS names are often just called **computer names**.)
- *Using a port address.* Recall from Chapter 10 that a port address is a number that identifies a program or service running on a computer to communicate over the network. These port addresses are not the same as the port addresses, also called I/O addresses, discussed in previous chapters. Port addresses will be covered in the next chapter.

Refer back to Figure 11-5, which shows examples of each of these addresses and at what layer of the network they are used. The sections that follow explain the different address types in more detail.

MAC Addresses

MAC addresses are used at the lowest (physical) networking level for NICs and other networking devices on the same network to communicate. If a host does not know the MAC address of another host on the same network, it uses the operating system to discover the MAC address. Because the hardware protocol (for example, Ethernet) controls traffic only on its own network, computers on different networks cannot use their MAC addresses for communication. In order for the host to communicate with a host on another LAN across the corporate intranet or Internet, it must know the

11

address of the host used by the TCP/IP protocols. These addresses are IP addresses (see Figure 11-7).

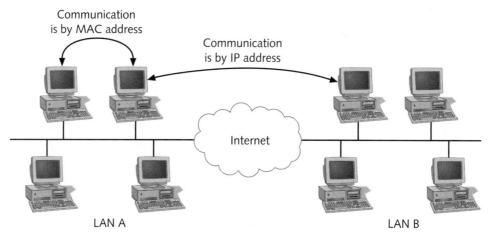

Figure 11-7   Computers on the same LAN use MAC addresses to communicate, but computers on different LANs use IP addresses to communicate over the Internet

If your PC is connected to the Internet or any other TCP/IP network, follow these directions to display the IP address and the NIC's MAC address in Windows NT/2000/XP:

1. Click **Start**, **Programs** (for Windows XP, **All Programs**), **Accessories**, and then **Command Prompt**. A command prompt window appears.

2. At the command prompt, type **ipconfig/all |more**. The screen shown in Figure 11-8 appears.

3. The |more option causes the results to appear one screen at a time instead of scrolling by so fast you cannot read them. Press **Enter** to see each screen.

4. To exit the command prompt window, type **Exit** at the command prompt.

A+
OS
4.1
4.2

Windows 2000 IP Configuration

Host Name ....: JEAN2000
Primary DNS Suffix ....:
Node Type.................................: Hybrid
IP Routing Enabled ....: No
WINS Proxy Enabled..................: No
DNS Suffix Search List ....: prestige.net

Ethernet adapter Local Area Connection:

Connection-specific DNS Suffix .: prestige.net
Description ....: Intel(R) PRO/100+ MiniPCI
Physical Address ....: 00-10-A4-90-1B-AA
DHCP Enabled...........................: Yes
Autoconfiguration Enabled ....: Yes
IP Address ....: 192.168.1.101
Subnet Mask ....: 255.255.255.0
Default Gateway ....: 192.168.1.1
DHCP Server ....: 192.168.1.1
DNS Servers..............................: 208.220.88.13
                                                      64.8.16.13
Lease Obtained ....: Wednesday, August 01, 2006 2:14:06 AM
Lease Expires ....: Tuesday, August 07, 2006 2:14:06 AM

Figure 11-8   Results of Windows 2000 ipconfig /all |more command show the current IP configuration
for this network

11

Windows 9x uses Winipcfg instead of Ipconfig. If you are using Windows 9x, follow these instructions to see your MAC address and IP address:

1. Click **Start** and then click **Run**. In the Run dialog box, type **winipcfg** and then
   press **Enter**. The IP Configuration window opens (see Figure 11-9).

2. Click the NIC in the drop-down list of network devices. The Adapter Address
   that appears is the MAC address; in this case, it is 00-20-78-EF-0C-5A.

3. Click **OK**.

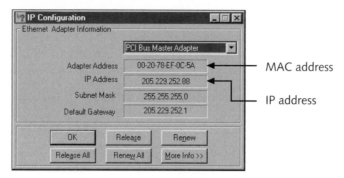

Figure 11-9   Use the Windows 9x Winipcfg utility to display a PC's IP address and MAC address

IP Addresses

All protocols of the TCP/IP suite identify a device on the Internet or an intranet by its IP address. An IP address is 32 bits long, made up of 4 bytes separated by periods, as in this address: 190.180.40.120. The largest possible 8-bit number is 11111111, which is equal to 255 in decimal, so the largest possible IP address in decimal is 255.255.255.255, which in binary is 11111111.11111111.11111111.11111111. Each of the four numbers separated by periods is called an **octet** (for 8 bits) and can be any number from 0 to 255, making a total of 4.3 billion potential IP addresses (256 × 256 × 256 × 256). Because of the allocation scheme used to assign these addresses, not all of them are available for use.

The first part of an IP address identifies the network, and the last part identifies the host. It's important to understand how the bits of an IP address are used in order to understand how routing happens over interconnected networks such as the Internet, and how TCP/IP can locate an IP address anywhere on the globe. When data is routed over interconnected networks, the network portion of the IP address is used to locate the right network. Once the data arrives at the local network, the host portion of the IP address is used to identify the one computer on the network that is to receive the data. Finally, the IP address of the host must be used to identify its MAC address so the data can travel on the host's LAN to that host. The next section explains this in detail.

Classes of IP Addresses

When a business, college, or some other organization applies for IP addresses, a range of addresses appropriate to the number of hosts on the organization's networks is assigned. IP addresses that can be used by companies and individuals are divided into three classes: Class A, Class B, and Class C, based on the number of possible IP addresses in each network within each class. IP addresses are assigned to these classes according to the scheme outlined in Table 11-1.

You can determine the class of an IP address and the size or type of company to which an address is licensed by looking at the address. More importantly, you also can determine what portion of an IP address is dedicated to identifying the network and what portion is used to identify the host on that network.

Class	Network Octets (Blanks in the IP address stand for octets used to identify hosts.)	Total Number of Possible Networks or Licenses	Host Octets (Blanks in the IP address stand for octets used to identify networks.)	Total Number of Possible IP Addresses in Each Network
A	0.__.__.__ to 126.__.__.__	127	__.0.0.1 to __.255.255.254	16 million
B	128.0.__.__ to 191.255.__.__	16,000	__.__.0.1 to __.__.255.254	65,000
C	192.0.0.__ to 223.255.255.__	2 million	__.__.__.1 to __.__.__.254	254

Table 11-1   Classes of IP addresses

Figure 11-10 shows how each class of IP address is divided into the network and host portions. A Class A address uses the first (leftmost) octet for the network address and the remaining octets for host addresses. A Class A license assigns a single number that is used in the first octet of the address, which is the network address. The remaining three octets of the IP address can be used for host addresses that uniquely identify each host on this network. The first octet of a Class A license is a number between 0 and 126. For example, if a company is assigned 87 as its Class A network address, then 87 is used as the first octet for every host on this one network. Examples of IP addresses for hosts on this network are 87.0.0.1, 87.0.0.2, and 87.0.0.3. (For class A, the last three octets cannot be all 0s or all 255s—0.0.0 or 255.255.255, so 87.0.0.0 would not be valid.) In the example address 87.0.0.1, the 87 is the network portion of the IP address, and 0.0.1 is the host portion. Because three octets can be used for Class A host addresses, one Class A license can have approximately $(256 \times 256 \times 256)$ -2 host addresses, or about 16 million IP addresses. Only very large corporations with heavy communication needs can get Class A licenses.

A Class B address uses the first two octets for the network portion and the last two for the host portion. A Class B license assigns a number for each of the two leftmost octets, leaving the third and fourth octets for host addresses. How many host addresses are there in one Class B license? The number of possible values for two octets is about (256×256) -2, or about 65,000 host addresses in a single Class B license. (Some IP addresses are reserved, so these numbers are approximations.) The first octet of a Class B license is a number between 128 and 191, which gives about 63 different values for a Class B first octet. The second number can be between 0 and 255, so there are approximately 63×256, or about 16,000, Class B networks. For example, suppose a company is assigned 135.18 as the network address for its Class B license. The first two octets for all hosts on this network are 135.18, and the

11

company uses the last two octets for host addresses. Examples of IP addresses on this company's Class B network are 135.18.0.1, 135.18.0.2, and 135.18.0.3. In the first example listed, 135.18 is the network portion of the IP address, and 0.1 is the host portion.

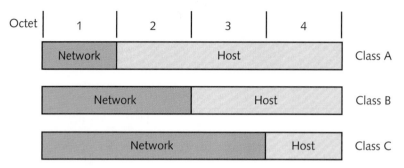

Figure 11-10   The network portion and host portion for each class of IP addresses

A Class C license assigns three octets as the network address. With only one octet used for the host addresses, there can be only 254 host addresses on a Class C network. The first number of a Class C license is between 192 and 223. For example, if a company is assigned a Class C license for its network with a network address of 200.80.15, some IP addresses on the network would be 200.80.15.1, 200.80.15.2, and 200.80.15.3.

Class D and Class E IP addresses are not available for general use. Class D addresses begin with octets 224 through 239 and are used for **multicasting**, in which one host sends messages to multiple hosts, such as when the host transmits a video conference over the Internet. Class E addresses begin with 240 through 254 and are reserved for research.

Different Ways of Assigning IP Addresses

When a small company is assigned a Class C license, it obtains 254 IP addresses for its use. If it has only a few hosts (say, less than 25 on a network), many IP addresses go unused, which is one reason there is a shortage of IP addresses. But suppose that the company grew, now has 300 workstations on the network, and is running out of IP addresses. There are two approaches to solving this problem: use private IP addresses and use dynamic IP addressing. Many companies combine both methods. An explanation of each of these solutions follows.

Public, Private, and Reserved IP Addresses   When a company applies for a Class A, B, or C license, it is assigned a group of IP addresses that are different from all other IP addresses and are available for use on the Internet. The IP addresses available to the Internet are called **public IP addresses**.

One thing to consider, however, is that not all of a company's workstations need to have Internet access, even though they may be on the network. So, while each workstation may need an IP address to be part of the TCP/IP network, those not connected to the Internet don't need addresses that are unique and available to the Internet; these workstations can use private IP addresses. **Private IP addresses** are IP addresses used on private intranets that are isolated from the Internet. Because the hosts are isolated from the Internet, no conflicts arise.

In fact, a small company most likely will not apply for a license of public IP addresses at all, but instead rely solely on private IP addresses for its internal network. A company using TCP/IP can make up its own private IP addresses to use on its intranet. IEEE recommends that the following IP addresses be used for private networks:

- 10.0.0.0 through 10.255.255.255
- 172.16.0.0 through 172.31.255.255
- 192.168.0.0 through 192.168.255.255

NOTE   IEEE, a nonprofit organization, is responsible for many Internet standards. Standards are proposed to the networking community in the form of an RFC (Request for Comment). RFC 1918 outlines recommendations for private IP addresses. To view an RFC, visit the Web site *www.rfc-editor.org*.

When assigning isolated IP addresses, also keep in mind that a few IP addresses are reserved for special use by TCP/IP and should not be used. They are listed in Table 11-2.

IP Address	How It Is Used
255.255.255.255	Broadcast messages
0.0.0.0	Currently unassigned IP address
127.0.0.1	Indicates your own workstation

Table 11-2   Reserved IP addresses

All IP addresses on a network must be unique for that network. A network administrator may assign an IP address to a standalone computer (for example, if someone is testing networking software on a PC that is not connected to the network). As long as the network is a private network, the administrator can assign any IP address, although a good administrator avoids using the reserved addresses.

Dynamically Assigned IP Addresses   If an administrator must configure each host on a network manually, assigning it a unique IP address, the task of going from PC to PC to make these assignments and keeping up with which address is assigned to which PC can be an administrative nightmare. The solution is to have a server

11

automatically assign an IP address to a workstation each time it comes onto the network. Instead of permanently assigning IP addresses (called **static IP addresses**) to workstations, an IP address (called a **dynamic IP address**) is assigned for the current session only. When the session terminates, the IP address is returned to the list of available addresses. Because not all workstations are online at all times, fewer IP addresses than the total number of workstations can satisfy the needs of the network. Also, you can use private IP addresses for the range of IP addresses that can be assigned to workstations. When a workstation has an IP address assigned to it, it is said that the workstation is leasing the IP address. **Internet service providers (ISPs)**, organizations through which individuals and businesses connect to the Internet, use dynamic IP addressing for their subscribers.

The server that manages these dynamically assigned IP addresses is called a **DHCP (Dynamic Host Configuration Protocol)** server. In this arrangement, workstations are called DHCP clients. DHCP software resides on both the client and the server to manage the dynamic assignments of IP addresses. DHCP client software is built into Windows NT/2000/XP and Windows 9x.

A+ EXAM TIP

The A+ OS exam expects you to know what a DHCP server is and understand when APIPA addressing is used.

When you configure a DHCP server, you specify the range of IP addresses that can be assigned to clients on the network. Figure 11-11 shows the configuration window for a DHCP server embedded as firmware on a router. (Routers are devices used to connect networks.) Access the configuration window using a Web browser on the network and then enter the IP address of the router in the Web browser address box. In the figure, you can see that the router's IP address is 192.168.1.1, and the starting IP address to be assigned to clients is 192.168.1.100. Because the administrator specified that the server can have up to 50 clients, the range of IP addresses is therefore 192.168.1.100 to 192.168.1.149. Also shown in the figure is a list of currently assigned IP addresses and the MAC address of the computer that currently leases that IP address.

When a PC first connects to the network, it attempts to lease an address from the DHCP server. If the attempt fails, it uses an **Automatic Private IP Address (APIPA)** in the address range 169.254.x.x.

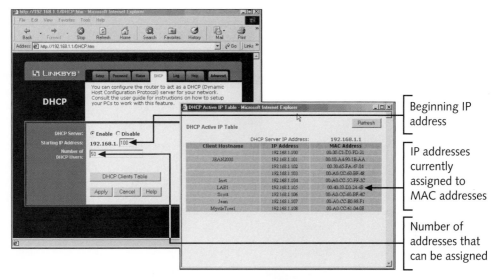

Beginning IP address

IP addresses currently assigned to MAC addresses

Number of addresses that can be assigned

Figure 11-11 A DHCP server has a range of IP addresses it can assign to clients on the network

Network Address Translation If hosts on a network using private IP addresses need to access the Internet, a problem arises because the private IP addresses are not allowed on the Internet. The solution is to use **NAT (Network Address Translation)**, which uses a single public IP address to access the Internet on behalf of all hosts on the network using other IP addresses. Using NAT, a networked computer trying to access the Internet must go through a server, router, or other device that substitutes its own IP address for that of the computer requesting the information. Because the device is standing in proxy for other hosts that want Internet access, it is called a **proxy server**. Figure 11-12 shows how a proxy server stands between the network and the Internet. This proxy server has two network cards installed. One card connects to the LAN, and the other connects to a cable modem and then to the ISP and the Internet.

NOTE

Windows 98 SE, Windows Me, Windows 2000, and Windows XP offer a NAT service called Microsoft Internet Connection Sharing (ICS). With it, two or more PCs on a home network can share the same IP address when accessing the Internet. Under ICS, one PC acts as the proxy server for other PCs on the home network.

Because a proxy server stands between a LAN and the Internet, it often does double duty as a firewall. Recall from Chapter 10 that a firewall is software or hardware that protects a network from illegal entry. Because networks are so often attacked by worms and hackers from the Internet, even a small LAN often has a router or other device between the LAN and the Internet that serves as a proxy server, DHCP server, and firewall. As a firewall, it filters out any unsolicited traffic coming from the Internet. Chapter 12 gives more information about firewalls.

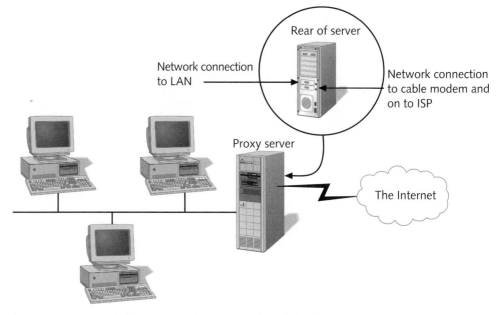

Figure 11-12 A proxy server stands between a private network and the Internet

Host Names and NetBIOS Names

Each computer on a TCP/IP network is assigned an IP address, but these numbers are hard to remember. Host names and NetBIOS names use characters rather than numbers to identify computers on a network and are easier to remember and use than IP addresses. In addition, a company might have a **domain name** that can be used to identify the network. An example of a domain name is *amazon.com*. Domain names are covered in the next chapter.

A+ EXAM TIP

The A+ OS exam expects you to be able to distinguish between DNS and WINS.

Recall that NetBEUI is a proprietary, legacy Windows network protocol used for Windows LANs that are not connected to the Internet. NetBEUI supports NetBIOS, a protocol that applications use to communicate with each other. Before TCP/IP became such a popular protocol, Windows assumed that the protocol of choice would be Net-BEUI and that all computers on a network would be assigned a Net-BIOS name such as *joesmith* or *Workstation12*. These names usually are assigned when the operating system is installed. In contrast, TCP/IP identifies computers by IP addresses, but TCP/IP also allows a computer to be assigned a character-based host name such as *joesmith*. The host name can also have a domain name attached that identifies the network: *joesmith.mycompany.com*. On a TCP/IP network, the NetBIOS name or host name must be associated with an IP address before one computer can find another on the network. This process of associating a character-based name with an IP address is called **name resolution**.

Two name resolution services track relationships between character-based names and IP addresses: **DNS** (**Domain Name System**, also called **Domain Name Service**) and Microsoft **WINS** (**Windows Internet Naming Service**). DNS tracks host names and WINS tracks NetBIOS names. A **DNS server** and a WINS server are computers that can find an IP address for another computer when only the host name and domain name are known, using either the DNS or WINS system. Windows networks sometimes use a combination of DNS and WINS; DNS is the more popular method.

Windows 98 assumes that a computer name is a NetBIOS name, which can have only 15 characters, but Windows 2000 and Windows XP assume that the computer name is a host name that uses the TCP/IP convention for host names. If the name is 15 characters or fewer, it works as a NetBIOS name or a TCP/IP name. If a host name is used, it can be up to 63 characters including letters, numbers, and hyphens, as long as the computer is not part of a workgroup. If the computer is part of a workgroup, the host name should not exceed 15 characters. Microsoft now considers the default naming convention to be TCP/IP host names rather than NetBIOS names.

Now that you know about the operating system protocols used on a network and how various types of addresses identify computers and devices on the network, let's turn our attention to how to install and configure a NIC and how to configure the OS to access and use resources on a network.

How Computers Find Each Other on a LAN

11

When an application wants to communicate with another computer on the same TCP/IP LAN, the requesting computer knows the name of the remote computer. Before TCP/IP communication can happen between the two computers, the first computer must discover the IP address of the remote PC. For Windows 98 using NetBIOS names, the computer runs through the following checklist in the order shown to discover the IP address. (A Windows 2000/XP computer using just TCP/IP and not NetBEUI uses DNS to resolve the name, not WINS, and begins at Step 5. If NetBEUI is running on this Windows 2000/XP computer, it tries DNS first, beginning at Step 5, and then turns to NetBEUI in Steps 1 through 4 to resolve the name.)

1. The computer checks the NetBIOS name cache. This cache is information retained in memory from name resolutions made since the last reboot.

2. If the computer has the IP address of a WINS server, it queries the server. A WINS server is a Windows NT/2000 server on the network that maintains a database of NetBIOS names and IP addresses.

3. The computer sends a broadcast message to all computers on the LAN asking for the IP address of the computer with the broadcasted NetBIOS name.

4. The computer checks a file named **LMHosts**, which is stored on the local computer. This file, called a host table, contains the NetBIOS names and associated IP addresses of computers on the LAN if someone has taken the time to manually make the entries in the file.

5. If the IP address is still not discovered, the computer assumes that the network is using DNS instead of WINS, so it checks the file named **Hosts** stored on the

A+
OS
4.1

local computer. The Hosts file is another host table that contains host names and associated IP addresses, and is similar to the information kept by DNS servers.

6. If the computer has the IP address of a DNS server, it queries the DNS server.

Both the LMHosts and Hosts host tables are stored in the \Windows\System32 \drivers\etc folder of a Windows 2000/XP computer or in the \Windows folder of a Windows 9x computer. LMHosts serves as a local table of information similar to that maintained by a WINS server for NetBIOS names, and Hosts serves as a local table of information similar to that kept by a DNS server.

If you look in the \Windows\System32\drivers\etc folder of a Windows 2000/XP computer or in the \Windows folder of a Windows 9x computer, you will see a sample of each file named LMHosts.SAM and Hosts.SAM, where the SAM stands for sample. Open each file with Notepad to examine it. Entries in a host table file beginning with the # symbol are comments and are not read by the name resolution process. The sample files contain many commented lines. You can add your entries to the bottom of the file without the # symbol. Then save the file in the same folder as the sample file, naming it Hosts or LMHosts with no file extension. An example of a Hosts file is shown in Figure 11-13. It tells this computer the IP address of the domain name *apache.test.com*. Recall that a domain name is a name of a network. In the example, apache is the host name, and the domain name is test.com. The **fully qualified domain name (FQDN)** is *apache.test.com*, which is often loosely called the domain name.

In this example, the computer named *apache.test.com* is used as a Web server for a private network. In order for people on the network to use this domain name, the Hosts file on each PC must have the entry shown in Figure 11-13, and the Web server must have the same IP address at all times. One way to accomplish this is to assign a static IP address to the server. Alternately, if your DHCP server supports this feature, you can configure it to assign the same IP address to your Web server each time if you tell the DHCP server your Web server's MAC address.

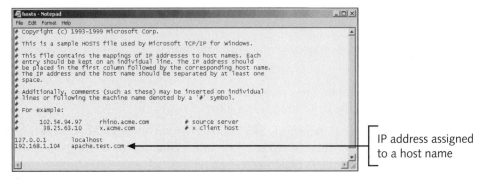

IP address assigned to a host name

Figure 11-13   An entry in your client Hosts file will tell the client the IP address of an intranet Web site when no DNS service is running in Windows 98

Configuring a Network Card and Connecting to a Network

Connecting a PC to a network requires a NIC, a patch cable, and a device for the PC to connect to, such as a hub. (Wireless PCs require a wireless NIC and require the PC to be within range of an access point.)

A+ EXAM TIP

The A+ Core and OS exams expect you to know how to configure a network connection.

Installing a network card and connecting the PC to a network involves three general steps: (1) put the NIC in the PC, and install the NIC's drivers, (2) configure the NIC using Windows, so that it has the appropriate addresses on the network and the correct network protocols, and (3) test the NIC to verify that the PC can access resources on the network. This section discusses these steps using Windows 2000/XP and Windows 9x. In the following sections you will also learn how to manage resources on the network and how to troubleshoot a failed network connection.

Installing a NIC Using Windows 2000/XP

11

To install a NIC using Windows 2000/XP, do the following:

1. Physically install the network card in the PC. (If the card is Plug and Play, it most likely has no jumpers or DIP switches to set.)

2. Turn on the PC. The Found New Hardware Wizard launches to begin the process of loading the necessary drivers to use the new device. It is better to use the manufacturer's drivers, not the Windows drivers. When given the opportunity, click Have Disk and insert the floppy disk or CD that came bundled with the NIC.

NOTE

Sometimes Windows XP will install its own drivers without asking if you want to use manufacturer-provided drivers. To prevent this from happening, you can run the setup program on the CD that comes bundled with the network adapter card before you install the card. Then, after you boot with the new card installed, Windows will find the already-installed manufacturer drivers and use those drivers.

3. After the Windows desktop loads, verify that the drivers installed successfully. Open **Device Manager**, right-click the card from the list of devices, and click **Properties**. The card's Properties window appears (see Figure 11-14). Look for any conflicts or other errors reported by Device Manager. If errors are reported, try downloading updated drivers from the Web site of the network card's manufacturer.

4. Connect a network patch cable to the NIC port and to the network hub or a wall jack connected to a hub. You are now ready to configure the NIC to access the network.

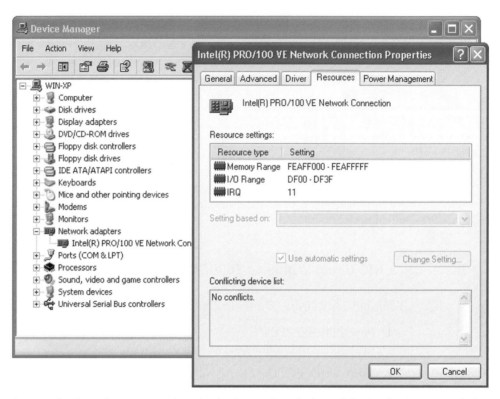

Figure 11-14   A network adapter's resources show in the Properties window of the Device Manager window

Incidentally, there are three ways to access the network adapter Properties window:

- As described earlier, open Device Manager, right-click the network adapter, and select Properties from the shortcut menu.
- From the Control Panel, launch the Windows XP Network Connections applet or the Windows 2000 Network and Dial-up Connections applet. Right-click the Local Area Connection icon and select Properties from the shortcut menu. Click Configure.
- Right-click My Network Places and select Properties from the shortcut menu. The Windows XP Network Connections applet or Windows 2000 Network and Dial-up Connections applet launches. Right-click the Local Area Connection icon and select Properties from the shortcut menu. Click Configure.

The first step to configure the OS for the network is to give the computer a name. Remember that if you plan to use NetBEUI as a networking protocol instead of

TCP/IP, limit the computer name to 15 characters. For Windows 2000/XP, the protocol is TCP/IP by default. Follow these directions to name a computer:

1. Right-click **My Computer** and select **Properties** from the shortcut menu. The System Properties window appears.

2. For Windows XP, click the **Computer Name** tab, then click the **Change** button. The Computer Name Changes dialog box appears (see Figure 11-15). For Windows 2000, click the **Network Identification** tab, and then click the **Properties** button. The Identification Changes window appears.

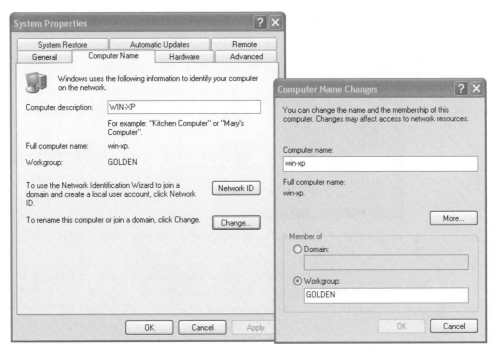

Figure 11-15   Windows XP uses the Computer Name Changes dialog box to assign a host name to a computer on a network

3. Enter the Computer name (**win-xp** in the example shown in Figure 11-15). Each computer name must be unique within a workgroup or domain.

4. Select **Workgroup** and enter the name of the workgroup (**GOLDEN** in this example). Recall that a workgroup is a group of computers on a network that share files, folders, and printers. All users in the workgroup must have the same workgroup name entered in this window. If the PC is to join a domain (a network where logging on is controlled by a server), enter the name of the domain here, such as *mycompany.com*. When configuring a PC on a network, always follow the specific directions of the network administrator responsible for the network.

5. Click **OK** to exit the Windows XP Computer Name Changes dialog box or the Windows 2000 Identification Changes window, and click **OK** to exit the System Properties window. You will be asked to reboot the computer for changes to take effect.

6. After rebooting a Windows XP system, click **Start**, **My Network Places**, and then click **View workgroup computers** to view this computer and others on the network. On the Windows 2000 desktop, open **My Network Places**, and double-click **Computers Near Me**. Figure 11-16 shows an example of My Network Places.

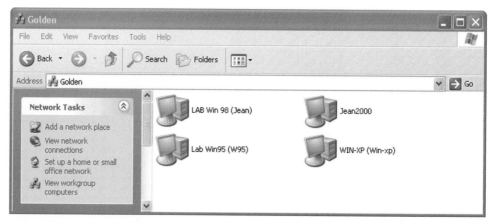

Figure 11-16   Windows XP My Network Places shows all computers on the LAN in a common workgroup

My Network Places for Windows 2000/XP and Network Neighborhood for Windows 9x can be viewed on the desktop and in Windows Explorer. By default, Windows XP puts My Network Places only in Windows Explorer, Windows 2000 puts My Network Places in both places, and Windows 98 puts Network Neighborhood in both places.

Installing and Configuring TCP/IP Using Windows 2000/XP

When a network card is installed in Windows 2000/XP, TCP/IP is installed by default. However, if TCP/IP has been uninstalled or gives you problems, you can install it again. Also, Windows makes some assumptions about how TCP/IP is configured, and these settings might not be appropriate for your network. This section addresses all these concerns.

A+
OS
4.1
4.2

Before you install and configure TCP/IP, you might need to ask the network administrator the following questions:

1. Will the PC use dynamic or static IP addressing?

2. If static IP addressing is used, what are the IP address, subnet mask, and default gateway for this computer?

3. Do you use DNS? If so, what are the IP addresses of your DNS servers?

4. Is a proxy server used to connect to other networks (including the Internet)? If so, what is the IP address of the proxy server?

In dynamic addressing the computer asks a DHCP server for its IP address each time it connects to the network. The server also gives the PC its subnet mask and default gateway so that the computer knows how to communicate with other hosts that are not on its own network. A **gateway** is a computer or other device that allows a computer on one network to communicate with a computer on another network. A **default gateway** is the gateway a computer uses to access another network if it does not have a better option. A **subnet mask** is a group of four dotted decimal numbers that tells TCP/IP if a remote computer's IP address is on the same or a different network.

Most likely, you will be using dynamic IP addressing, and the computer will obtain the DNS server address automatically. The DHCP server might also act as the proxy server so that computers inside the network can make connections to computers outside the network using the proxy server's public IP address.

To set the TCP/IP properties for a connection, follow these steps:

1. For Windows XP, open the **Network Connections** applet, and for Windows 2000 open the **Network and Dial-up Connection** applet. Right-click the **Local Area Connection** icon, and then select **Properties** from the shortcut menu. See Figure 11-17.

2. Select **Internet Protocol (TCP/IP)** from the list of installed components, and then click the **Properties** button. The Internet Protocol (TCP/IP) Properties dialog box opens, which is also shown in Figure 11-17.

3. For dynamic IP addressing, select **Obtain an IP address automatically**. (This is the most likely choice.) For static IP addressing, select **Use the following IP address,** and enter the IP address, Subnet mask, and Default gateway.

11

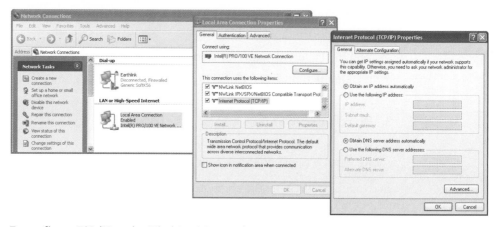

Figure 11-17   To configure TCP/IP under Windows XP, use the Internet Protocol (TCP/IP) Properties
dialog box

4. To disable DNS until the DHCP server gives the computer the DNS server
address, select **Obtain DNS server address automatically.** (This is the most
likely choice.) If you have the IP addresses of the DNS servers, click **Use the following DNS server addresses,** and enter the IP addresses. Click **OK** twice to
close both windows.

5. Open **My Network Places** and verify that your computer and other computers
on the network are visible. If you don't see other computers on the network,
reboot the PC.

To connect a Windows 2000 computer to a network using NetBEUI, use the Properties window of
the local area connection to install the NetBEUI Protocol, which automatically binds itself to the
NIC providing this local network connection. Then assign a name to the computer. Remember to
limit the name to 15 characters. Windows XP does not support NetBEUI. However, you can manually install it using the Windows XP setup CD. For directions, see the Microsoft Knowledge Base
Article 301041 at *support.microsoft.com.*

Installing a NIC Using Windows 9x

After a NIC is physically installed and the PC is turned on, Windows 9x automatically detects the card and guides you through the process of installing drivers. After
the installation, verify that the card is installed with no errors by using Device Manager. In Device Manager, the network card should be listed under Network adapters.
Right-click the card and select Properties to view the card's properties.

Connect a network patch cable to the NIC port and to the network hub or a wall
jack connected to a hub. You are now ready to configure the NIC to access the
network.

Assigning a Computer Name

A+
OS
4.1
4.2

To assign a name to a Windows 9x computer, follow these directions:

1. Access the **Control Panel** and double-click the **Network** icon.

2. Click the **Identification** tab (see Figure 11-18).

3. Enter the name of the workgroup (Golden in this example). Enter the computer name (Patricia in this example). Each computer name must be unique within the workgroup.

4. Click **OK** to exit the window. You will be asked to reboot the system.

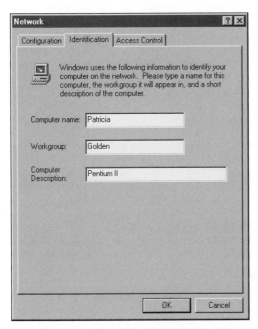

Figure 11-18   Each computer in a workgroup in Windows 98 must be assigned a name that other users on the network will see in their Network Neighborhood window

11

After you have rebooted, open Network Neighborhood on the Windows desktop. You should be able to see this computer and others on the network. Figure 11-19 shows an example of Network Neighborhood. If you cannot see other computers, you might have to install and configure TCP/IP, as described next.

Figure 11-19   Windows 98 Network Neighborhood shows all computers on the LAN in a common workgroup

Installing and Configuring TCP/IP Using Windows 98

If TCP/IP is not already installed, you must install it. For Windows 98, do the following:

1. Access the **Control Panel** and double-click the **Network** icon. The Network window opens.

2. Click **Add** to display the Select Network Component Type window, as shown in Figure 11-20.

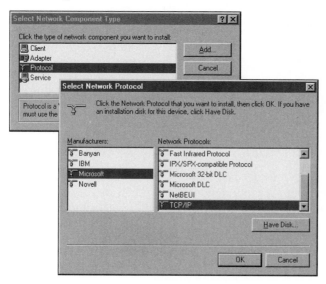

Figure 11-20   To install TCP/IP in Windows 98, use the Select Network Protocol window

A+
OS
4.1
4.2

3. Select **Protocol** and click **Add**. The Select Network Protocol window opens. Select **Microsoft** on the left and **TCP/IP** on the right (see Figure 11-20). Click **OK**. The system asks for the Microsoft Windows 98 CD and requests that you reboot the system.

4. When you return to the Network window, notice that TCP/IP is automatically bound to any network cards or modems that it finds installed.

The next step is to configure TCP/IP. Most likely, you will be using dynamic IP addressing, and the DNS service is initially disabled (later the DHCP server will tell the PC to enable it). In Windows 98, do the following to configure TCP/IP bound to a NIC to communicate over a local network:

1. In the Network window, select the item where TCP/IP is bound to the NIC. (In Figure 11-21, that item is TCP/IP->NETGEAR FA311 Fast Ethernet PCI Adapter.) Then, click **Properties**. The TCP/IP Properties window appears.

2. If static IP addressing is used, click **Specify an IP address**, and then enter the IP address and subnet mask supplied by your administrator. If dynamic IP addressing is used, click **Obtain an IP address automatically**. Most likely this will be your selection.

11

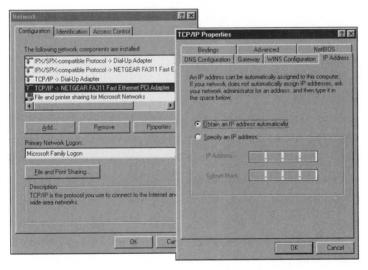

Figure 11-21   To configure TCP/IP in Windows 98, select the binding and click Properties to view the TCP/IP Properties window

3. Click the **DNS Configuration** tab, and choose to enable or disable DNS (see Figure 11-22). If you enable DNS, enter the IP addresses of your DNS servers. If your network administrator gave you other specific values for the TCP/IP

A+
OS
4.1
4.2

configuration, you will find the tabs for these settings on this window. But in most cases, the preceding steps are sufficient to configure TCP/IP.

4. When finished, click **OK** to exit the Properties window, and then click **OK** to exit the Network window.

5. On the desktop, verify that you can see your computer and others on the network in Network Neighborhood. If you don't see others on the network, reboot the PC.

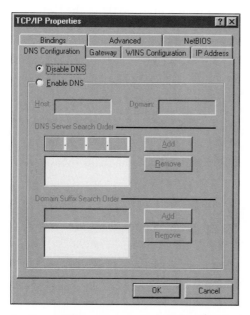

Figure 11-22   Configure DNS service under TCP/IP for Windows 98

NOTE

To use NetBEUI on a Windows 9x network, first verify that NetBEUI is installed or install it as you do TCP/IP. It should automatically bind itself to any network adapters installed. NetBEUI needs no other configuration.

Installing a Wireless NIC

A+
OS
4.2

Installing a wireless NIC works the same way as installing a regular NIC, except you must use the NIC's configuration software to specify wireless network parameters. A wireless connection requires the computer to be within an acceptable range of an access point or another wireless device that it will communicate with directly. Thisdis-tance is determined by the type of wireless technology used, which most likely will be 802.11b. This wireless standard supports ranges from 100 meters to more than 500 meters, depending on the speed at which the access point or other computer is configured to run. Generally, the higher the speed, the shorter the range is between devices.

Do the following to install and configure a wireless NIC in a PC or notebook:

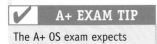

1. Install the wireless NIC and turn on the computer. A wireless NIC uses an internal or external antenna. If it has an external antenna, raise it. The computer immediately detects the device and launches the Found New Hardware Wizard. Follow the wizard to load the device drivers using the CD that came bundled with the NIC. If Windows prompts you to restart the computer, do so.

2. Configure the NIC to use the same wireless parameters as the access point or other computer. Run a setup program on the CD that came with the NIC to install the NIC configuration software, and then launch the software.

3. Consult the documentation to find out how to use the software. Figure 11-23 shows an example of the configuration window for a wireless NIC, but yours might look different. Using the configuration software, you can view the status of the wireless connection and change the wireless parameters.

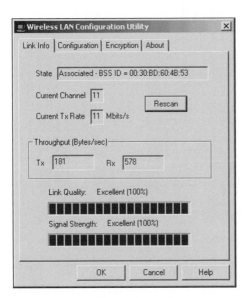

Figure 11-23   Wireless NIC configuration software reports the status of the current connection

Figure 11-23 shows an example of wireless configuration software reporting the following information about the connection:

■ *State.* The state is the status of the current connection and reports the BSS ID (basic service set identifier), which is the MAC address of the access point device that the NIC is currently using.

■ *Current Channel.* 802.11b uses 14 different channels. The United States can use channels 1 through 11. The access point device is configured to use one of these 11 channels, which is reported by the NIC software.

■ *Current Tx Rate.* Current transmission rate, which is 11 Mbits/sec in the figure.

■ *Throughput, Link Quality*, and *Signal Strength*. These values indicate throughput rate and how strong the signal is.

Figure 11-23 also shows a Rescan button. You can click this button to tell the NIC to scan for a new access point.

4. Click the **Configuration** tab to change how the NIC functions (see Figure 11-24). Most likely, you will not need to change any defaults.

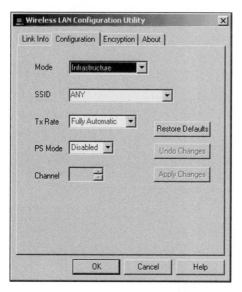

Figure 11-24   Configure how a wireless NIC will connect to a wireless LAN

Changes you can make on this screen include:

■ *Mode.* The mode indicates if the computer is to communicate through an access point (Infrastructure mode) or if the computer is to communicate directly with another wireless device (Ad Hoc mode).

■ *SSID.* The SSID (service set identifier) is currently set to ANY, which means the NIC is free to connect to any access point it finds. You can enter the name of an access point to specify that this NIC should connect only to a specific access point. If you don't know the name assigned to a particular access point, ask the network administrator responsible for managing the wireless network.

A+
OS
4.2

▪ *Tx Rate.* You can specify the transmission rate or leave it at fully automatic so that the NIC is free to use the best transmission rate possible.

▪ *PS Mode.* When this setting is disabled, the PC is not allowed to enter sleep mode; network communication continues uninterrupted. Enable PS Mode to allow the PC to go into sleep mode.

5. This NIC supports encrypted wireless transmission. To enable encryption, click the **Encryption** tab (see Figure 11-25). Select 64-bit or 128-bit encryption, and enter a secret passphrase. This passphrase is a word, such as "ourpassphrase," which generates a digital key used for encryption. Every computer user on this wireless network must enter the same passphrase, which can be changed at any time. Click **OK** to close the configuration software.

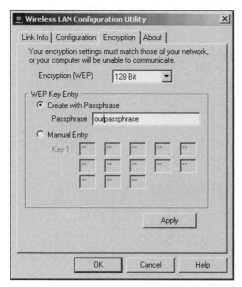

11

Figure 11-25   Enter a passphrase that generates a key to be used for 128-bit encryption to secure a wireless LAN

6. The next step is to configure the NIC to use TCP/IP or NetBEUI. This step is covered earlier in the chapter; it works the same way for wireless NICs as it does for regular NICs.

After the NIC is configured to use the OS network protocol, you should immediately see network resources in My Network Places or Network Neighborhood. If you don't, then try rebooting the PC.

Also, it is possible that the access point has been configured for MAC address filtering in order to control which wireless NICs can use the access point. Check with the network administrator to determine if this is the case; if necessary, give the administrator the NIC's MAC address to be entered into a table of acceptable MAC addresses.

Using Resources on the Network

A+
OS
1.1
4.1

Now you have learned how networks are structured, how to install NICs, and how to set up Windows networking. Let's look next at how to use resources on a network once it's been set up. This section covers how to share folders, files, applications, and even entire hard drives. In Chapter 13 you will learn how to share printers on a network.

Sharing Files, Folders, and Applications

If users on a LAN working on a common project need to share applications, files, or printers, then all these users must be assigned to the same workgroup or domain on the LAN. Recall that Windows 2000/XP makes shared resources available by way of My Network Places, and Windows 9x uses Network Neighborhood. Open either applet to see the names of all computers on the network. Figure 11-26 shows Windows 2000 My Network Places. Drill down to see shared files, folders, and printers in your workgroup. Using Network Neighborhood or My Network Places, you can copy files from one computer to another, use shared applications installed on one computer from another computer, and share printers.

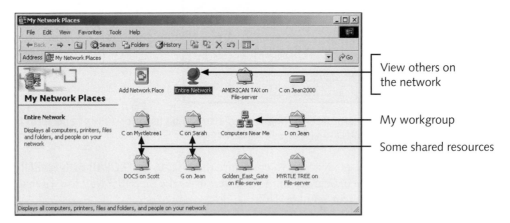

Figure 11-26   View and access shared resources on the network using My Network Places in Windows 2000

Workgroups can be effective when several people work on a common project. For example, if a group of people is building a Web site, sharing resources on the LAN is an effective method of passing Web pages around as they are built. Or one computer on the LAN can be designated as the file server. The user of this computer makes a portion of hard drive space available for the Web site files. All users have access to this one resource, and the Web site files are kept neatly in a single location. When

A+
OS
1.1
4.1
using workgroups, each user is responsible for protecting shared resources by using password protection for read and write privileges to files and folders.

To share resources over a peer-to-peer network, you must first install Client for Microsoft Networks and File and Printer Sharing. Client for Microsoft Networks is the Windows component that allows you to use resources on the network made available by other computers, and File and Printer Sharing allows you to share resources on your computer with others in your workgroup. After these components are installed, the last thing to do is to share the folders, files, or printers that you want others to be able to access. All these steps are covered in this section.

Installing Windows 2000/XP Components Needed to Share Resources

A+
OS
4.1
Client for Microsoft Networks and File and Printer are installed by default during a Windows 2000/XP installation. However, if you have a problem sharing resources on a LAN, you can try to uninstall and reinstall them. Do the following to install these components:

✔ A+ EXAM TIP

The A+ OS exam expects you to know how to share resources on a LAN and control who has access to these resources.

1. Open the Windows XP **Network Connections** applet or the Windows 2000 **Network and Dial-up Connections** applet. Right-click the **Local Area Connection** icon and select **Properties** from the shortcut menu. The Local Area Connection Properties dialog box appears (see Figure 11-27).

11

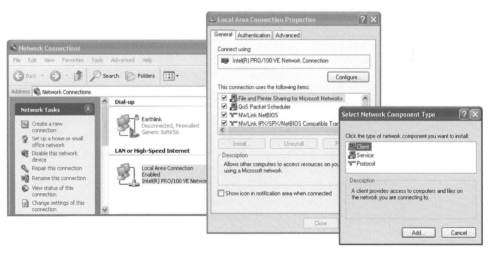

Figure 11-27   Use the Network Connections applet to install a network client, service, or protocol using Windows XP

2. Click **Install** on the **General** tab. The Select Network Component Type window appears, which is also shown in Figure 11-27. Select **Client** and then click **Add**. The Select Network Client window opens. Select **Client for Microsoft Networks.** You will need the Windows 2000 or Windows XP CD or other access to the installation files.

3. Also install the service for sharing files and printers with others on the Microsoft network. In the Select Network Component Type window, select **Service** and click **Add**. The Select Network Service dialog box opens. Select **File and printer sharing for Microsoft Networks,** and then click **OK**. You might need the Windows XP CD.

NOTE

When trying to secure a PC, you can take some preventive measures to ensure that other network users will not be allowed access. Windows 2000/XP installs File and Printer Sharing by default. To help secure the PC, you can disable this feature; open the Local Area Connection Properties dialog box, uncheck "File and printer sharing for Microsoft Networks," and click OK.

To further secure a Windows 2000/XP PC, you can prevent it from showing in the My Network Places windows of other network users. From the Control Panel, open the Administrative Tools applet and double-click Service. Right-click the Computer Browser service and select Properties from the shortcut menu. Under Startup type, select Disabled and click Apply. When you restart the PC, it will not be visible in My Network Places over the network.

Installing Windows 98 Components Needed to Share Resources

To install Client for Microsoft Networks and File and Printer in Windows 98, open the Network applet in the Control Panel and click Add. Select Client and then click Add. The Select Network Client window opens. Select Microsoft on the left and Client for Microsoft Networks on the right. You might need the Windows 9x CD. Using the same method, install File and Printer Sharing for Microsoft Networks.

Once these two components are installed, you must choose to enable file and printer sharing. On the Network window, click the File and Print Sharing button (see Figure 11-28). The File and Print Sharing window opens. Check both options to share both files and printers, and then click OK.

When they are installed, Client for Microsoft Networks and File and Print Sharing should automatically bind themselves to the TCP/IP protocol. You can verify this by accessing the TCP/IP Properties window and clicking the Bindings tab. Verify that Client for Microsoft Networks and File and Print Sharing are checked.

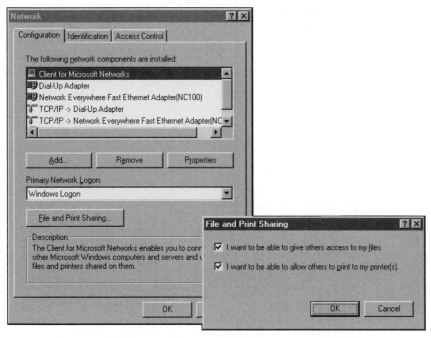

11

Figure 11-28   Turn on Windows 98 File and Printer Sharing so others on the LAN can access resources on
this PC

Sharing Files and Folders with the Workgroup

After the computer is configured for File and Print sharing, use Windows 2000/XP or
Windows 9x to make a folder or file available to others on the LAN:

1. Using Windows Explorer, select the folder or file. In this example, we are using
   a folder named **C:\data**. Right-click the folder name. If the Windows 98 or
   Windows 2000 system is configured for file and printer sharing, the shortcut
   menu lists **Sharing**. For Windows XP, select **Sharing and Security** (see Figure
   11-29). The data Properties dialog box opens, as shown in Figure 11-30.

2. For Windows 2000 or Windows 98, click the **Shared As** option button, and for
   Windows XP, check **Share this folder on the network**. Enter a name for the
   shared folder. In the figure, the name is JEAN'S DATA. This action makes the
   folder available to others on the network. They can see the folder when they
   open My Network Places or Network Neighborhood on their desktop.

3. For Windows 98 or Windows 2000, click the **Depends on Password** option
   button in the Access Type section.

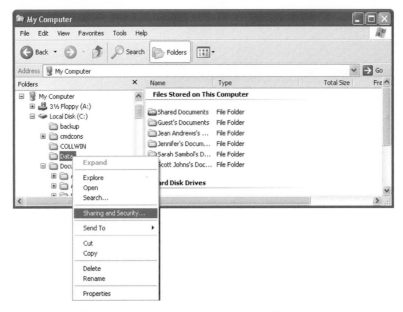

Figure 11-29 In Windows XP, use Windows Explorer to share a file or folder with others on a network

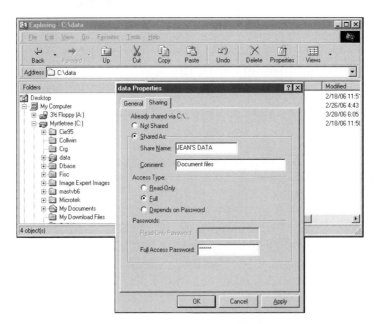

Figure 11-30 Using Windows 98, a user on a network can share a folder with others on the network

4. To allow others the right to make changes to the folder, enter a password under **Full Access Password**. For read-only access, enter a different password. Click **OK** to exit the window.

For Windows XP, you can allow others the right to change your files by checking **Allow network users to change my files.** Click **OK** to exit the window.

5. For added security when using Windows 2000/XP, set up a user account and password for each user who will have access to shared resources. This added security requires that a user give a valid password before accessing shared files, folders, or printers on the Windows 2000/XP PC.

When using the Depends on Password option, be sure to enter a password in both the Read-Only Password and Full Access Password fields. If you leave a password field empty, then no password is required for a user to have the corresponding read-only or full access to the folder. Distribute the two passwords to people who need to access the folder. You control the access rights (permissions) by selecting which password(s) you give.

NOTE Applications can also be shared with others in the workgroup. If you share a folder that has a program file in it, a user on another PC can double-click the program file in My Network Places or Network Neighborhood and execute it remotely on their desktop. This is a handy way for several users to share an application that is installed on a single PC.

11

Network Drive Maps

A **network drive map** is one of the most powerful and versatile methods of communicating over a network. By using network file service (NFS) client/server software, the network drive map makes one PC (the client) appear to have a new hard drive, such as drive E, that is really hard drive space on another host computer (the server). Even if the host computer uses a different OS, such as Unix, the drive map still functions. Using a network drive map, files and folders on a host computer are available even to network-unaware DOS applications. The path to a file simply uses the remote drive letter instead of a local drive such as drive A or drive C. To set up a network drive under Windows 2000/XP or Windows 9x, follow these steps:

1. On the host computer, using directions given earlier in the chapter, share the drive or folder on a drive to which you want others to have access.

2. On the remote computer that will use the network drive, connect to the network and access **Windows Explorer.** Click the **Tools** menu shown in Figure 11-31. Select **Map Network Drive.**

A+
OS
4.1

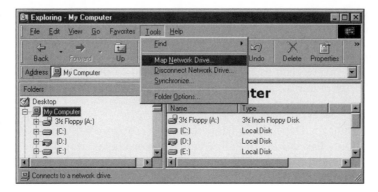

Figure 11-31   Mapping a network drive to a host computer in Windows 98, using Windows Explorer

3. The Map Network Drive dialog box appears, as shown in Figure 11-32. Select a drive letter from the drop-down list.

4. Enter a path to the host computer. Use two backslashes, followed by the name of the host computer, followed by a backslash and the drive or folder to access on the host computer. For example, to access the Public folder on the computer named Scott, enter **\\Scott\Public** and then click **OK**.

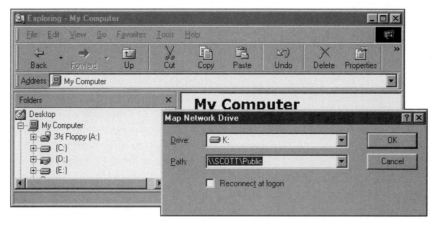

Figure 11-32   To map a network drive in Windows 98, enter a drive letter to use on your PC and the path to the host computer

NOTE

If a network drive does not work, go to My Network Places or Network Neighborhood, and verify that the network connection is good.

Figure 11-33 shows the results of the drive mapping. Windows Explorer displays a new drive K. Folders listed on the right side of the figure are on the host PC.

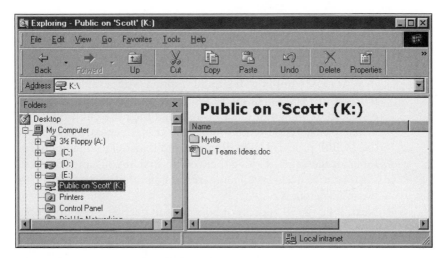

Figure 11-33   Content on the right side of Windows Explorer belongs to the host computer. This computer sees the content as belonging to its drive K

Troubleshooting a Network Connection

11

A+
OS
3.3
4.1

Sometimes you might have trouble with a network connection due to a TCP/IP problem. Windows TCP/IP includes several diagnostic tools that are useful in troubleshooting problems with TCP/IP. You will learn about several of these in the next chapter. The most useful is **Ping (Packet Internet Groper)**, which tests connectivity and is discussed here.Ping sends a signal to a remote computer. If the remote computer is online and hears the signal, it responds. Ipconfig under Windows NT/2000/XP and Winipcfg under Windows 9x test the TCP/IP configuration. Try these things to test TCP/IP configuration and connectivity:

✔ **A+ EXAM TIP**

The A+ OS exam expects you to know how to use Ping, Ipconfig, and Winipcfg.

- For Windows NT/2000/XP, enter *Ipconfig /all* at the command prompt. For Windows 9x, click Start, click Run, enter *Winipcfg* in the Run dialog box, and then click OK. If the TCP/IP configuration is correct and an IP address is assigned, the IP address, subnet mask, and default gateway appear along with the adapter address. For dynamic IP addressing, if the PC cannot reach the DHCP server, then it assigns itself an IP address. This is called IP autoconfiguration and the IP address is called an Automatic Private IP Address (APIPA). The Winipcfg window and the results of the Ipconfig command both show the IP address as the IP Autoconfiguration Address, and the address begins with 169.254. In this case, suspect that the PC is not able to reach the network or the DHCP server is down.
- Try to release the current IP address and lease a new address. To do this with Winipcfg, select the network card, click the Release button, and then click the

A+
OS
3.3
4.1

Renew button. For Ipconfig, first use the *Ipconfig /release* command, and then use the *Ipconfig /renew* command.

- Next, try the loopback address test. At a command prompt, enter the command *Ping 127.0.0.1* (with no period after the final 1). This IP address always refers to your local computer. It should respond with a reply message from your computer. If this works, TCP/IP is likely to be configured correctly. If you get any errors up to this point, then assume that the problem is on your PC. Check the installation and configuration of each component such as the network card and the TCP/IP protocol suite. Remove and reinstall each component, and watch for error messages, writing them down so that you can recognize or research them later as necessary. Compare the configuration to that of a working PC on the same network.

- Next, Ping the IP address of your default gateway. If it does not respond, then the problem may be with the gateway or with the network to the gateway.

- Now try to Ping the host computer you are trying to reach. If it does not respond, then the problem may be with the host computer or with the network to the computer.

- If you have Internet access and substitute a domain name for the IP address in the Ping command, and Ping works, then you can conclude that DNS works. If an IP address works, but the domain name does not work, the problem lies with DNS. Try this command: *ping www.course.com*.

CHAPTER SUMMARY

▶ The most popular physical network architecture for LANs is Ethernet.

▶ Ethernet can be configured as a bus or star arrangement. In a star arrangement, all nodes connect to a centralized hub. In a bus arrangement, all nodes connect in a line and there is no central connection point.

▶ Wireless LANs make connections using radio or infrared technology. A wireless LAN can be used in combination with a wired LAN.

▶ A PC connects to a network using a NIC (network interface card) or network adapter, which communicates with NICs on other PCs using a set of hardware protocols (such as Ethernet or Token Ring). The OSs on the two computers use a different set of protocols (such as TCP/IP or NetBEUI) to communicate.

▶ NICs and the device drivers that control them are designed to work with a particular network architecture and are the only PC components that are aware of the type of physical network being used. A NIC can be designed to use more than one type of cabling.

▶ A NIC is identified by a MAC address, a physical address unique to the device that is assigned at the factory and generally does not change.

▶ The three protocols that Windows supports for network communication are TCP/IP (the protocol suite for the Internet), IPX/SPX (designed for use with Novell NetWare), and NetBEUI (a proprietary Windows protocol for use on networks isolated from the Internet). Only TCP/IP is supported on the Internet.

▶ When an OS protocol is installed on a computer, it automatically binds itself to any NICs it finds. More than one OS networking protocol can be associated with a single NIC.

▶ The four types of addresses on a Windows network are MAC addresses, IP addresses, character-based names (such as NetBIOS names, host names, domain names), and port addresses.

▶ MAC addresses are used only for communication within a network.

▶ IP addresses identify devices on the Internet and other TCP/IP networks. They consist of four numbers separated by periods. The first part of an IP address identifies the network, and the last identifies the host. The class of an IP address determines how much of the address is used as the network identifier and how much is used for the host identifier.

▶ IP addresses can either be public or private. For private IP addresses to be able to access the Internet, they must go through NAT (network address translation) so that their requests all appear to be coming from a single public IP address for that network.

▶ Character-based names, such as fully qualified domain names, are used as an easy way to remember IP addresses.

▶ The IP address associated with a host name can change. DNS (Domain Name Service) and WINS (Windows Internet Naming Service) track the relationship between host names and IP addresses. DNS is more popular because it works on all platforms.

▶ Windows 98 assumes that a computer name is a NetBIOS name, which can have up to 15 characters. Windows 2000 and Windows XP assume that a computer name is a host name, which follows the TCP/IP convention and can have up to 63 characters.

▶ When installing a NIC, physically install the card, install the device drivers, install the OS networking protocol you intend to use (might already be installed by default), configure the OS protocol, and give the computer a name.

▶ NetBEUI is a fast network protocol that can be used on an isolated network. For Internet access, use TCP/IP. TCP/IP requires that the PC be assigned an IP address.

▶ When configuring TCP/IP, you must know if IP addresses are statically or dynamically assigned.

11

▶ Two files on a PC track IP addresses and related NetBIOS or host names. LMHosts tracks NetBIOS names on a NetBEUI network, and Hosts tracks host names on a TCP/IP network.

▶ Before users on a network can view or access resources on a PC, Client for Microsoft Networks and File and Print Sharing must be installed, and the resources must be shared.

▶ Network drive mapping makes one PC appear to have a new hard drive when that hard drive space is actually on another host computer. Use Windows Explorer to map a network drive.

▶ Ping is a useful TCP/IP utility to check network connectivity.

▶ Two other useful troubleshooting tools are Ipconfig (Windows NT, Windows 2000, and Windows XP) and Winipcfg (Windows 9x), which test TCP/IP configuration.

KEY TERMS

For explanations of key terms, see the Glossary near the end of the book.

802.11b
access point (AP)
adapter address
AirPort
Automatic Private IP Address (APIPA)
binding
Bluetooth
client
client/server
combo card
computer name
default gateway
DHCP (Dynamic Host Configuration Protocol)
DNS (Domain Name System, also Domain Name Service)
DNS server
domain name
dynamic IP address
Ethernet
fully qualified domain name (FQDN)

gateway
hardware address
host
host name
Hosts (file)
hub
Internet service provider (ISP)
intranet
IP address
IPX/SPX (Internetwork Packet Exchange/Sequenced Packet Exchange)
LAN (local area network)
LMHosts
MAC (Media Access Control) address
multicasting
name resolution
NAT (Network Address Translation)
NetBEUI (NetBIOS Extended User Interface)
NetBIOS (Network Basic Input/Output System)

network adapter
network drive map
network interface card (NIC)
network operating system (NOS)
network printer
node
octet
peer-to-peer network
physical address
Ping (Packet Internet Groper)
private IP address
proxy server
public IP address
RJ-45 connector
server
static IP address
subnet mask
TCP/IP (Transmission Control Protocol/Internet Protocol)
Wi-Fi
WINS (Windows Internet Naming Service)
wireless LAN (WLAN)

REVIEWING THE BASICS

1. What is the most popular network technology used on LANs?

2. Can a NIC be designed to use more than one network architecture? More than one type of cabling? Explain.

3. Describe the structure of an IP address. How is it different from a MAC address?

4. How many potential IP addresses are there?

5. How many networks and addresses are available for Class A IP addresses? Class B? Class C?

6. Why are Class D and E addresses not available to individuals and companies?

7. Which octets are used for the network address and for host addresses in Class A? Class B? Class C?

8. In what class is the IP address 185.75.255.10?

9. In what class is the IP address 193.200.30.5?

10. Describe the difference between public and private IP addresses. If a network is using private IP addresses, how can the computers on that network access the Internet?

11. Why is it unlikely that you will find the IP address 192.168.250.10 on the Internet?

12. Which operating system does not automatically include the NetBEUI protocol?

13. What are the two ways an IP address can be assigned to a PC? What is one advantage of each?

14. What are the Ping, Ipconfig, and Winipcfg utilities used for?

15. What two Windows components are required to share resources on a network and access those shared resources?

11

THINKING CRITICALLY

1. You work in the Accounting Department and have been using a network drive to post Excel spreadsheets to your workgroup as you complete them. When you attempt to save a spreadsheet to the drive, you see the error message, "You do not have access to the folder 'J:\'. See your administrator for access to this folder." What should you do first? Second?

   a. Ask your network administrator to give you permission to access the folder.

   b. Check My Network Places to verify that you can connect to the network.

   c. Save the spreadsheet to your hard drive.

   d. Using Windows Explorer, remap the network drive.

   e. Reboot your PC.

2. Your job is to support the desktop computers in a small company of 32 employees. A consulting firm is setting up a private Web server to be used internally by company employees. The static IP address of the server is 192.168.45.200. Employees will open their Web browser and enter *personnel.mycompany.com* in the URL address box to browse this Web site. What steps do you take so that each computer in the company can browse the site using this URL?

HANDS-ON PROJECTS

HANDS-ON
PROJECTS

PROJECT 11-1: Investigating Your PC

If you are connected to the Internet or a network, answer these questions:

1. What is the hardware device used to make this connection (modem or network card)? List the device's name as Windows sees it.

2. If you are connected to a LAN, what is the MAC address of the NIC? Print the screen that shows the address.

3. What is the IP address of your PC?

4. What Windows utilities did you use to answer the first three questions?

5. Print the screen that shows which network protocols are installed on your PC.

PROJECT 11-2: Researching IP Address Classes

Use the Web site *www.flumps.org/ip/* by Paul Rogers to answer these questions:

1. List three companies that have a Class A IP address.

2. List three companies that have a Class B IP address.

3. Who owns IP address class license 9.x.x.x?

4. Find another Web site on the Internet that gives similar information. How does the information on the new site compare with the information on the *www.flumps.org/ip/* site?

PROJECT 11-3: Using Windows XP Help and Support Center

Using Windows XP Help and Support Center, search for information on the Net View command. What specific information does the command produce? If you are connected to a network, use the command to test for connectivity. What command line did you use? What were the results of the command?

PROJECT 11-4: Practicing Networking Skills

11

Do the following to practice networking skills using either Windows 2000/XP or Windows 98:

1. On a PC connected to a network, write down the TCP/IP configuration settings for the network.

2. Uninstall, reinstall, and configure TCP/IP.

3. Share a folder on the hard drive.

4. Mount a network drive to a folder shared by someone else on the network.

Windows on the Internet

In earlier chapters, you learned how different versions of Windows work on a single PC. In Chapter 11, you learned about connecting PCs to a network. This chapter takes the next logical step in effectively using PCs by discussing connections to the Internet using Windows. You will learn how the TCP/IP suite of protocols is used, how to create and troubleshoot dial-up and broadband connections to the Internet, and how to support popular applications that use the Internet, such as Web browsers, email clients, and FTP software.

The TCP/IP Suite of Protocols

In Chapter 11, you learned how the operating system uses TCP/IP to make resources on a network available to the user, and how to install and configure the hardware and software necessary for networking. This chapter focuses on the applications on a desktop computer that use TCP/IP to access resources on a local network and on the Internet.

Most applications that use the Internet are **client/server applications**, which means the application has two components. The application (client) software makes a request for data from server software running on another computer. The World Wide Web itself is probably the most popular client/server application: The client is a Web browser, and the server is a Web host. The requested data is called a Web page, which can have graphics, sound, and video embedded as part of the requested data (see Figure 12-1).

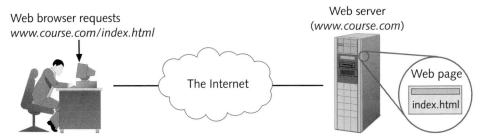

Web browser requests
www.course.com/index.html

The Internet

Web server
(*www.course.com*)

Web page

index.html

Figure 12-1   A Web browser (client software) requests a Web page from a Web server (server software); the Web server returns the requested file or files to the client

A PC support technician must know how to connect PCs to the Internet and support common client/server applications used on the Internet. Before we turn our attention to these applications, you will learn more about how the protocols in the TCP/IP suite are used on intranets and the Internet to support these applications. First, we look at how a client addresses a server application on another computer.

Using IP and Port Addresses to Identify Services

A server on the Internet or an intranet might be running a Web server application, an email server application, and an FTP server application, all at the same time. (**FTP, the File Transfer Protocol**, is a quick and easy way to move files over a TCP/IP network.) Each service is an executable program running under the OS on that server. For example, one Web server is Apache HTTP Server by the Apache Software Foundation (*www.apache.org*), and an email server is Ntmail by Gordano LTD (*www.ntmail.co.uk*). The Apache and Ntmail programs can both be running as background services on a computer. How does a Web browser on a client PC say, "I want to speak with the Web server" and an email program say, "I want to speak with the email server," if both programs are running on the same computer using the same IP address? The answer is by using an identifying number, called a **port, port address,** or **port number,** that has been assigned to each service when it is started. (Don't confuse these port numbers or addresses with I/O addresses assigned to hardware devices, which were also discussed in previous chapters.)

Each service "listens" at its assigned port. A network administrator can assign any port number to a server, but there are established port numbers for common services and protocols. A Web server is normally assigned port 80, and an email server receiving mail is normally assigned port 25, as shown in Figure 12-2. Port assignments are shown at the end of an IP address, following a colon. Using these default port assignments, the Web server would communicate at 138.60.30.5:80, and the email server would communicate at 138.60.30.5:25. Another example of a port number assigned to a common service is the use of port 119 for **NNTP (Network News Transfer Protocol),** the protocol used for newsgroups.

Figure 12-2   Each server running on a computer is addressed by a unique port number

 **A+ EXAM TIP**

The A+ OS exam expects you to know about the different protocols used on the Internet listed in Table 12-1.

Unless the administrator has a good reason to do otherwise, he or she uses the common port assignments listed in Table 12-1. (One reason not to use the default port assignments is concern about security. Some malicious software targets systems using default port assignments.) If a Web server is assigned a different port number, it can be accessed by entering the server's IP address in the address box

A+
OS
4.2

of the Web browser, followed by a colon and the port number of the Web server, like this: 138.60.30.5:8080.

Port	Protocol	Service	Description
20	FTP	FTP	File transfer data
21	FTP	FTP	File transfer control information
23	Telnet	Telnet	Telnet, an application used by Unix computers to control a computer remotely
25	SMTP	Email	Simple Mail Transfer Protocol; used by client to send email
80	HTTP or HTTPS	Web browser	World Wide Web protocol
109	POP2	Email	Post Office Protocol, version 2; used by client to receive email
110	POP3	Email	Post Office Protocol, version 3; used by client to receive email
119	NNTP	News server	News servers
143	IMAP	Email	Internet Message Access Protocol, a newer protocol used by clients to receive email

Table 12-1   Common TCP/IP port assignments for well-known services

The Web browser initiates a request using an IP address and port number but is unaware of all that happens in order for the request to reach the Web server. Also notice in Table 12-1 that each service has one or more designated protocols. These protocols are the rules of communication between the client and server components of the applications. We now have yet another layer of communication protocols used in networking. Recall from the last chapter that at the lowest networking level, the network or hardware protocol controls communication among physical networking devices such as Ethernet NICs and hubs. The next layer up is the OS protocol used on the network, such as TCP/IP, AppleTalk, or NetBEUI. Now, on top of the hardware and OS protocols, we add a third level of protocols that control how applications such as those listed in Table 12-1 communicate using the network. These applications protocols are all supported by TCP/IP and are discussed in the next section, together with other protocols that are part of the TCP/IP suite. Figure 12-3 shows all these different layers of protocols and how they relate to one another. Note in the figure that each protocol can be classified as a TCP/IP protocol, including the OS and applications protocols, or it is classified as a network (hardware) protocol used by networking hardware such as a phone line, NIC, or hub. As you read this section, this figure can serve as your roadmap to the different protocols.

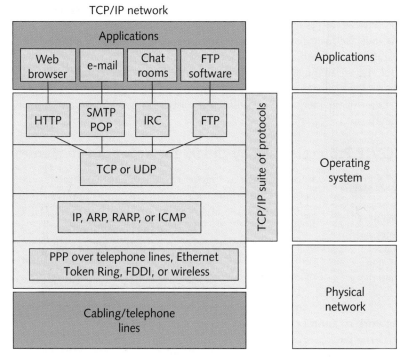

Figure 12-3   How software, protocols, and technology on a TCP/IP network relate to each other

12

TCP/IP Protocol Layers

Within the TCP/IP suite, several protocols operate; the more significant ones are introduced in this section, from the top layer down. However, you should know that the TCP/IP protocol suite includes more protocols than just these.

Applications Protocols

Four of the most common applications that use the Internet are Web browsers, email, chat rooms, and FTP. When one of these applications wants to send data to a counterpart application on another host, it makes an API (application programming interface) call to the operating system, which handles the request. (An API call is a common way for an application to ask an operating system to do something.) The API call causes the OS to generate a request. For Web browsers, the request will be an HTTP request. **HTTP (Hypertext Transfer Protocol)** is the protocol used for the World Wide Web and used by Web browsers and Web servers to communicate. In other words, HTTP formats the request, and encrypts and compresses it as necessary. It adds an HTTP header to the beginning of the data that includes the HTTP version being used and how the data is compressed and encrypted, if that was done.

Later, when the response is received from the server, it decrypts and decompresses the data as necessary before passing it on to the browser.

Once the response is passed to the browser, a session is established. **Sessions** (established communication links between two software programs), sometimes called **sockets**, are managed by the browser and Web server using HTTP. However, TCP/IP at the OS level can also create a limited type of session.

Later in the chapter, you will learn more about Web and email protocols and how they work.

TCP/IP Protocols Used by the OS for Network Communication

✓ A+ EXAM TIP

The A+ OS and Core exams expect you to be familiar with the TCP/IP protocol suite. The OS exam goes deeper into the different TCP/IP protocols than the Core exam.

Looking back at Figure 12-3, you can see three layers of protocols between the applications protocols and the physical network protocols. These three layers make up the heart of TCP/IP communication. In the figure, TCP or UDP manages communication with the applications protocols above them as well as the protocols shown underneath TCP and UDP, which control communication on the network.

Remember from the last chapter that all communication on a network happens by way of packets delivered from one location on the network to another. When a Web browser makes a request for data from a Web server, a packet is created and an attempt is made to deliver that packet to the server. In TCP/IP, the protocol that guarantees packet delivery is **TCP** (**Transmission Control Protocol**). TCP makes a connection, checks whether the data is received, and resends it if it is not. TCP is therefore called a **connection-oriented protocol**. TCP is used by applications such as Web browsers and email.

On the other hand, **UDP** (**User Datagram Protocol**) does not guarantee delivery by first connecting and checking whether data is received; thus UDP is called a **connectionless protocol** or a **best-effort protocol**. Guaranteed delivery takes longer and is used when it is important that data reach its destination accurately. UDP is primarily used for broadcasting and other types of transmissions, such as streaming video or sound over the Web, where guaranteed delivery is not as important as fast transmission.

Moving down the protocol layers, TCP and UDP pass a request to **IP** (**Internet Protocol**), which is responsible for breaking up and reassembling data into packets and routing them to their destination (see Figure 12-4).

Up to this point, the data with its header information is one long stream of bytes, sometimes too much data for transmission over a network. IP looks at the size of the data and breaks it into individual packets, which can be up to 4K in size. IP adds its own IP header, which includes the IP address of its host (source IP address) and that of the server (destination IP address), and then passes the packet off to the hardware.

If TCP is used to guarantee delivery, TCP uses IP to establish a session between client and server to verify that communication has taken place. When a TCP packet reaches its destination, an acknowledgment is sent back to the source (see Figure 12-5). If the source TCP does not receive the acknowledgment, it resends the data or passes an error message back to the higher-level application protocol.

Figure 12-4 TCP turns to IP to prepare the data for networking

12

Figure 12-5 TCP guarantees delivery by requesting an acknowledgment

Other protocols that operate in this part of the transmission process include the following:

- **ARP (Address Resolution Protocol)** is responsible for locating a host on a local network.
- **RARP (Reverse Address Resolution Protocol)** is responsible for discovering the Internet address of a host on a local network.

A+
OS
4.2

■ **ICMP (Internet Control Message Protocol)** is responsible for communicating problems with transmission. For example, if a packet exceeds the number of routers it can pass through on its way to its destination, called a **time to live** (TTL) or a **hop count,** a router kills the packet and returns an ICMP message to the source, saying that the packet has been killed.

Network Protocols Used by Hardware

As you learned in earlier chapters, network protocols used by PC hardware to communicate on a network are included in the firmware and drivers on a single NIC; for phone-line connections, these protocols are included on a modem and its drivers. The protocol used depends on the type of physical network that the data is traveling on. For example, for a regular phone line, the most popular protocol today is **PPP** (**Point-to-Point Protocol**), and the device managing that protocol is a modem. PPP is sometimes called a **line protocol** or, less commonly, a **bridging protocol**. You will learn more about PPP later in the chapter. An earlier version of a line protocol is **SLIP (Serial Line Internet Protocol)**, which does not support encrypted passwords and is seldom used today. As you learned in the last chapter, Ethernet is the most popular network technology used for LANs, and its network or hardware protocol is also called Ethernet.

TCP/IP Utilities

A+
OS
4.1

When TCP/IP is installed as a Windows 9x or Windows NT/2000/XP component, a group of utility tools are also installed that can be used to troubleshoot problems with TCP/IP. The most commonly used TCP/IP utilities are Ping, Winipcfg, and Ipconfig, which you learned about in the last chapter. Table 12-2 lists these and other TCP/IP utilities, and lists the purpose for each. The program files are found in the \Windows or \Winnt folder.

 A+ EXAM TIP

The A+ OS exam expects you to know about the following TCP/IP utilities listed in Table 12-2: Ipconfig, Winipcfg, Ping, Tracert, NSLookup, and Telnet. Where applicable, know the filename of the utility's program file as well as how and when to use the utility.

Utility	Description
ARP (Arp.exe)	Manages the IP-to-Ethernet address translation tables used to find the MAC address of a host on the network when the IP address is known
Getmac (Getmac.exe)	Windows utility (new in Windows XP) that displays the NIC's MAC address

Table 12-2 (continued)

Utility	Description
Ipconfig (Ipconfig.exe)	Displays the IP address of the host and other configuration information (A command similar to Ipconfig used by Unix is config.) Some parameters are: Ipconfig /all Displays all information about the connection Ipconfig /release Releases the current IP address Ipconfig /renew Requests a new IP address Ipconfig /? Displays information about Ipconfig
FTP (Ftp.exe)	Transfers files over a network
Nbtstat (Nbtstat.exe)	Displays current information about TCP/IP and NetBEUI when both are being used on the same network
Netstat (Netstat.exe)	Displays information about current TCP/IP connections
NSLookup (Nslookup.exe)	Displays information about domain names and their IP addresses
Ping (Ping.exe)	Verifies that there is a connection on a network between two hosts
Route (Route.exe)	Allows you to manually control network routing tables
Telnet (Telnet.exe)	Allows you to communicate with another computer on the network remotely, entering commands to control the remote computer
Tracert (Tracert.exe)	Traces and displays the route taken from the host to a remote destination; Tracert is one example of a trace-routing utility
Winipcfg (Winipcfg.exe)	Displays IP address and other configuration information in a user-friendly window (not available under Windows NT/2000/XP). In the Winipcfg window, use Release and Renew to cause the system to release the current IP address and request a new one, which can some-times solve TCP/IP connectivity problems when using a DHCP server.

Table 12-2   Utilities installed with TCP/IP on Windows

NOTE

To cause a network connection to release and renew its IP address in Windows XP, right-click My Network Places and select Properties from the shortcut menu. The Network Connections window appears. Select the network connection you want to repair and click "Repair this connection". You can also right-click the network connection you want to repair and select Repair from the shortcut menu.

Microsoft SNMP Agent

In addition to the utilities that are automatically installed with TCP/IP, another useful utility is Microsoft SNMP Agent. This utility can be installed after you install TCP/IP; use the Add or Remove Programs applet in the Control Panel. **SNMP**

A+
OS
4.1

(**Simple Network Management Protocol**) provides system management tools for networks. A system administrator can monitor remote connections to computers running Windows clients with SNMP Agent. The administrator will most likely use the utility sparingly because it can be a security risk. For more information about SNMP, see RFC 1156 (*www.rfc-editor.org*).

APPLYING CONCEPTS

Using NSLookup

An interesting tool that lets you read information from the Internet name space is NSLookup, which requests information about domain name resolutions from the DNS server's zone data. Zone data is information about domain names and their corresponding IP addresses kept by a DNS server. The NSLookup utility program is included in Windows 2000/XP. For example, to use Windows 2000 to retrieve what the DNS server knows about the domain name *www.microsoft.com*, follow these directions:

1. Click **Start**, **Programs**, **Accessories**, and **Command Prompt**. A command window appears.
2. Enter the command **Nslookup www.microsoft.com**. Figure 12-6 shows the results. Notice that the DNS server knows about three IP addresses assigned to *www.microsoft.com*. It also reports that this information is nonauthoritative, meaning that it is not the authoritative, or final, name server for the *www.microsoft.com* computer name.

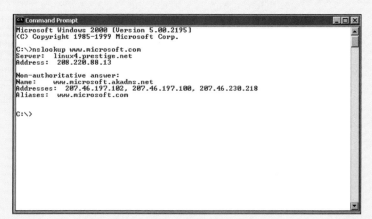

Figure 12-6   The Nslookup command reports information about the Internet name space

Connecting to the Internet

This section covers three ways to connect to the Internet: via a standard dial-up connection, DSL, and cable modem. You will learn how each type of connection is made as well as some advantages and disadvantages of each.

A+ EXAM TIP

The A+ OS exam expects you to know how to connect to the Internet using a dial-up, cable modem, DSL, LAN, ISDN, satellite, and wireless connection. All these connections have many things in common. Skills learned in making one type of connection can be used when making another type.

Dial-up Networking

To connect to the Internet over a phone line using a dial-up connection, you need to have a modem installed on your PC, as well as drivers to control the modem. In the last chapter, you learned how to install TCP/IP and bind it to your NIC; the same procedure is used for binding TCP/IP to a modem. This section assumes that TCP/IP is installed and bound to the modem. It covers how to connect to the Internet, beginning with how to install and configure the Dial-up Networking feature in Windows, and continuing with how to create and test the connection to your Internet service provider (ISP).

When a Windows PC connects to a network using a modem and regular phone line, the process is called **dial-up networking**. In effect, the modem on the PC acts like a network card, providing the physical connection to the network and the firmware at the lowest level of communication. After the dial-up connection is made, the PC's application software relates to the network as though it were directly connected using a network card, but a network card is not needed. The modems and phone lines in between are transparent to the user, although transmission speeds with direct network connections are much faster than those of dial-up connections.

This section covers how to use dial-up networking utilities in Windows 2000/XP and Windows 9x. Note that in Windows 9x, Dial-up Networking and Network Connections are two different applets located under My Computer. In Windows 2000, a single applet in the Control Panel called Network and Dial-up Connections combines both functions, and in Windows XP, this single Control Panel applet is called Network Connections.

How Dial-up Networking Works

Dial-up networking works by using PPP to send packets of data over phone lines. The network protocol (TCP/IP, NetBEUI, or IPX/SPX) packages the data, making it ready for network traffic, and then PPP adds its own header and trailer to these packets. Figure 12-7a shows how this works. The data is presented to the network protocol, which adds its header information. Then the packet is presented to the line protocol, PPP, which adds its own header and trailer to the packet and presents it to the modem for delivery over phone lines to a modem on the receiving end.

12

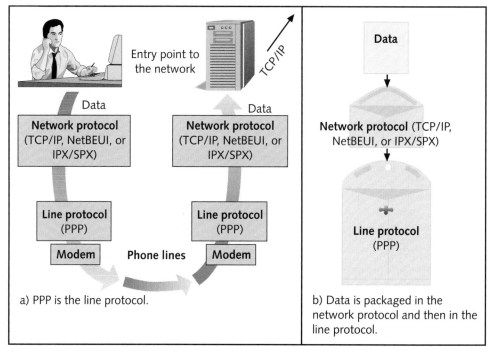

Entry point to the network

TCP/IP

Data

Data

Data

Network protocol (TCP/IP, NetBEUI, or IPX/SPX)

Network protocol (TCP/IP, NetBEUI, or IPX/SPX)

Network protocol (TCP/IP, NetBEUI, or IPX/SPX)

Line protocol (PPP)

Line protocol (PPP)

Line protocol (PPP)

Modem

Phone lines

Modem

a) PPP is the line protocol.

b) Data is packaged in the network protocol and then in the line protocol.

Figure 12-7   PPP allows a PC to connect to a network using a modem

The modem on the receiving end is connected to a PC or server. The receiving computer strips off the PPP header and trailer information and sends the packet on to the network still packaged in the TCP/IP protocols, or whatever protocols the network is using. In Figure 12-7b, you can see how these two protocols act like envelopes. Data is put in a TCP/IP envelope for travel over the network. This envelope is put in a PPP envelope for travel over phone lines. When the phone line segment of the trip is completed, the PPP envelope is discarded.

APPLYING CONCEPTS

Creating a Dial-up Connection in Windows 2000/XP

In order for your PC to connect to your ISP and use the Internet, you need answers to the following questions:

- What is the phone number of the ISP?
- What is your user ID and password for the ISP?
- Will DNS servers be assigned at connection (most likely, yes)? If not, what is the IP address of one or two DNS servers?
- How will your IP address be assigned (most likely dynamically)?

A+
OS
4.2

Creating a dial-up connection in Windows 2000/XP is easy because a wizard steps you through the process. For Windows XP, do the following:

1. To launch the New Connection Wizard in Windows XP, right-click **My Network Places** and select **Properties** from the shortcut menu. (Alternately, you can open **My Computer** and double-click **Dial-up Networking**.) The Network Connections window appears (see Figure 12-8). Click **Create a new connection**.

Figure 12-8   Using Windows XP, connect to the Internet by launching the New Connection Wizard

2. The New Connection Wizard opens. Click **Next** to skip the welcome screen. On the next screen, select **Connect to the Internet** and click **Next**.

3. On the next screen, select **Set up my connection manually** and click **Next**. On the following screen, select **Connect using a dial-up modem**. Click **Next**.

4. Enter a name to identify the connection, such as the name and city of your ISP. Click **Next**. In the following screen, enter the access phone number of your ISP. Click **Next**.

5. On the next screen (shown in Figure 12-9), enter your username and password at the ISP. This screen also gives you the options to make the logon automatic, make this the default connection to the Internet, and turn on Internet Connection Firewall for this connection. Make your choices and click **Next**.

6. On the next screen, you are given the opportunity to add a shortcut to the connection on the desktop. Make your choice and click **Finish** to complete the wizard. A connection icon is added to the Network Connections window; if you selected the option, a shortcut is added to the desktop.

12

A+
OS
4.2

Figure 12-9   The New Connection Wizard asks how you want to configure the connection

To use the connection, double-click the connection icon. The Connect dialog box appears. Click Dial. You will hear the modem dial up the ISP and make the connection.

Windows XP makes some assumptions about how your connection is configured. To view or change the configuration, do the following:

1. Use your desktop shortcut or the Network Connections window to open the Connect dialog box. Click **Properties**. The connection Properties window appears, as shown in Figure 12-10. Click the **Networking** tab.

Figure 12-10   Configure an Internet connection using the Properties windows of the connection icon

2. Select **Internet Protocol (TCP/IP)** and click **Properties**. The Internet Protocol (TCP/IP) Properties window appears, also shown in Figure 12-10.

3. Windows XP assumes that you are using dynamic IP addressing ("Obtain an IP address automatically") and that the ISP will give your PC DNS information when you first log on ("Obtain DNS server address automatically"). Most likely these are the correct options, but if necessary, you can change them and then click **OK** to apply the

changes. From this Properties window, you can also change the ISP's access phone number and control how the phone call is made.

> **NOTE**
>
> To launch the connection wizard in Windows 2000, right-click My Network Places and select Properties from the shortcut menu. The Network and Dial-up Connections window appears. Click Make New Connection. The wizard launches and steps you through the process to create a connection. The process is similar to that of Windows XP.

Creating a Dial-up Connection in Windows 98

To use Windows 98 or Windows NT to communicate with a network over phone lines, Dial-up Networking must be installed as an OS component on your PC using the Add/Remove Programs applet in the Control Panel. (Network and Dial-up Connections in Windows 2000 and Network Connections in Windows XP are installed by default.)

When Windows 98 installs Dial-up Networking, it also "installs" a dial-up adapter. In terms of function, think of this dial-up adapter as a virtual network card. Remember that in the last chapter, you learned how TCP/IP is bound to a network interface card. A dial-up adapter is a modem playing the role of a network card for dial-up networking. After Dial-up Networking is installed, open the Device Manager to see your "new" dial-up adapter listed under Network adapters, as shown in Figure 12-11. You can also see it listed as an installed network component in the Network window of the Control Panel.

Figure 12-11   After Dial-up Networking is installed, a new virtual network device, a dial-up adapter, is listed as an installed hardware device

A+
OS
4.2

You are now ready to create a Dial-up Networking connection. To create the connection in Windows 98:

1. After Dial-up Networking is installed, click **Start**, point to **Programs**, **Accessories**, and **Communications**, and then click **Dial-up Networking**. The Dial-Up Networking window appears, as shown in Figure 12-12.

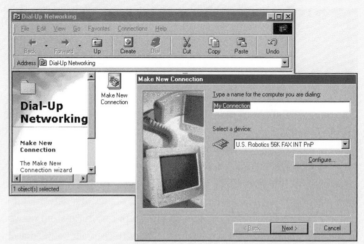

Figure 12-12   Creating a Windows 98 Dial-up Networking Connection icon

2. Double-click **Make New Connection**. The Make New Connection Wizard appears, also shown in Figure 12-12. Click **Next** to move past the first screen.
3. Enter a name for the connection. If your modem is already installed, it appears in the modem list.
4. In the next dialog box, type the phone number to dial, and then click **Next** to continue.
5. Click **Finish** to build the icon. The icon appears in the Dial-Up Networking window.

Next you will configure the connection. In Windows 98, do the following:

1. Right-click the icon you created for the connection, and select **Properties** from the shortcut menu.
2. Click the **General** tab. Verify that the correct phone number is entered for your ISP.
3. Click the **Server Types** tab. Figure 12-13 shows the resulting dialog box. Verify that these selections are made:

- Type of Dial-up Server: **PPP: Internet, Windows NT Server, Windows 98**
- Advanced Options: Select **Enable software compression** (software compression is most likely enabled, but this option really depends on what the ISP is doing). Also, click **Log on to network**.
- Allowed Network Protocols: **TCP/IP**

A+
OS
4.2

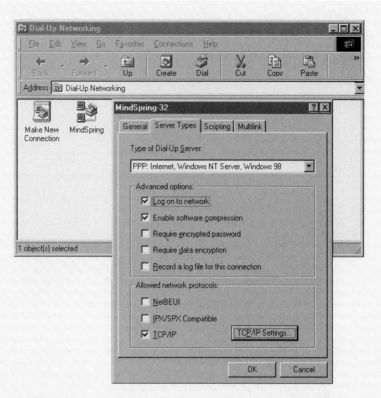

Figure 12-13   Configuring the server type for a connection to the Internet in Windows 9x

4. Click **TCP/IP Settings** to open the TCP/IP Settings dialog box, as shown in Figure 12-14. Most likely you will specify:

- **Server assigned IP address**
- **Server assigned name server addresses**
- **Use IP header compression**
- **Use default gateway on remote network**

5. Click **OK** twice to complete the Dial-up Networking connection.
6. To connect to your ISP, double-click the icon you created for it, which is now correctly configured. The first time you use the icon, enter the user ID and password to connect to your ISP. Check the option to remember the username and password if you don't want to have to enter them every time, but remember that this selection might not be wise if others who cannot be trusted have access to your PC.
7. Click **Connect**. You should hear the modem making the connection.

12

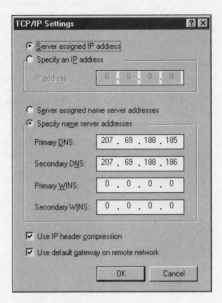

Figure 12-14 TCP/IP settings for a connection to the Internet in Windows 9x

Dial-up Networking Problems

In this section, you learn about some of the most common problems and errors that you may encounter with dial-up networking and what to do about them. As always, check the simple things first before trying more difficult solutions.

NOTE

To help troubleshoot problems with modems, Windows creates a modem log file of errors. For Windows 2000/XP, this file is named ModemLog*modemname*.txt. To view this file, click the Diagnostics tab in the modem's Properties dialog box and then click View log. For Windows 9x, you must tell Windows to turn on logging. On the Connection tab of the modem's Properties dialog box, click Append to Log to turn on logging and click View Log to see the log file, which is named Modemlog.txt.

In addition to these log files, you can create a log file to help troubleshoot problems with a Windows 9x dial-up adapter. To create the log file, open the Network applet in the Control Panel. Select Dial-Up Adapter and then click Properties. In the Properties dialog box, click the Advanced tab and select "Record A Log File". In the Value box, select Yes and click OK. The file, Ppplog.txt, is created in the Windows folder; it can get very large, so turn off dial-up adapter logging when you don't need it. For tips on how to interpret the file, see the Microsoft Knowledge Base Article 156435, at *support.microsoft.com*.

You cannot make a connection   If you have a problem connecting to the Internet using a dial-up connection, first find out what works and what doesn't work. Try the following:

- Find out the answers to these questions: At what point does the connecting process fail? Do you hear the modem hissing? If so, the problem is probably with the user ID and password. If not, then the problem might be the phone number, phone line, or modem. Is the phone line plugged in? Does the phone line work? Can you hear a dial tone?
- Check the Dial-up Networking connection icon for errors. Is the phone number correct? Does the number need to include a 9 to get an outside line? Has a 1 been added in front of the number by mistake?
- Try dialing the number manually from a phone. Do you hear beeps on the other end?
- Try another phone number.
- Does the modem work? Check Device Manager for reported errors about the modem.
- Print the Modemlog or Ppplog text file from a successful connection on another computer and the same file from the unsuccessful connection on the problem computer. Compare the two printouts to identify the point in the connection at which an error occurs.
- Are all components installed? Check for the dial-up adapter and TCP/IP, and check the configuration of each.
- Reboot your PC and try again.
- Try removing and reinstalling each network component. Begin with TCP/IP.

You can connect, but you get the message "Unable to resolve hostname"
This error message means that TCP/IP cannot determine how to route a request to a host. Right-click the Dial-up Networking connection icon, select Properties, and check for the following:

- Under Server Types, try making TCP/IP the only network protocol allowed.
- If your ISP provides the IP addresses of the DNS servers, enter them in the TCP/IP Settings dialog box (see Figure 12-14).
- Make sure "Use default gateway on remote network" is selected in the TCP/IP Settings dialog box.
- Try *not* selecting "Use IP header compression".

After connecting, you get the error message "Unable to establish a compatible set of network protocols"   This error is most likely caused by a problem with the installation and configuration of Dial-up Networking or TCP/IP. Try the following:

- Verify that the dial-up adapter and TCP/IP are installed and configured correctly.
- Remove and reinstall TCP/IP. Be sure to reboot after the installation.

12

- For Windows 9x, try putting the PC in a different workgroup.
- Compare the modem log file (Modemlog *modemname*.txt or Ppplog.txt) with one created during a successful connection.

When you double-click the Web browser, the modem does not dial automatically   When this error occurs, go to the Control Panel and open the Internet Connections applet or Internet Options applet. Click the Connections tab and check "Dial whenever a network connection is not present."

DSL and Cable Modem Connections

Recall that DSL and cable modems are called broadband technologies because they support the transmission of more than one kind of data at once. These connections can carry voice, data, sound, and video simultaneously. When using cable modem or DSL (as well as ISDN or satellite), if you are connecting a single PC to the Internet using an ISP, then the TCP/IP settings are no different from those used by a modem-to-phone line connection. In most cases, cable modem and DSL, like LANs, use a network card in the PC for the physical connection to the network, which in this case is the Internet. The network card provides a network port for a network cable. (Some newer cable modems use USB to connect to a PC.) For cable modem service to the Internet, the network or USB cable connects to a cable modem. For DSL, the phone line connects to a DSL box, which might also be a small router. The connection between the NIC and the broadband device most likely uses **PPPoE (Point-to-Point Protocol over Ethernet)**, a protocol specifically designed to support broadband connections. PPPoE is included in Windows XP.

For cable modem and DSL Internet connections, generally the installation goes like this:

1. Install the network card and the drivers to control the card.
2. Use a network cable to connect the PC to a cable modem or DSL box.
3. Install TCP/IP and bind TCP/IP to the card.
4. Configure TCP/IP to connect to the Internet or LAN.
5. Install the application software (for example, a browser) to use the connection.

In the following section, you'll learn about the different ways to connect to the Internet using these faster-than-phone-line connections and the details of installing these services.

Cable Modem

A cable modem uses a regular TV cable to connect to a TV cable wall outlet. Figure 12-15 illustrates what the arrangement looks like. The cable modem also has an electrical connection to provide power to the box. A cable modem connects to a

A+
OS
4.2

network card or USB port in your PC. Your cable modem company will provide you with the TCP/IP settings to use to configure TCP/IP. For a home installation, some cable modem companies will do the entire installation for you. You might need to purchase the cable modem and NIC, or they might be included in the installation fee. A service technician comes to your home, installs the network card if necessary, and configures your PC to use the service.

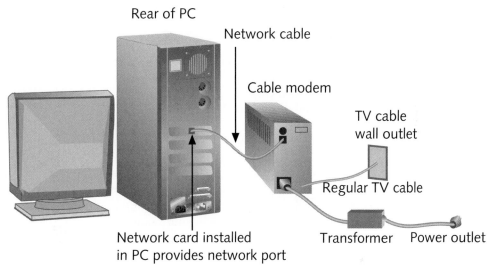

Rear of PC

Network cable

Cable modem

TV cable wall outlet

Regular TV cable

Network card installed in PC provides network port

Transformer   Power outlet

12

Figure 12-15   Cable modem connecting to a PC through a network card installed on the PC

If you don't have on-site service from the cable modem company, follow these instructions to install the cable modem:

1. Install the network card and drivers. For most cable modem companies, the MAC address of the network card in the PC or the MAC address of the NIC in the cable modem must be entered in an online list of valid addresses that identify your PC or cable modem as a subscriber to the cable modem service. When the PC first connects to the service, the system recognizes the PC and assigns it a valid IP address, subnet mask, IP address of the default gateway, and IP address of a domain name server. If the cable company help desk technician needs the MAC address of the PC, use Winipcfg or Ipconfig to display it. If the technician needs the MAC address of the cable modem, look for it printed somewhere on the back of the cable modem.

2. Configure TCP/IP to use the network card, using the TCP/IP configuration information provided by the cable modem company.

A+
OS
4.2

3. Shut down the PC and connect one end of the network or USB cable to the network or USB port on the back of the PC. Connect the other end of the cable to the cable modem. Be sure the cable modem is plugged in and turned on. There is usually a switch on the back of the box. Connect the TV cable from the TV cable outlet to the cable modem. (Refer back to Figure 12-15.) Turn on the PC.

4. When the PC starts, you should immediately be connected to the Internet. Test the connection using your Web browser or email client. If you are not connected, try the following:

   ▪ For Windows 2000/XP, use Ipconfig /release and Ipconfig /renew to lease a new IP address, and then check for connectivity again. (Alternately, for Windows XP, you open the Network Connections window, select the connection, and then click "Repair this connection" under Network Tasks to release and renew the IP address.) For Windows 9x, use Winipcfg to access the IP Configuration window. Select the network card and click **Release All**. Wait a moment, click **Renew**, and check for Internet connectivity again.

   ▪ If this doesn't work, turn off the PC and the cable modem. Wait a full five minutes until all connections have timed out at the cable modem company. Turn on the cable modem, and then turn on the PC. After the PC boots up, again check for connectivity.

   ▪ Try another cable TV jack in your home.

   ▪ If this doesn't work, call the cable modem help desk. The technician there can release and restore the connection at that end, which should restore service.

DSL and ISDN

DSL/ISDN service is provided by the local telephone company. The telephone company's responsibility for the phone system ends at your house. Inside your house, you are responsible for your home phone network. A DSL/ISDN connection uses a DSL/ISDN converter box that is sometimes combined with a router as a single device so that more than one PC can use the DSL/ISDN line. A DSL connection most likely will use a DSL router and an ISDN connection will use a device called a Terminal Adapter (TA) or an ISDN router. The device connects to the PC by way of a network cable and card.

As with a cable modem, a technician from the phone company most likely will install DSL/ISDN for you. The installation process on the PC works the same as that of a cable modem.

12

Sharing Internet Connections

A+
OS
4.2

There are several ways that computers on a LAN or WLAN can share an Internet connection. Here are a few options:

- If one computer on the LAN has a direct connection to the Internet by way of a phone line, cable modem, or DSL, it can serve as a host computer for others on the LAN. Windows XP and Windows 98 **ICS (Internet Connection Sharing)** is designed to manage this type of connection. Using ICS, the host computer uses NAT and acts as the proxy server for the LAN. Windows XP ICS also includes a firewall. However, enabling this firewall will prevent others on the LAN from accessing resources on this PC.

- For broadband connections (cable modem and DSL), the broadband converter box can connect to a network device such as a router that manages the connection for the entire network. The router has a network connection to the converter box and one or more network ports for devices on the network. In this situation, the router is also likely to have firewall software embedded in it and is controlled by way of a Web browser. A user on any computer on the network can enter the IP address of the router in a Web browser and bring up the software on the router to configure it. The router can serve as a DHCP server, a NAT proxy server, and a firewall.

- The router can also serve as a wireless access point for computers to connect wirelessly to the Internet. An example of a router that is also a wireless access point is the AirPlus D1-714P+ by D-Link (*www.dlink.com*) shown in Figure 12-16. It has one port for the converter box, four ports for computers on the network, and a parallel printer port designed to manage a network printer. The router can also support several computers with wireless adapters.

12

Figure 12-16 This D-Link router allows computers on a LAN to share a broadband Internet connection and is an access point for computers with wireless adapters

APPLYING CONCEPTS

Windows Internet Connection Sharing

To use Internet Connection Sharing in Windows XP or Windows 98, the computer that has a direct connection to the Internet by way of a phone line, cable modem, or DSL is the host computer. Follow these general directions to configure the LAN for Internet Connection Sharing using Windows XP:

1. Following directions earlier in the chapter, configure the hardware (modem, cable modem, or DSL) to connect to the Internet, and verify that the connection is working.
2. Open the Network Connections window in the Windows XP Control Panel, and click the link to **Set up a home or small office network**. The Network Setup Wizard opens. Click **Next** in this window and the next.
3. Select the connection method for your host computer, which is **This computer connects directly to the Internet. The other computers on my network connect to the Internet through this computer.** Click **Next**.
4. The wizard looks at your hardware connections (NIC or modem) and selects the one that it sees as a "live" connection. Verify that the wizard selected correctly and then follow the wizard to enter a description for your computer, your computer name, and your workgroup name.
5. The next screen of the wizard offers you the option of creating a Network Setup Disk that you can use to quickly configure every other computer on the LAN that is to use the Internet connection (see Figure 12-17). Select the option to **Create a Network Setup Disk**, insert a blank floppy disk in the drive, and click **Next**.

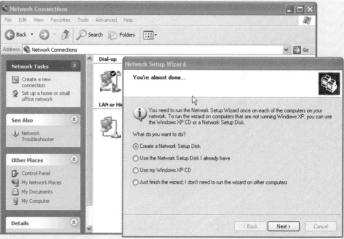

Figure 12-17   Create a Network Setup Disk to configure other computers on the LAN

6. The next screen gives you the option to format the disk. If it needs formatting, click **Format Disk**. Otherwise, click **Next**.

7. The wizard tells you that to use the disk, you must insert it into the next computer on the network, and run the program named Netsetup.exe from the disk. Click **Next** and then click **Finish**.

8. Use the Network Setup Disk on each computer on the LAN that is to use the shared connection.

Implementing a Firewall

Recall from previous chapters that one of the more important things to do when setting up access to the Internet is to install a good firewall. A firewall can function in several ways:

- Firewalls can filter data packets, examining the destination IP address or source IP address or the type of protocol used (for example, TCP or UDP).
- Firewalls can filter ports so that outside clients cannot communicate with inside services listening at these ports.
- Firewalls can filter applications such as FTP so that users inside the firewall cannot use this service over the Internet.
- Some firewalls can filter information such as inappropriate Web content for children or employees.

There are several variations of firewalls, from personal firewalls to protect a single PC to expensive firewall solutions for large corporations. A firewall is implemented either as software installed on a computer or as embedded firmware on a hardware device, as explained in the following sections.

Hardware Firewalls   The best firewall solution is a hardware firewall that stands between a LAN and the Internet (see Figure 12-18). A hardware firewall is better than software on each PC because it protects the entire network. For most home and small-office LANs, a router is used as a hardware firewall. You can buy a router with enough ports to connect several computers and perhaps a network printer to it. Some routers also serve double duty as a wireless access point to the network, DHCP server, and proxy server. The router connects directly to the cable modem or DSL converter. Note that some DSL devices are also routers and include embedded firewall firmware. Three companies that make routers suitable for small networks are D-Link (*www.dlink.com*), Linksys (*www.linksys.com*), and NetGear (*www.netgear.com*). You saw an example of a router in Figure 12-16.

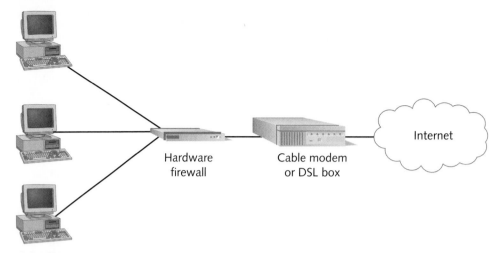

Figure 12-18   A hardware firewall stands between the Internet and a local network

Software Firewalls   Firewall software can be installed on a PC that is connected directly to the Internet or, for a network, you can install firewall software on each PC on the LAN. Some examples of firewall software are ZoneAlarm (see Figure 12-19) by Zone Labs (*www.zonelabs.com*), Norton Personal Firewall by Symantec (*www.symantec.com*), Check Point Software by Check Point Software Technologies (*www.checkpoint.com*), McAfee Personal Firewall by McAfee (*www.mcafee.com*), Personal Firewall Pro by Sygate (*www.sygate.com*), and Internet Connection Firewall, which is part of Windows XP. When evaluating firewall software, look for its ability to control traffic coming from both outside and inside the network. Also, you should know that some software firewalls, such as Windows XP Internet Connection Firewall (ICF), can prevent others on a LAN from accessing resources on the Windows XP PC, which is one reason that a hardware firewall is the best solution to protect a LAN.

Always use firewall software on a single computer that connects to the Internet by a dial-up connection and on a notebook computer used for travel. But know that a firewall does not substitute for antivirus software, which should also be installed and running.

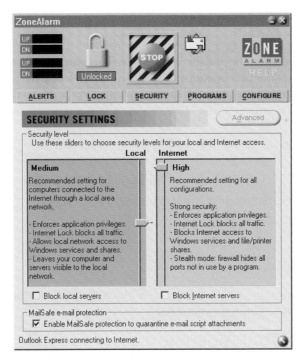

Figure 12-19　ZoneAlarm allows you to determine the amount of security the firewall provides

12

Supporting Internet Clients

Now that you've learned how to connect to the Internet, let's look at some ways of using it. Earlier in the chapter in Table 12-1, you saw a list of application services that use the Internet. In this section, you will learn how to support some of the most common Internet clients: Web browsers, email, and FTP.

Supporting Web Browsers

A Web browser is a software application on a user's PC that is used to request Web pages from a Web server on the Internet or an intranet. A Web page is a text file with an .htm or .html file extension. It can include text coded in **HTML (Hypertext Markup Language)** that can be interpreted by a Web browser to display formatted text and graphics, as well as play sounds. If the HTML code on the Web page points to other files used to build the page, such as a sound file or a photograph file, these files are also downloaded to the browser. In this section, you will learn about the addresses that Web browsers use to locate resources on a Web server and how to troubleshoot common problems that occur with Web browsers.

How a URL Is Structured

Earlier in the chapter you saw that a Web browser requests a Web page by sending an IP address followed by an optional port number. This works well on an intranet, but on the Internet, a more user-friendly address is preferred. A **URL (Uniform Resource Locator)** is an address for a Web page or other resource on the Internet. Figure 12-20 shows the structure of a URL.

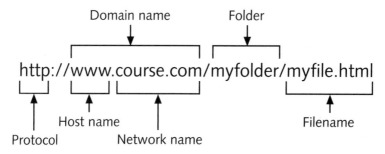

Figure 12-20   A URL contains the protocol used, the host name of the Web server, the network name, and the path and filename of the requested file

The first part of the URL shown in Figure 12-20 indicates the protocol, which in this case is HTTP. The protocol part of the URL specifies the rules, or protocol, the Web server should use when transmitting the page to the browser. A Web server is sometimes called an HTTP server.

Recall from Chapter 11 that a host name identifies a server or another computer within a network. In this example, the host name is *www* (a Web server), and *course.com* is the name of the Course Technology network, sometimes called the domain name. A name that contains not only the network name (in this case, *course.com*) but also the host on that network is called a fully qualified domain name (FQDN), as you learned in Chapter 11. In this case, the FQDN is *www.course.com*. The Web page requested is located in the folder *myfolder* on the *www* server, and the file within that folder is named *myfile.html*. The FQDN must be resolved to an IP address before the request can happen.

The last segment, or suffix, of a domain name is called the **top-level domain** (*.com* in our example) and tells you something about the organization or individual that owns the name. Some domain names in the United States end in the suffixes listed in Table 12-3. There are other endings as well, including codes for countries, such as .uk for the United Kingdom. With the growth of the Internet, there has been a shortage of available domain names; because of this shortage, additional suffixes are being created.

Domain Suffix	Description
.air	Aviation industry
.biz	Businesses
.com	Commercial institutions
.coop	Business cooperatives
.edu	Educational institutions
.gov	Government institutions
.info	General use
.int	Organizations established by international treaties between governments
.mil	U.S. military
.museum	Museums
.name	Individuals
.net	Internet providers or networks
.org	Nonprofit organizations
.pro	Professionals

Table 12-3 Suffixes used to identify top-level domain names

Domain names stand for IP addresses and provide an easy way to remember them, but domain names and IP addresses are not necessarily permanently related. A host computer can have a certain domain name, can be connected to one network and assigned a certain IP address, and then can be moved to another network and assigned a different IP address. The domain name can stay with the host while it connects to either network. It is up to a name resolution service, such as DNS or WINS, to track the relationship between a domain name and the current IP address of the host computer.

A+ EXAM TIP

The A+ OS exam expects you to know about HTTPS and SSL.

When banking or doing some other private business on the Web, you might have noticed HTTPS in the address box of your browser. To ensure privacy between the Web server and the browser, the data can be encrypted before transmission. In this case, the browser address box shows the protocol to be **HTTPS (HTTP secure)**. The secure protocol being used is SSL or TLS. **SSL (secure socket layer)** is the de facto standard developed by Netscape and used by Microsoft and Netscape browsers; it uses an encryption system that uses a digital certificate. Public keys are secret codes used to encrypt and later decrypt the data, and are exchanged before data is sent (see Figure 12-21). A **digital certificate**, also called a **digital ID** or **digital signature**, is a code assigned to you by a certificate authority such as VeriSign (*www.verisign.com*) that uniquely identifies you on the Internet and includes a public key. Recall from Chapter 7 that Microsoft uses digital certificates to validate or

12

A+
OS
4.2

digitally sign device drivers certified by Microsoft. **TLS (Transport Layer Security)** is an improved version of SSL.

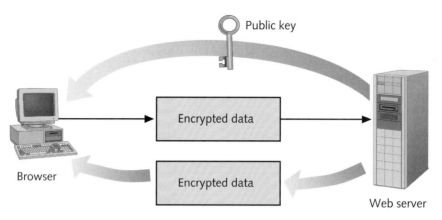

Figure 12-21   Using secure HTTP, a Web server and browser encrypt data using a public key before the data is transmitted

Configuring a Browser

The two most popular browsers are Internet Explorer and Netscape Navigator. Using Internet Explorer, you can control support options using the Internet Options window. Using Netscape Navigator, you control the browser options by clicking Edit on the menu bar and then clicking Preferences. There are three ways to access the Internet Options window to control Internet Explorer:

- Open the Internet Options applet in the Control Panel.
- From Internet Explorer, click Tools on the menu bar and then click Internet Options.
- Right-click the Internet Explorer icon and select Properties from the shortcut menu.

To control how and if scripts are executed, click the Advanced tab. Scripts are small programs embedded inside a Web page that control how the Web page functions. Under the Security tab, you can also click the Custom Level button (see Figure 12-22) to control how scripts are run as well as other security settings. Under the Connections tab of the Internet Options window, you can control proxy settings for an Internet Connection, giving the browser the IP address of the proxy server to use. However, if you only have one proxy server on your LAN, the browser should find the server without your having to give it an IP address.

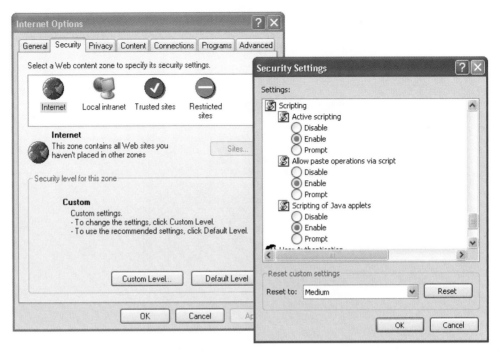

Figure 12-22   Security settings, Web content, Internet connections, and other browser functions are controlled from the Internet Options window

12

Solving Browser Performance Problems

If you notice poor browser performance, use the tools you have seen in earlier chapters, such as Defrag, ScanDisk, and System Information, to make sure that you have enough free hard drive space, that the hard drive is clean, and that the virtual memory settings are optimized. If you perform these tasks and the browser is still slow, try the following procedure using the most popular browser, Internet Explorer (IE), as an example:

1. Use the instructions from the previous section to open the Internet Properties window, as shown in Figure 12-23 for Windows 2000. (In Windows XP, this window is called Internet Options.)

2. Click **Delete Files** under the Temporary Internet files heading to clean out the IE cache. The Delete Files dialog box appears, asking you to confirm the deletion. Click **OK**. IE must search the entire cache each time it accesses a Web page. If the cache is too big, performance is affected.

3. Click **Clear History** under the History heading to clean out the shortcuts cache. The Internet Options dialog box appears, asking you to confirm the deletions. Click **OK**. If this cache gets too big, performance slows down. Also, if you reduce the number of days that Internet Explorer keeps pages in the history

A+
OS
4.2

folder, performance might improve because there will be less material for Internet Explorer to search. For example, change the number of days to keep pages in history from the default value of 20 to 7.

4. Click **OK** to close the window.

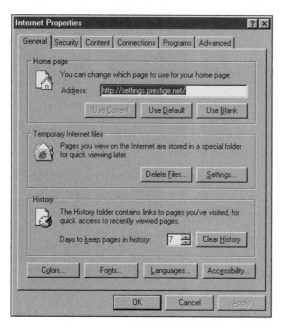

Figure 12-23   Use the Internet Properties window to control the Internet Explorer environment

Suppress Image Downloading   Slow browser performance can be caused by a slow Internet connection. In this case, one thing you can do is to suppress the downloading of images. Image files can be large and account for most of the downloaded data from Web sites. For Internet Explorer 5.x, you can download and install Web Accessories for Internet Explorer 5.x, which can be used to suppress the downloading of images from Web sites. (IE version 6 includes the ability to suppress downloading images without added software.) If the Microsoft site has been updated since the writing of this book, you may need to search for the Web Accessories for Internet Explorer. Follow these directions:

1. Go to this Microsoft Web site: *www.microsoft.com/windows/ie/downloads/ archive/default.asp*.

2. Scroll down and click the **Web Accessories** heading, and then scroll down, find Web Accessories from Microsoft, and click the **Download it now** link.

3. Another page opens, with more information about the Internet Explorer 5.x Web Accessories. On the right side of the page, locate the box labeled Download, and click the link to the file **ie5wa.exe**.

4. Click **Save** to save the file on disk. When the download window opens, choose to download the file to a location on your hard drive, and then click **Save**. Remember where you saved the file.

5. After you download the file ie5wa.exe, double-click it, then click **Yes** to install accessories.

6. Close the IE browser, and reopen it.

7. To use the IE Web Accessories to suppress downloading images, right-click the IE menu bar. If Favorites is already checked and on your menu bar, you can move on to Step 8. If it is not, click **Links** on the shortcut menu. This action adds the Links menu to the menu bar items.

8. Click **Favorites** on the menu bar, click **Links**, and then click **Toggle Images**. Web pages should now download without their images. You may have to click the **Refresh** button on your toolbar for the changes to take effect on an open page.

9. To reset the browser to download images, click **Favorites**, click **Links**, and then click **Toggle Images** again.

IE version 6 includes the option to suppress images, sound, animation, and video. Use the following procedure:

1. Open the **Tools** menu and then click **Internet Options**.

2. The Internet Options window opens. Click the **Advanced** tab.

3. Scroll down to the multimedia section of the check box list, and clear the check box or boxes for the feature or features that you do not want to display (**Show pictures**, **Play animations**, **Play videos**, or **Play sounds**).

To display an individual video or picture when you have cleared the related check boxes, right-click the icon with which it has been replaced on the Web page.

NOTE

Browser Updates and Patches

Browser manufacturers are continually improving their products, and generally speaking, you should use the most current version of the browser to take advantage of the latest features and fixes to known problems. However, if you have an older computer or operating system, you might not want to update a browser that requires a lot of system resources, because your older PC might not be able to support it. In this case, it's better to keep an older version on your PC unless you are having problems with your version.

If you are using Internet Explorer, check the Windows support Web site at *support.microsoft.com* to find information about specific problems with Internet Explorer. Search for the product and the error message for articles that describe the

12

problem and possible solutions. Also check the Windows update Web site at *windowsupdate.microsoft.com* for updates or patches for known Internet Explorer problems. Download the patch and install it following the same general instructions you have seen in earlier chapters.

If you are not using the latest version of your Web browser, try downloading the latest version. If you use your browser for banking on the Internet, be sure to download a version that supports 128-bit encryption for better security features. If the new version creates problems on your system, you can revert to your original version by uninstalling the new version.

Supporting Email

Email is a client/server application used to send text messages to individuals and groups. When you send an email message, it travels from your computer to your email server. Your email server sends the message to the recipient's email server. The recipient's email server sends it to the recipient's PC, but not until the recipient asks that it be sent by logging in and downloading email. Different parts of the process are controlled by different protocols.

Figure 12-24 shows the journey made by an email message as well as the protocols that control the different parts of the journey. The sender's PC and email server both use **SMTP (Simple Mail Transfer Protocol)** to send an email message to its destination. Once the message arrives at the destination email server, it remains there until the recipient requests delivery. The recipient's email server uses one of two protocols to deliver the message: either **POP (Post Office Protocol)** or **IMAP4 (Internet Message Access Protocol, version 4)**, a newer email protocol. The current version of POP is version 3, often abbreviated as POP3. IMAP is slowly replacing POP for receiving email.

NOTE

SMTP is defined in RFC 821 and RFC 822 (see *www.rfc-editor.org*). When email experts speak of error messages created during email transactions, they sometimes call these messages 822 messages.

Email client software communicates with an email server when it sends and receives email. Two common email clients are Eudora and Microsoft Outlook Express. Figure 12-24 shows a user with one email server. In fact, it's possible to have two email servers, one for sending email and the other for receiving email. Figure 12-25 shows this arrangement.

The email server that takes care of sending email messages (using the SMTP protocol) is often referred to as the SMTP server. The email server from which you collect messages sent to you is often referred to as the POP server, because it uses the POP protocol.

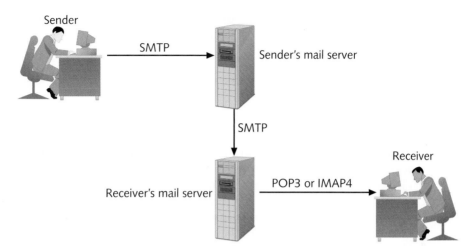

Figure 12-24 The SMTP protocol is used to send email to a recipient's mail server, and the POP3 or IMAP4 protocol is used to download email to the client

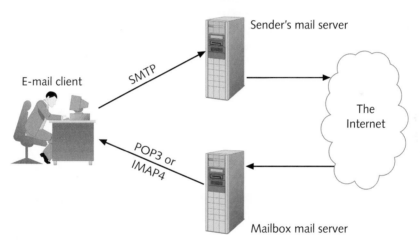

Figure 12-25 An email client can use one server to send email and another to receive email

When you configure your email client software for the first time, you need to enter the addresses of your email servers. If you are connecting to email via an Internet service provider, the ISP can tell you these addresses. For example, if your ISP is *MyISP.net*, you might have an outgoing mail server address of *smtp.myISP.net* and an incoming mail server address of *pop3.myISP.net*.

In most email client software, you enter the addresses of your POP or IMAP server and your SMTP server in a dialog box when setting up the program, along with the email address you will use when sending email. Look for menus or icons labeled Options, Preferences, Configuration, Setup, or similar names. After you enter the addresses, the software saves this and other configuration information in an initialization file, the Windows registry, or some other location. When you first log on to the email server, you will be asked for your user ID and password, which are used to validate your right to access the account.

Supporting FTP

A common task of communications software is file transfer, the passing of files from one computer to another. For file transfer to work, the software on both ends must use the same protocol. The most popular way to transfer files over the Internet is with FTP, which can transfer files between two computers using the same or different operating systems. For example, when upgrades for software become available, software vendors often provide files for customers to download to their PCs via FTP. This service is commonly provided by Windows NT/2000/2003 or Unix servers that offer access to files using FTP, and are called FTP servers or FTP sites. These commercial FTP sites only provide the ability to download a file to your PC. However, the FTP utility itself offers remote users the ability to copy, delete, and rename files, make directories, remove directories, and view details about files and directories, provided the user has the appropriate permissions on the FTP site.

Most communications applications provide an FTP utility that has a unique look and feel, but the basics of file transfer are the same from one utility to another. If you don't have graphical FTP software installed on your PC, you can use FTP commands from a command prompt.

FTP from a Command Prompt

FTP can be initiated at a Windows NT/2000/XP, Windows 9x, or DOS command prompt, if a connection to a network or the Internet is established. A sample set of FTP commands entered at the command prompt is shown in Table 12-4.

Command Entered at the Command Prompt	Description
FTP	Execute the FTP program, ftp.exe.
OPEN 110.87.170.34	Open a session with a remote computer having the given IP address.
LOGIN: XXXXXX	The host computer provides a prompt to enter a user ID for the computer being accessed.
PASSWORD: XXXXXX	The host computer requests the password for that ID. Logon is then completed by the host computer.
CD /DATA	Change directory to the /DATA directory.

Table 12-4 (continued)

Command Entered at the Command Prompt	Description
GET YOURFILE.DAT	Copy the file YOURFILE.DAT (or whatever file you want) from the remote computer to your computer.
PUT MYFILE.DAT	Copy the file MYFILE.DAT (or whatever file you want) from your computer to the remote computer.
BYE	Disconnect the FTP session.

Table 12-4   A sample FTP session from a command prompt

File Transfer Using FTP Software

FTP client software can be downloaded from the Internet or directly from your ISP. This example looks at how to use FTP using such software:

1. Start the FTP utility software. In this example we are using WS_FTP Pro by Ipswitch (*www.ipswitch.com*). The FTP utility screen that appears is similar to the one in Figure 12-26. Note that more recent versions of WS_FTP Pro might look and work slightly differently.

2. Click **Connect** to log on to an FTP site. A Session Profile dialog box appears, similar to the one in Figure 12-26.

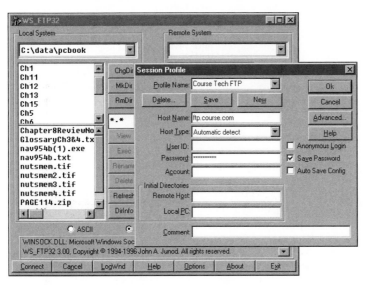

Figure 12-26   A typical FTP utility provided by an Internet service provider

3. Enter the Host Name, for example *ftp.course.com*. Enter the User ID and Password for this host computer, and then click **OK**.

4. The connection is made and your ID and password are passed to the host. After you have been authenticated by the host computer, a screen similar to that in Figure 12-27 appears.

5. The files on the left belong to you, and the files on the right belong to the remote host computer. You can drag and drop files either to or from the other computer, or you can use the commands at the bottom of the window. Notice in Figure 12-27 the choices near the bottom of the window: ASCII, Binary, or Auto. These choices refer to the format to be used to transfer the files. Text files are written in ASCII code; therefore, use ASCII for text files, and use Binary for all others. If you are not sure which to use, choose **Auto**.

6. When the transfer of files is complete, click **Exit** to leave the utility.

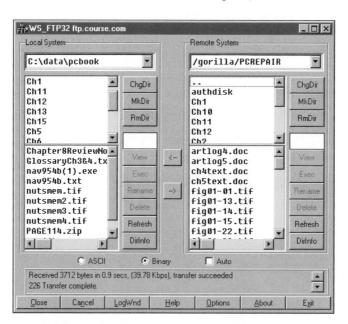

Figure 12-27   An FTP utility screen showing local and remote files

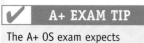

Many Web pages provide a link on the page offering you the ability to download a file. Click the link to download the file. This file is probably not being downloaded from the Web server, but from an FTP server. When you click the filename on the Web page, the program controlling the page executes FTP commands to the FTP server to download the file to you. If you receive an error, you can sometimes solve the problem by going directly to the company's FTP server and using an FTP utility (such as the one in the previous procedure) to download the file, or even see a list of other files that you might also like to download.

NOTE

A Web browser can also serve as an FTP client. Enter the URL of the FTP server in the address box (for example, *ftp.course.com*). The browser changes menu options to become an FTP client. For example, the Login As command is added to the File menu. To log on to the FTP server in Internet Explorer, click File on the menu bar, and then click Login As. The Log On As dialog box appears for you to enter a user ID and password. Files and folders on the FTP server then display in the browser.

CHAPTER SUMMARY

▶ Ports are used to address particular software or services running on a computer. Common port assignments are port 80 for HTTP (Web browser requests), port 25 for SMTP (sending email), port 110 for POP3 (receiving email), and port 20 for FTP.

▶ Generally, an API call is a way for an application to ask an operating system to do something. A browser uses an API call to access a Web server and make its request for information.

▶ TCP guarantees that a packet reaches its destination and so is called a connection-oriented protocol. UDP does not guarantee delivery and so is called a connection-less or best-effort protocol.

▶ IP is responsible for breaking data into packets and passing them from TCP or UDP to the hardware.

▶ PPP is used in dial-up networking to send packets of data over phone lines. It manages network transmission from one modem to another.

▶ Winipcfg and Ipconfig report configuration information about the current TCP/IP connection for a device and can release and renew the IP address. Winipcfg is supported in Windows 9x, and Windows NT/2000/XP supports Ipconfig.

▶ Other TCP/IP utilities useful in solving networking problems are Tracert, Ping, and Nbtstat.

▶ Before you can create a dial-up connection to the Internet, you need to have a modem installed along with the drivers to run it, as well as TCP/IP installed and bound to the modem.

▶ The Windows Dial-up Networking utility is used to connect to a network using a modem and a phone line. When a dial-up connection is made, a PC's application

12

software relates to the network as though the computer were directly connected to the network using a network card.

▶ You can create a dial-up networking connection through the Network Connections applet in the Control Panel of Windows XP, through the Network and Dial-up Connections applet in the Control Panel of Windows 2000, and in Windows 9x and Windows NT through the Dial-up Networking applet in My Computer.

▶ When experiencing problems with dial-up networking, make sure the modem is working, all necessary components are installed, and the phone number to dial and other settings are configured correctly.

▶ DSL and cable modems are broadband Internet connections that use a converter box connected to a NIC in a PC by way of a network cable. The connection can use the PPPoE protocol.

▶ Computers can share an Internet connection. Windows XP and Windows 98 use Internet Connection Sharing (ICS) to manage the connection on the host computer, or you can use a router that stands between the converter box and the network.

▶ Use a firewall on the host computer or router to protect the network from unsolicited activity from the Internet.

▶ A URL consists of a protocol, a host name, a network or domain name, and a top-level domain extension. Common top-level domains include .com for commercial institutions, .gov for divisions of government, and .org for nonprofit organizations.

▶ When you experience poor browser performance, try cleaning up your hard drive and making sure your system settings are optimized. If that doesn't work, try clearing your browser cache, clearing the Web page history, suppressing image downloads, or downloading updates.

▶ Email uses SMTP to send messages and POP3 to receive messages. POP3 is being replaced by IMAP. Your ISP will provide you with information on the server types and addresses that it uses to send and receive email.

▶ FTP is used to transfer files from one computer to another, whether or not the computers are using the same operating system. Both computers must have an FTP utility installed. It can be executed from user-friendly GUI software or from a command prompt.

KEY TERMS

For explanations of key terms, see the Glossary near the end of the book.

ARP (Address Resolution Protocol)
best-effort protocol
bridging protocol
client/server application
connectionless protocol
connection-oriented protocol
dial-up networking
digital certificate
digital ID
digital signature
FTP (File Transfer Protocol)
hop count
HTML (Hypertext Markup Language)
HTTP (Hypertext Transfer Protocol)
HTTPS (HTTP secure)

ICMP (Internet Control Message Protocol)
ICS (Internet Connection Sharing)
IMAP4 (Internet Message Access Protocol, version 4)
IP (Internet Protocol)
line protocol
NNTP (Network News Transfer Protocol)
POP (Post Office Protocol)
port
port address
port number
PPP (Point-to-Point Protocol)
PPPoE (Point-to-Point Protocol over Ethernet)

RARP (Reverse Address Resolution Protocol)
session
SLIP (Serial Line Internet Protocol)
SMTP (Simple Mail Transfer Protocol)
SNMP (Simple Network Management Protocol)
socket
SSL (secure socket layer)
TCP (Transmission Control Protocol)
time to live (TTL)
TLS (Transport Layer Security)
top-level domain
UDP (User Datagram Protocol)
URL (Uniform Resource Locator)

12

REVIEWING THE BASICS

1. Explain how a single physical computer can be a Web server and an email server at the same time.

2. Give the service and protocol for the following ports: port 21, port 25, port 80, and port 110.

3. What are API calls used for? Why are they necessary?

4. Which protocol used by Web browsers and Web servers is responsible for guaranteeing delivery? For breaking data into packets? For decrypting and decompressing data as necessary?

5. Explain the difference between a connection-oriented protocol and a connectionless protocol, and give an example of each.

6. What TCP/IP utility would you use to display the route taken over the Internet by a communication between a Web browser and Web server?

7. What utility would you use to display information about the name space kept by a DNS server for a particular domain name?

8. Explain the functions of the following TCP/IP utilities: NSLookup, Winipcfg, Ipconfig, and Microsoft SNMP agent.

9. What is the full command line to use Ipconfig to release the current IP address?

10. What utility new to Windows XP can be used to display a NIC's MAC address?

11. What must you do to get your system ready for creating a dial-up networking connection?

12. If TCP/IP is bound to a modem on your system, does it also need to be bound to a network card? Why or why not?

13. Explain how PPP is used by dial-up networking.

14. Place these stages of creating a dial-up networking connection in Windows 9x in the correct order: creating a connection, verifying installation of the dial-up adapter, installing the Dial-up Networking feature, entering configuration information for your ISP.

15. How is the process for creating a dial-up connection in Windows XP different from the process for Windows 9x?

16. Explain at least four things you can try if you cannot make a connection to the Internet using a dial-up networking connection.

17. What should you try if you can connect but you get the error message "Unable to resolve hostname"? If you get the error message "Unable to establish a compatible set of network protocols"?

18. What protocol is commonly used to manage the connection between a broadband converter box and a PC?

19. What Windows XP and Windows 98 component can be used to share an Internet connection with other computers on the LAN?

20. Label the component parts of this URL: *http://www.companyabc.com/Reports/december2001.doc.*

21. Give the type of organization that would use the following top-level domains: .mil, .net, .air, .com, .org, .gov.

22. What are three things you can do to improve slow browser performance?

23. What protocol is used for sending email? For receiving it?

24. Explain what FTP is used for.

25. What is defined in RFC 1156? RFC 822?

THINKING CRITICALLY

1. You are trying to connect to the Internet using a Windows XP dial-up connection. You installed a modem card and tested it, so you know it works. Next you create a dial-up connection icon in the Network Connections window. Then you double-click the icon and the Connect dialog box opens. You click Dial to make the connection. An error message displays saying, "There was no dial tone." What is the first thing you do?

   a. Check Device Manager for errors with the modem.

   b. Check with the ISP to verify that you have the correct phone number, username, and password.

   c. Check the phone line to see if it's connected.

   d. Check the properties of the dial-up connection icon for errors.

2. You connect to the Internet using a cable modem. When you open your browser and try to access a Web site, you get the error, "The Web page you requested is not available offline. To view this page, click Connect". What might be the problem(s) and what do you do? (Choose all that apply.)

   a. The browser has been set to work offline. On the File menu, verify that Work Offline is not checked.

   b. The cable modem service is down. In the Network Connections window, right-click the LAN connection and select Repair from the shortcut menu.

   c. Internet Connection Firewall is enabled on your PC. Disable it.

   d. The cable modem is down. Go to Device Manager and check for errors with the cable modem.

3. This question combines skills learned in this and previous chapters. You have set up a small LAN in your home with two Windows XP PCs connected to the Internet using a DSL connection. You have a DSL router box connected to the DSL line and to a small hub. Your two PCs connect to the hub. You have enabled Internet Connection Firewall on the LAN connection on both PCs, and you can browse the Internet from either PC. However, you discover that each PC cannot use the resources on the other PC. What is the problem and what do you do?

   a. The network hub is not working. Try replacing the hub.

   b. The NICs in each PC are not working. Try replacing one NIC and then the next.

12

c. The LAN connections in the Network Connections window are not working. Delete the connections and recreate them.

d. Internet Connection Firewall on each PC is preventing the PC from providing resources to others on the LAN. Disable Internet Connection Firewall.

HANDS-ON PROJECTS

PROJECT 12-1: Practicing TCP/IP Networking Skills

While connected to the Internet or another TCP/IP network, answer these questions:

1. What is your current IP address?

2. Release and renew your IP address. Now what is your IP address?

3. Are you using dynamic or static IP addressing? How do you know?

4. What is your adapter address for this connection?

5. What is your default gateway IP address?

6. What response do you get when you Ping the default gateway?

PROJECT 12-2: Practicing Dial-up Networking Skills with Windows 9x

This project requires you to have a modem installed and working.

1. Open **My Computer** and open the **Dial-up Networking** folder.

2. Double-click the **Make New Connection** option.

3. Enter the name **TEST** for the name of the computer that you are dialing. Click **Next**.

4. Enter your home phone number. Click **Next**.

5. Click the **Finish** button to create the Test dial-up.

6. Double-click the newly created **Test dial-up** icon and confirm that it dials correctly. Describe what happens.

PROJECT 12-3: Using a Browser Help Utility

Using your browser's help utility, print instructions for changing the size of the browser cache and cleaning out the cache.

PROJECT 12-4: Solving Browser Problems

Follow these instructions to solve problems with Netscape Navigator:

1. List the steps to access the Netscape Web site and search for information about a problem. Search the site for information about Error 403.6, IP Restriction error. Print any information you find about the error.

2. Print the Netscape Web site page that allows you to use SmartUpdate to download the latest fixes for Netscape Navigator. Download the update and apply it to your browser.

3. Perform the procedures to clean out the browser cache.

Now do the same three steps for Microsoft Internet Explorer:

1. List the steps to access the Microsoft Web site and search for information about a problem. Search the site for information about Error 403.6, IP Restriction error. Print any information you find about the error.

2. Print the Microsoft Web site page that allows you to use the Update wizard to download the latest fixes for Internet Explorer. Download the update and apply it to your browser.

3. Perform the procedures discussed in the chapter to clean out the browser cache.

PROJECT 12-5: Using Web Accessories for Internet Explorer

Using the instructions in the chapter, download and install Web Accessories for Internet Explorer. Use the tool to display and print the links on the Web page *www.foxnews.com*.

PROJECT 12-6: Using FTP

Practice using FTP by downloading the latest version of Netscape, a Web browser. Do the following:

1. Using your current browser as an FTP client, locate the latest version of Netscape at the Netscape FTP site (*ftp.netscape.com*) and download it to your PC.

2. Repeat the process to download Netscape, this time using FTP commands from a command prompt window.

Printers, the Mac OS, and Linux

In this chapter, you will learn:

- How to use Windows to support printers

- About starting up, using, and supporting hardware in the Mac OS

- About the file structure of the Linux OS and how to use some Linux commands

This chapter discusses how to use Windows operating systems to install a printer, to share a printer with others on a network, and to troubleshoot Windows printer problems. So far in this book we have focused on Microsoft operating systems, because they are the most popular OSs for the desktop. However, as a software technician, you will need to be familiar with a variety of operating systems, including the Mac OS and Linux. This chapter gives you a general introduction to the Mac OS and Linux.

Supporting Printers Using Windows

The section discusses how to use Windows operating systems to install a local printer, to share a networked printer, and to troubleshoot Windows printer problems. We first look at how to install and share a printer.

Installing and Sharing a Printer

A printer can be connected to a port on a computer, and then the computer can share the printer with others on the network. There are also network printers with Ethernet ports that can connect the printer directly to the network. Each computer on the network that uses the printer must have printer drivers installed so the OS on each computer can communicate with the printer and provide the interface between applications it supports and the printer. This section covers how to install a local printer, how to share that printer with others on the network, and how a remote computer on the network can use a shared printer. A printer connected to a computer by way of a port on the computer is called a **local printer**, and a printer accessed by way of a network is called a **network printer**. A computer can have several printers installed. Windows designates one printer to be the **default printer**, which is the one Windows prints to unless another is selected.

Installing a Local Printer

A+ EXAM TIP

The A+ Core and OS exams expect you to know how to install a local and network printer.

Follow these steps to install a local printer:

1. Physically attach the printer to the computer by way of a parallel port, serial port, 1394 port, USB port, SCSI port, IEEE 1394 port, PC Card connection, infrared connection, or wireless access point. Recall from Chapter 8 that you should use an IEEE 1284-compliant printer cable for a parallel port connection. For wireless printers, verify that the software for the wireless port on your PC is installed and the port is enabled. For infrared wireless printers, place the printer in line of sight of the infrared port on the PC. (Most wireless printers have a status light that stays lit when a wireless connection is active.)

2. Install the printer drivers using one of two approaches. You can have Windows install the driver, or you can use the printer manufacturer's installation program. In most cases, it is best to use the printer manufacturer's method. The exception is if you have several similar printers installed. Windows does a better job of preventing files used by one printer installation from being overwritten by files from another installation.

   a. To use the manufacturer's installation process, insert the printer driver
      CD that comes bundled with the printer in the CD-ROM drive, and
      follow directions onscreen to install the printer.

   b. Alternately, you can use the Windows printer windows to install the
      printer drivers. For Windows XP, open the Printers and Faxes window by
      clicking **Start, Control Panel,** and **Printers and Faxes** (in Classic view) or
      Printers and Other Hardware (in Category view). For Windows 2000 and
      Windows 98, click **Start, Settings,** and **Printers** to open the Printers
      window. Click **Add a Printer** and follow the Add Printer Wizard to install
      the printer drivers.

3. After you install the printer drivers, test the printer. Open the Printers and
   Faxes window or Printers window and right-click the printer. Select **Properties**
   from the shortcut menu. Click the **General** tab and then click the **Print Test
   Page** button.

From the Printers window (called the Printers and Faxes window for Windows
XP), you can also delete printers, change the Windows default printer, purge print
jobs to troubleshoot failed printing, and perform other printer maintenance tasks. If
a printer is giving you problems or you want to upgrade the printer drivers to add
new functionality, search the printer manufacturer's Web site for the latest drivers for
your printer and operating system. Download the drivers to a folder on the hard
drive such as C:\Downloads\Printer, and then double-click the driver file to extract
files and launch the installation program to update the printer drivers.

Sharing a Printer with Others in a Workgroup

To share a local printer using Windows, File and Printer Sharing must be installed,
and to use a shared printer on a remote PC, Client for Microsoft Networks must be
installed. In most cases, it is easiest to simply install both components on all computers on the network. How to install the components under Windows 2000/XP and
Windows 98 was covered in Chapter 11.
   To share a local printer connected to a Windows 2000/XP workstation, do the
following:

1. Open the Printers window or Printers and Faxes window by clicking **Start, Control Panel,** and **Printers and Faxes**. Right-click the printer you want to share,
   and select **Sharing** from the shortcut menu. The printer's Properties dialog box
   opens, as shown in Figure 13-1 for Windows XP; the dialog box in Windows
   2000 is similar. Select **Share this printer** and enter a name for the printer.

2. If you want to make drivers for the printer available to remote users who are
   using an operating system other than the OS being used, click **Additional Drivers.**

3. The Additional Drivers window appears, as shown in Figure 13-1. Select the
   OS. In the figure, Windows 95, 98, 2000, Me, and XP are selected so that users

13

of these OSs will have the printer drivers they need. Click **OK** twice to close both windows. You might be asked for the Windows installation CD or other access to the installation files. A shared printer shows a hand icon under it in the Printers window, and the printer is listed in My Network Places or Network Neighborhood of other PCs on the network.

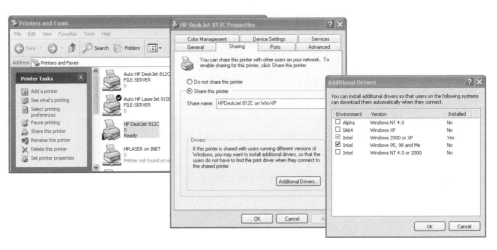

Figure 13-1   Sharing a printer on a Windows XP PC

To share a local printer with others in the workgroup connected to a Windows 98 computer, do the following:

1. Open the Printers window by clicking **Start**, **Settings**, and **Printers**.

2. Right-click the printer you want to share. From the shortcut menu, select **Sharing**. (This Sharing option is grayed out if File and Printer Sharing is not available.)

3. The Properties dialog box opens with the Sharing tab selected (see Figure 13-2).

4. Select **Shared As** and give the printer a **Share Name**. Click **OK** to exit.

The printer is listed in Network Neighborhood or My Network Places.

Using a Shared Printer   Recall that for a remote PC to use a shared network printer, the drivers for that printer must be installed on the remote PC. There are two approaches to installing shared network printer drivers on a remote PC. You can perform the installation using the drivers on CD (either the Windows CD or printer manufacturer's CD), or you can perform the installation using the printer drivers on the host PC. The installations work about the same way for Windows 2000/XP and Windows 98. The Windows XP installation is shown here, but differences for Windows 2000 and Windows 98 are noted.

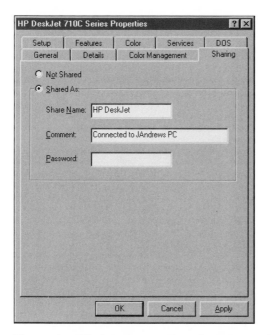

Figure 13-2   When using Windows 98, use the printer Properties dialog box to share a connected printer with other computers on the network

To use a shared printer on the network by installing the manufacturer's printer drivers from CD, do the following using Windows XP:

13

1. Open the Printers and Faxes window and double-click **Add a printer**. The Add Printer Wizard opens. Click **Next**.

2. In response to, "Select the option that describes the printer you want to use:" select **A network printer, or a printer attached to another computer**. Click **Next**. The wizard window in Figure 13-3 opens.

3. Enter the host computer name and printer name. Begin with two backslashes and separate the computer name from the printer name with a backslash. Or, you can click **Browse**, search the list of shared printers on the network, and select the printer to install. (If your network is using static IP addressing and you know the IP address of the host PC, you can enter the IP address instead of the host name in this step.) Click Next.

4. Windows XP searches for Windows XP drivers on the host computer for this printer. If it finds them (meaning that the host computer is a Windows XP machine), then the wizard skips to Step 6. If it doesn't find the drivers (the host computer is not a Windows XP machine), a message asks if you want to search for the proper driver. Click **OK**.

5. Click **Have Disk** to use the manufacturer's drivers, or to use Windows drivers, select the printer manufacturer and then the printer model from the list of supported printers. Click **OK** when you finish.

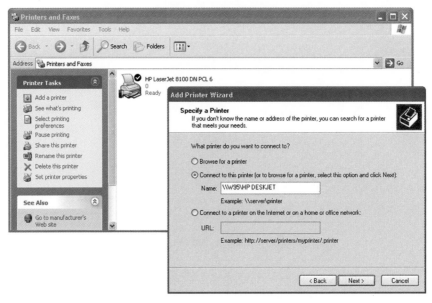

Figure 13-3   To use a network printer under Windows XP, enter the host computer name followed by the printer name, or have Windows XP browse the network for shared printers

6. In response to the question, "Do you want to use this printer as the default printer?", answer **Yes** if you want Windows to send documents to this printer until you select a different one. Click **Next**. Click **Finish** to complete the wizard.

7. The printer icon appears in the Printers and Faxes window. To test the printer installation, right-click the icon and select **Properties** from the shortcut menu. Click the **General** tab and then click **Print Test Page**.

Here are some additional things to know about installing a network printer using the Windows 98 Add Printer Wizard:

- When the wizard asks, "Do you print from MS-DOS-based programs?", answer Yes if you have any intention of ever doing so.
- The wizard gives you the opportunity to name the printer. You might include the location of the printer, such as 3rd Floor Laser or John's Laser.
- Sometimes a DOS-based program has problems printing to a network printer. You can choose to associate the network printer with a printer port such as LPT1 to satisfy the DOS application. Click Capture Printer Port, and then select the port from the drop-down menu in the Capture Printer Port dialog box (see Figure 13-4).

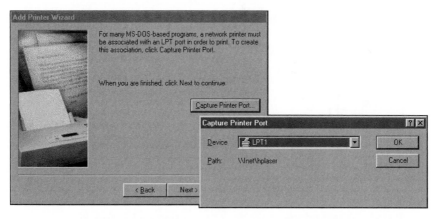

Figure 13-4   Associate a network printer with a printer port to help DOS applications in Windows 98

- The Windows 98 Add Printer Wizard gives you the opportunity to print a test page on the last window of the wizard. It's always a good idea to print this test page to verify that the printer is accessible.
- Know that the Windows 98 Add Printer Wizard does not attempt to use the printer drivers on the host PC, but always installs local Windows 9x drivers or uses the manufacturer CD.

Another way to install a shared printer is to first use My Network Places or Network Neighborhood to locate the printer on the network. This method is faster when one Windows 9x PC is providing a shared printer to be installed on other Windows 9x PCs, because the remote PCs can use the printer drivers on the host PC. Do the following:

1. On a remote PC that uses Windows 2000/XP, open **My Network Places** and find the printer. Right-click the printer and select **Connect** from the shortcut menu. See Figure 13-5. (For Windows 9x, open **Network Neighborhood** and find the printer. Right-click the printer and select **Install** from the shortcut menu.)

2. If the host computer is using the same OS as you are, or if you have a Windows NT/2000/XP host computer and the additional drivers for your OS have been installed, you can use those drivers for the installation. If Windows cannot find the right drivers, it sends you an error message and gives you the opportunity to install the drivers from your Windows CD or the printer manufacturer's CD.

13

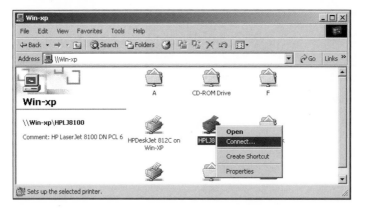

Figure 13-5   Install a shared printer in Windows 2000 using My Network Places

> When installing a shared printer on a Windows 9x PC where the host computer is also a Windows 9x PC, you must first share the \Windows folder on the host PC so the remote PC can access the printer drivers. This is a security risk, so remove the share status on this important folder as soon as all remote PCs have the printer installed.

Other Methods of Sharing Printers over a Network   You have just seen how a printer can be installed as a local printer on one PC and then shared with others in a workgroup. The three ways to make a printer available on a network are summarized here:

- A regular printer can be attached to a PC using a port on the PC, and then that PC can share the printer with the network. (This method was described in the previous section.)
- A network printer with embedded logic to manage network communication can be connected directly to a network with its own NIC.
- A dedicated device or computer called a print server can control several printers connected to a network. For example, HP has software called HP JetDirect, designed to support HP printers in this manner. For more information, see the HP Web site, *www.hp.com*.

If printers are available on the network using one of the last two methods, follow the printer manufacturer's directions to install the printer on each PC. If you don't have these directions, do the following:

1. Download the printer drivers from the printer manufacturer's Web site and decompress the downloaded file, if necessary.

2. Open the Printers window and start the wizard to add a new printer. Select the option to install a local printer but do not ask Windows to automatically detect the printer.

3. When given the opportunity, choose to create a new port rather than use an existing port (such as LPT1: or LPT2:). Choose to create a standard TCP/IP port. To create the port, you will need the IP address of the printer or the name of the printer on the network.

4. When given the opportunity, click **Have Disk** so you can point to and use the downloaded driver files that will be used to complete the printer installation.

One shortcut you might take to speed up the process of installing a printer connected directly to the network is to install the printer on one PC and then share it on the network. Then, you can install the printer on the other PCs by using My Network Places for Windows 2000/XP or Network Neighborhood for Windows 98, following the directions given earlier. Find the printer, right-click it, and then select Connect (for Windows 2000/XP) or Install (for Windows 9x) from the shortcut menu. The disadvantage of using this method is that the computer sharing the printer must be turned on when other computers on the network want to use the printer.

NOTE   Because a network printer has no OS installed, the printer's NIC contains all the firmware needed to communicate over the network. For a PC, some of this software is part of Windows, including the network protocols, TCP/IP and IPX/SPX. A network printer's NIC firmware usually supports TCP/IP and IPX/SPX. The network printer documentation will tell you which protocols are supported. One of these protocols must be installed on a PC using the printer.

How Windows Handles Print Jobs

When supporting printers using Windows, it is helpful to understand how Windows manages print jobs, using one of these methods:

- For Windows NT/2000/XP or Windows 9x using a PostScript printer, the print job data is converted to the PostScript language. PostScript, a language used to communicate how a page is to print, was developed by Adobe Systems. PostScript is popular with desktop publishing, the typesetting industry, and the Macintosh OS.
- For Windows 2000/XP, a printer language that competes with PostScript is PCL (Printer Control Language). PCL was developed by Hewlett-Packard but is considered a de facto standard in the printing industry. Many printer manufacturers use PCL.
- For Windows 9x applications using a non-PostScript printer, the print job data is converted to Enhanced Metafile Format (EMF). This format embeds print commands in the data to help speed printing.
- Text data that contains no embedded control characters is sent to the printer as is. When DOS applications use this type of printing, the data is called raw data and the print job is sent directly to the printer, bypassing the printer queue.

Normally, when Windows receives a print job from an application, it places the job in a queue and prints from the queue, so that the application is released from the

13

printing process as soon as possible. Several print jobs can accumulate in the queue, which you can view in the Printers window. This process is called **spooling**. (The word *spool* is an acronym for *simultaneous peripheral operations on line*.) Most printing from Windows uses spooling.

If the printer port, printer cable, and printer all support bidirectional communication, the printer can communicate with Windows. For example, Windows 2000 can ask the printer how much printer memory is available and what fonts are installed. The printer can send messages to the OS, such as an out-of-paper or paper-jam message.

Troubleshooting Printers Using Windows

Printing problems can be caused by the printer, the PC hardware or OS, the application using the printer, the printer cable, or the network. This section addresses problems caused by the OS or the application using the printer. Follow the steps in Figure 13-6 to isolate a printer problem. If you cannot print from an application, the next step is to print a test page using the OS. If that works, then the problem is with the application. If you can print a self-test page at the printer, but you cannot print an OS test page, then the problem is with connectivity between the PC and the printer or with the OS and printer drivers.

Verify that a Printer Self-Test Page Can Print

To eliminate the printer as the problem, first check that the printer is on, and then print a self-test page. For directions to print a self-test page, see the printer's user guide. For example, you might need to hold down a button or buttons on the printer's front panel. If this test page prints correctly, then the printer works correctly. A printer test page generally prints some text, some graphics, and some information about the printer, such as the printer resolution and how much memory is installed. Verify that the information on the test page is correct. For example, if you know that the printer should have 2 MB of on-board printer memory, but the test only reports 1 MB, then there is a problem with memory. Also, some printers allow you to flash BIOS on the printer.

APPLYING CONCEPTS

Jill is the PC support technician responsible for supporting 10 users, their peer-to-peer network, printers, and computers. Everything was working fine when Jill left work one evening, but the next morning three users meet her at the door, complaining that they cannot print to

A+
OS
3.3

the network printer and that important work must be printed by noon. What do you think are the first three things Jill should check?

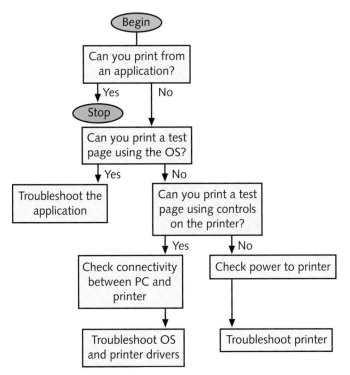

Figure 13-6   How to isolate a printer problem

Verify Connectivity Between PC and Printer

If the printer self-test worked, but the OS printer test did not work, the problem might be with the printer cable or the port the printer is using. Check these things:

- Enter CMOS setup of the PC and check how the printer's parallel port, serial port, or USB port is configured. Is it disabled? For a parallel port, is the port set to ECP or bidirectional? Try setting the port to bidirectional.
- Turn off the printer and disconnect the cable to the computer.
- Turn on the printer. If it now displays a Ready message, the problem is communication between the printer and computer.
- Verify that the cable is connected to the correct printer port.
- Verify that data to the installed printer is being sent to the correct port. For example, if the printer is using a parallel port, open the Properties dialog box of the installed printer. Verify that the print job is being sent to LPT1, as shown in Figure 13-7.

13

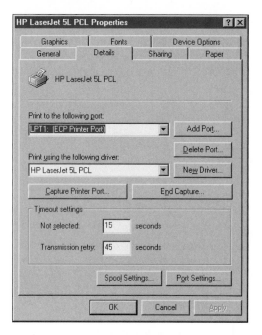

Figure 13-7   Verify that print data is being sent to the correct parallel port

Verify an OS Test Page Can Print

To verify you can print from the OS, try to print a test page using the Printers window. Right-click the printer you want to test, and choose Properties on the shortcut menu. Click the Print Test Page button to send a test page to the printer. If a self-test page works, but an OS test page to a local printer does not work, try the following:

- The print spool might be stalled. Try deleting all print jobs in the printer's queue. Double-click the printer icon in the Printers window. Select Printer on the menu bar, and then select Purge Print Documents. (It may take a moment for the print jobs to disappear.)
- Verify that the correct default printer is selected.
- Verify that the printer is online. See the printer documentation for information on how to determine the status from the control panel of the printer.
- If you still cannot print, reboot the PC. Verify that the printer cable or cable connections are solid.
- Verify that the printer is configured for the correct parallel port.
- Try removing and reinstalling the printer driver. To uninstall the printer driver, right-click the printer icon in the Printers window, and select Delete. Then reinstall the printer.
- In CMOS setup, check the configuration of the USB, serial, or parallel port that the printer is using.

- Check the parallel port mode in CMOS setup. If ECP mode is selected, verify that a DMA channel is available and not conflicting with another device. Try setting the port to bidirectional.
- Check the Web site of the printer manufacturer for an updated printer driver. Download and install the correct driver.
- In the printer Properties dialog box, click "Disable bidirectional support for this printer". The PC and printer might have a problem with bidirectional communication.
- Check the resources assigned to the printer port. Open Device Manager, select LPT1, and click Properties. Verify that the resources are assigned correctly for LPT1 (I/O addresses are 0378 to 037B) and that Device Manager reports "No conflicts".
- In the printer Properties dialog box, try disabling "Check Port State Before Printing".
- Try a different cable.
- Verify printer properties. Try lowering the resolution.
- If you can print from DOS, but not from Windows, try disabling printer spooling. Go to the printer Properties dialog box, and select Print Directly to the Printer. Spooling holds print jobs in a queue for printing, so if spooling is disabled, printing from an application can be slower.
- If you have trouble printing from an application, you can also bypass spooling by selecting Print from the File menu in the application, selecting the option to print to a file, and then dragging that file to the icon representing your printer.
- If you have trouble printing from an application in Windows 9x, the application may be incompatible with Windows. One way to try to solve this problem is to click Start, click Run, and type mkcompat.exe. This utility enables you to troubleshoot and solve problems that may make an application incompatible with a certain version of Windows.
- Verify that enough hard drive space is available for the OS to create temporary print files.
- Use Chkdsk, Error-checking (Windows 2000/XP), or ScanDisk (Windows 9x) to verify that the hard drive does not have errors. Use Defragmenter to optimize the hard drive.
- Boot Windows into Safe Mode and attempt to print. If this step works, then there might be a conflict between the printer driver and another driver or application.
- If you have access to a port tester device, test the parallel port.
- Check the printer documentation for troubleshooting steps to solve printer problems.
- Try the printer on another PC. Try another power cable and another printer cable.

13

Troubleshooting Printing from Applications

If you can print a Windows test page, but you cannot print from an application, try the following:

- Verify that the correct printer is selected in the Print Setup dialog box.
- Try printing a different application file.
- Delete any files in the print spool. From the Printers window, double-click the printer icon. Click Printer on the menu bar of the window that appears, and then click Purge Print Documents.
- Reboot the PC. Immediately enter Notepad or WordPad, type some text, and print.
- Reopen the application giving the print error and attempt to print again.
- Try creating data in a new file and printing it. Keep the data simple.
- Try printing from another application.
- If you can print from other applications, consider reinstalling the problem application.
- Close any applications that are not being used.
- Add more memory to the printer.
- Remove and reinstall the printer drivers.
- For DOS applications, you may need to exit the application before printing will work. Verify that the printer is configured to handle DOS printing.

Troubleshooting Networked Printers

When troubleshooting problems with connectivity between a PC on the network and a network printer, try the following:

- Is the printer online?
- Check that you can print a test page from the computer that has the printer attached to it locally. Right-click the printer you want to test, and choose Properties from the shortcut menu. Click the Print Test Page button to send a test page to the printer. Verify that the correct default printer is selected.
- If you cannot print from the local printer, solve the problem there before attempting to print over the network.
- Return to the remote computer and verify that you can access the computer to which the printer is attached. Go to Network Neighborhood or My Network Places and attempt to open shared folders on the printer's computer. Perhaps you have not entered a correct user ID and password to access this computer; if so, you will be unable to use the computer's resources.
- Using the Printers window, delete the printer, and then use Windows 2000/XP My Network Places or Windows 9x Network Neighborhood to reconnect the printer.
- Is the correct network printer selected on the remote PC?
- Can you print to another network printer? If so, there may be a problem with the printer. Look at the printer's configuration.

- Is enough hard drive space available on the remote PC?
- For DOS applications, you may need to exit the application before printing will work. Verify that the printer is configured to handle DOS printing over the network.
- If a PC cannot communicate with a network printer connected directly to the network, try installing a second network protocol that the network printer supports, such as IPX/SPX. If this works, then suspect that the firmware on the NIC is having a problem with TCP/IP. Try flashing the network printer's BIOS. Go to the printer manufacturer's Web site to read directions for flashing BIOS and to download the latest BIOS updates.

APPLYING CONCEPTS

Now back to Jill and her company's network printer problem. Generally, Jill should focus on finding out what works and what doesn't work, always remembering to check the simple things first. Jill should first go to the printer and check that the printer is online and has no error messages, such as a Paper Out message. Then Jill should ask, "Can anyone print to this printer?" To find out, she should go to the closest PC and try to print a Windows test page. If the test page prints, she should next go to one of the three PCs that do not print and begin troubleshooting that PC's connection to the network. If the test page did not print at the closest PC, the problem is still not necessarily the printer. To eliminate the printer as the problem, the next step is to print a self-test page at the printer. If that self-test page prints, then Jill should check other PCs on the network. Is the entire network down? Can one PC see another PC on the network? Perhaps part of the network is down (maybe because of a hub serving one part of the network).

13

Introducing the Mac OS

✔ **A+ EXAM TIP**

The A+ exams do not cover the Mac OS.

Recall from Chapter 1 that Mac OS X is the latest version of the proprietary OS for Apple Macintosh computers. This section covers the basic file and folder organization and startup process for the Mac OS. It is not intended to qualify you to support Macs but rather to give you a passing familiarity with them, so that you will recognize some of the main features of the OS and know where to go for more information.

Starting Up a Mac

When the Mac starts up, you see a graphical record of some of the events occurring in the startup process, such as the loading of the desktop and system applets, including the **Finder window** (which is used to explore the Mac system). Most of the startup process, however, is hidden from the user. Here are the main steps in the process:

1. Self-test controlled from ROM

2. PRAM (parameter RAM) settings retrieved

3. System folder located

4. Mac OS ROM file loaded

5. Smiling Mac icon and welcome screen displayed

6. Enablers loaded

7. Disk First Aid runs if the Mac was not shut down properly

8. Other System folder contents located

9. Mac desktop displayed

10. Finder and startup programs loaded

Each of these steps is described in more detail here, and major differences between Mac OS X and Mac OS 9 are noted.

1. *Self-test is controlled from ROM.* When you press the power button on a Mac and power is sent to the motherboard, the ROM signals the Mac to perform a self-test. Components tested include the hard drive, the processor, ports, controllers, and expansion cards. The self-test ensures that they are operating correctly. Once this is confirmed, the Mac tests its RAM and halts the startup process if major damage or incorrect installations of RAM modules are detected. Minor damage to RAM might not be detected during the startup test of RAM but might show up in system malfunctions later.

2. *PRAM settings are retrieved.* In the Mac, **PRAM**, or **parameter RAM**, stores configuration information for the Mac OS. After tests of components and RAM are completed, the Mac looks at the PRAM for settings that tell the system which drive is presently designated as the bootable drive (the startup disk). If it looks in that drive and does not find the Mac OS, it keeps looking in drives until it finds a bootable drive. If it cannot find one, the system displays a flashing question mark and pauses the startup process.

3. *The System folder is located.* After the Mac locates a bootable disk, it looks for an active **System folder**, which is the folder that the system designates as the one from which the Mac OS is to be loaded. A System folder is required for a disk to be bootable. In Mac OS 9, the System folder is named System Folder, and in Mac OS X, the System folder is named System. See Figure 13-8.

4. *The Mac OS ROM file is loaded.* The first item that the Mac loads into memory from the System folder is the **Mac OS ROM file**, which contains commands

required for interaction with hardware and the lower levels of the Mac OS. Before the iMac, these commands were stored in ROM on the motherboard in the Mac.

5. *The smiling Mac icon and welcome screen are displayed.* When the smiling Mac icon is displayed, the system is loading the OS into RAM, beginning with the **System file** containing the libraries and commands that make up the core of the OS.

6. *The system loads enablers for hardware components.* If Mac hardware is put on the market before the instructions to control it are included with the OS, an **enabler file** will be included with it that will enable it to function with the version of Mac OS being used on the computer. The enabler files are loaded after the System file. Generally, each revision of the Mac OS incorporates information included in enabler files that were necessary with the previous version.

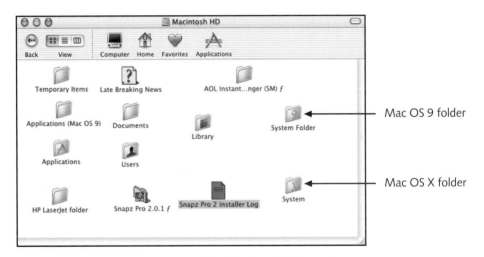

Mac OS 9 folder

Mac OS X folder

Figure 13-8   Mac OS 9 is stored in the System Folder, but Mac OS X uses System

7. *Disk First Aid runs if the system was not shut down properly.* If the system is not shut down properly, the next time the computer starts up the system will run **Disk First Aid**, a Mac disk utility, to search for and repair any problems that it finds with the hard drive. Disk First Aid runs after the System file and any enabler files are loaded.

8. *Other contents of the System folder are located.* In Mac OS 9, in addition to the System file and enabler files, the System folder also contains the Control Panels and Extensions folders (see Figure 13-9). The **Control Panels folder** controls system settings such as time and date, speaker volume, and the configuration of the Finder window and the desktop. The **Extensions folder** contains add-ons to provide new features to a Mac, as well as shared libraries and icons.

13

These no longer exist in Mac OS X; their functions are incorporated into a single **Library** folder, which is shown in Figure 13-10.

Figure 13-9   In OS 9, the Control Panels and Extensions folders are used to contain OS and applications utilities

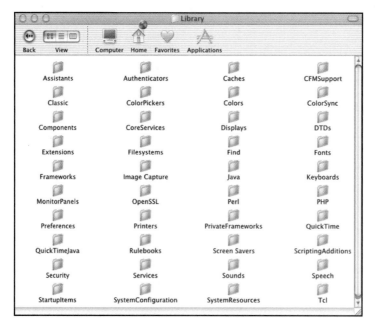

Figure 13-10   In OS X, the Library folder replaces the Control Panels and Extensions folders of OS 9

9. *The Mac desktop is displayed.* The Mac desktop is displayed after the necessary contents of the System folder have been loaded. All the required components of the Mac OS have been loaded at this point.

10. *The Finder window and startup programs are loaded.* After the Mac OS is completely loaded, the Finder window launches so that the user can access

programs and files. The Finder itself is an application that is loaded automatically during the startup process, not a part of the OS. When the Finder window has been loaded, the system loads items in the Startup Items folder, which contains items that the user wants to open immediately upon startup. In Mac OS 9, it also opens the Launcher, which provides easy access to commonly used folders, programs, and files, if the Launcher control panel has been installed.

Using the Mac

Now that you've had an overview of the Mac OS startup process, let's look at some major features of the Mac interface and learn some important procedures and hints for using the Mac. In this section, you'll learn about the Finder window, the Apple menu, and procedures to help you work with files and applications in a Mac environment.

The Mac Desktop

The Mac OS X desktop, with its major components labeled, is shown in Figure 13-11. The Finder application is open and active. Because it is the currently active application, the menu bar for the Finder window is displayed at the top of the screen. The menu bar provides pull-down menus that contain options for working with applications, files, and the interface. A new feature in the Mac OS X user interface is the **dock** that appears at the bottom of the desktop. It contains icons that provide access to frequently used applications. When you click the minus button to minimize a window, an icon representing that window appears in the dock. To open an application from its icon in the dock, just click it once. The icons in the dock that represent open applications have a small triangle underneath them. The Mac OS X desktop also includes shortcut icons that are usually located on the right side of the screen and provide quick access to files, folders, and programs.

The Mac OS X interface has been redesigned, and it does not use its own interface to run applications that were written for OS 9. Instead, it stores the Mac OS 9 applications in a separate folder and launches the OS 9 interface, which it calls the classic interface, whenever a user wants to use one of those applications. In this way, a user can still use older Mac applications with the newer Mac interface. In Figure 13-11 you can see the icon on the right side of the screen to launch the Desktop (Mac OS 9) classic interface.

Using the Finder

The Mac's Finder window functions something like Explorer or My Computer in Windows, enabling the user to navigate and access the Mac's files and applications. The Finder window at the computer level, which is the top level of the Mac OS X's hierarchical file structure, shows an icon for the computer's hard drive as well as a Network icon to provide access to any other workstations that the computer is connected to. The Finder window and other windows contain a toolbar that appears at

13

the top of the window and contains buttons that function much like the buttons in a Web browser, such as Back, Home, and Favorites. The Home button on the Mac OS X window toolbar takes the user back to the computer level.

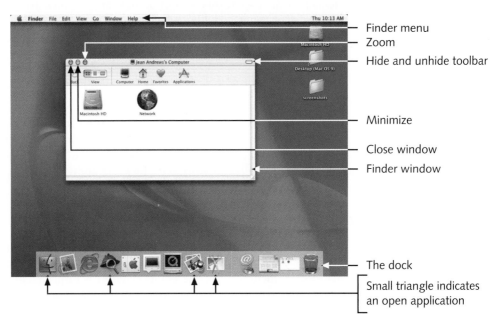

Figure 13-11   The Mac OS X desktop with a Finder window showing

NOTE   If you use a folder frequently, such as the Documents folder, you can keep it open all the time without having it in your way. In Mac OS 9, drag it down to the bottom of the screen until it becomes a tab on the title bar. In Mac OS X, drag it down to the dock, and it will become an icon on the dock.

Besides allowing you to access programs, files, and folders, the Finder window provides you with a way to organize and manage them. For instance, to create a new folder, locate the folder in which you want to create the new folder using the Finder. When you've reached the desired folder, go to the File menu and click New Folder. The new folder will appear with its name highlighted. Type its new name and press the Return key to rename the folder.

It is easier to locate a file or folder in the Finder window if you know exactly where it is, especially if there are several levels of folders inside each other. If you don't know the location of the file or folder you want to find, use the Sherlock utility to search for it. By default, the dock in Mac OS X contains an icon for Sherlock; it looks like a hat and a magnifying glass. The search screen for Sherlock is shown in Figure 13-12. Type the name of the file, folder, or text you want to find, click the check box next to the location you want to search, and then click the green magnifying glass button to begin the search. In the figure, you are searching the hard drive for a file that is named Myfile.

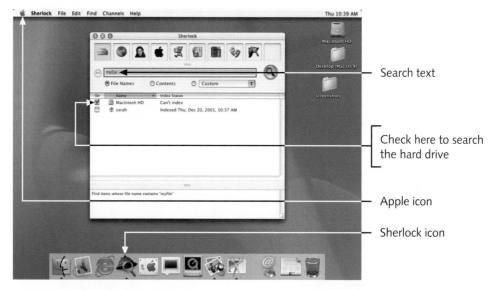

Search text

Check here to search the hard drive

Apple icon

Sherlock icon

Figure 13-12   Use Sherlock to search for files and folders

When you don't need a file or folder any more, just drag its icon to the Trash Can until the Trash Can is highlighted, and release the mouse button. Note that this is the only way you can delete icons from the Finder window. When an item is moved to the Trash Can, you can still recover it by double-clicking the Trash Can and locating the item. Items are not actually removed from the system until you chose File, Empty Trash from the menu.

Using the Apple Menu

The menu at the top of the Mac OS screen changes with each application that is active except for the Apple icon, which is always shown at the far left of the menu bar. The **Apple menu**, which opens when you click the Apple icon, and is similar to the Microsoft Windows Start menu, is present and is constantly accessible no matter what folder, window, or application you are using. It contains accessories to help you manage system tasks as well as programs such as media players, a calculator, search programs, and word-processing programs. The Mac OS X Apple menu is shown in Figure 13-13.

System Preferences on the Apple menu contains options for customizing the Mac interface. Click Apple and then click System Preferences to open the System Preferences window, shown in Figure 13-14. Control Panels, which you learned about earlier in the chapter, are also accessible from the Apple menu in OS 9. In Mac OS 9, you can customize the Apple menu to contain anything you want by adding items to or removing items from the Apple folder, which is located in the System folder. You

13

can create up to five levels of submenus under the Apple menu. In Mac OS X, the Apple menu is no longer customizable.

Apple icon

Figure 13-13 The Apple menu is always available no matter what application is active

Figure 13-14 The System Preferences window is used to customize the Mac interface

In Mac OS 9, there are three submenus on the Apple menu, called Recent Applications, Recent Documents, and Recent Servers. To customize these submenus, from the Apple menu, select Control Panels, Apple Menu Options. From this control panel, you can select whether to use recent menus and how many items to include on them. In Mac OS X, the Recent Items submenu on the Apple menu (shown in Figure 13-15) gives you access to recently accessed documents and applications.

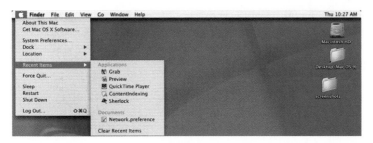

Figure 13-15 Using Mac OS X, the Recent Items menu under the Apple menu lists recently accessed documents and applications

Launching an Application

There are four ways to execute applications on the Mac:

- Double-click the icon for the application from the Finder window or another window or from the desktop.
- Choose the application from the Recent Applications submenu on the Apple menu.
- Double-click the icon of a file associated with that application, such as a text file saved from the Notepad application.
- Drag to the application's icon the icon of a document that you want to open with it.

The first two methods have already been discussed. The last option works well if you want to open a document with an application other than the one in which it was originally saved.

As you work with applications on the Mac, you may find that you want to have more than one open at a time. In Mac OS 9, the Applications menu, which you can access from the upper right-hand corner of your screen, allows you to switch between open applications easily. The menu will show the icon and name of the currently active application. To access other open applications, click the menu and choose the name of the application you want to access. Recall that in Mac OS X, open applications are shown as icons in the dock with a small triangle under them.

Supporting Hardware

In addition to working with files and applications, you will also need to know how to support hardware in a Mac system, such as monitors and hard drives, and including changing settings for video, understanding the file system used on the hard drive, and using system maintenance tools. Again, this section will not give you all you need to know to work with Mac hardware; it is simply intended to show you some important tools for working with the system. For more information specific to working with Mac hardware, study books devoted specifically to the Mac, documentation and

13

manuals that come with your system or with specific components, and the Apple Computer, Inc. Web site (*www.apple.com*).

Adjusting Display Settings

To change display settings such as color depth and resolution, double-click the Display icon under System Preferences. The Displays window appears, as seen in Figure 13-16. You can change the following settings in the Displays window:

Figure 13-16   The Displays icon in the System Preferences window is used to adjust the display settings

- *Resolution.* The resolution of a display affects how many pixels are shown on-screen. A resolution of 1024 × 768 means that there are 1,024 columns of pixels and 768 rows of pixels. When you change the resolution of your monitor, remember that the size of the items on the screen will change; the more pixels there are, the smaller items will be. This can be good if you want to see more items and space on your screen at one time, but it can be a drawback if you have vision problems. Two advantages to an 800 × 600 resolution are that it will produce a view close to what you will actually see in a printed document and that many Web pages are designed to be viewed at this resolution. A Web page optimized at 800 × 600 will look cramped at a lower resolution such as 640 × 480.
- *Contrast and brightness.* The sliders on the bottom of the Display tab of the Displays window enable you to control how much contrast there is between colors on your screen and how bright the overall display is. It is not a good idea to set a monitor to the highest brightness setting, because this can burn out the monitor prematurely.

▪ *Color depth.* Click the Color tab on the Displays window to view and change
the settings for depth of color. The Color Depth box allows you to change how
many colors can be shown on the screen: either 256, thousands, or millions.
More colors mean a more realistic and more detailed picture. Sometimes a picture will have been created using a certain setting and will not be displayed correctly in a different setting. If a picture appears blurred or too gray, change the
color depth until it appears correctly.

▪ *Display geometry.* Click the Geometry tab in the Displays window to reach
options for changing the shape of the display on the screen. On most monitors,
the display area is actually slightly smaller than the screen size, and you may see
some black space around the display area. Use the Geometry settings to change
the height, width, position, and shape of the display area.

Supporting the Hard Drive

As with other OSs, the Mac OS supports IDE and SCSI drive technologies and, for
hard drives, there is a choice of file systems to use.

Drive Technologies: IDE and SCSI   Recall from earlier chapters that IDE drives
follow an interface standard that allows for up to four IDE drives in a system. SCSI
drives are faster than IDE drives, and there can be up to 15 SCSI devices on a system.
It is possible to mix IDE and SCSI devices on a system.

NOTE

The terms *IDE* and *SCSI* refer not only to hard drives but also to other devices such as CD-ROM
drives, Zip drives, and DVD drives.

In the mid-1990s, IDE became the main technology for connecting internal devices
in a Mac, partially because it is less expensive than SCSI and is more widely used in
the computer industry. However, because it is faster and can support more devices,
SCSI can be a better choice for complex multimedia and graphics work. If you have a
Mac that uses IDE technology and want to convert to SCSI, you can purchase a SCSI
host adapter for that purpose. Choose a drive technology according to your needs,
your budget, and what technology your system supports.

File Systems on the Mac   Recall from Chapter 2 that a file system is the overall
structure that an OS uses to name, store, and organize files on a disk. The two main
choices for a file system on a Mac hard drive are **HFS (Hierarchical File System)**, also
called **Mac OS Standard Format**, and **HFS+**, also called the **Mac OS Extended Format**. HFS was the format used for Mac disks before 1998, when drives larger than
1 GB started to become more common. HFS limited the number of allocation units
on a disk to 65,536; how big each allocation unit was depended on the total size of
the drive. These allocation units are called **allocation blocks** or simply **blocks**, and
are similar to the Microsoft Windows file system's clusters; they are sets of hard drive

sectors where the Mac's file system stores files. Files smaller than the size of a block still take up an entire block, which can cause a significant amount of space to be wasted; this wasted space is called slack.

In 1998, with the release of Mac OS 8.1, HFS was updated to HFS+, which allows for smaller blocks and can format drives up to 2048 GB. Any drive larger than 1 GB should be formatted with HFS+. Hard drives or removable media disks (such as floppy disks) smaller than 1 GB should be formatted with HFS, as should any hard drive that you plan to use with a Mac running Mac OS 8.1 or earlier.

NOTE In Mac OS 9, the File Exchange control panel is a component that can be installed to allow the Mac to use Microsoft Windows FAT16 and FAT32 partitions. Macs can read some NTFS or Linux/ Unix file systems using utilities specially designed for that purpose. Mac OS X includes the ability to mount FAT drives but does not include a utility to format them as Mac OS 9 did.

The formatting of a hard drive with a file system creates blocks. It also creates a **directory structure** that allows the OS to access the drive. Some important elements of the directory structure are listed here.

- **Boot blocks** are the first two allocation blocks on the hard drive. They are initially empty, but once a System folder is installed on a computer, the boot blocks contain the location of the System folder so that the system can find and load the OS. You can correct damage to the boot blocks or replace erased boot blocks by installing a new System folder.
- Right after the boot blocks comes the **volume information block**, which holds information about the drive, including its format, name, number of files and folders, and allocation block size. This information must be present for a Mac to be able to access a drive. Because of the importance of the volume information block, a copy of it is stored in the next to last allocation block on the drive.
- A map of the allocation blocks on a hard drive is contained in the **volume bit map**, which uses a 1 to indicate that a block is storing files and a 0 to indicate that it is empty and is available for use. Damage to or corruption of the volume bit map does not prevent the Mac from being able to access the drive. However, when the Mac cannot determine from the volume bit map which allocation blocks are used, it might write new information to blocks that are full, overwriting the existing information. Regular disk maintenance (including use of the tools described in the next section) can help guard against this problem.
- The **catalog tree** is a database of the folders and files on a Mac hard drive, including information such as filenames and extensions, the application used to open a file, the creator of the file or folder, and the date the file or folder was created.
- The **extents tree** contains information about where the allocation blocks are located for files that take up more than one allocation block. When a file is larger than one allocation block, it is broken up into pieces called **extents**. One extent is stored in one allocation block. If a large proportion of the space on a

hard drive is being used, the extents that make up a file might not be stored next to each other. The catalog tree and the extents tree work together and are both necessary for the Mac to be able to access data stored on the hard drive. They are the closest thing in the Mac to the FAT and the root directory in Windows.

Drive Maintenance Tools

Now that you've learned about some of the components and structures created when a Mac hard drive is formatted, let's look at some utilities you can use to format, maintain, and repair hard drives on a Mac. This is not an exhaustive list but rather points you to a few common tools used for typical hard drive tasks.

In Mac OS 9, disk maintenance tools were accessed as separate applications. In Mac OS X, the Utilities folder (shown in Figure 13-17) contains various system tools, including **Disk Utility** (shown in Figure 13-18), which combines the functions of the Mac OS 9 tools Drive Setup and Disk First Aid.

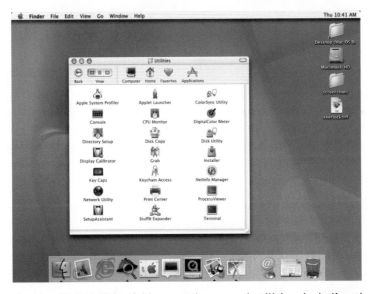

Figure 13-17   The Max OS X Utilities folder contains several utilities, including those used to manage a hard drive

Figure 13-18   The Mac OS X Disk Utility is in the Utilities folder and can be used to set up and repair a hard drive

Drive Setup   The **Drive Setup** function can be used to format a hard drive when it is initially installed or to reformat a damaged hard drive. Remember that reformatting a drive erases all data and programs on it because the format process creates new allocation blocks and directory structures. When you format a drive, you can choose whether or not to create partitions on it. Partitioning a drive is not required, but can be done to divide the drive into one or more logical drives. Drive Setup can format most IDE and SCSI drives. To use Drive Setup, on the Disk Utility window, click Drive Setup, select the disk you want to partition, and then click Partition. When you repartition a drive, all data on the current partitions is erased, and you cannot partition a drive that is currently used as the startup drive.

Defragmentation Utilities   Third-party software, such as Norton Utilities (*www.symantec.com*) or TechTool Pro, which is specifically designed for use with Macs (*www.micromat.com*), can be used to defragment your hard drive. These utilities copy the extents that make up a file into RAM on the Mac, reassemble the file, and save the complete file back onto the hard drive. One danger with these tools is that if a power failure occurs while they are running, any extents stored in the Mac's RAM will be lost. An alternate method, which is safer but much more time-consuming and cumbersome, is to back up the hard drive, reformat it, and then copy the files back onto the drive. You should always have a backup of your hard drive in case of any type of system failure.

Disk First Aid   As you learned earlier in the chapter, Disk First Aid is a disk repair tool that checks for errors on the hard drive and runs automatically on reboot when a Mac is not shut down properly. You can also run this tool manually as a preventive maintenance measure or as an attempt to address poor hard drive performance. Disk First Aid is part of the free Apple utility Disk Utility and is less powerful than third-party disk repair utilities such as Norton Disk Doctor, which is part of Norton Utilities, or Alsoft's Disk Warrior (*www.alsoft.com*). There are some problems that these utilities can repair that Disk First Aid can only detect.

Introducing Linux

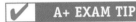

The A+ exams do not cover the Linux OS.

Generally, Windows and the Mac OS are very user-friendly and are ideal for many desktop computer uses. Linux is more often used as a file server, Web server, or email server than as a desktop OS; therefore, our approach to it will be different. This introduction to Linux is designed to give you a behind-the-scenes look at what a system administrator must know in order to manage the Linux OS in a corporate setting. In this section, you will learn about root and user accounts, file structure, some common commands, and how to use the vi editor.

NOTE   Recall from Chapter 1 that there are several different distributions of Linux. There are different versions within each distribution as well. The material in this section is meant as a general introduction to the OS. The organization of files and folders, the desktop's appearance, and the way each command works might be slightly different with the distribution and version of Linux you are using.

13

Root Account and User Accounts

Recall that an operating system is composed of a kernel, which interacts with the hardware and other software, and a shell, which interacts with the user and the kernel. Linux is a Unix-like operating system, and, just as with other versions of Unix, can use more than one shell. The default shell for Linux is the Bash shell. The name stands for "Bourne Again Shell" and takes the best features from two previous shells, the Bourne and the Korn shells.

For a Linux or Unix server, the system administrator is the person who installs updates to the OS (called patches), manages backup processes, supports the installation of software and hardware, sets up user accounts, resets passwords, and generally supports users. The system administrator has **root privileges**, which means that he or she can access all the functions of the OS and the principal user account called the **root account**. The administrator protects the password to the root account because this password gives full access to the system. When the administrator is logged on, he or she is logged on as the user root. You can use the *who* command to show a list of all users currently logged on to the system. In the example shown below, typing *who* shows that three users are currently logged on: the root, James, and Susan.

```
who
root tty1 Oct 12 07:56
james tty1 Oct 12 08:35
susan tty1 Oct 12 10:05
```

NOTE

The Linux command prompt for the root is different from the command prompt for ordinary users. The root command prompt is #, and other users have the $ command prompt.

Directory and File Layout

The main directory in Unix and Linux is the **root directory** and is indicated with a forward slash. (In Unix and Linux, directories in a path are separated with forward slashes, in contrast to the backward slashes used by DOS and Windows.) Use the *ls* command, which is similar to the DOS Dir command, to list the contents of the root directory. The command (*ls -l /*) and its results are shown in Figure 13-19. Notice that the *-l* parameter is added to the command, which displays the results using the long format, and that there are spaces included before and after the parameter of the command. Also notice in the figure the format used to display the directory contents. The *d* at the beginning of each entry indicates that the entry is a directory, not a file. The other letters in this first column have to do with the read and write privileges assigned to the directory and the right to execute programs in the directory. The name of the directory is in the last column. The rights assigned the directory can apply to the owner of the directory, to other users, or to an entire group of users.

Table 13-1 lists directories that are created in the root directory during a typical Linux installation. The actual list of directories for a Linux computer that you work with may be a little different, because the directories created in the root directory depend on what programs have been installed.

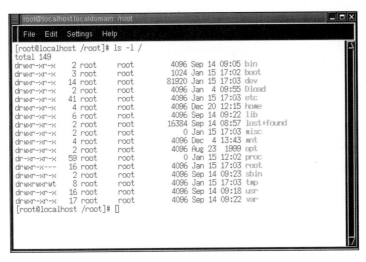

```
root@localhost.localdomain: /root                            _ □ ×
 File  Edit  Settings  Help
[root@localhost /root]# ls -l /
total 149
drwxr-xr-x    2 root     root       4096 Sep 14 09:05 bin
drwxr-xr-x    3 root     root       1024 Jan 15 17:02 boot
drwxr-xr-x   14 root     root      81920 Jan 15 17:03 dev
drwxr-xr-x    2 root     root       4096 Jan  4 09:55 Dload
drwxr-xr-x   41 root     root       4096 Jan 15 17:03 etc
drwxr-xr-x    4 root     root       4096 Dec 20 12:15 home
drwxr-xr-x    6 root     root       4096 Sep 14 09:22 lib
drwxr-xr-x    2 root     root      16384 Sep 14 08:57 lost+found
drwxr-xr-x    2 root     root          0 Jan 15 17:03 misc
drwxr-xr-x    4 root     root       4096 Dec  4 13:43 mnt
drwxr-xr-x    2 root     root       4096 Aug 23  1999 opt
dr-xr-xr-x   59 root     root          0 Jan 15 12:02 proc
drwxr-x---   16 root     root       4096 Jan 15 17:03 root
drwxr-xr-x    2 root     root       4096 Sep 14 09:23 sbin
drwxrwxrwt    8 root     root       4096 Jan 15 17:03 tmp
drwxr-xr-x   16 root     root       4096 Sep 14 09:18 usr
drwxr-xr-x   17 root     root       4096 Sep 14 09:22 var
[root@localhost /root]# []
```

Figure 13-19   A directory listing using the ls command

Directory	Description
/bin	Contains programs and commands necessary to boot the system and perform other system tasks not reserved for the administrator, such as shutdown and reboot.
/boot	Consists of components needed for the boot process, such as boot loaders.
/dev	Holds device names, which consist of the type of device and a number identifying the device. Actual device drivers are located in the /lib/modules/[kernel version]/directory.
/etc	Contains system configuration data, including configuration files and settings and their subdirectories. These files are used for tasks such as configuring a user account, changing system settings, and configuring a domain name resolution service.
/home	Contains user data. Every user on the system has a directory in the /home directory, such as /home/jean or /home/scott, and when a user logs on, that directory becomes the current working directory.
/lib	Stores common libraries used by applications so that more than one application can use the same library at one time. An example is the library of C programming code, without which only the kernel of the Linux system could run.
/lost+found	Stores data that is lost when files are truncated or when an attempt to fix system errors is unsuccessful.
/opt	Contains installations of third-party applications such as Web browsers that do not come with the Linux OS distribution.

Table 13-1 (continued)

13

Directory	Description
/root	The home directory for the root user; contains only files specific to the root user. Do not confuse this directory with the root directory, which contains all the directories listed in this table.
/sbin	Stores commands required for system administration.
/tmp	Stores temporary files, such as the ones that applications use during installation and operation.
/usr	Constitutes the major section of the Linux file system and contains read-only data.
/var	Holds variable data such as email, news, print spools, and administrative files.

Table 13-1   Directories in a typical Linux root directory

Linux Commands

This section describes some basic Linux and Unix commands, together with simple examples of how some are used. As you read along, be aware that all commands entered in Linux or Unix are case sensitive, meaning that uppercase and lowercase matter. Table 13-2 shows some common commands for Linux and Unix. This is not meant to be a comprehensive list of commands but simply to list some that might be useful to you in working with files, directories, network connections, and system configuration. In the rest of the section, you will learn how to use a few common commands. For all of these procedures, assume that you are in your home directory (which would be /home/*<yourname>*/).

Command	Description
cat	Lets you view the contents of a file. Many Linux commands can use the redirection symbol > to redirect the output of the command. For example, use the redirection symbol with the cat command to copy a file: cat/etc/shells > newfile The contents of the shells file are written to newfile.
cd	Change directory. For example, cd/etc changes the directory to /etc.
chmod	This command changes the attributes assigned to a file and is similar to the DOS Attrib command. For example, to grant read permission to the file myfile: Chmod +r myfile
clear	Clears the screen. This command is useful when the screen has become cluttered with commands and data that you no longer need to view.
cp	Used to copy a file: cp <source> <destination>

Table 13-2 (continued)

Command	Description
date	Entered alone, this command displays the current system date setting. Entered in the format date <mmddhhmmyy>, this command sets the system date. For example, to set the date to Dec 25, 2002 at 11:59 in the evening: Date 1225235902
echo	Displays information on the screen. For example, to display which shell is currently being used, enter this command: echo $SHELL
fdisk	Creates or makes changes to a hard drive partition table: fdisk <hard drive>
grep	Searches for a specific pattern in a file or in multiple files: grep <pattern> <file>
hostname	Displays a server's FQDN: hostname
ifconfig	Used to troubleshoot problems with network connections under TCP/IP. This command can disable and enable network cards and release and renew the IP addresses assigned to these cards. For example, to show all configuration information: ifconfig–a To release the given IP address for a TCP/IP connection named en0 (the first Ethernet connection of the system): ifconfig en0 -168.92.1.1
kill	Kills a process instead of waiting for the process to terminate: kill <process ID>
ls	The ls command is similar to the DOS Dir command, which displays a list of directories and files. For example, to list all files in the /etc directory, using the long parameter for a complete listing use: ls -l /etc
man	Displays the online help manual called the man pages. For example, to get information about the echo command: man echo The manual program displays information about the command. To exit the manual program, type q.
mkdir	This command makes a new directory: mkdir <directory>
|more	Appended to a command to display the results of the command on the screen one page at a time. For example, to page the ls command: ls |more
mv	Moves a file or renames it, if the source and destination are the same directory: mv <source> <destination>
netstat	Shows statistics and status information for network connections and routing tables: netstat
nslookup	Queries domain name servers to look up domain names: nslookup
ping	Used to test network connections by sending a request packet to a host. If a connection is successful, the host will return a response packet: ping <host>
ps	Displays the process table so that you can identify process IDs for currently running processes (Once you know the process ID, you can use the kill command to terminate a process): ps
pwd	Shows the name of the present working directory: pwd

13

Table 13-2 (continued)

Command	Description
reboot	Reboots the system: reboot
rm	Removes the file or files that are specified: rm <file>
rmdir	This command removes a directory: rmdir <directory>
route	Entered alone, this command shows the current configuration of the IP routing table. Entered in the format route [options], it configures the IP routing table.
traceroute	Shows the route of IP packets; used for debugging connections on a network: traceroute <host>
useradd	Adds a user to a system: useradd [option] <user>
userdel	Removes a user from a system: userdel <user>
vi	Launches a full-screen editor that can be used to enter text and commands: vi <file>
whatis	Displays a brief overview of a command. For example, to get quick information about the echo command: whatis echo
who	Displays a list of users currently logged in: who

Table 13-2   Some common Linux and Unix commands

Editing Commands

When you add options and file or directory names to a command, it can get quite long, and if you make a mistake while typing the command, you will want to edit it. Also, once the command has been entered, you can retrieve it, edit it, and press Enter to reissue the command. Some shells allow you to use the arrow, Backspace, Insert, and Delete keys to edit command lines, and other shells do not allow you to use these keys. Instead, use the following keystrokes to edit a command line:

- Alt+D   Delete a word
- Ctrl+K   Delete from the current position to the end of the line
- Ctrl+A   Move the cursor to the beginning of the command line
- Alt+B   Move the cursor left one word
- Alt+F   Move the cursor right one word

For example, follow these steps to edit a command line:

1. Type **who is this** but DO NOT press Enter.

2. To move one word to the left, press **Alt+B** so that your cursor is positioned on the word "is".

3. To delete the word "is", press **Alt+D**.

4. To delete the portion of the command line that follows the current cursor position, press **Ctrl+K**.

5. To move the cursor to the beginning of the command line, press **Ctrl+A**.

Viewing the Shells File

The shells file in the /etc directory contains a list of available shells to use on a Linux system. Each shell incorporates slightly different support for programming and scripting languages. Additionally, different Linux shells may use keystrokes other than the ones you just learned in supporting command line editing; the keystrokes in the procedure in the last section work in Bash, the default Linux shell. To determine whether you are using the Bash shell, type echo $shell and press Enter. If you see the output/bin/bash, you are using the Bash shell. If you are not using the Bash shell, type bash and press Enter to change to the Bash shell.

To view a list of available shells:

1. Type **cat /etc/shells**, and then press **Enter**.

2. A list of available shells appears. This list may include the entries /bin/bash, /bin/bsh, /bin/csh, /bin/sh, /bin/tcsh, and /bin/zsh. Notice that all these shells are stored in the /bin directory. Type **clear**, and then press **Enter** to clear the screen.

3. Type **cat –n /etc/shells**, and then press **Enter**. Notice that this time, the same list of shells is displayed with a number before each line because you used the –n option. (See Figure 13-20.) Notice in the figure that the current user is root.

Redirecting Output

Recall the list of available shells that you created using the cat command. When you entered the command cat /etc/shells, the list, which is the output of that command, was sent to the screen. What if you wanted to save that list? You would use the **redirection symbol**, which is the greater-than (>) sign, to direct the output to a file, perhaps with the name available_shells. Use these steps:

1. Go to the root directory by typing **cd /** and pressing **Enter**.

2. Type **cat /etc/shells > available_shells**, and then press **Enter**.

3. Notice that no command output appears on the screen, because the output has been saved to the new file available_shells (the file is created when the command is entered). To view the contents of the file, type **cat available_shells**, and then press **Enter**.

The file was created in the current directory, which is the root directory.

13

Figure 13-20   Use the Cat command to display a list of shells

Creating a Directory

It is not a good idea to store data files in the root directory, so let's create a directory to where the new file available_shells can be moved:

1. Type **mkdir myfiles**, and then press **Enter**. This creates a directory named myfiles under the current directory, which is root.

2. Type **cd myfiles** to change from the current directory to the new directory.

3. Type **mv /available_shells .** and then press **Enter** (don't overlook the period at the end of the command line; type it, too). This copies the file from the root directory to the current directory, which is /myfiles. The source directory is the root and the destination directory is /myfiles. The period in a command line means the current directory.

4. Type **ls** to see the contents of the myfiles directory. The available_shells file is listed. (See Figure 13-21.)

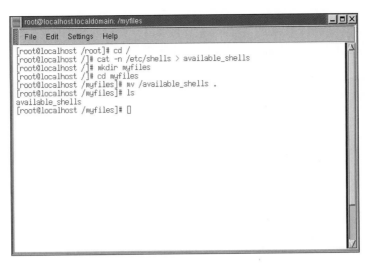

Figure 13-21   Creating and moving files to a directory

Using the vi Editor

Recall that you were introduced to the vi command in Table 13-2 earlier in the chapter. This command launches the **vi editor**, which got its name because it is a visual editor that was, at one time, the most popular Unix text editor. It is still used with shells that don't allow the use of the arrow, Delete, or Backspace keys. The editor can be used in **insert mode**, in which you can enter text, or **command mode**, which allows you to enter commands to perform editing tasks to move through the file. In this section, you will learn how to create and use commands on a text file in the vi editor. All of these commands are case sensitive.

Let's create and work with a file called mymemo.

1. To open the vi editor and create a file at the same time, type the command followed by the file name, as follows: **vi mymemo**

2. The vi editor screen is shown in Figure 13-22. Notice that the filename is shown at the bottom of the screen and that the cursor is at the top of the screen.

3. At this point, when you first open the vi editor, you are in command mode, which means that anything you type will be interpreted as a command by the vi editor. Type **i** to switch to insert mode. You will not see the command on the screen, and you do not need to press Enter to execute it. The command automatically switches you to insert mode. When you are in insert mode, the word INSERT will be shown at the bottom of the screen.

4. Type the first two sentences of Step 3 as the text for your memo. If your shell supports it, practice using the arrow keys to move the cursor through the

text, up, down, left, and right, one character at a time. You will see the keystrokes used to perform the same movements in Table 13-3; they can be used if the arrow keys are not supported.

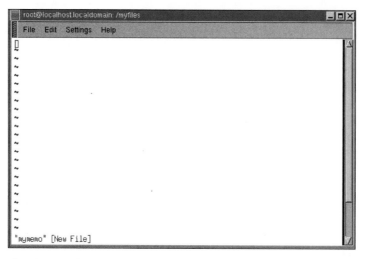

Figure 13-22   The vi text editor

5. To switch back to command mode, press the **Esc** key. Now you are ready to enter commands to manipulate your text. Type **H** to move the cursor to the upper-left corner of the screen. You must use an uppercase H, because all these commands are case sensitive.

6. Type **w** repeatedly until you reach the beginning of the word "first".

7. Type **dw** to delete the word "first". To delete one character at a time, you would use x; to delete an entire line, you would use dd.

8. To save the file and exit the vi editor, type **:x** and press **Enter**. This will save the file and close the editor.

Table 13-3 lists the vi editor commands to move the cursor. There are many more commands to manipulate text, set options, cancel, or temporarily leave a vi editor session. For a more complete list of vi editor commands, see a reference dedicated to Linux.

Command	Alternate	Description
Ctrl+B	Pg up	Back one screen
Ctrl+F	Pg down	Forward one screen

Table 13-3 (continued)

Command	Alternate	Description
Ctrl+U	--	Up half a screen
Ctrl+D	--	Down half a screen
k	Up arrow	Up one line
j	Down arrow	Down one line
h	Left arrow	Left one character
l	Right arrow	Right one character
W	--	Forward one word
B	--	Back one word
0 (zero)	--	Beginning of the current line
$	--	End of current line
NG	--	Line specified by number n
H	--	Upper left corner of screen
L	--	Last line on the screen

Table 13-3   vi editor commands

Window Managers

13

Because many users prefer a Windows desktop, several applications have been written to provide a GUI for Unix and Linux. These GUIs are called **window managers**. You saw a typical window manager screen for Linux in Chapter 1. One popular desktop environment software is GNU Network Object Model Environment (GNOME). GNOME (pronounced "guh-nome") provides a desktop that looks and feels like Windows 98, and is free software designed to use a Linux kernel. The major components of a GNOME window are shown in Figure 13-23. For more information about GNOME, see the organization's Web site at *www.gnu.org*.

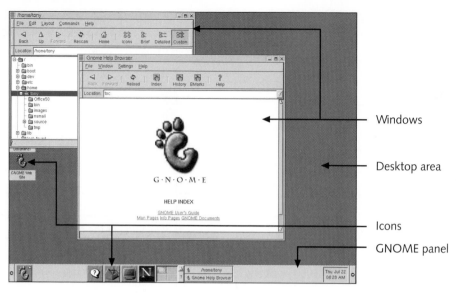

Figure 13-23   GNOME is popular desktop environment software used on Linux systems

CHAPTER SUMMARY

▶ Using Windows, printers are installed using the Windows 2000 and Windows 9x Printers window or the Windows XP Printers and Faxes window.

▶ Before users on a network can view or access resources on a PC, Client for Microsoft Networks and File and Printer Sharing must be installed, and these resources must be shared.

▶ When troubleshooting printers, first isolate the problem. Narrow the source to the printer, operating system including the device driver, application software, or network.

▶ The Finder Window in the Mac OS functions somewhat like Explorer or My Computer in Microsoft Windows. It allows you to navigate through the Mac's hierarchical file structure.

▶ The Mac OS boot process begins with ROM-initiated self-test of hardware components and ends with the loading of the interface after necessary components, including the Mac OS ROM file, enablers, and System folder contents, are loaded.

▶ The dock at the bottom of the Mac desktop is new to Mac OS X. It provides access to frequently used applications.

▶ The Apple menu contains options that are accessible no matter what application you are in. It is customizable in Mac OS 9 but not in Mac OS X.

▶ There are four ways to launch an application on the Mac: double-click its icon, choose it from Recent Applications under Recent Items on the Apple menu, double-click the icon of a file associated with it, and drag a document icon to the application icon.

▶ Use the Displays window, accessible from the System Preferences window, to change and monitor settings such as resolution, contrast, brightness, and geometry. Other system settings can also be accessed from System Preferences.

▶ The Drive Setup and Disk First Aid utilities, which are separate in Mac OS 9, have been combined into the Disk Utility in Mac OS X. This utility and other system tools are accessible in the Utilities folder, which is located under Applications.

▶ Macs can recognize, format, and support most IDE (Integrated Device Electronics) and SCSI (Small Computer System Interface) hard drives.

▶ The main file systems available for Mac are HFS and HFS+, but you can also mount FAT16, FAT32, and NTFS volumes on a Mac.

▶ Linux is based on Unix and uses many of the same commands.

▶ The default shell for Linux is the Bash shell.

▶ The system administrator for a Linux computer has root privileges and can access all the functions of the OS, support installations, manage backups, and make changes to system configuration.

▶ The root directory is the top level in the Linux file structure. The directory for each user is their /home directory, and unless a user has the root account, he or she is automatically in his or her home directory after logging on to the system.

▶ All commands in Linux and Unix are case sensitive. For example, in some of the text-editing commands, the same letter in lowercase and in uppercase can mean two different things.

▶ The vi editor is a text editor in Linux that runs in insert mode and command mode, allowing you to enter text and enter commands to manipulate that text.

▶ GUI interfaces for Linux are called window managers. One popular Linux window manager is GNOME.

13

KEY TERMS

For explanations of key terms, see the Glossary near the end of the book.

allocation block
Apple menu
block
boot blocks
catalog tree
command mode
Control Panels folder
default printer
directory structure
Disk First Aid
Disk Utility
dock
Drive Setup

enabler file
Extensions folder
extents
extents tree
Finder window
HFS (Hierarchical File System)
HFS+
insert mode
Library
local printer
Mac OS Extended Format
Mac OS ROM file
Mac OS Standard Format

network printer
PRAM (parameter RAM)
redirection symbol
root account
root directory
root privileges
spooling
System file
System folder
vi editor
volume bit map
volume information block
window manager

REVIEWING THE BASICS

1. What are two possible settings in CMOS for parallel port mode?

2. What two Windows components are used to share resources on a network and access those shared resources?

3. How do you share a local printer with others in the workgroup?

4. What are two ways to install a printer that is being shared by another computer on the network?

5. When would you want to enable Capture Printer Port while installing a network printer?

6. What company developed PostScript? PCL?

7. When you are unable to print from Windows, how can you eliminate the printer as being the source of the problem?

8. When you are unable to print from an application, how can you eliminate Windows as the source of the problem?

9. In Windows 98, what is the mkcompat.exe utility used for?

10. List at least five differences between Mac OS 9 and Mac OS X.

11. List the steps of the Mac OS startup process.

12. What role does the Mac OS ROM file play in the startup process?

13. Explain the four ways to access an application on a Mac.

14. Can you run Mac OS 9 applications from the Mac OS X interface? Explain.

15. How are open applications shown in Mac OS 9? In Mac OS X?

16. What is screen geometry, and how do you change it on a Mac?

17. Why is it a good idea to set your monitor's resolution to 800 × 600?

18. Name the two major hard drive technologies that Macs support.

19. What is the file system for the Mac? Name other, non-native file systems that Macs can support.

20. How did HFS+ improve HFS?

21. If you do not have any third-party defragmentation utilities available, what is one way that you can defragment your Mac hard drive?

22. What is the default Linux shell? What were the two shells that preceded it?

23. List some of the responsibilities of a system administrator for a Linux machine.

24. Explain the difference between the Linux root account and a regular user account.

25. What is contained in the Linux /etc directory? /opt? /sbin?

26. Under which directory are applications installed using Linux?

27. Which Linux command is used to copy a file? To clear the screen? To kill a process? To list the contents of a file with a number in front of each line?

28. What is the vi editor? Explain how to open it and close it. When might you use it?

29. Give two examples of background processes in Linux.

30. Explain what a Linux window manager is and give an example.

13

THINKING CRITICALLY

1. A Windows 98 computer has a locally installed printer that you must make available to eight other Windows 98 computers on the network. What is the best way to do this?

   a. Use the Add Printer icon in the Printers window for each of the eight PCs.

   b. Use Network Neighborhood to install the printer on each of the eight PCs.

c. Use the printer manufacturer's setup program from the printer's CD on each of the eight PCs.

d. Install the printer on each of the eight PCs while sitting at the host PC. Use Network Neighborhood on the host PC.

2. You are not able to print a Word document on a Windows XP computer to a network printer. The network printer is connected directly to the network, but when you look at the Printers and Faxes window, you see the name of the printer as \\SMITHWIN2K\HP LaserJet 8100. In the following list, select the possible sources of the problem.

a. The SMITHWIN2K computer is not turned on.

b. The HP LaserJet 8100 printer is not online.

c. The SMITHWIN2K printer is not online.

d. The Windows XP computer has a stalled printer spool.

e. The HP LaserJet 8100 computer is not logged on to the workgroup.

3. You are not able to print a test page from your Windows 2000 PC to your local HP DeskJet printer. Which of the following are possible causes of the problem?

a. The network is down.

b. The printer cable is not connected properly.

c. The Windows print spool is stalled.

d. You have the wrong printer drivers installed.

e. File and Printer Sharing is not enabled.

HANDS-ON PROJECTS

HANDS-ON PROJECTS

PROJECT 13-1: Sharing a Local Printer

Practice networking skills using Windows 2000/XP or Windows 9x:

1. Share a local printer with others on the network.

2. Install a shared printer on a remote PC. Verify that you can print to the printer.

PROJECT 13-2: Researching Mac Cross-compatibility

Using the Apple Web site (*www.apple.com*) and other Web sites as necessary, research whether you can do the following on a Mac:

1. Read Microsoft Word documents.

2. Mount a volume that is using FAT32.

3. Send documents to a Linux computer.

4. Use applications that were designed for Mac OS 8.1 when Mac OS X is installed.

Print the Web page showing the source of your information and instructions for accomplishing each task.

PROJECT 13-3: Using Mac Applications

On a Mac computer, locate the TextEdit application. Write a short memo and save it as myfile. Use this file and the instructions in this chapter to practice the four ways of accessing an application on the Mac.

PROJECT 13-4: Researching Linux

Recall from Chapter 1 that popular distributions of Linux include SuSE (*www.suse.com*), RedHat (*www.redhat.com*), and Caldera (*www.caldera.com*). For each distribution, find out the following:

1. Latest version number

2. File systems supported

3. Availability of free downloads and cost of any paid versions

4. Whether you can read Microsoft Word and Microsoft Excel documents, and if so, how

13

PROJECT 13-5: Practicing Linux Commands

From Linux without a GUI or from a terminal within a Linux window manager, create a text file using the vi editor. Save it to your home directory and then execute the commands to move it to another user's home directory. Refer to Table 13-2 in this chapter as necessary.

Error Messages and Their Meanings

A+
OS
3.1

The following table of error messages and their meanings can help you when you are diagnosing computer problems. For other error messages, consult your motherboard or computer documentation, or use a good search engine to search for the error message on the Internet.

Error Message	Meaning of the Error Message
Invalid partition table Error loading operating system Missing operating system Invalid boot disk Inaccessible boot device	The Master Boot program at the beginning of the hard drive displays these messages when it cannot find the active partition on the hard drive or the boot record on that partition. Use Diskpart or Fdisk to examine the drive for errors. Check the hard drive manufacturer's Web site for other diagnostic software.
Bad sector writing or reading to drive	Sector markings on the disk may be fading. Try ScanDisk or reformat the disk.
Beeps during POST	Before the video is checked, during POST, the ROM BIOS communicates error messages with a series of beeps. Each BIOS manufacturer has its own beep codes, but the following are examples of some BIOS codes. For specific beep codes for your motherboard, see the Web site of the motherboard or BIOS manufacturer.
One beep followed by three, four, or five beeps	Motherboard problems, possibly with DMA, CMOS setup chip, timer, or system bus.
Two beeps	The POST numeric code is displayed on the monitor.
Two beeps followed by three, four, or five beeps	First 64K of RAM has errors.
Three beeps followed by three, four, or five beeps	Keyboard controller failed or video controller failed.

(Table A-1 continued)

Error Message	Meaning of the Error Message
Four beeps followed by two, three, or four beeps	Problem with serial or parallel ports, system timer, or time of day.
Continuous beeps	Problem with power supply.
Configuration/CMOS error	Setup information does not agree with the actual hardware the computer found during boot. May be caused by a bad or weak battery or by changing hardware without changing setup. Check setup for errors.
Hard drive not found	The OS cannot locate the hard drive, or the controller card is not responding.
Fixed disk error	The PC cannot find the hard drive that setup told it to expect. Check cables, connections, power supply, and setup information.
Invalid drive specification	The PC is unable to find a hard drive or a floppy drive that setup tells it to expect. Look for errors in setup, or for a corrupted partition table on the hard drive.
No boot device available	The hard drive is not formatted, or the format is corrupted, and there is no disk in drive A. Boot from a bootable floppy and examine your hard drive for corruption.
Non-system disk or disk error Bad or missing Command.com No operating system found	The disk in drive A is not bootable. Remove the disk in drive A and boot from the hard drive. Command.com on drive C might have been erased, or the path could not be found. For Windows 9x or DOS, use the Sys command to restore system files.
Not ready reading drive A: Abort, Retry, Fail?	The disk in drive A is missing, is not formatted, or is corrupted. Try another disk or remove the disk to boot from the hard drive.
Numeric codes during POST	Sometimes numeric codes are used to communicate errors at POST. Some examples for IBM XT/AT error codes include:
Code in the 100 range	Motherboard errors
Code in the 200 range	RAM errors
Code in the 300 range	Keyboard errors
Code in the 500 range	Video controller errors

(Table A-1 continued)

A

Error Message	Meaning of the Error Message
Code in the 600 range	Floppy drive errors
Code in the 700 range	Coprocessor errors
Code in the 900 range	Parallel port errors
Code in the 1100–1200 range	Async (communications adapter) errors
Code in the 1300 range	Game controller or joystick errors
Code in the 1700 range	Hard drive errors
Code in the 6000 range	SCSI device or network card errors
Code in the 7300 range	Floppy drive errors
Track 0 bad, disk not usable	This usually occurs when you attempt to format a floppy disk using the wrong format type. Check the disk type and compare it with the type specified in the format command.
Missing operating system, error loading operating system	The MBR is unable to locate or read the OS boot sector on the active partition, or there is a translation problem on large drives. Boot from a bootable floppy and examine the hard drive file system for corruption.
Unknown error at POST	See the Web site of the system BIOS manufacturer: • AMI BIOS: *www.ami.com* • Award BIOS and Phoenix BIOS: *www.phoenix.com* • Compaq or HP: *www.hp.com* • Dell: *www.dell.com* • IBM: *www.ibm.com* • Gateway: *www.gateway.com*
Invalid directory	A command issued in the Autoexec.bat file references a working directory that does not exist. Check the Autoexec.bat file for errors.
Bad command or file not found	The OS command just executed cannot be interpreted, or the OS cannot find the program file specified in the command line. Check the spelling of the filename. When working with DOS or from a Windows startup disk, check that the path to the program file has been given to the OS in Autoexec.bat.

(Table A-1 continued)

A+
OS
3.1

Error Message	Meaning of the Error Message
Insufficient memory	This error happens during or after the boot under Windows when too many applications are open. Close some applications. A reboot might help.
Incorrect DOS version	When you execute a DOS external command, the OS looks for a program file with the same name as the command. It finds that this file belongs to a different version of the OS than the one that is now running. Use the Setver command in Autoexec.bat.
Write-protect error writing drive A:	Let the computer write to the disk by setting the switch on a 3½-inch disk or removing the tape from a 5¼-inch disk.
Error in Config.sys line xx	There is a problem loading a device driver or with the syntax of a command line. Check the command line for errors. Verify that the driver files are in the right directory. Reinstall the driver files.
Himem.sys not loaded, missing or corrupt Himem.sys	Himem.sys is corrupted, not in the right directory, or not the right version for the currently loaded OS. Verify Himem.sys.
Device not found	Errors in System.ini, Win.ini, or the registry. Look for references to devices or attempts to load device drivers. Use Device Manager to delete a device or edit System.ini or Win.ini.
Device/Service has failed to start	A hardware device or driver necessary to run the device or critical software utility is causing problems. This type of problem is best handled using OS troubleshooting methods and tools.

Table A-1   Error messages and their meanings

ASCII Character Set and Ansi.sys

A SCII (American Standard Code for Information Interchange) is a coding system used by personal computers to store character data, such as letters of the alphabet, numerals, some symbols, and certain control characters. There are 128 characters defined by the standard ASCII character set. Each ASCII character is assigned an 8-bit code that converts to a decimal number from 0 to 127, although in the standard set, the first bit is always 0. The first 31 values, which are nonprintable codes, are for control characters used to send commands to printers or other peripheral devices. Files that store data as ASCII characters are sometimes called ASCII files, ASCII text files, or simply text files. ASCII can be read by most text editors and word processors and is considered the universal file format for personal computers. Autoexec.bat is one example of an ASCII file.

In addition to the standard ASCII character set, some manufacturers use an extended ASCII character set that is specific to their equipment and is not necessarily compatible with other computers. The extended ASCII character sets use the codes 128 through 255.

The American National Standards Institute (ANSI), an organization responsible for many computer standards, developed an extended character set using codes 128 through 255 that includes special characters such as letters in an international alphabet and accents, currency symbols, and fractions. ANSI has also defined a series of control codes that can be used to control monitors. For example, a sequence of control codes can clear a monitor, cause characters to be displayed upside down, or put color on a DOS screen. Ansi.sys is a device driver that, when loaded in a DOS environment, provides these monitor and keyboard functions. Ansi.sys is loaded from the Config.sys file with this command:

```
Device=C:\DOS\Ansi.sys
```

Some DOS programs need Ansi.sys loaded in order to interpret the extended character set entered from the keyboard, display these characters on the screen, and control the monitor in other ways.

Table B-1 lists the standard ASCII character set. Note that items 2 through 32, the control characters, and the extended ASCII character set are not included.

Item Number	Symbol	Meaning	ASCII in Decimal Representation	ASCII in Binary Representation	ASCII in Hex Representation
1	.	Null	0	0000 0000	0
33	b/	Space	32	0010 0000	20
34	!	Exclamation point	33	0010 0001	21
35	"	Quotation mark	34	0010 0010	22
36	#	Number sign	35	0010 0011	23
37	$	Dollar sign	36	0010 0100	24
38	%	Percent sign	37	0010 0101	25
39	&	Ampersand	38	0010 0110	26
40	'	Apostrophe, prime sign	39	0010 0111	27
41	(	Opening parenthesis	40	0010 1000	28
42	)	Closing parenthesis	41	0010 1001	29
43	*	Asterisk	42	0010 1010	2A
44	+	Plus sign	43	0010 1011	2B
45	,	Comma	44	0010 1100	2C
46	-	Hyphen, minus sign	45	0010 1101	2D
47	.	Period, decimal point	46	0010 1110	2E
48	/	Slant	47	0010 1111	2F
49	0		48	0011 0000	30
50	1		49	0011 0001	31
51	2		50	0011 0010	32
52	3		51	0011 0011	33
53	4		52	0011 0100	34
54	5		53	0011 0101	35

(Table B-1 continued)

Item Number	Symbol	Meaning	ASCII in Decimal Representation	ASCII in Binary Representation	ASCII in Hex Representation
55	6		54	0011 0110	36
56	7		55	0011 0111	37
57	8		56	0011 1000	38
58	9		57	0011 1001	39
59	:	Colon	58	0011 1010	3A
60	;	Semicolon	59	0011 1011	3B
61	<	Less-than sign	60	0011 1100	3C
62	=	Equals sign	61	0011 1101	3D
63	>	Greater-than sign	62	0011 1110	3E
64	?	Question mark	63	0011 1111	3F
65	@	Commercial at sign	64	0100 0000	40
66	A		65	0100 0001	41
67	B		66	0100 0010	42
68	C		67	0100 0011	43
69	D		68	0100 0100	44
70	E		69	0100 0101	45
71	F		70	0100 0110	46
72	G		71	0100 0111	47
73	H		72	0100 1000	48
74	I		73	0100 1001	49
75	J		74	0100 1010	4A
76	K		75	0100 1011	4B
77	L		76	0100 1100	4C
78	M		77	0100 1101	4D
79	N		78	0100 1110	4E
80	0		79	0100 1111	4F

(Table B-1 continued)

Item Number	Symbol	Meaning	ASCII in Decimal Representation	ASCII in Binary Representation	ASCII in Hex Representation
81	P		80	0101 0000	50
82	Q		81	0101 0001	51
83	R		82	0101 0010	52
84	S		83	0101 0011	53
85	T		84	0101 0100	54
86	U		85	0101 0101	55
87	V		86	0101 0110	56
88	W		87	0101 0111	57
89	X		88	0101 1000	58
90	Y		89	0101 1001	59
91	Z		90	0101 1010	5A
92	[	Opening bracket	91	0101 1011	5B
93	\	Reverse slant	92	0101 1100	5C
94	]	Closing bracket	93	0101 1101	5D
95	^	Caret	94	0101 1110	5E
96	_	Underscore	95	0101 1111	5F
97	`	Acute accent	96	0110 0000	60
98	a		97	0110 0001	61
99	b		98	0110 0010	62
100	c		99	0110 0011	63
101	d		100	0110 0100	64
102	e		101	0110 0101	65
103	f		102	0110 0110	66
104	g		103	0110 0111	67
105	h		104	0110 1000	68
106	i		105	0110 1001	69

(Table B-1 continued)

B

Item Number	Symbol	Meaning	ASCII in Decimal Representation	ASCII in Binary Representation	ASCII in Hex Representation
107	j		106	0110 1010	6A
108	k		107	0110 1011	6B
109	l		108	0110 1100	6C
110	m		109	0110 1101	6D
111	n		110	0110 1110	6E
112	o		111	0110 1111	6F
113	p		112	0111 0000	70
114	q		113	0111 0001	71
115	r		114	0111 0010	72
116	s		115	0111 0011	73
117	t		116	0111 0100	74
118	u		117	0111 0101	75
119	v		118	0111 0110	76
120	w		119	0111 0111	77
121	x		120	0111 1000	78
122	y		121	0111 1001	79
123	z		122	0111 1010	7A
124	{	Opening brace	123	0111 1011	7B
125	|	Split vertical bar	124	0111 1100	7C
126	}	Closing brace	125	0111 1101	7D
127	~	Tilde	126	0111 1110	7E
128	Δ	Small triangle	127	0111 1111	7F

Table B-1   Standard ASCII character set

The Hexadecimal Number System and Memory Addressing

U nderstanding the number system and the coding system that computers use to store data and communicate with each other is fundamental to understanding how computers work. Early attempts to invent an electronic computing device met with disappointing results as long as inventors tried to use the decimal number system, with the digits 0–9. Then John Atanasoff proposed using a coding system that expressed everything in terms of different sequences of only two numerals: one represented by the presence of a charge and one represented by the absence of a charge. The numbering system that can be supported by the expression of only two numerals is called base 2, or binary; it was invented by Ada Lovelace many years before, using the numerals 0 and 1. Under Atanasoff's design, all numbers and other characters would be converted to this binary number system, and all storage, comparisons, and arithmetic would be done using it. Even today, this is one of the basic principles of computers. Every character or number entered into a computer is first converted into a series of 0s and 1s. Many coding schemes and techniques have been invented to manipulate these 0s and 1s, called **bits** for **bi**nary dig**its**.

The most widespread binary coding scheme for microcomputers, which is recognized as the microcomputer standard, is called ASCII (American Standard Code for Information Interchange). (Appendix B lists the binary code for the basic 127-character set.) In ASCII, each character is assigned an 8-bit code called a **byte**. The byte has become the universal single unit of data storage in computers everywhere. Table C-1 lists common terms used in the discussion of how numbers are stored in computers.

Term	Definition
Bit	A numeral in the binary number system: a 0 or a 1.
Byte	8 bits.
Kilobyte	1024 bytes, which is 2 to the 10th power, often rounded to 1000 bytes.
Megabyte	Either 1024 kilobytes or 1000 kilobytes, depending on what has come to be standard practice in different situations. For example, when calculating floppy disk capacities, 1 megabyte = 1000 kilobytes; when calculating hard drive capacity, traditionally, 1 megabyte = 1024 kilobytes.

Table C-1 (continued)

Term	Definition
Gigabyte	1000 megabytes or 1024 megabytes, depending on what has come to be standard practice in different situations.
ASCII	American Standard Code for Information Interchange coding scheme used for microcomputers, which assigns a 7- or 8-bit code to all characters and symbols. See Appendix B for more information.
Hex	Short for hexadecimal. A number system based on 16 values (called base 16), which is explained in this appendix. Uses the 16 numerals 0, 1, 2, 3, 4, 5, 6, 7, 8, 9, A, B, C, D, E, and F. Hex numbers are often followed by a lowercase h to indicate they are in hex (example: 78h).

Table C-1   Computer terminology

Computers convert binary data into the hexadecimal (hex) number system because it is much less complex than converting data into decimal numbers, and it is much easier for human beings to read hex numbers than to read binary numbers. This way, even though the actual processing and inner workings of computers use the binary system, they often display information using the hex system.

Learning to "Think Hex"

One skill a knowledgeable computer support person must have is the ability to read hex numbers and convert hex to decimal and decimal to hex. Once you understand one numbering system (decimal), you can understand any numbering system (including binary and hexadecimal), because they all operate on the same basic principle: place value. So we begin there.

Place Value

A key to understanding place value is to think of a number system as a method of grouping multiple small units together until there are enough of them to be packed into a single larger group, then grouping multiple larger groups together until there are enough of them to form an even larger group, and so on. In our (decimal) number system, once there are 10 units of any group, that group becomes a single unit of the next larger group. So, groups of 10 units are packed into groups of tens; groups of 10 tens are packed into groups of hundreds; groups of 10 hundreds are packed into groups of thousands, and so forth.

An easy way to understand number systems is to think of the numbers as being packaged for shipping, into boxes, cartons, crates, truckloads, and so on. For the decimal numbering system, consider packing widgets (units) into boxes (tens), which are packed into cartons (100s), which are packed into crates (1000s), and so forth. The same analogy works for binary, hexadecimal, and all other number systems.

Our friend Joe, in Figure C-1, is a widget packer in the shipping department of the ACE Widget Co. Joe can ship single widgets, or he can pack them in boxes, cartons, crates, and truckloads. He can fit three, and only three, widgets to a box; only three boxes into one carton ($3 \times 3 = 9$ widgets); only three cartons into one crate ($3 \times 9 = 27$ widgets); and only three crates into one truck ($3 \times 27 = 81$ widgets). He is not allowed to pack more widgets into boxes, cartons, crates, or truckloads than those specified. Neither is he allowed to send out a box, carton, crate, or truckload that is not completely filled.

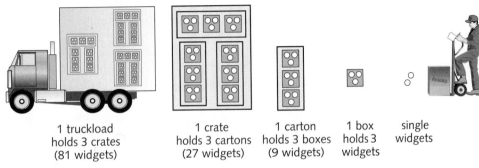

1 truckload
holds 3 crates
(81 widgets)

1 crate
holds 3 cartons
(27 widgets)

1 carton
holds 3 boxes
(9 widgets)

1 box
holds 3
widgets

single
widgets

Figure C-1   Joe in the shipping department groups widgets in singles, boxes, cartons, crates, and truckloads—all in groups of three

Joe receives an order to ship out 197 widgets. How does he ship them? The answer is shown in Figure C-2. Joe sends out 197 widgets grouped into 2 truckloads ($2 \times 81 = 162$ widgets), 1 crate (27 widgets), no cartons, 2 boxes ($2 \times 3 = 6$ widgets), and 2 single widgets. We can write this grouping of widgets as 21022, where the "place values" from left to right are truckloads, crates, cartons, boxes, and units, which in this case are (in decimal) 162 widgets, 27 widgets, 0 widgets, 6 widgets, and 2 widgets. Notice that each "place value" in our widget-packing system is a multiple of 3, because the widgets are grouped into three before they are packed into boxes; the boxes are grouped into three before they are packed into cartons, and so on. By grouping the widgets into groups of 3s in this manner, we converted the decimal number (base 10) 197 into the ternary number (base 3) 21022. Joe's widget-packing method is a base three, or ternary, system. The numerals in the ternary number system are 0, 1, and 2. When you get to the next value after 2, instead of counting on up to 3, you move one place value to the left and begin again with 1 in that position, which represents 3. So, counting in base 3 goes like this: 0, 1, 2, 10, 11, 12, 20, 21, 22, 100, 101, and so on. This is the same as Joe's never shipping out three of any one group unless they are packed together into one larger group. For example, Joe wouldn't ship three individual boxes, he would ship one carton.

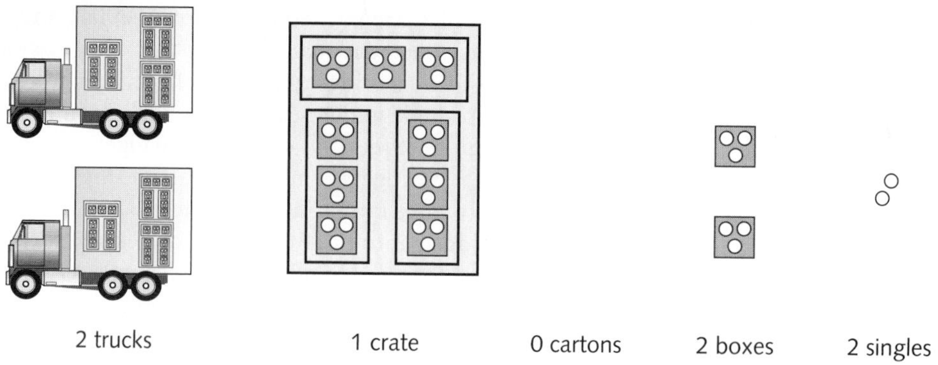

2 trucks   1 crate   0 cartons   2 boxes   2 singles

Figure C-2 Joe's shipment of 197 widgets: 2 truckloads, 1 crate, 0 cartons, 2 boxes, and a group of 2 singles

You can easily apply the widget-packing analogy to another base. If Joe used 10 instead of three, he would be using base 10 (decimal) rules. So, numbering systems differ by the different numbers of units they group together. In the hex number system, we group by 16. So, if Joe were shipping in groups of 16, as in Figure C-3, single widgets could be shipped out up to 15, but 16 widgets would make one box. Sixteen boxes would make one carton, which would contain 16 × 16, or 256, widgets. Sixteen cartons would make one crate, which would contain 16 × 256, or 4096, widgets.

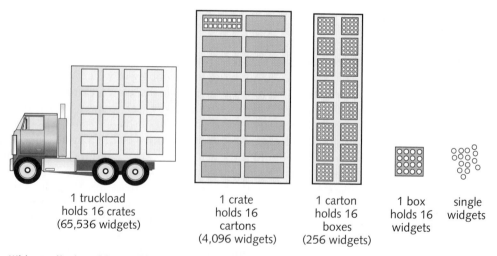

1 truckload
holds 16 crates
(65,536 widgets)

1 crate
holds 16
cartons
(4,096 widgets)

1 carton
holds 16
boxes
(256 widgets)

1 box
holds 16
widgets

single
widgets

Figure C-3 Widgets displayed in truckloads, crates, cartons, boxes, and singles grouped in 16s

Suppose Joe receives an order for 197 widgets to be packed in groups of 16. He will not be able to fill a carton (256 widgets), so he ships out 12 boxes (16 widgets each) and five single widgets:

12 × 16 = 192, and 192 + 5 = 197

You approach an obstacle if you attempt to write the number in hex. How are you going to express 12 boxes and 5 singles? In hex, you need single numerals to represent the numbers 10, 11, 12, 13, 14, and 15 in decimal. Hex uses the letters A through F for the numbers 10 through 15. Table C-2 shows values expressed in the decimal, hex, and binary numbering systems. In the second column in Table C-2, you are counting in the hex number system. For example, 12 is represented with a C. So you say that Joe packs C boxes and 5 singles. The hex number for decimal 197 is C5 (see Figure C-4).

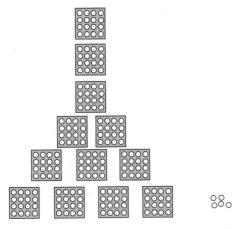

Figure C-4   Hex C5 represented as C boxes and 5 singles = 197 decimal

Decimal	Hex	Binary	Decimal	Hex	Binary	Decimal	Hex	Binary
0	0	0	14	E	1110	28	1C	11100
1	1	1	15	F	1111	29	1D	11101
2	2	10	16	10	10000	30	1E	11110
3	3	11	17	11	10001	31	1F	11111
4	4	100	18	12	10010	32	20	100000
5	5	101	19	13	10011	33	21	100001
6	6	110	20	14	10100	34	22	100010
7	7	111	21	15	10101	35	23	100011

Table C-2 (continued)

Decimal	Hex	Binary	Decimal	Hex	Binary	Decimal	Hex	Binary
8	8	1000	22	16	10110	36	24	100100
9	9	1001	23	17	10111	37	25	100101
10	A	1010	24	18	11000	38	26	100110
11	B	1011	25	19	11001	39	27	100111
12	C	1100	26	1A	11010	40	28	101000
13	D	1101	27	1B	11011			

Table C-2   Decimal, hex, and binary values

For a little practice, calculate the hex values of the decimal values 14, 259, 75, and 1024 and the decimal values of FFh and A11h.

How Exponents Are Used to Express Place Value

If you are comfortable with using exponents, you know that writing numbers raised to a power is the same as multiplying that number by itself the power number of times. For example, $3^4 = 3 \times 3 \times 3 \times 3 = 81$. Using exponents in expressing numbers can also help us easily see place value, because the place value for each place is really the base number multiplied by itself a number of times, based on the place value position. For instance, look back at Figure C-1. A truckload is really $3 \times 3 \times 3 \times 3$, or 81, units, which can be written as 34. A crate is really $3 \times 3 \times 3$, or 27, units. The numbers in Figure C-1 can therefore be written like this:

Truckload = 3^4 Crate = 3^3 Carton = 3^2 Box = 3^1 Single = 3^0

(Any number raised to the 0 power equals 1.) Therefore, we can express the numbers in Figure C-2 as multiples of truckloads, crates, cartons, boxes, and singles like this:

	Truckloads	Crates	Cartons	Boxes	Singles
21022 (base 3)	2×3^4	1×3^3	0×3^2	2×3^1	2×3^0
Decimal equivalent	162	27	0	6	2

When we sum up the numbers in the last row above, we get 197. We just converted a base 3 number (21022) to a base 10 number (197).

Binary Number System

It was stated earlier that it is easier for computers to convert from binary to hex or from hex to binary than to convert between binary and decimal. Let's see just how easy. Recall that the binary number system only has two numerals, or bits: 0 and 1. If our friend Joe in shipping operated a "binary" shipping system, he would pack like this: 2 widgets in a box, 2 boxes in one carton (4 widgets), two cartons in one crate (8 widgets), and two crates in one truckload (16 widgets). In Figure C-5, Joe is asked to pack 13 widgets. He packs 1 crate (8 widgets), 1 carton (4 widgets), no boxes, and 1 single. The number 13 in binary is 1101:

$$(1 \times 2^3) + (1 \times 2^2) + (0 \times 2^1) + (1 \times 2^0) = 8 + 4 + 0 + 1 = 13$$

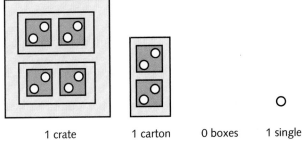

1 crate	1 carton	0 boxes	1 single

Figure C-5   Binary 1101 = 13 displayed as crates, cartons, boxes, and singles

Now let's see how to convert binary to hex and back again. The largest 4-bit number in binary is 1111. This number in decimal and hex is:

```
binary 1111 = 1 group of 8 = 8
              1 group of 4 = 4
              1 group of 2 = 2
                  1 single = 1

                     TOTAL = 15 (decimal)
     Therefore, 1111 (binary) = 15 (decimal) = F (hex)
```

This last calculation is very important when working with computers: F is the largest numeral in the hex number system and it only takes 4 bits to write this largest hex numeral: F (hex) = 1111 (binary). So, every hex numeral (0, 1, 2, 3, 4, 5, 6, 7, 8, 9, A, B, C, D, E, and F) can be converted into a 4-bit binary number. Look back at the first 16 entries in Table C-2 for these binary values. Add leading zeroes to the binary numbers as necessary.

When converting from hex to binary, take each hex numeral and convert it to a 4-bit binary number, and string all the 4-bit groups together. Fortunately, when working with computers, you will almost never work with more than two hex numerals at a time. Here are some examples:

1. To convert hex F8 to binary, do the following: F = 1111, and 8 = 1000. There-fore, F8 = 11111000 (usually written 1111 1000).

2. To convert hex 9A to binary, do the following: 9 = 1001, and A = 1010. There-fore, 9A = 1001 1010.

Now try converting from binary to hex:

1. To convert binary 101110 to hex, first group the bits in groups of 4, starting at the right and moving left, adding leading zeroes as necessary: 0010 1110.

2. Then convert each group of 4 bits in binary to a single hex numeral: 0010 = 2, and 1110 = E. The hex number is 2E.

Writing Conventions

Sometimes when you are dealing with hex, binary, and decimal numbers, it is not always clear which number system is being used. If you see a letter in the number, you know the number is a hex number. Binary numbers are usually written in groups of four bits. Sometimes a hex number is preceded by 0x, as in 0xFF. This book fol-lows the convention of placing a lowercase h after a hex number, like this: 2Eh.

Memory Addressing

Computers often display memory addresses in the hex number system. You must either "think in hex" or convert to decimal. It's really easier, with a little practice, to think in hex. Here's the way it works:

Memory addresses are displayed as two hex numbers. An example is C800:5.

The part to the left of the colon (C800) is called the *segment address*, and the part to the right of the colon (5) is called the *offset*. The offset value can have as many as four hex digits. The actual memory address is calculated by adding a zero to the right of the segment address and adding the offset value, like this:

C800:5 = C8000 + 5 = C8005.

The first 640K of Windows 9x or DOS memory is called conventional memory. Look at how that memory is addressed, first in decimal and then in hex (assuming 1 kilobyte = 1024 bytes):

640K = 640 × 1024 = 655,360

There are 655,360 memory addresses in conventional memory, where each mem-ory address can hold 1 byte, or 8 bits, of either data or program instructions. The decimal value 655,360 converted to hex is A0000 (10×16^4). So, conventional mem-ory addresses begin with 00000h and end with A0000h minus 1h or 9FFFFh.

Written in segment-and-offset form, conventional memory addresses range from 0000:0 to 9FFF:F.

Recall that upper memory is defined as the memory addresses from 640K to 1024K. The next address after 9FFF:F is the first address of upper memory, which is A0000, and the last address is FFFFF. Written in segment-and-offset terms, upper memory addresses range from A000:0 to FFFF:F.

Here is one way to organize the conversion of a large hex value such as FFFFF to decimal (remember F in hex equals 15 in decimal).

FFFFF converted to decimal:

```
15 × 16⁰ = 15 × 1 =                15
15 × 16¹ = 15 × 16 =              240
15 × 16² = 15 × 256 =          3,840
15 × 16³ = 15 × 4096 =        61,440
15 × 16⁴ = 15 × 65,536 =     983,040

            TOTAL = 1,048,575
```

Remember that FFFFF is the last memory address in upper memory. The very next memory address is the first address of extended memory, which is defined as memory above 1 MB. If you add 1 to the number above, you get 1,048,576, which is equal to 1024 × 1024, which is the definition of 1 megabyte.

Displaying Memory with DOS DEBUG

In Figure C-6 you see the results of the beginning of upper memory displayed. The DOS DEBUG command displays the contents of memory. Memory addresses are displayed in hex segment-and-offset values. To enter DEBUG, type the following command at the C prompt and press Enter:

```
C:\> DEBUG
```

You create a memory "dump" when you tell the system to record the contents of memory to a file or display it onscreen; a dump can be useful when troubleshooting. Type the following dump command to display the beginning of upper memory (the hyphen in the command is the DEBUG command prompt) and press Enter:

```
-d A000:0
```

Memory is displayed showing 16 bytes on each line. The A area of memory (the beginning of upper memory) is not used unless the computer is using a monochrome monitor or this area is being used as an upper memory block. In Figure C-6, the area contains nothing but continuous 1s in binary or Fs in hex. The ASCII interpretation is on the right side. To view the next group of memory addresses, you can type *d* at the hyphen and press Enter. DEBUG displays the next 128 addresses.

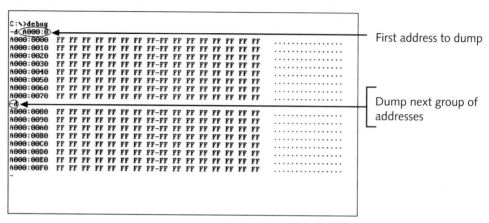

Figure C-6   Memory dump: -d A000:0

The A and B ranges of upper memory addresses (upper memory addresses that begin with A or B when written in hex) are used for monochrome monitors. The C range contains the video BIOS for a color monitor. Figure C-7 shows the dump of the beginning of the C range.

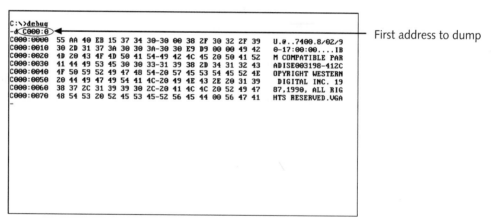

Figure C-7   Memory dump: -d C000:0

There is more than one way—in fact there are many ways—to identify the same segment-and-offset value. Try these commands to display the same upper memory addresses:

```
-d C000:0
-d BFF1:00F0
-d BFFF:0010
-d BEEE:1120
```

In summary, reading and understanding binary and hex numbers are essential skills for managing computers. All data is stored in binary in a computer and is often displayed in hex. Memory addresses are often displayed in hex segment-and-offset terms. An address in memory can be written in a variety of segment-and-offset values. The actual memory address is calculated by placing one zero to the right side of the segment address and adding the resulting value to the offset value. To exit DEBUG, type *q* for quit and press Enter at the hyphen prompt.

Fat Details

This appendix gives you the details of the FAT file system. The FAT file system for a floppy disk or HDD logical drive uses a boot record, FAT, and root directory table. The layout of each of these items is described, as well as how they work together.

OS Boot Record

An OS boot record at the beginning of a floppy disk or volume (logical drive) is used during the boot process to inform the OS how the disk or volume is organized. If the disk or volume is the boot device, the boot program at the end of the boot record loads the first Windows hidden file, Io.sys, or Ntldr. Table D-1 shows the complete layout for the boot record.

The eleventh item in Table D-1 is the number of heads, which is the number of surfaces allocated for the volume. The top and bottom of each disk equal two surfaces or heads. For a floppy disk, the number of heads is always two. The medium descriptor byte tells the OS what type of disk this is. Table D-2 gives the values of this descriptor byte.

Description	Number of Bytes
Machine code	11
Bytes per sector	2
Sectors per cluster	1
Reserved	2
Number of FATs	1
Number of root directory entries	2
Number of logical sectors	2
Medium descriptor byte	1
Sectors per FAT	2

Table D-1 (continued)

Description	Number of Bytes
Sectors per track	2
Heads	2
Number of hidden sectors	2
Total sectors in logical volume	4
Physical drive number	1
Reserved	1
Extended boot signature record	1
32-bit binary volume ID	4
Volume label	11
Type of file system (FAT12, FAT16, or FAT32)	8
Program to load operating system (bootstrap loader)	Remainder of the sector

Table D-1   Layout of the boot record on each logical drive or floppy disk

Disk Type	Descriptor Byte
3½-inch double-density floppy disk, 720K	F9
3½-inch high-density floppy disk, 1.44 MB	F0
Hard disk	F8

Table D-2   Disk type and descriptor byte

Root Directory Table

The root directory contains information about each file and subdirectory stored in it. Each directory entry is 32 bytes long, although only 22 bytes are used. Table D-3 lists how the 22 bytes are used. Although earlier versions of Windows did limit the number of entries in the root directory for a hard drive, Windows 98 and later Windows OSs do not. Note, however, that Microsoft recommends that you keep only about 150 entries in any one directory. Having any more entries slows access to the directory. A 3½-inch high-density floppy disk can have up to 224 entries in the root directory.

Root Directory	Bytes Usage
8	Name of file
3	File extension
1	Attribute byte (special meaning for each bit)
10	Not used
2	Time of creation or last update
2	Date of creation or last update
2	Starting cluster number in binary
4	Size of file in binary

Table D-3   Root directory information for each file

Note that the root directory has no provision for the period (often referred to as "dot") that we normally see between the filename and the file extension in OS command lines. The period is not stored in directories but is only used in OS command lines to indicate where the filename ends and the file extension begins.

File attributes are used for various purposes. One file attribute byte is broken into bits, and each bit has a specific meaning. The first two bits are not used. Table D-4 lists the meanings of the other six bits, beginning with the leftmost bit in the byte and moving to the right. Several of these bits can be changed using the Attrib command or Windows Explorer.

Bit	Description	Bit = 0	Bit = 1
1, 2	Not used		
3	Archive bit	Not to be archived	To be archived
4	Directory status	File	Subdirectory
5	Volume label	Not volume label	Is volume label
6	System file	Not system file	Is system file
7	Hidden file	Not hidden	Hidden
8	Read-only file	Read/write	Read-only

Table D-4   Meaning of each bit in the directory attribute byte for each file (reading from left to right across the byte)

NOTE

Bit 3, the archive bit, is a switch used to indicate whether the file has changed since the last backup and should be backed up next time a backup is made.

How the OS Uses the FAT and Directory Table

Notice that the root directory contains only the starting cluster number. To find out what other clusters store the file, look in the file allocation table. For example, suppose a file named Mydata.txt begins at cluster 5 and requires three clusters to hold the file. The OS takes the following steps to read the file. (The first three are numbered in Figure D-1.)

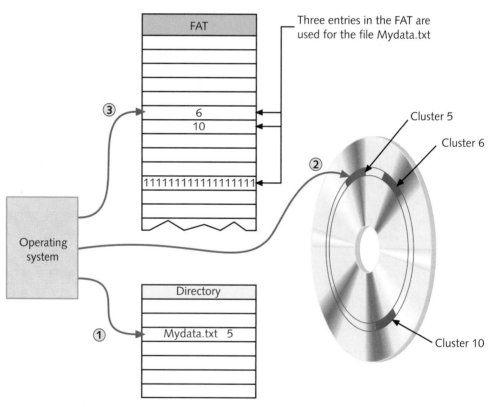

Figure D-1 How an OS reads a file from the hard drive or a floppy disk

1. The OS goes to the root directory and reads the name of the file (Mydata.txt) and the first cluster number (5).

2. The OS retrieves the contents of cluster 5 on the floppy disk, which is the first segment of the file.

3. The OS turns to the FAT, looks at the fifth position in the FAT, and reads 6, which says the next segment of the file is in cluster 6.

4. It retrieves the second segment of the file from cluster 6 on the floppy disk.

5. The OS turns to the sixth position in the FAT and reads 10, which says the next segment of the file is in cluster 10.

6. It retrieves the third segment of the file from cluster 10 on the floppy disk.

7. The OS turns to the tenth position in the FAT and reads all 1s in the FAT entry, which says this is the last cluster in the file. (If the FAT is FAT16, then an entry of 16 ones is written in the FAT. If it is FAT32, then an entry of 28 ones is written.)

NOTE By dividing the size of a file by the number of bytes per cluster and rounding up to the nearest whole number, you can determine how many clusters the file occupies.

The root directory and all subdirectories contain the same information about each file. Only the root directory has a limitation on the number of entries. Subdirectories can have as many entries as disk space allows. Because long filenames require more room in a directory than short filenames, assigning long filenames reduces the number of files that can be stored in the root directory.

The Professional PC Technician

As a professional PC technician, you can manage your career by staying abreast of new technology and striving for top professional certifications. In addition, you should maintain excellent customer relationships, behave with professionalism, and seek opportunities for joining professional organizations. As you know, PC technicians provide service to customers over the phone or online, in person on-site, and sometimes in a shop where they have little customer contact. Although each setting poses specific challenges, almost all of the recommendations in this appendix apply across the board.

What Customers Want: Beyond Technical Know-How

Probably the most significant indication that a PC technician is doing a good job is that customers are consistently satisfied. You should provide excellent service and treat customers as you would want to be treated in a similar situation. One of the most important ways to achieve customer satisfaction is to do your best by being prepared, both technically and nontechnically. Being prepared includes knowing what customers want, what they don't like, and what they expect from a PC technician.

Your customers can be "internal" (you both work for the same company) or "external" (your customers come to you or your company for service). Customers can be highly technical or technically naive, represent a large company or simply own a home PC, be prompt or slow at paying their bills, want only the best (and be willing to pay for it) or be searching for bargain service, be friendly and easy to work with or demanding and condescending. In each situation, the key to success is always the same: Don't allow circumstances or personalities to affect your commitment to excellence.

The following traits distinguish one competent technician from another in the eyes of the customer.

- *Have a positive and helpful attitude.* This helps to establish good customer relationships.
- *Own the problem.* Taking ownership of the customer's problem builds trust and loyalty, because the customer knows you can be counted on.
- *Be dependable.* Customers appreciate those who do as they say. If you promise to be back at 10:00 the next morning, be back at 10:00 the next morning.

If you cannot keep your appointment, never ignore your promise. Call, apologize, let the customer know what happened, and reschedule your appointment.

- *Be customer-focused.* When you're working with or talking to a customer, focus on him or her. Make it your job to satisfy this person, not just your organization, your boss, your bank account, or the customer's boss.
- *Be credible.* Convey confidence to your customers. Being credible means being technically competent and knowing how to do your job well, but credible technicians also know when the job is beyond their expertise and when to ask for help.
- *Maintain integrity and honesty.* Don't try to hide your mistakes from your customer or your boss. Everyone makes mistakes, but don't compound them by a lack of integrity. Accept responsibility and do what you can to correct the error.
- *Know the law with respect to your work.* For instance, observe the laws concerning the use of software. Don't use or install pirated software.
- *Act professionally.* Customers want a technician to look and behave professionally. Dress appropriately for the environment. Consider yourself a guest at the customer's site.
- *Perform your work in a professional manner.* If a customer is angry, allow the customer to vent, keeping your own professional distance. (You do, however, have the right to expect a customer not to talk to you in an abusive way.)

Support Calls: Providing Good Service

Customers want good service. Even though each customer is different and might expect different results, the following characteristics constitute good service in the eyes of most customers.

- The technician responds and completes the work within a reasonable time.
- For on-site visits, the technician is prepared for the service call.
- The work is done right the first time.
- The price for the work is reasonable and competitive.
- The technician exhibits good interpersonal skills.
- If the work extends beyond a brief on-site visit or phone call, the technician keeps the customer informed about the progress of the work.

Planning for Good Service

Whether you support PCs on the phone or online, on-site, or in a shop, you need a plan to follow when you approach a service call. This section surveys the entire service situation, from the first contact with the customer to closing the call. Follow these general guidelines when supporting computers and their users:

- Almost every support project starts with a phone call. Follow company policies to obtain the specific information you should take when answering an initial call.
- Don't assume that an on-site visit is necessary until you have asked questions to identify the problem and asked the caller to check and try some simple things while on the phone with you. For example, the customer can check cable connections, power, and monitor settings, and can look for POST error messages.
- Be familiar with your company's customer service policies. You might need to refer questions about warranties, licenses, documentation, or procedures to other support personnel or customer relations personnel. Your organization might not want you to answer some questions, such as questions about upcoming releases of software or new products, or questions about your personal or company experience with supporting particular hardware or software.
- After reviewing your company's service policies, begin troubleshooting. Take notes, and then interview the customer about the problem so you understand it thoroughly. Have the customer reproduce the problem, and carefully note each step taken and its results. This process gives you clues about the problem and about the customer's technical proficiency, which helps you know how to communicate with the customer.
- Search for answers. If the answers to specific questions or problems are not evident, become a researcher. Learn to use online documentation, expert systems, and other resources that your company provides.
- Use your troubleshooting skills. Isolate the problem. Check for user errors. What works and what doesn't work? What has changed since the system last worked? Reduce the system to its essentials. Check the simple things first. Use the troubleshooting guidelines throughout this book to help you think of approaches to test and try.
- If you have given the problem your best, but still haven't solved it, ask for help. You learn when to ask for help from experience. Once you have made a reasonable effort to help, and it seems clear that you are unlikely to be successful, don't waste a customer's time.
- After a call, create a written record to build your own knowledge base. Record the initial symptoms of the problem, the source of the problem you actually discovered, how you made that discovery, and how the problem was finally solved. File your documentation according to symptoms or according to solutions.

Making an On-site Service Call

When a technician makes an on-site service call, customers expect him or her to have both technical and interpersonal skills. Prepare for a service call by reviewing information given you by whomever took the call. Know the problem you are going to address, the urgency of the situation, and what computer, software, and hardware needs servicing. Arrive with a complete set of equipment appropriate to the visit, which might include a tool kit, flashlight, multimeter, grounding strap and mat, and bootable disks that have been scanned for viruses.

Set a realistic time for the appointment (one that you can expect to keep) and arrive on time. When you arrive at the customer's site, greet the customer in a friendly manner. Use Mr. or Ms. and last names rather than first names when addressing the customer, unless you are certain that the customer expects you to use first names. The first thing you should do is listen; save the paperwork for later.

As you work, be as unobtrusive as possible. Don't make a big mess. Keep your tools and papers out of the customer's way. Don't use the phone or sit in the customer's desk chair without permission. If the customer needs to work while you are present, do whatever is necessary to accommodate that.

Keep the customer informed. Once you have collected enough information, explain the problem and what you must do to fix it, giving as many details as the customer wants. When a customer must make a choice, state the options in a way that does not unfairly favor the solution that makes the most money for you as the technician or for your company.

After you have solved the problem:

- Allow the customer time to be fully satisfied that all is working before you close the call. Does the printer work? Print a test page. Does the network connection work? Can the customer log on to the network and access data on it?
- If you changed anything on the PC after you booted it, reboot one more time to make sure that you have not caused a problem with the boot.
- Review the service call with the customer. Summarize the instructions and explanations you have given during the call. This is an appropriate time to fill out your paperwork and explain to the customer what you have written.
- Explain preventive maintenance to the customer (such as deleting temporary files from the hard drive or cleaning the mouse). Most customers don't have preventive maintenance contracts for their PCs and appreciate the time you take to show them how they can take better care of their computers.

Phone Support

When someone calls asking for support, you must control the call, especially at the beginning. Follow these steps at the beginning of a service call:

- Identify yourself and your organization. (Follow the guidelines of your employer as to what to say.)
- Ask for and write down the name and phone number of the caller. Ask for spelling if necessary. If your help desk supports businesses, get the name of the business that the caller represents.

- Your company might require that you obtain a licensing or warranty number to determine if the customer is entitled to receive your support free of charge, or that you obtain a credit card number, if the customer is paying by the call. Get whatever information you need at this point to determine that you should be the one to provide service, before you start to address the problem.
- Open up the conversation for the caller to describe the problem.

Phone support requires more interaction with customers than any other type of PC support. To give clear instructions, you must be able to visualize what the customer sees at his or her PC. Patience is required if the customer must be told each key to press or command button to click. Help desk support requires excellent communication skills, good phone manners, and lots of patience. As your help desk skills improve, you will learn to think through the process as though you were sitting in front of the PC yourself. Drawing diagrams and taking notes as you talk can be very helpful.

If you spend many hours on the phone at a help desk, use a headset instead of a regular phone to reduce strain on your ears and neck. If your call is accidentally disconnected, call back immediately. Don't eat or drink while on the phone. If you must put callers on hold, tell them how long it will be before you get back to them. Don't complain about your job, your company, or other companies or products to your customers. A little small talk is okay and is sometimes beneficial in easing a tense situation, but keep it upbeat and positive. As with on-site service calls, let the user make sure that all is working before you close the phone call. If you end the call too soon and the problem is not completely resolved, the customer can be frustrated, especially if it is difficult to contact you again.

When the Customer Is Not Knowledgeable

A help desk call is the most difficult situation to handle when a customer is not knowledgeable about how to use a computer. When on-site, you can put a PC in good repair without depending on a customer to help you, but when you are trying to solve a problem over the phone, with a customer as your only eyes, ears, and hands, a computer-illiterate user can present a challenge. Here are some tips for handling this situation:

- Don't use computer jargon while talking. For example, instead of saying, "Open Windows Explorer," say, "Using your mouse, right-click the Start button and select Explore from the menu."
- Don't ask the customer to do something that might destroy settings or files without first having the customer back them up carefully. If you think the customer can't handle your request, then ask for some on-site help.
- Frequently ask the customer what the screen displays to help you track the keystrokes and action.
- Follow along at your own PC. It's easier to direct the customer, keystroke by keystroke, if you are doing the same things.
- Give the customer plenty of opportunity to ask questions.

- Compliment the customer whenever you can, to help the customer gain confidence.
- If you determine that the customer cannot help you solve the problem without a lot of coaching, you may need to tactfully request that the caller have someone with more experience call you.

NOTE

When solving computer problems in an organization other than your own, check with technical support instead of working only with the PC user. The user may not be aware of policies that have been set on the PC to prevent changes to the OS, hardware, or applications.

When the Customer Is Overly Confident

Sometimes customers are proud of their computer knowledge. Such customers may want to give advice, take charge of a call, withhold information they think you don't need to know, or execute commands at the computer without letting you know, so that you don't have enough information to follow along. A situation like this must be handled with tact and respect for the customer. Here are a few tips:

- When you can, compliment the customer's knowledge, experience, or insight.
- Ask the customer's advice. Say something like, "What do you think the problem is?" (However, don't ask this question of customers who are not confident, because they most likely don't have the answer and might lose confidence in you.)
- Slow the conversation down. You can say, "Please slow down. You're moving too fast for me to follow. Help me understand."
- Don't back off from using problem-solving skills. You must still have the customer check the simple things, but direct the conversation with tact. For example, you can say, "I know you've probably already gone over these simple things, but could we just do them again together?"
- Be careful not to accuse the customer of making a mistake.
- Use technical language in a way that conveys that you expect the customer to understand you.

When the Customer Complains

When you are on-site or on the phone, a customer might complain to you about your organization, products, or service, or the service and product of another company. Consider the complaint to be helpful feedback that can lead to a better product or service and better customer relationships. Here are a few suggestions on how to handle complaints and customer anger:

- Be an active listener, and let customers know that they are not being ignored. Look for the underlying problem. Don't take the complaint or the anger personally.
- Give the customer a little time to vent, and apologize when you can. Then start the conversation from the beginning, asking questions, taking notes, and

solving problems. If this helps, don't spend a lot of time finding out exactly who the customer dealt with and what happened to upset the customer.

■ Don't be defensive. It's better to leave the customer with the impression that you and your company are listening and willing to admit mistakes.

■ If the customer is complaining about a product or service that is not from your company, don't start off by saying, "That's not our problem." Instead, listen to the customer complain. Don't appear as though you don't care.

■ If the complaint is against you or your product, identify the underlying problem if you can. Ask questions and take notes. Then pass these notes on to people in your organization who need to know.

■ Sometimes simply making progress or reducing the problem to a manageable state reduces the customer's anxiety. As you are talking to a customer, summarize what you have both agreed on or observed so far in the conversation.

■ Point out ways that you think communication could be improved. For example, you might say, "I'm sorry, but I'm having trouble understanding what you want. Could you please slow down, and let's take this one step at a time."

When the Customer Does Not Want to End a Phone Call

Some customers like to talk and don't want to end a phone call. In this situation, when you have finished the work and are ready to hang up, you can ease the caller into the end of the call. Ask if anything needs more explanation. Briefly summarize the main points of the call, and then say something like, "That about does it. Call if you need more help." Be silent about new issues. Answer only with "yes" or "no." Don't take the bait by engaging in a new topic. Don't get frustrated. As a last resort, you can say, "I'm sorry, but I must go now."

When You Can't Solve the Problem

You are not going to solve every computer problem you encounter. Knowing how to escalate a problem to those higher in the support chain is one of the first things you should learn on a new job. When escalation involves the customer, generally follow these guidelines:

■ Before you escalate, first ask knowledgeable co-workers for suggestions for solving the problem, which might save you and your customer the time and effort it takes to escalate it.

■ Know your company's policy for escalation. What documents do you fill out? Who gets them? Do you remain the responsible "support" party, or does the person now addressing the problem become the new contact? Are you expected to keep in touch with the customer and the problem, or are you totally out of the picture?

■ Document the escalation. It's very important to include the detailed steps necessary to reproduce the problem, which can save the next support person lots of time.

- Pass the problem on according to the proper channels of your organization. This might mean a phone call, an online entry in a database, or an email message.
- Tell the customer that you are passing the problem on to someone who is more experienced and has access to more extensive resources. In most cases, the person who receives the escalation will immediately contact the customer and assume responsibility for the problem. However, you should follow through, at least to confirm that the new person and the customer have made contact.
- If you check back with the customer only to find out that the other support person has not called or followed through to the customer's satisfaction, don't lay blame or point fingers. Just do whatever you can to help within your company guidelines. Your call to the customer will go a long way toward helping the situation.

Recordkeeping and Information Tools

If you work for a service organization, it will probably have most of the tools you need to do your job, including forms, online recordkeeping, procedures, and manuals. In some cases, help desk support personnel may have software to help them do their jobs, such as programs that support the remote control of customers' PCs (one example is pcAnywhere), an online help utility, or a problem-solving tool developed specifically for their help desk.

Several types of resources, records, and information tools can help you support PCs, such as the following:

- Specific software or hardware that you support must be available to you to test, observe, study, and use to re-create a customer's problem whenever possible.
- You should have a copy of—and be familiar with—the same documentation that the user sees.
- Hardware and software products generally have more technical documentation than just a user manual. A company should make this technical documentation available to you when you support its product.
- Online help targeted to field technicians and help desk technicians is often available for a product. This online help will probably include a search engine that searches by topics, words, error messages, and the like.
- Expert systems software is designed and written to help solve problems. It uses databases of known facts and rules to simulate human experts' reasoning and decision-making. Expert systems for PC technicians work by posing questions about a problem, to be answered either by the technician or the customer. The response to each question triggers another question from the software, until the

expert system arrives at a possible solution or solutions. Many expert systems are "intelligent," meaning that the system will record your input and use it in subsequent sessions to select more questions to ask and approaches to try.

- Call tracking can be done online or on paper. Most organizations have a call-tracking system that tracks (1) the date, time, and length of help desk or on-site calls, (2) causes of and solutions to problems already addressed, (3) who did what, and when, and (4) how each call was officially resolved. Call-tracking software or documents can also help to escalate calls when necessary and track the escalation.

Professional Organizations and Certifications

The work done by PC technicians has been viewed as a profession only within the past few years. The most significant certifying organization for PC technicians is the Computing Technology Industry Association (CompTIA, pronounced "comp-TEE-a"). CompTIA sponsors the A+ Certification Program and manages the A+ Service Technician Certification Examination, which measures the knowledge of job tasks and behavior expected of entry-level technicians. To become certified, you must pass two test modules: the A+ Core Hardware exam and the A+ Operating System Technologies exam. A+ Certification has industry recognition, so it should be your first choice for certification as a PC technician. As evidence of this industry recognition, these companies now include A+ Certification in their requirements for employment:

- ENTEX Information Services requires that all service employees have A+ Certification.
- GE Capital Services requires that all service employees have A+ Certification one year after hire.
- Okidata requires that all field service technicians have A+ Certification.
- Packard Bell requires all employees to be A+ certified within 90 days of hire.

Some other organizations where A+ Certification is mandatory are Aetna U.S. Healthcare; BancTec, Inc.; Computer Data, Inc.; Computer Sciences Corp.; Delta Airlines; Dow Jones & Company; the FBI; the U.S. Department of Justice; Gateway; Tandy Corporation; TSS IBM; US Airways; and Wang.

CompTIA has over 13,000 members from every major company that manufactures, distributes, or publishes computer-related products and services. For more information about CompTIA and A+ Certification, see the CompTIA Web site at *www.comptia.org*.

Other certifications are more vendor-specific. For example, Microsoft, Novell, and Cisco offer certifications to use and support their products. These are excellent choices for additional certifications when your career plan is to focus on these products.

Why Certification?

Many people work as PC technicians without any formal classroom training or certification. However, by having certification or an advanced technical degree, you prove to yourself, your customers, and your employers that you are prepared to do the work and are committed to being educated in your chosen profession. Certification and advanced degrees serve as recognized proof of competence and achievement, improve your job opportunities, create a higher level of customer confidence, and often qualify you for other training or degrees.

In addition to becoming certified and seeking advanced degrees, the professional PC technician should also stay abreast of new technology. Helpful resources include on-the-job training, books, magazines, the Internet, trade shows, interaction with colleagues, seminars, and workshops. Probably the best-known trade show is COMDEX and Windows World, where you can view the latest technology, hear industry leaders speak, and network with vast numbers of organizations and people. For more information about COMDEX and Windows World, see the Web site *www.comdex.com.*

Protecting Software Copyrights

As a computer support technician, you will be faced with the legal issues and practices surrounding the distribution of software. When someone purchases software from a software vendor, that person has only purchased a license for the software, which is the right to use it. The buyer does not legally *own* the software, and therefore does not have the right to distribute it. The right to copy the work, called a copyright, belongs to the creator of the work or others to whom the creator transfers this right.

As a PC technician you will be called upon to install, upgrade, and customize software. You need to know your responsibilities in upholding the law, especially as it applies to software copyrights. Copyrights are intended to legally protect the intellectual property rights of organizations or individuals to creative works, which include books, images, and software. While the originator of a creative work is the original owner of a copyright, the copyright can be transferred from one entity to another.

The Federal Copyright Act of 1976 was designed in part to protect software copyrights by requiring that only legally obtained copies of software be used; the law also allows for one backup copy of software to be made. Making unauthorized copies of original software violates the Federal Copyright Act of 1976, and is called software piracy, or more officially, software copyright infringement. Making a copy of software and then selling it or giving it away is a violation of the law. Because it is so easy to do, and because so many people do it, many people don't realize that it's illegal. Normally, only the person who violated the copyright law is liable for infringement; however, in some cases, an employer or supervisor is also held responsible, even when the copies were made without the employer's knowledge.

The Business Software Alliance (a membership organization of software manufacturers and vendors) has estimated that 26 percent of the business software in the United States is obtained illegally.

Site licensing, whereby a company can purchase the right to use multiple copies of software, is a popular way for companies to provide software to employees. With this type of license, companies can distribute software to PCs from network servers or execute software directly off the server. Read the licensing agreement of any software to determine the terms of distribution.

One of two associations committed to the prevention of software piracy is the Software Information Industry Association, a nonprofit organization that educates the public and enforces copyright laws. Its Web address is *www.siia.net*, and its antipiracy hotline is 1-800-388-7478. Another organization is the Business Software Alliance, which manages the BSA Anti-Piracy Hotline at 1-888-NOPIRACY. The BSA can also be reached at its email address: *software@bsa.org*. Its Web site is *www.bsa.org*. These associations are made up of hundreds of software manufacturers and publishers in North and Latin America, Europe, and Asia. They promote software raids on large and small companies; in the United States, they receive the cooperation of the U.S. government to prosecute offenders.

What Does the Law Say?

The Federal Copyright Act of 1976 protects the exclusive rights of copyright holders. It gives legal users of software the right to make one backup copy. Other rights are based on what the copyright holder allows. In 1990, the U.S. Congress passed the Software Rental Amendment Act, which prevents the renting, leasing, lending, or sharing of software without the expressed written permission of the copyright holder. In 1992, Congress instituted criminal penalties for software copyright infringement, which include imprisonment for up to five years and/or fines of up to $250,000 for the unlawful reproduction or distribution of 10 or more copies of software.

What Are Your Responsibilities Under the Law?

Your first responsibility as an individual user is to use only software that has been purchased or licensed for your use. As an employee of a company that has a site license to use multiple copies of the software, your responsibility is to comply with the license agreement. It is also your responsibility to purchase only legitimate software. Purchasers of counterfeit or copied software face the risk of corrupted files, virus-infected disks, inadequate documentation, and lack of technical support and upgrades, as well as the legal penalties for using pirated software.

Glossary

This glossary defines the key terms listed at the end of each chapter and other terms related to managing and maintaining a personal computer.

16-bit mode — *See* real mode.

32-bit flat memory mode — A protected processing mode used by Windows NT/2000/XP to process programs written in 32-bit code early in the boot process.

32-bit mode — *See* protected mode.

822 messages — Error messages that occur during email transactions. 822 messages are named after RFC 822, which is the RFC that defines them.

ACPI (Advanced Configuration and Power Interface) — Specification developed by Intel, Compaq, Phoenix, Microsoft, and Toshiba to control power on notebooks and other devices. Windows 98 and Windows 2000/XP support ACPI.

Active Directory — A Windows 2000 and Windows 2003 directory database and service that allows for a single point of administration for all shared resources on a network, including files, peripheral devices, databases, Web sites, users, and services.

active partition — The primary partition on the hard drive that boots the OS. Windows NT/2000/XP calls the active partition the system partition.

adapter address — *See* MAC address.

administrator account — In Windows NT/2000/XP, an account that grants to the administrator(s) rights and permissions to all hardware and software resources, such as the right to add, delete, and change accounts and to change hardware configurations.

Advanced Options menu — A Windows 2000/XP menu that appears when you press F8 when Windows starts. The menu can be used to troubleshoot problems when loading Windows 2000/XP.

AGP (Accelerated Graphics Port) bus — A bus or slot on the motherboard used for a single video card.

allocation blocks — Sets of hard drive sectors used by a Macintosh computer where the Mac's file system stores files.

answer file — A text file that contains information that Windows NT/2000/XP requires in order to do an unattended installation.

antivirus (AV) software — Utility programs that prevent infection or scan a system to detect and remove viruses. McAfee Associates' VirusScan and Norton AntiVirus are two popular AV packages.

API (Application Program Interface) — *See* application program interface (API) call.

Apple menu — The Mac OS menu accessed by an apple icon in the upper-right corner of the desktop. The Apple menu contains options that are always available no matter what application you are in.

application program interface (API) call — A request from software to the OS to access hardware or other software using a previously defined procedure that both the software and the OS understand.

ARP (Address Resolution Protocol) — A protocol that TCP/IP uses to translate IP addresses into physical network addresses (MAC addresses).

Autoexec.bat — A startup text file once used by DOS and used by Windows 9x to provide backward-compatibility. It executes commands automatically during the boot process and is used to create a 16-bit environment.

Automated System Recovery (ASR) — The Windows XP process that allows you to restore an entire hard drive volume or logical drive to its state at the time the backup of the volume was made.

Automatic Private IP Address (APIPA) — An IP address in the address range 169.254.x.x, used by a computer when it cannot successfully lease an IP address from a DHCP server.

backup domain controller (BDC) — In Windows NT, a computer on a network that holds a read-only copy of the SAM (security accounts manager) database.

Backup Operator — A Windows 2000/XP user account that can back up and restore any files on the system regardless of its having access to these files.

backward-compatible — Refers to new hardware andsoftware that is able to support older, existing technologies. This is a common choice of hardware and software manufacturers.

baseline — The level of performance expected from a system, which can be compared to current measurements to determine what needs upgrading or tuning.

basic disk — A way to partition a hard drive, used by DOS and all versions of Windows, that stores information about the drive in a partition table at the beginning of the drive. Compare to dynamic disk.

batch file — A text file containing a series of OS commands. Autoexec.bat is a batch file.

best-effort protocol — *See* connectionless protocol.

binding — [new definition:] The process by which a protocol is associated with a network card or a modem card.

BIOS (basic input/output system) — Firmware that can control much of a computer's input/output functions, such as communication with the floppy drive and the monitor. Also called ROM BIOS.

block — *See* allocation blocks.

blue screen — A Windows NT/2000/XP error that displays against a blue screen and causes the system to halt. Also called a stop error.

bootable disk — For DOS and Windows, a floppy disk that can upload the OS files necessary for computer startup. For DOS or Windows 9x, it must contain the files Io.sys, Msdos.sys and Command.com.

boot blocks — The first two allocation blocks on a Macintosh computer's hard drive. They are initially empty, but once a System folder is installed on a computer, the boot blocks contain the location of the System folder so that the system can find and load the OS.

booting — The process that a computer goes through when it is first turned on to get itself ready to receive commands.

boot loader menu — A startup menu that gives the user the choice of which operating system to load such as Windows 98 or Windows XP which are both installed on the same system creating a dual boot.

boot partition — The hard drive partition where the Windows NT/2000/XP OS is stored. The system partition and the boot partition may be different partitions.

boot record — The first sector of a floppy disk or logical drive in a partition; it contains information about the disk or logical drive. On a hard drive, if the boot record is in the active partition, then it is used to boot the OS. Also called *boot sector*.

boot sector — *See* boot record.

boot sector virus — An infectious program that can replace the bootstrap loader program with a modified, infected version of the program, often causing boot and data retrieval problems.

bootstrap loader — A small program at the end of the boot record that can be used to boot an OS from the disk or logical drive.

bridging protocol — *See* line protocol.

Briefcase — A system folder in Windows 9x that is used to synchronize files between two computers.

buffer — A temporary memory area where data is kept before being written to a hard drive or sent to a printer, thus reducing the number of writes to the devices.

built-in user account — An administrator account and a guest account that are set up when Windows NT/2000/XP is first installed.

bus — Wires or printed circuits used to transmit electronic signals or voltage on the motherboard to other devices.

cabinet file — A file with a .cab extension that contains one or more compressed files and is often used to distribute software on disk. The Extract command is used to extract files from the cabinet file.

cache — A location in memory or some other place used to store frequently used data.

catalog tree — A database of the folders and files on a Macintosh computer's hard drive, including information such as filenames and extensions, the application used to open a file, the creator of the file or folder, and the date the file or folder was created. Works with the extents tree to allow the Mac to access hard drive data.

CD (change directory) command — A command given at the command prompt that changes the default directory, for example CD \Windows.

chain — A group of clusters used to hold a single file.

child directory — *See* subdirectory.

child, parent, grandparent backup method — A plan for backing up and reusing tapes or removable disks by rotating them each day (child), week (parent), and month (grandparent).

clean install — Installing an OS on a new hard drive or on a hard drive that has a previous OS installed, but without carrying forward any settings kept by the old OS including information about hardware, software, or user preferences. A fresh installation.

client — A software program or computer that requests information from another software program on another computer.

client/server — A computer concept whereby one computer (the client) requests information from another computer (the server).

cluster — One or more sectors that constitute the smallest unit of space on a disk for storing data (also referred to as a file allocation unit).

Cmd.exe — The 32-bit program that provides a command window.

CMOS configuration chip — A chip on the motherboard that contains a very small amount of RAM, enough to hold configuration (or setup) information about the computer. The chip is powered by a battery when the PC is turned off. Also called *CMOS setup chip or CMOS RAM chip.*

CMOS RAM chip — *See* CMOS configuration chip.

CMOS setup chip — *See* CMOS configuration chip.

cold boot — *See* hard boot.

Command.com — Along with Msdos.sys and Io.sys, one of the three files that are the core components of the real-mode portion of Windows 9x. Command.com provides a command prompt and interprets commands.

command mode — The Linux vi editor mode in which you can type commands to manipulate text or to change the status of the editor.

comment — A line or part of a line in a program that is intended as a remark or comment and is ignored when the program runs. A semicolon or an REM is often used to mark a line as a comment.

Compatibility mode — A Windows XP utility that provides an application with the older Microsoft OS environment it was designed to operate in.

compressed drive — A drive whose format has been reorganized in order to store more data. A compressed drive is really not a drive at all; it's actually a type of file, typically with a host drive called H.

Config.sys — A text file used by DOS and supported by Windows 9x that lists device drivers to be loaded at startup. It can also set system variables to be used by DOS and Windows.

Configuration Manager — A component of Windows Plug and Play that controls the configuration process of all devices and communicates these configurations to the devices.

connectionless protocol — A protocol such as UDP that does not require a connection before sending a packet and does not guarantee delivery. An example of a UDP transmission is streaming video over the Web. Also called a *best-effort protocol.*

connection-oriented protocol — In networking, a protocol that confirms that a good connection has been made before transmitting data to the other end. An example of a connection-oriented protocol is TCP.

console — A centralized location from which to execute commonly used tools.

Control Panels folder — In Mac OS 9, a folder that contains control panels for system settings such as time and date, speaker volume, and the configuration of the Finder window and the desktop. In Mac OS X, control panels no longer exist; their functions are incorporated into the Library folder.

conventional memory — Memory addresses between 0 and 640K. Also called base memory.

cooperative multitasking — A type of pseudo-multitasking whereby the OS switches back and forth between programs loaded at the same time. One program sits in the background waiting for the other to relinquish control. Also called *task switching*.

CPU (central processing unit) — The heart and brain of the computer, which receives data input, processes information, and executes instructions. Also called a *microprocessor or processor*.

cross-linked clusters — Errors caused when files appear to share the same disk space, according to the file allocation table.

CVF (compressed volume file) — The file on the host drive of a compressed drive that holds all compressed data.

data bus — *See* data path.

datagram — *See* packet.

data packet — *See* packet.

data path — That portion of a bus that carries data. A data bus is usually 32 or 64 bits wide. Also called a data bus.

default gateway — The gateway a computer on a network will use to access another network unless it knows to specifically use another gateway for quicker access to that network.

default printer — The printer Windows prints to unless another printer is selected.

defragment — To "optimize" or rewrite a file to a disk in one contiguous chain of clusters, thus speeding up data retrieval.

desktop — The initial screen that is displayed when an OS has a GUI interface loaded.

device driver — A program stored on the hard drive that tells the computer how to communicate with an input/output device such as a printer or modem.

DHCP (Dynamic Host Configuration Protocol) server — A service that assigns dynamic IP addresses to computers on a network when they first access the network.

dial-up networking — A Windows 9x and Windows NT/2000/XP utility that uses a modem and telephone line to connect to a network.

differential backup — Backup method that backs up only files that have changed or have been created since the last full backup. When recovering data, only two backups are needed: the full backup and the last differential backup.

digital certificate — A code used to authenticate the source of a file or document or to identify and authenticate a person or organization sending data over the Internet. The code is assigned by a certificate authority such as VeriSign and includes a public key for encryption. Also called *digital ID* or *digital signature*.

digital ID — *See* digital certificate.

digital signature — *See* digital certificate.

directory structure — Files created during formatting that allow a Macintosh computer to access its hard drive. Important directory include the boot blocks, the volume information block, the volume bit map, the catalog tree, and the extents tree.

directory table — An OS table that contains file information such as the name, size, time and date of last modification, and cluster number of the file's beginning location.

disk cache — A method whereby recently retrieved data and adjacent data are read into memory in advance, anticipating the next CPU request.

disk cloning — *See* drive imaging.

disk compression — Compressing data on a hard drive to allow more data to be written to the drive.

Disk First Aid — A free Mac OS disk repair utility included with Mac OS 9. In Mac OS X, Disk First Aid and Drive Setup are combined into the single Disk Utility.

disk imaging — *See* drive imaging.

Disk Management — A Windows 2000/XP utility used to display, create, and format partitions on basic disks and volumes on dynamic disks.

disk quota — A limit placed on the amount of disk space that is available to users. Requires a Windows 2000/XP NTFS volume.

disk thrashing — A condition that results when the hard drive is excessively used for virtual memory because RAM is full. It dramatically slows down processing and can cause premature hard drive failure.

Disk Utility — A Mac OS X utility that can be used to set up a drive, reformat a damaged drive, or detect and repair problems on it. It combines the functions of the Mac OS 9 tools Disk First Aid and Drive Setup.

distribution server — A file server holding Windows setup files used to install Windows on computers networked to the server.

distributions — Different versions of an OS by different vendors.

DLL (dynamic-link library) — A file with a .dll file extension that contains a library of programming routines used by programs to perform common tasks.

DMA (direct memory access) channel — Shortcut method whereby an I/O device can send data directly to memory, bypassing the CPU.

DNS (domain name service or domain name system) — A distributed pool of information (called the name space) that keeps track of assigned domain names and their corresponding IP addresses, and the system that allows a host to locate information in the pool. Compare to *WINS*.

DNS server — A computer that can find an IP address for another computer when only the domain name is known.

dock — A new feature of the Mac OS X interface that consists of icons representing frequently used and currently open applications on a bar at the bottom of the desktop.

docking station — A device that receives a notebook computer and provides additional secondary storage and easy connection to peripheral devices.

domain — In Windows NT/2000/XP, a logical group of networked computers, such as those on a college campus, that share a centralized directory database of user account information and security for the entire domain.

domain name — A unique, text-based name that identifies a network.

domain user account — An account for a user that has permission to access resources, folders, and files on a domain. A domain user can log on to a domain and access the network.

DOS box — A command window.

Dosstart.bat — A type of Autoexec.bat file that is executed by Windows 9x in two situations: when you select Restart the Computer in MS-DOS mode from the Shut down menu or you run a program in MS-DOS mode.

drive imaging — Making an exact image of a hard drive, including partition information, boot sectors, operating system installation, and application software to replicate the hard drive on another system or recover from a hard drive crash. Also called *disk cloning* or *disk imaging*.

Drive Setup — A Mac OS 9 tool that can be used to format a hard drive when it is initially installed or to reformat a damaged hard drive. In Mac OS X, Drive Setup and Disk First Aid are combined into the Disk Utility.

DriveSpace — A Windows 9x utility that compresses files so that they take up less space on a disk drive, creating a single large file on the disk to hold all the compressed files.

Dr. Watson — A Windows utility that can record detailed information about the system, errors that occur, and the programs that caused them in a log file. Windows 9x names the log file \Windows\Drwatson\WatsonXX.wlg, where XX is an incrementing number. Windows 2000 names the file \Documents and Settings\user\Documents\DrWatson\Drwtsn32.log. Windows XP calls the file Drwatson.log.

Drwatson.log — The log file for the Dr. Watson utility in Windows XP.

dual boot — The ability to boot using either of two different OSs, such as Windows 98 and Windows XP.

dump file — A file that contains information captured from memory at the time a stop error occurred.

dynamic disk — A way to partition one or more hard drives, introduced with Windows 2000, in which information about the drive is stored in a database at the end of the drive. Compare to basic disk.

dynamic IP address — An assigned IP address that is used for the current session only. When the session is terminated, the IP address is returned to the list of available addresses.

dynamic volume — A volume type used with dynamic disks for which you can change the size of the volume after you have created it.

dynamic VxD — A VxD that is loaded and unloaded from memory as needed.

EFS (Encrypted File System) — A way to use a key to encode a file or folder on an NTFS volume to protect sensitive data. Because it is an integrated system service, EFS is transparent to users and applications and is difficult to attack.

EIDE (Enhanced Integrated Drive Electronics) — A standard for managing the interface between secondary storage devices and a computer system. A system can support up to six serial ATA and parallel ATA IDE devices or up to four parallel ATA IDE devices, such as hard drives, CD-ROM drives, and Zip drives.

Emergency Repair Disk (ERD) — A Windows NT record of critical information about your system that can be used to fix a problem with the OS. The ERD enables restoration of the Windows NT registry on your hard drive.

Emergency Repair Process — A Windows 2000 process that restores the OS to its state at the completion of a successful installation.

emergency startup disk (ESD) — *See* rescue disk.

Emm386.exe — A DOS and Windows 9x utility that provides access to upper memory for 16-bit device drivers and other software.

enabler file — A file included with Macintosh hardware that is released before the instructions to control it are incorporated into the Mac OS. Enabler files allow a device to function with the version of Mac OS being used on the computer.

encrypting virus — A type of virus that transforms itself into a nonreplicating program in order to avoid detection. It transforms itself back into a replicating program in order to spread.

encryption — The process of putting readable data into an encoded form that can only be decoded (or decrypted) through use of a key.

enhanced metafile format (EMF) — A format used to print a document that contains embedded print commands. When printing in Windows 9x, EMF information is generated by the GDI portion of the Windows kernel.

environment — As related to OSs, the overall support that an OS provides to applications software.

executive services — In Windows NT/2000/XP, a group of components running in kernel mode that interfaces between the subsystems in user mode and the HAL.

extended memory — Memory above 1024K used in a DOS or Windows 9x system.

extended partition — The hard drive partition that can contain more than one logical drive.

Extensions folder — A Mac OS 9 folder that contains add-ons to provide new features to a Mac, as well as shared libraries and icons. Extensions no longer exist in Mac OS X; their functions are incorporated into the Library folder.

extents — On a Mac, the pieces into which a file is broken when it is larger than one allocation block.

extents tree — A Mac directory structure that contains information about where the allocation blocks are located for files that take up more than one allocation block.

external command — Commands that have their own program files.

FAT (file allocation table) — A table on a hard drive or floppy disk that tracks the clusters used to contain a file.

FAT12 — A file system used on floppy disks in which the width of each entry in the one-column table used to track clusters on the disk is 12 bits.

fatal system error — An error that prevents Windows from loading. An example is a damaged registry.

fault tolerance — The degree to which a system can tolerate failures. Adding redundant components, such as disk mirroring, is a way to build in fault tolerance.

file extension — A three-character portion of the name of a file that is used to identify the file type. In command lines, the file extension follows the filename and is separated from it by a period. For example, Msd.exe, where exe is the file extension.

filename — The first part of the name assigned to a file. In DOS, the filename can be no more than eight characters long and is followed by the file extension. In Windows, a filename can be up to 255 characters.

file system — The overall structure that an OS uses to name, store, and organize files on a disk. Examples of file systems are FAT32 and NTFS.

file virus — A virus that inserts virus code into an executable program file and can spread wherever that program is executed.

Finder window — A type of Mac window that allows a user to navigate the Mac OS hierarchical file structure. It functions something like My Computer or Explorer in Windows and includes buttons similar to those on a Web browser.

firmware — Programs permanently embedded on a microchip. The BIOS on a motherboard is an example of firmware.

folder — *See* subdirectory.

forgotten password floppy disk — A Windows XP disk created to be used in the event the user forgets the user account password to the system.

fragmentation — The distribution of data files on a hard drive or floppy disk such that they are stored in noncontiguous clusters.

fragmented file — A file that has been written to different portions of the disk so that it is not in contiguous clusters.

frame The header and trailer information added to data to form a data packet to be sent over a network.

front-side bus — *See* system bus.

FTP (File Transfer Protocol) — The protocol used to transfer files over a TCP/IP network such that the file does not need to be converted to ASCII format before transferring.

full backup — A complete backup, whereby all of the files on the hard drive are backed up each time the backup procedure is performed. It is the safest backup method, but it takes the most time.

fully qualified domain name (FQDN) — A host name and a domain name such as *jsmith.amazon.com*. Sometimes loosely referred to as a domain name.

gateway — A computer or other device that connects networks.

GDI (Graphics Device Interface) — A Windows 9x component that controls screens, graphics, and printing.

global user account — Sometimes called a domain user account, the account is used at the domain level, created by an administrator, and stored in the SAM (security accounts manager) database on a Windows 2000 Server or a Windows 2003 Server domain controller.

group profile — A group of user profiles. All profiles in the group can be changed by changing the group profile.

Guest user — A user who has limited permissions on a system and cannot make changes to it. Guest user accounts are intended for one-time or infrequent users of a workstation.

GUI (graphical user interface) — A user interface, such as the Windows interface, that uses graphics or icons on the screen for running programs and entering information.

HAL (hardware abstraction layer) — The low-level part of Windows NT/2000/XP, written specifically for each CPU technology, so that only the

HAL must change when platform components change.

hard boot — Restart the computer by turning off the power or by pressing the Reset button. Also called a *cold boot.*

hardware address — *See* MAC address. Also called a *buffer.*

hardware cache — A disk cache that is contained in RAM chips built right on the disk controller.

hardware interrupt — An event caused by a hardware device signaling the CPU that it requires service.

hardware profile — A set of hardware configuration information that Windows keeps in the registry. Windows can maintain more than one hardware profile for the same PC.

hardware tree — A database built each time Windows 9x starts up that contains a list of installed components and the resources they use.

HCL (hardware compatibility list) — The list of all computers and peripheral devices that have been tested and are officially supported by Windows NT/2000/XP. (See *www.microsoft.com/hcl/ default.mspx*.)

HFS (Hierarchical File System) — The file system used for Macintosh computer disks before 1998, when drives larger than 1 GB started to become more common. HFS limited the number of allocation units on a disk to 65,536. Also known as *Mac OS standard format.*

HFS+ — The file system used for Mac disks since the release of Mac OS 8.1 in 1998. HFS+ is an update of HFS, and can format drives up to 2,048 GB. Also called *Mac OS extended format.*

hidden file — A file that is not displayed in a directory list. Whether to hide or display a file is indicated by one of the file's attributes kept by the OS.

Himem.sys — The DOS and Windows 9x memory manager extension that allowed access to memory addresses above 1 MB.

hive — Physical segments of the Windows NT/ 2000/XP registry that is stored in a file.

HMA (high memory area) — The first 64K of extended memory.

host — Any computer or other device on a network that has been assigned an IP address. Also called a node.

host drive — Typically drive H on a compressed drive. *See* compressed drive.

host name — A name that identifies a computer, printer, or other device on a network.

Hosts — A text file located in the Windows folder that contains host names and their associated IP addresses. This file is used for name resolution for a TCP/IP network using DNS.

HTML (HyperText Markup Language) — A markup language used for hypertext documents on the World Wide Web. This language uses tags to format the document, create hyperlinks, and mark locations for graphics.

HTTP (HyperText Transfer Protocol) — The protocol used by the World Wide Web.

HTTPS (HTTP secure) — A version of the HTTP protocol that includes data encryption for security.

hub — A network device or box that provides a central location to connect cables.

hypertext — Text that contains links to remote points in the document or to other files, documents, or graphics. Hypertext is created using HTML and is commonly distributed from Web sites.

I/O addresses — Numbers that are used by devices and the CPU to manage communication between them. Also called *ports* or *port addresses.*

ICMP (Internet Control Message Protocol) — Part of the IP layer that is used to transmit error messages and other control messages to hosts and routers.

IDE (Integrated Drive Electronics or Integrated Device Electronics) — A hard drive whose disk controller is integrated into the drive, eliminating the need for a controller cable and thus increasing speed, as well as reducing price. Also see *EIDE.*

IEEE (Institute of Electrical and Electronics Engineers) — A nonprofit organization that develops standards for the computer and electronics industries.

IMAP4 (Internet Message Access Protocol version 4) — Version 4 of the IMAP protocol, which is an email protocol that has more functionality than its predecessor, POP. IMAP can archive messages in folders on the email server and can allow the user to choose not to download attachments to messages.

incremental backup — A time-saving backup method that only backs up files changed or newly created since the last full or incremental backup. Multiple incremental backups might be required when recovering lost data.

infestation — Any unwanted program that is transmitted to a computer without the user's knowledge and that is designed to do varying degrees of damage to data and software. There are a number of different types of infestations, including viruses, Trojan horses, worms, and logic bombs.

information (.inf) file — Text file with an .inf file extension, such as Msbatch.inf, that contains information about a hardware or software installation.

initialization files — Configuration information files for Windows. System.ini is one of the most important Windows initialization files.

insert mode — A Linux vi editor mode in which you can type text into the editor.

internal command — Commands that are embedded in the Command.com file.

Internet Connection Firewall (ICF) — Windows XP software designed to protect a PC from unauthorized access from the Internet.

interrupt handler — A program (either BIOS or a device driver), that is used by the CPU to process a hardware interrupt. Also called *request handler*.

intranet — A private network that uses the TCP/IP protocols.

Io.sys — Along with Msdos.sys and Command.com, one of the three files that are the core components of the real mode portion of Windows 9x. It is the first program file of the OS.

IP (Internet Protocol) — The rules of communication in the TCP/IP stack that control segmenting data into packets, routing those packets across networks, and then reassembling the packets once they reach their destination.

IP address — A 32-bit address consisting of four numbers separated by periods, used to uniquely identify a device on a network that uses TCP/IP protocols. The first numbers identify the network; the last numbers identify a host. An example of an IP address is 206.96.103.114.

IPX/SPX (Internetwork Packet Exchange/ Sequenced Packet Exchange) — A networking protocol suite first used by Novell NetWare, which corresponds to the TCP/IP protocols.

IRQ (interrupt request number) — A line on a bus that is assigned to a device and is used to signal the CPU for servicing. These lines are assigned a reference number (for example, the normal IRQ for a printer is IRQ 7).

ISA (Industry Standard Architecture) — An 8-bit or 16-bit slot first used in the 1980s on motherboards and sometimes still used today.

ISP (Internet service provider) — A commercial group that provides Internet access for a monthly fee. AOL, Earthlink, and CompuServe are large ISPs.

kernel — The portion of an OS that is responsible for interacting with the hardware.

kernel mode — A Windows NT/2000/XP "privileged" processing mode that has access to hardware components.

key — (1) In encryption, a secret number or code used to encode and decode data. (2) In Windows, a section name of the Windows registry.

LAN (local area network) — A computer network that covers only a small area, usually within one building.

laptop computer — *See* notebook.

legacy — A term used to refer to older computer devices or software that does not use the most current technologies.

Library — The Mac OS X folder that takes over the functions of the Mac OS 9 control panels and extensions, which do not exist in Mac OS X. System settings and add-ons are controlled from the Library folder.

Limited user — Windows XP user accounts known as Users in Windows NT/2000, which have limited access to other users' data.

line protocol — A protocol used to send data packets destined for a network over telephone lines. PPP and SLIP are examples of line protocols.

LMHosts — A text file located in the Windows folder that contains NetBIOS names and their associated IP addresses. This file is used for name resolution for a NetBEUI network.

local bus — A bus that runs synchronized with the system bus and CPU.

local printer — A printer connected to a computer by way of a port on the computer. Compare to *network printer*.

local profile — User profile that is stored on a local computer and cannot be accessed from another computer on the network.

local user account — A user account that applies only to a local computer and cannot be used to access resources from other computers on the network.

logic bomb — Dormant code added to software that is triggered by a predetermined time or event.

loopback device — A virtual device, which consists of the local system and has the IP address 127.x.x.x. It is used to test the TCP/IP configuration on a computer.

lost allocation units — *See* lost clusters.

lost clusters — Lost file fragments that, according to the file allocation table, contain data that does not belong to any file. The command Chkdsk/F can free these fragments.

MAC (Media Access Control) address — A 6-byte hexadecimal hardware address unique to each NIC card and assigned by themanufacturer. The address is often printed on the adapter. An example is 00 00 0C 08 2F 35. Also called a *physical address*, an *adapter address*, or a *hardware address*.

Mac OS extended format — *See* HFS+.

Mac OS ROM file — The first item that the Mac loads into memory from the System folder during the startup process. This file contains commands required for interaction with hardware and the lower levels of the Mac OS.

Mac OS standard format — *See* HFS.

macro — A small sequence of commands, contained within a document, that can be automatically executed when the document is loaded, or executed later by using a predetermined keystroke.

macro virus — A virus that can hide in the macros of a document file.

mandatory user profile — A roaming user profile that applies to all users in a group, and individual users cannot change that profile.

master file table (MFT) — The database used by the NTFS file system to track the contents of a logical drive.

MBR (Master Boot Record) — The first sector on a hard drive, which contains the partition table and a program the BIOS uses to boot an OS from the drive.

memory address A number assigned to each byte in memory. The CPU can use memory addresses to track where information is stored in RAM. Memory addresses are usually displayed as hexadecimal numbers in segment/ offset form.

memory bus — *See* system bus.

memory dump — The contents of memory saved to a file at the time an event halted the system. Support technicians can analyze the dump file to help understand the source of the problem.

memory extender — For DOS and Windows 9x, a device driver named Himem.sys that manages RAM giving access to memory addresses above 1 MB.

memory leak — Occurs when software unloads from memory but does not release the memory addresses that it was using for its data back to the OS.

memory paging — In Windows, swapping blocks of RAM memory to an area of the hard drive to serve as virtual memory when RAM is low.

memory-resident virus — A virus that can stay lurking in memory even after its host program is terminated.

microprocessor — *See* CPU.

Microsoft Management Console (MMC) — A utility to build customized consoles. These consoles can be saved to a file with a .msc file extension.

minifile system — In Windows NT/2000/XP, a simplified file system that is started so that Ntldr (NT Loader) can read files from any file system the OS supports.

mixed mode — A Windows 2000 mode for domain controllers used when there is at least one Windows NT domain controller on the network.

motherboard — The largest circuit board inside the computer; it holds the CPU, slots, connections, and ports for other devices and wires for communication called a bus. Also called system board.

Msdos.sys — In Windows 9x, a text file that contains settings used by Io.sys during booting. In DOS, the Msdos.sys file was a program file that contained part of the DOS core.

multicasting — A process in which a message is sent by one host to multiple hosts, such as when a video conference is broadcasted to several hosts on the Internet.

multipartite virus — A combination of a boot sector virus and a file virus. It can hide in either type of program.

multiprocessing — Having two or more CPUs in a system.

multitasking — Doing more than one thing at a time. A true multitasking system requires two or more CPUs, each processing a different thread at the same time. Compare to cooperative multitasking and preemptive multitasking.

multithreading — The ability to pass more than one function (thread) to the OS kernel at the same time, such as when one thread is performing a print job while another reads a file.

name resolution — The process of associating a NetBIOS name or host name to an IP address.

NAT (Network Address Translation) — A process that converts private IP addresses on a LAN to the proxy server's IP address before a data packet is sent over the Internet.

native mode — A Windows 2000 mode used by domain controllers when there are no Windows NT domain controllers present on the network.

NetBEUI (NetBIOS Extended User Interface) — A fast, proprietary Microsoft networking protocol used only by Windows-based systems, and limited to LANs because it does not support routing.

NetBIOS (Network Basic Input/Output System) — An API protocol used by some applications to communicate over a NetBEUI network. NetBIOS has largely been replaced by Windows Sockets over a TCP/IP network.

network drive map — Mounting a drive to a computer, such as drive E, that is actually hard drive space on another host computer on the network.

network printer — A printer that any user on the network can access, through its own network card and connection to the network, through a connection to a standalone printer server, or through a connection to a computer as a local printer, which is shared on the network.

NIC (network interface card) — A expansion card that plugs into a computer's motherboard and provides a port on the back of the card to connect a PC to a network. Also called a network adapter.

NNTP (Network News Transfer Protocol) — The protocol used by newsgroup server and client software.

non-memory-resident virus — A virus that is terminated when the host program is closed. Compare to memory-resident virus.

NOS (network operating system) — An operating system that resides on the controlling computer in the network. The NOS controls what software, data, and devices a user on the network can access. Examples of a NOS are Novell Netware and Windows 2003 Server.

notebook — A portable computer that is designed for travel and mobility. Notebooks use the same technology as desktop PCs, with modifications for conserving voltage, taking up less space, and operating while on the move. Also called a *laptop computer.*

NTFS (NT file system) — The file system for the Windows NT/2000/XP operating systems. NTFS cannot be accessed by other operating systems such as DOS. It provides increased reliability and security in comparison to other methods of organizing and accessing files. There are several versions of NTFS that might or might not be compatible.

NTHQ (NT Hardware Qualifier) — A utility found on the Windows NT installation CD-ROM that examines your system to determine if all hardware present qualifies for NT.

Ntldr (NT Loader) — In Windows NT/2000/XP, the OS loader used on Intel systems.

NTVDM (NT virtual DOS machine) — An emulated environment in which a 16-bit DOS application resides within Windows NT/2000/XP with its own memory space or WOW (Win16 on Win32).

octet — Term for each of the four 8-bit numbers that make up an IP address. For example, the IP address 206.96.103.114 has four octets.

operating system — Software that controls a computer. An operating system controls how system resources are used and provides a user interface, a way of managing hardware and software, and ways to work with files.

packet — Segment of network data that also include header, destination address, and trailer information that is sent as a unit. Also called data packet or datagram.

page fault — An OS interrupt that occurs when the OS is forced to access the hard drive to satisfy the demands for virtual memory.

page file — *See* swap file.

Pagefile.sys — The Windows NT/2000/XP swap file.

page-in — The process in which the memory manager goes to the hard drive to return the data from a swap file to RAM.

page-out — The process in which, when RAM is full, the memory manager takes a page and moves it to the swap file.

pages — 4K segments in which Windows NT/2000/XP allocates memory.

parallel port — A 25-pin female port on a computer that can transmit data in parallel, 8 bits at a time, and is usually used by a printer. The port is sometimes configured as LPT1 or LPT2.

partition table — A table at the beginning of the hard drive that contains information about each partition on the drive. The partition table is contained in the master boot record.

patch — An update to software that corrects an error, adds a feature, or addresses security issues. Also called an update or *service pack*.

path — (1) A drive and list of directories pointing to a file such as C:\Windows\command. (2) The OS command to provide a list of paths to the system for finding program files to execute.

PCI (Peripheral Component Interconnect) bus — A bus common on Pentium computers that runs at speeds of up to 33 MHz or 66 MHz, with a 32-bit-wide or 64-bit-wide data path. PCI-X, released in September 1999, enables PCI to run at 133 MHz. For some chip sets, it serves as the middle layer between the memory bus and expansion buses.

peer-to-peer network — A network of computers that are all equals, or peers. Each computer has the same amount of authority, and each can act as a server to the other computers.

physical address — *See* MAC address.

PIF (program information file) — A file used by Windows to describe the environment for a DOS program to use.

Ping (Packet Internet Groper) — A Windows and Unix command used to troubleshoot network connections. It verifies that the host can communicate with another host on the network.

pixel — Small spots on a fine horizontal scan line that are illuminated to create an image on a monitor.

Plug and Play (PnP) — A standard designed to make the installation of new hardware devices easier by automatically configuring devices to eliminate system resource conflicts (such as IRQ or I/O address conflicts). PnP is supported by Windows 9x, Windows 2000 and Windows XP.

Plug and Play BIOS — System BIOS that supports the Plug and Play standards and is designed to automatically recognize new devices when they are installed.

polling — A process by which the CPU checks the status of connected devices to determine if they are ready to send or receive data.

polymorphic virus — A type of virus that changes its distinguishing characteristics as it replicates itself. Mutating in this way makes it more difficult for AV software to recognize the presence of the virus.

POP (Post Office Protocol) — The protocol that an email server and client use when the client requests the downloading of email messages. The most recent version is POP3. POP is being replaced by IMAP.

port — (1) As applied to services running on a computer, a number assigned to a process on a computer so that the process can be found by TCP/IP. Also called a *port address* or *port number*. (2) Another name for an I/O address. *See also* I/O address. (3) A physical connector, usually at the back of a computer, that allows a cable from a peripheral device, such as a printer, mouse, or modem, to be attached.

port address — *See* I/O address and/or port.

port number — *See* port.

port replicator — A device designed to connect to a notebook computer in order to make it easy to connect the notebook to peripheral devices.

POSIX (Portable Operating System Interface) — A set of standards for Unix and similar operating systems used to create applications to comply with standards used by federal agencies for their software.

POST (power-on self test) — A self-diagnostic program used to perform a simple test of the CPU, RAM, and various I/O devices. The POST is performed by startup BIOS when the computer is first turned on and is stored in ROM-BIOS.

power scheme — A feature of Windows XP support for notebooks that allows the user to create groups of power settings for specific sets of conditions.

Power User — *See* standard user.

PPP (Point-to-Point Protocol) — A protocol that governs the methods for communicating via modems and dial-up telephone lines. The Windows Dial-up Networking utility uses PPP.

PRAM (parameter RAM) — A small amount of RAM on a Mac that contains configuration information for the Mac.

preemptive multitasking — A type of pseudo-multitasking whereby the CPU allows an application a specified period of time and then preempts the processing to give time to another application.

primary domain controller (PDC) — In a Windows NT network, the computer that controls the directory database of user accounts, group accounts, and computer accounts on a domain. Also see backup domain controller.

primary partition — A hard disk partition that can contain only one logical drive.

primary storage — Temporary storage on the motherboard used by the CPU to process data and instructions. Memory is considered primary storage.

private IP address — An IP address that is used on a private TCP/IP network that is isolated from the Internet.

process — An executing instance of a program together with the program resources. There can be more than one process running for a program at the same time. One process for a program happens each time the program is loaded into memory or executed.

product activation — The process that Microsoft uses to prevent software piracy. For example, once Windows XP is activated for a particular computer, it cannot be installed on another computer.

program file — A file that contains instructions designed to be executed by the CPU.

protected mode — An operating mode that supports preemptive multitasking, the OS manages memory and other hardware devices, and programs can use a 32-bit data path. Also called *32-bit mode*.

Protocol.ini — A Windows initialization file that contains network configuration information.

proxy server — A server that acts as an intermediary between another computer and the Internet. The proxy server substitutes its own IP address for the IP address of the computer on the network making a request, so that all traffic over the Internet appears to be coming from only the IP address of the proxy server.

public IP address — An IP address available to the Internet.

RAID (redundant array of inexpensive disks or redundant array of independent disks) — Several methods of configuring multiple hard drives to store data to increase logical volume size and improve performance, or to ensure that if one hard drive fails, the data is still available from another hard drive.

RAM (random access memory) — Memory modules on the motherboard containing microchips used to temporarily hold data and programs while the CPU processes both. Information in RAM is lost when the PC is turned off.

RAM drive — An area of memory that is treated as though it were a hard drive, but that works much faster than a hard drive. The Windows 98 startup disk uses a RAM drive. Compare to *virtual memory*.

RARP (Reverse Address Resolution Protocol) — A protocol used to translate the unique hardware NIC addresses (MAC addresses) into IP addresses (the reverse of ARP).

real mode — A single-tasking operating mode whereby a program has 1024K of memory addresses, has direct access to RAM, and uses a 16-bit data path. Using a memory extender (Himem.sys) a program in real mode can access memory above 1024K. Also called *16-bit mode*.

Recovery Console — A Windows 2000/XP command interface utility and OS that can be used to solve problems when the Windows cannot load from the hard drive.

redirection symbol — The greater than (>) symbol used in OS commands to redirect output to a file or printer instead of to a screen.

registry — A database that Windows uses to store hardware and software configuration information, user preferences, and setup information.

Remote Access Service (RAS) — The Windows NT service used to configure a computer to allow inbound calls.

Remote Assistance — A Windows XP feature that allows a support technician at a remote location to have full access to the Windows XP desktop.

request handler — *See* interrupt handler.

rescue disk — A floppy disk that can be used to start up a computer when the hard drive fails to boot. Also called *emergency startup disk (ESD)* or *startup disk*.

resolution — The number of pixels on a monitor screen that are addressable by software, such as 1024 × 768.

resource arbitrator — A Plug and Play component that decides which resources are assigned to which devices.

resource management — The process of allocating resources to devices at startup.

restore point — A snapshot of the Windows Me/XP system state, usually made before installation of new hardware or applications.

restricted user — *See* user.

RFC (Request for Comments) — A document that proposes a change in standards or protocols for the communications industry. An RFC can be presented by different organizations but is managed under the general guidance of the Internet Architecture Board (IAB).

roaming user profile — A user profile for a roaming user. Roaming user profiles are stored on a server so that the user can access the profile from anywhere on the network.

roaming users — Users who can move from PC to PC within a network, with their profiles following them.

root account — The principal user account in Linux, accessible by the system administrator. Only the owner of the root account has the ability to make certain alterations to the system and perform certain system tasks.

root directory — The main directory created when a hard drive or disk is first formatted. In Linux, indicated by a forward slash. In DOS and Windows, indicated by a backward slash.

root privileges — The privileges that the system administrator has on a Linux system, which allow the system administrator full access to the system.

run-time configuration — An ongoing Plug and Play process that monitors changes in system devices, such as the removal of a PC card on a notebook computer or the docking of a notebook computer to a docking station.

secondary storage — Storage that is remote to the CPU and permanently holds data, even when the PC is turned off, such as a hard drive.

sector — On a disk surface one segment of a track, which almost always contains 512 bytes of data.

security accounts manager (SAM) — A portion of the Windows NT/2000/XP registry that manages the account database that contains accounts, policies, and other pertinent information about local accounts.

serial port — A male 9-pin or 25-pin port on a computer system used by slower I/O devices such as a mouse or modem. Data travels serially, one bit at a time, through the port. Serial ports are sometimes configured as COM1, COM2, COM3, or COM4.

server — (1) A software program that interacts with client software in a client/server environment. (2) A computer that runs server software and responds to requests for information from client computers.

service pack — *See* patch.

session — An established communication link between two software programs. On the Internet, a session is created by TCP.

SFC (System File Checker) — A Windows tool that checks to make sure Windows is using the correct versions of system files.

shell — The portion of an OS that relates to the user and to applications.

shortcut — An icon on the desktop that points to a program that can be executed or to a file or folder.

Sigverif.exe — A Windows utility that allows you to search for digital signatures.

simple volume — A type of dynamic volume used on a single hard drive that corresponds to a primary partition on a basic disk.

single-tasking — When only one program is running at a time.

SLIP (Serial Line Internet Protocol) — A line protocol used by regular telephone lines that has largely been replaced by PPP.

SMARTDrive — A hard drive cache program that came with Windows 3.x and DOS and can be executed as a TSR from the Autoexec.bat file (for example, Device=Smartdrv.sys 2048).

SMTP (Simple Mail Transfer Protocol) — The protocol used by email clients and servers to send email messages over the Internet. *See* POP.

snap-ins — Components added to a console using the Microsoft Management Console.

SNMP (Simple Network Management Protocol) — A protocol used to monitor and manage network traffic on a workstation. SNMP works with TCP/IP and IPX/SPX networks.

socket — *See* session.

soft boot — To restart a PC without turning off the power, for example, in Windows XP, by clicking Start, Turn Off Computer, and Restart. Also called *warm boot*.

software cache — Cache controlled by software whereby the cache is stored in RAM.

software interrupt — An event caused by a program currently being executed by the CPU signaling the CPU that it requires the use of a hardware device.

spanned volume — A type of dynamic volume used on two or more hard drives that fills up the space allotted on one physical disk before moving to the next.

spooling — Placing print jobs in a print queue so that an application can be released from the printing process before printing is completed. Spooling is an acronym for simultaneous peripheral operations online.

SSL (secure socket layer) — A secure protocol developed by Netscape that uses a digital certificate including a public key to encrypt and decrypt data.

standard user — Standard users can read from and write to parts of the system other than their own local drive, install applications, and perform limited administrative tasks. Also called *Power User*.

startup BIOS — Part of system BIOS that is responsible for controlling the PC when it is first turned on. Startup BIOS gives control over to the OS once it is loaded.

startup disk — *See* rescue disk.

static IP address — An IP address permanently assigned to a workstation.

Static VxD — A VxD that is loaded into memory at startup and remains there for the entire OS session.

stealth virus — A virus that actively conceals itself by temporarily removing itself from an infected file that is about to be examined, and then hiding a copy of itself elsewhere on the drive.

stop error — An error severe enough to cause the operating system to stop all processes.

striped volume — A type of dynamic volume used for two or more hard drives that writes to the disks evenly rather than filling up allotted space on one and then moving on to the next. Compare to *spanned volume*.

subdirectory — A directory or folder contained in another directory or folder. Also called a *child directory* or *folder*.

subnet mask — A subnet mask is a group of four numbers (dotted decimal numbers) that tell TCP/IP if a remote computer is on the same or a different network.

subsystems — The different modules into which the Windows NT/2000/XP user mode is divided.

swap file — A file on the hard drive that is used by the OS for virtual memory. Also called *page file*.

Sysedit — The Windows System Configuration Editor, which is a text editor generally used to edit system files.

system BIOS — BIOS located on the motherboard.

system bus — The bus between the CPU and memory on the motherboard. The bus frequency in documentation is called the system speed such as 400 MHz. Also called the *memory bus*, *front-side bus*, *local bus*, or *host bus*.

system disk — Windows terminology for a bootable disk.

System file — The Mac OS file that contains the libraries and commands that make up the core of the OS.

System File Protection — A Windows feature that prevents system files from being deleted.

System folder — The folder that a Mac system designates as the one from which the OS is to be loaded.

System.ini — A text configuration file used by Windows 3.x and supported by Windows 9x for backward-compatibility.

system partition — The active partition of the hard drive containing the boot record and the specific files required to load Windows NT/2000/XP.

System Restore — A Windows Me/XP utility, similar to the ScanReg tool in earlier versions of Windows, that is used to restore the system to a restore point. Unlike ScanReg, System Restore cannot be executed from a command prompt.

system state data — In Windows 2000/XP, files that are necessary for a successful load of the operating system.

System Tray — An area to the right of the taskbar that holds the icons of small applets launched at startup.

task switching — *See* cooperative multitasking.

TCP (Transmission Control Protocol) — Part of the TCP/IP protocol suite. TCP guarantees delivery of data for application protocols and establishes a session before it begins transmitting data.

TCP/IP (Transmission Control Protocol/Internet Protocol) — The suite of protocols that supports communication on the Internet. TCP is responsible for error checking, and IP is responsible for routing.

Terminate-and-stay-resident (TSR) — A 16-bit program that is loaded into memory and remains dormant until called on, such as a screen saver or a memory-resident antivirus program.

thread — Each process that the CPU is aware of; a single task that is part of a longer task or program.

TIFF (Tagged Image File Format) — A bitmapped file format used to hold photographs, graphics, and screen captures. TIFF files can be rather large, and have a .tif file extension.

TLS (Transport Layer Security) — A protocol used to secure data sent over the Internet. It is an improved version of SSL.

top-level domain — The highest level of domain names, indicated by a suffix that tells something about the host. For example, .com is for commercial use and .edu is for educational institutions.

track — One of many concentric circles on the surface of a hard drive or floppy disk.

Trojan horse — A type of infestation that hides or disguises itself as a useful program, yet is designed to cause damage at a later time.

UDP (User Datagram Protocol) — A connectionless protocol that does not require a connection to send a packet and does not guarantee that the packet arrives at its destination. UDP works at the Transport layer and is faster than TCP because TCP takes the time to make a connection and guarantee delivery.

UMB (upper memory block) — In DOS and Windows 9x, a group of consecutive memory addresses in RAM from 640K to 1MB that can be used by 16-bit device drivers and TSRs.

unattended installation — A Windows NT/ 2000/ XP installation that is done by storing the answers to installation questions in a text file or script that Windows NT/2000/XP calls an answer file so that the answers do not have to be typed in during the installation.

upgrade install — The installation of an OS on a hard drive that already has an OS installed in such a way that settings kept by the old OS are carried forward into the upgrade, including information about hardware, software, and user preferences.

upper memory — In DOS and Windows 9x, the memory addresses from 640K up to 1024K, originally reserved for BIOS, device drivers, and TSRs.

URL (Uniform Resource Locator) — An address for a resource on the Internet. A URL can contain the protocol used by the resource, the name of the computer and its network, and the path and name of a file on the computer.

USB (universal serial bus) — A bus that is expected to eventually replace serial and parallel ports. USB is designed to make installation and configuration of I/O devices easy, providing room for as many as 127 devices daisy-chained together. The USB uses only a single set of resources for all devices on the bus.

user — In reference to Windows NT/2000/XP permissions, a restricted user who has read-write

access only on his or her own folders, read-only access to most system folders, and no access to other users' data.

user account — The information, stored in the SAM database, that defines a Windows NT/ 2000/XP user, including username, password, memberships, and rights.

user component — A Windows 9x component that controls the mouse, keyboard, ports, and desktop.

user mode — In Windows NT/2000/XP, a mode that provides an interface between an application and the OS, and only has access to hardware resources through the code running in kernel mode.

user profile — A personal profile about a user that enables the user's desktop settings and other operating parameters to be retained from one session to another.

User State Migration Tool (USMT) — A Windows XP utility that helps you migrate user files and preferences from one computer to another in order to help a user makes a smooth transition from one computer to another.

value data — In Windows, the name and value of a setting in the registry.

VCACHE — A built-in Windows 9x 32-bit software cache that doesn't take up conventional memory space or upper memory space as SMARTDrive does.

VFAT (virtual file allocation table) — A variation of the original DOS 16-bit FAT that allows for long filenames and 32-bit disk access.

vi editor — A text editor in Linux that operates in two modes: insert mode, in which you can type text into the editor, and command mode, in which you can enter commands to work with the text or change the status of the editor.

virtual device driver (VxD or VDD) — A Windows device driver that may or may not have direct access to a device. It might depend on a Windows component to communicate with the device itself.

virtual DOS machine (VDM) — Environment in which Windows runs a 16-bit DOS application. In a VDM, the application "thinks" it is running in real mode, but the OS is managing hardware resources using 32-bit drivers and providing virtual memory to the application.

virtual machine — One or more logical machines created within one physical machine by Windows, allowing applications to make serious errors within one logical machine without disturbing other programs and parts of the system.

Virtual Machine Manager (VMM) — A Windows 9x program that controls virtual machines and the resources they use, including memory. The VMM manages the page table used to access memory.

virtual memory — A method whereby the OS uses the hard drive as though it were RAM. Compare to *RAM drive*.

virtual real mode — An operating mode that works similarly to real mode provided by a 32-bit OS for a 16-bit program to work.

virus — A program that often has an incubation period, is infectious, and is intended to cause damage. A virus program might destroy data and programs or damage a disk drive's boot sector.

virus signature — A set of distinguishing characteristics of a virus used by antivirus software to identify the virus.

volume bit map — On a Macintosh computer, a map of the allocation blocks on a hard drive. It uses a 1 to indicate that a block is storing files and a 0 to indicate that it is empty and is available for use.

volume information block — On a Macintosh computer, the directory structure that comes right after the boot blocks on a hard drive. It holds information about the drive, including its format, name, number of files and folders, and allocation block size.

VxD — *See* virtual device driver.

warm boot — *See* soft boot.

WDM (Win32 Driver Model) — The only Windows 9x Plug and Play component that is found in Windows 98 but not Windows 95. WDM is the component responsible for managing device drivers that work under a driver model new to Windows 98.

WFP (Windows File Protection) — A Windows 2000/XP tool that protects system files from modification.

Win.ini — The Windows initialization file that contains program configuration information needed for running the Windows operating environment. Its functions were replaced by the registry beginning with Windows 9x, which still supports it for backward compatibility with Windows 3.x.

Win386.swp — The name of the Windows 9x swap file. Its default location is C:\Windows.

window manager — A graphical user interface for a Linux computer. A popular window manager is GNOME.

WINS (Windows Internet Naming Service) — A Microsoft resolution service with a distributed database that tracks relationships between NetBIOS names and IP addresses. Compare to *DNS*.

WinSock (Windows Sockets) — A part of the TCP/IP utility software that manages API calls from applications to other computers on a TCP/IP network.

WIS (Windows Installer Service) — A feature new to Windows 2000 that standardizes the installation process for applications.

workgroup — In Windows, a logical group of computers and users in which administration, resources, and security are distributed throughout the net- work, without centralized management or security.

worm — An infestation designed to copy itself repeatedly to memory, on drive space or on a network, until little memory or disk space remains.

WOW (Win16 on Win32) — A group of programs provided by Windows NT/2000/XP to create a virtual DOS environment that emulates a 16-bit Windows environment, protecting the rest of the OS from 16-bit applications.

Index

A+ PC Repair
Total Solution

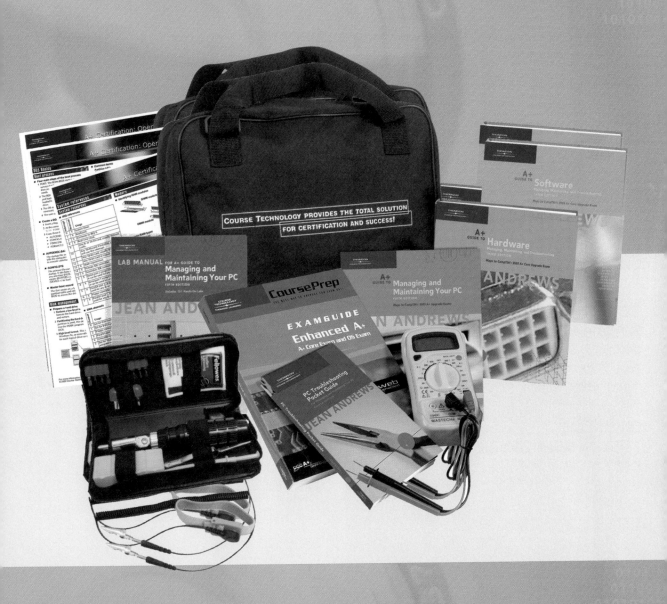

COURSE TECHNOLOGY offers *everything* you need to prepare for CompTIA's 2003 A+ Certification Exams and embark on a successful career as a computer technician.

All books are written by best-selling author and instructor Jean Andrews.

COMPREHENSIVE TEXTS

A+ Guide to Managing and Maintaining Your PC, Comprehensive, Fifth Edition
ISBN: 0-619-21324-8

A+ Guide to Hardware: Managing, Maintaining, and Troubleshooting, Third Edition
ISBN: 0-619-21327-2

A+ Guide to Software: Managing, Maintaining, and Troubleshooting, Third Edition
ISBN: 0-619-21326-4

HANDS-ON PRACTICE

Lab Manual for A+ Guide to Managing and Maintaining Your PC, Fifth Edition
ISBN: 0-619-18619-4

A+ Computer-Based Training (CBT), Third Edition by InfoSource
ISBN: 0-619-18621-6

PC Troubleshooting Pocket Guide, Fourth Edition
ISBN: 0-619-21364-7

EXAM PREPARATION

A+ PC Repair Flash Cards
ISBN: 0-619-21305-1

Prometric A+ Exam Voucher
ISBN: 0-619-25894-2

A+ CoursePrep ExamGuide, Second Edition
ISBN: 0-619-18623-2

A+ Hardware CourseCard
ISBN: 0-619-20362-5

A+ Software CourseCard
ISBN: 0-619-20363-5

ON THE JOB

22-Piece Toolset with ESD Strap
ISBN: 0-619-01655-8

Digital Multimeter
ISBN: 0-619-13101-2